MW01617789

VINCENT VAN GOGH
The Drawings

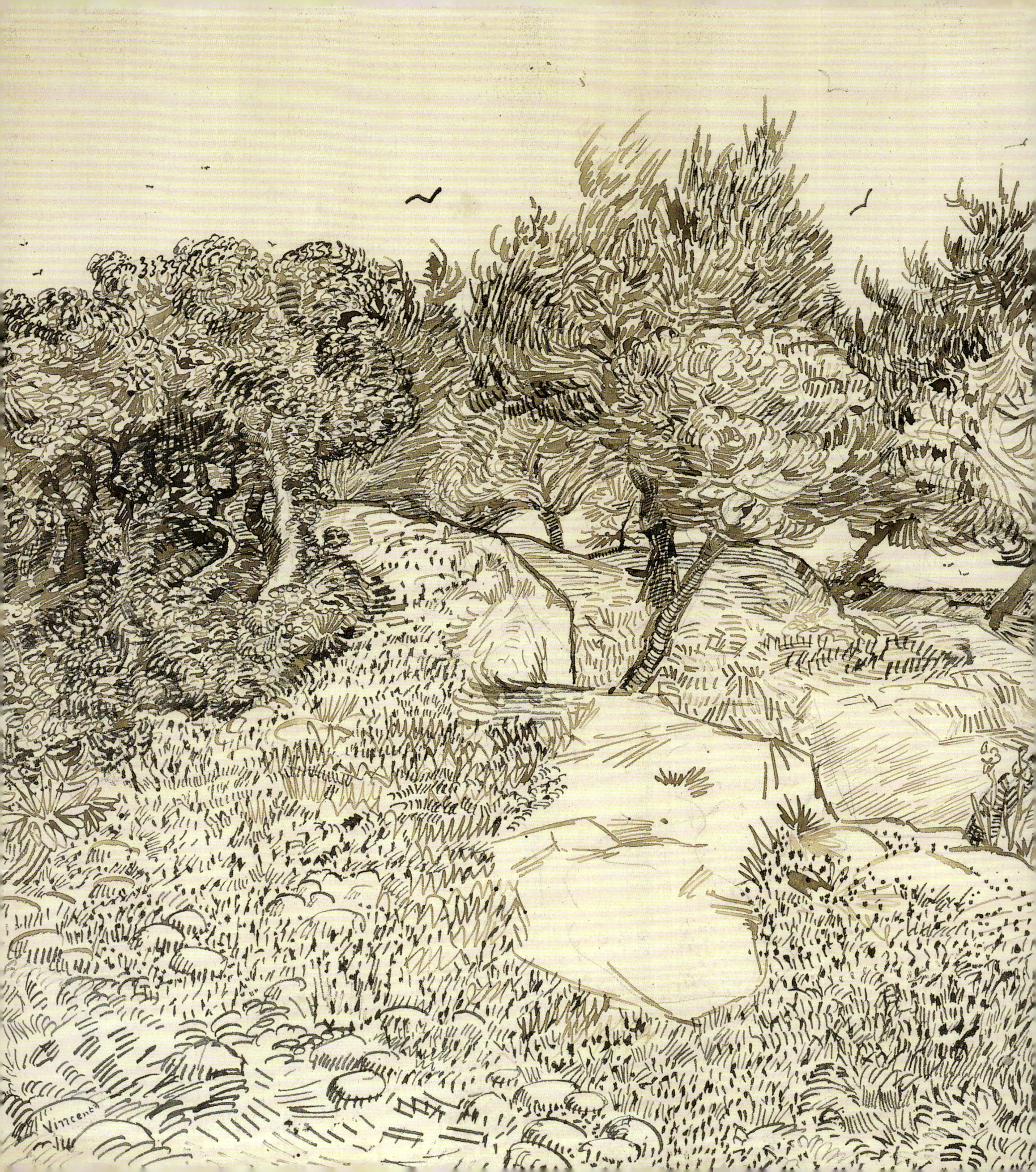
Vincent

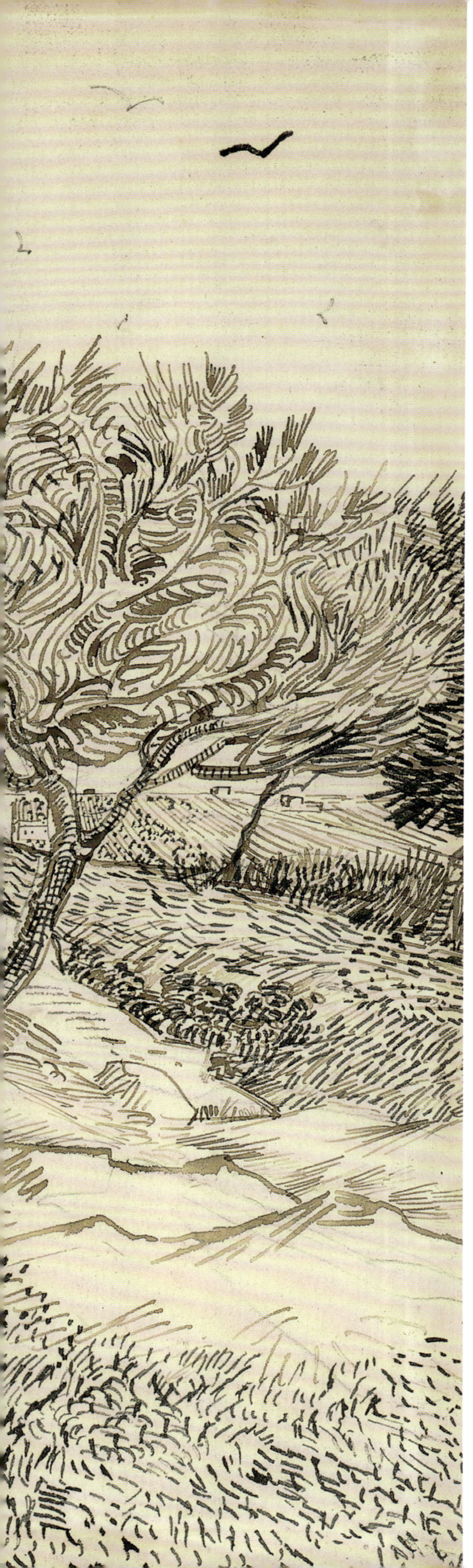

VINCENT VAN GOGH
The Drawings

Colta Ives, Susan Alyson Stein,
Sjraar van Heugten, and Marije Vellekoop

The Metropolitan Museum of Art, New York
Van Gogh Museum, Amsterdam
Yale University Press, New Haven and London

This catalogue is published in conjunction with the exhibition "Van Gogh Draftsman: The Masterpieces," on view at the Van Gogh Museum, Amsterdam, July 1–September 18, 2005; and "Vincent van Gogh: The Drawings," on view at The Metropolitan Museum of Art, New York, October 12–December 31, 2005.

The exhibition in New York is made possible by

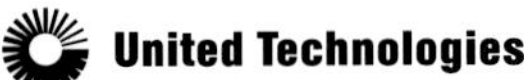

The exhibition catalogue is made possible in part by the Janice H. Levin Fund.

The exhibition was jointly organized by The Metropolitan Museum of Art, New York, and the Van Gogh Museum, Amsterdam.

Published by The Metropolitan Museum of Art, New York, and the Van Gogh Museum, Amsterdam

At the Metropolitan Museum
John P. O'Neill, Editor in Chief and General Manager of Publications
Gwen Roginsky, Associate General Manager of Publications
Margaret Rennolds Chace, Managing Editor
Margaret Aspinwall, Senior Editor
Bruce Campbell, Designer
Peter Antony and Sally Van Devanter, Production
Minjee Cho, Desktop Publishing
Jean Wagner, Bibliographic Editor

At the Van Gogh Museum
Suzanne Bogman, Publications Manager
Monique Hageman, Research and Documentation
Patricia Schuil, Documentation/Editorial Assistant, Images
Denise Willemstein, Publication Assistant

Unless otherwise specified, all photographs were supplied by the owners of the works of art, who hold the copyright thereto, and are reproduced with permission. Photographs of works in the Metropolitan Museum's collection are by The Photograph Studio, The Metropolitan Museum of Art. Photographs of works in the Van Gogh Museum's collection are by Thijs Quispel. Additional photograph credits: cat. 22, András Rázsó; cat. 44 (and figs. 116, 117), Joseph Levy; cats. 48, 49, 50, 52, 56, 61, Joseph Zehavi; cats. 57 (and fig. 179), 64, 73, Jörg P. Anders—Bildarchiv Preussischer Kulturbesitz/Art Resource, NY; cat. 69, Jean de Calan; cat. 74, R. Lorenzson; cat. 90, Hickey-Robertson, Houston; cat. 95, Matt Flynn; cat. 109, Malcolm Varon; cat. 116, Martina Bienenstein

Separations by Professional Graphics Inc., Rockford, Illinois
Printed and bound by Conti Tipocolor s.p.a., Florence

Jacket/cover illustrations: *Front,* detail of cat. 91, *Cottage Garden* (F1456), by August 8, 1888. Reed pen, quill, and ink over graphite on wove paper, 61 x 49 cm (24 x 19¼ in.). Private collection. *Back,* cat. 35, *Self-Portrait,* January–June 1887. Pen and ink, graphite on wove paper, 31.1 x 24.4 cm (12¼ x 9⅝ in.). Van Gogh Museum, Amsterdam (Vincent van Gogh Foundation)
Frontispiece: Detail of cat. 82, *Olive Trees, Montmajour* (JH Add. 3), July 1888. Reed pen and ink on wove paper, 48 x 60 cm (18⅞ x 23⅝ in.). Musée des Beaux-Arts, Tournai

Cataloging-in-Publication Data is available from the Library of Congress.
ISBN 1-58839-164-7 (hc: The Metropolitan Museum of Art)
ISBN 1-58839-165-5 (pbk: The Metropolitan Museum of Art)
ISBN 0-300-10720-X (Yale University Press)

Contents

Sponsor's Statement

In a letter to his brother in July 1885, Vincent van Gogh wrote, "I can't tell the future, Theo, but I do know the eternal law that all things change." During Van Gogh's lifetime, artists' portrayal of the world was transforming, like the world itself. Artistic trends were often at odds with each other, and with new trends came new subject matter. Scenes from industry and everyday life, with peasants and postmen, were fresh subject matter for the artist's imagination. At the center of Van Gogh's oeuvre was his drawing. It served as both form and tool and was the foundation for all his other work, including those most widely recognized today.

United Technologies Corporation (UTC) is delighted to sponsor "Vincent van Gogh: The Drawings" at The Metropolitan Museum of Art. We're pleased as well that this coincides with the twenty-fifth anniversary of our sponsorship of the arts. Starting with "Old Master Paintings from the Collection of Baron Thyssen-Bornemisza" in 1980, UTC's sponsorships include exhibitions with diversity ranging from "Johannes Vermeer" at the National Gallery in Washington to "A Spiritual Resonance: The Vernacular Dwellings of China" at the National Museum of Chinese History in Beijing.

In his letter to his brother, Van Gogh continued, "Think back 10 years, and things were different, the circumstances, the mood of the people, in short everything. And 10 years hence much is bound to have changed again. But what one does remains, and one does not easily regret having done it." We feel the same way about our support for the arts.

George David
Chairman and Chief Executive Officer
United Technologies Corporation

Directors' Foreword

Is there any significant aspect of Vincent van Gogh's life and art that remains little known and underresearched? From the time his work first began to attract serious interest from critics and scholars in the early twentieth century through to the present level of intense interest in the artist, every possible facet of his brief career would seem to have been subjected to rigorous scrutiny and exposure—perhaps even overexposure. However, with this exhibition and its accompanying catalogue we propose that there is indeed a major part of Van Gogh's production that remains comparatively unknown, at least to the general public. In quantity Van Gogh's drawings count for more than half of his artistic output. In quality they count as many of his finest and most dramatic creations. Yet the fame and familiarity of his painted oeuvre have long overshadowed his work as a draftsman. Van Gogh's drawings have often been cast in a supporting role, of interest for what they reveal about his career and his artistic processes, and subordinate to the demands of painting. Here we claim not only that his drawings are worthy of appreciation as great works of art in their own right but that Van Gogh should be counted as one of the finest draftsmen of his century.

From the hybrid techniques of his early drawings to the simplicity of his later compositions in reed pen and ink, from frantic experiment to easy virtuosity, Van Gogh's emergence as a brilliant draftsman is every bit as dramatic as his parallel development as a painter in oils. As the authors of this catalogue show, the activity of drawing came to fulfill many roles in his artistic production. At the outset of his career, before he dared to turn his hand to oil painting, Van Gogh first spent several years mastering the art of drawing. In sheet after sheet he teased out his reluctant talent, forcing his drawing tools to conform to his wishes. Later there would be other periods, of poverty or sickness, for example, when drawing again became his primary mode of expression. But drawing would always remain more than just training for hand and eye or a subordinate part of the process of painting. Van Gogh belonged to a generation of artists that worked happily and easily in various media on paper, creating self-sufficient works for exhibition and for sale. While some of his drawings are studies for or records of his painted work, there are others that he regarded as independent creations capable of holding their own as works of art.

We can be grateful that such a substantial number of Van Gogh's drawings have survived. His itinerant lifestyle, his experimentation with different techniques, and his lack of knowledge about the materials of his craft were all factors that threatened the preservation of fragile works on paper. Thankfully, the artist's family and descendants recognized the importance of his drawings at an early stage. Almost half of the surviving drawings remained in the family's possession and passed eventually to the present owners, the Vincent van Gogh Foundation, on permanent loan to the Van Gogh Museum. Over the past ten years the Van Gogh Museum has compiled a series of four scholarly catalogues of this entire collection of works on paper. The present exhibition marks both the completion and the culmination of this project and offers the public in Europe and America a chance to benefit from the many insights gained in studying this extensive body of drawings.

Our two institutions have enjoyed the benefit of working together on other exhibitions of mutual interest, most recently, *Cézanne to*

Van Gogh: The Collection of Doctor Gachet (1999) and *Signac: 1863–1935* (2001). Yet the present project represents a rather special instance of collaboration, for its realization, in exhibition and book form, depended on the unique resources of our two museums and, above all, on the generosity the Van Gogh Museum extended to the Metropolitan Museum throughout this venture. This spirit of cooperation has enabled the Metropolitan to bring to its public the first American retrospective of Van Gogh's achievement as a draftsman.

A great many people have been involved in bringing this project together. First and foremost we thank the many lenders to this show. The Vincent van Gogh Foundation has been exceptionally generous and we would like to express our thanks to the chairman, Vincent Willem van Gogh, and his fellow board members for their enthusiastic support. We are grateful, too, to the many institutions and private lenders who have for a time parted with their precious works. We are only too conscious of their sacrifice, knowing that in most cases these are works that can be displayed only briefly for reasons of conservation and it may be many years before some sheets may be shown in public again. In Amsterdam and New York, the staffs of our respective institutions have worked with their customary professionalism and devotion to develop this exhibition and its catalogue. Our thanks are due especially to the curatorial team, Sjraar van Heugten, Colta Ives, Susan Alyson Stein, and Marije Vellekoop, who evolved the concept and brought their expertise to bear on the selection and explanation of the exhibited works.

At the Metropolitan Museum, we are indebted to United Technologies Corporation, whose generous support of the exhibition's presentation in New York has significantly enriched the project. We are similarly grateful to the Janice H. Levin Fund for its vital contribution toward the realization of this publication.

Thanks to all of these people, this exhibition represents a unique opportunity to encounter the very best of Van Gogh's drawings. It may be that we all still harbor something of the clichéd image of Van Gogh as a crazed genius struggling to find an outlet for his emotions in pools of brightly colored oil paint. The power of these drawings will surely invoke not just our wonder at the intensity of his expression but also our admiration for the rigor and discipline that he applied to his artistic mission.

John Leighton
Director
Van Gogh Museum

Philippe de Montebello
Director
The Metropolitan Museum of Art

Lenders to the Exhibition

Public Collections

Amsterdam, Rijksmuseum, cats. 20, 66, 84

Amsterdam, Stedelijk Museum, cat. 41

Amsterdam, Van Gogh Museum (Vincent van Gogh Foundation), cats. 6, 7, 11, 12, 15–18, 19, 21, 23, 25–28, 31–35, 37–40, 42, 43, 49, 54, 63, 76, 78, 83, 85, 92, 94, 98, 99, 102–5, 107, 110, 112, 114, 115, 117, 118

Berlin, Kupferstichkabinett, Staatliche Museen zu Berlin, cats. 57, 64, 73

Boston, Museum of Fine Arts, cat. 13

Brussels, Musées Royaux des Beaux-Arts de Belgique—Koninklijke Musea voor Schone Kunsten van België, cat. 59

Budapest, Szépművészeti Múzeum, cat. 22

Chicago, The Art Institute of Chicago, cat. 100

Dallas Museum of Art, cat. 96

Essen, Museum Folkwang, cat. 29

Glens Falls, New York, The Hyde Collection, cat. 44

Houston, The Menil Collection, cat. 90

London, British Museum, cat. 86

London, Tate, cats. 24, 101, 119

Los Angeles, The J. Paul Getty Museum, cats. 72, 81

Los Angeles County Museum of Art, cat. 87

Moscow, Pushkin State Museum of Fine Arts, cat. 55

Munich, Staatliche Graphische Sammlung, cat. 116

New York, Brooklyn Museum, cat. 108

New York, Cooper-Hewitt, National Design Museum, Smithsonian Institution, cat. 95

New York, The Metropolitan Museum of Art, cats. 8, 53, 77, 109, 111, 113

New York, Thaw Collection, The Pierpont Morgan Library, cats. 48, 52, 56, 61

New York, Solomon R. Guggenheim Museum, Thannhauser Collection, cats. 58, 75, 79, 93

Oslo, Nasjonalmuseet/Nasjonalgalleriet, cat. 47

Ottawa, National Gallery of Canada, cat. 1

Otterlo, Kröller-Müller Museum, cats. 2–5, 9, 14, 30, 106

Paris, Musée Rodin, cat. 69

Philadelphia Museum of Art, cat. 67

Providence, Museum of Art, Rhode Island School of Design, cat. 46

Tournai, Musée des Beaux-Arts, cat. 82

Washington, National Gallery of Art, cats. 65, 70

Washington, The Phillips Collection, cat. 36

Winterthur, Kunstmuseum Winterthur, cat. 58

Zürich, Kunsthaus Zürich, Graphische Sammlung, cat. 45

Private Collections

Anonymous lenders, cats. 51, 60, 62, 71, 74, 91, 97

Sidney E. Frank, cat. 10

Miles, Sebastian, and Hugh Gibson, cat. 89

Private collection, courtesy of Thomas Gibson Fine Art Ltd., cat. 80

Private collection, courtesy of Wildenstein & Co., Inc., cat. 88

Private collection, on deposit at The Pierpont Morgan Library, New York, cat. 50

Preface and Acknowledgments

This book and the exhibition it documents were conceived by four curators from two museums, in Amsterdam and New York. Together, we envisioned celebrating Van Gogh's graphic genius in a presentation of his drawings of the most admirable quality and condition. Convinced that Van Gogh's achievements as a draftsman are equal to those he made as a painter, we have endeavored to demonstrate the extraordinary range and ingenuity of his production on paper as it evolved during his decade-long career. Recognizing the attraction of his linear invention, we have placed emphasis on the drawings of the artist's maturity, particularly those realized during his fifteen-month-long sojourn in Arles (1888–89), when an exceptionally dynamic dialogue between drawing and painting unfolded.

Every effort has been made in the present volume to expand an understanding of Van Gogh's drawings, especially as they developed within the context of his own activities and were stimulated by and forecast the achievements of other artists. Our aims have been to clarify issues of chronology, the artist's working methods, and the content and character of his drawing campaigns. Naturally, our catalogue builds upon the work of many authors, whose scholarly contributions we acknowledge under "summary of the literature" in each entry. These citations, supplemented by provenance, selected exhibition history, excerpts from the artist's letters, technical notes, and comparative images, provide the documentation that is so often missing from current studies of Van Gogh but remains essential as the firm foundation for present and future scholarship.

In all, our endeavors to honor and elucidate this exciting and original body of work have resulted in a book that is larger and more lavish than anticipated. In this regard, as in all other aspects of this project, we owe an enormous debt of gratitude for the support of the directors of our respective museums, Philippe de Montebello and John Leighton.

Since an exhibition focused on the delicacies of drawing materials cannot be realized without the wholehearted cooperation of those privileged to possess and care for such works, we must express our profound appreciation to the public and private lenders generous enough to contribute their own splendid drawings to the exhibition. Their loans enrich selections from the organizing museums, most notably those from the Van Gogh Museum (Vincent van Gogh Foundation), which account for more than one-third of the included works.

The extraordinary resources of the Van Gogh Museum, its collections, archives, libraries, and staff of experts, have been of inestimable value in the realization of this entire effort and are thus deserving of special thanks, especially Edwin Becker, Andreas Blühm, Suzanne Bogman, Monique Hageman, Ellen Jansen, Leo Jansen, Hans Luijten, Alex Nikken, Aly Noordermeer, Fieke Pabst, Patricia Schuil, Frans Stive, Chris Stolwijk, Serge Taal, Anita Vriend, Marije Wissink, and Roelie Zwikker. The curators at the Van Gogh Museum are grateful for the assistance of Denise Willemstein, who fulfilled her job as publication assistant with care.

At the Metropolitan Museum, we have enjoyed the support and commitment of many members of the staff, beginning with the chairmen of the departments responsible for nineteenth-century drawings and paintings, George Goldner and Gary Tinterow. In the publication of this book, we have been blessed with the clear-eyed constancy of our editor Margaret Aspinwall and the talents of Peter Antony, Bruce Campbell, Minjee Cho, Sally Van Devanter, Gwen Roginsky, and Jean Wagner, supported by editor in chief John P. O'Neill. Conservators Marjorie Shelley and Charlotte Hale made invaluable contributions to this project, assisted by Alison Gilchrest and Silvia Centeno. We were most fortunate to have been able to rely on the fine research and administrative skills of Alison Strauber and Kathryn Calley Galitz, and to count on assistance from other colleagues at the Metropolitan, including Susan Bresnan, Jeff Daly, Walter Liedtke, Patrice Mattia, Nina Maruca, Connie Norkin, Rebecca Rabinow, Deborah Vincelli, and Mary Zuber.

For their extraordinary helpfulness, we wish to recognize appreciatively the following individuals: Martin Bailey, Roy S. Berns, Renée Blok, Richard Brettell, David Brooks, Anne Clergue, Gail Davidson, Susan Davidson, Roland Dorn, Elizabeth Easton, Rhoda Eitel-Porter, Walter Feilchenfeldt, Michael Findlay, Jack Flam, Léonard Gianadda, Christine Giviskos, Lee Hendrix, Jan Howard, Ay-Whang Hsia, Dominique-Charles Janssens, Ryan Jensen, Stefan Koldehoff, Toos van Kooten, Elizabeth Kujawski, Diana Kunkel, Marilyn Kushner, Håkan Larsson, Philippe Latourelle, Sarah Lees, Nico Lingbeek, Teio Meedendorp, Charles S. Moffett, Steven Naifeh, Robert Parks, Robert Pettit, Anita Gruetzner Robins, Beate Schreiber, Bogomilia Welsh-Ovcharov, Gregory White Smith, Isabelle Taudière, Jennifer Tonkovich, and Peter Zegers.

Colta Ives, *Curator, Drawings and Prints*
The Metropolitan Museum of Art

Susan Alyson Stein, *Curator, Nineteenth-Century, Modern, and Contemporary Art*
The Metropolitan Museum of Art

Sjraar van Heugten, *Head of Collections*
Van Gogh Museum

Marije Vellekoop, *Curator of Drawings*
Van Gogh Museum

Notes to the Reader

Van Gogh's works are cited by their numbers in the catalogue raisonné De la Faille 1928/1970/1992 (F).

Quotations from the artist's correspondence rely on Van Gogh Letters 1958 and are followed by that publication's numerical designation for the letters enclosed in brackets. Translations have occasionally been modified in the interest of accuracy.

Dates given to the letters in the present volume have been furnished by Leo Jansen and Hans Luijten, who head the Letters Project Research at the Van Gogh Museum and are preparing a definitive edition of the letters for publication in 2008–9, which will incorporate and substantiate these assignments.

Selected exhibitions listed for the works on paper include all known exhibitions before World War I, and thereafter citations are limited to significant international loan shows devoted entirely or in large part to the artist's works. We have not included the many traveling exhibitions generated by the Vincent van Gogh Foundation during the mid-twentieth century; those are listed comprehensively in the entries in collection catalogues of drawings published by the Van Gogh Museum: Van Heugten 1996, Van Heugten 1997, Vellekoop and Van Heugten 2001, and Vellekoop and Zwikker 2006 (forthcoming).

VINCENT VAN GOGH

The Drawings

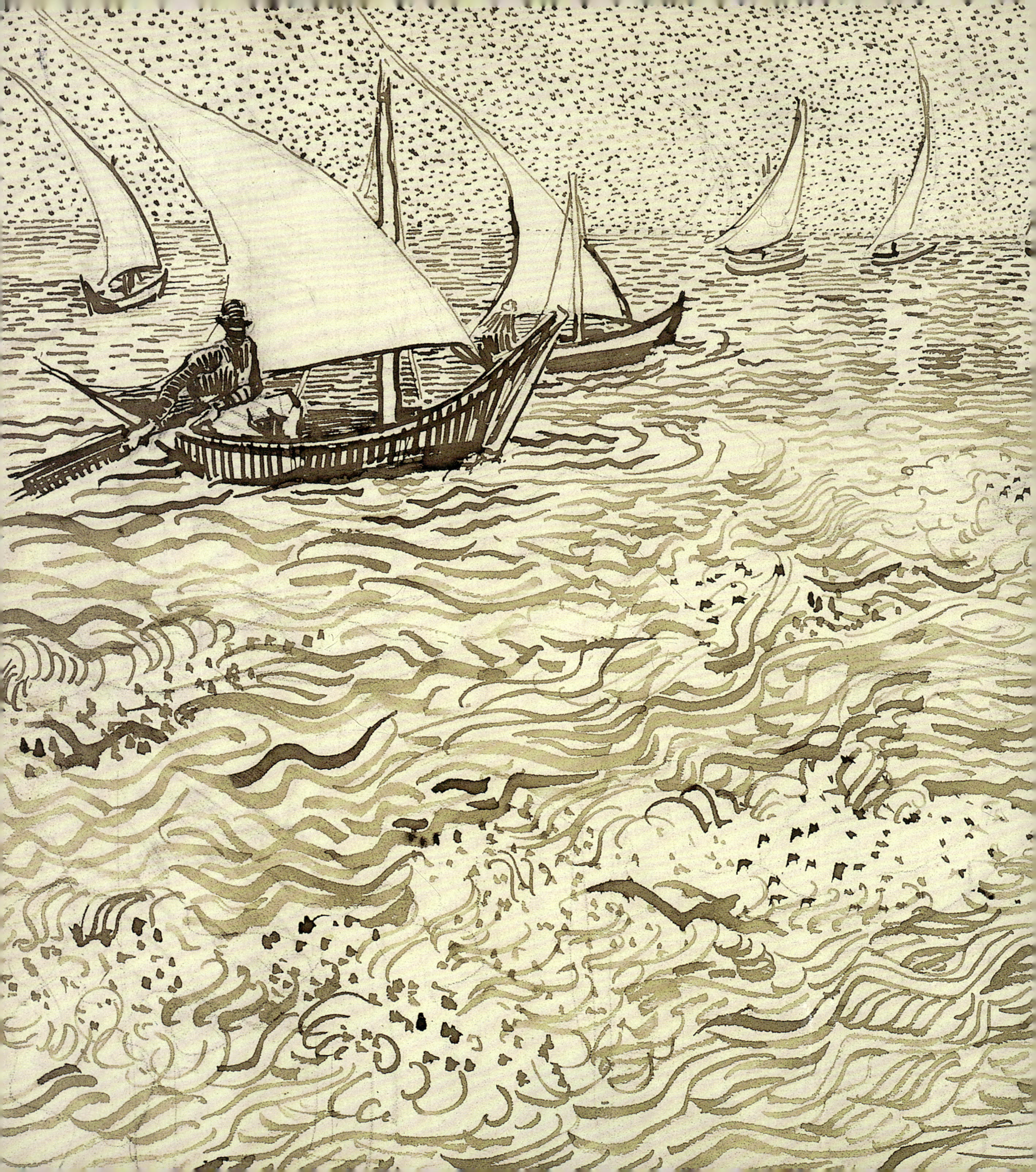

Out of Line: How Van Gogh Made His Mark

COLTA IVES

Drawing is the root of everything.

Vincent van Gogh,
letter to his brother Theo,
June 3, 1883 [290]

Vincent van Gogh (1853–1890) seldom employed the process of drawing in the most traditional way, to outline a painting, but instead pulled it from the periphery to the very center of his work. He was thus prepared to invest greatly in its success. There were periods when he wished to do nothing but draw and times when drawing was expedient: at the outset of his artistic career when he dared not begin to paint; at times, later, when he was between painting campaigns or ran short of oil pigments and canvas; and, near the end of his days, when his doctors thought it unhealthy for him to do otherwise. Sometimes Van Gogh spoke of his drawings as works to be exhibited or marketed, to be presented or exchanged with other artists or friends. But regardless of their stated function, he did not stint. His drawings, like his letters, were, importantly, regular and faithful records of what was on his mind. Often as soon as the ink dried, they sped through the mail to his brother Theo; others were delivered to family and friends to announce his achievements. The reed-pen drawings of finished paintings Van Gogh sent from Arles to Émile Bernard, John Russell, and Theo are at least as exquisite as the oils they announced. They are ingenious in their graphic vocabulary, bold in syntax, and subtly varied in style to suit the recipient or the message—rather like Vincent's handwritten letters where the script sometimes changed from line to line, in tempo with the author's thoughts. Astonishingly inventive, Van Gogh's drawings are an inextricable part of his development as a painter and had a tremendous impact on that outcome.[1]

One must travel far to find an artist whose drawings are so closely intertwined with their paintings as Van Gogh's are, in composition, style, and technique. Spirited pen scribbling crops up every now and then in the history of Western art, interestingly, in port cities with trade routes to the East, like Amsterdam and Venice. But seldom, until well into the nineteenth century, when artists' oil sketches began to be appreciated, was graphic fervor made a dominant constituent not only of drawing but also of painting. Of this trend, Van Gogh is a master.

The enthusiasm for Van Gogh's art is so enormous and his output so large (over 800 paintings; more than 1,100 drawings), it hardly seems possible that his career spanned only a decade and his best work materialized in the space of three years (1887–90). The Dutchman was twenty-seven when he declared his life's pursuit the practice of art. He made the commitment (admittedly) with little talent, but his desire was very great. He had spent time working at Goupil's galleries in The Hague, London, and Paris, but it was only after aborted efforts to be a teacher, a lay preacher, a bookshop assistant, a student of theology, and an evangelist in the Borinage mining district of Belgium that he discovered his true calling: to become an artist.

For the most part self-taught, Van Gogh built a career on the acuity of his vision and the profundity of his faith. His most closely held beliefs were rooted in the religion of his father, a Dutch Reformed pastor, but as orthodoxy dimmed in his mind, he came to embrace Nature rather than the Church as the governing order, the supreme power. Most

Fig. 1. *Boats at Sea, Saintes-Maries-de-la-Mer* (F1430a, cat. 58), detail, left side, showing Van Gogh's penwork held within the edges of his drawing sheet

importantly, Van Gogh believed resolutely in his own personal strengths, which fueled his dogged and solitary pursuit of artistic achievement despite scarce notice of it. Like another hardheaded artist, Paul Gauguin, whose path for some time paralleled his, he was determined to follow his raw instincts, wherever they led him.

Thanks to the law that required instruction in drawing for students in Holland's secondary schools, Van Gogh received some early art training.[2] However, among his juvenile endeavors one finds little to recommend either pupil or teacher. Not much facility and only a rudimentary understanding of the laws of perspective are evident in these earnest appreciations of nature. And yet there is an apparent fascination with making marks and an effect that is somehow haunting (fig. 2).

For the most part, Van Gogh steered clear of art academies and instead thumbed through art manuals for basic instruction, from time to time seeking the advice of other artists. The distinctive style of his production thus developed largely outside the mainstream. A voracious reader, he picked up ideas from texts and looked hungrily at pictures wherever he went. Without doubt, his greatest resource was his visual memory. By the time he began to think of himself as an artist, he had already developed an enviable grasp of the history of art, the result of visits to museums and galleries in cities in which he lived and reinforced by his handling of reproductions of artworks while in the employ of the Goupil firm, then the most active publisher and distributor of reproductive prints in Europe. Van Gogh had an insatiable appetite for prints and magazine illustrations, especially those whose gritty realism mirrored the miseries of the downtrodden. He recalled that, as an apprentice art dealer in London, he "used to go every week to the show windows of the printing offices of the *Graphic* and the *London News* to see the new issues. . . . [T]he drawings are [still] clear in my mind . . . my enthusiasm for those things is rather stronger than it was even then" [R20].[3]

Having been apprenticed to the pulpit, Van Gogh found his first ambition as an artist was to preach. He saw the possibilities of performing this activity by pictorial means and therefore resolved to become an illustrator for magazines and newspapers where he could address the masses with sympathy for their plight. Taking the traditional path laid for the instruction of artists, he began his practice by drawing in chalk, pencil, and pen, with the thought of progressing from there to the production of prints. For a few months in 1882 and 1883, he drew on treated paper with a lithographic crayon ("an excellent material"),

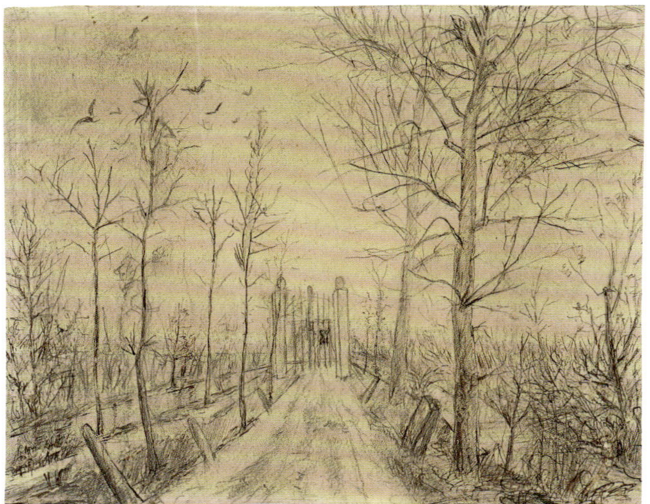

Fig. 2. *A Gated Driveway* (F836r), 1872–73. Pen and brown ink and graphite, 18.3 x 22.4 cm ($7\frac{1}{4}$ x $8\frac{7}{8}$ in.). Van Gogh Museum, Amsterdam (Vincent van Gogh Foundation)

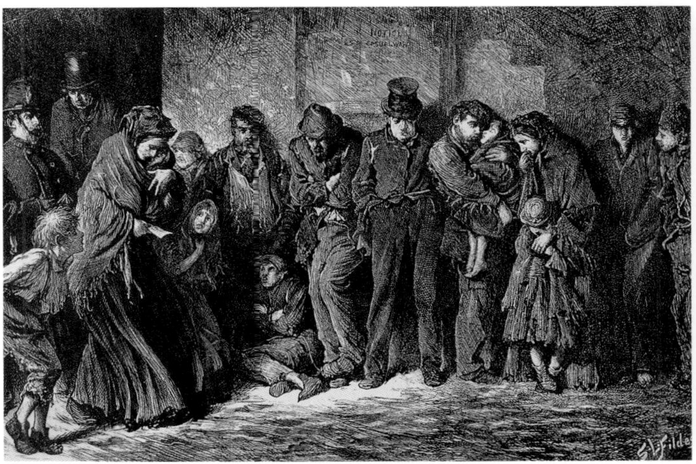

Fig. 3. Luke Fildes, *Houseless and Hungry*. Wood engraving. *Graphic*, December 4, 1869, from Van Gogh's collection of magazine illustrations. Van Gogh Museum, Amsterdam (Vincent van Gogh Foundation)

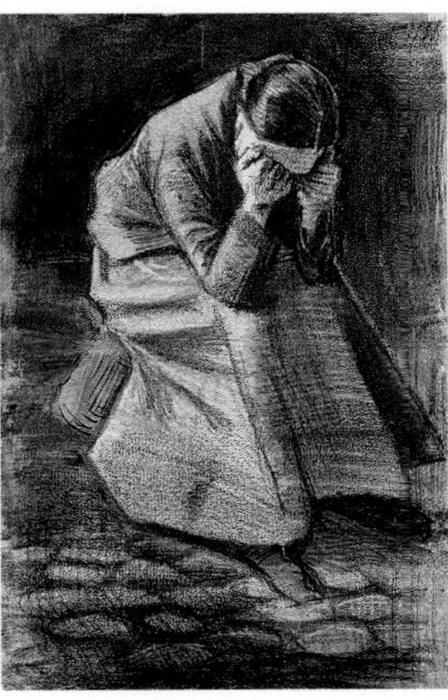

Fig. 4. *Woman Seated with Her Head in Her Hands* (F1069), 1883. Black chalk, heightened with white, 49 x 30.5 cm (19¼ x 12 in.). The Art Institute of Chicago

which allowed him to produce eight transfer prints, but he ventured only one further lithograph, a copy of his painting *The Potato Eaters* (F82, fig. 88) in 1885.[4] Some of Van Gogh's earliest efforts were modeled on engravings clipped from periodicals that he had stashed in portfolios. From these dark images rendered in an abbreviated system of marks that assured their survival in the mangle of industrial presses he adopted a distinct phraseology and pathos (see figs. 3, 4).

But mastery of the human figure did not come easily to Van Gogh and he met with continual frustration. "What is drawing?" he asked. "How does one learn it? It is working through an invisible iron wall that seems to stand between what one *feels* and what one *can do.* How is one to get through that wall—since pounding at it is of no use? In my opinion one has to undermine that wall, filing through it steadily and patiently" [237]. Perhaps seeking to fortify his efforts, Van Gogh at first populated his work with impoverished people, heroically surviving their backbreaking labor and hardscrabble lives. He saw the portrayal of peasants by Jean-François Millet and Jules Breton as a great innovation in contemporary art, redressing the failure of earlier masters to convey a reality that was basic and therefore profound.

In 1880, soon after launching his art career, Van Gogh made a pilgrimage to the village of Courrières, where the peasant-painter Breton lived, a visit he recalled as a turning point, for although he retraced his steps without venturing to call on the master, he decided then and there to devote himself to drawing [136]. His draftsmanship still lacked fluency and control, nonetheless he set as his goal the portrayal of workingmen and -women in ways that might measure up to the monumental drawings of Breton whose "genius," he said, like Millet's, "may be equaled, but it is impossible to surpass it" [241] (see figs. 5, 7).

From the start, Millet's staunch celebration of routine rural life proved to be the most profound and enduring influence on Van Gogh, for it was forthright in its focus on the toils of individuals and, at the same time, reflective of grander truths—earthy and yet ethereal. At both the beginning and toward the end of his career he made quantities of copies and variants of Millet's compositions, inspired by their content and by their openhandedness.[5]

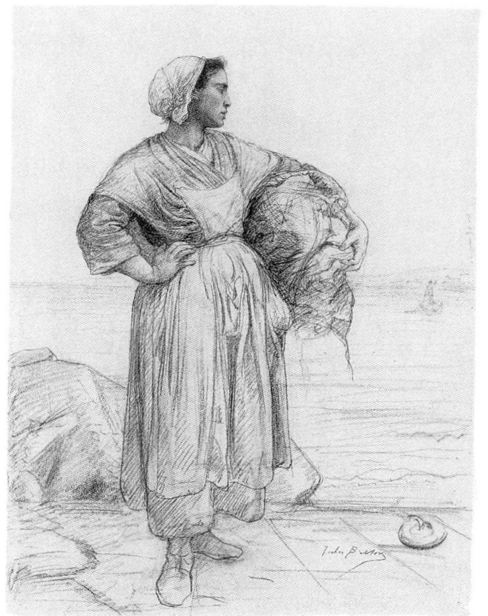

Fig. 5. Jules Breton, *A Breton Peasant Woman*, ca. 1870. Black chalk, 61.1 x 45.7 cm (24 x 18 in.). Private collection

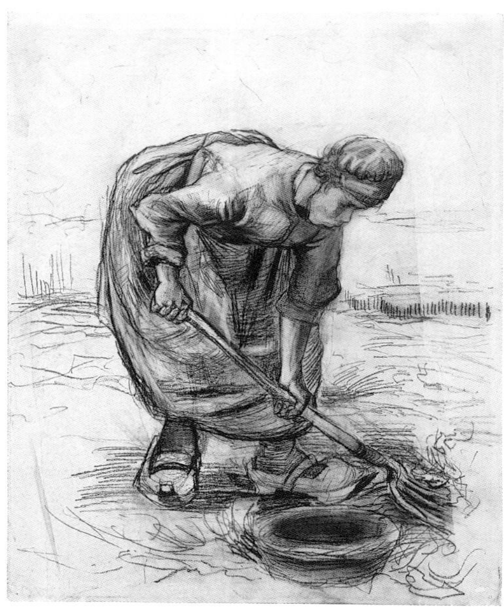

Fig. 6. *Peasant Woman Lifting Potatoes* (F1251), 1885. Black chalk, 49.2 x 40.2 cm (19 3/8 x 15 7/8 in.). Van Gogh Museum, Amsterdam (Vincent van Gogh Foundation)

Millet's reputation reached a high point just after his death in 1875. That year, Van Gogh saw the Gavet Collection of Millet's drawings prior to their sale in Paris and declared the exhibition "Holy Ground" [29]. He may also have seen the show of Millet's etchings at the Galeries Durand-Ruel the following March. By then, he had begun a collection of Millet's prints, which in 1880 totaled nearly fifty items. He tacked them to the walls of his Paris apartment and, later, his studio in Arles.

To jump-start his career as an artist, Van Gogh relied heavily on Millet's example, initially copying his compositions *The Diggers, The Angelus,* and *The Sower,* in which farmers plodded through work or stood silent as trees (see fig. 7). Van Gogh made it his own business to draw ditchdiggers, woodcutters, and farmers working the soil as if their lives depended upon it. And when he drew them plunging their hands into the earth, he did so with gestural efforts to match theirs and with

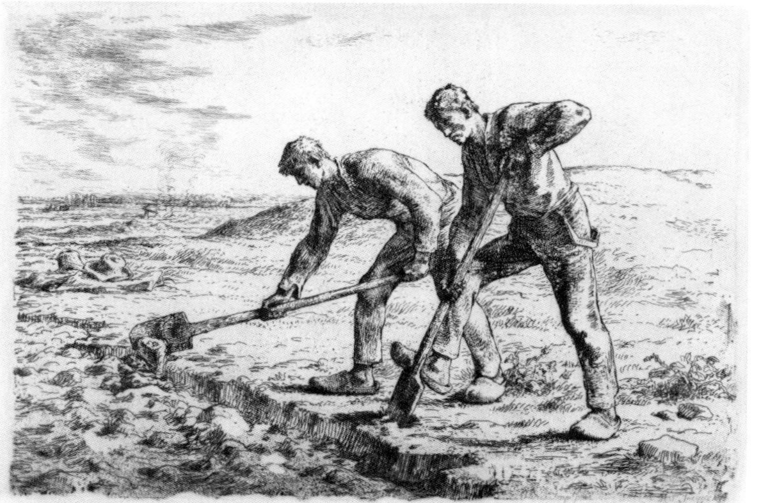

Fig. 7. Jean-François Millet, *The Diggers*, ca. 1855. Etching, 23.7 x 33.7 cm (9 5/16 x 13 1/4 in.). The Metropolitan Museum of Art, New York, Gift of Theodore de Witt, 1923 (23.65.12)

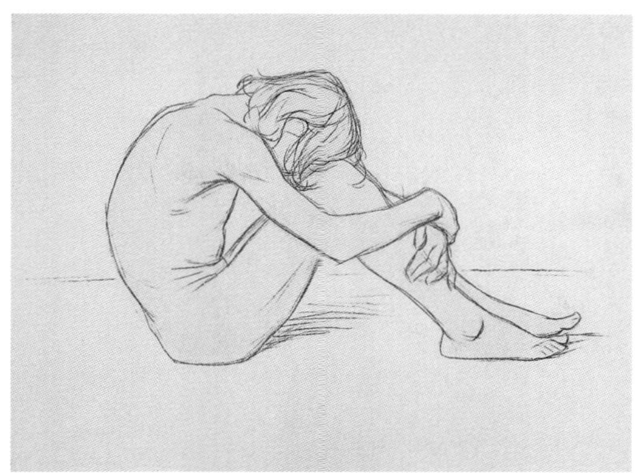

Fig. 8. Charles Bargue, *Boy Seated on the Ground, His Head on His Knees.* Lithograph. *Cours de dessin* (Paris, ca. 1873), pl. 24

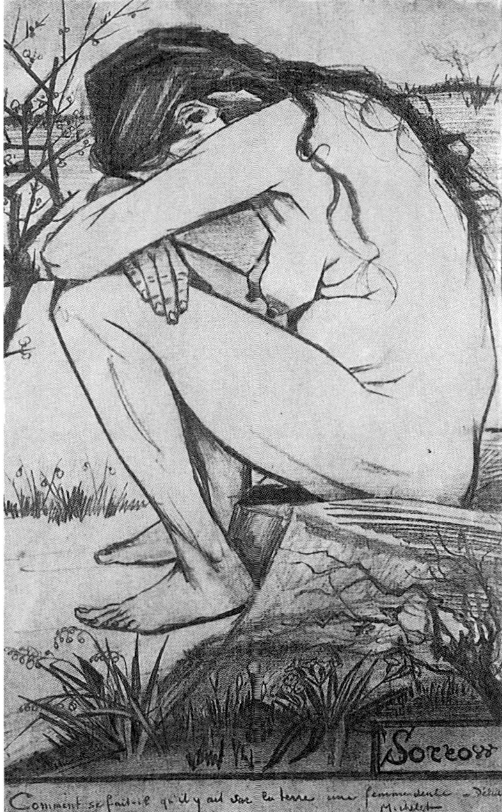

Fig. 9. *Sorrow* (F929a), 1882. Black chalk, 44.5 x 27 cm (17 1/2 x 10 5/8 in.). The New Art Gallery, Walsall, England

deep satisfaction in his own manual labor. He took pride in his self-proclaimed "dirty and difficult trade" [W1] and declared himself "delighted" to be mistaken for "an ironmonger" [442]. He meant to "paint peasants as if one were one of them, as if one felt and thought as they do" [404].

While Van Gogh avoided a regular course of formal instruction, he still felt bound to follow the traditional path by which artists had trained since the Renaissance, by learning first to draw and convincingly represent the human figure. But with live and willing models hard to find and costly to hire, Van Gogh was forced to teach himself. This he did by studying pictures and reading books. So important to him were a clutch of how-to manuals for artists that he continued to consult them right up to his final days—still hoping to improve his draftsmanship and holding fast to the conviction that in order to paint, an artist first needed to know how to draw.[6]

At the very outset of his career, and certainly by September of 1880, Van Gogh began to copy pictures from Charles Bargue's instructive *Cours de dessin,* which he had borrowed from the art dealer Tersteeg, a family friend. The volumes of large lithographs, published by Van Gogh's former employer Goupil and Company in the 1860s and 1870s, included exercises for drawing various parts of the body and for copying plaster casts, the works of old masters, as well as Bargue's own lithographs of nudes in various postures (fig. 8).[7] The aspiring artist worked through the exercises three times between 1880 and 1881. Nearly a decade later, in 1890, by then in Auvers, he requested delivery of Bargue's *Exercices au fusain* so he could run through them once more. Thus, only months before his death, Van Gogh was still trying to master the art of drawing according to academic practice.

The effects of Bargue's drawing course on Van Gogh seem to have been mixed. One result was that he trained himself to copy images graphically, a skill he later came to use frequently to translate his own paintings into works in pen and ink. Although at the time, he reported, "my hand and my mind are growing daily more supple and strong" [136], he appears to have gained rather little in confidence and command of the human figure. The sense of achievement he felt a short time later in having drawn convincingly the nude body of his lover, Sien (fig. 9)—"the best figure I have drawn yet" [186]—was apparently an isolated experience and brief. Having acknowledged "the great importance of the outline," he had taken "a great deal of trouble to make progress in that respect" [221]. And yet, four years later, weary and frustrated in his practice, he was prepared to abandon academic figure study and the restrictive dictates of drawing contours. A short stint of instruction in Antwerp during the winter of 1885–86 proved particularly exasperating, not least on account of the "nagging of those fellows at the academy" and their repeated insistence that one must "*prendre par le contour.*" "How flat, how lifeless and how insipid the results of that system are," Van Gogh declared, as he resigned himself to the bottom rung of the class, "because all the drawings of the others are exactly alike, and mine is absolutely different" [452].

More comfortable in Van Gogh's hands was the freer drawing style of Eugène Delacroix that relied, as the Greeks supposedly had, on building living forms from energy-charged masses. During the spring of 1885, Vincent wrote to Theo that he was "busy putting into practice, on the drawing of a hand and an arm, what Delacroix said about drawings: 'Ne pas prendre par la ligne mais par le milieu' [Work not from the outlines, but from the center]." Now, halfway through his decade-long career, Van Gogh understood his own art would have to be defined in ways other than realistic description. "And what I try to acquire," he explained to Theo, "is not to draw a *hand* but the *gesture,* not a mathematically correct head, but the general *expression.* For instance, when a digger looks up and sniffs the wind or speaks. In short, *life*" [408].

Perhaps because he believed it a professional imperative, Van Gogh remained committed to the study of the human figure throughout his career, even though he recognized the limits of his success. Certainly disappointed at his failure to render human beings as convincingly as an aspiring illustrator might have wished, he alternatively found in picturing landscape a way to consider the plights of humankind symbolically. Enduring ties between the land and the living were evidenced everywhere before him, and he saw "how the life and death of the peasants remain forever the same, budding and withering regularly, like the grass and the flowers" [411]. "Sometimes I have such a longing to do landscape," he wrote Theo, "just as I crave a long walk to refresh myself; and in all nature . . . I see expression and soul. . . . A row of pollard willows sometimes resembles a procession of almshouse men . . . the trodden grass at the roadside looks tired and dusty like the people of the slums" [242].

Van Gogh's avowed pursuit of the "expression" of life became realized in his depiction of landscape as a reflection of nature's enduring cycles. Grander, in every sense, than the individual, the landscape was ever present, universal, and with a perpetually renewing face. For an artist too short of cash to purchase costly oil paints and canvas or to hire human models, the landscape stood still, just outside the window or down the road, to be described on a sheet of paper with a pencil, a stick of chalk, or pen and ink. Landscape was, moreover, a singularly accommodating subject for an artist set on expressing abstract ideas.

Seeking rules to direct his practice, Van Gogh at first clung to lessons of perspective learned from books. Often guiding his hand were Armand Cassagne's manuals, first mentioned in the artist's letters in the spring of 1881 [146] and still a subject of comment seven years later when Van Gogh declared the *Abécédaire du dessin* "the *only* really practical book I know" [519]. Cassagne's method of studying motifs through a perspective frame—a rectangular opening divided into sections by strings—became the backbone of

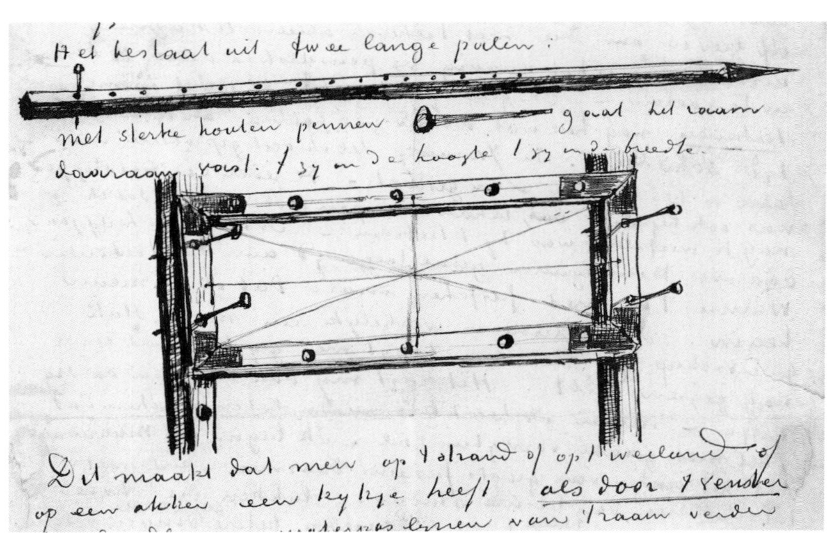

Fig. 10. *The Artist's Perspective Frame.* Pen-and-ink sketch in a letter to Theo van Gogh, August 5 or 6, 1882 [223]. Van Gogh Museum, Amsterdam (Vincent van Gogh Foundation)

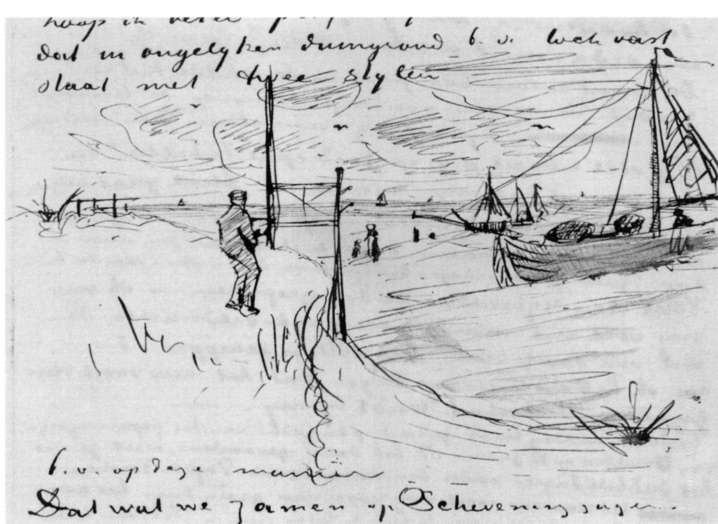

Fig. 11. *The Artist's Perspective Frame Installed by the Sea.* Pen-and-ink sketch in a letter to Theo van Gogh, August 5, 1882 [222]. Van Gogh Museum, Amsterdam (Vincent van Gogh Foundation)

Van Gogh's landscape study. Within the first year of his career and until at least the spring of 1888, he regularly employed a perspective frame made with the help of a blacksmith according to Cassagne's specifications. "So on the shore or in the meadows or in the fields one can look through it like a window," Vincent enthusiastically explained to Theo, illustrating the frame and its use in two 1882 letters: "I think you can imagine how delightful it is to turn this 'spy-hole' frame on the sea, on the green meadows, or on the snowy fields in winter, or on the fantastic network of thin and thick branches and trunks in autumn or on a stormy day" [223] (figs. 10, 11).

For six years the perspective frame anchored Van Gogh's gaze as it wandered over land and sea in Holland, Belgium, and France, regularly focusing his vision and organizing prospects into pictures. The frame's constant structure was a blessing. Without it, the artist might never have pulled together coherently and quite so tightly all the vagrant strands of energy he felt within himself and perceived threaded through nature. In a very early drawing of the placid waters of a marsh teeming with reeds, lily pads, and a clump of iris, he seems to have been striving frantically to convey the hum of life (fig. 12). One discovers, in even such early, halting landscape drawings, traits that characterize Van Gogh's latest, spontaneously cursive ones. His impulse appears to have been to blanket a sheet with marks, but to do so strictly within its limits, a keen awareness of the paper's edges holding penwork within bounds, like a charged fence. However, at this stage, the sum of his strokes represented little more than its many parts: merely a map of someplace, with no particular point given to go there.

How staggering the leap to seven years hence when, that summer of 1888 in Arles, everything clicked. There arose certitude, a system, a master plan guiding Van Gogh's hand, so that in his drawings, every element had a place of its own and was inextricably tied to the rest. By this time and for the most part, he had freed himself from dependence on the perspective frame, but in nearly all the years in between, it had trained him to find geometry underpinning every sight, to target the center of an image and tether it to its boundaries.

Even after Van Gogh gave up the perspective frame, he must have retained in his mind's eye the imprint of its strictures. But absent the device that had for so long intervened between his vision and the view, he was freed to establish a new and more immediate relationship with the object of his fascination and the canvas or paper on which he painted or drew. Reporting to Theo his sense of release in drawing the fishing boats on the beach at Saintes-Maries (F1428, cat. 60) without the usual safety net and in only "*an hour,*" Vincent marveled that this had been "done without measuring, just by letting my pen go" [500]. The discovery that he could draw "just by letting [his] pen go" was not only exhilarating but empowering, for in the two months that followed—July and August—the artist made nearly all of his greatest drawings.

Van Gogh often stated a desire to project in his drawings a "manliness," a vigor that, conveyed however awkwardly, would be so energetic that it would strike the viewer with force. When he started to draw, he told his brother, "I hope I shall be able to make some drawings with something human in them" [136], a thought he later expanded, insisting, "I want to progress so far that people will say of my work, He feels deeply, he feels tenderly—notwithstanding my so-called roughness, perhaps even because of it" [218]. Acknowledging the "rough" nature of his drawings, Van Gogh strove to make this characteristic a virtue, declaring, "I with my draftsman's fist [am] willing to work" [157].

Determined to express feelings about his subjects rather than simply picture them, Van Gogh chose coarse and tactile materials that would reinforce such an effort: carpenter's pencil, charcoal, and fabricated chalk. In the spring of 1883 he was glad to discover "black mountain chalk," which he called "gypsy crayon," in admiration of its dark and dramatic fluidity: "There is a soul and life in that crayon. . . . [It] knows what I want, it listens with intelligence and obeys . . ." [272]. And,

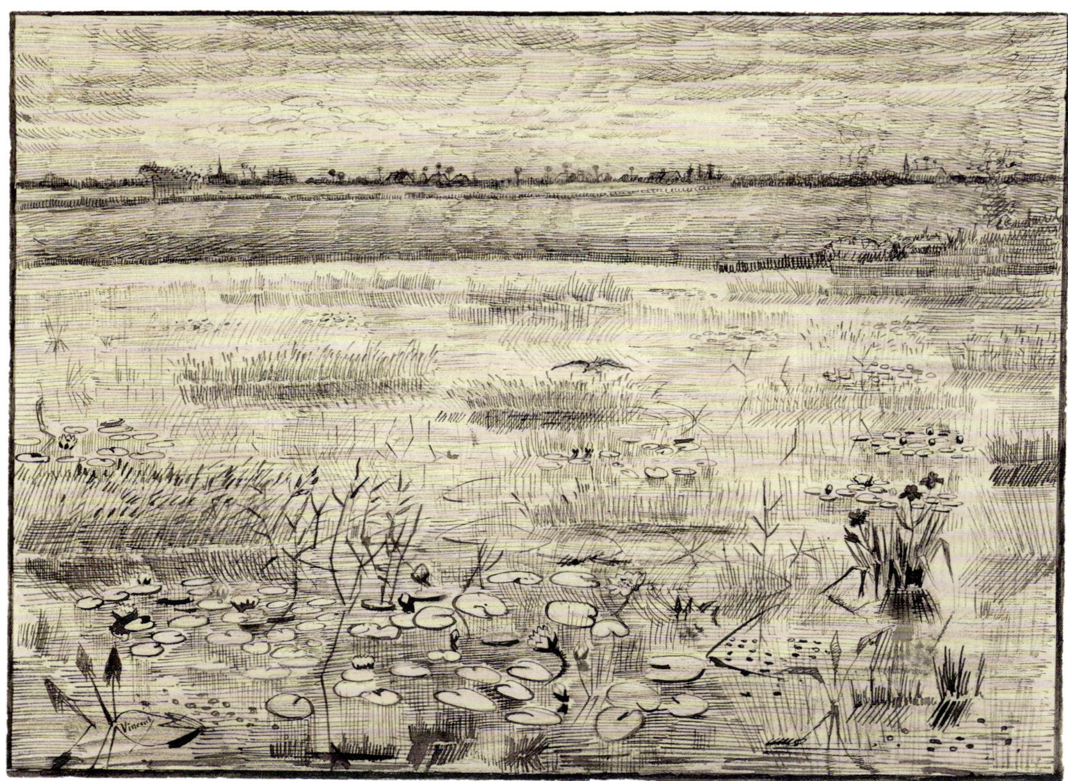

Fig. 12. *Marsh with Water Lilies* (F845), June 1881. Pen and ink over graphite, 23.5 x 31.4 cm (9¼ x 12⅜ in.). Virginia Museum of Fine Arts, Richmond, Collection of Mr. and Mrs. Paul Mellon (photo: Katherine Wetzel)

in Provence, encountering the local hollow-barreled grass that he found could be sharpened with a penknife "the way you would a goose quill" [478], Van Gogh adopted a drawing instrument entirely sympathetic to his needs: easy to acquire and use, bold and incisive in its statement.

In La Fontaine's *Fables,* the reed, unlike the oak tree, knew how to bend and thus survived the storm. In Van Gogh's hands, the reed bowed to an artist's urgency to fix an image while the experience of it still hung in the air. The reed pen allowed Van Gogh to draw pictures as freely as he penned thoughts in handwritten letters, fulfilling his persistent desire to report graphically what passed before his mind and eye. His vast production of letters and drawings suggests this was a very powerful compulsion. Indeed, experts in the symptoms of temporal-lobe epilepsy, the condition from which doctors believe Van Gogh suffered, have a term for such impulses: hypergraphia.[8] Even if he was no more hyper in his mark making than many a great artist, Van Gogh expressed himself graphically in especially distinctive ways, and his marks, their character, their rhythms are riveting. A fully worked drawing from the apex of his productivity presents a virtual fireworks of hatches, dots, and curlicues, methodically dispersed to the farthest edges of the paper, to hover there or recoil, just short of crossing bounds (see fig. 1).

The reed pen encouraged Van Gogh, as it had Rembrandt, Delacroix, and innumerable draftsmen since the beginning of recorded time, to execute simple and bold designs. Its knife-cut tip creates blunt, emphatic lines, but it runs out of ink quickly. It is thus useful only for brief and rapidly made marks, a limitation innately preferable to an artist who admired the dashed strokes with which Hals and Rembrandt finished their paintings and who himself wished "to draw, quick as lightning" [223]. Working swiftly, a draftsman could show spontaneity and shorten the gap between perception and execution. Accurate description would thus become pointless, where awkwardness and distortion carried far greater force.

Van Gogh began justifying "clumsiness" in his work relatively early in his career, reporting to fellow painter Anthon van Rappard that it was "not accidental but . . . *reasoned out* and *willed*" [R37]. More and more convinced of the value of the awkwardness he saw in his own pictures, he told Van Rappard in 1884. "I most decidedly expect that, as I gain in what I will call expressive force, people will not say *less* frequently, but on the contrary *even more* frequently, that I have *no* technique. . . . What I am expressing in my present work will have to be expressed more *vigorously* . . . but I don't care a damn whether my language is in conformity with that of the grammarians" [R43].

At the same time, however, Van Gogh the aspiring illustrator continued to make drawings carefully executed to approximate the appearance of prints, using a quill to lay in masses of finely penned lines like the hatching that creates tonal variation in etchings and engravings. Only after switching from quill pen to reed in Provence did he successfully inject into his designs the purposely rough, unstudied quality that became the primary source of their power, transforming otherwise static scenes into charged fields. Respecting the quirkiness of each mark and giving it room to be recognized, he came to appreciate and finally achieve that balance between blank paper and black lines that characterizes the superlative reed-pen drawings of his fellow countryman Rembrandt (fig. 16).

Van Gogh paid respect to the greatest of the old Dutch masters, whom he called "the magician of magicians" [442], throughout his life—in pictures he copied after Rembrandt and in frequent mention of the artist in his letters. He wrote of hanging Rembrandt's prints on his walls in Paris [30] and The Hague [213] and of visiting the Trippenhuis in Amsterdam to see the painter's etchings [110]. Initially, it

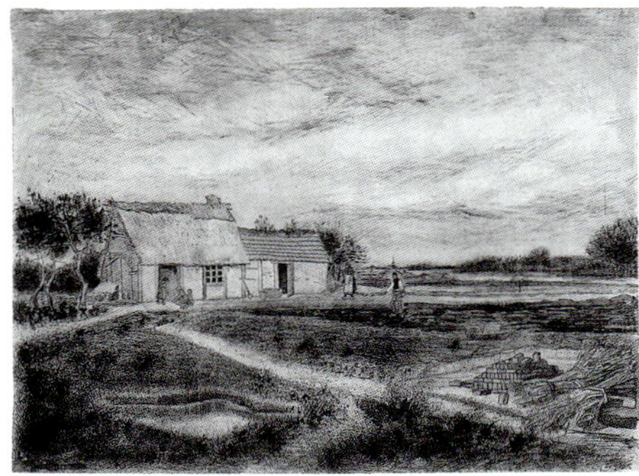

Fig. 13. *A Cottage on the Heath and "the Protestant barn"* (F842), 1881. Pen and ink, graphite, and paint, 47.3 x 62 cm (18⅝ x 24⅜ in.). Museum Boijmans Van Beuningen, Rotterdam

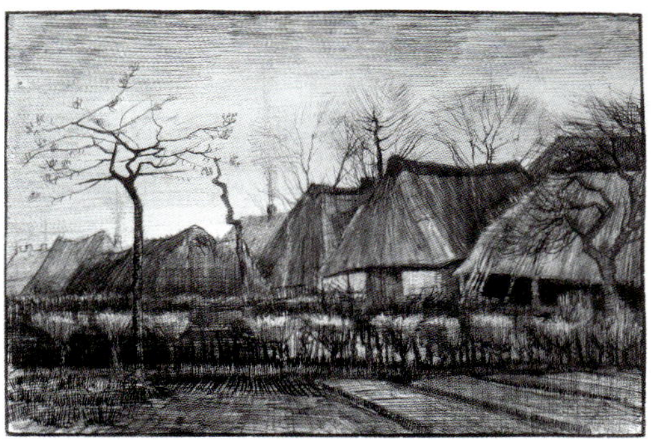

Fig. 14. *Houses with Thatched Roofs* (F1242, cat. 24)

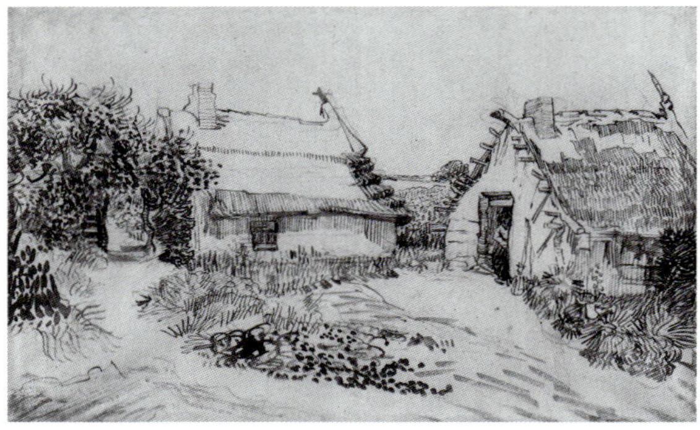

Fig. 15. *Two Cottages, Saintes-Maries-de-la-Mer* (F1440, cat. 48)

was the spirituality in Rembrandt's pictures that attracted his awe [133]; later, as he struggled to find his own way as an artist, he praised not only the master's "noble sentiment," but also his "fiery hand" [426].[9]

Van Gogh, however, was no Rembrandt. Not for long did he care to probe or caress his subjects with brush or pen, nor did he study patiently the singularity of their features or frame of mind. He strove instead to capture the sizzle of his own gaze. He admired Rembrandt, as he did Delacroix, Daumier, and Millet, for the quality of hand that conveyed a profound and forceful spirit.

It is fascinating to follow the arc of Van Gogh's evolving, increasingly iconoclastic graphic style from its tentative beginnings to the heights of daring and resolve, then the final, dizzying tumble—knowing that he remained conflicted all along about the worth of drawing by the rules (figs. 13–15, 17–19). In fact, by the time Van Gogh picked up pen and brush, constraints governing the practices of drawing and painting had long been under siege and the rebels continued to gain. By midcentury, the freewheeling drawings of Delacroix and Daumier were already famously inspiring, as they soon became also to Van Gogh. A spirit of revolt (not only political) had taken hold, encouraging the individual artist's free expression. Moreover, the verisimilitude offered by newfangled photography prodded

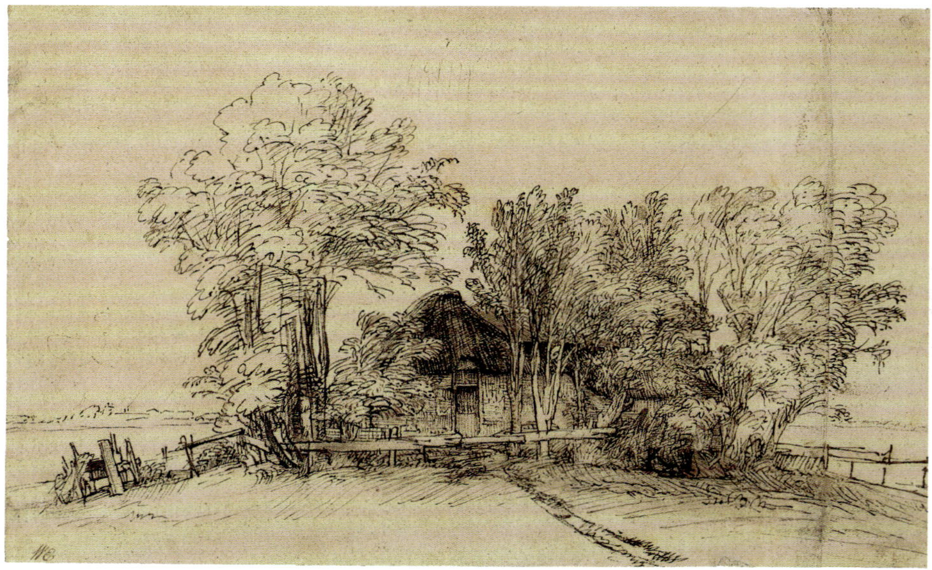

Fig. 16. Rembrandt van Rijn, *Cottage among Trees*, 1648–50. Pen and brown ink, brush and brown wash, 17.1 x 30.8 cm (6¾ x 12⅛ in.). The Metropolitan Museum of Art, New York, H. O. Havemeyer Collection, Bequest of Mrs. H. O. Havemeyer, 1929 (29.100.939) (photo: Malcolm Varon)

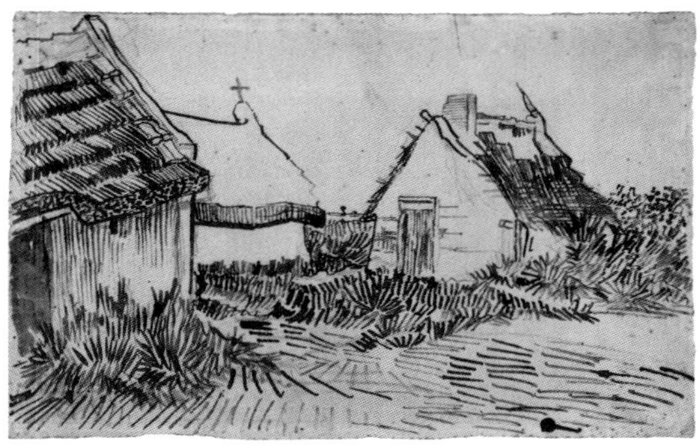

Fig. 17. *Three Cottages, Saintes-Maries-de-la-Mer* (F1438, cat. 49)

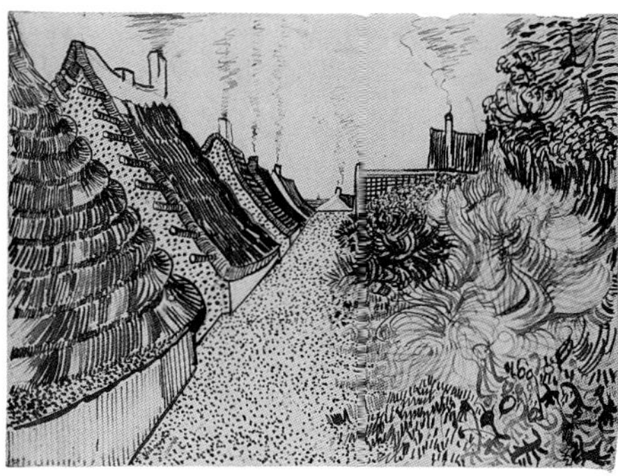

Fig. 18. *Street in Saintes-Maries-de-la-Mer* (F1435, cat. 53)

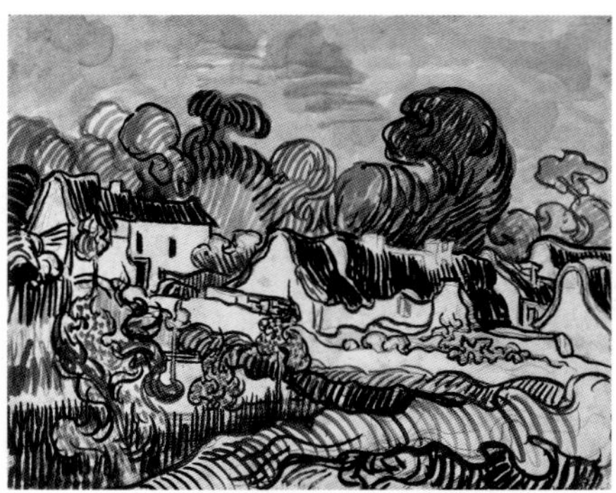

Fig. 19. *Landscape with Houses* (F1640r, cat. 118)

artists to create pictures in ways that mechanical devices could not. (Realistic exactitude could be left behind, for the camera.) Meanwhile, Victor Hugo began fashioning drawings from accidental ink blots, and toward the end of the century, Seurat and Signac experimented in making drawings out of dots. Always a somewhat sloppy draftsman, Manet had been pronounced a failure by his teacher, but he nonetheless turned into France's first great modern master. The academic painter who was his instructor, Thomas Couture, forbade his students to paint until they drew figures and folded drapery perfectly, and he expelled Manet from the studio, predicting, "You will never be anything more than another Daumier."[10]

Van Gogh's downright modern drawing style first saw light of day in his landscapes, probably because open-air vistas lend themselves more readily to abstraction than do, say, portraiture or figure studies. Indeed, in the nineteenth century, a liberal handling of landscape became increasingly the norm. Underscoring their affection for the complex glories of the simple countryside, painters of the Barbizon school—Millet, Charles-François Daubigny, Camille Corot, and Théodore Rousseau—scribbled unrestrainedly to indicate the lay of the land, foliar shapes and densities, the shimmer of atmosphere at sunset, or on starlit nights (figs. 20, 21). Even more dramatically than that first generation

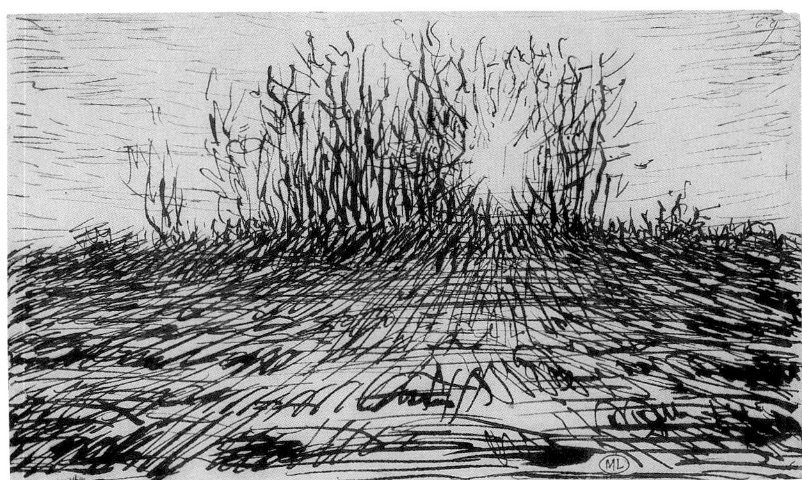

Fig. 20. Jean-François Millet, *Sunset through the Trees*, ca. 1870–74. Pen and brown ink, 9 x 15 cm (3½ x 6 in.). Musée du Louvre, Paris (photo: Michèle Bellot—RMN / Art Resource, NY)

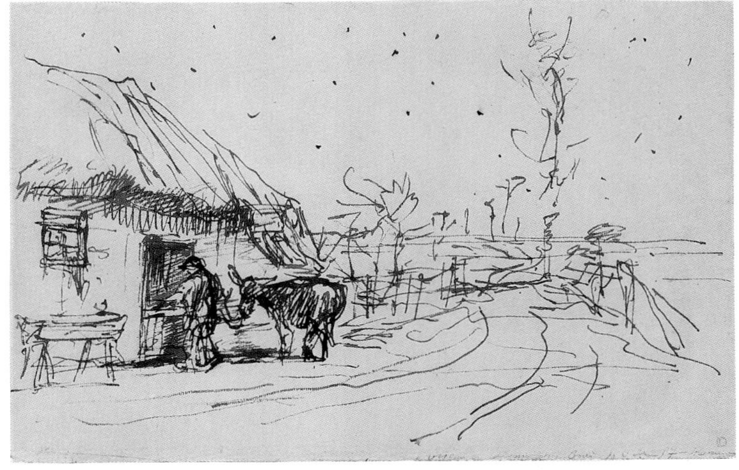

Fig. 21. Charles-François Daubigny, *A Peasant with a Donkey Returning Home on a Starry Night*, ca. 1860. Pen and brown ink, 24.2 x 37.3 cm (9½ x 14⅝ in.). Private collection

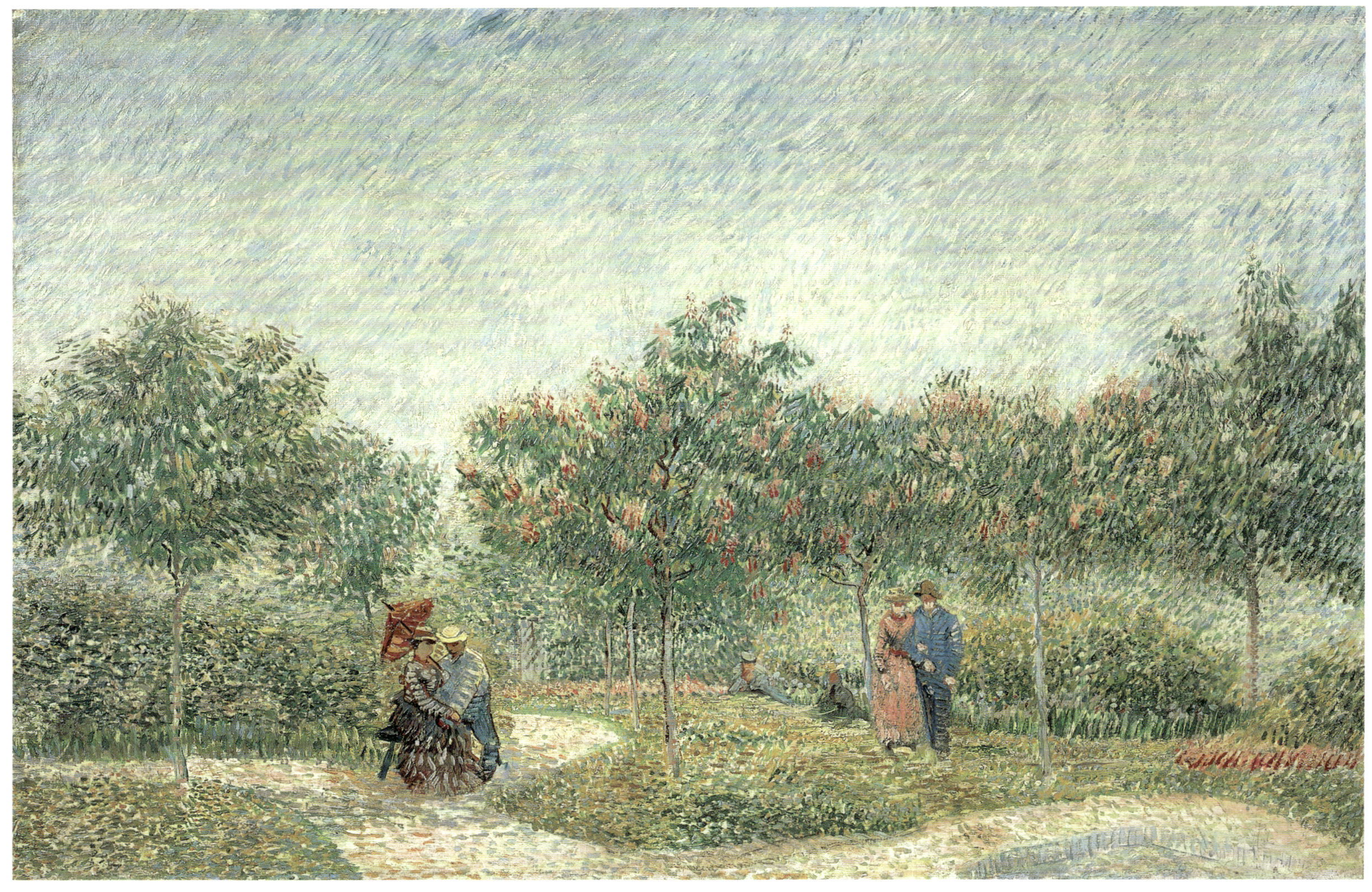

Fig. 22. *The Voyer d'Argenson Park, Asnières* (F314), 1887. Oil on canvas. Van Gogh Museum, Amsterdam (Vincent van Gogh Foundation)

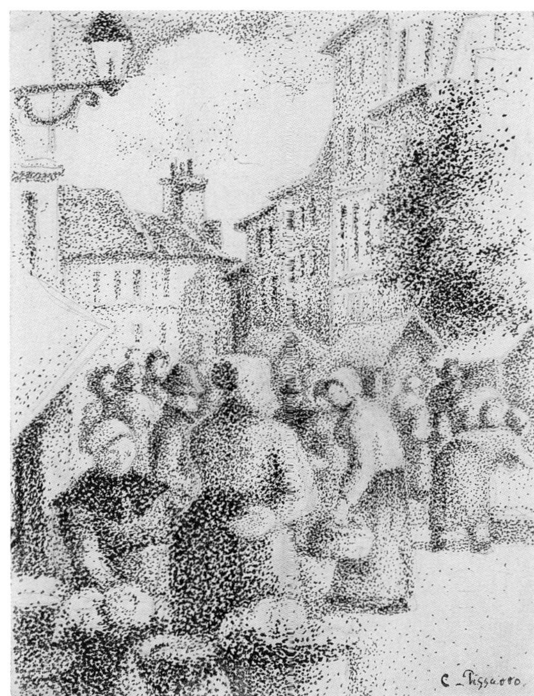

Fig. 24. Camille Pissarro, *Market Place in Pontoise*, 1886. Pen and ink over graphite, 16.8 x 12.7 cm (6⅝ x 5 in.). The Metropolitan Museum of Art, New York, Robert Lehman Collection, 1975 (1975.1.679) (photo: Schecter Lee)

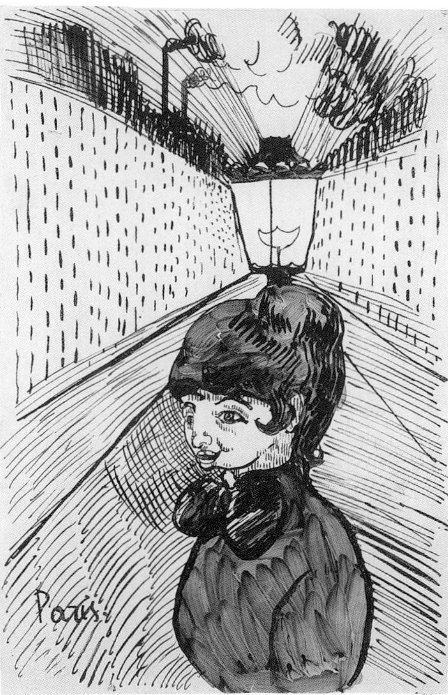

Fig. 25. Émile Bernard, *Girl in a Paris Street*, 1887–88 (probably sent to Van Gogh in April 1888). Pen and ink, 31 x 19.9 cm (12¼ x 7⅞ in.). Van Gogh Museum, Amsterdam (Vincent van Gogh Foundation)

of campstool painters, the Impressionists declared almost complete technical freedom and proceeded straight to painting landscapes without bothering to sketch them first, a shortcut that surely endeared them to Van Gogh. However, arriving in Paris in 1886, he had to admit, "I did not even know what the impressionists were" [459a]. When his brother Theo, who was an art dealer, introduced him to their work, Vincent at first was "bitterly disappointed," thinking the pictures "slovenly, ugly, badly painted, badly drawn, bad in color, everything that's miserable" [W4]. Yet, once inside their sphere, he saw "what is to be gained is *progress* . . . " [459a].

During the two years he spent in Paris (1886–88), sharing an apartment in Montmartre with Theo, Vincent eagerly absorbed all he could by visiting exhibitions and rubbing elbows with artists of his generation, including Paul Gauguin and fellow pupils in Cormon's studio, Henri de Toulouse-Lautrec, Louis Anquetin, and Émile Bernard. He saw the eighth and final group exhibition of the Impressionists and witnessed the launching of Neo-Impressionism by Seurat and Signac. Allying himself with the avant-garde in Paris, Van Gogh let social realism slide from his agenda and focused his sights instead on the city and its suburbs, mainly the latter, where he could find scenery that reminded him of home. He discarded the gloom of his peasant pictures and overcast landscapes and took up a much brighter palette. As most of the Impressionists had done, he put aside his practice of drawing and, in painting, adopted a shortened, semigraphic stroke close to that of the Neo-Impressionists, who strove to impose order over the "messy" brushwork of the Impressionists (fig. 22). The impulse to manufacture art according to a system prompted Seurat to draw in ways that did not reveal his hand—in layers of conté crayon on pebbly-surfaced paper (fig. 23), while Signac and

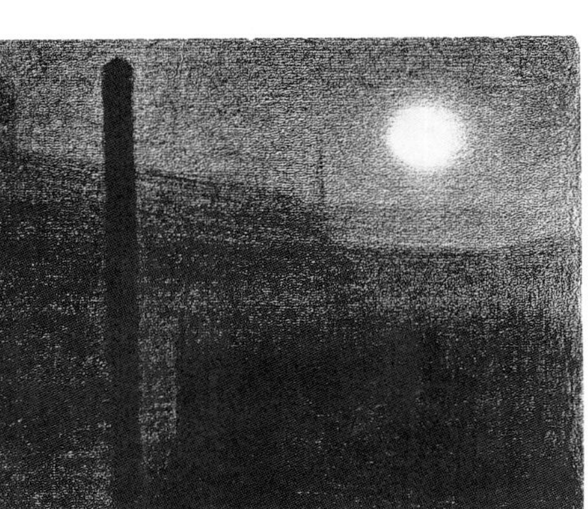

Fig. 23. Georges Seurat, *Courbevoie: Factories by Moonlight*, 1882–83 (exhibited, Salon des Indépendants, Paris, 1886). Conté crayon, 23.6 x 31.1 cm (9$^{5}/_{16}$ x 12¼ in.). The Metropolitan Mueum of Art, New York, Gift of Alexander and Grégoire Tarnopol, 1976 (1976.243)

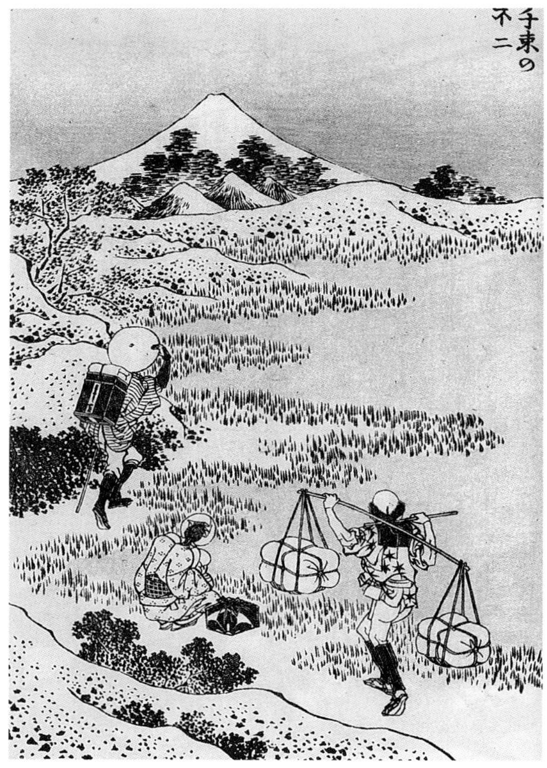

Fig. 26. Katsushika Hokusai, *Fuji from Senzoku.* Woodcut. *One Hundred Views of Mount Fuji,* ca. 1835, no. 98

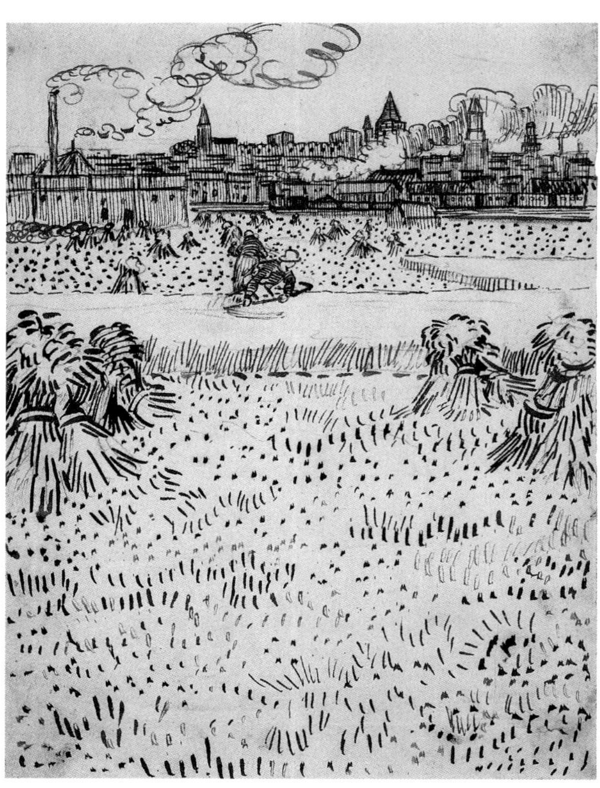

Fig. 27. *Arles: View from the Wheat Fields* (F1491, cat. 70)

Camille Pissarro took to drawing in stipples (fig. 24). Young Bernard, with whom Van Gogh often shared thoughts, sought to reinvigorate drawing and painting by reviving the rugged simplicity that characterized decoration in crafts like stained glass, weaving, and wood carving (fig. 25). Outbursts of the unconventional like these put Van Gogh well on the path to developing pictures out of dashes and dots.

Like many of the most innovative writers and artists of the time, Van Gogh became also fascinated with the enchanting exoticism of Japanese art, which flooded Europe after new trade routes to the East opened in 1854. The collection of ukiyo-e prints he first mentioned tacking to the walls of his studio in Antwerp in 1885 grew exponentially, as did his enthusiasm, prompting him to organize an exhibition of the color woodcuts in 1887 at the Café le Tambourin.[11]

The art of Japan's popular ukiyo-e, which, like Impressionism, focused on picturesque aspects of nature and daily life, offered Van Gogh alternatives to hidebound artistic traditions that were incompatible with his distinctive skills and aims. It was therefore with bold hope that he painted copies of prints by Kesai Eisen and Hiroshige (see fig. 133) in order to experiment with the novelties of Japanese woodcuts: the bird's-eye perspective, the vertical format (unusual in Western art, especially for landscapes), the garish hues, and the simplified outlines that made forms look puzzle-cut. He must have leafed many times through his copy of Hokusai's *One Hundred Views of Mount Fuji,* where he found exotic motifs to decorate his 1887 painting *Japonaiserie: Oiran* (F373). The small black-and-white woodcuts were brimming with energy, offering to Western eyes a bright, new perspective (fig. 26). The full extent of ukiyo-e's influence on him did not become clear until he took up drawing again in earnest, in Provence. Brandishing his newfound reed pen, the artist seized upon an ingenious and varied graphic vocabulary inspired by the flattened space and abbreviated calligraphy of the Japanese (fig. 27).

Van Gogh most certainly admired the way Rembrandt modeled fluid contours with delicately hatched lines, but the bolder, blunter systems of Impressionism, Pointillism, and Japonisme were much better suited to his self-styled "drawing fist" (see figs. 28, 29). The reed pen, which required frequent reinking, cooperated in this effort, since it necessitated briefer strokes. The regular interruptions encouraged the artist to construct an image in clear-cut stages and out of more or less uniform parts enabling him to chart terrain as difficult and varied as that of the human face.

Once Van Gogh had made his draftsmanship "more spontaneous, more exaggerated" [495] and "free" according to his terms, it seemed to matter little (least of all to the artist himself) whether it measured up to traditional standards. Indeed, having been influenced by non-Western models of cunning simplicity, his graphic language looked peculiarly foreign. Not only in their material, but also in their making, Van Gogh's drawings seemed to bypass linearity altogether, offering images that appeared to have been fully formed somewhere else before landing on paper—an effect more akin to printing than to drawing

Van Gogh frequently voiced the wish to convey spontaneity and speed in his drawings,

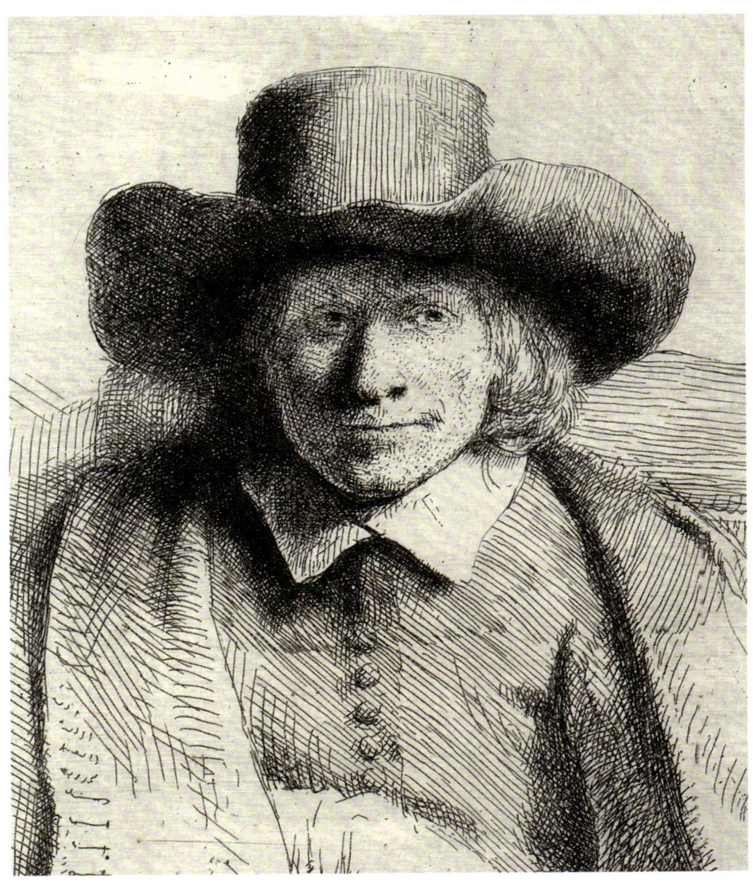

Fig. 28. Rembrandt van Rijn, *Clement de Jonghe* (?), 1651, detail. Etching, drypoint, and engraving, first state, 20.7 x 16.1 cm ($8\frac{1}{8}$ x $6\frac{5}{16}$ in.). The Metropolitan Museum of Art, New York, H. O. Havemeyer Collection, Bequest of Mrs. H. O. Havemeyer, 1929 (29.107.2)

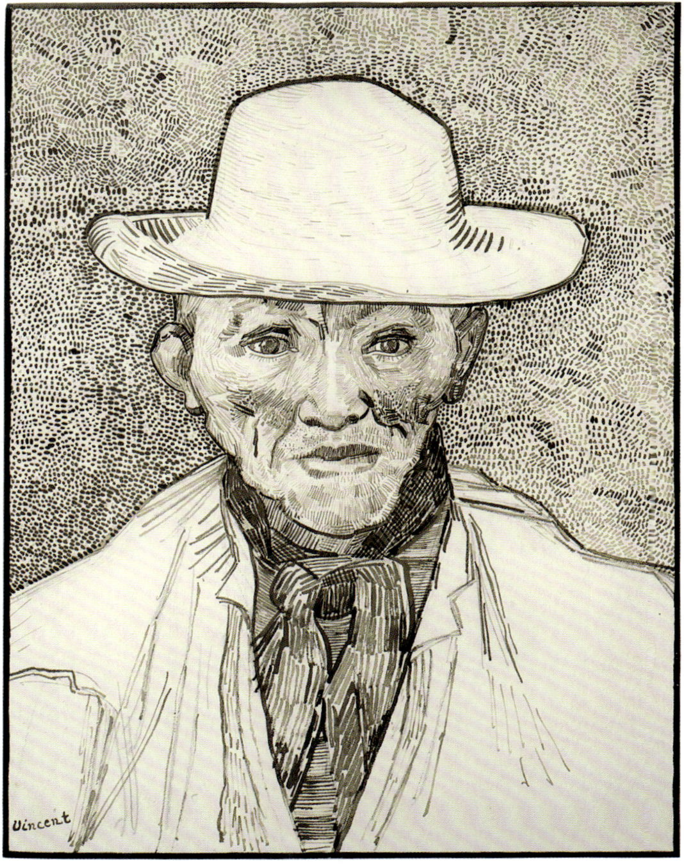

Fig. 29. *Portrait of Patience Escalier* (F1460), 1888. Reed pen and ink over graphite on paper, 49.4 x 38 cm ($19\frac{1}{2}$ x 15 in.). Fogg Art Museum, Harvard University Art Museums, Cambridge, Mass., Bequest of Grenville L. Winthrop (photo: Katya Kallsen)

but contradictorily, and perhaps even deliberately, he created a style that was laborious and time-consuming. It seems as if the Protestant preacher's son needed to produce a record of steady employment. If an amateur's attempt to copy one of Van Gogh's Arles drawings is any measure of this effort, more than two hours of uninterrupted penwork would have been required to complete one of the medium-sized sheets.[12] The Montmajour panoramas (F1420, cat. 85; F1424, cat. 86) no doubt consumed much greater time and, after they had been well developed on-site, must have been completed back in the studio.

By sidestepping academic strictures that might have restrained his drawing practice and by arming himself with tools and techniques of his own invention, Van Gogh gained the confidence to strike out on his own. And, as he mastered his signature drawing style, he came to recognize its power—to make black and white as expressive as color. It was then, perhaps intuitively, that he proceeded to reinvent his practice of painting. The impulses that charged his pen simply took over when he loaded his brush so that he delivered paint to canvas in dynamic, graphic strokes (figs. 30, 31). In ways he might never have anticipated, Van Gogh thus demonstrated the dictum he had framed: "drawing is the root of everything" [290].

1. The author expresses her gratitude to the J. Paul Getty Museum and Lee Hendrix, Curator of Drawings, for the appointment, Visiting Scholar, which provided inestimable resources in early 2002 for research leading to the realization of this catalogue and the exhibition it celebrates. Also, in appreciation, the following authors are acknowledged for their particularly lucid evaluations of Van Gogh's drawing style: Novotny 1953; Wadley 1969; and Elderfield 1983, pp. 22–23, 30–31.
2. The social context for Van Gogh's early development has been surveyed most recently in Silverman 2000, chap. 5, pp. 144–79.
3. See Pickvance in Nottingham and other cities 1974–75.
4. See letter R20 and works F1655–64, including Van Gogh's nine lithographs and one etching, a portrait of Dr. Gachet made with the encouragement and assistance of the sitter in Auvers, May 1890.
5. On Millet's role in Van Gogh's development, see Stein 1989; and Amsterdam 1988–89.
6. The importance to Van Gogh of the art manuals he consulted, particularly Cassagne's texts and the prescribed perspective frame, is discussed at length in Wylie 1970; Murray 1980; and Van Heugten 1996, pp. 17–25.
7. See Ackerman 2003.
8. The Internet contains general information regarding epilepsy, a neurological disorder that causes sudden bursts of electrical energy in the brain. See, for instance, www.epilepsy.com for a summary of views by Drs. Geschwind, Bear, and Fedio regarding "the epileptic personality." I am grateful to Steven Naifeh (now preparing with Greg Smith a new biography of Van Gogh), for sharing with me the following studies of the artist's illness: Henri Gastaut, "La maladie de Vincent van Gogh envisagée à la lumière des conceptions nouvelles sur l'épilepsie psychomotrice," *Annales médico psychologiques,* 1956, pp. 196–238; Michael R. Trimble, "Hypergraphia," in *Aspects of Epilepsy and Psychiatry* (Chichester and New York, 1986), pp. 75–87; and Dietrich Blumer, "The Illness of Vincent van Gogh," *American Journal of Psychiatry,* April 2002, pp. 519–26.
9. Rembrandt's place within the inherent Dutchness of Van Gogh's art is explored in Pollock 1980.
10. "Allez, mon pauvre garçon, vous ne serez jamais que le Daumier de votre temps"; quoted in Proust 1913, p. 22.
11. "My studio is not bad, especially as I have pinned a lot of little Japanese prints on the wall, which amuse me very much. You know, those little women's figures in gardens, or on the beach, horsemen, flowers, knotty thorn branches" [437]. See Luijten 2003, pp. 110–12, and Kōdera 1991, pp. 11–45.
12. This experiment was performed by tracing a scale copy of F1451 (cat. 90).

Fig. 30. *Starry Night* (F1540), ca. June 20–July 2, 1889. Reed pen, brush, and ink, over graphite, 47.1 x 62.2 cm (18½ x 24½ in.). Formerly Kunsthalle Bremen

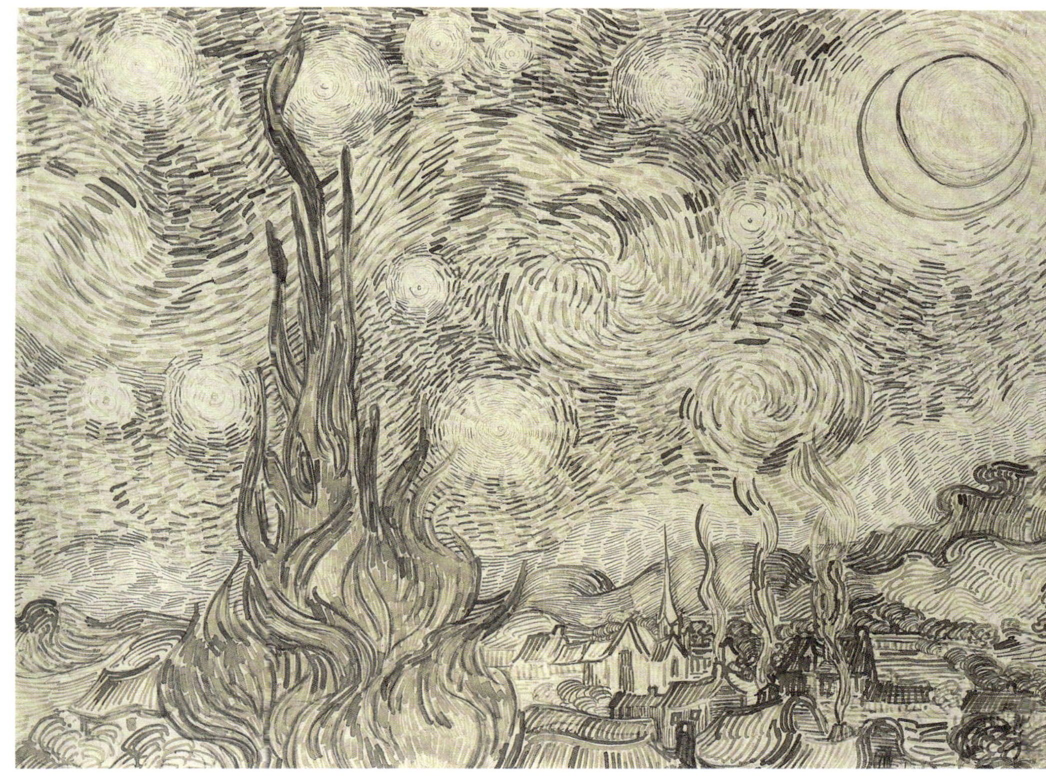

Fig. 31. *Starry Night* (F612), 1889. Oil on canvas, 73.7 x 92.1 cm (29 x 36¼ in.). Museum of Modern Art, New York, acquired through the Lillie P. Bliss Bequest (photo: SCALA / Art Resource, NY)

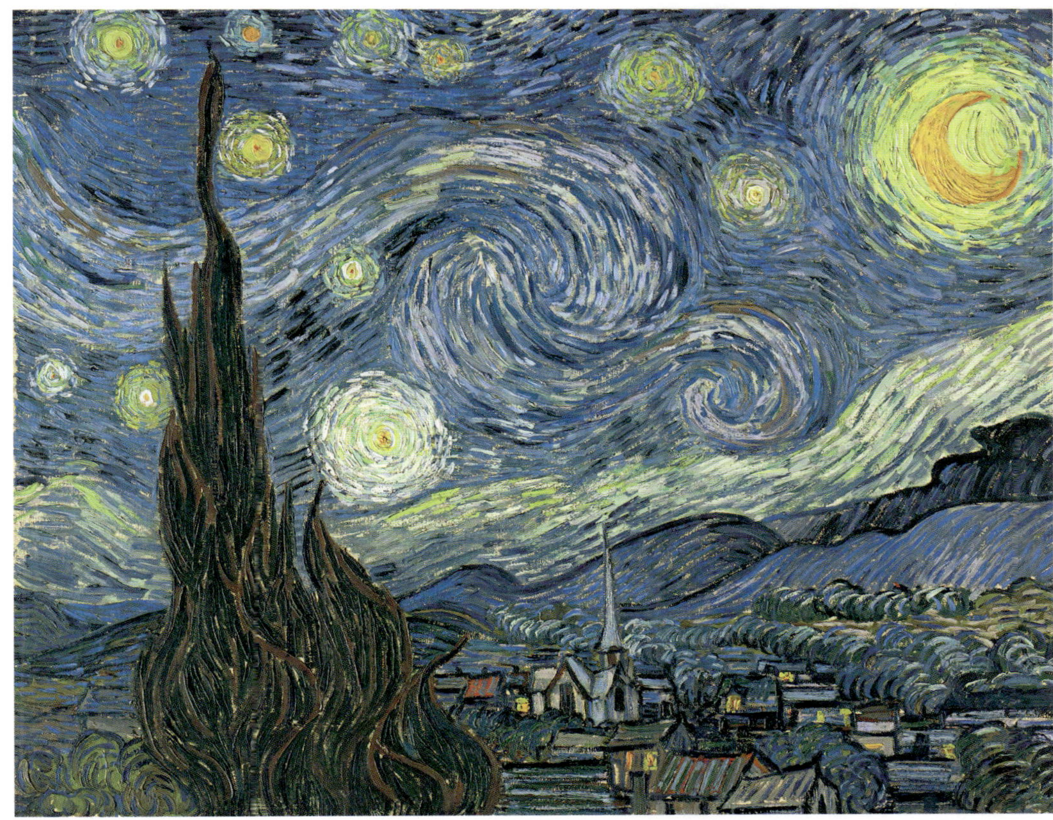

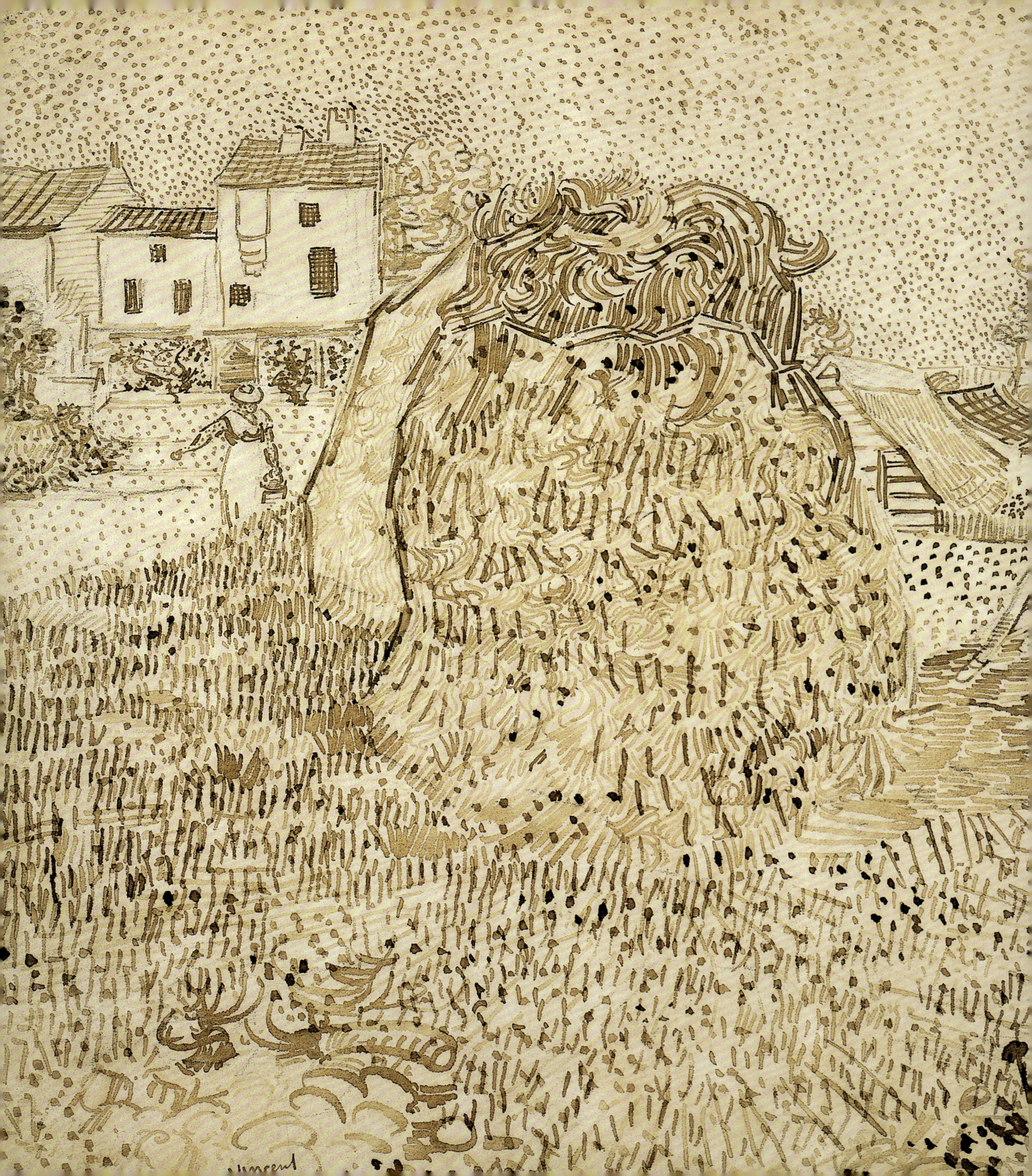

The Paper Trail: From Portfolios to Posterity

SUSAN ALYSON STEIN

Fig. 32. Detail of cat. 67, *Haystacks* (F1427)

"It may be accepted as certain that, in the future, the artist who died young will receive attention primarily for his drawings."[1] So wrote the Dutch critic Johan de Meester in 1892, just two years after Vincent van Gogh's death. This art-world correspondent assumed that the artist's achievement as a draftsman would triumph over the vibrant canvases and the painter's equally dramatic suicide. Yet as time went on and Van Gogh's fame as colorist and martyr to the cause of modernism took hold and gained momentum, the drawings, rather than guaranteeing his renown, failed to keep pace with other aspects of Van Gogh's decade-long career that have continued to sustain the public's imagination. While his present-day celebrity owes curiously little to his originality as a draftsman, this was not always the case. The drawings Van Gogh left behind soon became known at large, attracting enough interest on the part of an ever-growing circle of admirers to predict that their posthumous fate, if not their greater glory, was assured as early as 1892. By this date, the sheets were emerging from the safekeeping of brimming portfolios kept by his devoted brother Theo and from an album put together by Émile Bernard to hang in exhibitions in Brussels, The Hague, Amsterdam, Antwerp, Rotterdam, and Paris; to illustrate avant-garde journals; and to find new homes with collectors from Dordrecht to Copenhagen. That these works did not suffer neglect or worse as a consequence of Theo's demise in 1891 makes the early prominence they enjoyed even more surprising. Theo's widow, Johanna van Gogh-Bonger, turned a deaf ear to those who advised her to abandon the "worthless" lot and instead seems to have taken to heart something Vincent once said:

> It is really done for you—the public. . . . Of course a drawing must have artistic value, but in my opinion this doesn't prevent the man in the street from finding something in it [245].

Married to Theo in 1889, Johanna went from bride to widow in less than two years and from being a quiet if astute observer of the talent of a brother-in-law she hardly knew and the public was just beginning to discover, to playing a guiding role in the revelation of his multisided genius. Johanna's enterprise and her dedication to making this legacy known were matched by her sensitivity and foresight. For example, she did not rush the artist's correspondence into print (a project she completed in 1914) because she did not want to "create interest in his personality before the work to which he gave his life was recognized and appreciated as it deserved."[2] Similarly, as she put Van Gogh's art before the public, she sought recognition for his production as a whole, bringing early Dutch figure studies and late pen-and-ink landscapes to bear on the perception of an artist who might otherwise have been appreciated strictly as an "intense and fantastic colorist."[3] The artist's drawings were invariably among the loans she selected for exhibitions, and they were the exclusive focus of nearly twenty shows she organized during her lifetime, mostly in the Netherlands, beginning with three in the early 1890s in The Hague, Amsterdam, and Leiden. She routinely offered drawings even when they were not requested for an exhibition, for example, when the artist's works debuted in Copenhagen in 1893 and in London in 1910–11 at the Grafton Galleries' "Manet and the Post-Impressionists" show. Indeed, Johanna seems to have made it her mission to ensure that Van Gogh's drawings would not remain the exclusive privilege of "connoisseurs [who] had always considered [them] as important as his paintings."[4]

While Van Gogh's paintings had been shown during his lifetime, at the annual exhibitions of the Salon des Indépendants in Paris from 1888 to 1890 and with Les XX in Brussels in 1890, his drawings had not. Van Gogh had second thoughts about participating in the 1888 show of the Dutch Etching Society after initially being receptive enough to Theo's suggestion to produce a series devoted to Montmajour for the venue. For the 1890 exhibition of Les XX, Van Gogh had selected six paintings but had not yet chosen the drawings, which organizer Octave Maus was keen to include, when he suffered a breakdown. Thus, not until the following year, thanks to loans Maus secured from Johanna, were Van Gogh's works as a draftsman first shown—in the context of a memorial tribute.

Maus's enthusiasm for Van Gogh's drawings, which he had first seen and "greatly admired" on a visit to Theo's apartment in 1889 [T21], prompted him—a year later, when Theo was confined to a mental facility—to prevail on Johanna to lend drawings to the 1891 Les XX exhibition in order to present "le plus grand cas" of the artist's genius to Belgian artists and the public.[5] Undeterred by circumstance, Johanna offered her cooperation. On December 31, 1890, she advised Maus that she had sent fifteen of the "most important" drawings: eleven late works ("of the midi"), as well as "four that date from the first period in Holland which [he] might wish to show"; eight paintings were also lent. Apologizing to Maus that the drawings were not properly mounted or framed ("given the unfortunate position I find myself with my poor husband's illness"), she welcomed being "able to contribute to the success of Vincent's works" and looked forward to receiving reviews.[6] On February 5, 1891, Maus wrote Johanna, offering condolences on Theo's death and assuring her that the display made an "excellent effect." Space had allowed him to exhibit only the "seven most beautiful" of the fifteen drawings, all from Provence.[7] Notwithstanding such notable outtakes as *Portrait of Patience Escalier* (F1460, fig. 29) and *The Country on the Banks of the Rhône Viewed from Montmajour* (F1424, cat. 86), the selection was impressive. It included *The Courtyard of the Hospital in Arles* (F1467, cat. 99) and *Fountain in the Garden of the Asylum* (F1531, cat. 103); three views of Montmajour, of which one *Olive Trees, Montmajour* (JH Add. 3, cat. 82), was sold to the Belgian collector Henri van Cutsem;[8] and *Boats at Sea, Saintes-Maries-de-la-Mer* (F1430b, cat. 59), which Johanna presented to Maus as a token of gratitude. Her sense of the importance of the Montmajour drawings and the two large-format hospital gardens seems to have guaranteed that this core group, which typically also featured a "View of Arles" and at least one of the Rhône, played a leading role in introducing Van Gogh's efforts as a draftsman to an ever-widening public.

The seven drawings shown in Brussels in 1891 elicited far more favorable commentary (though considerably less press coverage) than the eight paintings. One writer wondered why, given the strength of such images as *The Courtyard of the Hospital in Arles,* the artist had even bothered to express himself in color and went on to characterize the drawings as "powerful, original, superb, absolutely unique [works] executed with brio by a skilled hand."[9] The impatient yet confident quality of Van Gogh's touch intrigued the Belgian Symbolist poet Émile Verhaeren, who likened

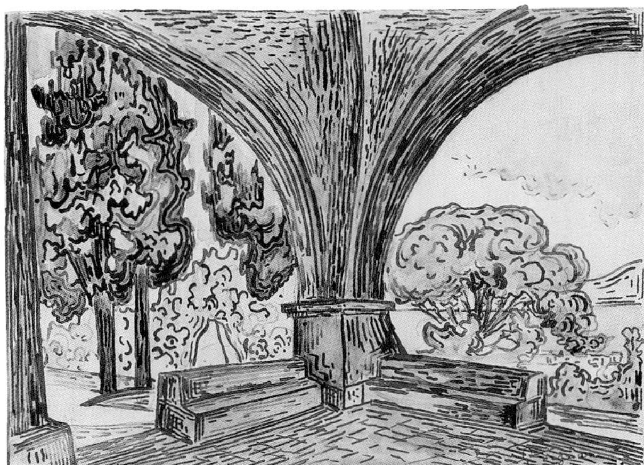

Fig. 33. Paul Signac, *The Chapel of Sainte-Anne at Saint-Tropez,* ca. 1895. Watercolor and ink on paper, 21 x 28.5 cm (8¼ x 11¼ in.). Arkansas Arts Center Foundation Collection, Little Rock, Gift of James T. Dyke, 1999

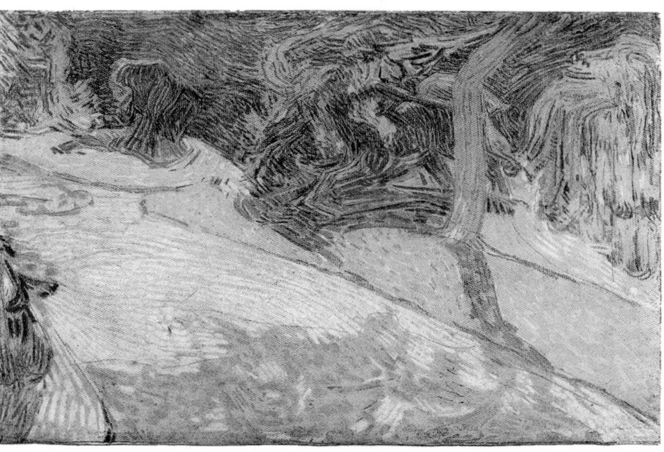

Fig. 34. Henry van de Velde, *Garden Study (Vogelenzang),* ca. 1892. Pastel on paper, 29 x 44 cm (11⅜ x 17⅜ in.). Grafische Sammlung, Museum für Gestaltung, Zürich

the drawings to "those of a very practiced, very assured wood-engraver" He added, "They are marvelous—all of them."[10]

Artists were equally open in their admiration. Paul Signac immediately penned a note to the critic Félix Fénéon praising these "fantastic drawings made with a bamboo reed, [as] having rare power and vigorous style."[11] But the "watercolors heightened with ink" that Signac began producing in the 1890s show that the impression they made on him proved more indelible; *The Chapel of Sainte-Anne at Saint-Tropez* (fig. 33), for one, invites comparison with the cloistered hospital gardens by Van Gogh (F1467, cat. 99; F1531, cat. 103) that were shown. Signac was not alone among adherents to Neo-Impressionism who found Van Gogh's graphic approach seductive. For the Belgian painter and architect Henry van de Velde, the spell of Seurat's "hopelessly peaceful and slow technique" was broken by Van Gogh's "dynamic lines in which [he] recognized—after almost ten years of academic design—the real sense of drawing."[12] In a series of pastels, including several garden views of 1892 that recall those he had seen by Van Gogh (see fig. 34), Van de Velde reconciled competing tendencies in his art, investing Van Gogh's linear style with a more decorative sensibility that would be the hallmark of his Art Nouveau architectural design. In 1892, Van de Velde approached Johanna for permission to publish letters and drawings by Van Gogh in a commemorative issue of the avant-garde journal *Van nu en straks,* and two years later he paid her a visit. Though he found it a treat to see so many paintings by Van Gogh, the highlight of the visit was seeing "[t]hose random sheets, unframed, rough-edged [that] were so charged with electricity that as we took each in turn they seemed to be intent on

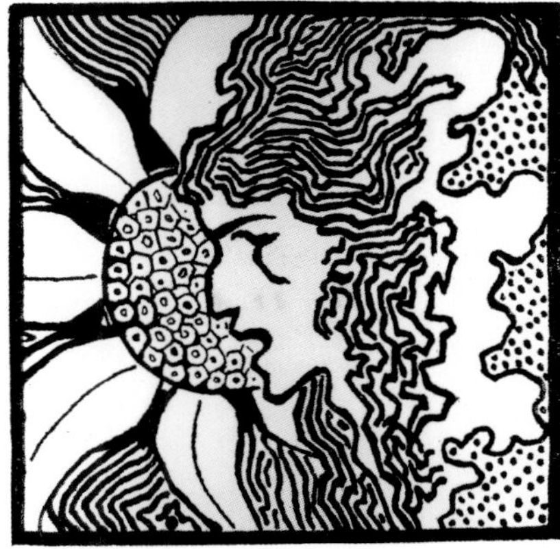

Fig. 35. Richard Roland-Holst, vignette for *Van nu en straks,* no. 3 (1893), p. [37]. Woodcut, 8.7 x 8.7 cm (3⅜ x 3⅜ in.). Van Gogh Museum, Amsterdam (Vincent van Gogh Foundation)

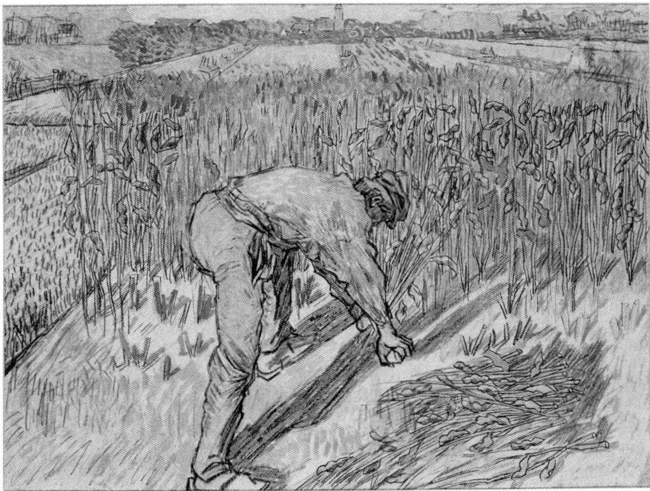

Fig. 36. Jan Toorop, *Man Harvesting Beans,* 1903. Black chalk, pastel, and oil paint on paper, 48 x 61 cm (18⅞ x 24 in.). Private collection

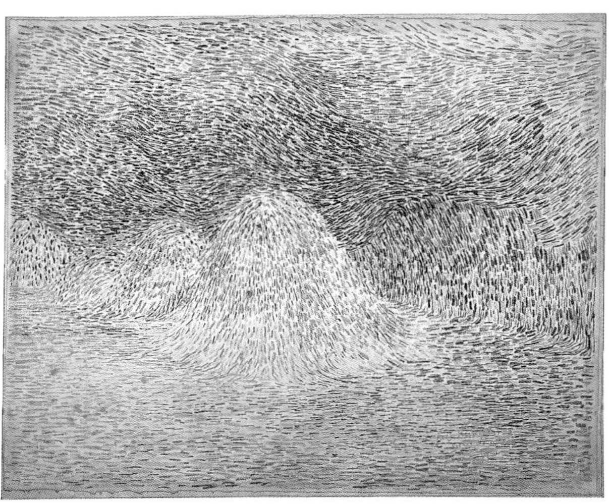

Fig. 37. Johan Thorn Prikker, *Haystacks (Soleil du midi),* ca. 1904. Chalk and paint on paper, 48.7 x 59 cm (19⅛ x 23¼ in.). Kröller-Müller Museum, Otterlo

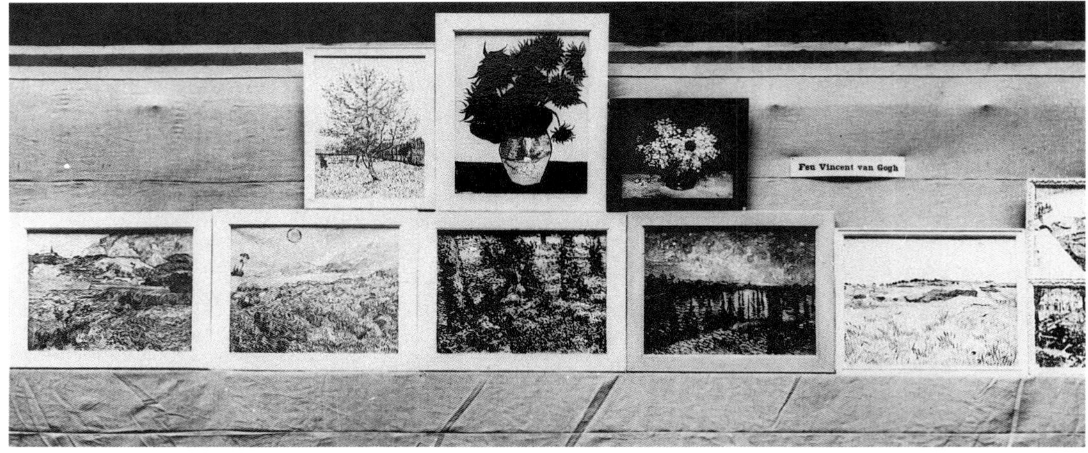

Fig. 38. Installation view of works by Van Gogh at the Association pour l'Art exhibition, Antwerp, 1892. Two drawings, *Sand Barges on the Rhône* (F1462) and *The Courtyard of the Hospital in Arles* (F1467), are shown at far right (photo: Van Gogh Museum, Amsterdam)

wriggling out of our hands, like prisoners long immured in darkness, frantic to escape into the light of day."[13] He purchased *Field with Poppies* (F1494) from Johanna on May 30, 1894.[14]

The list of contributors to the special issue of *Van nu en straks,* published in Antwerp in 1893, may be seen as a "who's who" of Van Gogh's most devoted followers among Belgian and Dutch members of Les XX. Beyond Van de Velde's contribution, there were dedicatory prints by other artists who were especially receptive to Van Gogh's graphic style, including vignettes by Richard Roland-Holst (fig. 35), Jan Toorop, and Johan Thorn Prikker, whose drawings would later show an even greater debt to their Dutch contemporary. Toorop's work came to reflect his sympathy not only for the linear invention of Van Gogh's Provençal landscapes but also, in his monumental workers with their sturdy bearing and emphatically contoured forms, for the earlier Nuenen figure studies (fig. 36). Van Gogh's influence is perhaps even more obvious in the series of drawings Prikker made in the Ardennes between 1900 and 1904, in which

Dutch Critical Response, 1891–92: The Debut of Van Gogh's Drawings at the Pulchri Studio, The Hague, December 1891, and at the Kunstzalen Oldenzeel, Rotterdam, March 1892

Sat evening there was an opening for members of Pulchri Studio to see a number of black and white drawings displayed, mostly pen drawings, by Vincent van Gogh.

This art show, as we were informed by letter from The Hague, has lots of success. The talent of this recently deceased artist is a talent that stands exceptionally apart from the norm of the Dutch school; it is therefore not unimportant to note that various artists who previously doubted the talent of Van Gogh now recognize that he not only strived to achieve something extraordinary but that he indeed arrived at that goal.

Powerful and personal is his work. Among the drawings there was one of a fountain [F1531, cat. 103], also a pair of rocky landscapes [F1446, cat. 84; F1447, cat. 83], a harbor with a pair of boats [F1462, cat. 95]; also among Brabant drawings there were some fine things; figures were scarce, only a man's head from the late period [F1460, fig. 29]; the distance between the Brabant and later drawings was great. There were many small drawings, most from the south of France, of enormously great character (Anonymous, "Letteren en Kunst," Haarlems dagblad *[December 1891], press clipping, Andries Bonger Plakboek BVG 311, Van Gogh Museum, Amsterdam).*

How an artist can err to the point of madness, art-loving residents of The Hague have been able to see in Pulchri Studio for a fortnight. Drawings were exhibited there by Vincent van Gogh, a man little known here, but a Dutchman by birth and spirit. . . . The drawings he made during those years were now to be seen for the first time. . . . True, there were not masterpieces, but from practically each work arose a sigh: If only he could straighten himself out! That was not allowed to happen (P. A. M. Boele van Hensbroek, "De van Goghs," De Nederlandsche spectator, *January 9, 1892, quoted in translation in Stein 1986, p. 286).*

It may be accepted as certain that, in the future, the artist who died young will receive attention primarily for his drawings. Mr. Oldenzeel temporarily has a beautiful collection of them. Some are in portfolio, some are shown to their advantage in the quiet hallway on the second floor of the art dealer's beautiful home. . . . In those drawings, from the very beginning, as well in what Vincent produced later, one sees very clearly the effort to immediately achieve the expression that synthesized what was represented. He was preeminently modern in this effort. Indeed, many young artists in Paris have begun to see in him a chef d'école. *He went through all the stages of their impatient seeking and striving. He took part in Pointillism, he let himself be counted among the Symbolists, . . . but compared to the often childish formation of schools, he always stood out by the personal nature of his work . . . (Johan de Meester, "Letteren en kunst: Vincent van Gogh,"* Nieuwe Rotterdamsche courant, *March 6, 13, 1892, quoted in translation in Stein 1986, p. 289).*

"streams of multicolored parallel chalk lines" on cream-colored paper captured his impression of the picturesque countryside (see fig. 37).[15]

These artistic homages to Van Gogh were made in the wake of a series of local exhibitions that followed the influential 1891 show in Brussels. Word traveled quickly among this close-knit art circle, and the most fervent admirers took initiative in arranging, through Johanna, for opportunities to see Van Gogh's work on their home turf. The first, devoted exclusively to drawings, was held in December 1891 at the Pulchri Studio, an artist's association in The Hague. In May 1892, Toorop helped to organize a retrospective of forty-five paintings and forty-four drawings at the Kunstkring, The Hague. At the end of that year, a 106-work exhibition, engineered by Roland-Holst, opened in Amsterdam at the Kunstzaal Panorama. Johanna lent her support to projects of varying ambition. In the spring of 1892, at the time of the large-scale Hague Kunstkring show, she also contributed a small but fine selection of a dozen works to the Association pour l'Art in Antwerp, including the two hospital gardens that had commanded such attention in Brussels (F1467, F1531) and *Sand Barges on the Rhône* (F1462, cat. 95), which had been admired by a reviewer when it was shown in 1891 at the Pulchri Studio in The Hague (see fig. 38, and review quoted above). Given the interest in the drawings expressed not only by artists' groups but also the trade, there was even competition among different venues. When the secretary of the Amsterdam art association, Art et Amicitiae, who asked Johanna "to lend drawings of the late Vincent van Gogh" for a February 1892 showing, she was unable to respond immediately because the works requested were in Rotterdam for a March exhibition at the gallery of the dealer Oldenzeel. The dealer, however, recognizing how important it was to Johanna "to exhibit the watercolors" at "Arti in

Amsterdam," ensured that they were sent in time,[16] and as she awaited this opening with keen anticipation, Johanna recorded in her diary: "It is a feeling of indescribable triumph—when I think that it has come at last—the appreciation" from "those who used to laugh at Vincent and poke fun of him."[17]

Johanna succeeded in organizing some two dozen Van Gogh exhibitions in various cities and towns in the Netherlands prior to World War I, half of which were devoted to drawings: two in The Hague (1891, 1912), four in Amsterdam (1892, 1901, 1906, 1914–15), four in Leiden (1893, 1901, 1909, 1913), and two in Rotterdam (1900–1901, 1907–8). She created a climate that fostered widespread appreciation of the artist's manifold talent, and perhaps it is not coincidental that the earliest and single largest Van Gogh collection of note, formed by the wealthy Dordrecht manufacturer Hidde Nijland, was devoted exclusively to drawings, all from the Dutch years (1880–85). Nijland began buying works in 1892 and in 1905 published a portfolio illustrating one hundred of the sheets he owned by then. In the interim, he promoted the artist's drawings in an exhibition held in The Hague in 1895 and in a long-term loan to the Dordrecht Museum (1904–10), while ensuring that the draftsman would be permanently represented in a Dutch public institution: his 1899 gift of a *Peasant Woman* (F1270) to the Museum Boijmans Van Beuningen in Rotterdam was the first Van Gogh to enter a museum collection. In 1906, a year after the artist's genius was extolled in a 474-work retrospective at the Stedelijk Museum, Johanna and Nijland each presented drawings to Amsterdam's Rijksmuseum, respectively, F1129 (cat. 20) and F1478 (cat. 66), and F1312.

The exposure the artist's work received in the 1890s had the effect of nurturing the sympathies of admirers and of bringing around skeptics, which was of no small consequence considering that several of the greatest champions of Van Gogh's art, such as critics Jan Veth and Albert Plasschaert and art adviser H. P. Bremmer, had not been immediate fans. Bremmer, a mediocre painter who found his calling in edifying society matrons in art appreciation, became *the* arbiter of taste and aesthetic judgment for the moneyed Dutch by the turn of the twentieth century. Bremmer's courses, advisory services, and publications attracted a devoted following, and his passion for Van Gogh's work proved contagious. In 1899 he was one of the earliest, and by 1911 one of the most committed, collectors, with thirty-nine drawings and seventeen paintings. Bremmer had a penchant for the artist's Dutch period, particularly the drawings, owning some fine examples, such as the *The Fish-Drying Barn at Scheveningen* (F945, cat. 10). When "unknown Van Goghs" made headline news in 1903, the artist and Bremmer, as the expert of note, became household names.

By 1903, a cache of early works that Van Gogh had abandoned in 1885, when he abruptly left Nuenen for Antwerp, had found its way from the hands of a carpenter, who had stored the crates for fifteen years, to a secondhand dealer to a buyer named Mouwen, who brought them to the attention of the art world and marketplace. The subsequent dispersal of these newfound and highly publicized paintings and drawings proved a windfall to collectors of the artist's works: Nijland's holdings doubled with his purchase of sixty early drawings; amateurs and dealers alike availed themselves of the opportunity to acquire such gems as two of the finest Drenthe watercolors (F1099, cat. 16; F1104, cat. 15). Much of the spirited buying was attributed to Bremmer's influence; alluding to him, a critic sneered, "Now, everybody, higgledy-piggledy, has to have a Van Gogh. Why? Because one person happens to be leading the flock who recognizes Vincent's beauty."[18] The most illustrious member of Bremmer's flock was Helene Kröller-Müller, who became his pupil in 1905

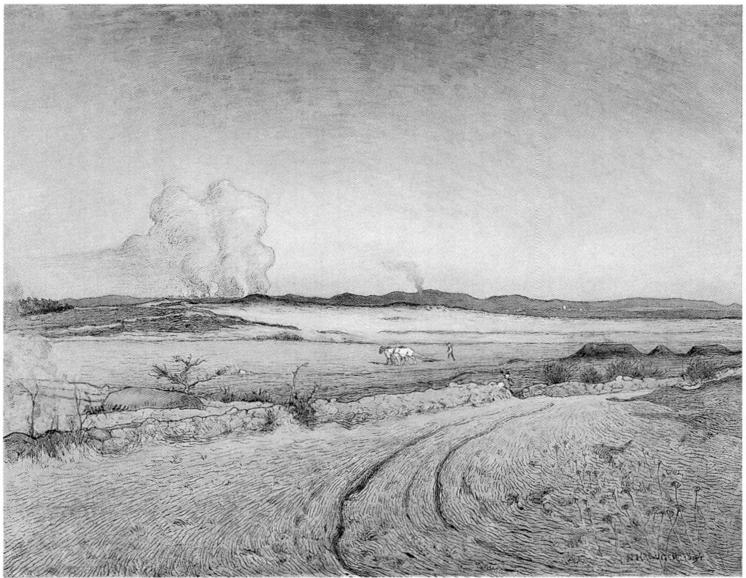

Fig. 39. Nils Kreuger, *Spring in Halland* (center panel of a triptych), 1894. Oil on wood, 50 x 60 cm (19¾ x 23⅝ in.). Nationalmuseum, Stockholm (photo: Åsa Lundén)

and hired him as her adviser in 1907. She and her husband eventually amassed a collection numbering over 270 paintings and drawings by Van Gogh. Their largest single acquisition was the purchase of most of the Nijland collection, some 120 sheets, including the four splendid examples from 1881–85 represented in the present exhibition (F851, cat. 3; F868, cat. 5; F939, cat. 9; F1326, cat. 30).

Johanna has been called "the heart and soul of the Dutch discovery of Van Gogh,"[19] but she was no less instrumental in satisfying interest in his work abroad. Van Gogh's art reached Denmark earlier than most other countries. Danish artist Christian Mourier-Petersen returned to his homeland not only with paintings that vaguely recall his association with Van Gogh in Arles but with enough enthusiasm to prompt compatriot artist Johan Rohde to seek out Van Gogh's works on his yearlong travels in France and the Netherlands in 1892.[20] Rohde, for his part, returned to Denmark with a drawing by Van Gogh (F1450, cat. 88) and a desire to bring to Copenhagen some measure of the genius he had seen at galleries in Paris and at the Kunstkring retrospective in The Hague. On February 4, 1893, Rohde wrote to Johanna asking for the loan of ten to twenty pictures for an exhibition of work by Van Gogh and Gauguin at the Frie Udstilling in Copenhagen. She agreed to lend twenty pictures and characteristically offered drawings as well to give a fuller sense of Van Gogh's oeuvre. The selection of loans was entrusted to Rohde's traveling companion, Georg Seligmann, whose initial reluctance at the task was assuaged by the "young and charming widow" whose "paintings and drawings" proved "what an extraordinarily fine artist [Van Gogh] was."[21] Johanna's guiding sensibility is reflected in the selection. The drawings she sent to Copenhagen were those she had routinely favored in the early 1890s to demonstrate the artist's gifts as a draftsman: *The Courtyard of the Hospital in Arles* (F1467, cat. 99) and *Fountain in the Garden of the Asylum* (F1531, cat. 103), a view of the Rhône (perhaps F1462, cat. 95, since it was certainly present in both The Hague in 1891 and Antwerp in 1892), and *View of Arles from Montmajour* (F1452, cat. 47), which was bought by Hans Christian Christiansen. Had Johanna been willing to part with the *Fountain* at a reduced price, this, too, would have remained in Copenhagen after the close of the show.[22] (By 1906, when Johanna lent that drawing to the Berliner Secession, it was "not for sale," and *View of Arles from Montmajour* had entered the collection of the Nasjonalgalleriet, Oslo.)

Even in the company of Gauguin's provocative Tahitian paintings and Van Gogh's dazzling Provençal canvases, the works on paper held their own. Danish author Johannes Jørgensen exclaimed, "One feels the same lust for life in Van Gogh's drawings. Look at the sunshine over the stubble field in the picture called A Garden in Arles [F1450, cat. 88]! Feel the refreshing coolness of the fountain and the leafy shade in the drawing entitled A Fountain [F1531, cat. 103]! Then you will understand that this man's power of feeling was too deep

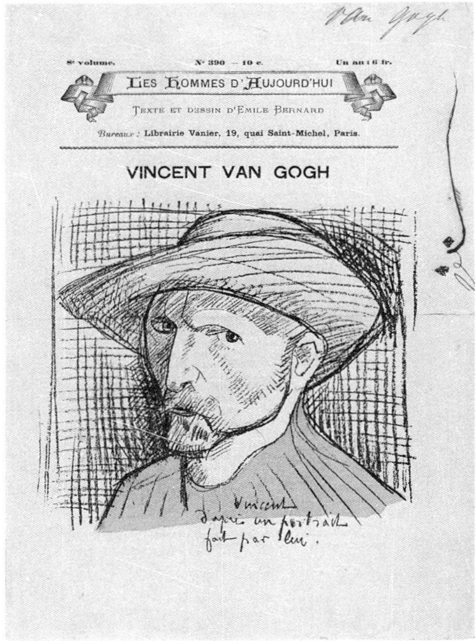

Fig. 40. Émile Bernard, *Portrait of Van Gogh* (after a self-portrait), cover of *Les hommes d'aujourd'hui* 8, no. 390 (1891). Lithograph, 28.2 x 20.3 cm (11 1/8 x 8 in.). Van Gogh Museum, Amsterdam (Vincent van Gogh Foundation)

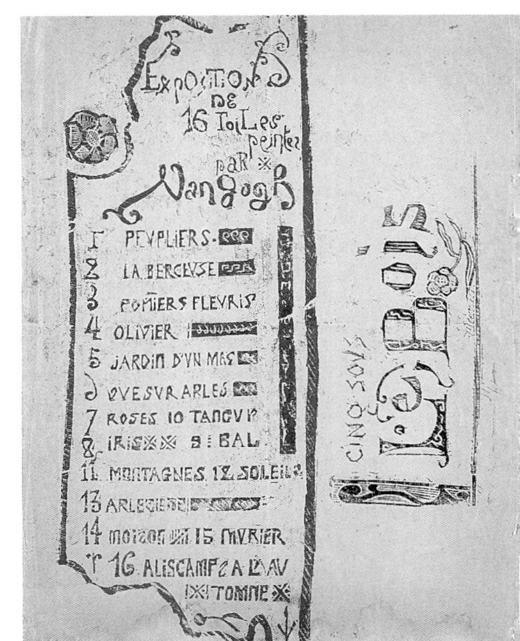

Fig. 41. Émile Bernard, flyer for the Van Gogh exhibition at Le Barc de Boutteville, Paris, April 1892. Woodcut, 40 x 31 cm (15 3/4 x 12 1/4 in.). Van Gogh Museum, Amsterdam (Vincent van Gogh Foundation)

and great to suffer for long the burden of an impoverished and sorrowful life."[23] As for the effect on Scandinavian artists, Nils Kreuger's exploration of a technique that depended on lines and dots drawn in ink to invigorate the surface of his canvases undoubtedly found inspiration if not its origins in Van Gogh's reed-pen drawings (fig. 39). Yet in addition to the Frie Udstilling exhibition, interest in Van Gogh's work reached Denmark in such other ways as the photographs that Ivan Aguéli brought back from France and showed to other Swedish artists in the spring of 1891, and friendships, for example, between Rohde and Edvard Munch, who met in Copenhagen in the fall of 1891 and moved on to Paris in the spring of 1892, where thanks to Émile Bernard they may well have discovered Van Gogh's talent as a draftsman.

In Paris, Bernard almost single-handedly kept Van Gogh's drawings in the public eye in the first years after his death. Largely responsible

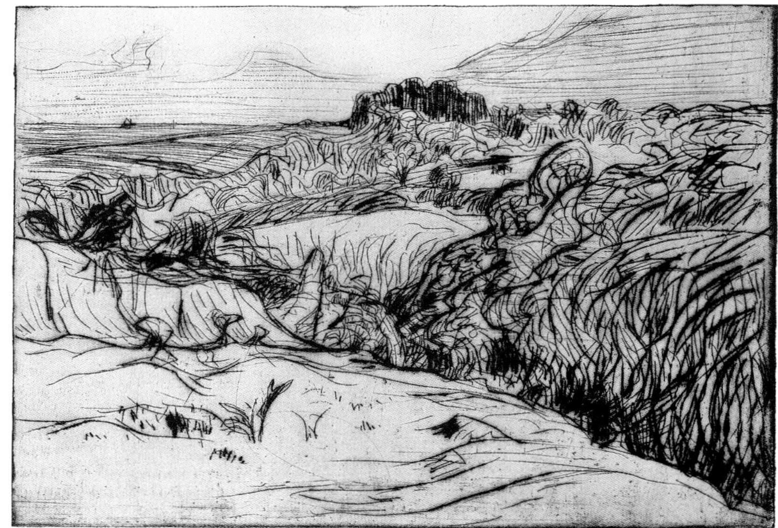

Fig. 42. Roderic O'Conor, *Dunes,* 1893. Ink drypoint on paper, sheet 30.5 x 44.8 cm (12 x 17 5/8 in.). Indianapolis Museum of Art, Gift of Samuel Josefowitz in tribute to Bret Waller and Ellen Lee

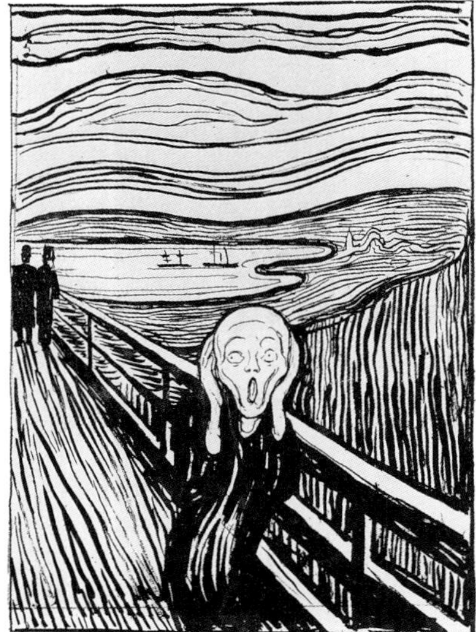

Fig. 43. Edvard Munch, *The Scream,* 1895. Lithograph, 35.7 x 23.6 cm (14 x 9 1/4 in.). The Metropolitan Museum of Art, New York, Bequest of Scofield Thayer, 1982 (1984.1203.1)

French Critical Response, 1891–92: Preview and Debut of Van Gogh's Drawings in Paris

I met Van Gogh for the first time at Cormon's studio. . . . [W]e quickly became friends, and he opened up boxes from Holland and his portfolio of studies. What surprising sketches! Gloomy processions under gray skies, the "common grave"; views of the [Paris] fortifications in rectilinear perspective; the Moulin-de-la-Galette with its sinister arms (over which still lingered a hazy, sober northern fog); then scraggy gardens, roads at dusk, and faces of peasant women with African eyes and mouths (Émile Bernard, "Vincent van Gogh," Les hommes d'aujourd'hui *8, no. 390 [1891], quoted in translation in Stein 1986, p. 283 [see fig. 40]).*

Enamored by the art of the Japanese, Indians, Chinese, with everything that sings, laughs, vibrates, he found in these born artists his astounding technique for achieving harmonies and the extraordinary flights of his drawings . . . (Émile Bernard, "Vincent van Gogh," La plume, *September 1, 1891, quoted in translation in Stein 1986, p. 282).*

He left behind, the poor deceased, with all the hopes that such an artist could inspire, a considerable body of work, close to four hundred canvases and an enormous quantity of drawings, of which many are absolute masterpieces. . . . One rediscovers in his numerous drawings not resemblances [to Rembrandt] but a similar exasperated worship of the same forms and a parallel richness of linear invention. Van Gogh does not always adhere to the discipline nor to the sobriety of the Dutch master; but he often equals his eloquence and his prodigious ability to render life (Octave Mirbeau, "Vincent van Gogh," L'echo de Paris, *March 31, 1891, quoted in translation in Stein 1986, p. 269).*

I must admit to seeing Van Gogh until now only as a colorist, so I am very interested in the drawings that show Vincent from another angle. Van Gogh, whom no professor taught the art of drawing, has nevertheless executed some drawings of the highest order. Isn't that an undeniable example of what I advanced just now concerning inspiration?

They are landscapes, almost always without figures and very simple in composition: an immense plain, a few sheaves of hay [F1488, cat. 73]—that suffices the artist.

Let those who deride him go to Le Barc [de Boutteville]. They will be forced to admit that many so-called serious artists would be incapable of doing landscapes in pen like those on exhibit (Francis, "Exposition van Gogh chez le Barc de Boutteville," La vie moderne, *April 24, 1892, quoted in translation in Stein 1986, p. 294).*

Here are exhibited seventeen canvases and several drawings by Vincent van Gogh. . . . The awkwardness of design merges with bizarre observation in the studies of beings, and the drawings are of a somewhat outdated Japanese mannerism. All of it by a great, yet incomplete, artist, who appeared like a meteor and disappeared too soon, like Monticelli, like Seurat perhaps, to long-standing regret (Camille Mauclair [Séverin Faust], "Galerie Le Barc de Boutteville," La revue indépendante *23 [April 1892], quoted in translation in Stein 1986, pp. 294, 303).*

[Van Gogh's] special idealism took pleasure in symbolic compositions inspired by Rembrandt's etchings or Delacroix's drawings. Hence . . . these ink sketches with the simplicity of woodcuts. At times the exacting and levelheaded observer asserted itself in drawings enhanced with watercolor (see, at Le Barc's, a precise study of a Zouave [F1482, cat. 77]), in psychological portraits . . . (Charles Saunier, "Vincent van Gogh," L'endehors, *April 24, 1892, quoted in translation in Stein 1986, pp. 304–5).*

---

for installing the memorial show in Theo's Montmartre apartment in the fall of 1890, Bernard wrote tributes to Van Gogh in 1891 (see fig. 40), published excerpts from the letters along with illustrations of seventeen drawings in avant-garde journals between 1892 and 1895,[24] and placed works from his personal collection on view at the gallery Le Barc de Boutteville in 1892. The catalogue, a woodcut flyer designed by Bernard (fig. 41), lists, in decorative text, only paintings, but from reviewers' accounts we know that the exhibition included "several drawings" as well (see reviews quoted above). While an intimate circle of friends and visitors to Theo's flat, such as the writer Octave Mirbeau, had seen Van Gogh's drawings before this date, those who had followed his career through recent work shown at the Salon des Indépendants between 1888 and 1891 had known only half the story: his genius as a painter, but not as a draftsman.[25] Thus, the public debut of Van Gogh's drawings in Paris at Le Barc de Boutteville in the spring of 1892 came as a revelation to critics, who recorded these sentiments in print and to various artists who left Paris richer for the experience, from Johan Rohde (who probably acquired his drawing [F1450, cat. 88] from this venue) to Roderic O'Conor of the Pont-Aven circle (see fig. 42), and perhaps even Edvard Munch (see fig. 43) if he happened to visit the show just before his return to Norway later that year.

Those who missed the Barc de Boutteville exhibition would have been able to see some of its highlights in the pages of the *Mercure de France* over the next three years (see note 24). Others might have stopped by Bernard's studio or made the short trip to Auvers to see Dr. Paul Gachet, whose collection included eighteen drawings (several of which he lent to the 1905 Indépendants annual).[26] Yet, with the death of color merchant Julien Tanguy in 1894 and the return to Johanna in 1895 of ten unsold canvases that the dealer Durand-Ruel held on consignment, opportunities to appreciate Van Gogh's work in Paris dimmed. Ambroise Vollard, a sharp young dealer who had recently set up shop on the rue Laffitte, sought to capitalize on this situation and applied to Johanna in 1895 for several loans. She sent him ten paintings and four drawings that summer—a glimmer of things to come. At the end of 1896, Vollard secured from Johanna a 113-work retrospective comparable to the shows she had mounted in the 1890s in the Netherlands. Works on paper included forty-three drawings, thirteen watercolors, and a lithograph, *Sorrow* (F1655)—half the exhibition.[27]

The selection at Vollard ranged in date from an Etten *Digger* of 1881 (F866) to an 1890 view of Auvers (F1624, cat. 117), striking a balance between Van Gogh's early and later triumphs as a draftsman and affording a sense of his accomplishments in various genres. His efforts at figure drawing were represented by twenty-eight sheets, mainly from the period he worked in Nuenen, and an equal number illustrated major motifs he had covered as a landscapist in Holland and France. Featured were pen-and-ink winter gardens of 1884 (F1135, cat. 23, and probably F1130, cat. 22); several watercolors made in and around Paris in 1887, ranging from street scenes in Montmartre (F1393; F1411, cat. 40) to a view of the fortifications; and from the period he worked in Arles, two views of Montmajour (F1424, cat. 86; F1447, cat. 83), *Harvest in Provence* (F1483, cat. 62), *View of Saintes-Maries* (F1439, fig. 130), *Garden with Flowers* (F1455, fig. 163), and *Café Terrace on the Place du Forum* (F1519, cat. 96). In addition to these large-format works, smaller sheets were shown (e.g., F1470, fig. 169). There were a number of impressive drawings from Saint-Rémy, depicting both the asylum garden (F1532, cat. 102; F1533, cat. 104; and two unidentified watercolors listed as "jardin") and the hilly Provençal terrain (F1540, fig. 30; F1542, cat. 112; and F1547).

The show was neither a financial nor a critical success. Curiously, it was ignored by the press. "The newspapers contrary to every hope," Vollard lamented to Johanna, "won't concern themselves with this exhibition."[28] And, were it not for Degas's acquisition of an 1885 peasant drawing (see fig. 44)[29]—of the kind that had prompted Renoir to remark, "What a fine thing that is! What would Millet's sniveling peasant look like beside it!"[30]—one would imagine that every one of the artists who had flocked to Cézanne's show at Vollard's a year before had this time stayed home. Vollard did not give up promoting Van Gogh's works. However, he was forced to find other sources to stock his gallery because Johanna effectively refused to do business with the hard-bargaining dealer after relinquishing to him a half-dozen canvases and ten drawings for a paltry sum in March 1897.[31] While Vollard favored the late paintings, he seems to have bought drawings of various dates. Possibly the interest that Degas and Renoir expressed in the early figure studies encouraged Vollard to stock a few examples, but outside the Netherlands, the Dutch-period works never quite took hold (as the dealer himself may have come to realize if it took him more than a decade to dispose of various sheets from this cache [see note 31]). Among the later drawings Vollard purchased were an unidentified view of Arles and, almost certainly, the ambitious watercolor study for *Harvest in Provence* (F1483, cat. 62), which was next owned briefly by the influential German critic Julius Meier-Graefe, who published a lithograph of the image in *Germinal* in 1899 (fig. 45), and subsequently by the dealer Jos Hessel, who lent it to exhibitions in Paris in 1901 and 1909.

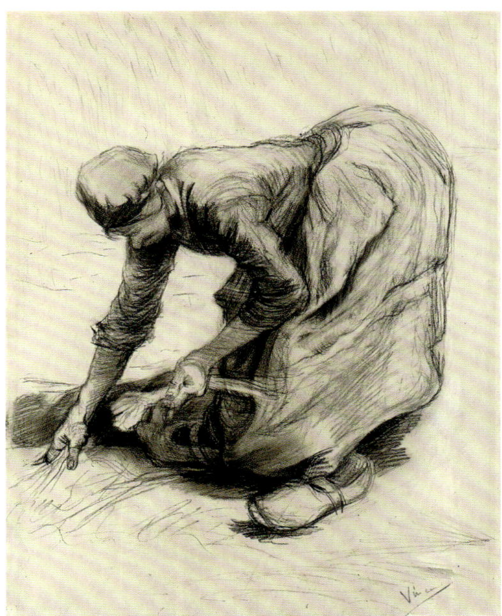

Fig. 44. *Peasant Woman Gleaning* (F1262a), 1885. Black chalk, gray wash heightened with white on paper, 53.3 x 42.5 cm (21 x 16¾ in.). Private collection (photo: Christie's Images)

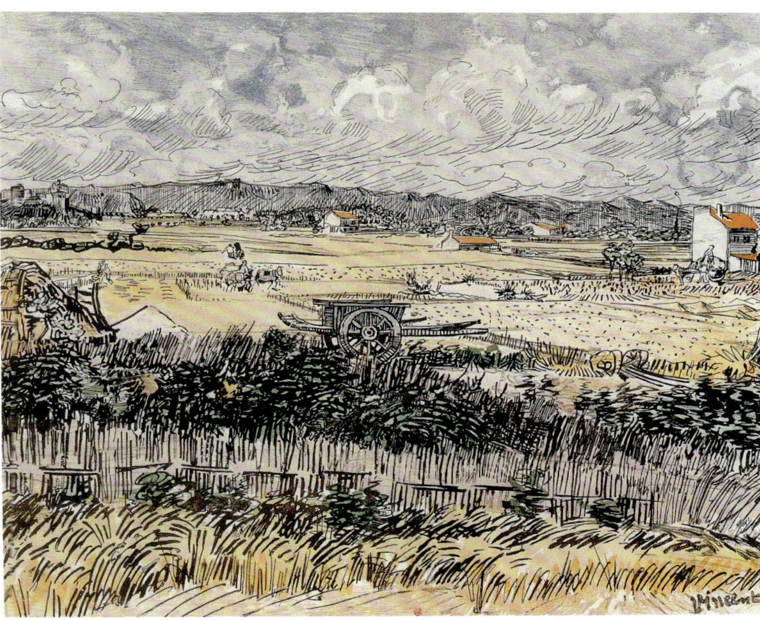

Fig. 45. Color lithograph after Van Gogh's *Harvest in Provence* (F1483, cat. 62), pl. XVI in *Germinal,* a portfolio of twenty prints published by J. Meier-Graefe, La Maison Moderne, 1899, with a preface by Gustave Geffroy. Bibliothèque Nationale de France, Paris (photo: courtesy David Nash)

Van Gogh's drawings claimed very little wall space in exhibitions in Paris during the first decade of the twentieth century; in fact, fewer than twenty examples were included in the major monographic shows of 1901, 1905, 1908, and 1909 combined. There was, however, one prime opportunity to appreciate this aspect of the artist's oeuvre—just down the block from Vollard's gallery, in 1902: Johanna, though soured by her experiences with French dealers, was persuaded to lend a group of drawings to Léonce Moline, who ran the Galerie Laffitte. Moline was eager to have the display of thirty drawings on view for a client "very susceptible to buying," who was due shortly to pass through Paris, and urged Johanna, in February 1902, to send the shipment posthaste.[32]

At least eight of the drawings, including *Rocks and Trees, Montmajour* (F1447, cat. 83) and *Café Terrace on the Place du Forum* (F1519, cat. 96), had been shown at Vollard's six years earlier.[33] Here, however, they were seen in a context that focused on the artist's mature works, with two-thirds of the drawings dating to 1888–89. This well-chosen selection included single sheets of great merit such as *A Farmhouse in Provence* (F1478, cat. 66) and the highly stylized *Public Garden in the Place Lamartine* (F1477, cat. 94), as well as pairings and groups of related subjects. For example, the artist's late May–early June 1888 visit to Saintes-Maries was illustrated by three sheets a view of thatched huts (F1440, cat. 48), a "marine" (possibly F1432), and the triumphant boats on the beach (F1428, cat. 60); his late summer 1888 gardens by two drawings in contrasting vertical and horizontal formats (F1457, cat. 92; F1455, fig. 163); and his campaign to capture the "obelisk-like" form of the cypresses in 1889 by three Saint-Rémy landscapes of differing scale and time of day (F1525a; F1538, cat. 110; and F1540, fig. 30). Of figure studies, there were some from Nuenen, such as the fine *Head of a Woman* (F1182, cat. 27), and two prime examples from Arles, *The Seated Zouave* (F1443, fig. 151) and *Portrait of Patience Escalier* (F1460,

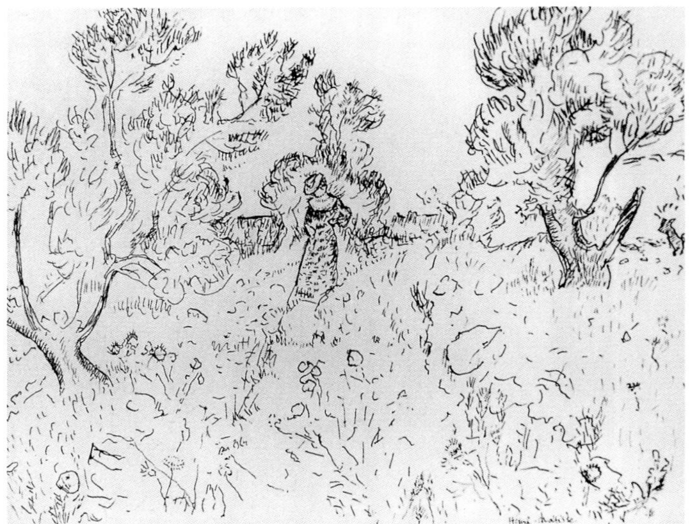

Fig. 46. Henri Matisse, *Madame Matisse among Olive Trees,* 1905. Pen and ink on paper, 20.3 x 26.7 cm (8 x 10½ in.). Private collection (photo: courtesy Jack Flam)

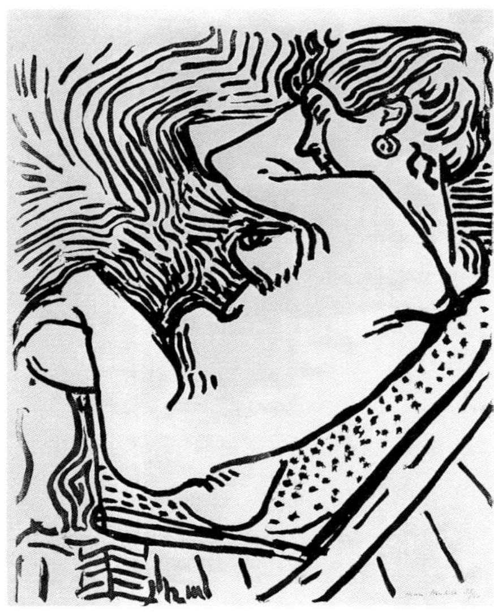

Fig. 47. Henri Matisse, *Seated Nude,* 1906. Brush and ink on paper, 46.3 x 36.8 cm (18¼ x 14½ in.). Private collection (photo: courtesy Jack Flam)

fig. 29). Moline seems to have bought three large-format drawings from this group: two early peasants at work and the striking bust-length peasant portrait from Arles (on Johanna's list, nos. 8, 28, and 14 and priced at 280, 250, and 300 francs, respectively, tallied twice at the bottom, for a total of 830 francs). The sale of the Escalier portrait to Moline in 1902 would not only explain the drawing's conspicuous absence from the comprehensive 1905 exhibition at the Stedelijk Museum in Amsterdam and from any number of the major shows held in Germany during that decade, but it would resolve the riddle of how the Scandinavian collector Klas Fåhræus came to acquire the drawing in Paris in December 1911. Fåhræus had purchased from Johanna two grand drawings, *Sand Barges on the Rhône* (F1462, cat. 95) and *Cypresses* (F1524, fig. 230), and advised her of this acquisition: "I have bought another beautiful drawing in Paris: the large head in a hat and a large scarf," adding that he got the Escalier portrait ("The Bull Watcher") "quite inexpensively" from the "amateur dealer" Alphonse Kann, "nephew to the earlier Rembrandt collector."[34]

That same year, 1911, the Budapest collector Pál Majovszky purchased four drawings by Van Gogh from Vollard. Two, including *Winter Garden* (F1130, cat. 22), may well have come from the group Vollard bought from Johanna in 1897 (see note 31), but the two others, *Haystacks* (F1426, fig. 185) and *A Summer Evening* (F1514, cat. 68), were among the cache of drawings Vollard acquired from Émile Bernard at the turn of the century. Just as Johanna explored more friendly avenues for marketing Vincent's work in Paris—Moline in 1902 and, later, Bernheim-Jeune—Vollard discovered that he could cheaply replenish his stock by turning to various artists and friends, such as M. and Mme Ginoux in Arles. For drawings, Vollard's main supplier was Bernard, who between 1899 and 1904 sold him more than twenty sheets for a pittance, about 50 francs each (half the price Bernard got for the three [F1430, cat. 57; F1485, cat. 64; F1488, cat. 73] he sold privately in 1904 to Hugo von Tschudi, director of the Nationalgalerie Berlin; see "*Répétitions:* Drawings after Paintings"). These drawings had acquired a certain cachet from their publication in the *Mercure de*

France, and their graphic appeal and cost (relative to the paintings) proved irresistible. Henri Matisse bought two (F1461, fig. 154; F1491, cat. 70), which he proudly lent to the 1905 Salon des Indépendants along with the one given to him by John Russell (F1427, cat. 67), whom he befriended on summer trips to Belle-Île-en-Mer, Brittany, in 1896–97.[35]

Introduced to Van Gogh's work at close hand through the suite of drawings Russell owned (see *"Répétitions"*) and those Vollard had in stock, Matisse took in the great 1901 Van Gogh retrospective at Galerie Bernheim-Jeune in the company of André Derain and Maurice Vlaminck; having absorbed its impact by the time of the memorial tribute held at the Indépendants in 1905, they emerged as the Dutch artist's heirs under the banner of "Fauves" (wild beasts). Yet while Matisse, perhaps above all, epitomized Van Gogh's belief that "the painter of the future will be a *colorist such as has never yet existed*" [482], neither he nor his friends ignored Van Gogh's achievement as a draftsman. When Matisse put pen and ink to paper between 1905 and 1906, he seems to have drawn inspiration, quite literally, from the works he owned. Van Gogh's *Haystacks* of 1888 (F1427, cat. 67) may be seen as a point of departure for his idyllic *Madame Matisse among Olive Trees* of 1905 (fig. 46), which adapts its delicate, agitated linearity within a similarly composed landscape, whereas the bold, defiant character and heavily outlined contours of Van Gogh's portrait drawing (F1461, fig. 154) anticipate his 1906 *Seated Nude* (fig. 47). Derain, who had come to appreciate Van Gogh's graphic works on his own, joined Matisse in emulating their spirit in his pen-and-ink views of Collioure (for example, see fig. 48).

During his service in the military between 1901 and 1904, Derain seems to have thought a good deal about Van Gogh. On one occasion, he asked Vlaminck if he had "seen any new Van Goghs,"[36] and lamented on another, "Almost a year has gone by since we saw Van Gogh[s], yet the memory continues to haunt me. I am increasingly aware that he really makes sense."[37] Beyond counting on his friends to keep him informed, Derain apparently depended on past issues of the *Mercure de France*, freely quoting from what he had read in Albert Aurier's article "Vincent van Gogh" (January 1890) and various letters

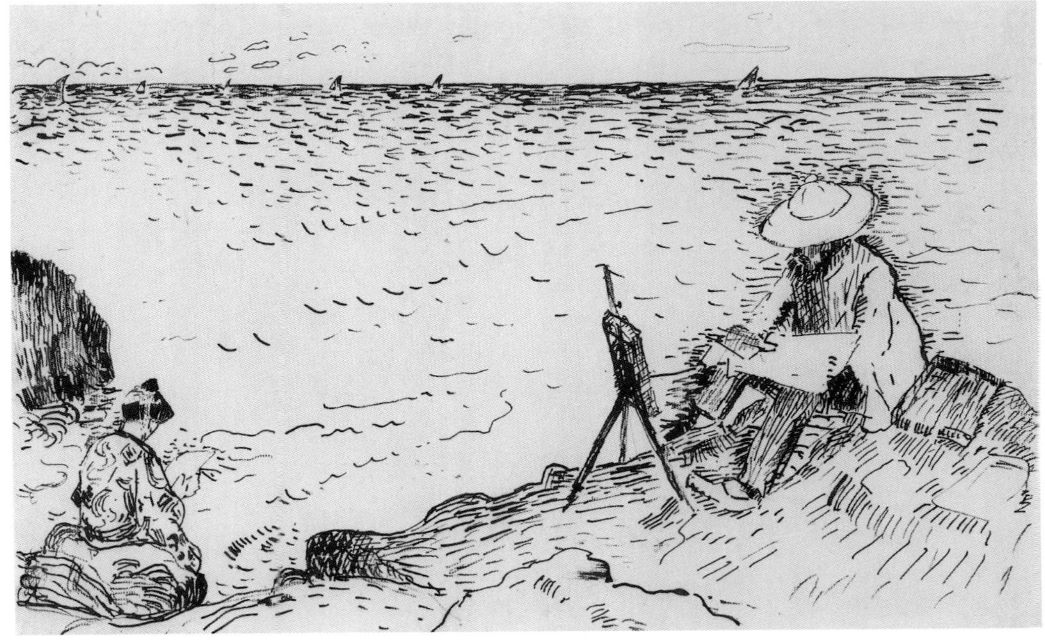

Fig. 48. André Derain, *Matisse and His Wife at Collioure*, summer 1905. Pen and ink on laid paper, 30.2 x 47.9 cm (11⅞ x 18⅞ in.). The Metropolitan Museum of Art, New York, Hermina, Movses, Charles and David Allen Devrishian Fund, 2004 (2004.60)

published by Bernard (1893–95).[38] The reproductions of drawings in these issues (see note 24) could certainly explain why Derain, who had perhaps heard of the show at Moline's Galerie Laffitte, was so keen to see "Van Gogh's drawings" in Vlaminck's company during his Easter leave in 1902.[39] Important as this exhibition may have been as a unique opportunity to appreciate Van Gogh's work in Paris between 1901 and 1905, the drawings illustrated in the *Mercure de France*—whether as stimulus or as fallback—doubtless contributed to Derain's interest in this aspect of Van Gogh's oeuvre and to his experimentation along similar lines in the summer of 1905 alongside Matisse.

The role of reproductions in establishing Van Gogh's reputation as a draftsman should not be underestimated. In the 1890s, Bernard set an example in the *Mercure de France*, and in 1893 and 1895 drawings were reproduced in *Van nu en straks*. Albert Plasschaert, through his Arts and Crafts Gallery in The Hague, issued a portfolio of ten reproductions accompanied by notes in 1898. In 1904 came W. Versluys's forty "Photo Collographs" after works by Van Gogh, followed in 1907 by a set devoted to twenty-four drawings. The well-publicized portfolio illustrating the one hundred drawings owned by Hidde Nijland, published in 1905, brought Van Gogh's earliest efforts as a draftsman to an international audience. Advertisements appeared, for example, in the Parisian journal *La plume*, and the portfolio exerted a wide influence, extending from the Belgian critic Ad van Bever to the German poet Rainer Maria Rilke.[40] During the 1910s Van Gogh's drawings were featured in editions of the artist's correspondence, including the 1911 luxury volume of *Lettres de Vincent van Gogh à Émile Bernard*, published by Vollard, and by this date, also in the Japanese cultural magazine *Shirakaba*.[41] At the same time, remarkably high-quality reproductions of the drawings were produced for sale, from the set of "Isographieën" put out by Willem Jan Gerritt van Meurs in 1910 to the stunning facsimiles issued by the Marées-Gesellschaft in 1919 and 1928.

Interest in the work of Van Gogh spread to Germany at the beginning of the twentieth century. Between 1901 and 1914, Johanna, who had reaped some personal satisfaction but little financial reward from most of her international ventures, enjoyed both by lending her support to over thirty major exhibitions held in more than a dozen German cities.[42] Half of these presentations, whether by a few well-chosen examples within the context of group shows or as a key part of ambitious monographic surveys, featured drawings; and they were the focus of several venues, notably the Berlin Secession's "Works on Paper" ("Zeichnende Künste") exhibitions of 1906, 1907, and 1909, and the thirty-five-work "Drawings by Vincent van Gogh" ("Zeichnungen von Vincent van Gogh") exhibition in Cologne and Frankfurt in 1910.

The artist's drawings debuted in Germany in a fourteen-work display in Hagen in 1905 that Johanna had arranged with Karl Ernst Osthaus, founder and director of the Folkwang Museum. He purchased three (F1419, F1539, F1550), the first acquired in Germany, for the museum's fledgling collection (which would find its permanent home in Essen). The following year, Hugo von Tschudi, director of Berlin's Nationalgalerie, donated anonymously to that institution the three drawings he had bought from Bernard (F1430, cat. 57; F1485, cat. 64; F1488, cat. 73). His foresight matched only by his unerring eye, Tschudi immediately sought out further examples, acquiring twice as many drawings (at twice the scale) in 1906–7, including *Boats on the Beach, Saintes-Maries-de-la-Mer* (F1428, cat. 60), *Cottage Garden* (F1456, cat. 91), *Café Terrace on the Place du Forum* (F1519, cat. 96), and *Walled Wheat Field with Rising Sun* (F1552, cat. 116). These

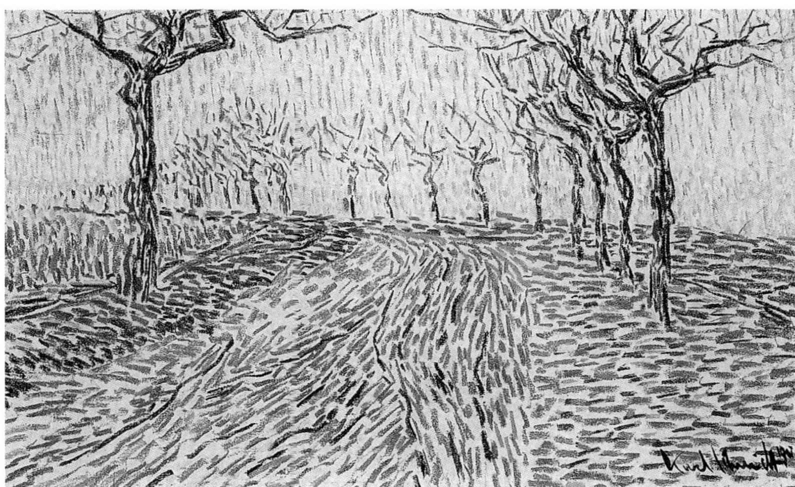

Fig. 49. Karl Schmidt-Rotluff, *Country Road in Spring*, 1905. Colored crayon on paper, 29 x 46.8 cm (11⅜ x 18⅜ in.). Private collection

two enlightened museum directors numbered among the sixteen German collectors who availed themselves of the opportunity to acquire Van Gogh drawings locally largely thanks to the initiative of Paul Cassirer, a dealer and the secretary of the Berlin Secession.

Cassirer, benefiting from his close relationship with Johanna, established a strong and lively market for Van Gogh's works in Germany in the early twentieth century, and he published the first German edition of the correspondence in 1914. Following Cassirer's lead, gallery owners and representatives of arts organizations solicited—and received—Johanna's support. Among the dealers were Emile Richter in Dresden, Marie Held in Frankfurt, Commenter in Hamburg, and Brakl and Thannhauser in Munich. Johanna regularly contributed loans to the Kunstverein displays held in various cities over the years, as well as to the famous 1912 Sonderbund exhibition in Cologne.

Although Van Gogh's works on paper found favor among those who pioneered the appreciation of his art in Germany, they did not command the same degree of interest as his paintings, particularly those of 1888–90. Approximately one drawing was bought for every three paintings acquired in Germany in the years before World War I, and with few exceptions, these dated to the artist's maturity. Van Gogh's aggressive color combinations and loaded brushstrokes were mainly what sustained the fascination of collectors, critics, and artists. Virtually no member of Die Brücke or Die Blaue Reiter remained untouched by the intensity and the freedom of expression in Van Gogh's richly saturated canvases, though some—for example, Karl Schmidt-Rotluff in his 1905 *Country Road in Spring* (fig. 49)—were responsive to Van Gogh's linear invention as well. Paul Klee stands apart among German artists, for, as he noted in diary entries between 1908 and 1911, his rapt attention was captured by Van Gogh's realization of the expressive potential of line.

While certain landscape and figure studies by Klee (see figs. 50, 51) record something of a debt to Van Gogh's ink drawings, Klee's diary offers more compelling proof of their profound impact on him. Klee was awe-struck at first by this towering genius, whose "pathos" and fervor seemed "alien," even downright disturbing, to him. In April 1908, he saw two shows of the artist's work in Munich at Brakl's Moderne Kunsthandlung and the W. Zimmermann gallery, and by that November—during the run of a third—he recognized that "[a] work of art goes beyond naturalism the instant the line enters in as an independent pictorial element, as in Van Gogh's drawings and paintings."[43] Three years later, Klee was able to fully appreciate the value of

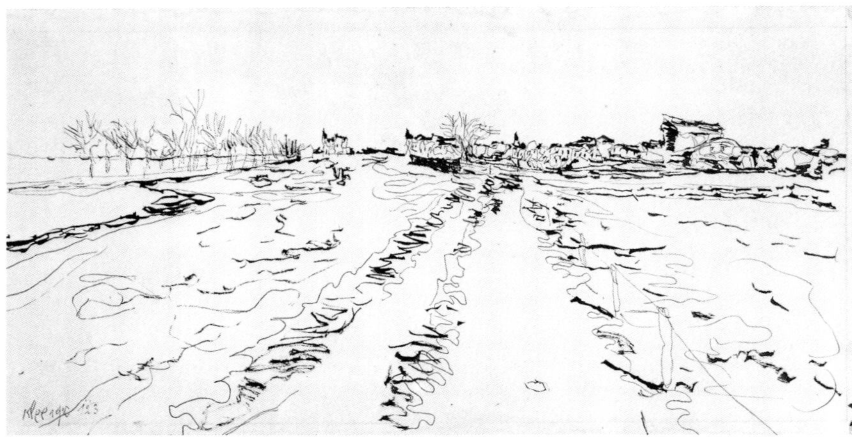

Fig. 50. Paul Klee, *Houses on the Oberwiesenfeld Parade Ground near Munich,* 1910. Pen, brush, and ink on paper, mounted on cardboard, 21.1 x 40.7 cm (8¼ x 16 in.). Paul-Klee-Stiftung, Kunstmuseum Bern (photo: ARS, New York)

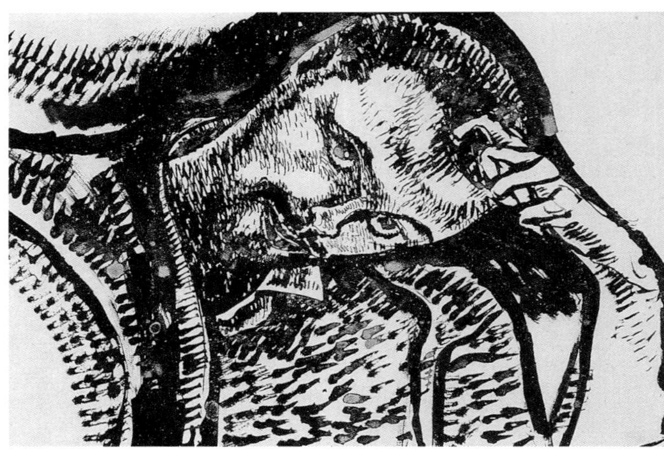

Fig. 51. Paul Klee, *Young Man Resting,* 1911. Brush and ink on writing paper, 13.8 x 20.2 cm (5⅞ x 8 in.). Private collection

Van Gogh's formidable achievement, convinced from his reading of the Dutch artist's letters of the sincerity behind his forceful manner:

> His line is new and yet very old, and happily not a purely European affair. It is more a question of reform than of revolution.
>
> The realization that there exists a line that benefits from Impressionism and at the same time conquers it has a truly electrifying effect on me. "Progress possible in the line!"
>
> The possibility ripened in me of harmonizing my swarming scribbles with firmly restraining linear boundaries. And this will bear for me a further fruit: the line that eats and digests scribbles. Assimilation. The spaces still look a bit empty, but not for much longer![44]

By the outbreak of World War I, Van Gogh's efforts as a draftsman had played a consequential role in the aesthetic development of a circle of artists that extended from Paul Signac to Henri Matisse and from Jan Toorop to Piet Mondrian, and his reputation as a trailblazer in modern art had been confirmed on an international front. His work was introduced amid much fanfare in London at the influential exhibition "Manet and the Post-Impressionists" held at the Grafton Galleries in 1910–11, and in New York at the historic Armory Show of 1913; however, it was not until after the war that his achievement as both painter and draftsman was shown in retrospective breadth in England and the United States. Yet long before Johanna furnished London's Leicester Gallery with a monographic survey in 1923, she helped to flesh out the selection that initially brought Van Gogh's genius to the British public: in 1910, a month after the opening of the Grafton Galleries Post-Impressionist show, she sent four drawings and *Self-Portrait with an Easel* (F522) to London in the hope that these additions would invite the public to be more attentive to the twenty-one paintings on view. Her effort was not in vain. Desmond MacCarthy, secretary for the venue, wrote to her on December 10, 1910, "The drawings look splendid. They have done a good deal to make people look at the pictures."[45] Quite conceivably, these supplemental loans had a larger influence on collectors and artists alike. Just after the close of the show in March 1911, C. Frank Stoop, a Dutch-born stockbroker living in London, purchased three drawings through the firm of C. M. van Gogh in The Hague: *Houses with Thatched Roofs* (F1242, cat. 24), *Pine Trees in the Walled Garden of the Asylum* (F1497, cat. 101), and *Landscape with a Bridge over the Oise* (F1639, cat. 119), which

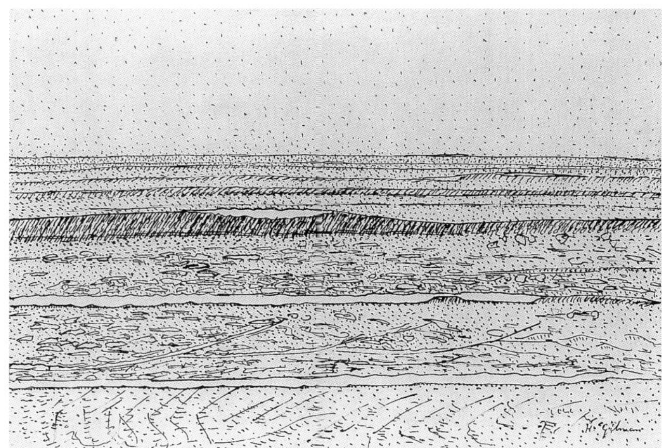

Fig. 52. Harold Gilman, *Seascape: Breaking Waves,* 1917. Pen and ink on paper, 29.8 x 43 cm (11¾ x 16⅞ in.). Ashmolean Museum, Oxford

he bequeathed to the Tate Gallery.[46] For Sir Michael Sadler, who took in the Grafton Galleries show—and later wrote the introduction to the 1923 Van Gogh exhibition catalogue and acquired three drawings for his collection (F1516, cat. 44; F1525, cat. 108; and F1544)[47]—the occasion may have kindled sympathies that grew stronger in time. And this may also have been true for British artist Harold Gilman, who during the war succeeded in making reed-pen drawings in the spirit of Van Gogh's panoramic views of Montmajour (fig. 52).

Organizers of the "International Exhibition of Modern Art," held at the Sixty-ninth Regiment Armory in New York in 1913, taking their cue from the Grafton Galleries and Sonderbund exhibitions in Europe, offered American viewers their first glimpse of work by an artist already recognized abroad as one of the "great immortals." Among the eighteen works by Van Gogh, there was, however, but a single drawing, lent by French dealer Émile Druet: the *Zouave* watercolor (F1482, cat. 77), which had debuted in Paris a decade earlier as part of the 1892 memorial show organized by Bernard. Then, as in 1913, it served to introduce the public to Van Gogh's lesser-known works on paper. The watercolor later found a permanent home in New York at the Metropolitan Museum, which led the way among American public institutions in exhibiting drawings by Van Gogh. After the close of the sixty-eight-work Van Gogh retrospective that Johanna organized in late 1920 for the Montross Gallery in New York, she agreed to lend three of the some thirty drawings on view to the Metropolitan. Thus, in the spring of 1921, *Winter Garden* (F1128, cat. 21), *Cottages, Saintes-Maries-de-la-Mer* (F1437, cat. 54), and *Rocks and Trees, Montmajour* (F1447, cat. 83) were shown in a works-on-paper display held in conjunction with the Metropolitan's "Loan Exhibition of Impressionist and Post-Impressionist Paintings,"[48] the institution's first nod to modernism. Eight decades later, these three great drawings, which remained part of the family legacy preserved in the Van Gogh Museum, return to the Metropolitan to take their place in the first monographic survey in the United States of Van Gogh's triumphs as a draftsman.

1. Johan de Meester, "Letteren en kunst: Vincent van Gogh," *Nieuwe Rotterdamsche Courant,* March 6, 13, 1892, quoted in translation in Stein 1986, p. 289.
2. Johanna van Gogh-Bonger, preface to *Brieven aan zijn broeder* (Amsterdam, 1914), reprinted in Van Gogh Letters 1958, vol. 1, p. xiii.
3. G.-Albert Aurier, "Les isolés: Vincent van Gogh," *Mercure de France,* January 1890, pp. 24–29, quoted in translation in Stein 1986, p. 192.
4. Letter from Johanna van Gogh-Bonger, agreeing to lend works on paper to the 1891 exhibition of Les XX in Brussels, to Octave Maus, December 26, 1890, A.A.C.B. Fonds Octave Maus, no. 5756, quoted in Daloze 1982, p. 35.
5. Letter from Octave Maus to Johanna van Gogh-Bonger, [December 1890], A.A.C.B. Fonds Vincent van Gogh, no. 4956, quoted in Daloze 1982, p. 35.
6. Letter from Johanna van Gogh-Bonger, enclosing a list of fifteen drawings, to Octave Maus, December 31, 1890, Archives, Van Gogh Museum, Amsterdam, Bd 61.
7. Letter from Octave Maus to Johanna van Gogh-Bonger, February 5, 1891, Archives, Van Gogh Museum, Amsterdam, b 1349 V/1962.
8. The sale, March 21, 1891, is the first entered in Johanna's account book (100 gulden); see Stolwijk and Veenenbos 2002, pp. 18, 140 no. 11/2. The drawings were shown with Les XX as nos. 9–15; the *Fountain* (no. 15), the only one from Saint-Rémy, was erroneously listed among the Arles drawings.
9. A. J. W., "Aux XX," *La gazette,* February 20, 1891, quoted in Daloze 1982, p. 39.
10. Émile Verhaeren, "Les XX," *La nation,* February 14, 1891, cited in Daloze 1982, p. 39; the quotations are from Verhaeren's piece in La Société Nouvelle's *Chronique artistique* 1, no. 7 (1891), p. 248, as translated in A. M. Hammacher, "Van Gogh and the Words," in De la Faille 1970, p. 19.
11. Letter from Paul Signac to Félix Fénéon, February 10, 1891, Signac Archives, Paris; quoted in Marina Ferretti-Bocquillon, *Signac Watercolors* (Paris, 2001), p. 30.
12. Henry van de Velde, "Mémoires" (manuscript), quoted in Susan Marie Canning, *Henry van de Velde (1863–1957): Schilderijen en tekeningen / Paintings and Drawings,* exh. cat. (Antwerp and Otterlo, 1987), pp. 88–89 n. 41; and in English translation in Essen–Amsterdam 1990, p. 238.
13. Quoted in Canning, *Henry van de Velde,* p. 93.
14. The purchase is recorded in Stolwijk and Veenenbos 2002, p. 142 no. 12/1 (for 50 gulden).
15. As observed by Leeman in Essen–Amsterdam 1990, p. 234.
16. Johanna's correspondence with Oldenzeel is quoted in translation in Han van Crimpen, "Johanna van Gogh: A Legacy, A Mission," in Kōdera 1993, pp. 358–59.
17. Johanna van Gogh-Bonger, diary entry of February 24, 1892, quoted in translation in V. W. van Gogh, "Introduction," in Van Gogh Letters 1958, vol. 1, p. lxi.
18. Albert Plasschaert, "Vincent van Gogh (Oldenzeel)," *De Kroniek,* November 7, 1903, p. 355, quoted in translation in the valuable essay on this subject by Hildelies Balk, "'All the nobility of his soul': Bremmer's Passion for the Work of Vincent van Gogh," in Kröller-Müller Museum 2003, p. 433.
19. Hammacher in De la Faille 1970, p. 19.
20. Johan Rohde kept a diary of his travels, which was published as *Journal fra en rejse i 1892* (Copenhagen, 1955); excerpts are reprinted in translation in Stein 1986, pp. 290–92.
21. Quoted in translation in Kirsten Olesen, "From Amsterdam to Copenhagen," in Copenhagen 1984–85, pp. 29–30.
22. See Olesen in Copenhagen 1984–85, p. 122. In the catalogue of Copenhagen 1893, the drawings by Van Gogh are listed as nos. 193–97.
23. Johannes Jørgensen, exhibition review in *Politiken,* April 16, 1893, quoted in translation in Copenhagen 1984–85, p. 116.
24. Mark Roskill (1971, pp. 174–75) was the first to recognize the significance of the drawings reproduced by Bernard, and he provided valuable documentation on their appearance in French journals between 1892 and 1895. The following summary incorporates his findings: the drawings *Boats at Sea, Saintes-Maries-de-la-Mer* (F1430, cat. 57) and *La Mousmé Sitting in an Armchair* (F1504, as "Jeune fille à la fleur") reproduced in *Le livre d'art,* June–July 1892, p. 8; *A Summer Evening* (F1514, cat. 68) reproduced in G.-Albert Aurier, *Oeuvres posthumes* (Paris, 1893), p. 203, with the caption "Dessiné par Vincent van Gogh"; Bernard published extracts from Van Gogh's letters in installments in the *Mercure de France,* accompanied by reproductions of *The Sower* (F1442 [fig. 189], May 1893, p. 15), *Wheat Field* (F1481 [fig. 186], June 1893, p. 113); *The Trinquetaille Bridge* (F1507 [fig. 182], July 1893, p. 213), *A Farmhouse in Provence* (F1478 [cat. 66], August 1893, p. 307), *Portrait of Patience Escalier* (F1460 [fig. 29], August 1893, p. 313), *A Summer Evening* (F1514 [cat. 68], September 1893, p. 71), *Field with Cemetery of Saintes-Maries in the Background* (F1479, October 1893, p. 111), *The Yellow House* (F1453 [cat. 97], October 1893, p. 117), *Provençal Orchard* (F1414 [fig. 118], November 1893, p. 267), *Trunk of a Tree* (F1509, January 1894, p. 31), *Street in Saintes-Maries-de-la-Mer* (F1436, March 1894, p. 225), *Street in Saintes-Maries-de-la-Mer* (F1434 [cat. 50], July 1894, p. 251), *A Park in Arles* (F1465, September 1894, p. 21), *Rhône Bank, Starry Night* (F1515, February 1895, p. 213).
25. After the close of the 1891 exhibition in Brussels, Johanna instructed Octave Maus to send five drawings shown—of the seven, minus the one sold and the one she gave to Maus—to Paris (as noted in Stolwijk and Veenenbos 2002, p. 26). Perhaps they were intended for inclusion in the Indépendants show, which opened a month later. The correspondence does not clarify why she made this request, and it appears from reviewers' accounts that no drawings were shown in the 1891 Salon des Indépendants.
26. The drawings in Gachet's collection are documented in the "Summary Catalogue of Works by Major Artists," in Anne Distel and Susan Alyson Stein, *Cézanne to Van Gogh: The Collection of Doctor Gachet,* exh. cat. (New York: Metropolitan Museum of Art, 1999), nos. P.G. III-27–40, pp. 222–28. Gachet's loans were nos. 23–25 in the 1905 Indépendants show and included F1648 and F1653; see ibid., PG. III-28, p. 222.
27. The contents of the Vollard exhibition, which opened in late November 1896 and ran for almost two months, has yet to be documented in the Van Gogh literature; indeed, the exhibition itself is not recorded in any of the editions of De la Faille. The list of loans Johanna sent to Vollard is preserved in the Van Gogh Museum (b 1437 V/1962), however, along with her correspondence with the dealer. The fifty-seven works on paper were listed by title and inventory number and grouped by medium (drawings, nos. 1–41 [with three items under no. 16]; watercolors, nos. 42–54; and "a lithograph Sorrow"). Because the inventory numbers Johanna assigned to drawings in her collection were inscribed on the reverse of the sheets, it is possible to identify many of these loans. Monique Hageman of the Van Gogh Museum graciously placed at my disposal her documentation on drawings inscribed with inventory numbers, and, thanks to the cooperation of owners, who allowed us to look at the back of their works or did so on our behalf, additional loans may be confirmed. On this basis, the following drawings, listed in order by their number in De la Faille, were lent to Vollard in 1896 (those in bold are catalogued in the present volume): F866, 1006, 1024, **1135**, 1165, 1170, 1184, 1186, 1192, 1250, 1251, 1273, 1288, 1316, 1317, **1327**, 1393, **1411**, 1439, **1447**, 1455, 1470, **1519**, **1532**, **1533**, **1542**, 1547, **1624**. In addition, we may assume that the following other drawings, which do not bear visible inscriptions but are either the only candidate or the most likely for works described on her list, were also lent: **F1130** (as

no. 14, "Jardin de village"), F1244r (as no. 44, under watercolors, "vue à vol d'oiseau"), **F1424** (as no. 13, "campagne des bords du Rhone," an adaptation of the title Van Gogh inscribed on the sheet; listed with a price of 200 francs in accordance with other large-scale drawings); **F1483** (as no. 49, under watercolors, "Moisson en Provence"); F1540 (as no. 37, "étoiles tournantes," listed with a price of 100 francs). Less certain is which watercolor, from among F1400–1403, was lent as no. 42, "fortifications."

28. Letter from Ambroise Vollard to Johanna van Gogh-Bonger, February 3, 1897, Archives, Van Gogh Museum.
29. Undoubtedly the drawing Degas acquired from Vollard was one of the half-dozen gleaners on display and among the "dix dessins" that Vollard bought from Johanna after the close of the show (see note 31, below). On her list, these works, titled "arracheusse de carottes" or "d'herbe," appeared as nos. 18, 19, 20, 30 31, along with an "arracheuse de pommes de terre," no. 32 (F1273). Figure 44 (F1262a) reproduced here was identified as probably the "Glaneuse" owned by Degas, in *The Private Collection of Edgar Degas: A Summary Catalogue,* exh. cat. (New York: Metropolitan Museum of Art, 1997), no. 597, p. 66. See also Christie's, London, sale cat., June 22, 2004, no. 3.
30. Renoir's remark, which he made at the gallery "one day" on seeing "some charcoal drawings by Van Gogh of farm laborers at work," is quoted in Ambroise Vollard, *Recollections of a Picture Dealer,* trans. Violet M. Macdonald (New York, 1978), p. 64.
31. Vollard confirmed his purchase of "ten drawings selected among those which were not catalogued according to price," in a letter to Johanna of March 29, 1897, Van Gogh Museum, Amsterdam; see also Stolwijk and Veenenbos 2002, pp. 142–43, no. 12/7. It is not possible to definitively identify these ten drawings, though some reasoned proposals can be made on the basis of works that have supporting (or at least not conflicting) subsequent provenances.

    Vollard may have purchased two or three peasant women gleaning from the half-dozen loans listed as "arracheusse," namely, F1265a and F1690 (relying on De la Faille's documentation that Vollard handled these two works) and F1262a (relying on the identification of this drawing as the gleaner that Degas purchased from Vollard; see note 29 above). Two works that Vollard later sold to Pál Majovszky could have come from this group: F1130 (cat. 22), a Nuenen view of the parsonage garden (listed as "Jardin de village"), and perhaps even the Nuenen interior, F1207a, as one of the "untitled" drawings. Other possible candidates include the two drawings of old men that Vollard sold to Cassirer in 1912, F965 and F972a (according to Feilchenfeldt and Veenenbos 1988, p. 127), although they cannot be associated with specific titles on Johanna's list; and other early figure drawings (a "Head of a Woman," a "Sheaf Binder," a "Woman with Corn Sheaf," or a "Mower"), "Village (watercolor)," as well as a "landscape" or two. Later drawings, in addition to a "Vue d' Arles," likely included "Moisson en provence (watercolor)," F1483 (cat. 62).
32. Postcard from Moline to Johanna van Gogh-Bonger (Van Gogh Museum, Amsterdam, b 3463 V/1984), postmarked February 1902, thus providing an indication of when the show was held. This card and the list of drawings Johanna sent to Moline (b 2188 VF/1982) were kindly placed at my disposal by Monique Hageman of the Van Gogh Museum. Johanna listed each of thirty loans by title and inventory number (which makes it possible to identify the majority of the works, as described in note 27, above), and all were for sale, with prices ranging from 175 to 400 francs. The following drawings, in order by their number in De la Faille, were shown by Moline (those in bold are catalogued in the present volume): **F1182**, 1186, 1214, 1249, 1288, 1316, **1428**, **1440**, 1443, **1447**, 1455, **1457**, 1460, **1477**, **1478**, **1519**, **1522**, 1525a, **1538**, 1540, 1547; in addition, there were three other Dutch figure studies, a Brabant landscape, and five later views, including a "Vue de la Crau" and a "Marine" (possibly F1474 and F1432, respectively).
33. Other loans previously shown at Vollard's include F1186, F1288, F1316, F1455, F1540, F1547.
34. Letters from Klas Fåhræus to Johanna van Gogh-Bonger, December 12 and 29, 1911, Archives, Van Gogh Museum, Amsterdam; quoted in Håkan Larsson, *Flames from the South: On the Introduction of Vincent van Gogh to Sweden* (Eslöv, 1996), p. 227.
35. Matisse's loans to the 1905 Indépendants show were listed in the catalogue as nos. 29–31.
36. André Derain, *Lettres à Vlaminck* (Paris, 1955), p. 29, late 1901.
37. Ibid., p. 59, early 1902.
38. As Fred Leeman astutely recognized in his insightful discussion on Derain in "Reflections of Van Gogh in the Work of Some Masters of Early Modern Art," in Kōdera 1993, p. 51. For Aurier's 1890 article, see note 3, above.
39. Derain, *Lettres à Vlaminck,* p. 60, ca. early spring 1902. The exact dates of this show are not known, but since Moline asked Johanna to send the works in February (see above and note 32), there is a good possibility that it ran through Easter, which fell on March 30, 1902.
40. On this subject, see Hammacher in De la Faille 1970, p. 22.
41. See Kinoshita Nagahiro, "Van Gogh in Modern Japanese Literature," *Shirakaba* 2, no. 6 (1911), p. 176; and Takashina Shūji, "The Formation of the 'Van Gogh Mythology' in Japan," *Shirakaba* 2, no. 6 (1911), p. 152.
42. The works by Van Gogh exhibited and collected in Germany during these years have been thoroughly documented in the invaluable publication by Walter Feilchenfeldt, *Vincent van Gogh and Paul Cassirer, Berlin: The Reception of Van Gogh in Germany from 1901 to 1914* (1988), which includes a catalogue of the drawings compiled by Han Veenenbos. Their findings have served as the backbone for the observations made in this section of my text and should be consulted for further information.
43. *The Diaries of Paul Klee, 1898–1918,* ed. Felix Klee (Berkeley, 1964), Munich diary entries, pp. 224, 232.
44. Ibid., p. 260.
45. This letter (Archives, Van Gogh Museum, b 5868 V/1996) and the fact that Johanna sent these supplemental loans to London in late 1910 were brought to light in Anna Gruetzner-Robins, *Modern Art in Britain, 1910–1914,* exh. cat. (London, 1997), p. 37.
46. See Stolwijk and Veenenbos 2002, p. 151 no. 18/11.
47. See ibid., p. 164 no. 101/13–15, p. 197 no. 101/14.
48. These three drawings, on view at the Metropolitan, May 17–September 15, 1921, are recorded in a "List of Exhibitions" ledger in the Department of Drawings and Prints, The Metropolitan Museum of Art. In the 1920 Montross Gallery exhibition catalogue, they appeared as nos. 3 (F1128), 5 (F1447), and 13 (F1437).

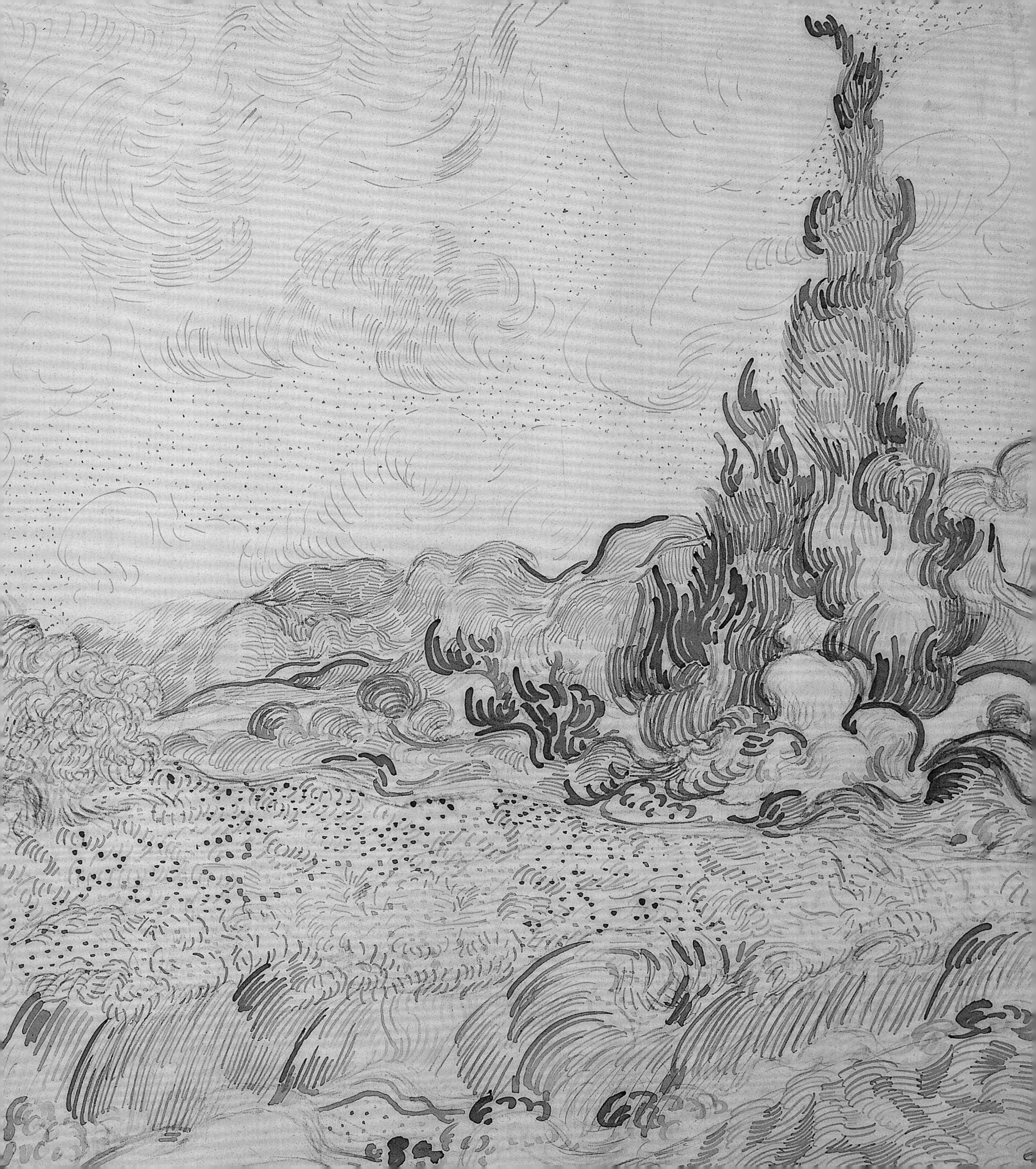

Metamorphoses: Van Gogh's Drawings Then and Now

SJRAAR VAN HEUGTEN

Fig. 53. Detail of cat. 110, *Wheat Field with Cypresses* (F1538)

Like any other man-made objects, works of art are subject to change over time. Humidity, oxidation, ultraviolet rays, and microorganisms are just some of the menaces facing curators and restorers. Today, new insights and techniques make it increasingly possible to conserve and, if necessary, restore damaged works. Often, however, it is already too late: the storage and exhibition practices so widely accepted today have not been in effect for very long. Many works of art have thus sustained changes that can no longer be reversed and which have fundamentally altered their original appearance. In such cases, the work no longer conforms to the artist's original intentions.

Many of Van Gogh's drawings have undergone such metamorphoses. Although no comprehensive inventory has ever been made, for several reasons it seems safe to assume that his works have suffered more—particularly from exposure to light—than those of most other Impressionists and Post-Impressionists. First, the drawings play an extremely important role in Van Gogh's oeuvre; they are equal partners to his paintings—far more so than is the case with the work of many of his contemporaries. This is widely recognized, and the resulting demand for works on paper to include in exhibitions has been detrimental to them. Moreover, many of Van Gogh's most significant drawings were executed in pen and often highly light-sensitive ink. No other modernist gave this technique such prominence in the creative process. Thus Van Gogh's drawn oeuvre is extremely vulnerable to damage, in a way comparable only to works by artists who specialized in the equally sensitive medium of watercolor, such as Paul Cézanne.

The following essay is not intended, however, as a simple account of disaster; most of the metamorphoses in Van Gogh's drawings can hardly be described as dramatic. A work executed in black ink that has changed to brown still retains most of its original character, and a drawing in black chalk on blue paper now turned off-white has not necessarily forfeited its artistic power. All the same, there *are* works that have changed radically, ranging from compositions that have become unbalanced or had their color schemes spoiled to a small number of sheets on which the ink has faded so badly that the image must be considered lost.

To comprehend Van Gogh's drawn oeuvre, and to come to an understanding of the artistic intentions behind it, one must approach the aging process with common sense. Ironically, it is often through these transformations that one becomes aware of the extraordinary refinement of Van Gogh's technique. For example, many pen-and-ink drawings, both from Nuenen and from the south of France, employ a combination of pen and pencil. The pen strokes themselves have frequently faded from black to brown, while the pencil work has retained its gray-black tone. More than was ever possible before, we can now see that the pencil not only served for the underdrawing but also played a role in the overall composition that was unusually prominent for a pen drawing. Such mutations can almost be described as serendipitous, and their study can prove genuinely enlightening.

This overview of the metamorphoses in Van Gogh's drawings aims to provide insight into the artist's creative intentions with regard to both style and meaning. The latter refers to the expressive power that, for whatever reasons, Van Gogh sought to give his work by employing a variety of techniques. The essay is presented chronologically rather than by medium, although within the different periods each medium is considered separately. This chronological organization allows us to trace the leitmotifs in Van Gogh's drawn oeuvre and to demonstrate that, as revolutionary as his approach was, there were still important constants. To render the picture as complete as possible, I took into consideration not just the works in the catalogue and exhibition (these sheets, after all, are the artist's masterworks, and were chosen at least in part because of their excellent condition) but also representative examples from the artist's entire output.[1]

The Early Work

Van Gogh's earliest drawings, executed in 1880–81 in Belgium and in Etten in Brabant, are relatively well preserved. They were generally done with a graphite pencil, occasionally combined with ink, on a fair-quality off-white laid paper. The most common alteration is a yellowing or browning of the paper, which can affect the sense of contrast in the work. Considering that Van Gogh was devoted to using paper the color of "unbleached linen" [164]—that is, a somewhat yellowish off-white—this is indeed important. However, in certain cases the discoloration can be reversed to some extent through restoration, and it is rarely genuinely problematic.

In The Hague, where he worked from the end of December 1881 to September 1883, Van Gogh initially drew mainly with a pencil, later employing the robust type favored by carpenters. From the late summer of 1882, he began developing a preference for a kind of heavy-duty watercolor paper—called *torchon* in French—that had a number of advantages. It was very strong, and the artist was now in the habit of drawing both with great verve and on wet sheets, which allowed him to model his material. As a result, the paper is often blistered and creased, an effect that enhances the works' somewhat raw expressivity. There has sometimes been a tendency to try to flatten these drawings during restoration, but this is a mistake: the state of the paper results from Van Gogh's working method. The excellent quality of the *torchon* paper (chiefly with the watermark HALLINES) and the use of graphite, which never ages, mean that these works have remained in good condition and have preserved their original vibrancy. Where this is no longer the case, close examination reveals it to be the result of poor restoration.[2]

Among several groups of technically related drawings from The Hague, we begin to find an aging phenomenon that has had an important effect on Van Gogh's drawn oeuvre: a "browning" of the originally black ink—as in *Country Road* of March–April 1882 (F1089, cat. 7). Ink and graphite were the primary materials, and taken together they once created a subtle play of black and somewhat polished gray tones. The change in the color of the ink undermines this effect and now gives the drawing a less vivid, warmer aura than Van Gogh originally intended. Other pen-and-pencil drawings of the same period make a similar impression. Among them is *The Entrance to the Pawn Bank* (JH126, cat. 6). A number of elements in the composition were executed with highly thinned and now-faded black ink and today have all but disappeared—for example, the texts on the posters on the wall announcing, among others, several estate sales. These undoubtedly once gave the work an anecdotal quality that is now far less explicit.

At no other time in his career did Van Gogh experiment with his materials as he did in The Hague. A highlight among these trials is a

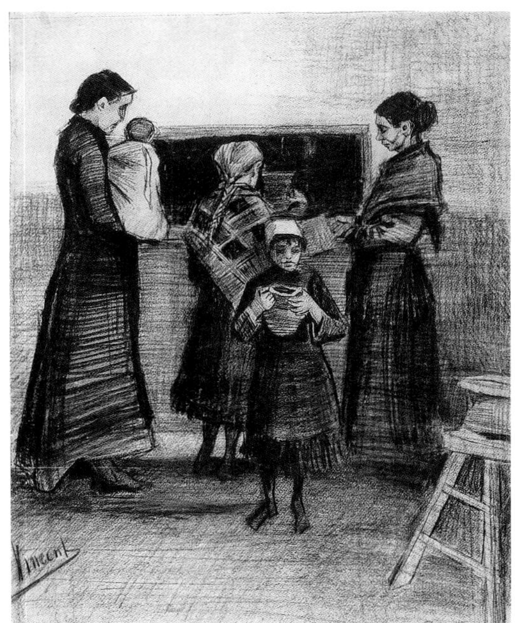

Fig. 54. *Soup Distribution in a Public Soup Kitchen* (F1020a), March 1883. Natural black chalk, brush and black paint, opaque white watercolor, scratched, on watercolor paper, 56.5 x 44.4 cm (22¼ x 17½ in.). Van Gogh Museum, Amsterdam (Vincent van Gogh Foundation)

group of sheets from 1882 that resulted from what he called "painting with black." The idea was borrowed primarily from English black-and-white magazine illustrations. Van Gogh was a great admirer of these cleverly executed wood engravings and collected them avidly. Although printed only in black, they employ a wide variety of graphic techniques, which give them a striking character. As he did not yet feel ready to work in color—his self-invented learning program insisted on taking things a step at a time—Van Gogh decided to try something similar in his drawings. He sought out a variety of blacks, employing, among others, graphite pencil, lithographic crayon, and ink—printer's and India ink. These sober materials, applied in combination with forceful contrast of light and dark, produced a number of studies of heads and genre scenes of a melancholy cast appropriate to the kind of socially conscious, realist themes the artist favored at the time. The majority of these subjects have remarkably little facial expression in themselves; Van Gogh's use of materials and angular style, however, create the perfect portrait of these obvious and introverted working-class types.

Here, too, we find that the ink has faded. Although rarely truly disturbing within the broader range of materials employed, the works no longer reflect Van Gogh's intention to "paint with black." A brown tone has now replaced the finishing black accents, and this, of course, is contrary to his aims. The phenomenon can be seen clearly in *Old Man with a Top Hat* (F985, cat. 12).

In March and April of 1883, Van Gogh worked with a natural black chalk that he referred to as *bergkrijt* (literally mountain chalk). He was extremely fond of this material, particularly for the quality of its black—a warm tone tending toward brown that he described as the color "of a plowed field on a summer's evening" [R30]. As he explained to Theo, there was "something dead" about other types of chalk, but this one had a "gypsy soul" that had charmed him.

One of his most ambitious figure compositions, *Soup Distribution in a Public Soup Kitchen* (F1020a, fig. 54), is executed in natural chalk on hefty watercolor paper that has yellowed slightly. The subtle tone of the chalk—the most important medium—is still clearly evident and is highly appropriate to the modest scene. Three other images Van Gogh made with the same material are explicitly domestic in character.[3] The choice of this type of chalk, with its warmer feel, was, of course, no accident. Today, however, such fine points have been entirely lost. Van Gogh here employed a cheap, woody paper that has browned badly over the years. Since the other materials are water soluble and any treatment would require the use of water, the discoloration cannot be reversed. The brown tone is thus permanent, depriving the work forever of its original nuances. Moreover, the once-white color of the paper must have played a role in the chiaroscuro; today such contrasts have been drastically reduced.

Nuenen

There is little to say about the aging process with regard to the small number of drawings Van Gogh executed during his three-month stay in Drenthe. The multifaceted drawn oeuvre from Nuenen, on the other hand, exhibits a number of striking metamorphoses.

In general, neither the watercolors nor the drawings Van Gogh made in Nuenen using dry black or colored drawing materials have changed radically. The pen drawings, on the other hand, have undergone important transformations. The ink employed for most of the Nuenen pen drawings has now turned brown; in a large number of cases it can be either demonstrated or presumed with great certainty that its color was originally black, or at least much darker than it is today. A number of sheets have suffered from corrosion, which

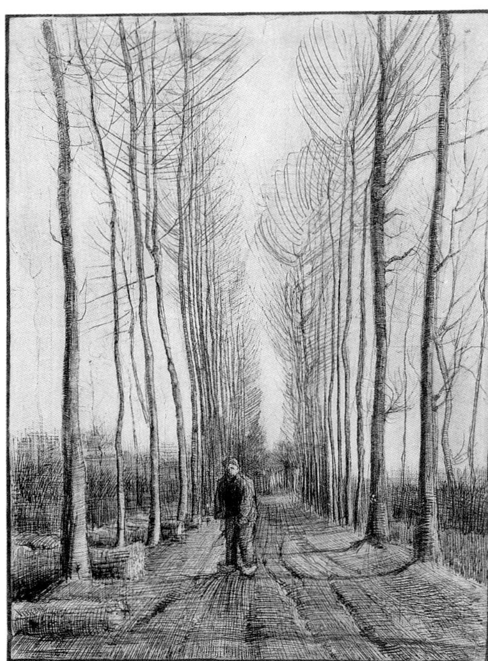

Fig. 55. *Avenue of Poplars* (F1239), March 1884. Pen and brown (originally black) ink, graphite on wove paper, 54.2 x 39.3 cm (21 3/8 x 15 1/2 in.). Van Gogh Museum, Amsterdam (Vincent van Gogh Foundation)

proves that Van Gogh used iron-gall ink;[4] over time, this type of ink, originally black or a very dark brown, discolors to brown. Another clear indication that the ink was once much darker than it is today is the combination with graphite, already mentioned above: in the present color scheme, dominated by brown, the use of pencil is illogical, while with black it would have harmonized perfectly.

The combination of pen and pencil, whereby the graphite serves as more than merely the material for the underdrawing, is unusual. Even in the case of underdrawings, draftsmen generally erase the traces of their pencil in order to allow the pen lines to work to maximum effect. Van Gogh rarely made the effort to efface his preliminary sketches and, moreover, liked to apply graphite together with ink. Ink is naturally the most important material in these drawings, but the graphite appears to have had an important function. This can be seen, for example, in *Pollard Birches* (F1240, cat. 19), which belongs to a group of impressive pen drawings from the spring of 1884 (cats. 19–22, fig. 55). The graphite adds volume and definition to the tops of several of the trees; it gives more weight to portions of the ground; and it indicates shadow. Pencil work plays an even greater role in *Avenue of Poplars* (F1239, fig. 55), where we find it used again for the ground but above all for the branches of the trees. In the drawing's original state, this must have made the branches appear quite fragile, particularly in comparison to the trunks and heavier boughs; this effect has now been lost. In essence, this combining of materials is a more refined form of the "painting in black" experiments of The Hague. Despite the unintended shift in emphasis, however, the Nuenen sheets still have enormous power.

Van Gogh left for Antwerp in November of 1885. Only a few drawings from his three-month sojourn there have been preserved, and none of them has undergone changes of the kind discussed here.

Paris: Modernist Experiments in Color

The disconcerting discovery that the style of painting he had practiced for the last three years was hopelessly old-fashioned and the realization that he needed to reconsider both his use of color and his brushwork led Van Gogh to concentrate mainly on painting in 1886. The drawings from that year are primarily studies in graphite or black chalk and are generally well preserved. Pen drawings from the artist's second year in Paris were mostly executed in good-quality carbon ink that has maintained its color.

In early 1887 Van Gogh once again took up drawing seriously, completing a series of ambitious cityscapes. In a number of them, color—the subject to which he had devoted himself the previous year—plays an important role. They are *A Guinguette* (F1407, cat. 37), *Window in the Bataille Restaurant* (F1392, fig. 56), and *Boulevard de Clichy* (F1393, fig. 58). In contrast to the latter two, the first sheet employs only black and white materials, but all three are executed on a gray-blue paper that has almost completely lost its color (with the exception of a few areas along the edges), now varying from a dirty yellow to a yellowish brown. The consequences are significant, and in *Window in the Bataille Restaurant*—the only drawing in the group to have retained some of its original blue—they are frankly disconcerting.

A Guinguette is the sheet that has suffered least from the discoloration. It is also the only one of the three works to be included in the present exhibition. Set against a blue background, the scene must certainly once have made a fresher impression and more accurately captured the atmosphere of a bright winter's day, thanks in particular to the contrast of the white clouds against the sky. Today, the mood is more that of a gray autumn afternoon, but the power of the artist's drawing style still makes it an attractive work.

Window in the Bataille Restaurant has clearly lost much in terms of coloration.

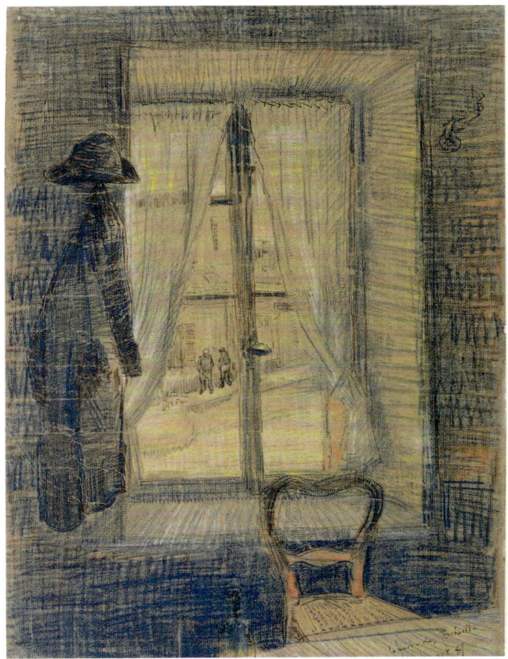

Fig. 56. *Window in the Bataille Restaurant* (F1392), February–March 1887. Pen and brown (originally black) ink, blue, yellow, orange, and white chalk on laid paper that was originally blue-gray, 54 x 39.8 cm (21¼ x 15⅝ in.). Van Gogh Museum, Amsterdam (Vincent van Gogh Foundation)

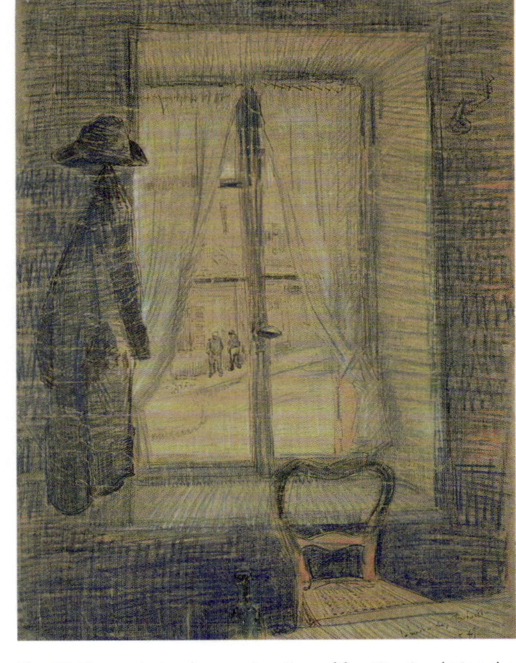

Fig. 57. Computerized reconstruction of fig. 56, simulating the original color of the drawing paper

Thanks to computer technology, we can now simulate the original color of the paper and thus gain insight into Van Gogh's color experiments.[5] The present state and a reconstruction of the drawing as it probably originally appeared are here set side by side for the sake of comparison (figs. 56, 57). Using the original blue of the paper, Van Gogh drew in a darker blue chalk in a variety of tones: heavier for the walls, the jacket, and the mullions; lighter for the table and the window frame; and a vague, almost delicate hue for the scene outside. This created a subtle simultaneous contrast—an effect achieved through the use of closely related colors—of two shades of blue. He further enlivened the drawing with a few accents of complementary orange and by adding still lighter tones of white and yellow. Today, little evidence of these color relationships remains: against the dirty yellow background, the lines of blue chalk seem coarse and all sense of harmony has disappeared; it has become nearly impossible to grasp the once-so-intelligently constructed balance of simultaneous and complementary contrasts. Incidentally, at an early stage, various elements of the composition were sketched in with a fine pen: the chair, the jacket, and an almost invisible bottle in the foreground. These were later gone over with chalk, and the already rather fine pen strokes—which, moreover, have lost some of their intensity over the years—have mostly vanished under the artist's robust chalk strokes.

In *Boulevard de Clichy*, too, the balance of colors has been upset, although here the sheet is somewhat less affected than in the previous example (see figs. 58, 59). In this street scene Van Gogh once more worked in blue-on-blue: he applied the color quite heavily to the sky, more thinly in the street, and still more discreetly in the buildings. He again used touches of orange chalk—originally redder than they are today—to create elements of complementary contrast within the overall scheme of simultaneous contrast that appears

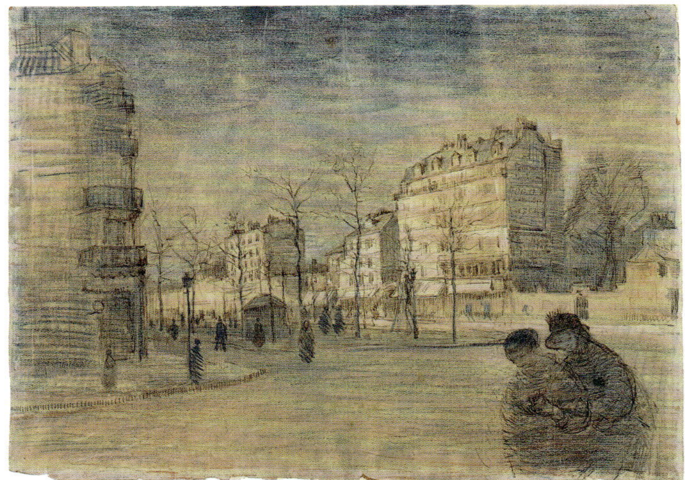

Fig. 58. *Boulevard de Clichy* (F1393), February–March 1887. Pen and brown (originally black) ink, orange and blue chalk, opaque white watercolor, graphite on laid paper that was originally blue-gray, 40.1 x 54.4 cm (15¾ x 21⅜ in.). Van Gogh Museum, Amsterdam (Vincent van Gogh Foundation)

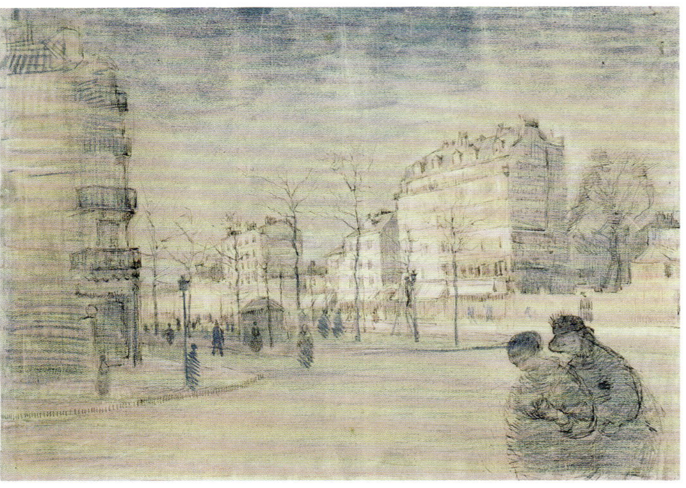

Fig. 59. Computerized reconstruction of fig. 58, simulating the original color of the drawing paper

to have been the goal of the experiment. He used white to highlight various details, and the pen was also employed.

With the fading of the paper, these unique color experiments in Van Gogh's drawn oeuvre have been lost. A direct link with the paintings has also disappeared: there is a version of the Boulevard de Clichy motif on canvas, painted over a background of very light blue (F292).[6] This demonstrates once again that the drawings discussed here were part of the well-planned investigation of the potentials of color that Van Gogh undertook while in Paris.

Summer Cityscapes and Parisian Ukiyo-e

Further color experiments on paper took place between June and September 1887, and clearly establish the ever-increasing clarity of Van Gogh's works (F1410, cat. 41; F1401, cat. 38; F1411, cat. 40; F1406, cat. 39). Three watercolors of the ramparts on the outskirts of Paris (F1400, fig. 60; F1402; F1403, fig. 61) and a view of the city from Montmartre (F1410, cat. 41), each measuring about 40 by 54 centimeters, show that despite his emphasis on painting, Van Gogh was still very interested in drawing. The works are all striking in composition and in the choice of viewpoint, and they explicitly make reference to the art of the Impressionists. Van Gogh here worked on a type of laid paper that subsequently turned rather brown. In *View from Montmartre* (cat. 41) and the sheet from the Whitworth Art Gallery (fig. 61), the consequences are limited, as the paper is more or less completely covered with watercolor; the bare areas now create a different contrast than intended, but on the whole the works are still very striking. A sheet in the Van Gogh Museum, on the other hand, reveals more of the paper underneath (fig. 60). Moreover, in the foreground, the artist painted over the lines of chalk with a gouache of the same color as the original paper. The latter has discolored, while the former has not, resulting in a strongly contrasting white area that is completely unintentional. The brown in the sky further diminishes the sense of a sunny summer's day.

An attractive group of smaller watercolors was produced in the same months (F1406, cat. 39; F1401, cat. 38; F1411, cat. 40). Thanks to the good quality of the paper and drawing materials, they are still in exemplary condition. Their size, brilliant coloration, and rather playful character clearly demonstrate

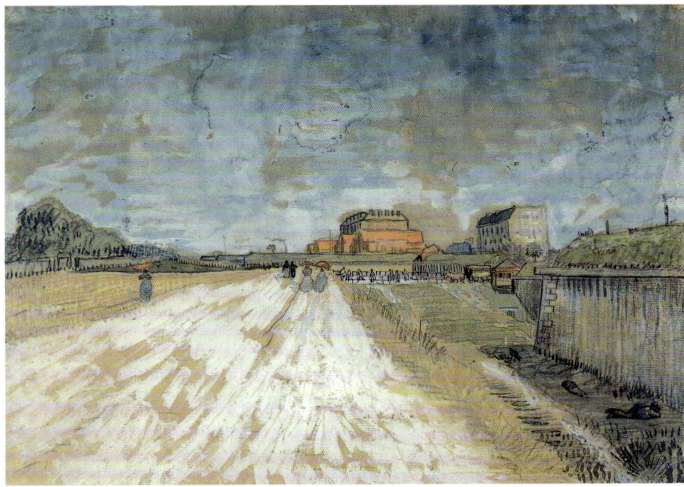

Fig. 60. *Road Running beside the Paris Ramparts* (F1400), June–September 1887. Transparent and opaque watercolor, yellow, green, orange, ocher, and blue chalk, brush and blue (oil?) paint, pen and blue ink, graphite on laid paper, 39.7 x 53.8 cm (15⅝ x 21⅛ in.). Van Gogh Museum, Amsterdam (Vincent van Gogh Foundation)

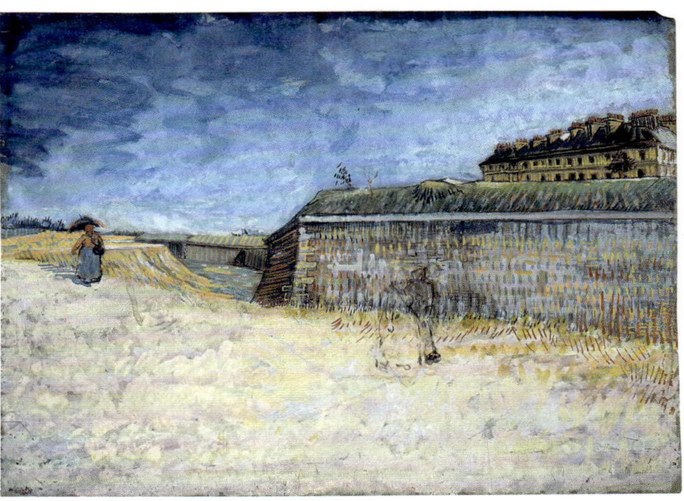

Fig. 61. *The Ramparts of Paris* (F1403), June–September 1887. Transparent and opaque watercolor, pen and brown ink, white gouache, graphite on laid paper, 39.5 x 53.5 cm (15½ x 21⅛ in.). Whitworth Art Gallery, Manchester

that they were made under the influence of the Japanese ukiyo-e prints Van Gogh so admired. Comparisons with early reproductions confirm their excel ent state of preservation (see cat. 38 and fig. 62); only here and there can one point to mutations of color, a fate from which many watercolors unfortunately suffer. On the little wall at the left, for example, we find several light-colored patches that were once strokes of pale pink, and in the sky there are now several white streaks that formerly dissolved into their surroundings—metamorphoses, however, that hardly detract from the overall charm of the work.

Arles: The Inspired Line

There are only a few large sheets among the pen drawings Van Gogh made in Paris (see F1407, cat. 37). The real focus of his experiments was color, and the most important drawings of the period are thus vibrant watercolors. In Arles, on the other hand, pen and line became central. It was here that Van Gogh discovered the type of reed pen he found most useful for drawing. A small role for watercolor remained, though, and in several cases he combined watercolor and pen.

The watercolors of this period have undergone some discoloration, which, as noted above, is almost inherent in the medium; others,

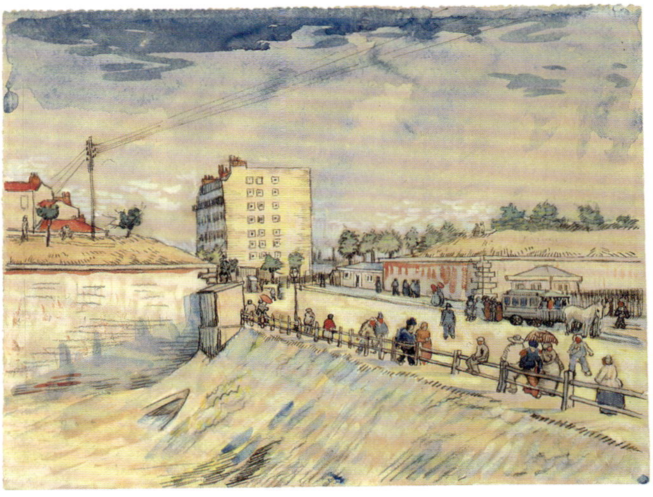

Fig. 62. Reproduction of *Gate in the Paris Ramparts* (F1401, cat. 38) in Julius Meier-Graefe, *Vincent van Gogh: Faksimiles nach Aquarellen und Zeichnungen* (Munich, 1928), no. 1

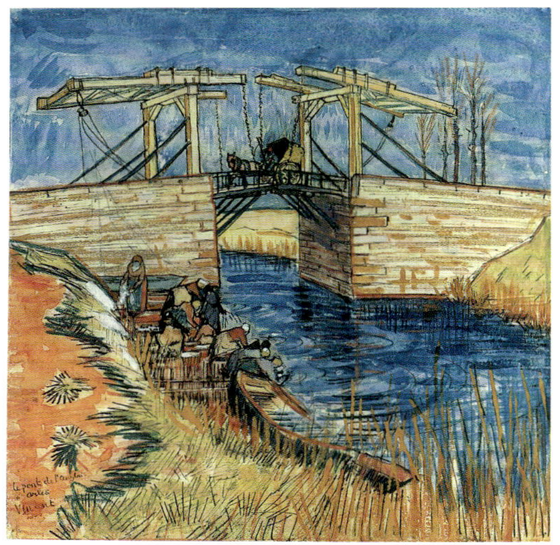

Fig. 63. *The Langlois Bridge* (F1480), April 1888. Transparent and opaque watercolor, wax crayon, pen and ink, graphite on paper, 30.5 x 30.2 cm (12 x 11⅞ in.). Private collection

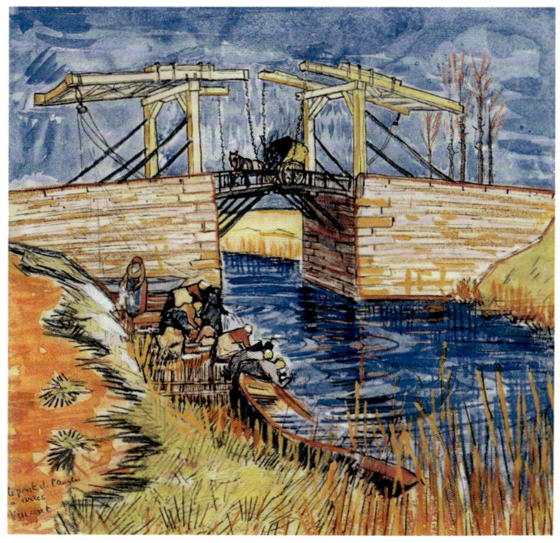

Fig. 64. Reproduction of fig. 63 in Julius Meier-Graefe, *Vincent van Gogh: Faksimiles nach Aquarellen und Zeichnungen* (Munich, 1928), no. 7

however, are extraordinarily well preserved. *The Langlois Bridge* (F1480, fig. 63) and *Boats on the Beach, Saintes-Maries-de-la-Mer* (F1429, fig. 135) have retained their almost brazen coloration, despite the fact that the former has lost some of the green along the canal banks, as an older reproduction (fig. 64) shows. A number of the watercolors were made after paintings, such as *The Langlois Bridge* (fig. 63), *The Yellow House* (F1413, cat. 98), and *The Night Café* (F1463, fig. 217); none of these has suffered unduly. Also among this group, however, is a watercolor after *Pink Peach Trees (Souvenir de Mauve)* (F1469, fig. 65), a painting (F394) now in the Kröller-Müller Museum. Just as in the artist's own painted replica in the Van Gogh Museum (F404, fig. 66), the pink pigment of the blossoms in the drawing has faded. On canvas, the blossoms have at least remained visible as daubs of white impasto against the blue sky. But there is no impasto in a watercolor, and here nothing is left but a few traces of pink, making the trees look bare and the white flecks almost like clouds.

For his pen drawings in Arles, Van Gogh employed a number of different types of ink. Their stability varies from very good to inordinately poor. He also occasionally combined two kinds of ink on the same sheet, one of which was more stable than the other.

In certain cases, works have lost some of their expressivity due to fading of the ink or because the paper has browned. There is, however, a category of sheets, which, although some were undoubtedly once masterpieces, can now no longer play a credible role in the drawings oeuvre. They are part of the so-called first Montmajour series, views Van Gogh made in May 1888 from atop the hill of that name. Two of these are drawings in the collection of the Van Gogh Museum that depict the ruins of the former monastery on Montmajour and were executed in pen and aniline ink (F1423, figs. 67, 68; F1417, figs. 69, 70).[7] Where the passe-partout covered parts of the scene in figure 67 the drawing has preserved its purple color; the rest of the pen lines have faded almost to invisibility. Figure 69 was also once purple in tone. Jo van Gogh-Bonger recorded the color of the drawings in 1907 and 1909 in two lists she made of the works; and even earlier an art critic had expressed his enthusiasm for the use of purple ink in five sheets on display at the Rotterdamsche Kunstkring in 1901.[8] In any case, in the early twentieth century the works still had a convincing purple tint, although one cannot therefore deduce with absolute certainty that this was exactly their original color.[9] Aniline ink comes in a variety of shades, some of which are known to discolor to purple and, with further exposure to light, to fade or turn brown. In theory, the sheets could have been executed with a number of different inks, all of which turned the same purple and then later brown. The browning and fading did not occur with the same intensity in all the sheets, but we do not know what caused these variations. To determine this, research would have to be done into such aspects as their exhibition history, the combination of materials, and the circumstances under which they were stored.

In addition to the aforementioned groups, there are, however, a number of sheets from Arles that have changed over time but which have nonetheless remained artistically and aesthetically convincing. As in the case of the Nuenen pen drawings, these works provide an insight into aspects of Van Gogh's working method that would never have come to light were the works still in pristine condition. In a number of other sheets belonging to the first Montmajour series, intriguing drawings in graphite or black chalk have now been revealed: Van Gogh apparently first sketched in the broad lines of the composition, as well as the incidental detail; later, when working with the pen, he sometimes followed his own prescriptions, but also on occasion deviated from his original idea. It seems clear that here, as in the Nuenen sheets, the dry materials were meant to play a visual role in the finished work. They were used to intensify areas of shadow—sometimes before the ink was applied and once afterward, but always with a purpose and not simply as a kind of underdrawing—and to give numerous other elements in the landscape more emphasis. In a rather faded sheet in Essen (F1419, fig. 71), some of the pencil lines have been drawn with such force that it is hard to imagine they were intended to function as nothing more than a preliminary sketch; had that been the case, finer lines would have sufficed. We find something similar in two fairly degraded works also made at Montmajour (F1448; F1493, fig. 72). Old black-and-white photographs show a large number of chalk or graphite lines that undoubtedly played an important part in these compositions even before the ink began to fade. Notable here is that we know that the ink used in the sheet in the Van Gogh Museum was once purple—and this was most certainly also the case with F1448. What we are dealing with, then, is probably a kind of experiment, whereby Van Gogh sought to give the purple pen lines more weight and definition through the use of dark chalk. Some caution is in order, however, as the combination of materials might also be an indication that the ink was not in fact originally purple, but rather a darker tint that would have harmonized better with the dry medium.[10]

In July 1888 Van Gogh once again began exploring the plains of La Crau for suitable motifs. This led to a group of large pen drawings that are a high point in his career. They are extremely well thought out, without, however, losing any of their spontaneity. Some of these works still illustrate his artistic qualities to the fullest: *Rocks and Trees, Montmajour* (F1447, cat. 83) is executed in black and dark gray ink, which appears to be in almost

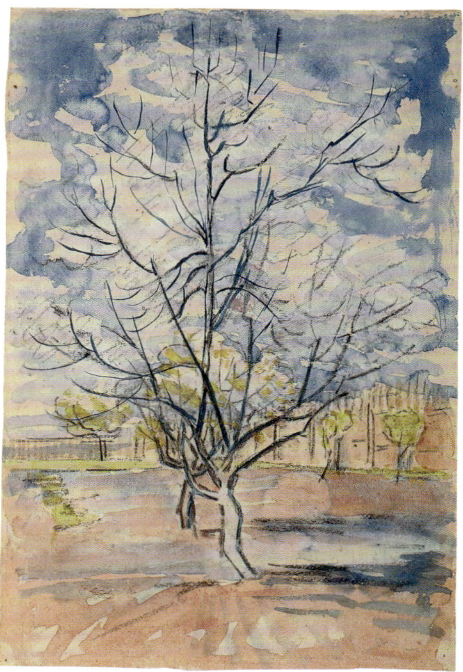

Fig. 65. *Pink Peach Trees (Souvenir de Mauve)* (F1469), April 1888. Transparent and opaque watercolor, black chalk on wove paper, 45.4 x 30.7 cm (17⅞ x 12⅛ in.). Van Gogh Museum, Amsterdam (Vincent van Gogh Foundation)

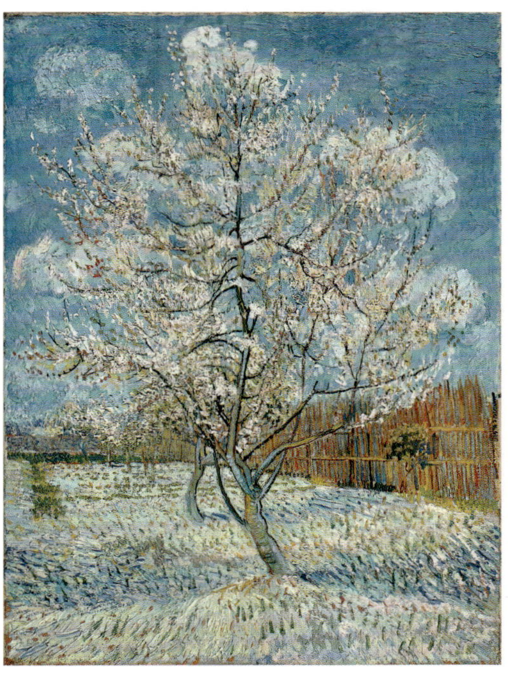

Fig. 66. *Pink Peach Trees* (F404), May 1888. Oil on canvas, 80.5 x 59.5 cm (31¾ x 23⅜ in.). Van Gogh Museum, Amsterdam (Vincent van Gogh Foundation)

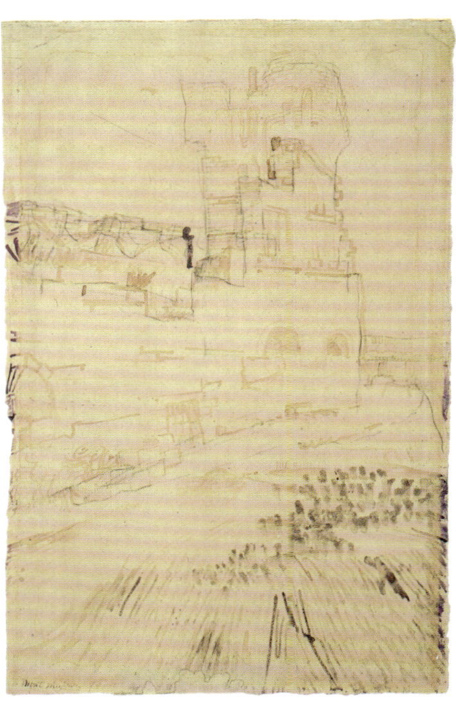

Fig. 67. *Montmajour* (F1423), May 1888. Pen, reed pen, brush, and aniline ink, graphite on laid paper, 48.1 x 31.4 cm (19 x 12⅜ in.). Van Gogh Museum, Amsterdam (Vincent van Gogh Foundation)

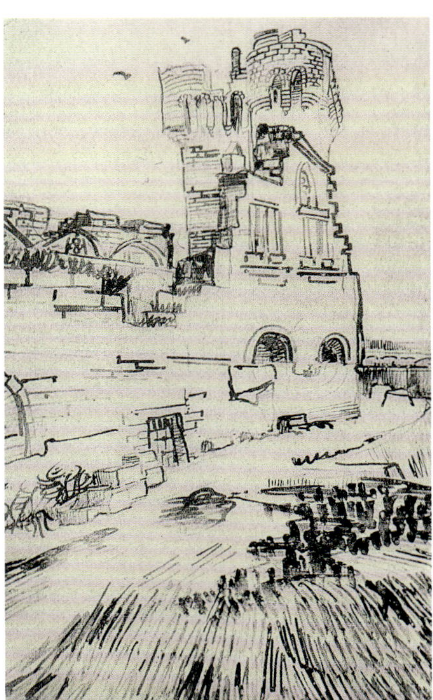

Fig. 68. Reproduction of fig. 67 in De la Faille 1928, pl. CL

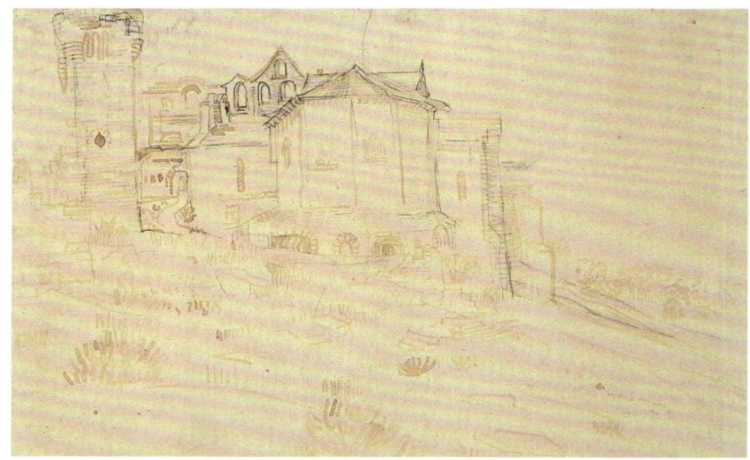

Fig. 69. *The Ruins of Montmajour* (F1417), May 1888. Reed pen, brush, and aniline ink, graphite on laid paper, 31.3 x 47.8 cm (12⅜ x 18⅞ in.). Van Gogh Museum, Amsterdam (Vincent van Gogh Foundation)

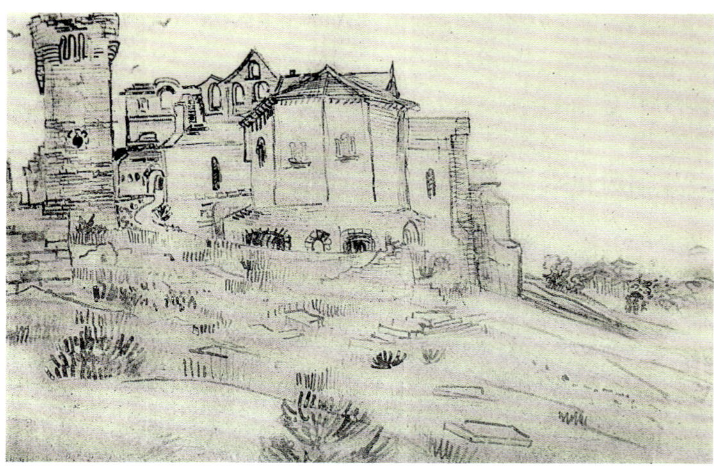

Fig. 70. Reproduction of fig. 69 in De la Faille 1928, pl. CL

perfect condition. Other inks have suffered more, as is the case with *Rock and Ruins, Montmajour* (F1446, cat. 84) and *La Crau: The View from Montmajour* (F1420, fig. 73). The ink in the former is now considerably lighter than it once was. The second sheet has undergone a more complex metamorphosis: here, Van Gogh drew with two inks that appear to have once been only slightly different in tone, creating a subtle variegation. One of the two is today predominantly light brown, and is even quite faded in places; the other, by contrast, has turned dark brown. Van Gogh used the now-faded ink for the area just under the horizon, among others. He applied it with a fine pen, which released the ink in thin lines; these sections were thus covered only by a small amount of ink. The consequences of the fading are thus quite severe, as it gives the (false) impression Van Gogh sought to create an effect of atmospheric perspective by making the scene appear to dissolve into the distance. An early reproduction reveals that the entire sheet was once covered with pen strokes in two tones—and therefore in two kinds of ink (fig. 74). In addition, it seems the differently faded inks have unbalanced the composition, as a comparison of details in the original and

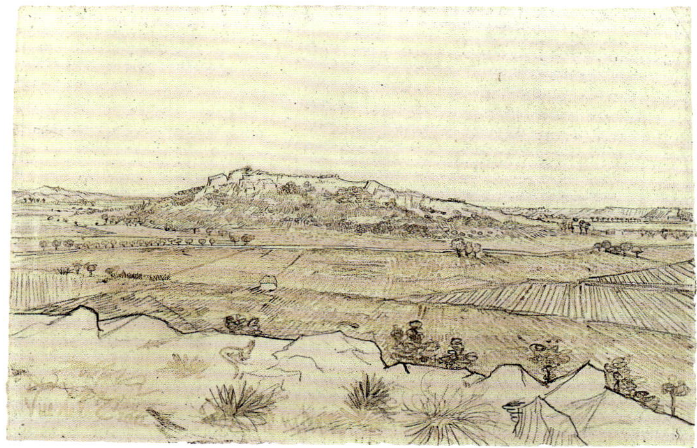

Fig. 71. *The Plain of La Crau* (F1419), May 1888. Reed pen and ink, graphite on laid paper, 30.9 x 47.7 cm (12⅛ x 18¾ in.). Museum Folkwang, Essen

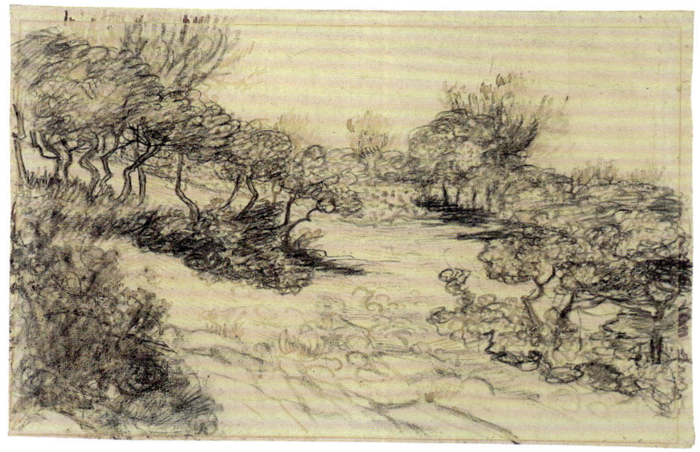

Fig. 72. *Meadow* (F1493), May 1888. Reed pen and aniline ink, graphite, washed with brush, on laid paper, 31.3 x 48.1 cm (12⅜ x 19 in.). Van Gogh Museum, Amsterdam (Vincent van Gogh Foundation)

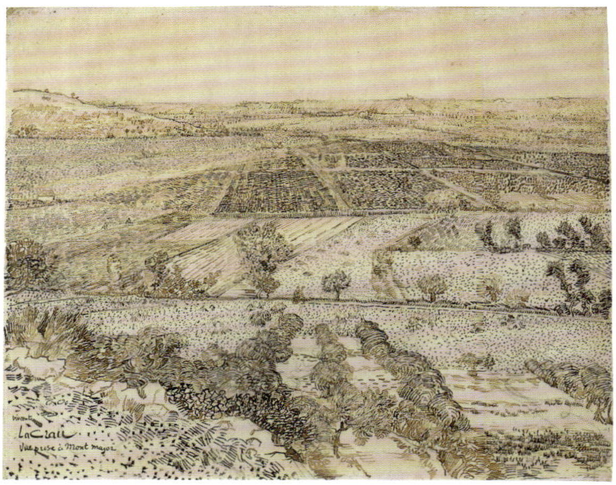

Fig. 73. *La Crau: The View from Montmajour* (F1420, cat. 85)

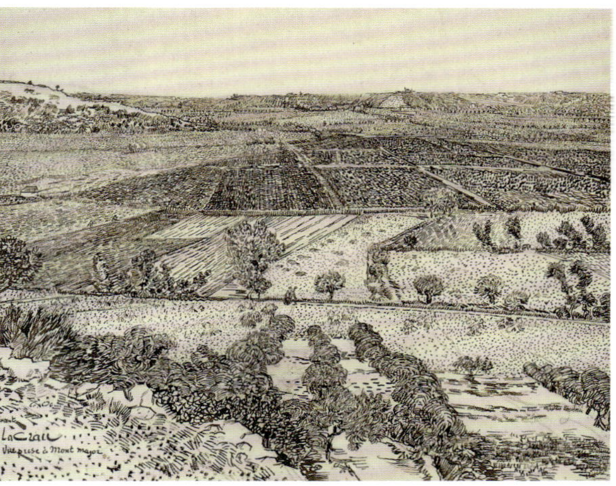

Fig. 74. Reproduction of fig. 73 in Julius Meier-Graefe, *Vincent van Gogh: Faksimiles nach Aquarellen und Zeichnungen* (Munich, 1928), no. 3

the reproduction illustrates (figs. 75, 76, the group of trees in the center right).

In several of the sheets in this series a role has been assigned to the graphite pencil as well, albeit a much smaller one than discussed above. It no longer has any essential function in drawings JH Add. 3, F1447, and F1446 (cats. 82–84), but the case is somewhat different in the compositionally and technically related panoramas of La Crau in the Van Gogh Museum and the British Museum, respectively (F1420, fig. 73; F1424, cat. 86). In these sheets, Van Gogh used the graphite to indicate volume and shadow, albeit rather prudently—especially when compared with the previous group. It appears, then, that in the works from July the artist was striving for a greater clarity of execution; based on an unadulterated application of the ink, certainly in comparison with the series from May, this aspect has now come very much to the fore.

Saint-Rémy: Rhythm and Cohesion

Although while in Saint-Rémy Van Gogh continued to make pen drawings in which his pencil played an important role, such as F1497 (cat. 101), the large sheets from this period mostly continue along the path first

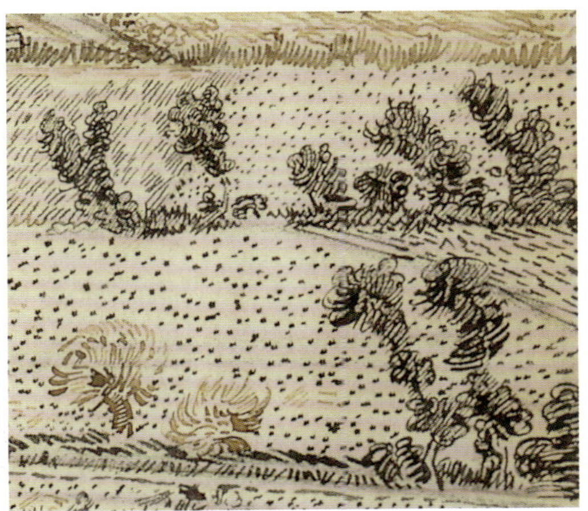

Fig. 75. Detail of fig. 73

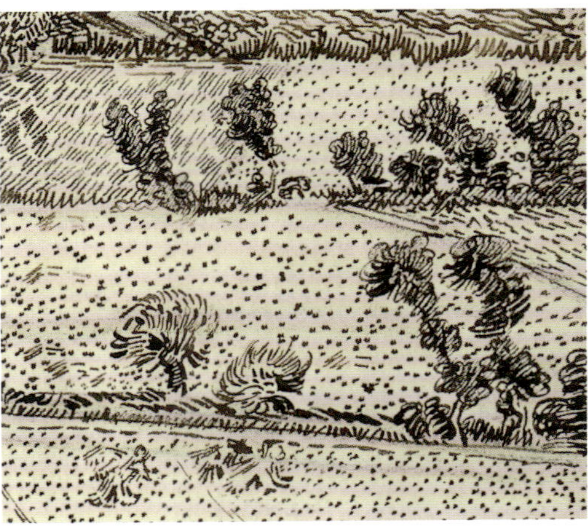

Fig. 76. Detail of fig. 74

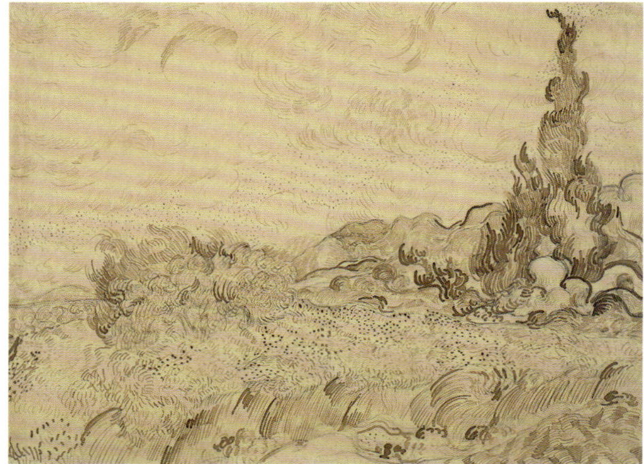

Fig. 77. *Wheat Field with Cypresses* (F1538, cat. 110)

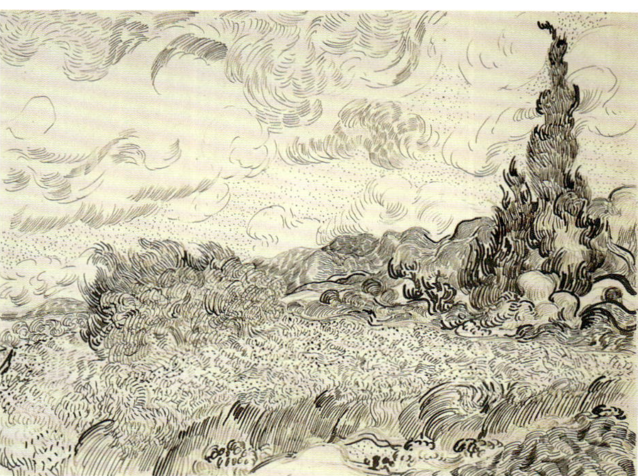

Fig. 78. Reproduction of fig. 77 in Julius Meier-Graefe, *Vincent van Gogh: Faksimiles nach Aquarellen und Zeichnungen* (Munich, 1928), no. 9

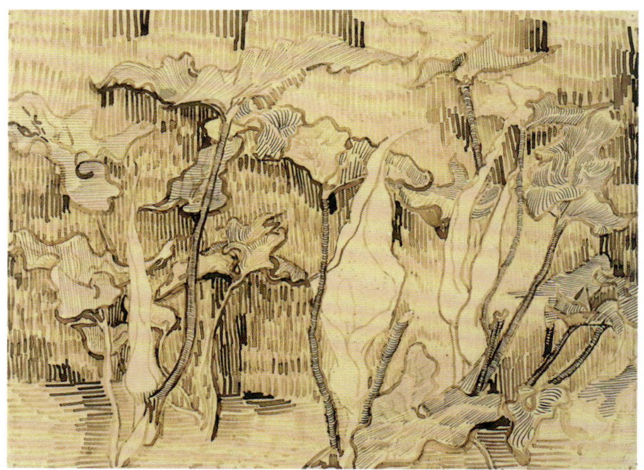

Fig. 79. *Arums* (F1613), 1889. Pen, reed pen, and ink (originally darker) on wove paper, 31.4 x 41.3 cm (12 ⅜ x 16¼ in.). Van Gogh Museum, Amsterdam (Vincent van Gogh Foundation)

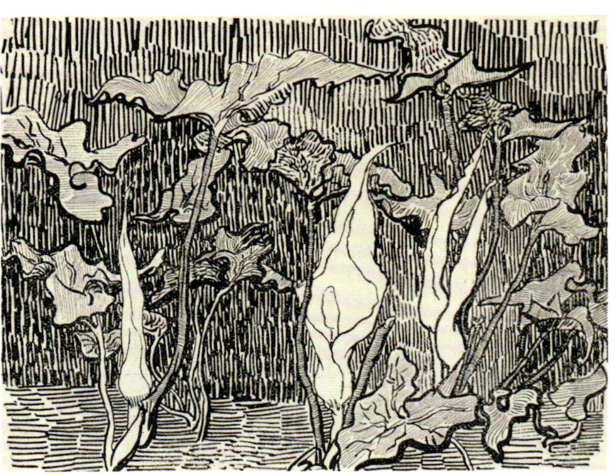

Fig. 80. Reproduction of fig. 79 in *Lettres de Vincent van Gogh à Émile Bernard publiées par Ambroise Vollard* (Paris, 1911), pl. LXV

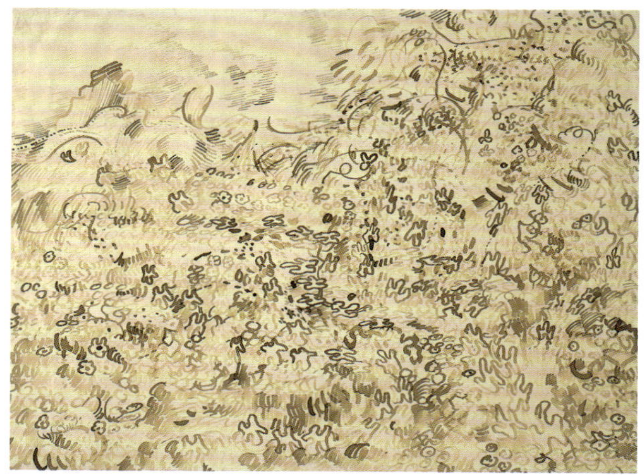

Fig. 81. *Wild Vegetation* (F1542, cat. 112)

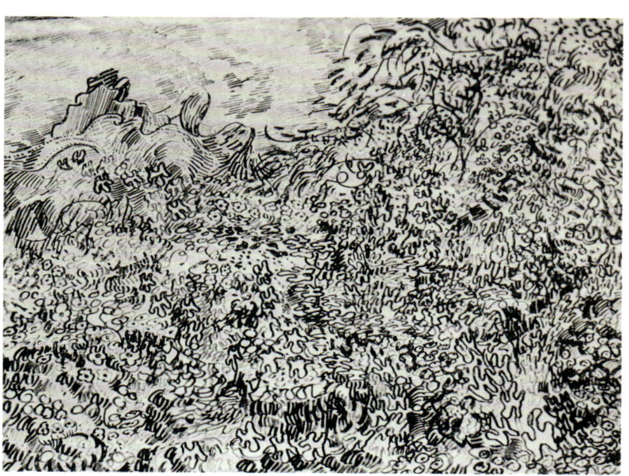

Fig. 82. Reproduction of fig. 81 in De la Faille 1928, pl. CLXXXI

taken in Arles. Purity of line became the artist's main concern, a result of his experiments in Arles. More than ever before, Van Gogh used his pen to create a rhythm of lines, forming patterns that lend coherence to the composition (we see a similar development in the paintings, effected through the brushwork). To achieve this goal, the pen strokes needed to stand out perfectly against the paper; indistinctness caused by other materials was undesirable.[11]

Van Gogh's pen drawings from Saint-Rémy are thus quite different from those made in Arles. The emphasis on rhythm, the focusing of composition, and a reduction in detail make these drawings significantly more abstract than the more or less realistic works of 1888. In instances in which the sheets have (partially) faded—and this has occurred to an extent similar to those from Arles—the result can be quite serious, as the already highly abstracted composition begins to lose its cohesion and becomes almost illegible and certainly far more conceptual than the artist ever intended. This is the case with three drawings from the Van Gogh Museum: *Wheat Field with Cypresses* (F1538, fig. 77), *Arums* (F1613, fig. 79), and *Wild Vegetation* (F1542, fig. 81). Comparison with early reproductions reveals that the fading process has indeed had far-reaching consequences (figs. 77–82). In order to understand Van Gogh's intentions, one must aim to apprehend the works in their original state as closely as possible. *Arums,* for example, still exudes a certain charm but has clearly lost much of the audacity of its original conception.

The summer of 1889 saw the creation of two small groups of color experiments. Three interior views of the asylum, executed in ocher, brown, blue, and green tones, were mostly painted in oil and are still surprisingly powerful (F1529, cat. 113; F1528, cat. 114; F1530, cat. 115). A series of seven sheets, all views of the asylum garden, among them F1533 and F1535 (cats. 104, 105),[12] were done mainly in green and blue—once again probably with thinned-down oil paint—and include contrasting elements in purple and red. The red likely contained an organic, somewhat unstable pigment, as it has lost much of its original strength. The purple, applied here and there, has also faded considerably, making the original, rather daring color contrast far less pronounced in character.

Auvers-sur-Oise: Subtle Experiments in Color

Van Gogh's drawings from the last three months of his life, spent in Auvers-sur-Oise, are mainly small studies executed in chalk and have changed little over time. In a handful of large, ambitious sheets, however, he did add several strikingly new aspects to his draftsmanship.

In two works created shortly after his arrival (late May 1890), he experimented once again with the potential of simultaneous contrast (F1624, fig. 83; F1640r, cat. 118). If we compare the *Old Vineyard with Peasant Woman* with an early reproduction, we can see that the color effect—which is still quite remarkable—must once have been even subtler (F1624, figs. 83, 84). Today, the sheet appears to be mainly an exercise in shades of blue: light green-blue in the sky; dark, almost purplish blue in the houses and central areas; and light blue in the lower part of the composition. As the reproduction shows, the light blue tone under the arbor was once violet, creating an effective suggestion of shadow and making the simultaneous contrast both deeper and stronger. Moreover, the roofs of the houses were not originally brown, but rather orange, thereby creating a complementary contrast with the predominant blues. There is no complementary contrast in the second sheet, which seems to have been intended as an experiment in pure simultaneous contrast.

Van Gogh tested other, equally refined contrasts in two other works. *Landscape with*

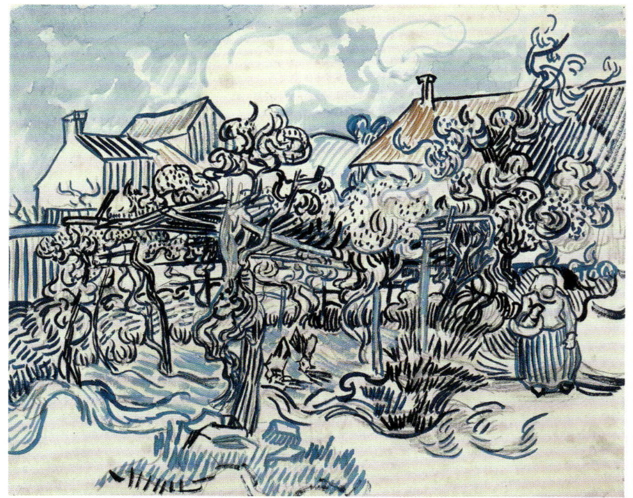

Fig. 83. *Old Vineyard with Peasant Woman* (F1624, cat. 117)

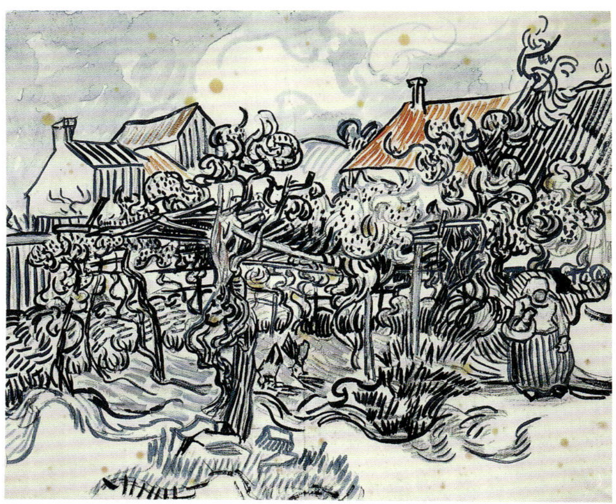

Fig. 84. Reproduction of fig. 83 in Julius Meier-Graefe, *Vincent van Gogh: Faksimiles nach Aquarellen und Zeichnungen* (Munich, 1928), no. 12

a Bridge over the Oise (F1639, cat. 119) is fairly well preserved and is drawn in shades of green and purplish blue on pink paper. An old reproduction indicates that the roofs of the factories and several of the cows were once a bright orange.[13] The simultaneous contrast of the green and purple-blue tones thus found a rather mellow complementary contrast in the pink (i.e., light red) of the paper and the now-vanished orange.

The aforementioned sheets have nothing in common with the works Van Gogh created in Paris, either stylistically or technically, but as color experiments they are certainly related to *Window in the Bataille Restaurant* (figs. 56, 57) and *Boulevard de Clichy* (figs. 58, 59), which were also investigations of simultaneous contrast. Van Gogh's paintings from Auvers reveal a fairly broad range of color experiments, varying from quite adventurous (F802) to very subtle (fig. 85). The modest group of large drawings from the last three months belongs above all to the latter category, and reveals an artist who had obviously not yet grown tired of exploring the world of color.

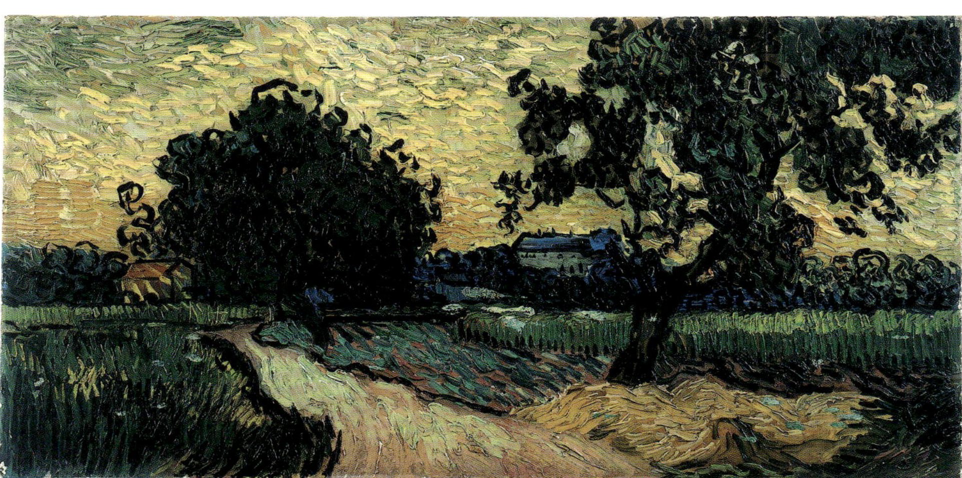

Fig. 85. *Landscape at Twilight* (F770), June 1890. Oil on canvas, 50 x 101 cm (19¾ x 39¾ in.). Van Gogh Museum, Amsterdam (Vincent van Gogh Foundation)

Conclusion

The study of the aging processes of Van Gogh's work provides both detailed knowledge of and insight into the leitmotifs of his career as a draftsman. With regard to the latter, one of the most striking discoveries is that in many cases Van Gogh remained faithful to both the techniques and the theories that had occupied him in his early years. During a period of experimentation in The Hague, he developed a gamut of techniques and color-theoretical ideas that he would continue to pursue. This constancy did not stand in the way of his extraordinary stylistic development but was one of the things that made it possible in the first place.[14]

1. The ideas presented here were first formulated during the preparation of the four-volume catalogue of the Van Gogh drawings in the Van Gogh Museum (Van Heugten 1996, Van Heugten 1997, Vellekoop and Van Heugten 2001, Vellekoop and Zwikker 2006). The works in this collection thus play an important role in the essay. Aspects of the aging process are regularly discussed in these catalogues, but only in the individual entries. As it has become clear that a systematic overview of these metamorphoses can provide significant new insights, the dispersed information has here been gathered together and is analyzed in depth.
2. While still in private hands, *Old Man Drinking Coffee* (F1682), now in the Van Gogh Museum, was restored without any understanding of Van Gogh's practice. The sheet has become too pale in the areas where milk was used as a fixative and smudged where this was not the case. Moreover, the sheet was mistakenly flattened and smoothed out.
3. *Child Kneeling in Front of the Cradle* (F1024), *Woman Sewing, with a Girl* (F1072), and *Woman with a Child on Her Lap* (F1067).
4. Corrosion is caused by a chemical process in which sulfuric acid is produced in the ink, which eats away at the fiber of the paper. Given the right conditions, iron-gall ink can be kept more or less stable, but corrosion can also lead to the complete destruction of the sheet.
5. I am grateful to Roy S. Berns, R. S. Hunter Professor of Color Science, Appearance, and Technology, Munsell Color Science Laboratory, Center for Imaging Science, Rochester Institute of Technology, who used his expertise to make these color reconstructions.
6. This work, which is now in the Van Gogh Museum, is currently undergoing intensive scrutiny in connection with the second volume of the complete catalogue of the paintings collection (forthcoming). With thanks to Ella Hendriks.
7. There is yet another sheet (F1448) in this group that I have seen neither with my own eyes nor in good color reproductions. Black-and-white photographs lead me to believe that large areas of the paper are badly browned.
8. The two lists in the archives of the Van Gogh Museum are b 2182 V/1962 (perhaps intended for the Berlin Secession exhibition of 1907) and b 2201 V/1962 (which refers to Munich and other cities 1909–10). The review, written in conjunction with the exhibition "Tentoonstelling van teekeningen van Vincent van Gogh" (Rotterdam 1900–1901), appeared in the February 6, 1901, *Nieuwe Rotterdamsche Courant,* under "Letteren en Kunst. Kunstkring. II."
9. The Instituut Collectie Nederland (ICN) in Amsterdam is currently working with the Van Gogh Museum on research into these inks.
10. In two other works that are part of this series, F1475 (Museum Boijmans Van Beuningen, Rotterdam) and F1418 (private collection), the black drawing material is somewhat less emphatically applied, but here, too, its function appears to be more than that of a simple preparatory sketch.
11. Browning of the paper can also spoil this contrast, as, for example, in *Fountain in the Garden of the Asylum* (F1531, cat. 103), now in the Van Gogh Museum.
12. The other works in this series are F1526, F1527, F1534, F1536, and F1537. I have seen F1534 only in black-and-white photographs.
13. See Cooper 1955, no. 30.
14. On this, see also Van Heugten 2003, passim.

The Dutch Years, 1880–85

Van Gogh's career followed an erratic course, reaching a critical low point in July 1879, when his contract as an evangelist in the Belgian Borinage was not renewed. Within a decade, he had foundered as an art dealer, a teacher, a clergyman, a bookseller, and a student of religion, and there seemed little prospect of further employment. After months of worrying about his future, in late 1880 he decided to follow the advice of his brother Theo and devote himself to art. He had long had a love of painting but otherwise almost no experience. Indeed, although he had drawn regularly in the past, his talent seemed negligible (see fig. 86), and his first efforts following this momentous decision were equally unpromising (see fig. 87). Van Gogh himself realized that he would have to work extremely hard and study intensely if he was to succeed in his newly chosen métier.

He approached his studies with characteristic enthusiasm, following a self-designed "academic" program. In the first years, until late 1883, he limited himself mainly to drawing, well aware that this was the necessary basis for painting. He copied from model books and pored over treatises on anatomy and perspective, as well as various other materials on the principles of draftsmanship. Of particular importance were the publications of the painter Armand Cassagne, the author of a number of lucid manuals for beginning artists.

Van Gogh deliberately followed in the footsteps of the painters he admired most: masters of the peasant genre such as Jules Breton and, above all, Jean-François Millet. Although he would ultimately excel at landscape painting, Van Gogh's great ambition in all the ten years of his career was to become a figure or genre painter.

After living in Brussels for about six months, in April 1881 Van Gogh moved into his parents' house in Etten, in Brabant. The rustic character of the village provided him with numerous opportunities to train his hand at peasant motifs.

Since the starting point for the choice of works in this catalogue and exhibition was to bring together the finest and most artistically outstanding sheets in Van Gogh's drawn oeuvre, much of his early work was necessarily excluded. Van Gogh had a long way to go to become an accomplished artist, and the difficulties he encountered in representing his subjects are often reflected in the drawings. The figures done in Etten are bony and their gestures wooden. They are frequently depicted in profile, which allowed Van Gogh to avoid the complex problems of foreshortening. Sometimes, however, the fledgling artist rose above himself, with surprising results (see F851, cat. 3; F868, cat. 5). *Man at the Fireplace* (cat. 5), in particular, indicates that he was also capable of depicting more complicated poses.

If Van Gogh had natural talent, it was for the art of landscape, and even in the early years of his career he was quite able to capture its various aspects. From boyhood onward he had a particular bond with nature and was a great admirer of landscape painting. Even his earliest efforts in this genre have a masterful quality, and some of them exhibit a sensitivity akin to that of the later works, without, of course, sharing in their virtuosity. *A Marsh* (F846, cat. 1) is the high point of his first year as an artist. In addition to revealing Van Gogh's talent for landscape, this drawing also shows his gift for using pen and ink. While he often had great difficulties with other techniques, throughout his career the pen drawings are almost always among the best of his productions.

Van Gogh struggled with perspective and anatomy and with mastering the various media and techniques available to the draftsman. His first works were done mainly in graphite pencil; following the advice of his cousin-by-marriage the painter Anton Mauve, he also investigated the potential of colored chalk, watercolor, and charcoal. In November–December 1881, Mauve taught him to work in watercolor, but initially Van Gogh preferred to avoid color, concentrating on overcoming a variety of other technical problems.

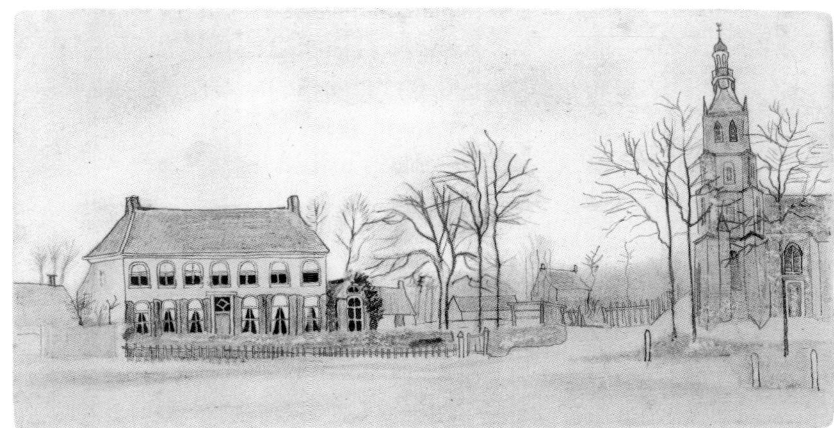

Fig. 86. *Vicarage and Church at Etten* (Juv. XXI), April 1876. Pen and ink, graphite on wove paper, 9.5 x 17.8 cm (3¾ x 7 in.). Van Gogh Museum, Amsterdam (Vincent van Gogh Foundation)

The Hague and Drenthe

In the last week of 1881, Van Gogh settled in The Hague, where he remained until September 1883. One can argue that overall during this period he was mainly concerned with studying the human figure. While he had his first commercial success in The Hague—the commissions he received for two series of city views from his uncle Cornelis Marinus van Gogh, a well-known art dealer in Amsterdam—most of his effort was focused on working as often as possible from a live model. Initially he had trouble finding people to pose for him, and until September 1882 he alternated between figure studies, in which Sien Hoornik, his lover at the time, played an important role, and city- and landscapes (F1089, cat. 7). From September onward, however, Van Gogh found enough models among the aged inhabitants of the Nederlands Hervormde Oude Mannen- en Vrouwenhuis, a local hospice. With their features and bodies marked by the hard lives they had led, these men and women were in many ways the ideal subjects for Van Gogh's realist drawing style.

During this time he drew much inspiration from English and French illustrated magazines, which had a predominantly social-realist character. Van Gogh was moved by the expressive manner of the illustrations' execution, using only black and white and with much attention paid to the effects of light and shadow. He developed a strikingly angular and powerful style of modeling and increased the drawings' expressivity by employing a variety of media in black. Occasionally he also attempted a multifigure composition, but he felt he had insufficient artistic skill to bring such works to successful completion. This would never be his forte.

The high point of Van Gogh's years in The Hague is a group of landscapes and village or city views. The neighborhood around his house on Schenkweg provided the motifs for several surprising and innovative compositions (see F930, cat. 8; F939, cat. 9), and the picturesque fishing village of Scheveningen inspired him as well (see F945, cat. 10).

Following the end of his relationship with Sien Hoornik, Van Gogh left The Hague on September 11, 1883, and settled in rural Drenthe in the northern Netherlands. He spent three months there, months that were filled with disappointment. Once again, he had trouble finding models, and he suffered from a chronic shortage of supplies for both drawing and painting. Nonetheless, he was extremely taken with the unspoiled ambience of the province, particularly at twilight, which he sought to capture in several impressive drawings in ink and watercolor (see F1104, cat. 15; F1099, cat. 16).

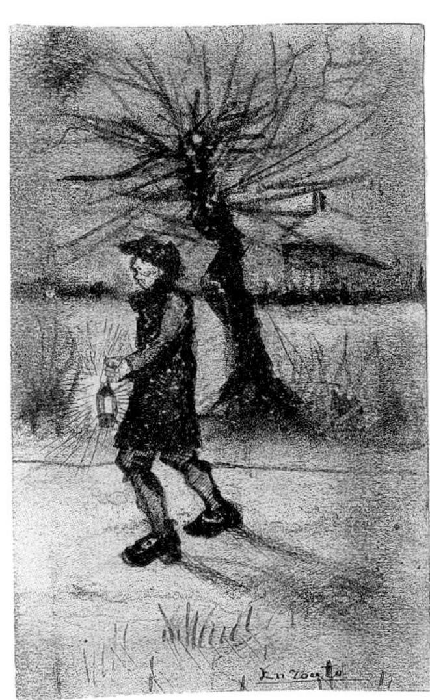

Fig. 87. *En route* (Juv. XV), January 1881. Pen and ink, graphite on wove paper, 9.8 x 5.8 cm (3⅞ x 2¼ in.). Van Gogh Museum, Amsterdam (Vincent van Gogh Foundation)

Nuenen: Masterful Landscapes, Commercial Ambitions, and Disappointment

Van Gogh never explicitly mentioned his evidently intuitive talent for landscape, but he was certainly very much aware of it. In late December 1883 he settled in Nuenen in the southern Netherlands, where he would remain for two years, and he quickly began to explore its environs for material to draw. Following several hesitant "finger exercises" completed shortly after his arrival, in March and April 1884 this led to a series of pen drawings that are entirely exceptional within his Dutch oeuvre. The talent already announced in his early landscapes in pen here culminated in a moving, almost poetic, and highly personal vision of the countryside of the southern Netherlands (F1128, cat. 21; F1129, cat. 20; F1130, cat. 22; F1135, cat. 23; F1240, cat. 19). Van Gogh well understood that he had created something special with this group of six works (probably originally seven), and, hoping for commercial success, he sent a number of the sheets to Theo. Once it became apparent that nothing was to come of this—Theo's precarious relationship with his superiors at the gallery Boussod, Valadon et Cie in Paris meant he was unable to promote his brother's work as he would have liked—Van Gogh sought to sell them to members of the circle around his friend Anthon van Rappard, also an artist. Despite Van Rappard's enthusiasm for the drawings, this effort failed as well.

Van Gogh must have been extremely disappointed at this lack of success. In any case, he would not attempt any more such ambitious drawings while in the Netherlands.

Drawing the Human Figure

The industrious study of the live model to which Van Gogh had applied himself while in The Hague gave him the confidence to begin working on compositions with more than one figure. His first "campaign," begun in early 1884, was devoted to a long series of drawings and paintings of weavers. These are often intriguing works of the craftsmen and their machines, frequently with a rather somber air (see F1115, cat. 17; F1118, cat. 18).

In April 1884, drawing began to take second place to painting, which Van Gogh now attempted to master. Not until the end of the year would he take up his drawing materials again. He began to make a number of carefully planned series of drawn and painted peasant heads and, somewhat later, studies—mainly on paper—of hands. All these efforts were preparations for what he intended as his "masterwork": a complex, multifigure peasant scene, a plan that resulted in *The Potato Eaters* (F82, fig. 88). The preliminary drawings are sometimes powerful representations of the objects and people observed, but they have no pretension to being anything but studies. Only a few sheets stand out from the rest, for example the head of a peasant woman whose difficult life is clearly etched on her features (F1182, cat. 27). There is also a group of small pen-and-ink drawings that were obviously executed with some ambition: a few are highly worked up and even signed, which leads one to suspect the artist thought them salable (F1177, cat. 26; F1198, cat. 25).

Despite all his intense preparation, *The Potato Eaters* earned Van Gogh nothing but criticism. He was able to rebuff this to a degree, but he also accepted that he still had much to learn about depicting the human figure. He rededicated himself to figure drawing: borrowing the principles of Eugène Delacroix and breaking the human body down into circles, ovals, and ellipses, Van Gogh hoped to come to a better understanding of its fundamental volumes and thereby achieve a more exact representation. This turned out to have a spectacular result, for the figure studies of working peasant men and women from the summer of 1885 are almost overwhelming in their monumentality and expressivity and are among the most successful figures in Van Gogh's entire oeuvre (see F1279, cat. 29; F1326, cat. 30; F1327, cat. 31).

The end of the summer also put an end to Van Gogh's figure studies. He was unjustly accused of having impregnated a young girl from Nuenen, and the local priest spoke out against the artist to such a degree that it became impossible for him to find models. Van Gogh had already considered the possibilities of going to Antwerp to further his studies, and the situation in which he now found himself pushed him to make this move.

SvH

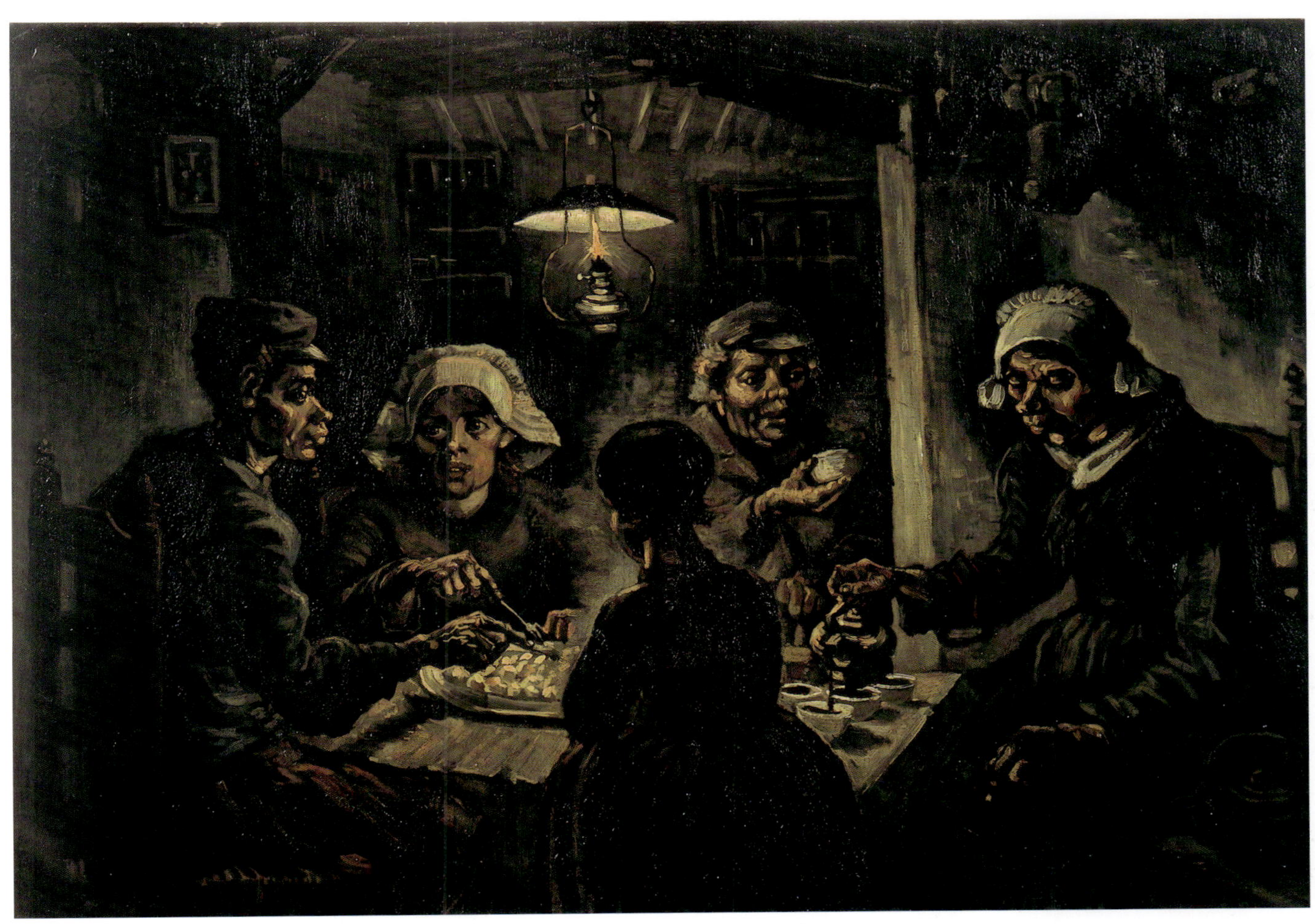

Fig. 88. *The Potato Eaters* (F82), April 1885. Oil on canvas, 82 x 114 cm (32¼ x 44⅞ in.). Van Gogh Museum, Amsterdam (Vincent van Gogh Foundation)

1. *A Marsh*

June 1881
Pen and ink, graphite on laid paper watermarked
PL BAS
42.5 x 56.5 cm (16¾ x 22¼ in.)
National Gallery of Canada, Ottawa, purchased 1967 (15461)
F846, JH8

Provenance: Probably left by the artist with his mother, Anna Cornelia van Gogh-Carbentus, Nuenen, November 1885; deposited by her, along with other works, with Schrauwen, Breda, 1886; sold by Schrauwen to J. C. Couvreur, Breda, 1902; sold to C. Mouwen and W. van Bakel, Breda, 1902; sold from an exhibition at Kunstzalen Oldenzeel, Rotterdam, to H. Tutein Nolthenius (d. 1944), Delft, 1903; Kunstzalen d'Audretsch, The Hague; Myrtil Frank, The Hague and New York; Mrs. Martin Nachmann, New York, by 1948; sold by her through Myrtil Frank to Walter Feilchenfeldt, Zürich, 1967; acquired from him by the National Gallery of Canada, Ottawa, 1967.

Selected exhibitions: Rotterdam 1903b; Rotterdam 1904, no. 52; New York 1955, no. 79; Otterlo 1990, no. 4; Ottawa 1999, unnumbered; Sapporo–Kōbe 2002, no. 1.

Summary of the literature: De la Faille (1928, no. 846) dated the sheet to June 1881 on the evidence of letter 146. Vanbeselaere 1937, pp. 52, 59, 124, 407. Hulsker (1980, no. 8), again on the basis of the letter, specified the date as June 13. Van der Wolk (in Otterlo 1990, no. 4) dated the work more generally to the summer of 1881. Heenk (1995, pp. 33, 34) suggested the fall on the evidence of the vegetation. Pickvance in Martigny 2000, p. 285. Op de Coul (2002, pp. 118, 119) discussed the exhibition at the Oldenzeel gallery in 1903, where the sheet was on display.

While in Etten, Van Gogh focused mainly on figural works, but he occasionally also sought motifs in the surrounding countryside. In June 1881 he received a visit from his friend Van Rappard. Van Gogh wrote to Theo about their meeting and their trip to the nearby Passievaart, close to the village of Seppe, to the west of Etten. Van Rappard executed several drawings there, as well as a now-lost painting, while Van Gogh concentrated solely on drawing [146]. He specifically mentioned a spot with many water lilies, presumably the site represented in the sheet now in Virginia (F845, fig. 89). As it is not mentioned in the letter, the large drawing from Ottawa was probably executed not during the visit to the Passievaart but nonetheless about the same time.

SvH

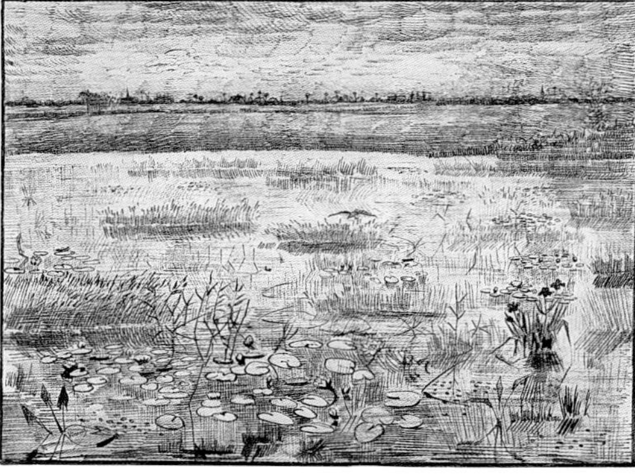

Fig. 89. *Marsh with Water Lilies* (F845), June 1881. Pen and ink over graphite on paper, 23.5 x 31.4 cm (9¼ x 12⅜ in.). Virginia Museum of Fine Arts, Richmond, Collection of Mr. and Mrs. Paul Mellon (photo: Katherine Wetzel)

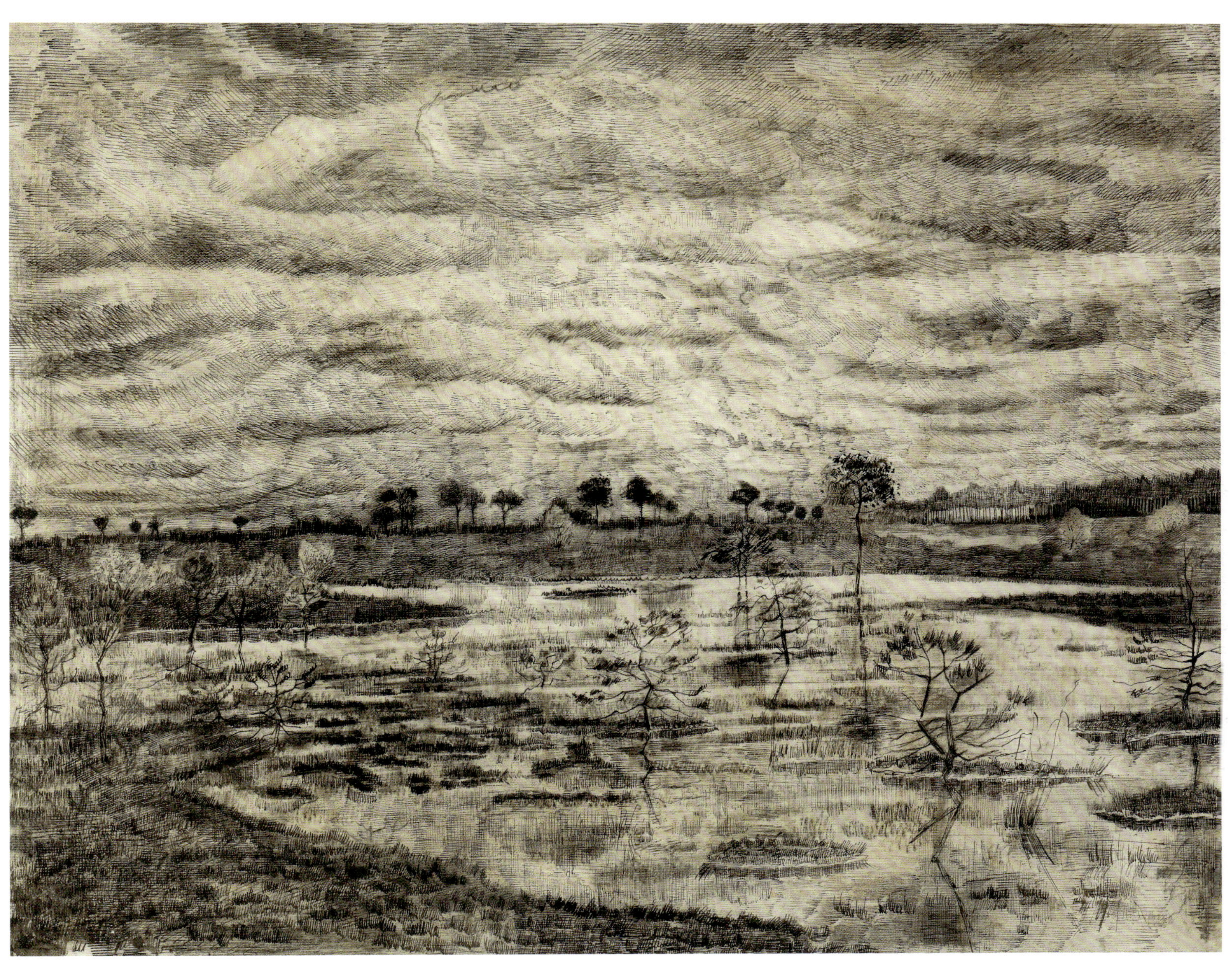

2. *Windmills near Dordrecht (Weeskinderendijk)*

August 25 (?), 1881
Opaque watercolor, pen and ink, graphite, black chalk on laid paper watermarked ED & CIE and PL BAS
25.7 x 69.8 cm (10⅛ x 27½ in.)
Signed lower left: *Vincent*
Kröller-Müller Museum, Otterlo (KM 126.249)
F850, JH15
Letter 149

Provenance: L. C. Enthoven, Voorburg, possibly a purchase or a gift from the artist, until 1920; his sale, Frederik Müller, Amsterdam, May 18, 1920, no. 256; purchased at that sale (for 1,000 gulden) by Helene Kröller-Müller (with five other drawings and twenty-six paintings); Kröller-Müller Foundation, 1928; Kröller-Müller Museum, Otterlo, 1937.

Selected exhibitions: 's Hertogenbosch 1987–88, no. 6; Otterlo 1990, no. 15.

Summary of the literature: Bremmer 1921–28, no. 176. Bremmer (1926, vol. 8, no. 59) referred to the work as "De molens." Fels 1928, p. 1. De la Faille (1928, no. 850) specified the location as Dordrecht and dated the drawing August 1881. Vanbeselaere 1937, pp. 53, 61, 407. Cooper (1955, p. 16) believed the drawing demonstrated that Van Gogh had begun to master the medium. Elgar 1958, no. 4; De Gruyter 1961, p. 89. In De la Faille 1970 (no. 850) the location was designated as "windmills on the Weeskinderendijk at Dordrecht" and the drawing dated to early autumn 1881. Kress 1973, pp. 14, 15. Hulsker (1980, no. 15) dated the work to July–September 1881. Kröller-Müller Museum 1980, p. 18. In De la Faille 1992 (no. 850) the editors suggested the drawing was made after a now-lost sketch. Heenk (1995, pp. 34, 58, 225) believed Van Gogh sketched the motif on the spot, later working it up in the studio.

Van Gogh stayed in The Hague from August 23 to 25, 1881, seeing a number of exhibitions and visiting his cousin-by-marriage Anton Mauve and Théophile de Bock, an artist he had known for some time. On the way there, he was much taken with the windmills near Dordrecht that he glimpsed from the train. On the return trip he made a special stop in Dordrecht to see them again, executing a drawing despite the pouring rain. It is not entirely certain it was this sheet, but the satisfied tone in which Van Gogh remarked on his "souvenir" [149] indicates a certain degree of finish. It is of course possible that the drawing was further worked up at a later stage.

SvH

Letter to Theo van Gogh, August 26, 1881 [149]: Then I went to Dordrecht because from the train I had seen a spot I wanted to draw—that row of windmills. Though it was raining, I managed to finish it, and so at least I have a souvenir from my little trip.

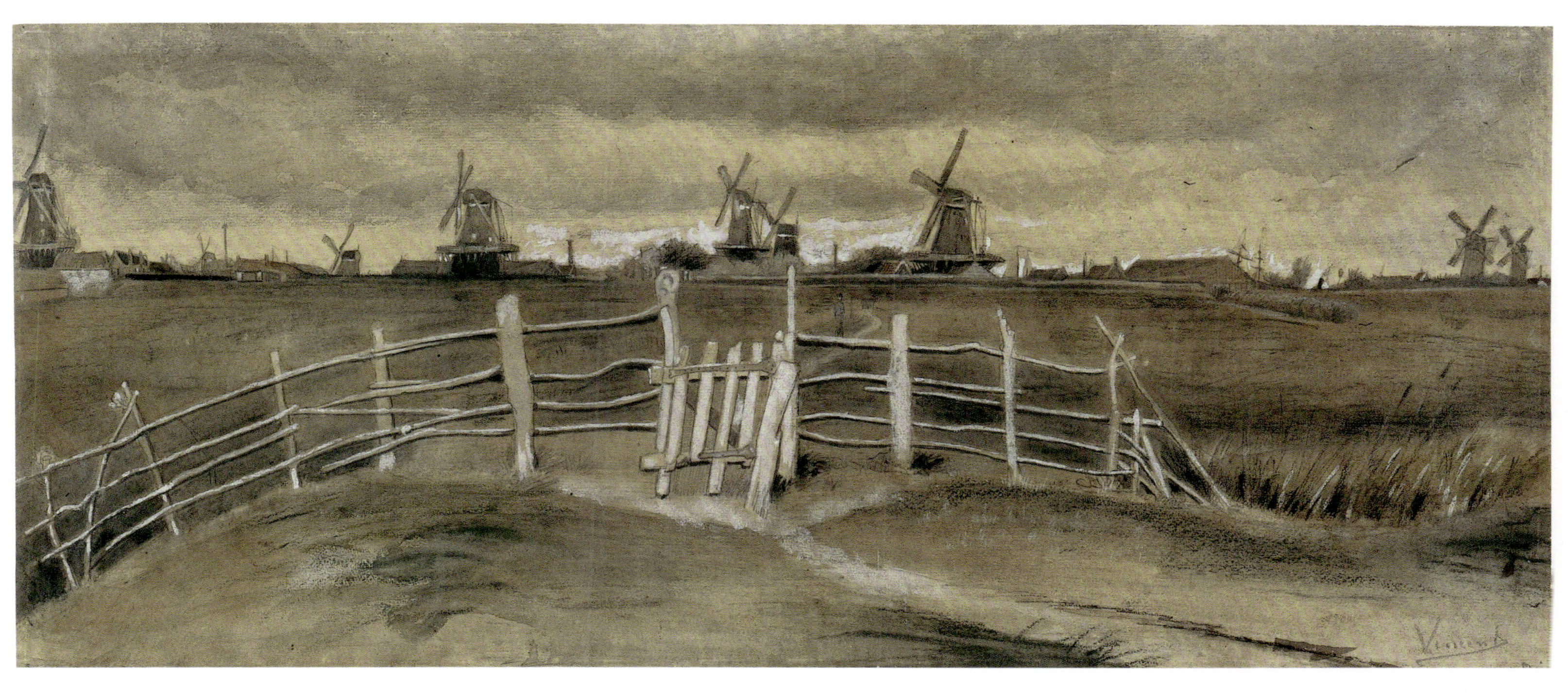

3. *Boy with a Sickle*

Last week of October–November 1, 1881
Black chalk, charcoal, opaque watercolor, washed, on laid paper watermarked ED & CIE and PL BAS
46.5 x 60.4 cm (18¼ x 23¾ in.)
Signed lower left: *Vincent*
Kröller-Müller Museum, Otterlo (KM 111.847)
F851, JH61
Letter R3

Provenance: J. Hidde Nijland, Dordrecht and The Hague, before 1904, until 1928; lent by him to the Dordrechts Museum, 1904–10; acquired by Helene Kröller-Müller, The Hague, 1928; Kröller-Müller Foundation, 1932; Kröller-Müller Museum, Otterlo, 1937.

Selected exhibitions: Dordrecht 1905; The Hague 1918, unnumbered; Amsterdam 1924, no. 96; London–Birmingham–Glasgow 1947–48, no. 102; New York–Chicago 1949–50, no. 14; 's Hertogenbosch 1987–88, no. 6; Rome 1988, no. 53; Otterlo 1990, no. 12.

Summary of the literature: The first reproduction was published in Nijland 1905 (fig. 44). Bremmer n.d., fig. 19; Bremmer 1911, pp. 87–97. De la Faille (1928, no. 851) gave the drawing the title "Jeune paysan à la faucille," identifying the model as Piet Kaufman; he dated the work to October 1881, a date that has been accepted by all subsequent authors. Fels 1928, p. 39; Vanbeselaere 1937, pp. 55, 63, 64, 66–67, 407; Weisbach 1949–51, vol. 1, p. 147; Elgar 1958, p. 15; De Gruyter 1961, p. 93; Gans 1961, p. 34; Leymarie 1968, p. 17; Wadley 1969, p. 24. In De la Faille 1970 (no. 851), the work was titled "Young Peasant with Sickle." Hulsker (1980, no. 61) referred to it as "Boy Cutting Grass with a Sickle." Kröller-Müller Museum 1980, pp. 15, 16. In 's Hertogenbosch 1987–88 (pp. 137, 138), the model's name was spelled incorrectly. Kerstens 1990, pp. 24, 25. Heenk (1995, p. 40) was the first to suggest that the model's clothes indicate he posed indoors.

Since Van Gogh wrote to Anthon van Rappard on November 2, 1881, that, among other things, he had recently made a drawing of "a boy cutting grass with a sickle" [R3], the sheet must have been executed in the last week of October or, at the latest, November 1. It is highly worked up and the pose is well captured. The model was the Van Gogh family gardener, the seventeen-year-old Piet Kaufmann. His lightweight clothing suggests that he posed indoors. In the rather clumsily drawn clumps of grass and surroundings a lack of direct observation can be detected; they were probably inventions of the artist, added later.

SvH

Letter to Anthon van Rappard, November 2, 1881 [R3]: Today, I drew another digger. And also since your visit, a boy cutting grass with a sickle.

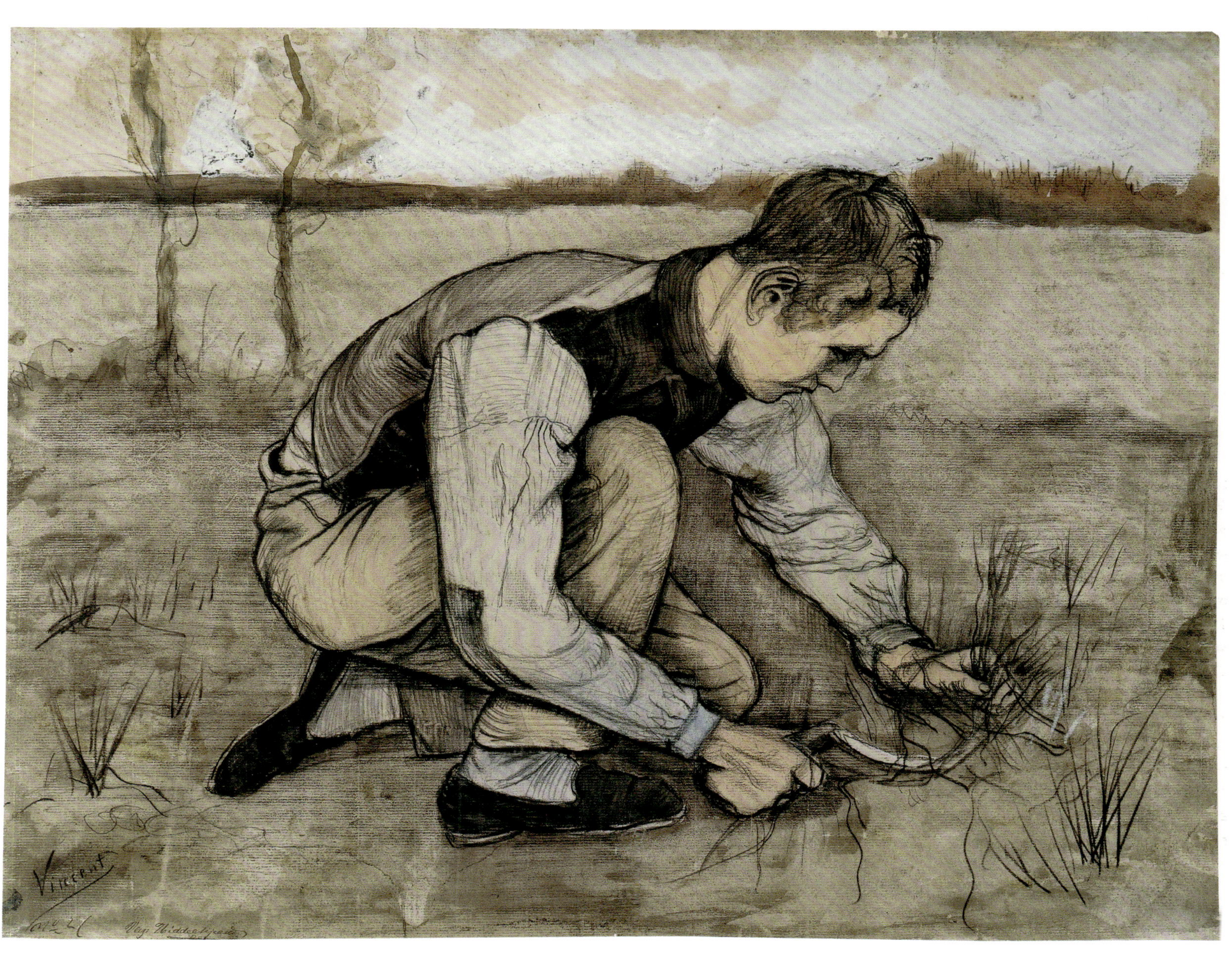

4. *Woman Sewing*

October–November 1881
Opaque watercolor, wash, black chalk on laid paper
61.8 x 47 cm (24⅜ x 18½ in.)
Kröller-Müller Museum, Otterlo (KM 122.653)
F1221, JH70

New York only

Provenance: L. C. Enthoven, Voorburg, possibly a purchase or a gift from the artist, until 1920; his sale, Frederik Müller, Amsterdam, May 18, 1920, no. 256; purchased at that sale (for 800 gulden) by Helene Kröller-Müller (with five other drawings and twenty-six paintings); Kröller-Müller Foundation, 1928; Kröller-Müller Museum, Otterlo, 1937.

Selected exhibitions: 's Hertogenbosch 1987–88, no. 7; Otterlo 1990, no. 8.

Summary of the literature: *Lettres* 1911, pl. LXVII, was the first published reproduction. Bremmer 1921–28, no. 211. De la Faille (1928, no. 1221) dated the work to Nuenen. Vanbeselaere 1937, pp. 58, 279, 412; Wadley 1969, p. 24. In De la Faille 1970 (no. 1221) the date was corrected to November 1881. Hulsker (1980, no. 70) dated the sheet to October–early November 1881. Kröller-Müller Museum 1980, p. 12. In 's Hertogenbosch 1987–88 (pp. 138–39) it was confirmed that the drawing was made in Etten based on the woman's typical West Brabant cap, and a further interpretation of content was given. In Otterlo 1990 (pp. 39, 54) late 1881 was suggested as the date. Soth (1994, p. 106) related the domesticity of the scene to Van Gogh's love for his cousin Kee Vos. Heenk 1995, pp. 43, 225.

Following a short visit to Anton Mauve in The Hague during the summer of 1881, Van Gogh returned to Etten full of new ideas. Among other things, Mauve suggested to Van Gogh that he "try [drawing] with charcoal and chalk and brush and stump" [169]. This depiction of a woman sewing, executed in a mix of techniques in October–November, clearly shows that Van Gogh followed his advice. Women at their needlework was a favorite theme among the artists of the Hague school, including Mauve, and was therefore also well known to Van Gogh. In December, again under Mauve's supervision, he made three watercolors of the subject, two of which strongly resemble the sheet illustrated here (F869, fig. 90).

SvH

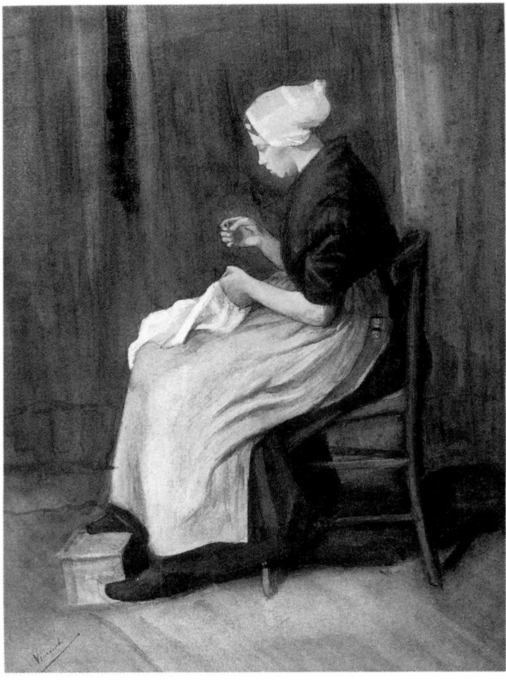

Fig. 90. *Scheveningen Woman Sewing* (F869), December 1881. Watercolor, 48 x 35 cm (18⅞ x 13¾ in.). P. and N. de Boer Foundation, Amsterdam

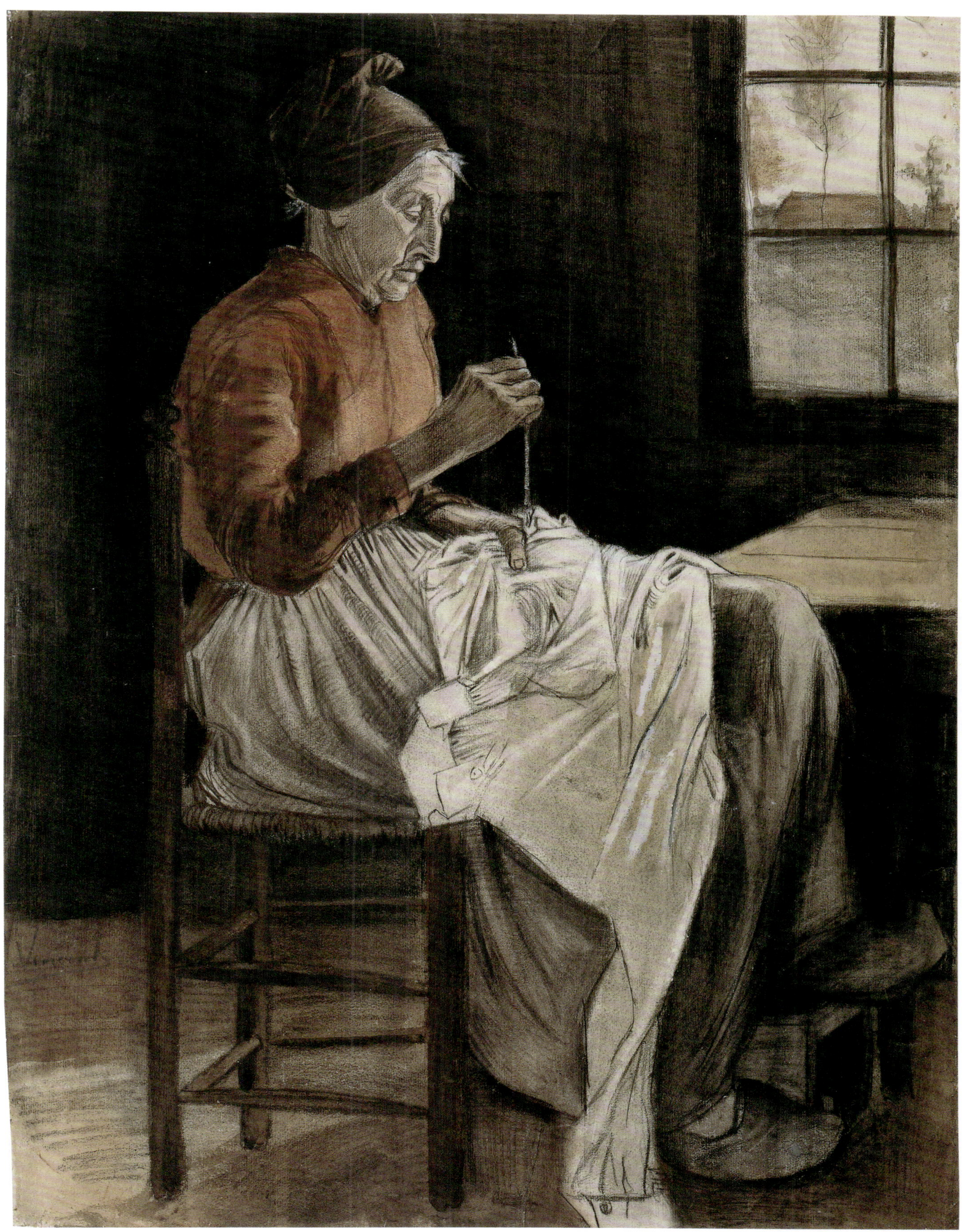

5. *Man at the Fireplace*

November 17, 1881
Black and red chalks, opaque watercolor, wash on laid paper
55.7 x 44.5 cm (21⅞ x 17½ in.)
Signed lower right: *Atelier Vincent*
Kröller-Müller Museum, Otterlo (KM 120.849)
F868, JH80
Letter 158

Amsterdam only

Provenance: A. Terhell, The Hague, until 1892; perhaps exhibited at Kunstzalen Oldenzeel, 1892; J. Hidde Nijland, Dordrecht and The Hague, before 1904 (possibly acquired at Oldenzeel, 1892), until 1928; lent by him to the Dordrechts Museum, 1904–10; purchased by Helene Kröller-Müller, The Hague, 1928; Kröller-Müller Foundation, 1932; Kröller-Müller Museum, Otterlo, 1937.

Selected exhibitions: Dordrecht 1905; The Hague 1918, unnumbered; Amsterdam 1924, no. 68; Amsterdam 1980–81, no. 40; 's Hertogenbosch 1987–88, no. 8; Otterlo 1990, no. 7.

Summary of the literature: The first reproduction was published in Nijland 1905 (fig. 95). De la Faille (1928, no. 868) dated the sheet to November 1881 on the evidence of letter 158 and called it "Vieux paysan près du foyer." This date was adopted by all later authors, although the title changed slightly. Vanbeselaere 1937, pp. 57, 73, 74, 126, 137, 192, 407; Elgar 1958, no. 6. In De la Faille 1970 (p. 324) it was pointed out in reference to F863 that the same model was used for this drawing; Schuitemaker was mentioned in the letters discussed in the entry for F863. J. Joosten (1970, p. 101, n. 49) suggested on the basis of an old description that the sheet was exhibited at Kunstzalen Oldenzeel in 1892. Hulsker 1980/1996, no. 80; Kröller-Müller Museum 1980, pp. 14, 15; Heenk 1995, pp. 41, 209. In Breda 2003–4 (pp. 77, 81, 82) further details on the Oldenzeel show and on A. Terhell, the owner of the works on view, were given.

Van Gogh described this drawing—"an old man laying twigs in a fireplace"—as made "yesterday" in his letter to Theo of November 18, 1881. As in *Woman Sewing* (F1221, cat. 4), he worked in a variety of techniques, as Mauve had suggested to him. Particularly striking is the brown wash, added to give the scene the dusky feel of the interior of a peasant hut. Van Gogh drew a number of figures at the fireplace in this period and later, but among the variations done in Etten this one is the liveliest. The model is the sixty-eight-year-old peasant Cornelis Schuitemaker. The foreshortening is very convincing, as are details such as the way the arms and legs are depicted.

Although the paper is somewhat yellowed, the main cause of the sheet's overall brown tone is the brown wash Van Gogh used to evoke a dim interior.

SvH

Letter to Theo van Gogh, November 18, 1881 [158]:* Have my drawings arrived? *I made another yesterday, a peasant boy in the morning lighting the fire in the hearth with a kettle hanging over it, and another, an old man laying twigs in a fireplace. I am sorry to say there is still something harsh and severe in my drawings, and I think that she, that is, her influence, is needed to soften that.

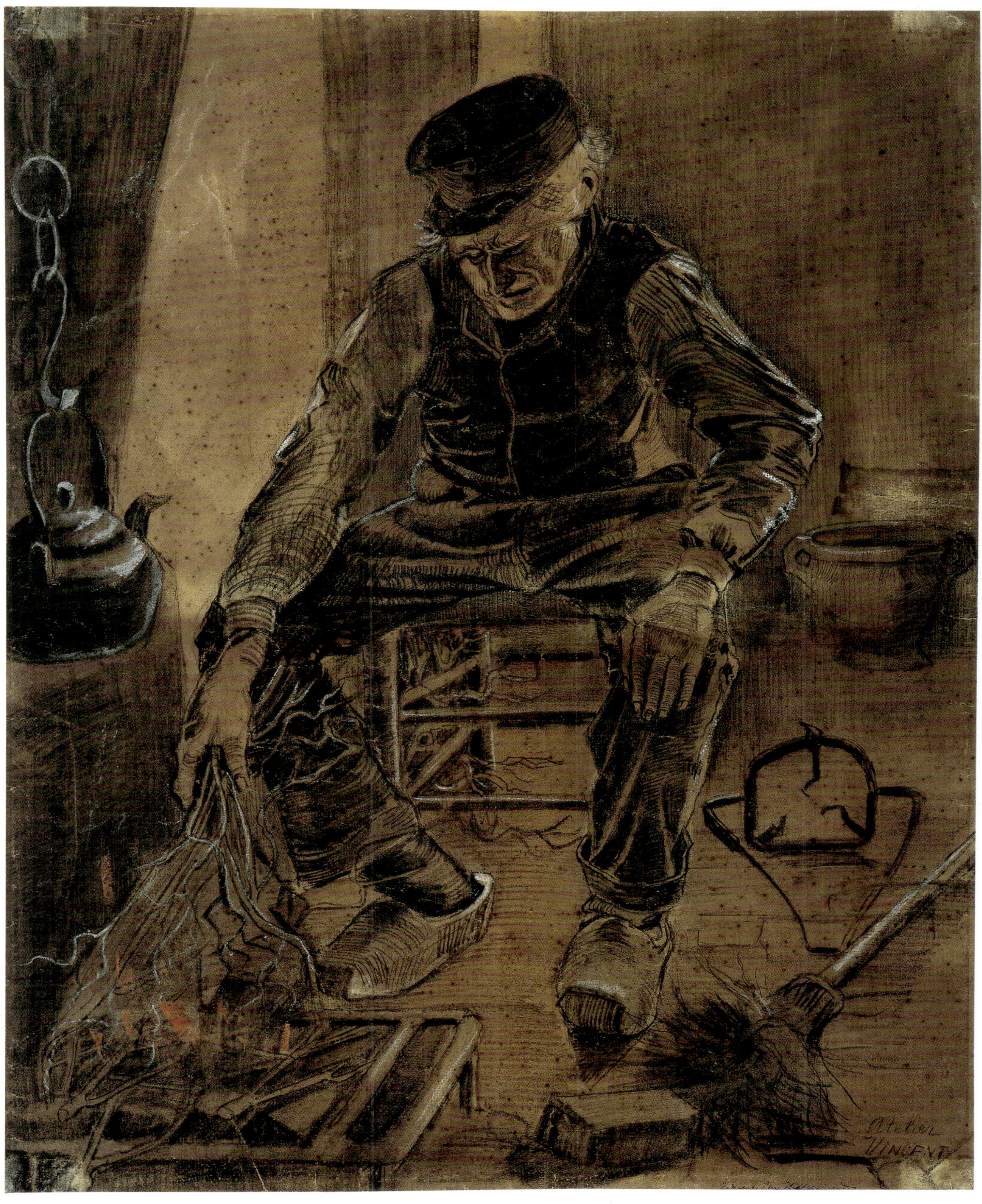
Atelier
VINCENT

6. *The Entrance to the Pawn Bank*

March 1882
Pen and ink, graphite, brush and wash, opaque white watercolor on laid paper watermarked with an illegible trace along the top edge
23.9 x 33.7 cm (9⅜ x 13¼ in.)
Signed lower left: *Vincent*
Inscribed on verso, in another hand: *Ingang bank van Leening*
Traces of squaring
Van Gogh Museum, Amsterdam (Vincent van Gogh Foundation) (d 374 V/1975)
F1679a, JH126

Provenance: Purchased from the artist (as part of a commission) by his uncle C. M. van Gogh, Amsterdam, 1882; auctioned (along with others from this group) at M. Nijhoff/R. W. P. de Vries, The Hague, May 13–15, 1902, no. 434, but remained unsold; acquired at some point after the 1902 sale by Coenraad 't Lam; to his son Arie 't Lam (d. 1975); to his son Coenraad 't Lam, Rijswijk, 1975; purchased from him by the Vincent van Gogh Foundation, 1975; on permanent loan to the Van Gogh Museum, Amsterdam.

Selected exhibitions: Rotterdam 1900–1901, no. 68; Amsterdam 1980–81, no. 69; Otterlo 1990, no. 22; Amsterdam 1996, unnumbered.

Summary of the literature: Not in De la Faille 1928 or 1970. The drawing was first published by Op de Coul (1975, pp. 28–30) as "Entrance to the Bank van Leening [Pawnshop]" and dated to March 1882. Both title and date have been accepted by all later authors. Op de Coul identified the location (Korte Lombardstraat) and noted that F913 served as the model for the woman in the composition. She demonstrated that the sheet belongs to the first set of drawings made for C. M. van Gogh. Hulsker (1976, pp. 18, 19) discussed this group in depth. Op de Coul (1976, pp. 65–68) called attention to the drawings that served as models for the composition (F913, F914, F934, F935, F936). Hulsker 1980/1996, no. 126. Op de Coul (1983, pp. 199, 200) related the drawing to a newly discovered and similarly awkward sheet (JH Add. 19). Pollock (1983, p. 335) noted Van Gogh's preference for nonpicturesque city views, probably inspired by his reading of modern literature; the sheet depicts poverty. Van Uitert and Hoyle 1987, p. 388, no. 2.134; Dorn 1987, pp. 64–66. Van der Mast and Dumas (in The Hague 1990, pp. 50, 53, 54) related the sheet to F930a; they gave an account of the history of the Bank van Leening (p. 170). De la Faille 1992, no. 1679a; Heenk 1995, pp. 52, 53, 55. Van Heugten (1996, pp. 105–9) noted that many of the drawings for C. M. van Gogh have a title on the verso, all written in the same hand. These works were all exercises in perspective, with the figures added later. The texts on the walls were also identified.

This drawing of the entrance to the Hague Pawn Bank is one of the twelve city views Van Gogh executed in March 1882 for his uncle the art dealer Cornelis Marinus van Gogh. Uncle C.M., as he was known in the family, paid the artist 2.50 gulden (the equivalent then of about $1.30) per sheet. The bank was under municipal supervision, and was founded in 1673 in order to prevent private pawnshops, which still existed in Van Gogh's day, from making exorbitant profits. The work is an excellent example of the type of socially concerned, realistic themes that are the leitmotif of Van Gogh's early oeuvre. Above all, however, it is an exercise in perspective. It is one of the earliest drawings in which we find a penciled grid, indicating the use of the perspective frame, which the artist began to employ about this time. Here, it helped him render the architecture in particular; the figures were added later, in the studio, and their size and relative relationships are unconvincing in the overall perspectival scheme.

SvH

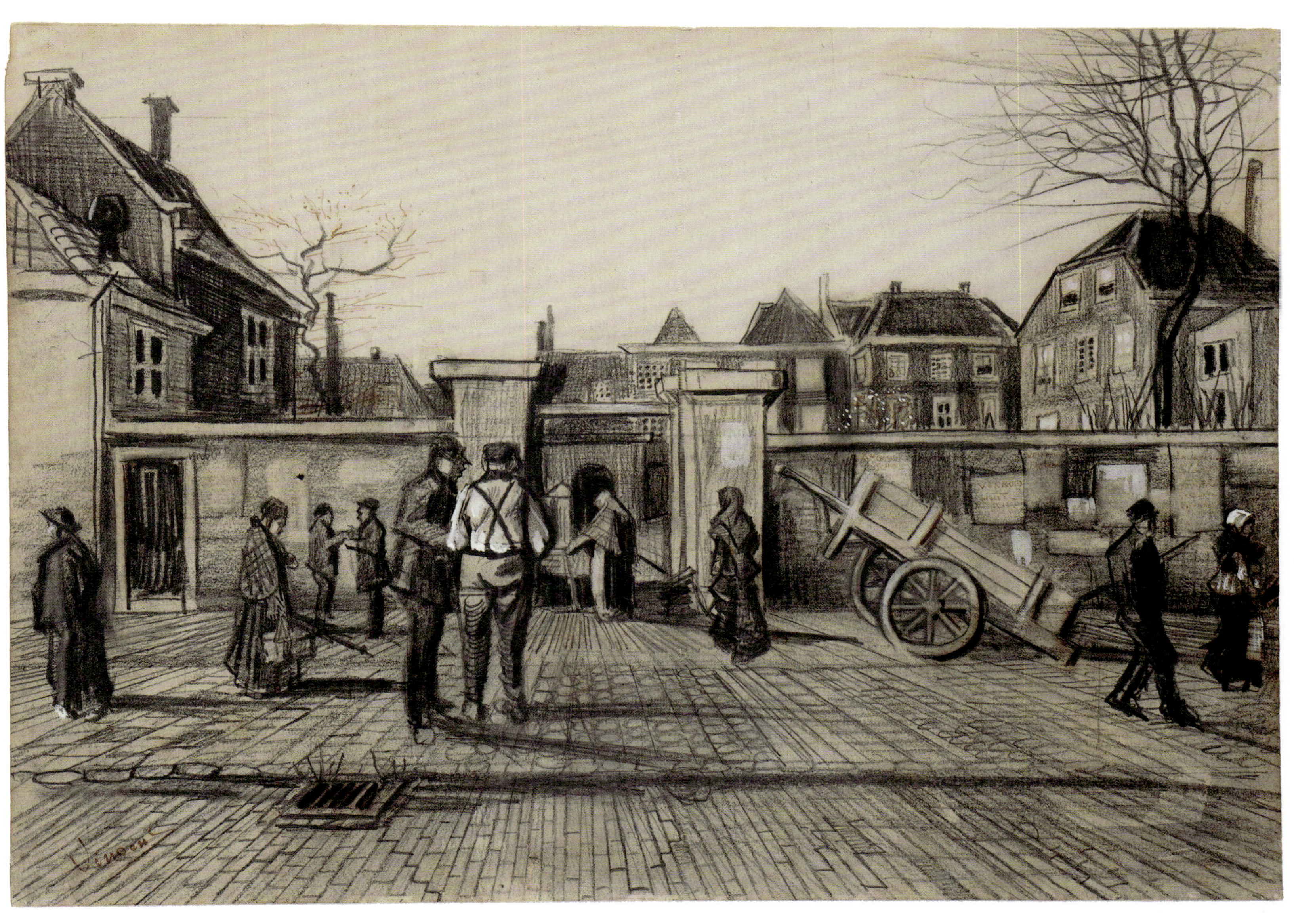

7. Country Road

March–April 1882
Pen, brush, and ink, graphite, opaque white watercolor on laid paper
24.6 x 34.4 cm (9¾ x 13½ in.)
Signed lower right: *Vincent*
Van Gogh Museum, Amsterdam (Vincent van Gogh Foundation) (d 428 V/1962)
F1089, JH124

Provenance: Theo van Gogh (d. 1891); by inheritance to his son, Vincent Willem van Gogh (1890–1978), as part of his collection, administered by his widow, Johanna van Gogh-Bonger (d. 1925), 1891; placed on loan at the Stedelijk Museum, Amsterdam, 1931–73; ownership transferred to the Vincent van Gogh Foundation, 1962; placed on permanent loan at the Van Gogh Museum, Amsterdam, 1973.

Selected exhibitions: Amsterdam 1905, no. 261; The Hague–Amsterdam 1912, no. 10; Amsterdam 1914–15, no. 18; New York 1920, no. 18; Berlin 1927–28, no. 6; New York–Chicago 1949–50, no. 28; London 1968–69, no. 7; Amsterdam 1980–81, no. 55; Rome 1988, no. 56; Otterlo 1990, no. 69.

Summary of the literature: Van Meurs 1910, p. 19; early reproductions in *Lettres* 1911, pl. II, and Bremmer 1926, vol. 11, no. 84. De la Faille (1928, no. 1089) gave the title as "Route près de Loosduinen"—which was to become the most commonly used—and dated the work to the Hague period. Vanbeselaere (1937, pp. 85, 148, 410) referred to it as "Weg langs de moestuinen," July 1882. Cooper (1955, pp. 18–21) dated it to April–May 1882; Bowness (in London 1968–69, p. 24), to March 1882, as part of the first series made for C. M. van Gogh. In De la Faille 1970 (no. 1089) it was dated to early 1882. Visser (1973, pp. 110, 111) identified the location as Het Nieuwe Slag, now Groen van Prinstererlaan, and noted the function of the wind screens. Hulsker (1980, no. 124) dated the sheet to March 1882; Van Uitert and Hoyle (1987, p. 389, no. 2.141) followed Hulsker. Van der Mast and Dumas (in The Hague 1990, pp. 71, 72) mentioned Visser's identification of the site and suggested Laan van Eik en Duinen as an alternative. Heenk 1995, pp. 55, 59. Van Heugten (1996, pp. 116–19) gave the title "Country Road" and dated the sheet to March–April 1882; it does not belong to the first group of works commissioned by C. M. van Gogh but resembles them in size and technique, and is also an exercise in perspective drawing; the location cannot be identified with any certainty. Te Rijdt (in Amsterdam 1997–98, p. 296) noted the influence of Mauve and illustrated magazines. Tokyo 2000, pp. 42, 165.

The exact location of this country road near The Hague, bordered by market gardens, has never been pinpointed convincingly. Reed or wind screens, erected to protect the crops from wind and drifting sand, surround the plots at the left. Van Gogh used the long, linear elements so typical of this landscape to produce a successful exercise in two-point perspective. Here was a chance to put into practice what he had learned from Armand Cassagne's *Traité pratique de perspective* (Paris, 1879). For example, Cassagne's suggestions proved extremely helpful in determining the relative distance between the alders as they move into the distance (fig. 91).

SvH

62 PERSPECTIVE ÉLÉMENTAIRE.

81. — Allée d'arbres en perspective.

Opération. — Pour l'avenue fuyante (fig. 99), la hauteur AB et la première distance AA' étant prises à volonté, conduire les parallèles fuyantes AP — BP — et CP; du sommet B conduire la diagonale BC' prolongée en A"; le point A" déterminera la place

Fig. 99.

du troisième arbre; conduire la diagonale B'C"; le point E sera la base du quatrième arbre. On opérera de même pour les arbres suivants; puis, de chaque base, conduisant des horizontales, on aura sur la fuyante DP les arbres de l'autre côté de l'avenue aux points opposés D'D", etc.

(Voir, pour l'application de cette règle, la figure 98 et la figure 100.)

Il est facile d'observer que cette règle s'applique également à une suite de colonnes ou à tous autres objets également espacés entre eux.

Fig. 91. *Allée d'arbres en perspective*, in Armand Cassagne, *Traité pratique de perspective* (Paris, 1879), p. 62

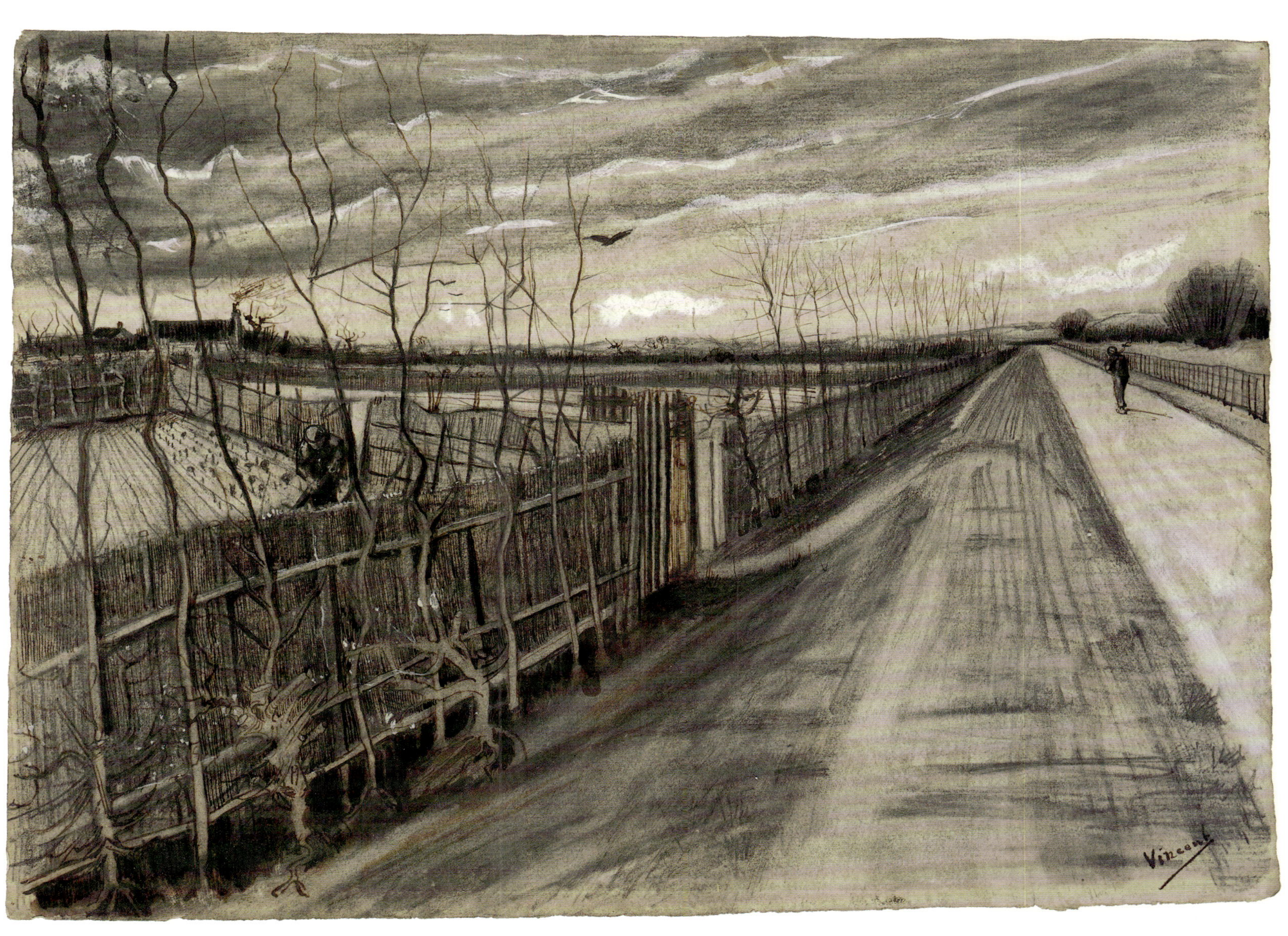
Vincent

8. *Nursery on Schenkweg*

April–May 1882
Black chalk, graphite, pen, brush, and ink, heightened with white body color on laid paper watermarked ED & CIE (in a cartouche)
29.6 x 58.5 cm (11⅝ x 23 in.)
Signed lower left: *Vincent*
The Metropolitan Museum of Art, New York, Bequest of Walter C. Baker, 1971 (1972.118.281)
F930, JH138
Letters 183, R8

Provenance: Purchased from the artist (as part of a commission) by his uncle C. M. van Gogh, Amsterdam, 1882; art dealer J. H. de Bois, Haarlem, until February 1914; sold (for 4,000 marks) to J. Cook (or Cock), Alkmaar; Kunstzalen d'Audretsch, The Hague; Myrtil Frank, The Hague and New York; J. H. de Bois, Haarlem; sold to Walter C. Baker (d. 1971), New York, by 1953; his bequest to The Metropolitan Museum of Art, 1971.

Selected exhibitions: Otterlo 1990, no. 28; Vienna 1996, no. 14.

Summary of the literature: De la Faille (1928, no. 930) dated the sheet to April 1882 on the basis of letter 183. Vanbeselaere (1937, pp. 81, 82, 128, 129, 131) suggested that the subject is the kitchen gardens on Laan van Meerdervoort in The Hague. De la Faille 1970 (no. 930) dated the work to May 1882, now correctly identifying it with a passage in letter R8, and gave the location as Schenkweg. Visser (1973, pp. 51–54) named a different site, the nursery on Javastraat. Hulsker 1980/1996, no. 138; Amsterdam 1980–81, p. 53. Van der Mast and Dumas (in The Hague 1990, pp. 35, 36, 172, 173) provided more concrete information on the location, identifying it as the Van der Putte nursery on Schenkweg. On the basis of the still-bare trees, they suggested it was begun in April and finished in May. Heijbroek and Wouthuysen (1993, p. 200) discussed the sale by De Bois. Heenk 1995, pp. 57, 58; Loos in Amsterdam 2002, pp. 70, 71.

Satisfied with the first group of cityscapes (see F1679a, cat. 6), Vincent's Uncle C.M. (Cornelis Marinus van Gogh) commissioned the artist for a second series, to which this sheet belongs. Van Gogh regarded these works as exercises in perspective. As the writing in the background indicates, the subject is P. van der Putte's nursery, located at Schenkweg 37 in The Hague. Van Gogh wrote to Van Rappard that he had followed the latter's advice and concentrated his efforts on the ditch and the surrounding greenery [R8]. The effect, in his eyes, was one of a tranquil spring day. The drawing is indeed very good, a striking combination of landscape and city view. At the end of May, Van Gogh sent it to his uncle, together with six other drawings.

SvH

Letter to Theo van Gogh, March 24, 1882 [183]: I am busy drawing figures and also a few landscapes of a nursery here on Schenkweg.

Letter to Anthon van Rappard, May 28, 1882 [R8]: Then there is the florist's garden; this I changed the way you suggested, i.e. I studied the side of the ditch more carefully, as well as the water in the foreground, and only now it shows to its full advantage, I feel, and expresses "Spring" and a gentle silence.

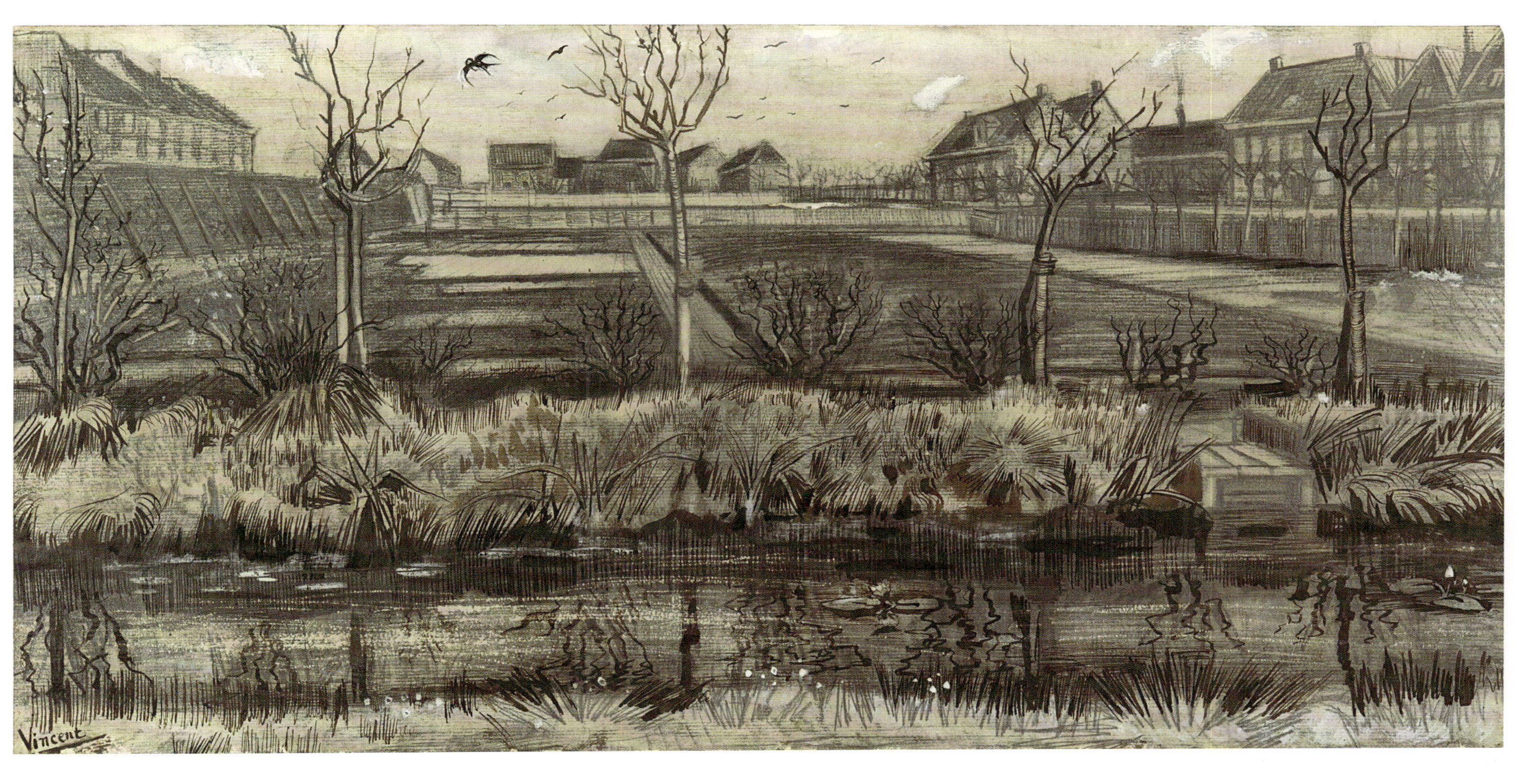
Vincent

9. *Carpenter's Yard and Laundry*

April–May 1882
Black chalk, graphite, pen, brush, and black ink, watercolor, washed, scratched, on laid paper watermarked PL BAS
28.4 x 46.2 cm (11⅛ x 18¼ in.)
Signed lower left: *Vincent del* [*delineavit*]
Kröller-Müller Museum, Otterlo (KM 116.039)
F939, JH150
Letter R8

Provenance: Acquired from the artist by his uncle C. M. van Gogh, Amsterdam, 1882; sold by him to J. Hidde Nijland, Dordrecht and The Hague, before 1904; acquired from him by Helene Kröller-Müller, The Hague, 1928; Kröller-Müller Foundation, 1932; Kröller-Müller Museum, Otterlo, 1937.

Selected exhibitions: Dordrecht 1905; The Hague 1918, unnumbered; Amsterdam 1924, no. 25; New York and other cities 1935–36, no. 79; London–Birmingham–Glasgow 1947–48, no. 104; New York–Chicago 1949–50, no. 19; Amsterdam 1980–81, no. 75; Otterlo 1990, no. 31.

Summary of the literature: First reproduction appeared in Nijland 1905 (fig. 6). De la Faille (1928, no. 939) referred to the sheet as "Derrière le Schenkweg," a title maintained by many authors. He also dated the work to May 1882. Douwes 1930, p. 71; Vanbeselaere 1937, pp. 82, 83, 131, 408; Weisbach 1949–51, vol. 1, pp. 161, 162; Leymarie 1951, p. 21; Cooper 1955, pp. 22, 23; Elgar 1958, no. 9; De Gruyter 1961, p. 94; London 1962, p. 33; Wadley 1969, p. 26. Visser (1973, pp. 24, 36, 44–48) identified the washerwoman as Simonis-De Mol and suggested the sheet was completed before April 20, 1882, the day she died. Chetham 1976, pp. 25, 89, 272. Hulsker (1980, no. 150) referred to the work as "Carpenter's Yard and Laundry" and identified it as one of the drawings sent to C. M. van Gogh. Kröller-Müller Museum 1980, pp. 21, 22. Van der Mast and Dumas (in The Hague 1990, pp. 24–26) claimed that it was not this sheet but F944 that Van Gogh sent to his uncle; they also suggested it was executed in April–May, on the evidence of the still rather bare trees. Heenk 1995, p. 59; Kröller-Müller Museum 2003, p. 21.

Van Gogh drew this view of the area behind his house on Schenkweg in two more or less identical variants; the second sheet, F944, is less neatly composed and somewhat sketchier in execution. The rear of the row of houses figures in a number of drawings. In the foreground lies the laundry owned by Van Gogh's neighbor widow Simonis-De Mol with, behind, a carpenter's workshop. The artist sent the sheet, together with six other cityscapes, to his uncle Cornelis Marinus van Gogh. It has been suggested that F944 was the work dispatched to C.M., but its more sketchlike character and the fact that it was the sheet shown here that was acquired by Helene Kröller-Müller from Hidde Nijland (who purchased several of Van Gogh's views from Uncle C.M.) make this seem unlikely.

At the end of May, Van Gogh sent seven sheets to his uncle, among them this one. Visser (1973) suggested it must have been executed before April 20, as the washerwoman in the scene died on that day. Since Van Gogh could have added her from sketches made earlier rather than drawing her directly from life, the date "April–May" has been maintained.

SvH

Letter to Anthon van Rappard, May 28, 1882 [R8]: And then the one of the carpenter's shed—taken from the window of my studio—by working on it with pen I have brought a new kind of black into it, and now "the sun is shining," because the lights show up more strongly.

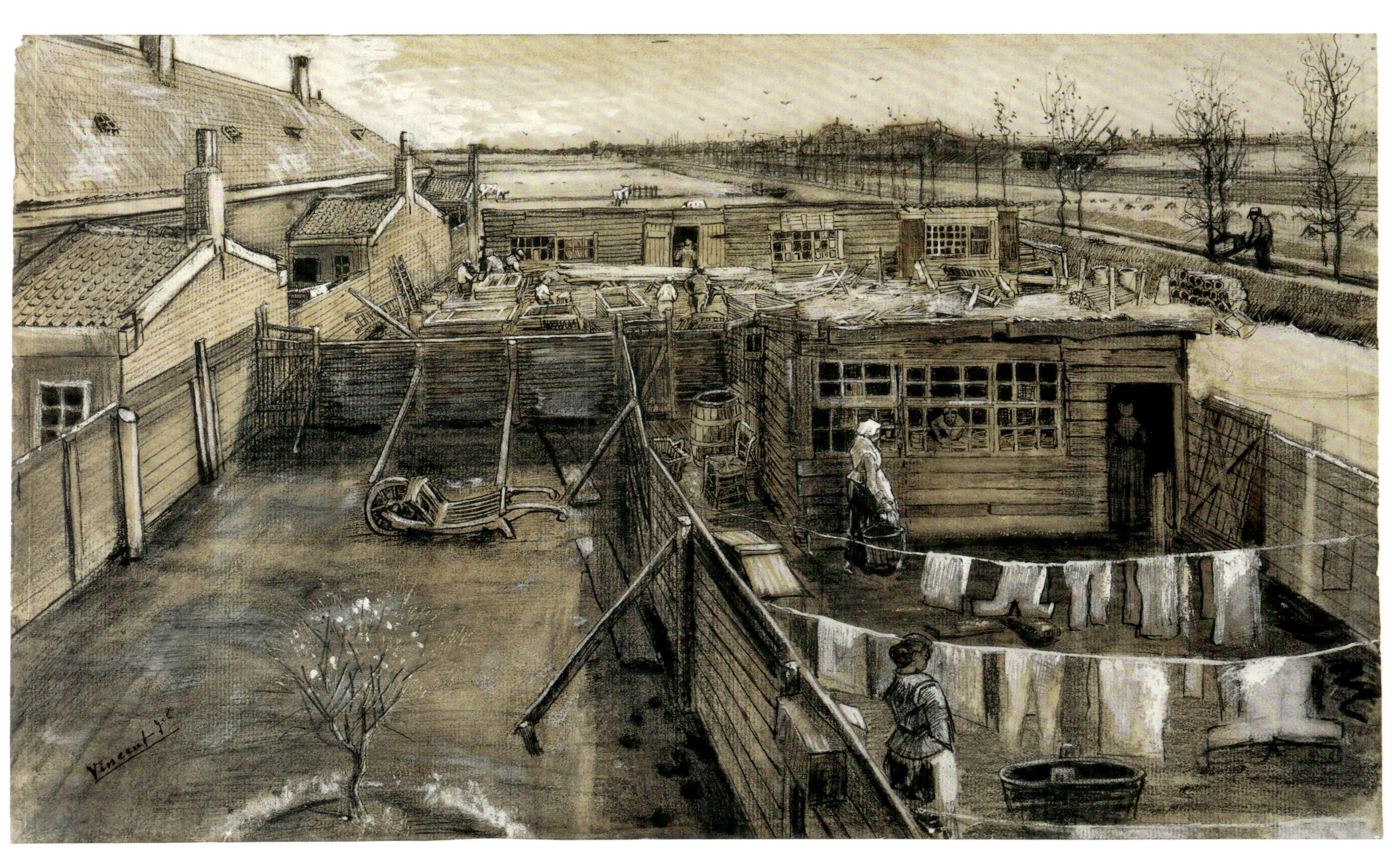
Vincent

10. *The Fish-Drying Barn at Scheveningen*

July 1882
Opaque and transparent watercolor, graphite, pen and ink on wove paper pasted on cardboard
36.4 x 52.6 cm (14⅜ x 20¾ in.)
Sidney E. Frank, Chairman, Sidney Frank Importing Co., Inc.
F945, JH160
Letter 220

Provenance: Acquired by H. P. Bremmer (d. 1956), The Hague, before 1928, possibly by 1911; his heirs, The Hague, after 1956; Floris Bremmer, The Hague; E. J. van Wisselingh and Co., Amsterdam; Myrtil Frank, The Hague and New York; E. V. Thaw and Co., New York; Benjamin Edward Bensinger, Chicago, from 1969; private collection, Tokyo, by 1975, until at least 1986; private collection, until 2001; sold, Sotheby's, New York, November 7, 2001, no. 9; private collection; to present owner.

Exhibition: Tokyo–Nagoya 1985–86, no. 38.

Summary of the literature: De la Faille (1928, no. 945) gave the date as July and identified the building as the fish-drying barn in Scheveningen; these facts have never been disputed. Douwes 1930, p. 71; Vanbeselaere 1937, pp. 84, 143, 145, 148, 408. Visser (1973, p. 95) identified the location as Kolenwagenslag in Scheveningen. Hulsker 1980/1996, no. 160; Van der Mast and Dumas in The Hague 1990, pp. 64, 66; Heenk 1995, pp. 63, 76.

Van Gogh knew the fishing village Scheveningen well from the many walks he had taken there in 1869–73, when he had a job at Goupil's gallery in The Hague. From the very beginning of his career as an artist he was determined to spend time working there, and he was able to realize his plan in the summer and autumn of 1882.

The picturesque fish-drying barn on Kolenwagenslag is depicted in three further drawings, one of which shows the building from the side (F940, fig. 92). The angle is somewhat different, since the structure is viewed from the dunes. The sheet is a little earlier than the work in the exhibition, in which the baskets in the foreground are empty. Van Gogh was extremely pleased with the luxuriant greenery he found there in July and sought to capture its effect in this watercolor.

In terms of technique, the watercolor typifies Van Gogh's working method. He rarely drew with brush and watercolor, using instead gouache, thinned to various degrees.

SvH

Letter to Theo van Gogh, July 26, 1882 [220]: I have now made three of Scheveningen, again the Fish drying barn, which you know—drawn as elaborately—but now there is color too. I am sure you know, Theo, that it is not more difficult to work in color than in black and white; indeed, perhaps the reverse, for as far as I can see, three-fourths of it depends on the original sketch, and almost the whole watercolor rests on its quality. It is not sufficient to give an à peu près; it was and is my aim to intensify it. In the black-and-white Fish drying barn that is already apparent, I think, for in them you can follow everything and trace the composition of the whole. And look here, I think the reason for my working so much more easily in watercolors is that I have tried so hard and for such a long time to draw more correctly. . . .

When I returned to that fish drying barn, a wonderfully bright fresh green of turnips or rapes had sprouted in those baskets full of sand in the foreground which serve to prevent the sand from drifting off the dunes. Two months ago everything was bare except the grass in the little garden, and now this rough, wild, luxuriant growth forms a very pretty effect in contrast to the bareness of the rest.

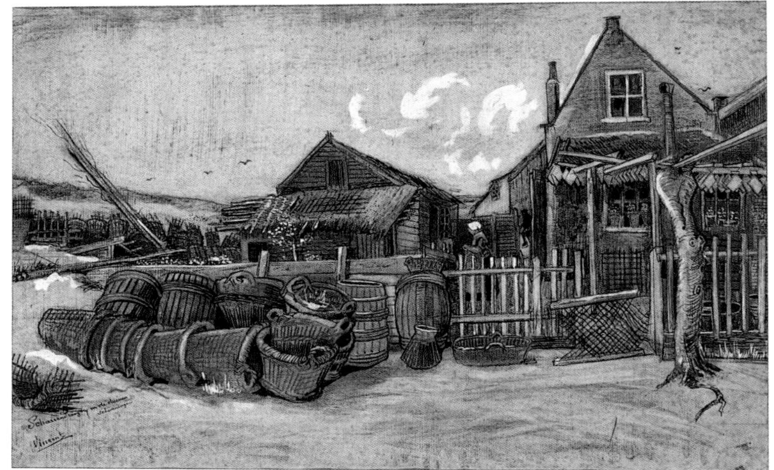

Fig. 92. *Fish-Drying Barn* (F940), June 1882. Pen, brush, and ink, opaque watercolor, graphite, 28.5 x 45 cm (11¼ x 17¾ in.). Private collection

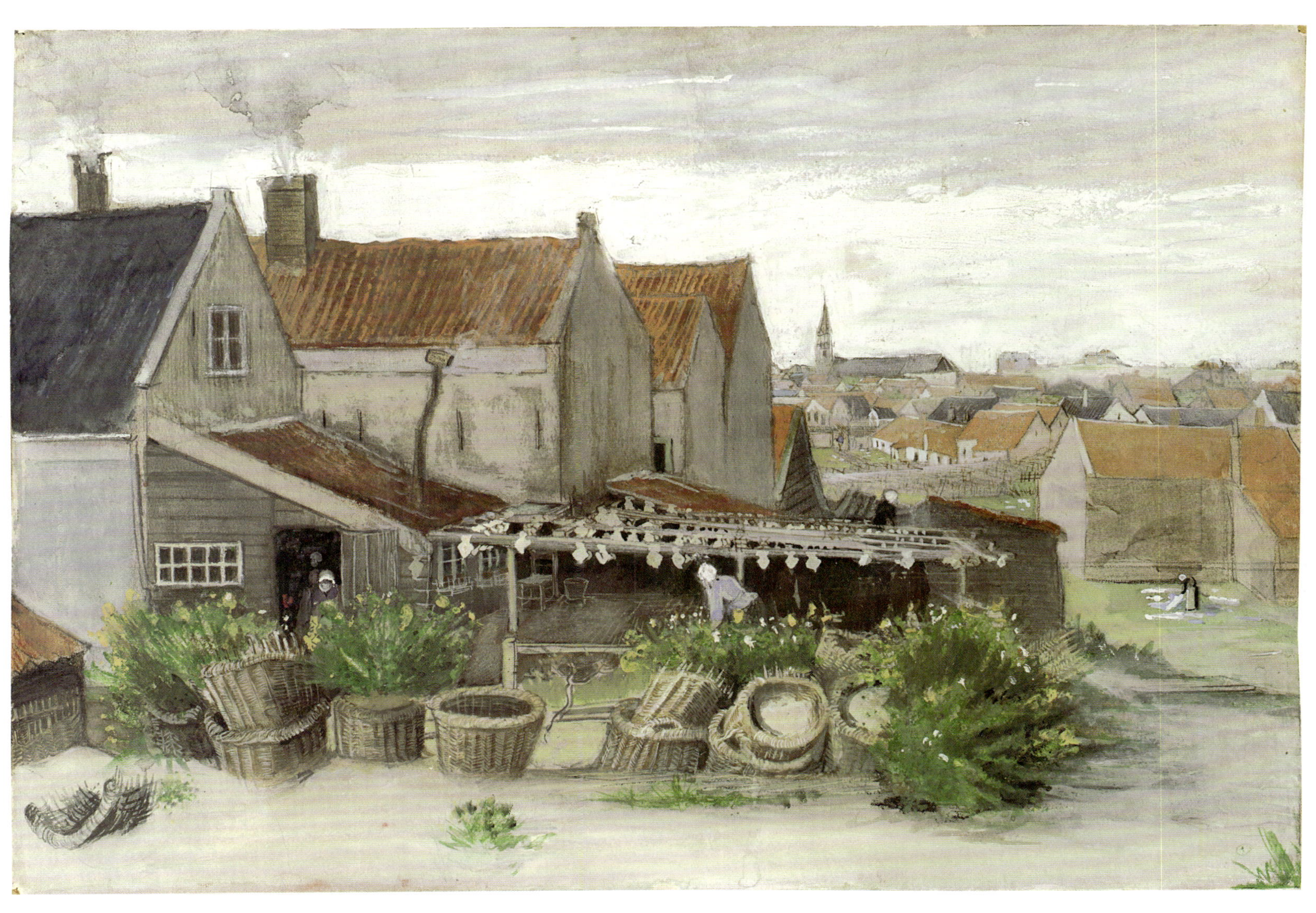

11. *Worn Out*

November 1882
Graphite on watercolor paper
50.4 x 31.6 cm (19⅞ x 12⅜ in.)
Signed in black chalk, lower left: *Vincent*
Traces of squaring
Van Gogh Museum, Amsterdam (Vincent van Gogh Foundation) (d 378 V/1962)
F997, JH267
Letters 247, R18, 248, 250, 251, 253

Provenance: Theo van Gogh (d. 1891); by inheritance to his son, Vincent Willem van Gogh (1890–1978), as part of his collection, administered by his widow, Johanna van Gogh-Bonger (d. 1925), 1891; placed on loan at the Stedelijk Museum, Amsterdam, 1931–73; ownership transferred to the Vincent van Gogh Foundation, 1962; placed on permanent loan at the Van Gogh Museum, Amsterdam, 1973.

Selected exhibitions: Amsterdam 1905, no. 246; Cologne–Frankfurt 1910; Amsterdam 1914–15, no. 29; Rotterdam 1923, hors cat.; London–Birmingham–Glasgow 1947–48, no. 109; London 1968–69, no. 14; Otterlo 1990, no. 41; Amsterdam 1995, hors cat.; Amsterdam 1996; Florence 1997, no. 29.

Summary of the literature: Bremmer 1904, vol. 6, cover ill. De la Faille (1928, no. 997) called the sheet "Vieillard pleurant"—a title maintained, with some variation, by most later authors—and dated it to November 1882, which has also remained unchanged. Vanbeselaere (1937, pp. 94, 96, 185, 192, 409) mentioned the lithograph F1662 and letters 247 and 248. De Gruyter (1961, p. 96, fig. 14) made a connection to the Etten version of the motif and the painted variation from Saint-Rémy, F702. The themes of the work are the existence of God and eternity. Wadley (1969, p. 28) associated the work with *Sorrow* (F929a). De la Faille 1970 (no. 997) summarized the older literature. Chetham (1976, p. 26) pointed out that nineteenth-century artists produced many works on this motif and that Van Gogh had some of these in his print collection. Hulsker (1980, no. 267) referred to letter 253. Van Uitert and Hoyle 1987, p. 393, no. 2.160. Feilchenfeldt and Veenenbos (1988, p. 127) indicated that the sheet was on display at Amsterdam 1905 under the title "Oudejaarsavond." In Otterlo 1990 (pp. 65, 93) the title was mistakenly given as "At Eternity's Gate," the title Van Gogh used for the lithograph, F1662. Heenk 1995, pp. 70, 73. Van Heugten and Pabst (1995, p. 52) discussed the relationship between the drawing and the print and the influence of Thomas Faed's print *Worn Out*. Van Heugten (1996, pp. 160–64) titled the sheet "Worn Out," listed all the related letters, and discussed the history of the motif and Van Gogh's different versions, as well as their varying interpretations.

This image of a sorrowing man belongs to a large group of figure studies executed between September and November 1882. The model was Adrianus Zuyderland, one of the residents of the Nederlands Hervormde Oude Mannen- en Vrouwenhuis, where Van Gogh often found people to pose for him. The motif of the weary and disenfranchised had a long and respectable artistic tradition, which Van Gogh first sought to tackle in September 1881 (F863, fig. 93). As before, he called his new work *Worn Out*. A few days later, he made a lithograph of it, which he titled *At Eternity's Gate*. *Sorrowing Woman* (F1060, cat. 14) is a closely related reworking of the same theme.

Van Gogh used a carpenter's pencil for the group of drawings to which this sheet belongs. He worked on heavy watercolor paper and treated the graphite with milk to create a more velvety, less shiny black. This effect can be seen clearly in the drawing, as can the stain around the figure left by the fixative. There are also traces of a grid, indicating that the artist here once again made use of his perspective frame. SvH

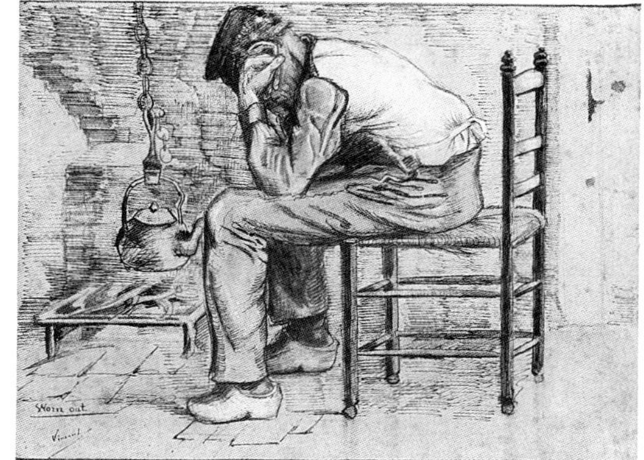

Fig. 93. *Worn Out* (F863), September 1881. Pen and ink, transparent and opaque watercolor on laid paper, 23.5 x 31 cm (9¼ x 12¼ in.). P. and N. de Boer Foundation, Amsterdam

Letter to Theo van Gogh, November 24, 1882 [247]: Today and yesterday I drew two figures of an old man sitting with his elbows on his knees and his head in his hands. Long ago Schuitemaker sat for me, and I kept the drawing because I wanted to make a better one someday. Perhaps I will also make a lithograph of it. How beautiful such an old workman is, with his patched fustian clothes and his bald head.

Letter to Anthon van Rappard, November 24, 1882 [R18]: You may remember the drawing "Worn out"; I did it all over again the other day—actually three separate times, with two models—and I am going to toil on it a lot more. For the present I have one which will be the subject of the fifth stone; it shows an old workman sitting lost in thought, his elbows on his knees, and his hands clasping his head (this time with a bald crown).

Letter to Theo van Gogh, November 26 and 27, 1882 [248]: As to the lithography, I hope to get a proof tomorrow of a little old man. I hope it will turn out well. I made it with a kind of chalk especially patterned for this process, but I am afraid that after all the common lithographic crayon will prove to be the best, and that I shall be sorry I did not use it.

Letter to Theo van Gogh, ca. December 3, 1882 [250]: The hands and the head are bad, but in the print of the other old man they were the parts which were best. I again witnessed the transferring to the stone and the printing and I must tell you that I think great things can be done with this process. Today I was at Van der Weele's, who was rather pleased with the little old man with his head in his hands; he intends to try it himself.

Letter to Theo van Gogh, between December 4 and 9, 1882 [251]: Now in these drawings I have tried to show my meaning even more clearly than in the old man with his head in his hands. These fellows are all in action, and this fact especially must be kept in mind in the choice of subjects, I think. You know yourself how beautiful the numerous figures in repose, which are done so very, very often, are. They are done more often than figures in action. It is always very tempting to draw a figure at rest; it is very difficult to express action, and in many people's eyes the former effect is more "pleasant" than anything else. But this

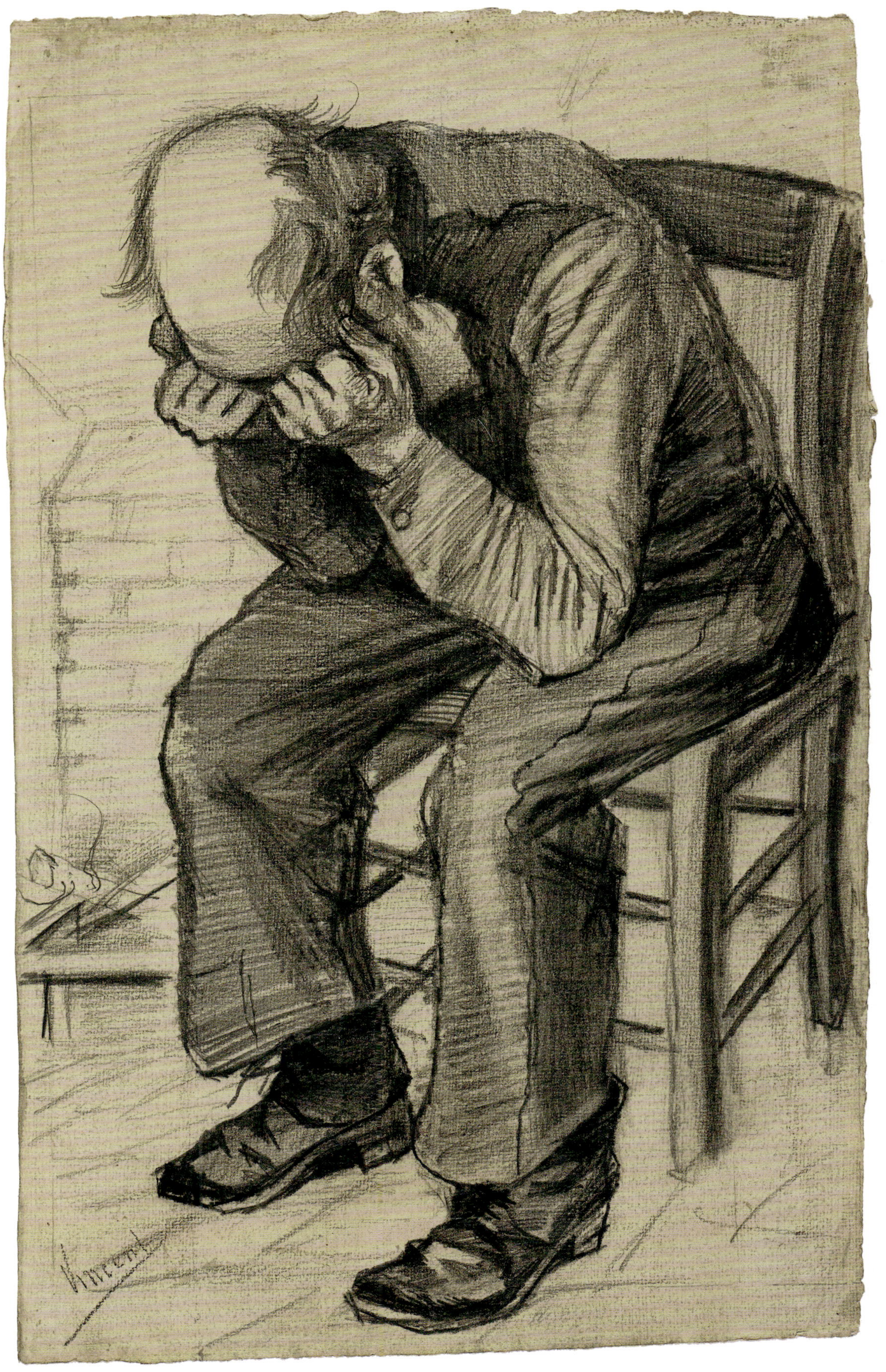
Vincent

"pleasant" aspect must not detract from the truth, and the truth is that there is more drudgery than rest in life.

Letter to Theo van Gogh, between ca. December 13 and 18, 1882 [253]: I have two new drawings now, one of a man reading his Bible, and the other of a man saying grace before his dinner, which is on the table. Both are certainly done in what you may call an old-fashioned sentiment—they are figures like the little old man with his head in his hands. The "Bénédicité" [Grace] is, I think, the best, but they complement each other. In one there is a view of the snowy fields through the window. My intention in these two, and in the first little old man, is one and the same, namely to express the peculiar sentiment of Christmas and New Years Eve.

12. *Old Man with a Top Hat*

December 1882–January 1883
Lithographic crayon, graphite, pen, brush, and ink, scratched, on watercolor paper watermarked HALLINES (cut in half lengthwise by the right edge)
60 x 36 cm (23⅝ x 14⅛ in.)
Signed (incised) lower left: *Vincent*
Traces of squaring
Van Gogh Museum, Amsterdam (Vincent van Gogh Foundation) (d 183 V/1962)
F985, JH286

Provenance: Theo van Gogh (d. 1891); by inheritance to his son, Vincent Willem van Gogh (1890–1978), as part of his collection, administered by his widow, Johanna van Gogh-Bonger (d. 1925), 1891; placed on loan at the Stedelijk Museum, Amsterdam, 1931–73; ownership transferred to the Vincent van Gogh Foundation, 1962; placed on permanent loan at the Van Gogh Museum, Amsterdam, 1973.

Selected exhibitions: Groningen 1897; Amsterdam 1905, no. 258; Amsterdam 1914–15, no. 25; London 1968–69, no. 12; Amsterdam 1980–81, no. 60; Otterlo 1990, no. 45; Amsterdam 1996; Detroit–Boston–Philadelphia 2000–2001, unnumbered (not shown in Philadelphia).

Summary of the literature: De la Faille (1928, no. 985) gave the title "Vieillard coiffé d'un chapeau haut de forme"—a title maintained by most later authors—and dated the sheet to October 1882. Vanbeselaere (1937, pp. 91, 99, 189, 409) suggested a date of December 1882. De la Faille 1970 (no. 985) called the work "Orphan Man with Top Hat," a mistranslation, as there is no English equivalent for the word Van Gogh himself used ("weesman"); dated it to early winter 1882; and noted that F961 shows the same model. Hulsker (1980, no. 286) dated the sheet to December 1882. Pollock (1983, p. 352) noted that the drawing was not intended as a portrait, although the strong characterization of the figure makes it seem like one. Van Uitert and Hoyle (1987, p. 395, no. 2.168) followed Hulsker. In Otterlo 1990 (pp. 32, 97) the problem of distinguishing the various drawing materials was discussed using this sheet (among others) as an example; the drawing was dated to late 1882. Heenk (1995, p. 73) agreed with Pollock (1983). Van Heugten (1996, pp. 176–78) dated the sheet more broadly, to December 1882–January 1883, and viewed it as part of the series of heads Van Gogh was working on at the time, all of which are similar in technique; this technique, which Van Gogh referred to as "painting in black," and the link with magazine illustrations were described in detail.

In December 1882–January 1883 Van Gogh executed a series of studies of heads of working-class people, among them this *Old Man with a Top Hat.* His source of inspiration was a suite of wood engravings entitled *Heads of the People*, published in the English periodical *The Graphic.* In terms of technique, Van Gogh also took his cue from the English artists who, since 1872, had exhibited their works at so-called Black and White Exhibitions. Following their example, he executed his group of heads in an array of black media, such as chalk, lithographic crayon, various inks, opaque watercolor, and graphite. Like the weary old man in *Worn Out* (F997, cat. 11), this striking figure was undoubtedly a resident of the Nederlands Hervormde Oude Mannen- en Vrouwenhuis.

SvH

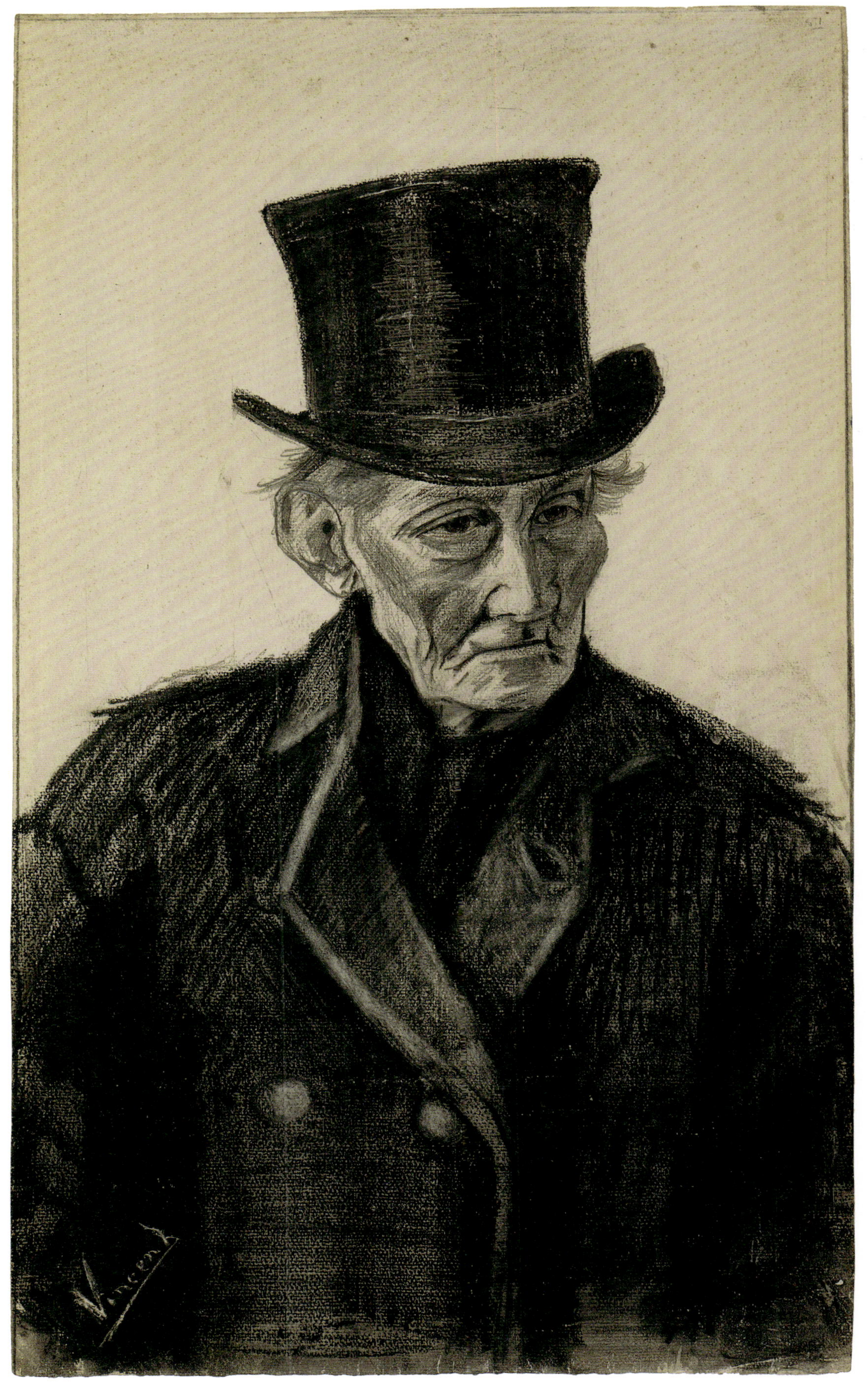
Vincent

13. *Girl with a Pinafore*

December 1882–January 1883
Lithographic crayon, graphite, pen and brush, ink, and opaque watercolor, scratched, on watercolor paper watermarked DAMBRICOURT FRERES HALLINES 1877
48.5 x 25.5 cm (19⅛ x 10 in.)
Museum of Fine Arts, Boston, William Francis Warden Fund (1970.468)
F1685, JH300

Provenance: Theo van Gogh (d. 1891); by inheritance to his son, Vincent Willem Van Gogh, as part of his collection, administered by his widow, Johanna van Gogh-Bonger, 1891, until at least 1897; subsequent whereabouts unknown; sold at auction, Mak van Waay, April 15, 1969, no. 204; purchased at that sale by a Dutch collector; with the art dealer John Streep, Amsterdam and New York, 1969; purchased from him by E. V. Thaw and Co., New York; sold by him to the Museum of Fine Arts, Boston, 1970.

Selected exhibitions: Groningen 1897; Vienna 1996, no. 41; Detroit–Boston–Philadelphia 2000–2001, unnumbered (not shown in Detroit).

Summary of the literature: Not in De la Faille 1928; in De la Faille 1970 (no. 1685), the drawing was given the title "Young Girl: Half Figure" and dated to 1883. Museum of Fine Arts 1976, pp. 382, 383. Hulsker (1980, no. 300) called it "Girl with Pinafore, Half-Figure" and dated it to mid-January 1883. He identified the girl as Sien's daughter, making this (or possibly F1008) the sheet Van Gogh sent to Theo in January. Wadley 1991, pp. 264, 265. Heenk (1995, p. 74) gave a description of the technique and the watermark. Van Heugten (1996, pp. 184–86) rejected the notion that this is the same child as the one in F1007 and F1008; she can be seen, however, in F1024.

The shy-looking child in this drawing is probably Sien Hoornik's daughter, Maria Wilhelmina. She was born on May 7, 1877, and was thus five years old when she posed for Van Gogh. Hulsker suggested that she appears in other drawings—F1007 and F1008—but the child in those works is older and thinner, and is thus probably not the same. It seems likely, however, that she is the girl in a drawing in the Van Gogh Museum (F1024, fig. 94), shown kneeling by her brother's cradle, although we cannot be sure of her identity, as she is seen from behind. The drawing belongs to the series of works depicting popular types that Van Gogh worked on from December 1882 to January 1883, all executed in lithographic crayon over graphite on heavy watercolor paper.

Van Gogh drew a frame around the drawing in black ink, a rarity in his Hague oeuvre and an indication that he valued the work highly.

SvH

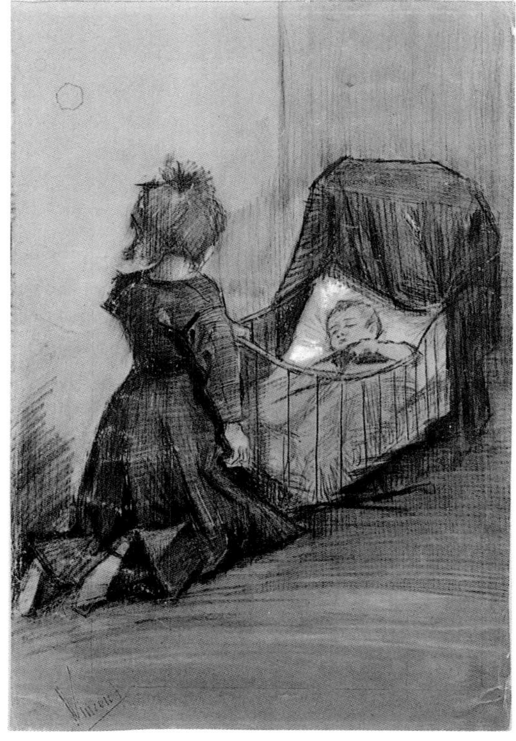

Fig. 94. *Girl Kneeling by a Cradle* (F1024), March 1883. Natural black chalk, graphite, opaque watercolor, wash on wove paper, 48 x 32.3 cm (18⅞ x 12¾ in.). Van Gogh Museum, Amsterdam (Vincent van Gogh Foundation)

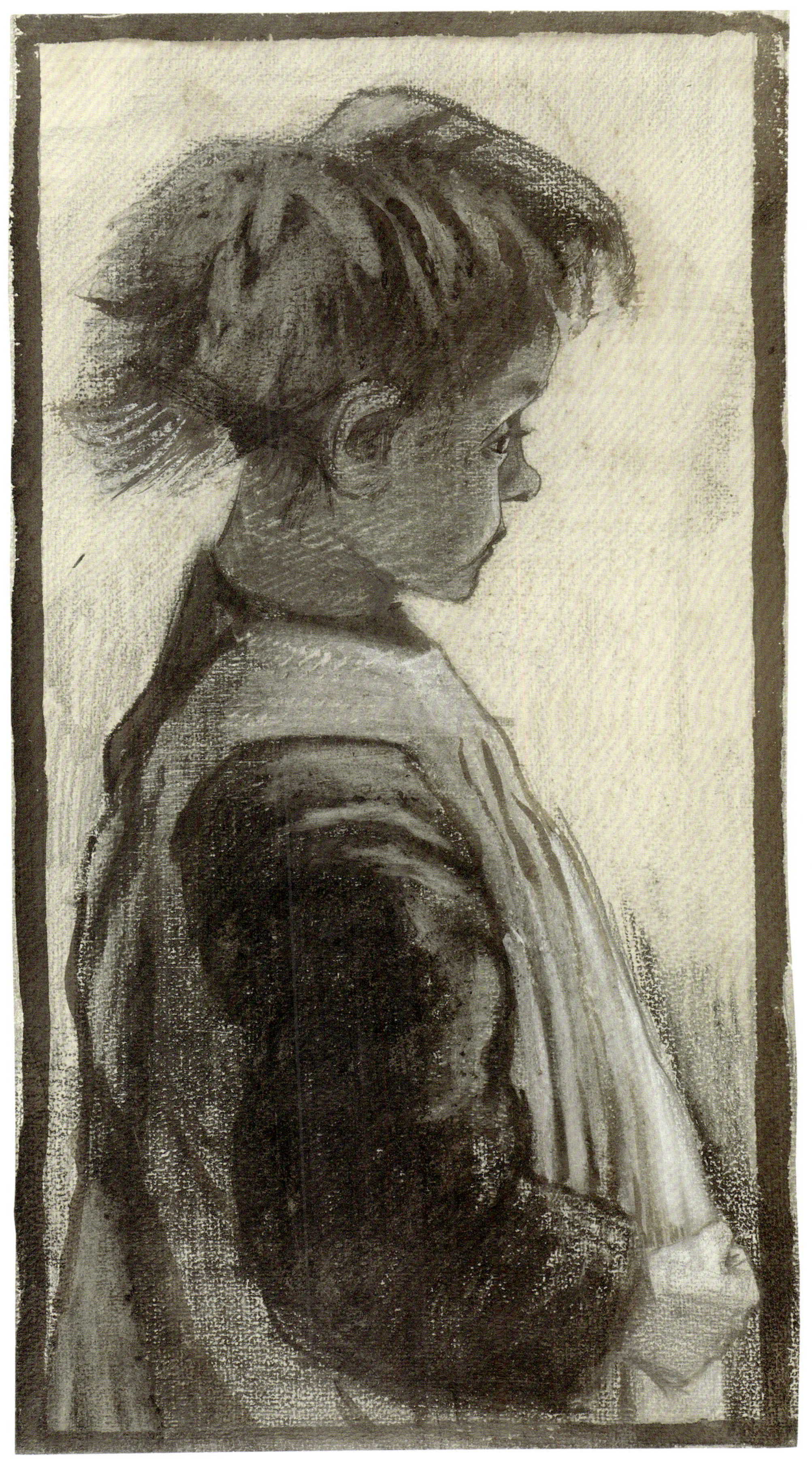

14. *Sorrowing Woman*

February–March 1883
Lithographic crayon, scratched, brush and wash, opaque watercolor on watercolor paper watermarked HALLINES 1877
47.4 x 29.5 cm (18⅝ x 11⅝ in.)
Traces of squaring
Kröller-Müller Museum, Otterlo (KM 123.495)
F1060, JH326

Provenance: Probably sent by the artist to his uncle C. M. van Gogh (d. 1908), Amsterdam; sold by Kunsthandel C. M. van Gogh, Amsterdam, to Helene Kröller-Müller, 1911; Kröller-Müller Foundation, 1928; Kröller-Müller Museum, Otterlo, 1937.

Selected exhibitions: Cologne 1912, no. 110; London 1992, no. 20.

Summary of the literature: Bremmer 1917, no. 114; Bremmer 1919, pl. 20; Bremmer 1921–28, no. 167. De la Faille (1928, no. 1060) gave the sheet the title "Femme Pleurant" and dated it to the Hague period. Fels 1928, p. 67; Vanbeselaere 1937, pp. 105, 207, 410. In De la Faille 1970 (no. 1060) the work was dated to March–April 1883. Chetham (1976, pp. 27, 101, 273) saw a connection with a print by H. Harral in *The Graphic* of September 24, 1870, *Summoned to the War*, which featured a similar figure type. Hulsker (1980, no. 326) dated the sheet to 1883. Kröller-Müller Museum 1980, pp. 28, 29; Zemel 1987, pp. 362, 363; Feilchenfeldt and Veenenbos 1988, p. 128. Bailey (in London 1992, no. 20) proposed a link to a print by Edward Dalziel, *London Sketches—Sunday Afternoon, 1 pm: Waiting for the Public House to Open* (*The Graphic*, January 10, 1874). Van Gogh mentioned that engraving in a letter of late February 1883 [R29], leading Bailey to date the drawing to the same month. Heijbroek and Wouthuysen 1993, p. 202. Heenk (1995, p. 76) also mentioned the Dalziel print but dated the drawing to March–April 1883. Kröller-Müller Museum 2006 (parts of the manuscript supplied to the authors, with thanks to Teio Meedendorp) suggests that the drawing was sent to C. M. van Gogh with a number of others (see letter 326, ca. September 21, 1883).

Sorrowing Woman is a new variation on one of Van Gogh's favorite themes (see F997, cat. 11), the weary working-class figure, head buried in hands. Here, for the first time, the artist depicted a woman in the role. In another version we see her more from the front (F1069, fig. 4). Although prints were once thought to have provided Van Gogh with inspiration for the drawing (see Summary of the literature), he had been experimenting with the subject—very popular among artists of the period—since 1881.

In terms of technique, this work is a marked improvement on the group of drawings executed in December 1882–January 1883. Those were mostly done in lithographic crayon over detailed graphite sketches. Here, by contrast, the lithographic crayon is the primary drawing material, and there are no traces of graphite whatsoever. Given both the technical skill exhibited and the naturalness of the figure, a date of February–March 1883 seems the most plausible.

SvH

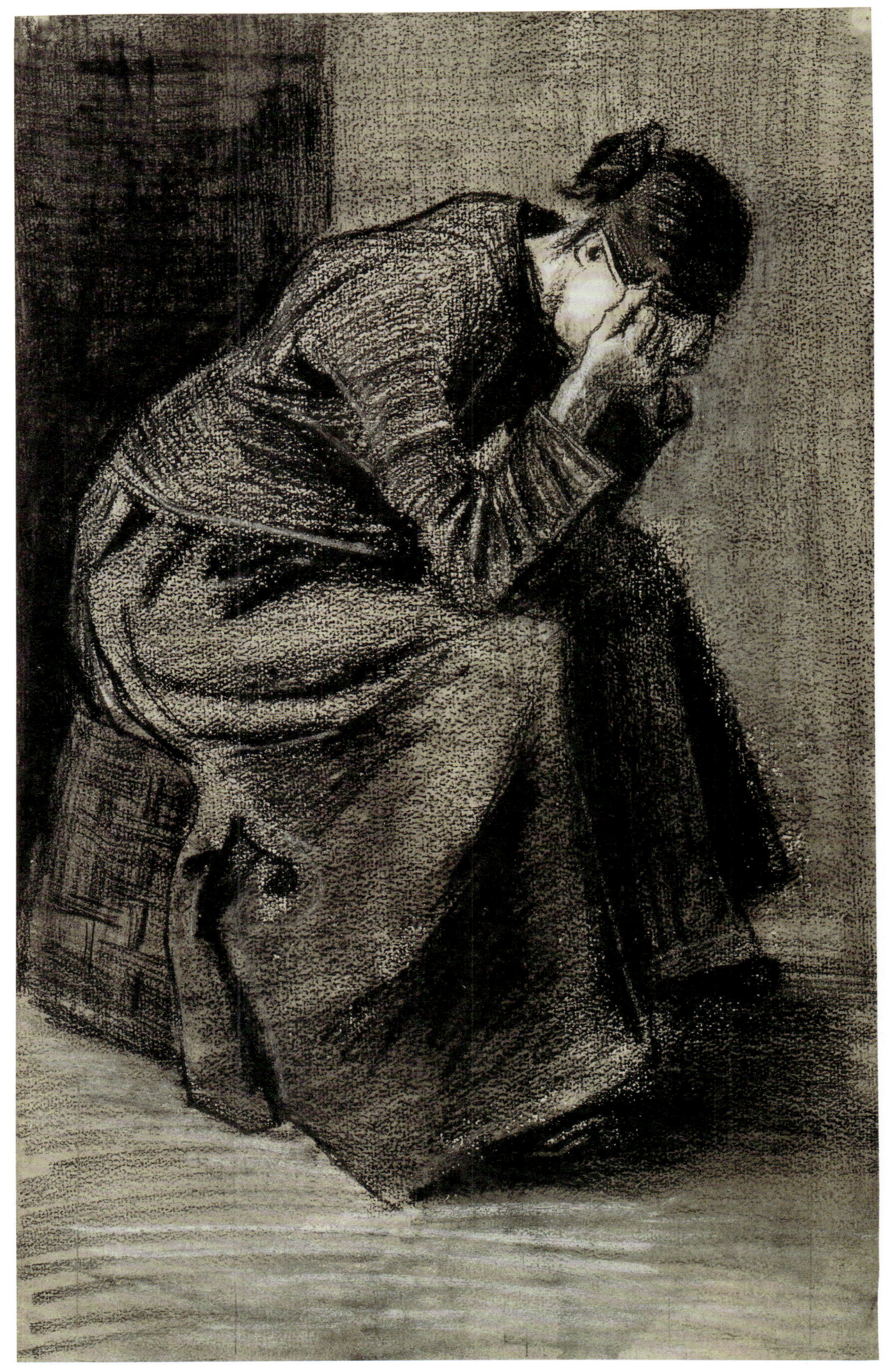

15. *Landscape in Drenthe*

Second half of September–early October 1883
Pen, brush, and ink, graphite, opaque watercolor on laid paper watermarked VDL; a coat of arms with a lion with a sword bordered by the inscription PRO PATRIA EENDRAGT MAAKT MAGT
31.4 x 42.1 cm (12⅜ x 16⅝ in.)
Van Gogh Museum, Amsterdam (Vincent van Gogh Foundation) (d 810 M/1986)
F1104, JH424

Provenance: Probably left by the artist with his mother, Anna Cornelia van Gogh-Carbentus, Nuenen, November 1885; deposited by her with Schrauwen, Breda, 1886; sold by Schrauwen to J. C. Couvreur, Breda, 1902; sold to C. Mouwen and W. van Bakel, Breda, 1902; offered for sale at an exhibition at the Kunstzalen Oldenzeel, Rotterdam, 1903, no. 78, but remained unsold; acquired by art dealers Buffa, Amsterdam, 1904; sold, Frederik Müller, Amsterdam, May 3, 1904, no. 34; purchased at that sale (for 62 gulden) by the poet Herman Gorter (d. 1927), Bussum; Kunstzalen d'Audretsch, The Hague, before 1928; G. H. E. van Suchtelen, The Hague; A. L. J. Einthoven-van Suchtelen, The Hague; art dealers Huinck and Scherjon, Amsterdam, 1953; Wilhelm Weinberg (d. 1957), Amsterdam and Scarsdale, New York; his sale, Sotheby's, London, July 10, 1957, no. 54; purchased at that sale by Philip J. Goldberg (d. 1969), London; his wife, Aimée Ethel Goldberg (d. 1986), London; her sale, Christie's, London, December 2, 1986, no. 127; purchased at that sale by the Van Gogh Museum, with the support of the Vincent van Gogh Foundation and the Vereniging Rembrandt.

Selected exhibitions: Rotterdam 1900–1901, no. 52? (or possibly F1099); Rotterdam 1903b, no. 78; New York 1955, no. 92; Rome 1988, no. 64; Otterlo 1990, no. 74; Amsterdam 1996; Tokyo 2000, no. 10.

Summary of the literature: De la Faille (1928, no. 1104) regarded the drawing as a depiction of a sunrise ("Lever de soleil dans la plaine"), made in Drenthe at an unknown date. Vanbeselaere (1937, pp. 237, 410) gave the title "Landschap" and dated the work to October–November 1883. Tralbaut (1959, pp. 215, 224) adopted the title "Zonsopgang" from De la Faille and dated the sheet to October 1883. Tralbaut 1969, p. 122. In De la Faille 1970 (no. 1104) it was called "Landscape in Drenthe with Canal and Sailboat"—a title maintained by most later authors—and Tralbaut's dating to November 1883 was followed. Hulsker (1980, no. 424) followed De la Faille. Pollock (in Amsterdam 1980–81, p. 71) saw the sheet as one of the works in which Van Gogh expressed his disgust with modernization and his love of such traditional things as transportation via local waterways and barges; she regarded it as a typical Hague school image. Van Crimpen (1986, p. 70) made an inventory of the Drenthe works and regarded this work as a depiction of a sunrise. Van Uitert and Hoyle (1987, p. 496, no. 2.789) followed De la Faille. Van Crimpen 1987. Van der Wolk (in Otterlo 1990, pp. 121, 126) linked the drawing to letter 326 and viewed it as preparing the way for paintings (which were never executed). In Amsterdam 1991 (pp. 40, 41), the title was given as "Drents landschap bij vallende avond" and the work was dated rather early, to late September–early October 1883, on the evidence of the still-leafy trees. Heenk (1995, pp. 93, 94 ,110) followed the opinions in Amsterdam 1991 but dated the sheet to October 1883. Van Heugten (1996, pp. 235–36) adopted the conclusions in Amsterdam 1991 but gave an abbreviated title, "Landschap in Drenthe." Dijk and Van der Sluis (2001, pp. 238–41, 327, 331) believed the location was the northern bank of the Verlengde Hoogeveense Vaart (Lengthened Hoogeven Canal), which would mean that Van Gogh was facing west and the scene does indeed depict a sunset. Op de Coul (2002, p. 117) identified the sheet as no. 78 in the exhibition at Kunstzalen Oldenzeel in November–December 1903 (Rotterdam 1903b).

This sheet is one of the sixteen drawings preserved from Van Gogh's brief sojourn in Drenthe. Anthon van Rappard had described the area to him, and he had high expectations regarding the landscape of this province in the northeastern Netherlands. In the end, however, he was rather disappointed: during the day, he found the extensive moors monotonous, although at twilight they took on an impressive and sublime character. It is precisely the latter effect Van Gogh sought to capture in this drawing. The work forms the overture for the series of drawings in pen and ink the artist would execute in Nuenen—works that are among the best produced in the Dutch period. The Drenthe sheet, however, is somewhat more modest in terms of both technique and mood.

The last remains of daylight hang above the horizon, an effect created by the pencil hatching, which becomes heavier toward the vanishing point and near the edges of the sheet. The effect is further underlined by the addition of thinned white gouache (opaque watercolor) in the lighter central area. The contrast has become stronger than originally intended, as the paper has yellowed and the gouache retained its color. The drawing suffered severe damage at some point. The paper was torn at the left along the entire length; even after restoration—during which the paper was lined—this damage is still visible.

SvH

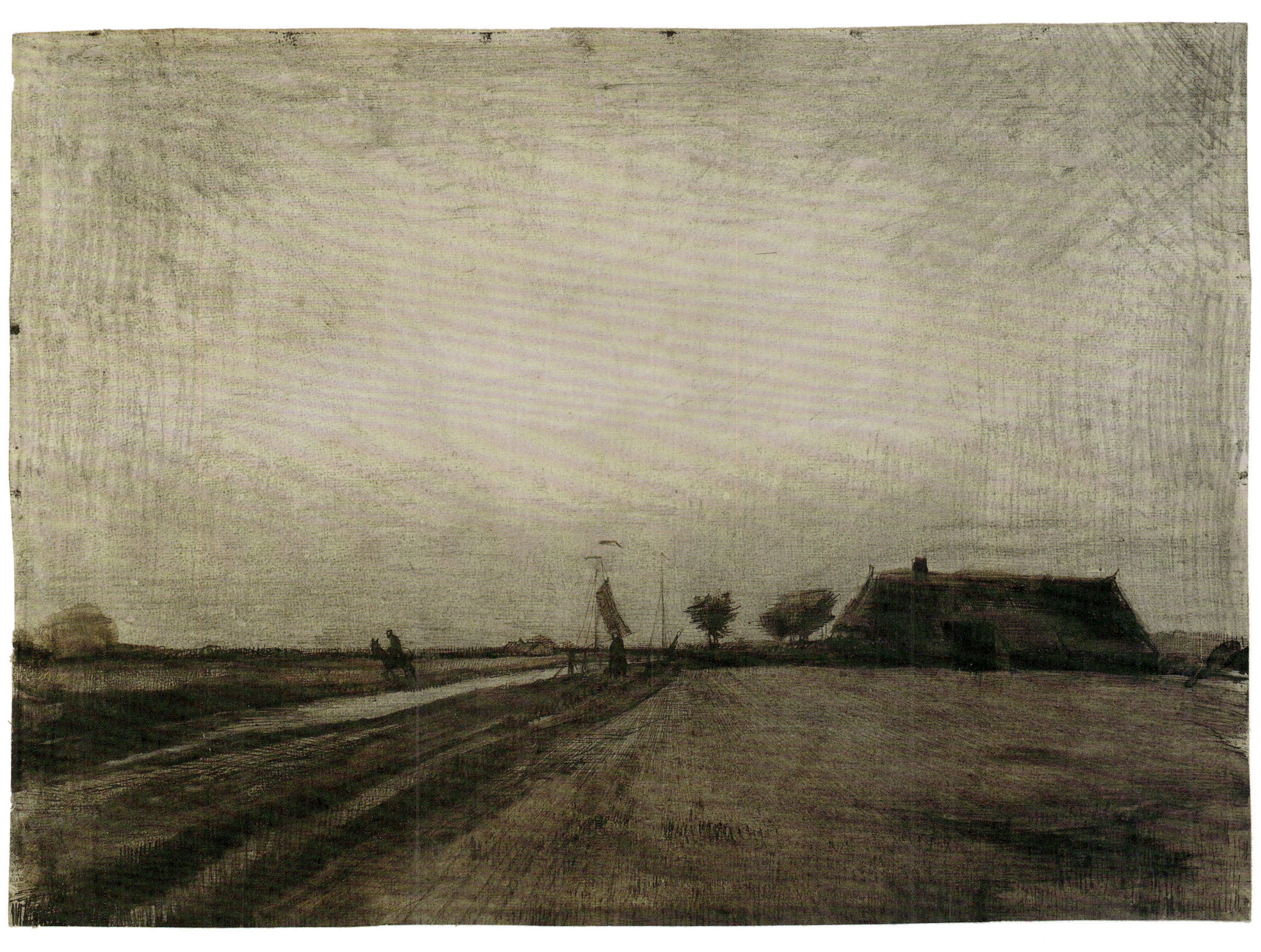

16. *Landscape with a Stack of Peat and Farmhouses*

September–December 1883
Brush and opaque watercolor on wove paper
41.7 x 54.1 cm (16$\frac{3}{8}$ x 21$\frac{1}{4}$ in.)
Van Gogh Museum, Amsterdam (Vincent van Gogh Foundation) (d 386 M/1977)
F1099, JH399

Amsterdam only

Provenance: Probably left by the artist with his mother, Anna Cornelia van Gogh-Carbentus, Nuenen, November 1885; deposited by her with Schrauwen, Breda, 1886; sold by Schrauwen to J. C. Couvreur, Breda, 1902; sold to C. Mouwen and W. van Bakel, Breda, 1902; sold from an exhibition at the Kunstzalen Oldenzeel, Rotterdam (no. 88), to the collector M. Gieseler (d. 1925), Rotterdam and The Hague, 1903; his sale, Mak van Waay, October 27, 1925, no. 28; purchased at that sale (for 1,000 gulden) by W. G. van Beuningen (d. 1948), Utrecht; to C. E. van Beuningen-Fentener van Vlissingen (d. 1976), Wassenaar; to W. van Beuningen, Zutphen, 1976; acquired by the Van Gogh Museum, Amsterdam, 1977.

Selected exhibitions: Rotterdam 1900–1901, no. 52? (or possibly F1104); Rotterdam 1903a, no. 88; Amsterdam 1980–81, no. 105; Otterlo 1990, no. 73; Amsterdam 1996.

Summary of the literature: De la Faille (1928, no. 1099) gave the title as "Paysage au déclin du jour" and no date, but he referred to letter 326 (which mentions a group of drawn studies of the heath, although none specifically). Vanbeselaere (1937, pp. 236, 410) titled the work "Heide," and dated it to September 1883 (p. 236) and to October–December 1883 (p. 410). Tralbaut (1959, pp. 214, 223) referred to the sheet as "Heide," and dated it to September 1883. In De la Faille 1970 (no. 1099), the title was given as "Landscape towards Evening," the date September 1883, again with reference to letter 326. Hulsker (1980/1996, no. 399) followed De la Faille. Van Uitert and Hoyle (1987, pp. 120–21, 400, no. 2.197) gave a title of "Heath at Nightfall" and a date of September 1883, and mistakenly identified the stack of peat as a hut. Van der Wolk (in Otterlo 1990, pp. 121, 125) dated the sheet to 1883. Heenk (1995, pp. 96, 97, 225) pointed out the work's similarities to F1094, from October 1883. Van Heugten (1996, pp. 238–40) contended that it was impossible to give a more precise date within the Drenthe period than September–December 1883, said that what appears to be a building is actually a stack of peat, and recorded that the sheet was sold at Kunstzalen Oldenzeel as "Landschap bij avond" in November 1903. Dijk and Van der Sluis (2001, pp. 130–33, 325, 330) believed they had identified the location depicted, but given the lack of detail in the drawing this is not convincing; they interpreted the shape in the middle ground as a pile of rye straw. Op de Coul (2002, p. 118) corrected Van Heugten 1996: the drawing was at Oldenzeel in January–February 1903.

As in *Landscape in Drenthe* (F1104, cat. 15), in this watercolor Van Gogh aimed to seize the twilight effects that so fascinated him on the Drenthe moors. At the center is a large stack of peat, similar in shape to a house and occasionally mistaken for one. Such stacks appear in several of the drawings from this period, as well as in a letter sketch, about which Van Gogh noted, "These were the people I saw at the peat cuttings, who were sitting eating their lunch behind a stack of peat, with a fire in the foreground" [335] (fig. 95). On his departure to Antwerp, Van Gogh probably left this sheet with his mother. The Van Gogh Museum acquired it in 1977 from a private collector.

SvH

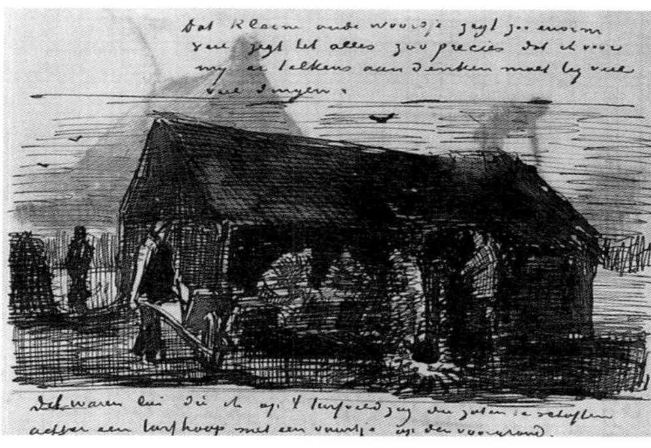

Fig. 95. Sketch in a letter to Theo van Gogh, ca. October 22, 1883 [335]. Van Gogh Museum, Amsterdam (Vincent van Gogh Foundation)

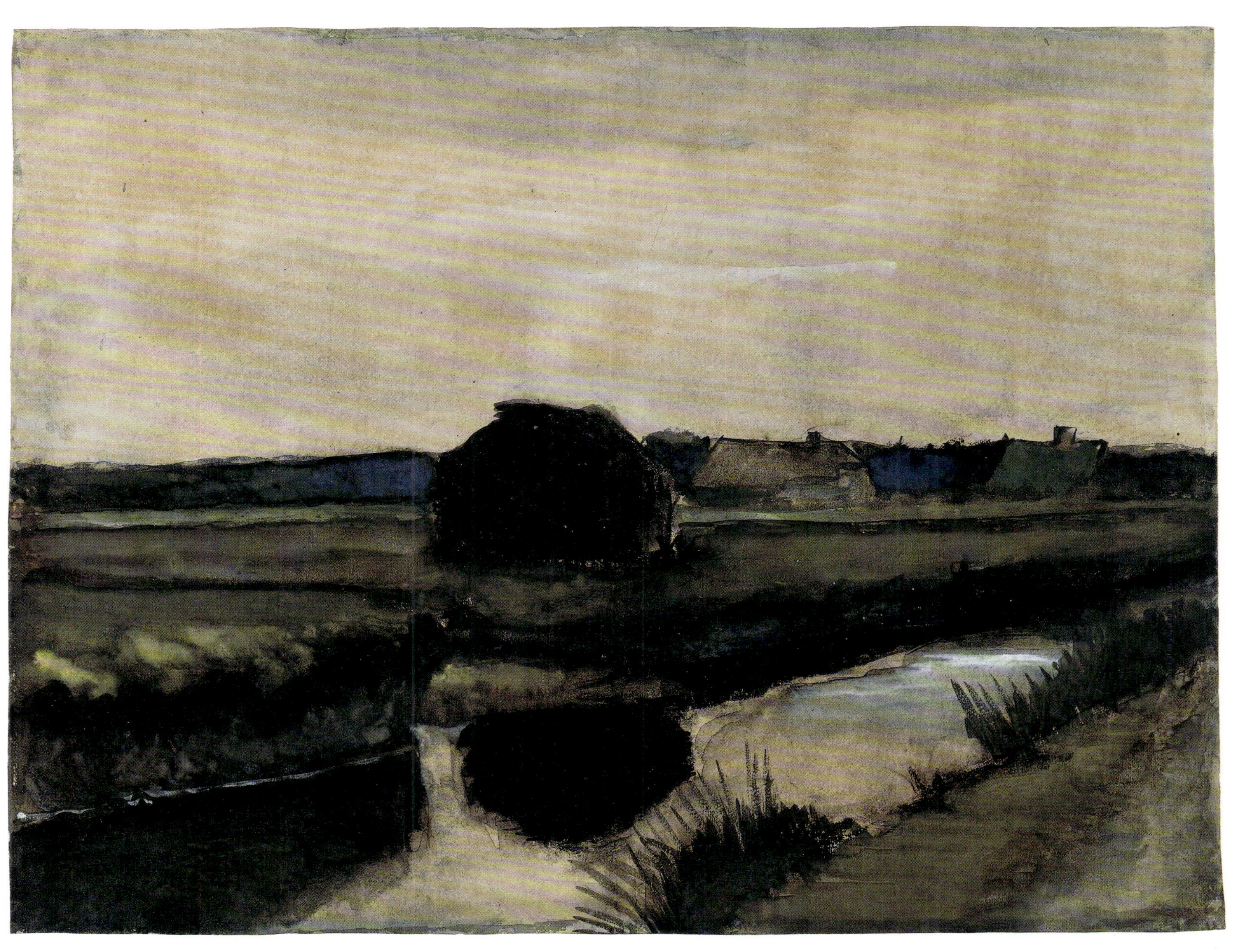

17. *Weaver*

December 1883–August 1884
Transparent and opaque watercolor, pen and ink, graphite on laid paper watermarked HFDC
35.5 x 44.6 cm (14 x 17½ in.)
Signed lower left: *Vincent*
Van Gogh Museum, Amsterdam (Vincent van Gogh Foundation) (d 423 V/1962)
F1115, JH502

Provenance: Theo van Gogh (d. 1891); by inheritance to his son, Vincent Willem van Gogh (1890–1978), as part of his collection, administered by his widow, Johanna van Gogh-Bonger (d. 1925), 1891; placed on loan at the Stedelijk Museum, Amsterdam, 1931–73; ownership transferred to the Vincent van Gogh Foundation, 1962; placed on permanent loan at the Van Gogh Museum, Amsterdam, 1973.

Selected exhibitions: Amsterdam 1905, no. 323; Amsterdam 1914–15, no. 54; Rotterdam 1923; Tokyo–Kyōto–Nagoya 1976–77, no. 17; Paris 1977, unnumbered; Otterlo 1990, no. 77; Amsterdam 1997.

Summary of the literature: De la Faille (1928, no. 1115) gave the title as "Le tisserand"—subsequently the title was occasionally more descriptive but otherwise deviated little—and dated the sheet to January–April 1884. Vanbeselaere (1937, pp. 257, 318, 411) maintained a date of June 1884. In De la Faille 1970 (no. 1115) the date was given as June 1884. Hulsker (1980, no. 502) believed the drawing was executed in July 1884 on the evidence of letter 372, in which Van Gogh described a very similar painting. Van Uitert and Hoyle (1987, pp. 128, 129, 405, no. 2.225) followed De la Faille 1970. Pey (in Otterlo 1990, pp. 37, 128) discussed the technique. Heenk (1995 pp. 103, 104) stated that it is almost impossible to date these watercolors of weavers with any precision. Van Heugten (1997, pp. 66, 67, 73) assumed a wider time span, i.e., between the time Van Gogh first began making images of weavers and the time he stopped, December 1883–August 1884.

There were 440 weavers working in Nuenen in Van Gogh's time, providing him with ample models. He was convinced that images of weavers would prove popular on the market and executed sixteen full-fledged ink and watercolor drawings, as well as ten paintings of the subject. When he first encountered weavers in 1879 (see F1118, cat. 18), Van Gogh saw in the figures a certain romantic dreaminess. In Nuenen, however, he discovered that they were actually hardworking, poor, and rather exploited craftsmen. Van Gogh found there was "often something agitated and restless" about them [392], and the grim reality of their lives is reflected in many of his images, such as the one shown here.

SvH

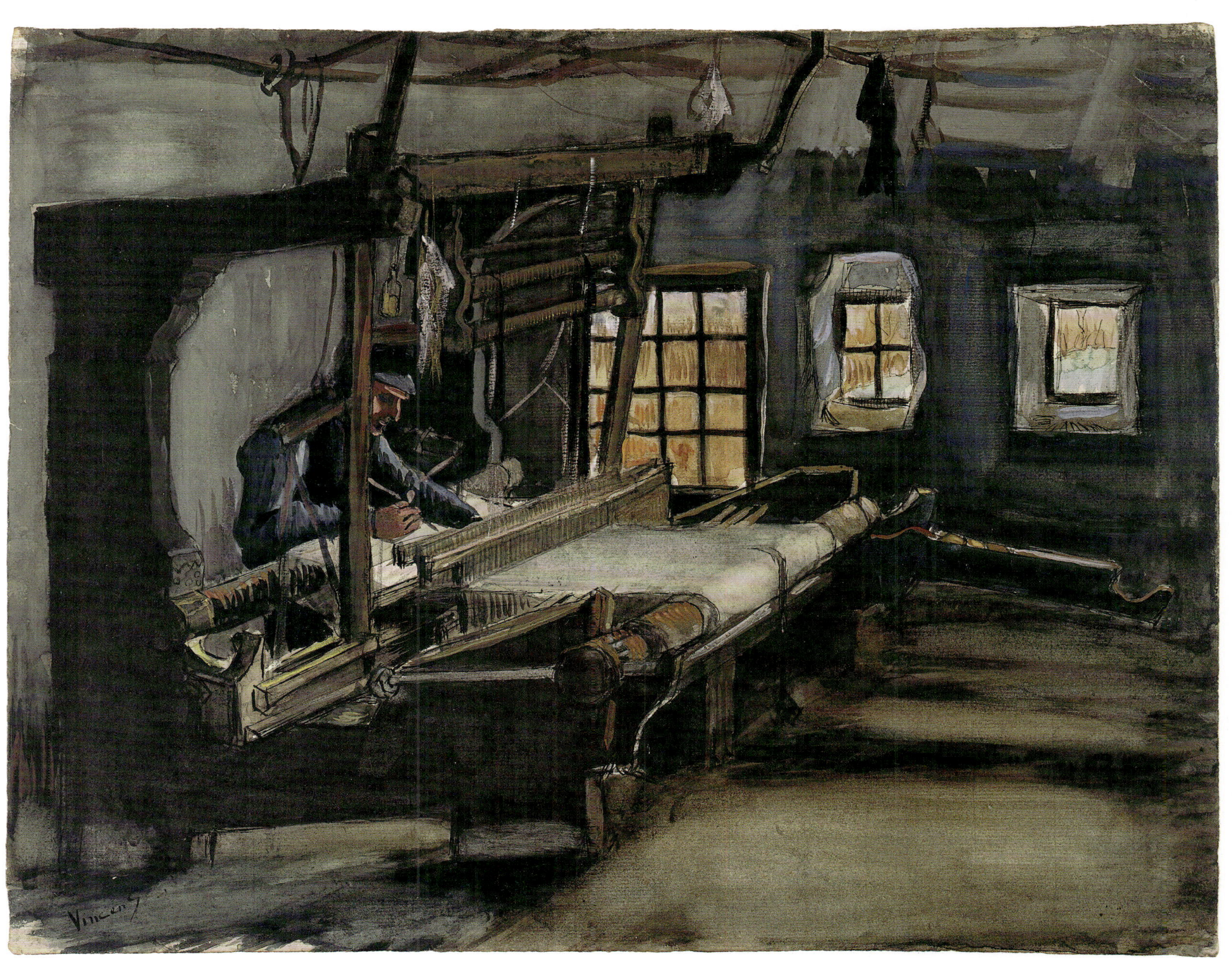
Vincent

18. *Weaver, with a Baby in a Highchair*

Late January–early February 1884
Pen and ink, heightened with opaque watercolor, graphite on wove paper
31.5 x 39.9 cm (12⅜ x 15¾ in.)
Signed lower left: *Vince[nt]*
Van Gogh Museum, Amsterdam (Vincent van Gogh Foundation) (d 82 V/1962)
F1118, JH452
Letter 357

Provenance: Theo van Gogh (d. 1891); by inheritance to his son, Vincent Willem van Gogh (1891–1978), as part of his collection, administered by his widow, Johanna van Gogh-Bonger (d. 1925), 1891; ownership transferred to the Vincent van Gogh Foundation, 1962; placed on permanent loan at the Van Gogh Museum, Amsterdam, 1973.

Selected exhibitions: Leiden 1893; Groningen 1897; Amsterdam 1905, no. 303; Amsterdam 1914–15, no. 64; Amsterdam 1980–81, no. 142; 's Hertogenbosch 1987–88, no. 15; Amsterdam 1991, no. 35; Amsterdam 1997.

Summary of the literature: De la Faille (1928, no. 1118) gave the title as "Intérieur de tisserand"—subsequent titles summarized the various objects seen in the interior, either with or without the baby in the highchair—and dated the drawing to February 1884. Vanbeselaere (1937, pp. 256, 316, 411) gave a date of January 1884. Leurs and Tralbaut (1957, pp. 52, 53) interpreted the scene (on the basis of the similar painting, F24) as illustrating work in the home, work in the field (visible through the window), and faith (the old church tower, also discernible through the window). In De la Faille (1970, no. 1118) the sheet was dated to January–February and letter 355, which mentions F24, was referred to; watercolor F1119, identical in composition, was also mentioned. Hulsker (1980, no. 452) dated the sheet to February–March 1884, called attention to letters 355 and 357, and concluded from the latter that it was not until February that Van Gogh began making pen drawings of weavers. Zemel (1985, pp. 124, 125, 135) saw the continuity of tradition reflected in the scene, suggesting the child would also one day become a weaver. Van Uitert and Hoyle (1987, p. 402, no. 2.210) dated the work to January–February 1884. Kōdera (1990, pp. 29–30) saw the influence of Jozef Israëls in Van Gogh's decision to combine an interior with a view of a church through the window, a motif he had encountered in Israëls's work in 1873. Blotkamp (in Glasgow–Amsterdam 1990–91, no. 35 [Amsterdam only]) accepted Zemel's interpretation and noted that Van Gogh was probably inspired by Anthon van Rappard, who had made studies of the weavers of Drenthe in 1883. Heenk 1995, pp. 103, 105. Hulsker (1996, no. 452) now dated the sheet to ca. January 24, 1884, on the evidence of letter 355. Van Heugten (1997, pp. 56–59) situated the work at the end of January to early February on the basis of the same letter and suggested that Van Gogh may have been inspired by George Eliot's *Silas Marner*. De Brouwer (2000, pp. 47, 96) saw the drawing as an exercise in preparation for the painting F24 and identified a possible location for the house of the weaver depicted.

Van Gogh wanted to make images of weavers from the time of his long walking tour in 1879 through Belgium and northern France. There he had passed through villages of weavers and was deeply impressed by what he saw as the craftsmen's almost meditative aura. His interest was rekindled in 1882, when he learned that there were many weavers in Nuenen, the Van Gogh family's new home. Weavers thus appear repeatedly in his work from the time he himself settled in Nuenen in December 1883 until August 1884. Van Gogh took his inspiration for *Weaver, with a Baby in a Highchair* from George Eliot's novel *Silas Marner*, in which a lonely weaver finds happiness when a foundling enters his life.

This drawing is also a study of light effects: the light coming through the window is suggested by the white highlights on various elements in the composition. The sheet has been damaged and is now missing a small and a large piece of the paper at the lower right, as well as most of the last two letters of the signature. Van Gogh also treated the motif in a watercolor, F1119.

SvH

Letter to Theo van Gogh, between February 18 and 23, 1884 [357], possibly among the works referred to: I can send you 5 such drawings of weavers, which I drew after my painted studies, and which are a little different—and I think more vigorous of technique, than the pen drawings of mine you have seen up to now. I am working at them early and late, for except the painted studies, and the pen-and-ink drawings, I have also some new watercolors of them.

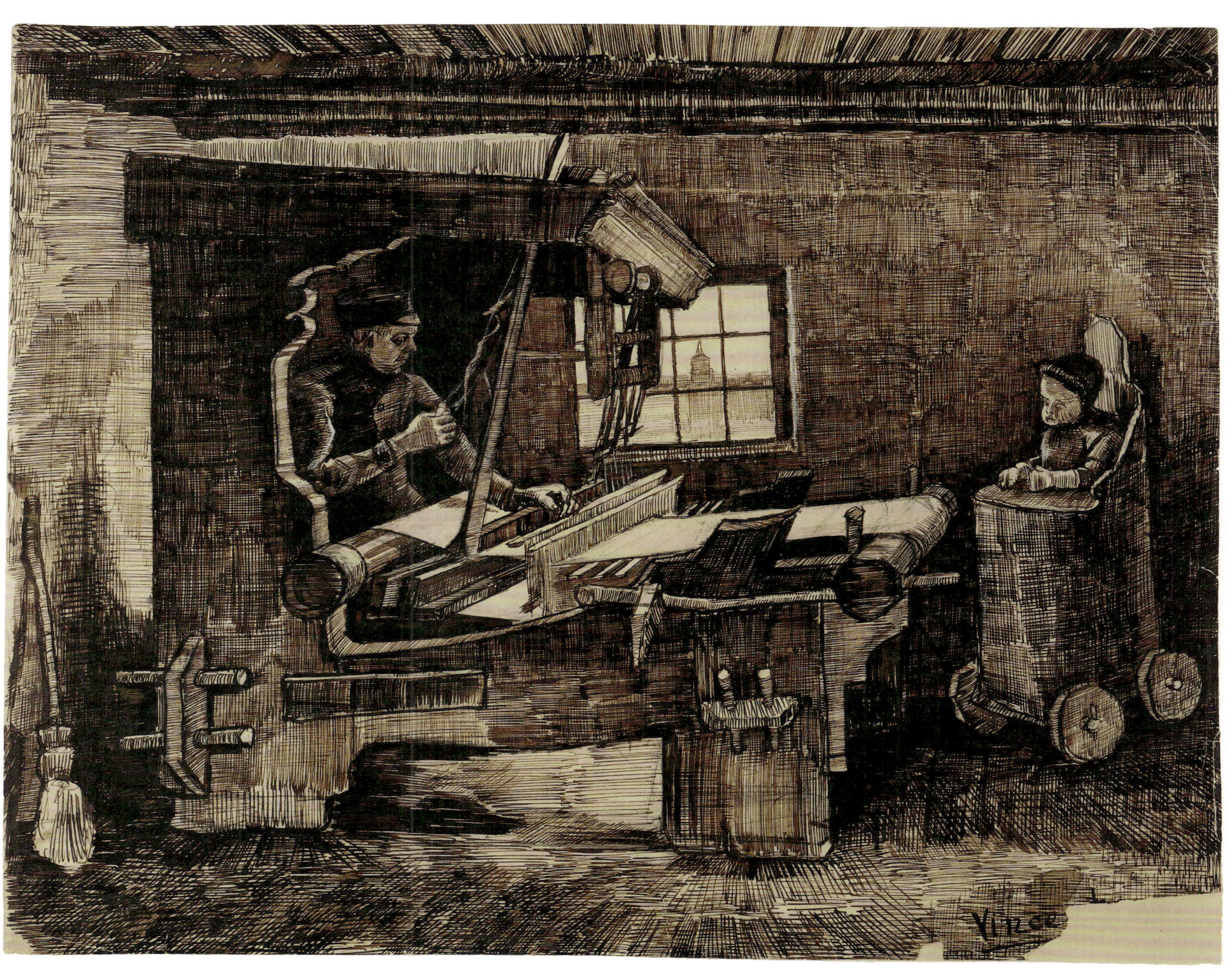

19. *Pollard Birches*

First half of March 1884
Pen and ink, graphite, heightened with opaque watercolor, on wove paper
39.5 x 54.2 cm (15½ x 21⅜ in.)
Signed lower left: *Vincent*
Horizontal pencil line, possibly part of a grid
Van Gogh Museum, Amsterdam (Vincent van Gogh Foundation) (d 364 V/1968)
F1240, JH469
Letter R44

Provenance: Theo van Gogh (d. 1891); by inheritance to his son, Vincent Willem van Gogh (1890–1978), as part of his collection, administered by his widow, Johanna van Gogh-Bonger (d. 1925), 1891; acquired at an unknown date by Van Gogh's sister Anna van Houten-van Gogh (d. 1930), Dieren; her friend the painter Hendrik Joan Calkoen, Velsen, 1930–63; acquired by the Theo van Gogh Foundation, 1963; placed on loan at the Stedelijk Museum, Amsterdam, 1963–73; ownership transferred to the Vincent van Gogh Foundation, 1968; placed on permanent loan at the Van Gogh Museum, Amsterdam, 1973.

Selected exhibitions: Leiden 1893; Amsterdam 1980–81, no. 139; 's Hertogenbosch 1987–88, no. 73; Otterlo 1990, no. 94; Amsterdam 1997; Tokyo 2000, no. 12.

Summary of the literature: De la Faille (1928, no. 1240) referred to the work as "L'allée des saules" but gave no date. Vanbeselaere (1937, pp. 263, 353, 412) provided the correct title, "Knotberken," which has remained virtually unchanged, and he dated it to February–March 1885. De la Faille 1970 (no. 1240) again described the trees as willows and dated the sheet to the spring of 1884. Hulsker (1980, no. 469) dated it March–April 1884. Van Uitert and Hoyle (1987, p. 404, no. 2.219) dated it to March 1884. Van Heugten (1997, pp. 87, 88) specified the date to the first half of March 1884.

Trees play an important role in Van Gogh's landscapes, and are often even their principal subject. He was especially fond of pollard oaks, willows, and birches. For him, a pollard birch was a living being [152], and he once described a row of them as a "procession of almshouse men" [242]. One can easily detect such anthropomorphic sentiments in the expressive, almost melancholy trees in this drawing. The shepherd with his flock at the right and the woman with a rake over her shoulder at the left give the scene an anecdotal character. Van Gogh often yearned for Brabant when he was in Saint-Rémy, and in a letter to his mother of July 1889 he mentioned the Nuenen pollard birches and how pretty he had found them [598].

SvH

Letter to Anthon van Rappard, ca. March 13, 1884 [R44]: Well, I was pleased to hear that you liked my winter garden a little. Indeed, this garden sets me dreaming, and since then I have made another one of the same subject, also with a little black spook in it, which this time too appears in it not as an example, worthy of imitation, of the correct drawing of the structure of the human body, but as a spot. I am sending you these and a few others too—sepia sketch / in the broeck—pen-and-ink drawings / Pollard Willows—Poplar Avenue—Behind the Hedges—the Kingfisher and Winter Garden. I send them rolled up, but please put them into the portfolio along with the others, especially when you return them, in order to keep them as flat as possible. I added a piece of gray paper; they will show up better if you place them against that.

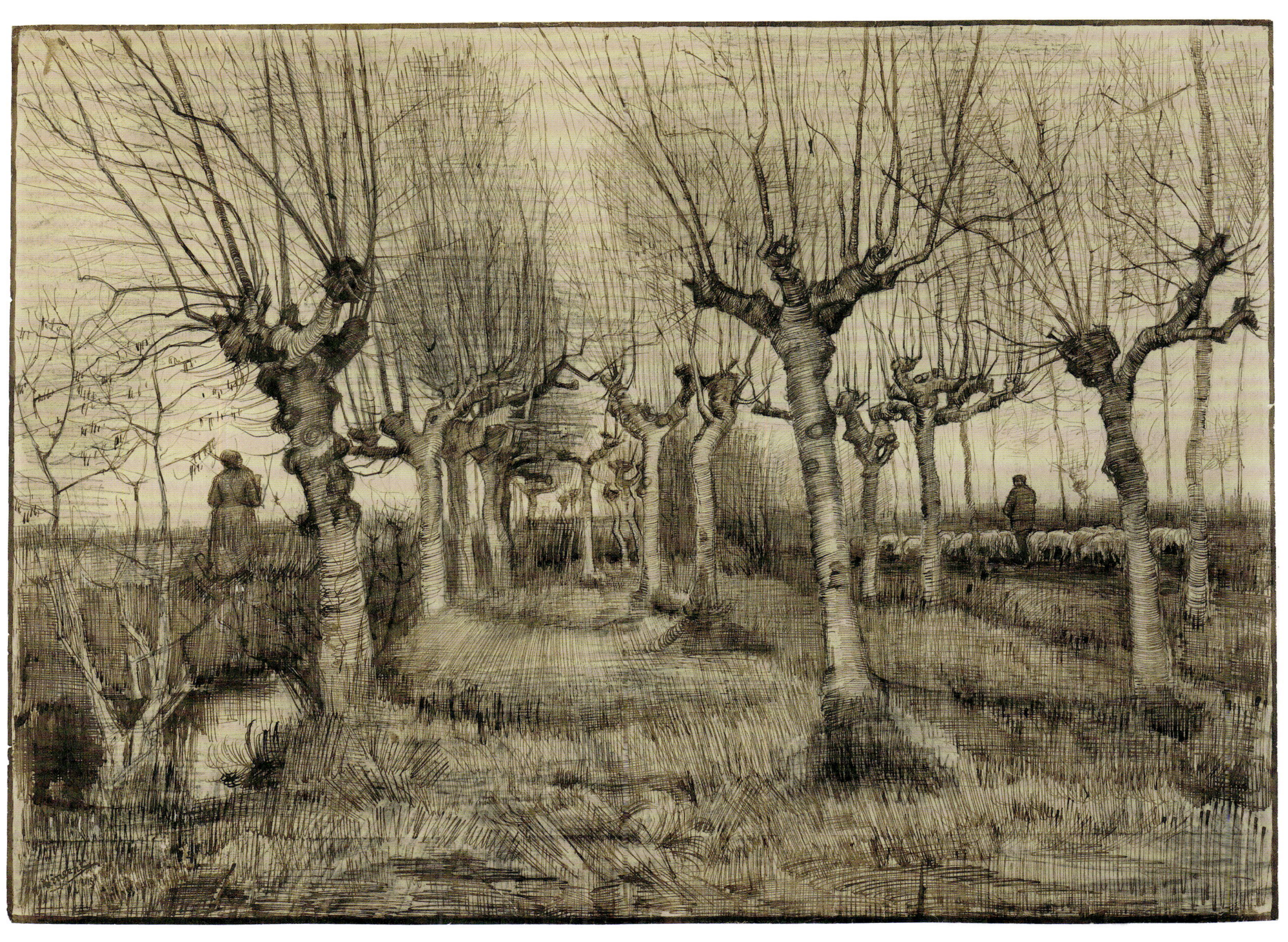

20. *Behind the Hedges*

March 1884
Pen and ink, graphite on wove paper
40 x 53 cm (15¾ x 20⅞ in.)
Signed lower left: *Vincent*
Rijksmuseum, Amsterdam (SK-A-2225)
F1129, JH461
Letters R44, 364

Provenance: Sent by the artist to Theo van Gogh (d. 1891), May 1884; by inheritance to his son, Vincent Willem van Gogh, as part of his collection, administered by his widow, Johanna van Gogh-Bonger, 1891; given by her to the Rijksmuseum, Amsterdam, 1906.

Selected exhibitions: Leiden 1893; Groningen 1897; Amsterdam 1905, no. 286; 's Hertogenbosch 1987–88, no. 70; Otterlo 1990, no. 92; Vienna 1996, no. 53.

Summary of the literature: *Lettres* 1911, pl. xv; Bremmer 1918, vol. 2, no. 16. De la Faille (1928, no. 1129) referred to the sheet as "Derrière le jardin" and dated it to March 1884. Vanbeselaere (1937, pp. 259, 322, 411) followed this dating but changed the title to "Achter de heggen" and pointed out that the trees, which he identified as pollard oaks and a pollard birch, also figure in F44. De la Faille 1970 (no. 1129) changed the title to "Road with Pollard Willows and a Man with a Wheelbarrow." Hulsker (1980, no. 461) dated the work to the middle of March. Van der Wolk (in Otterlo 1990, pp. 129, 149) dated the sheet to early 1884. Heijbroek (1991, p. 183) described how the work entered the Rijksmuseum. Heenk 1995, p. 114.

Behind the Hedges—the title Van Gogh himself gave to the sheet in a letter to Van Rappard [R44]—depicts an area along the road behind the vicarage garden in Nuenen. Here, once again, a group of pollard trees plays an important role (see F1240, cat. 19), in this case three oaks and a birch. The man with a wheelbarrow and the woman walking in the background give the drawing an anecdotal character. The sun sets behind the trees, adding to the overall melancholy mood. In November 1885, Van Gogh made a painting of the same trees (F44, fig. 96); there, however, he stood with his back to the hedges, with a view of the fields behind the trees.

SvH

Letter to Anthon van Rappard, ca. March 13, 1884 [R44]: I am sending you these [two drawings of the garden] and a few others too—sepia sketch / in the broeck—pen-and-ink drawings / Pollard Willows—Poplar Avenue—Behind the Hedges—the Kingfisher and Winter Garden.

Letter to Theo van Gogh, ca. March 20, 1884 [364]: For this month I have some pen-and-ink drawings for you, in the first place those that are at Rappard's for the moment, about which I had a letter from him, telling me that he liked them all, and especially admired the sentiment in Behind the Hedges and The Kingfisher.

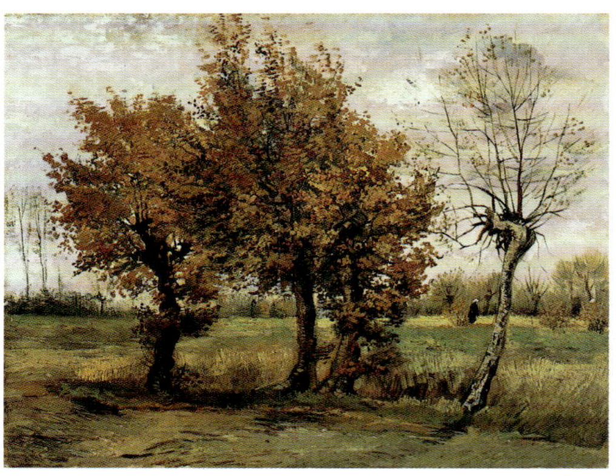

Fig. 96. *Autumn Landscape* (F44), November 1885. Oil on canvas, 69 x 87.8 cm (27⅛ x 34⅝ in.). Kröller-Müller Museum, Otterlo

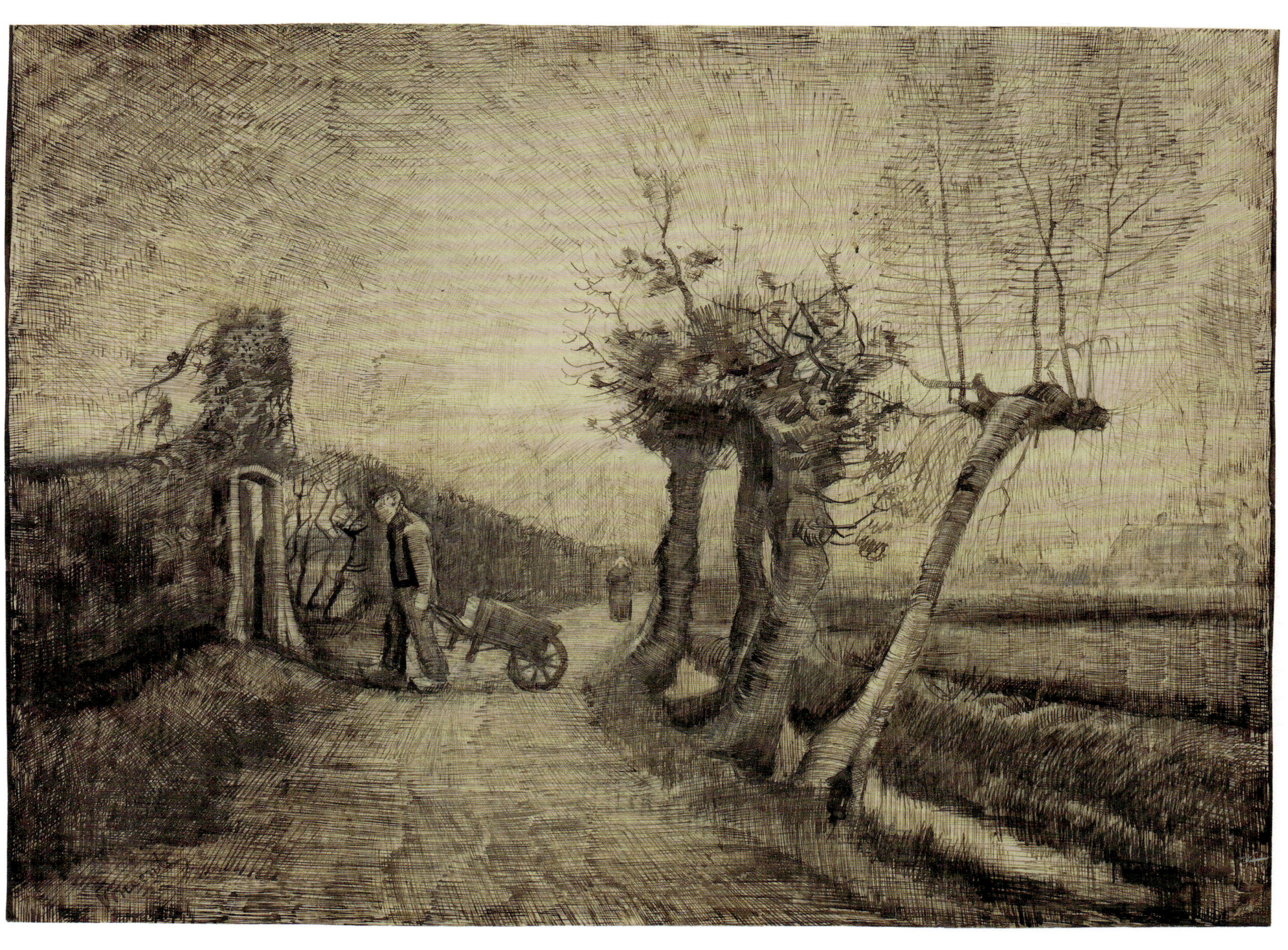

21. *Winter Garden*

March 1884
Pen and ink, graphite on wove paper
40.3 x 54.6 cm (15⅞ x 21½ in.)
Signed lower left: *Vincent*
Van Gogh Museum, Amsterdam (Vincent van Gogh Foundation) (d 365 V/1962)
F1128, JH466
Letters R44, 364, 363a, 366, 369

Provenance: Theo van Gogh (d. 1891); by inheritance to his son, Vincent Willem van Gogh (1890–1978), as part of his collection, administered by his widow, Johanna van Gogh-Bonger (d. 1925), 1891; placed on loan at the Stedelijk Museum, Amsterdam, 1931–73; ownership transferred to the Vincent van Gogh Foundation, 1962; placed on permanent loan at the Van Gogh Museum, Amsterdam, 1973.

Selected exhibitions: Groningen 1897; Amsterdam 1905, no. 336; Berlin 1906, no. 57; Leiden 1910; Antwerp 1914, no. 12; Berlin 1914, no. 11; Amsterdam 1914–15, no. 107; New York 1920, no. 3; The Hague 1925; Paris 1937, no. 60; London–Birmingham–Glasgow 1947–48, no. 114; New York–Chicago 1949–50, no. 32; Amsterdam 1980–81, no. 140; 's Hertogenbosch 1987–88, no. 71; Otterlo 1990, no. 89; Amsterdam 1997.

Summary of the literature: Van Meurs 1910, no. 5; Vogelsang 1905, facing p. 66; *Lettres* 1911, pl. XVI; Havelaar 1915, fig. 1; Bremmer 1918, pp. 17–19, no. 12. De la Faille (1928, no. 1128) gave the title, "Jardin de presbytère en hiver," and date (March 1884), which were subsequently followed by most authors. Meier-Graefe 1928a, vol. 2, no. 12. Vanbeselaere (1937, pp. 259, 322, 411) saw the sheet as a second version, made after F1130 (cat. 22). Leurs and Tralbaut (1957, p. 46) remarked on the liberties the artist took in his rendering of the old tower. De Gruyter 1961, p. 97. Chetham (1976, p. 31) pointed to the influence of prints from illustrated magazines. Hulsker 1980/1996, no. 466. Blotkamp (in The Hague 1978, p. 99) saw a symbolic meaning in the garden motif and proposed that the sheet contains references to paradise or heaven. Van Uitert and Hoyle 1987, p. 403, no. 2.218; Feilchenfeldt and Veenenbos 1988, p. 128. Van Heugten (1997, pp. 82–86) noted that here, as well as in F1240 and F1135, some of the pencil lines resulted from a ridge in Van Gogh's drawing board, which he had purchased on March 8, indicating that the works must have been executed after that date. Van Heugten also suggested that Van Gogh very likely used his perspective frame in making the series of landscapes to which this sheet belongs, although there are no traces of squaring. De Brouwer 2000, pp. 35, 52, 96.

Van Gogh was especially fond of the garden behind his father's vicarage. He depicted it in a number of drawings, and when he decided to create a series of large-scale landscapes in pen and ink in March 1884 he devoted two of the six sheets to the motif (see also F1130, cat. 22). Although the view is the same in both, they differ in format—one is vertical, the other horizontal—and in their attention to detail. The drawing in the Van Gogh Museum is the more accomplished of the two. Van Gogh was clearly interested in the vegetation, such as the rosebush and the young trees, at the right, packed in straw to protect them from the cold. He also added "a little black spook" [R44] in the form of a woman carrying a pitcher, seen from behind.

The suite of landscapes probably consisted of seven sheets. Van Gogh's correspondence indicates that there was a third image of the garden in winter, but it has since been lost (see Van Heugten 1997, no. 89).

SvH

Letter to Anthon van Rappard, ca. March 13, 1884 [R44]: Well, I was pleased to hear that you liked my winter garden a little. Indeed, this garden sets me dreaming, and since then I have made another one of the same subject, also with a little black spook in it, which this time too appears in it not as an example, worthy of imitation, of the correct drawing of the structure of the human body, but as a spot. I am sending you these and a few others too—sepia sketch / in the broeck—pen-and-ink drawings / Pollard Willows—Poplar Avenue—Behind the Hedges—the Kingfisher and Winter Garden. I send them rolled up, but please put them into the portfolio along with the others, especially when you return them, in order to keep them as flat as possible. I added a piece of gray paper; they will show up better if you place them against that.

Letter to Theo van Gogh, ca. March 20, 1884 [364]: For this month I have some pen-and-ink drawings for you, in the first place those that are at Rappard's for the moment, about which I had a letter from him, telling me that he liked them **all, and especially** ***admired the sentiment in Behind the Hedges and The Kingfisher, and the first Winter Garden which he also liked very much.***

Letter to Theo van Gogh, ca. March 24, 1884 [363a]: I did not send you the sixth pen drawing because . . . that drawing was at Rappard's, and I should have had it back, but up to now he has kept it, along with two other pen drawings, Winter Garden.

Letter to Theo van Gogh, early April 1884 [366]: What struck me in reality was the remarkably quaint, half old-fashioned, half rustic character of that garden. And I made three pen-and-ink drawings of that same nook, besides several studies which I destroyed, just because I wanted to render that character in some intimate details, which are not expressed easily or without effort or by chance.

Letter to Theo van Gogh, ca. May 28, 1884 [369]: As [Van Rappard] has brought the pen-and-ink drawings with him, I can send them to you now.

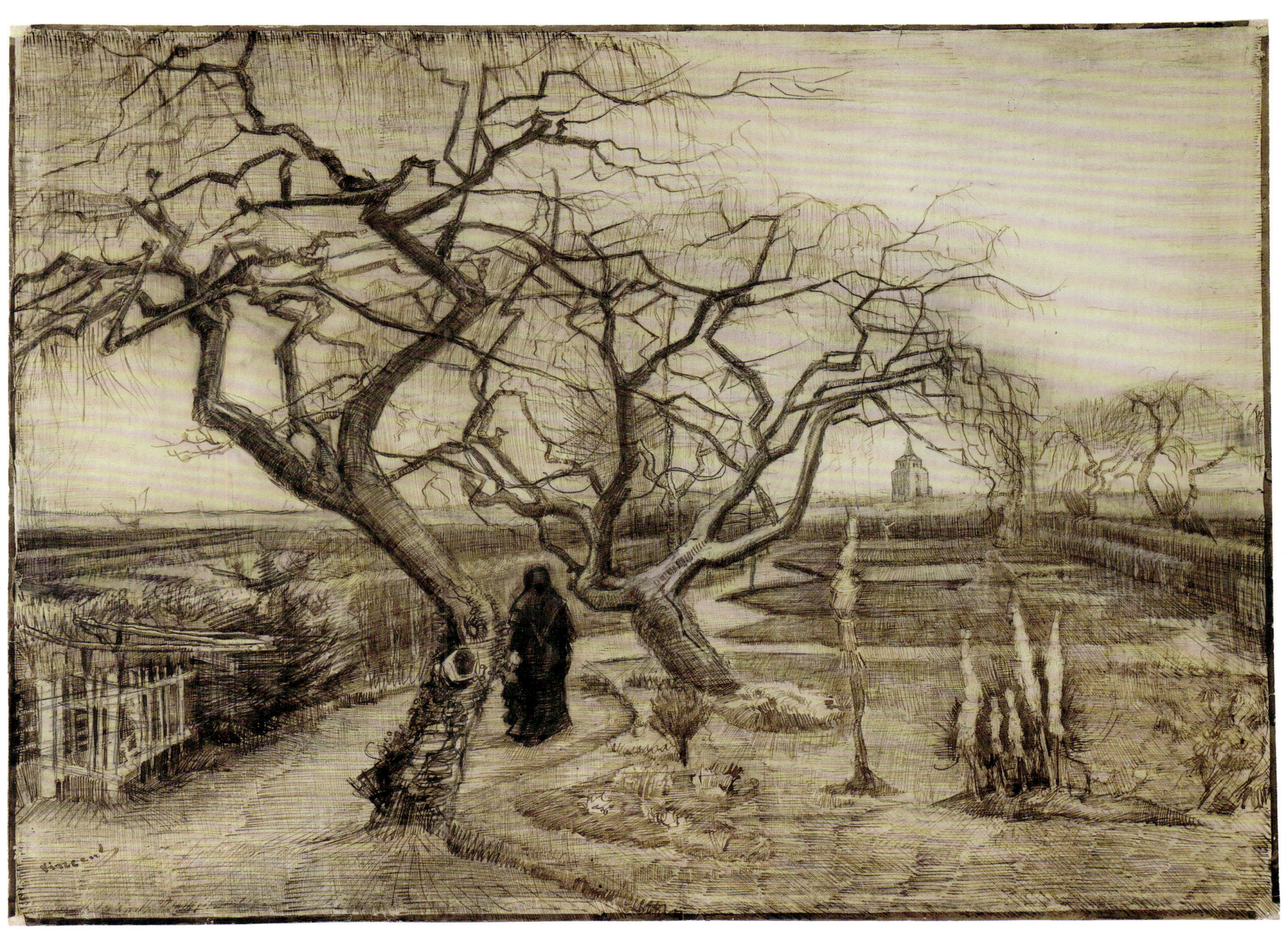

22. *Winter Garden*

March 1884
Pen and ink, graphite on wove paper
51.5 x 38 cm (20¼ x 15 in.)
Signed lower left: *Vincent*
Szépművészeti Múzeum, Budapest (1935-2791)
F1130, JH465
Letters R44, 364, 363a, 366, 369

Provenance: Probably sent by the artist to Theo van Gogh (d. 1891), May 1884; his collection inherited by his son, Vincent Willem van Gogh, administered by his widow, Johanna van Gogh-Bonger, 1891; possibly sold by her to Ambroise Vollard, March 1897; sold by Vollard to Pál Majovszky (d. 1935), Budapest, between May 31 and July 21, 1911 (for 300 francs); his bequest to the Szépművészeti Múzeum, Budapest, 1935.

Selected exhibitions: Paris 1896–97 (possibly no. 14 on Johanna's list of loans); Otterlo 1990, no. 90.

Summary of the literature: The first reproduction was published in *Lettres* 1911, pl. XXXII. De la Faille (1928, no. 1130) gave the title "Jardin de presbytère en hiver" and dated the work to March 1884; subsequent literature on this sheet and F1128 (cat. 21) deviates little from this interpretation. Vanbeselaere 1937, pp. 259, 322, 411; Pataky 1959, p. 26; Wadley 1969, p. 30; Hulsker 1980/1996, no. 465; Washington–Chicago–Los Angeles 1985, no. 90; Heenk 1995, p. 114; De Brouwer 2000, pp. 48, 49, 96; Findhammer 2002, p. 21.

In this vertical version of the vicarage garden in winter, Van Gogh left out some of the vegetation that he included in F1128 (cat. 21), such as the wrapped trees and the rosebushes. The addition of a chicken prevents the scene from seeming too barren. The pen strokes create a striking sense of perspective, stretching toward the old tower in the background. Van Gogh clearly wanted to draw attention to this landmark, leaving its view unobscured by details of the garden. The artist was very fond of this medieval structure, including it in numbers of his drawings and paintings. Here it is still almost complete, but during the course of Van Gogh's stay in Nuenen it would be slowly dismantled.

SvH

For Van Gogh's letters about this drawing to Anthon van Rappard, ca. March 13, 1884 [R44], and to Theo van Gogh, ca. March 20, 1884 [364], ca. March 24, 1884 [363a], early April 1884 [366], and ca. May 28, 1884 [369], see cat. 21 (F1128).

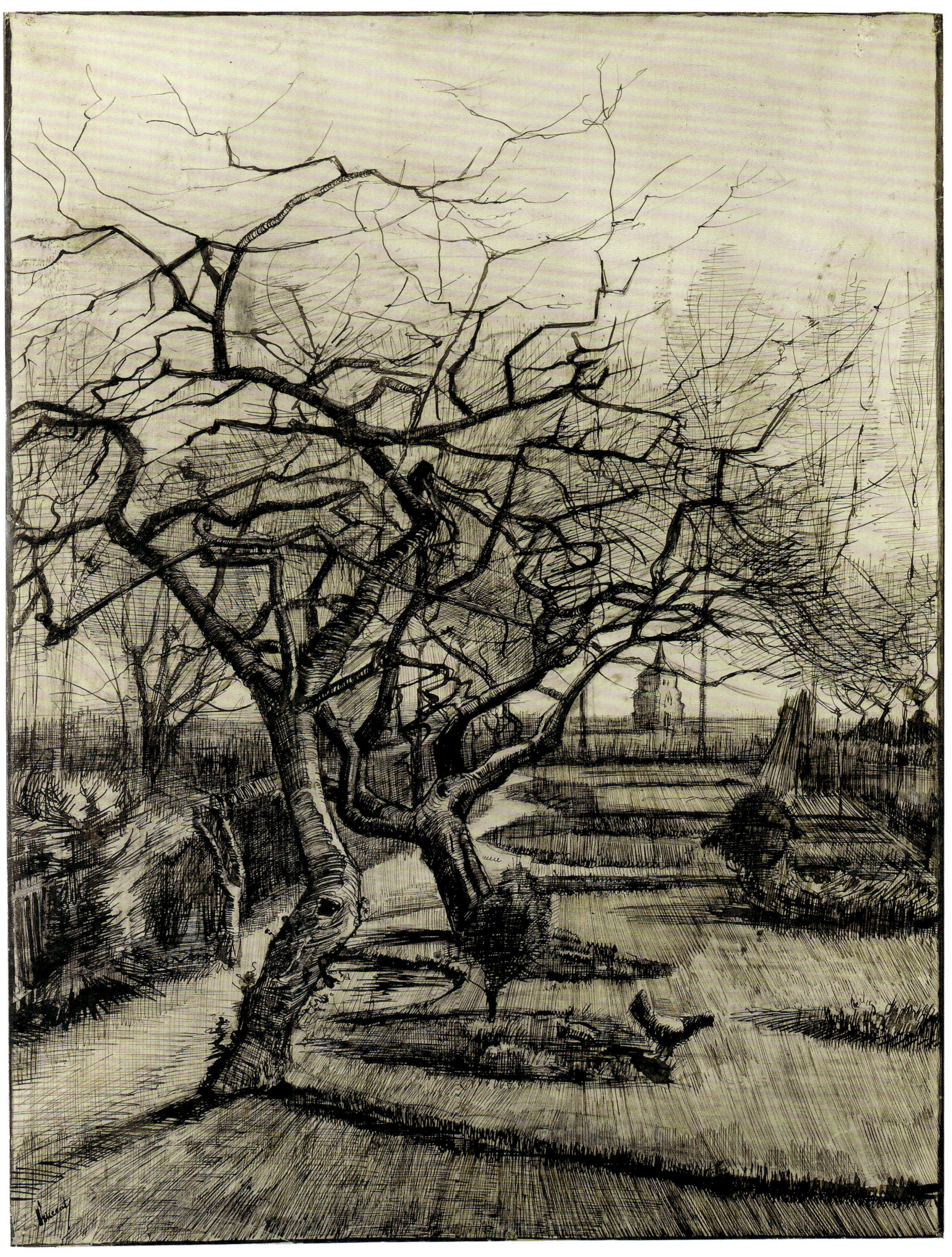
Vincent

23. *The Kingfisher*

March 1884
Pen, brush, and ink, graphite, heightened with opaque white paint, on wove paper
40.2 x 54.2 cm (15⅞ x 21⅜ in.)
Signed lower left: *Vincent*
Van Gogh Museum, Amsterdam (Vincent van Gogh Foundation) (d 775 M/1982)
F1135, JH468
Letters R44, 364

Provenance: Theo van Gogh (d. 1891); by inheritance to his son, Vincent Willem van Gogh, as part of his collection, administered by his widow, Johanna van Gogh-Bonger, 1891; purchased from her by J. J. Polak (d. 1920), Rotterdam, at the Rotterdamsche Kunstkring, 1901 (for ca. 150 gulden); to his son, H. Polak (d. 1969), Wassenaar, 1920; to his widow, M. M. M. Polak-Leyden (d. 1980), Wassenaar, 1969; lent by her to the Van Gogh Museum, Amsterdam, 1975–80; to her son, M. E. Polak, Hillegom, 1980; purchased from him by the Van Gogh Museum, with the support of the Vincent van Gogh Foundation, the Theo van Gogh Foundation, and the Ministry of Culture, 1982.

Selected exhibitions: The Hague 1892; Leiden 1893; Paris 1896–97; Rotterdam 1900–1901, no. 28; Amsterdam 1905, no. 344 bis; London–Birmingham–Glasgow 1947–48, no. 118; Osaka 1986, no. 7; 's Hertogenbosch 1987–88, no. 72; Rome 1988, no. 67; Otterlo 1990, no. 91; Amsterdam 1997.

Summary of the literature: Van Meurs 1910, no. 2; *Lettres* 1911, pl. x. De la Faille (1928, no. 1135) gave the title "Une mare à Nuenen" and dated the sheet to 1884, from which few subsequent authors have deviated. Vanbeselaere (1937, pp. 259, 322, 411) gave the title as "IJsvogel." Leurs and Tralbaut 1957, pp. 48–51. De Gruyter (1961, p. 98) described the technique as "time-consuming" and noted that Van Gogh would rarely use it again. De la Faille 1970 (no. 1135) gave the date as March–April 1884 and the title as "The Pond in the Vicarage Garden, with a Kingfisher"; the pond's location has been adopted by most authors. Hulsker 1980/1996, no. 468; Van Uitert and Hoyle 1987, p. 403, no. 2.217. Van der Wolk (in Otterlo 1990, pp. 129, 148) dated the sheet to early 1884. In De la Faille 1992 (no. 1135), the date assigned was April 1884. Heenk 1995, p. 114. Van Heugten (1997, pp. 90–94) suggested the scene was inspired by Jules Breton's poem "Automne" and argued that the pond was not actually in the vicarage garden but at another, still unknown location. Stolwijk and Veenenbos (2002, pp. 144, 193) provided the provenance.

Van Gogh drew his inspiration for this somber landscape from Jules Breton's poem "Automne" (Autumn). The poem and the drawing are similarly melancholic in tone, and Van Gogh followed Breton's description of the tall trees, the pool, and the diving kingfisher almost to the letter. The body of water has often been identified as the pond at the bottom of the vicarage garden, but as the two versions of *Winter Garden* (F1128, cat. 21; F1130, cat. 22) clearly show, the vegetation there was far less wild. Van Gogh undoubtedly directly observed many of the elements in the landscape, but the drawing itself was most likely composed and executed in the studio on the basis of sketches. The church in the background resembles Saint-Clement's in Nuenen, but is so different in detail that it, too, must have been modeled on a sketch.

SvH

Letter to Anthon van Rappard, ca. March 13, 1884 [R44]: Well, I was pleased to hear that you liked my winter garden a little. Indeed, this garden sets me dreaming, and since then I have made another one of the same subject, also with a little black spook in it, which this time too appears in it not as an example, worthy of imitation, of the correct drawing of the structure of the human body, but as a spot. I am sending you these and a few others too—sepia sketch / in the broeck—pen-and-ink drawings / Pollard Willows—Poplar Avenue—Behind the Hedges—the Kingfisher and Winter Garden. I send them rolled up, but please put them into the portfolio along with the others, especially when you return them, in order to keep them as flat as possible. I added a piece of gray paper; they will show up better if you place them against that.

Letter to Theo van Gogh, ca. March 20, 1884 [364]: For this month I have some pen-and-ink drawings for you, in the first place those that are at Rappard's for the moment, about which I had a letter from him, telling me that he liked them all, and especially admired the sentiment in Behind the Hedges and The Kingfisher, and the first Winter Garden which he also liked very much.

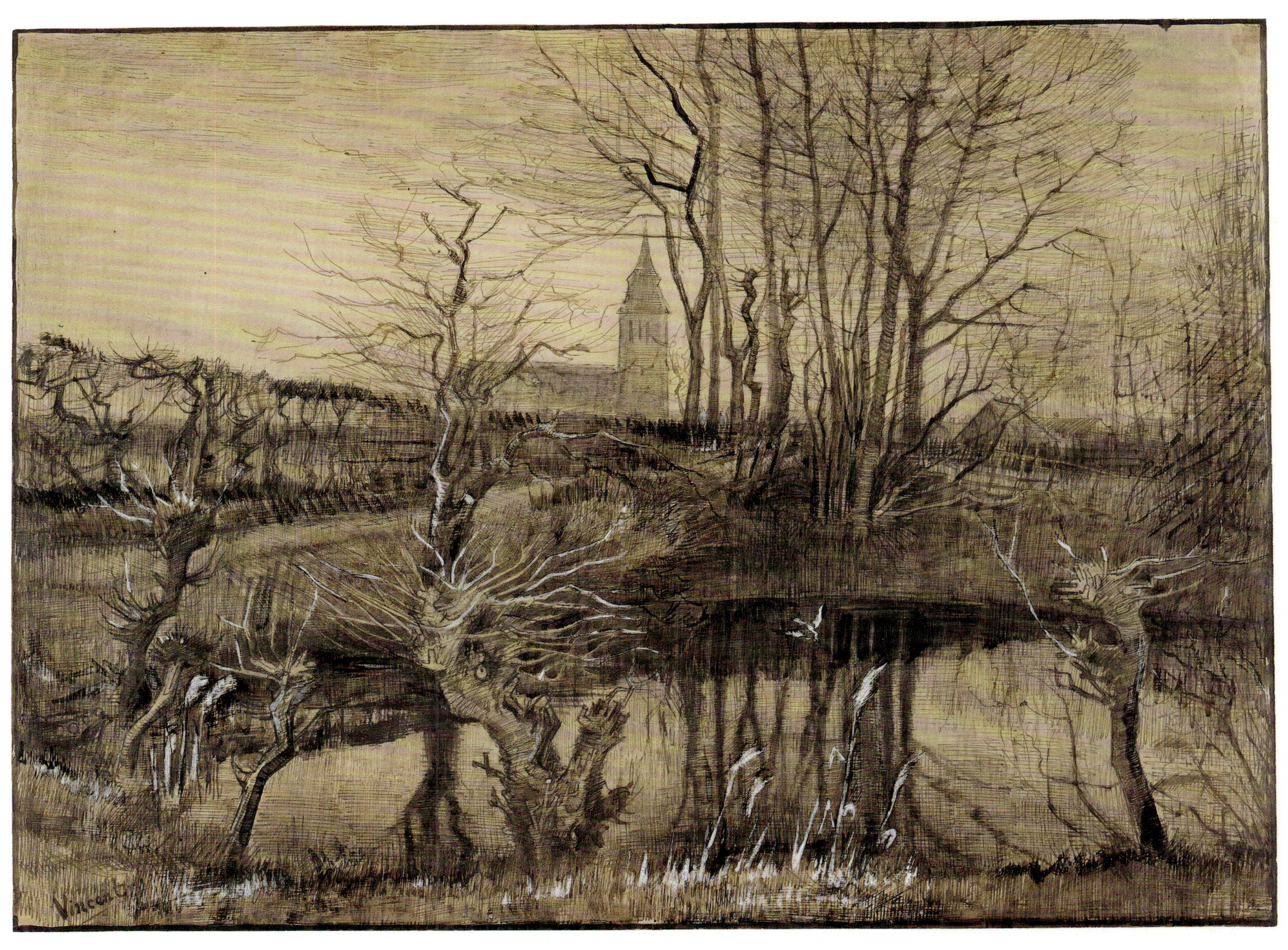
Vincent

24. *Houses with Thatched Roofs*

March 1884
Pen and ink, graphite, watercolor on wove paper
30.5 x 44.8 cm (12 x 17⅝ in.)
Tate, London, Bequeathed by C. Frank Stoop, 1933 (NO 4715)
F1242, JH474
Letter R45

Provenance: Theo van Gogh (d. 1891); by inheritance to his son, Vincent Willem van Gogh, as part of his collection, administered by his widow, Johanna van Gogh-Bonger, 1891; sold by her, through Kunsthandel C. M. van Gogh, to C. F. Stoop (for 650 gulden), 1911; his bequest to the Tate Gallery, London, 1933.

Selected exhibitions: Leiden 1893; Groningen 1897; Amsterdam 1905, no. 299; Frankfurt 1970, no. 34; 's Hertogenbosch 1987–88, no. 74; Otterlo 1990, no. 96; Vienna 1996, no. 54; Martigny 2000, no. 13.

Summary of the literature: Bremmer 1910, vol. 11, no. 84. De la Faille (1928, no. 1242) listed the title of the work as "Les chaumières" and dated it to the Nuenen period. Vanbeselaere (1937, pp. 259, 322, 412) referred to the sheet as "Rietdaken," a title generally followed by subsequent authors, and dated it to May 1884. Hulsker (1980, no. 474) claimed the drawing was executed in April 1884. Alley (1981, pp. 290, 291) pointed to the work's similarities to F190 and suggested it might have been inspired by Jules Breton's poem "Seule." Heijbroek and Wouthuysen (1993, pp. 32, 203) mentioned the sale by J. H. de Bois at Kunsthandel C. M. van Gogh to C. F. Stoop. Baer 1994, p. 144; Heenk 1995, p. 114. Stolwijk and Veenenbos (2002, pp. 53, 129, 151, 163, 193) recorded that Jo van Gogh-Bonger's account book indicates the sheet was sold in March 1911 to C. F. Stoop for 650 gulden.

Van Gogh initially sent this sheet to Van Rappard in late March 1884, together with two others (F1249, fig. 97; F1243, fig. 98) and then to Theo late that spring. In it, he sought to capture the sober character of the landscape—"the effect of light and brown" [R45]. The three drawings are somewhat less worked up than the larger sheets executed in March (F1129, cat. 20; F1130, cat. 22; F1135, cat. 23) and are thus more spontaneous and instinctive. Van Gogh was very fond of the thatched-cottage motif. He regarded the artlessness of the dwellings as a reflection of the lives of the simple people who inhabited them. He would return to the subject whenever possible throughout his career, both in paintings and in drawings.

That Van Gogh's stated aim here was to depict "the effect of light and brown" indicates that the original ink was in fact brown, rather than a black that has now faded.

SvH

Letter to Anthon van Rappard, between ca. March 24 and 29, 1884 [R45]: The trees are blossoming outside, and at the moment the weather is still not too hot for long rambles. A few days ago I sent you three more pen-and-ink drawings, Little Ditch, Norway Pines in the Fen, Thatched Roofs; I thought you would like the subjects. As for the execution, I should have wished with all my heart that the direction of the pen scratches had followed the forms more expressively, and that the forces which render the tone of the masses expressed their shape more clearly at the same time. I think you will admit that I did not systematically or intentionally neglect the composition of things, their shape, but I had to take a shot at it in a rough sort of way in order to render the effect of light and brown—the atmosphere of the scenery as it was at that moment—the general aspect—as well as I could. For at present one can see these three things only at special moments.

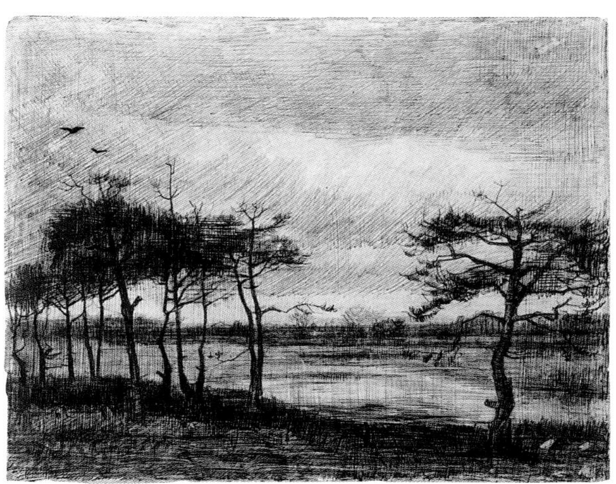

Fig. 97. *Pine Trees in the Fen* (F1249), April 1884. Graphite, pen, brush, and ink on wove paper, 35.8 x 45 cm (14⅛ x 17¾ in.). Van Gogh Museum, Amsterdam (Vincent van Gogh Foundation)

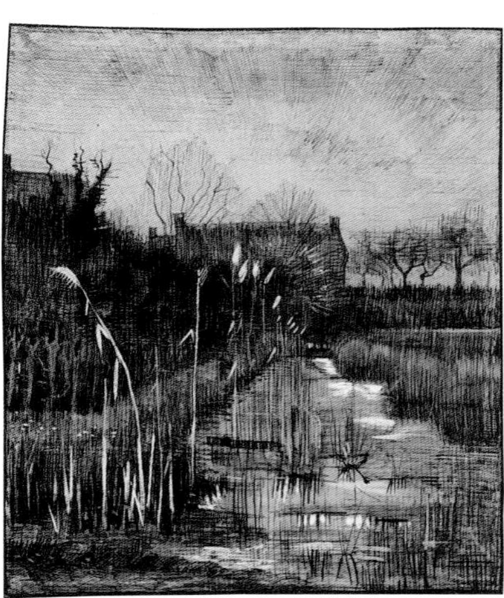

Fig. 98. *Ditch* (F1243), April 1884. Pen and ink heightened with paint on wove paper, 42.3 x 34.5 cm (16⅝ x 13⅝ in.). Van Gogh Museum, Amsterdam (Vincent van Gogh Foundation)

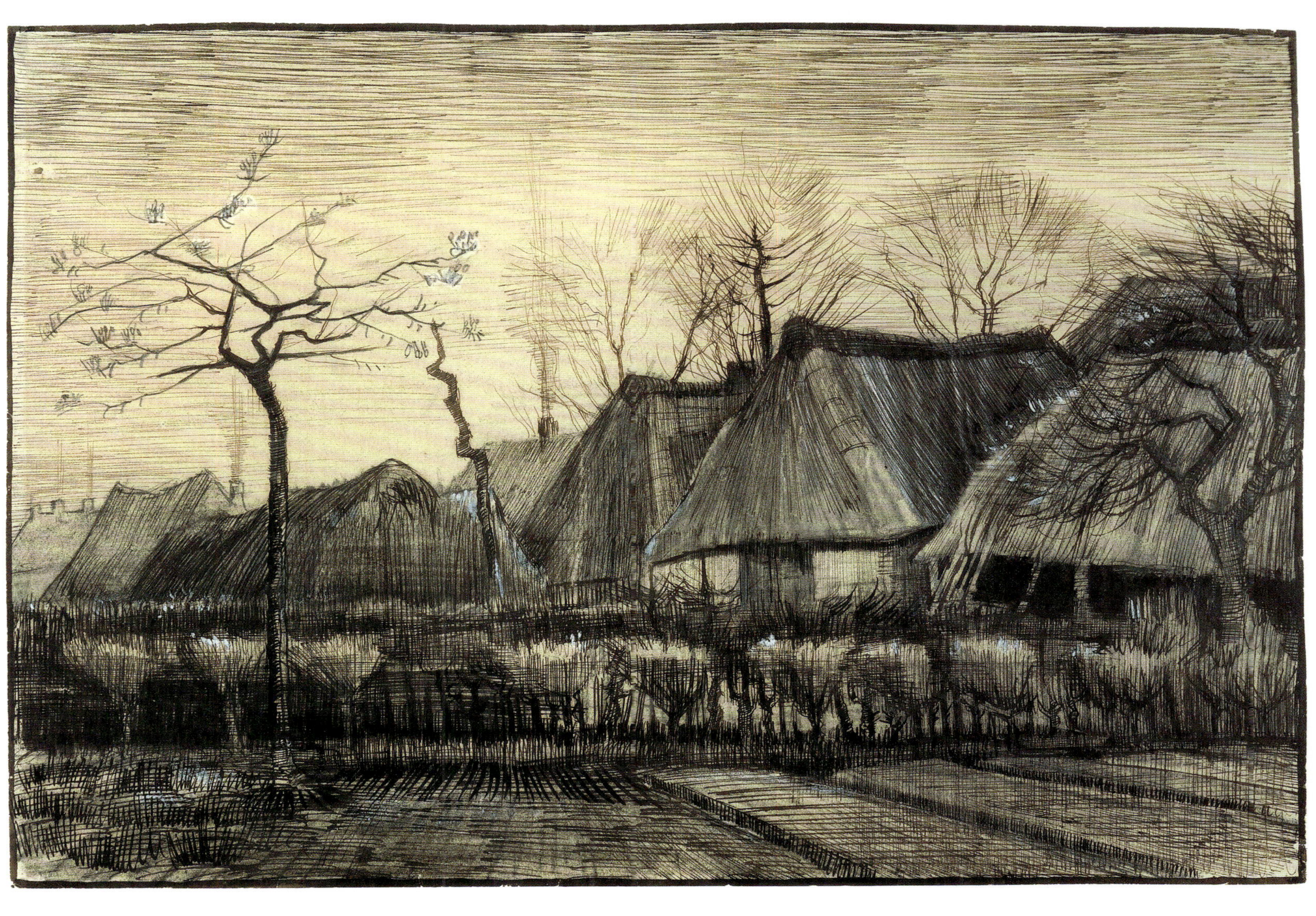

25. *Head of a Man*

December 1884–January 1885
Pen, brush, and coarse brush (?) with ink and wash, graphite on laid paper with remnant of watermark, possibly of a shield with a crowned lion holding a scimitar, encircled by the words CONCORDIA RES PARVAE CRESCUNT
14.8 x 10.4 cm (5⅞ x 4⅛ in.), the framed scene 14 x 10.4 cm (5½ x 4⅛ in.)
Signed lower left: *Vincent*
Van Gogh Museum, Amsterdam (Vincent van Gogh Foundation) (d 274 V/1962)
F1198, JH564

Provenance: Sent by the artist to Theo van Gogh (d. 1891), between December 1884 and January 1885 [389–92]; by inheritance to his son, Vincent Willem van Gogh (1890–1978), as part of his collection, administered by his widow, Johanna van Gogh-Bonger (d. 1925), 1891; ownership transferred to the Vincent van Gogh Foundation, 1962; placed on permanent loan at the Van Gogh Museum, Amsterdam, 1973.

Selected exhibitions: Groningen 1897; Amsterdam 1905, no. 270; Amsterdam 1914–15, no. 110; Amsterdam 1997.

Summary of the literature: De la Faille (1928, no. 1198) dated this "Tête de paysan" (the title adopted by most subsequent authors) to February–April 1885. Vanbeselaere (1937, pp. 264, 341, 344, 411) dated it to April 1885 and noted that the model is the same old man seen in *The Potato Eaters* (F82). Van Gelder (1949, p. 11) saw the drawing as a study for that painting. The editors of De la Faille 1970 (no. 1198) accepted Van Gelder's interpretation and dated the sheet to April 1885; added that the model is seen in F160a as well; and noted the existence of the series of small-sized pen drawings. Hulsker (1980, no. 564), on the evidence of letter 391, which announces to Theo a shipment of small pen drawings of heads, suggested a date of December 1884 and identified the man as the father of the De Groot family, also depicted in F82 (*The Potato Eaters*) and F160a (from which the drawing was done). Van Uitert and Hoyle (1987, p. 406, no. 2.236) followed Hulsker's dating. Heenk (1995, p. 117) noted that it is highly unusual for such small examples of Van Gogh's work to be signed. Hulsker (1996, no. 564) changed his earlier dating to December 1884–January 1885. Van Heugten (1997, pp. 124–32) employed the neutral title "Head of a Man" and suggested that since Van Gogh sent the small studies in several letters during December 1884–January 1885 [389–92] they should be dated then. Within the larger group of fifteen small pen drawings, he considered that this one (for which the model was F160a) belongs to a subset of five signed sheets, whose importance is also suggested by their somewhat larger size and greater finish.

Between December 1884 and January 1885, Van Gogh sent Theo several packages containing a total of twenty small studies of peasant heads; about fifteen of these have survived. Some are little more than pencil drawings worked up in pen, others are more elaborate. Five appear to have been executed with some degree of ambition; they are drawn with care and attention to detail, and all are signed. Among these five striking likenesses are this head of a man and *Head of a Woman* (F1177, cat. 26). Several of the fifteen works are based on paintings, including the one shown here (F160a, fig. 99). The male model is also depicted in *The Potato Eaters* (F82, fig. 88).

In *Head of a Man* and *Head of a Woman*, Van Gogh used an unusual technique in the background: little spots of ink, almost like splashes, help render the dusky surroundings. The effect may have been achieved by moistening a rather coarse brush with a relatively small amount of ink and then pressing it directly onto the paper.

SvH

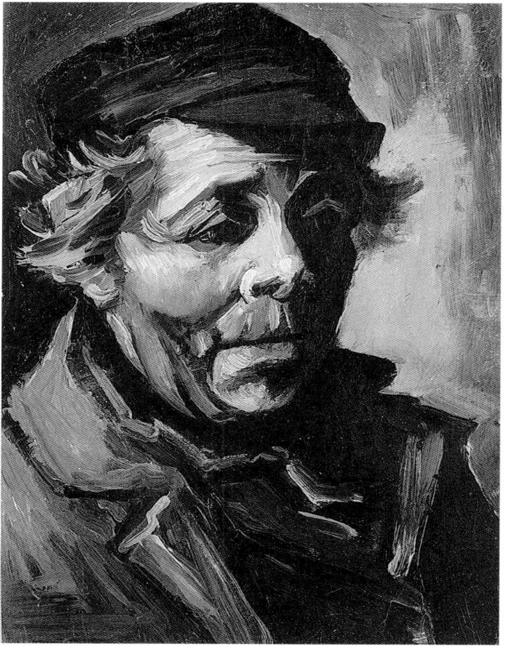

Fig. 99. *Head of a Man* (F160a), December 1884–January 1885. Oil on canvas, 39.4 x 30.2 cm (15½ x 11⅞ in.). Art Gallery of New South Wales, Sydney, Art Gallery of New South Wales Foundation Purchase, 1990

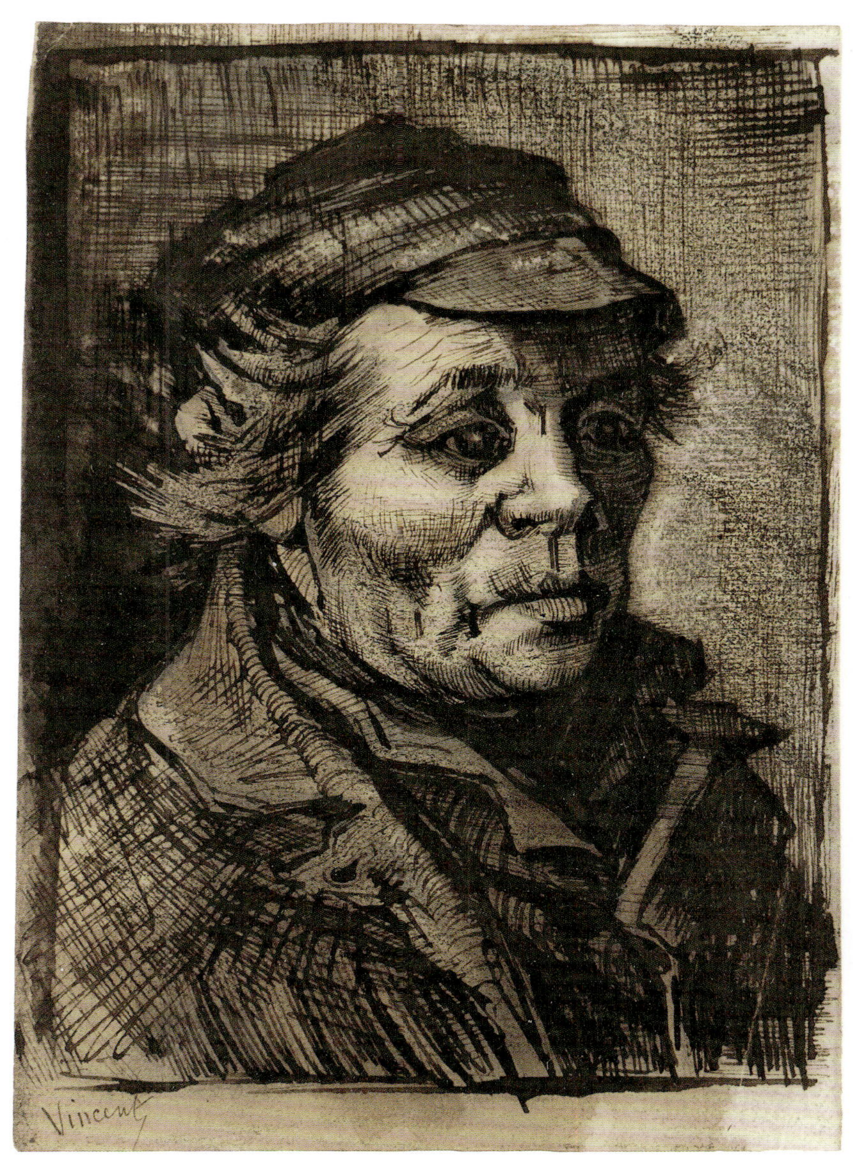
Vincent

26. *Head of a Woman*

December 1884–January 1885
Pen and brush with ink and wash, graphite on laid paper with an illegible watermark truncated along left edge
14.2 x 10.4 cm (5⅝ x 4⅛ in.), the framed scene 13.2 x 10 cm (5¼ x 4 in.)
Signed lower left: *Vincent*
Van Gogh Museum, Amsterdam (Vincent van Gogh Foundation) (d 270 V/1962)
F1177, JH609

Provenance: Sent by the artist to Theo van Gogh (d. 1891), between December 1884 and January 1885 [389–92]; by inheritance to his son, Vincent Willem van Gogh (1890–1978), as part of his collection, administered by his widow, Johanna van Gogh-Bonger (d. 1925), 1891; ownership transferred to the Vincent van Gogh Foundation, 1962; placed on permanent loan at the Van Gogh Museum, Amsterdam, 1973.

Selected exhibitions: Amsterdam 1905, no. 269; Amsterdam 1914–15, no. 47; Amsterdam 1997.

Summary of the literature: Bremmer 1926, vol. 11, cover ill. De la Faille (1928, no. 1177) gave the title "Tête de paysanne," adopted without variation by all later authors, and dated the sheet to February–April 1884. Vanbeselaere (1937, pp. 264, 341, 344, 411) saw a relationship to *The Potato Eaters* (F82) and thus dated the work to April 1885. De la Faille 1970 (no. 1177) assumed it was executed in December 1884. Hulsker (1980, no. 609) gave January 1885 and viewed F154 as the model. Van Uitert and Hoyle (1987, p. 407, no. 2.240) followed Hulsker's dating. Heenk 1995, p. 117. Hulsker in 1996 (no. 609) now dated the sheet one month later, to February 1885. Van Heugten (1997, pp. 124–32) dated it more broadly, to the period of the other small drawings, i.e., December 1884–January 1885. Five of the fifteen surviving works are signed and fully worked up, indicating they were important to Van Gogh.

Like *Head of a Man* (F1198, cat. 25), this pen-and-ink drawing is based on a painting (F154, fig. 100). In December 1884 Van Gogh embarked on a series of painted and drawn studies of heads in preparation for an ambitious, multifigure genre scene (see F1182, cat. 27), but the small pen-and-ink drawings were not part of this group. Van Gogh sent them to Theo, among other reasons to give him an impression of the paintings he was then working on. Given their small size, Van Gogh probably did not intend these signed sheets for sale on the art market but instead saw them as potential magazine illustrations, a source of income whose possibilities he hoped to exploit.

SvH

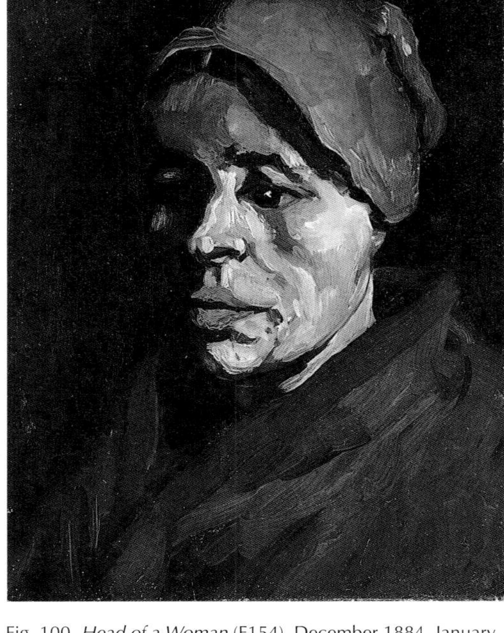

Fig. 100. *Head of a Woman* (F154), December 1884–January 1885. Oil on canvas, 42.5 x 33.1 cm (16¾ x 13 in.). Kröller-Müller Museum, Otterlo

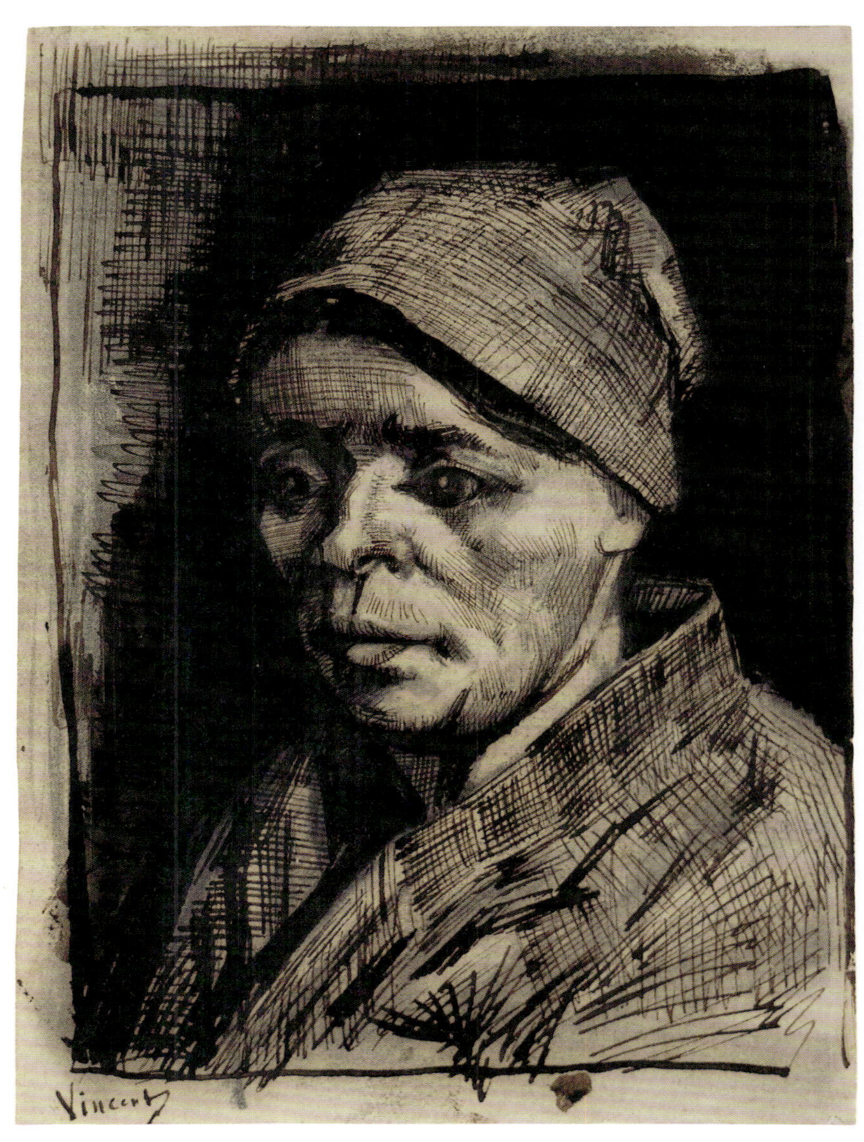
Vincent

27. *Head of a Woman*

December 1884–May 1885
Black chalk on wove paper
40.2 x 33.3 cm ($15^{7}/_{8}$ x $13^{1}/_{8}$ in.)
Van Gogh Museum, Amsterdam (Vincent van Gogh Foundation) (d 362 V/1962)
F1182, JH590

Provenance: Theo van Gogh (d. 1891); by inheritance to his son, Vincent Willem van Gogh (1890–1978), as part of his collection, administered by his widow, Johanna van Gogh-Bonger (d. 1925), 1891; placed on loan at the Stedelijk Museum, Amsterdam, 1931–73; ownership transferred to the Vincent van Gogh Foundation,1962; placed on permanent loan at the Van Gogh Museum, Amsterdam, 1973.

Selected exhibitions: Groningen 1897; Paris 1902; Amsterdam 1905, no. 298; Munich 1908, no. 82; Dresden 1908, no. 86; Frankfurt 1908, no. 93; Amsterdam 1914–15, no. 89; New York 1920, no. 24; New York and other cities 1935–36, no. 98; London–Birmingham–Glasgow 1947–48, no. 119; New York–Chicago 1949–50, no. 35; Amsterdam 1980–81, no. 149; 's Hertogenbosch 1987–88, no. 27; Otterlo 1990, no. 97; Amsterdam 1997.

Summary of the literature: Bremmer (1910, vol. 11, no. 82) discussed the ugliness of the woman in detail ("monstermensch"). De la Faille (1928, no. 1182) dated this "Tête de paysanne" (a title varied only slightly by later authors) to February 1885. Meier-Graefe 1928a, pl. 9. Vanbeselaere (1937, pp. 264, 342, 411) dated it to March 1885. Hulsker (1980, no. 590) suggested it was executed about January 1885. Pollock (in Amsterdam 1980–81, pp. 119, 121, 126) claimed Van Gogh sought neither to make a portrait nor to illustrate a certain type, but rather to render the unrefined peasant of the modern era; she gave pencil and pen in brown ink as the drawing materials. Van Uitert (in Van Uitert and Hoyle 1987, p. 407, no. 2.242) followed Hulsker's dating. Trappeniers (in 's Hertogenbosch 1987–88, pp. 158–62) referred to the woman's cap as an under-cap. Feilchenfeldt and Veenenbos (1988, p. 128) suggested that the sheet was shown at the Stedelijk Museum in 1905 under the title "Vrouwenkop met zwarte muts." Van der Wolk (in Otterlo 1990, pp. 130, 154) dated it to early 1885. Van Tilborgh (1993, p. 36) discussed physiognomy and Van Gogh's interest in this pseudoscience. Heenk (1995, pp. 119, 225) believed the sheet belonged to a group of studies of heads, together with F1180 and F1199. Hulsker (1996, no. 590) dated the work to December 1884–January 1885. Van Heugten (1997, pp. 122, 123) regarded it as a sheet intended only for Van Gogh's own use but suggested it shows some ambition nonetheless; he felt that no other drawing of Van Gogh's expresses the difficulties of peasant life as strongly. Since it has proven impossible to establish a precise date, he suggested the period December 1884–May 1885, the quality of the drawing indicating that it might well belong to the later months.

In December 1884 Van Gogh began work on a large group of peasant portraits, which he referred to as "heads of the people" [390]—a reference to the series of the same name that had appeared in the English illustrated magazine *The Graphic*. The images convey Van Gogh's idea of the peasant character, which he saw as rough, uncultivated, even animal-like, but also—precisely because of this—intimately bound to life and the cycles of nature. This was a widely accepted view in the nineteenth century and found its reflection in both literature and the fine arts. The detailed execution and format (the majority of the studies in this series are only half as big) give this striking head of a woman a special place in Van Gogh's oeuvre.

SvH

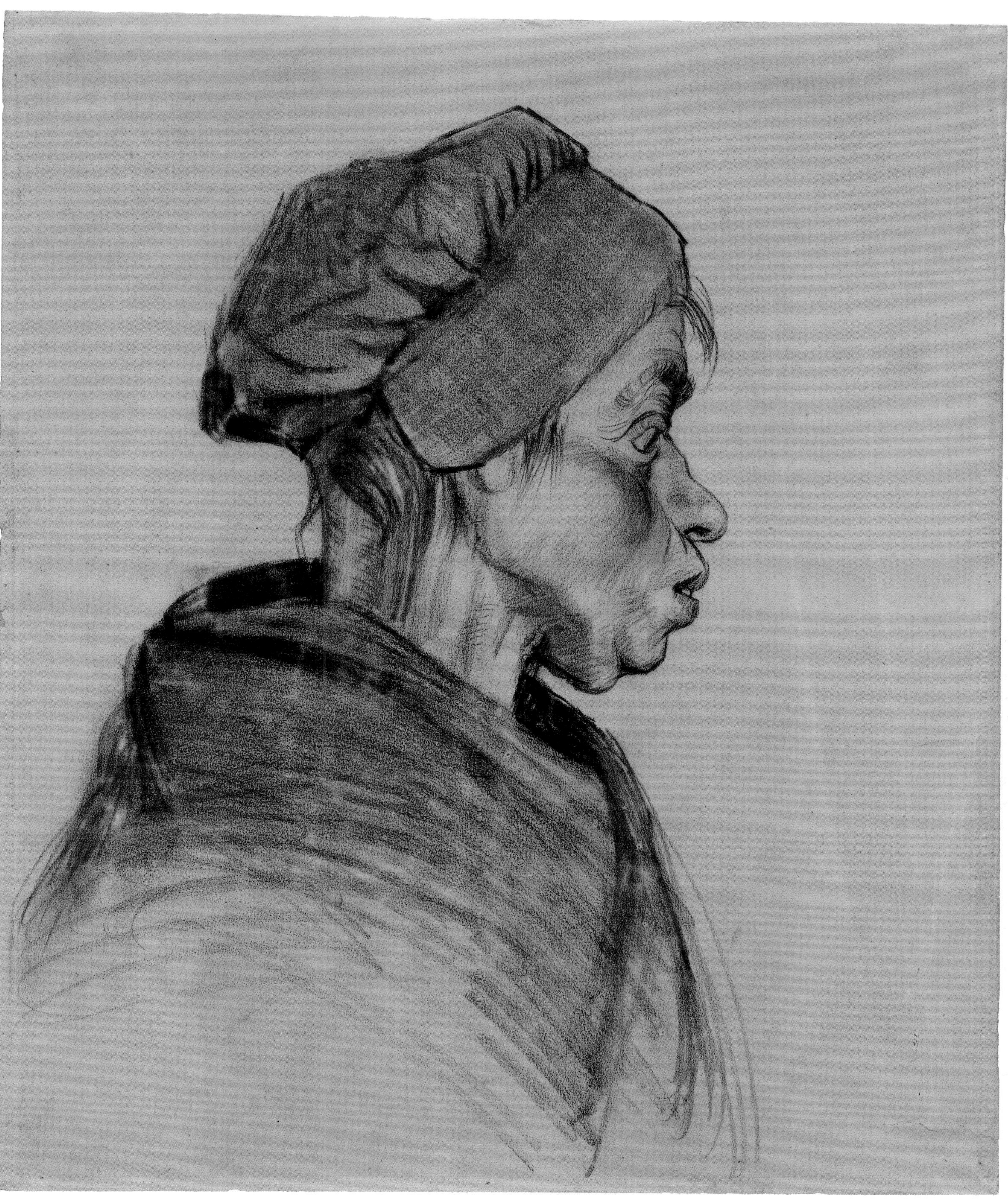

28. *Sale of Building Scrap*

May 1885
Transparent and opaque watercolor, black chalk or charcoal on watercolor paper
38 x 55.4 cm (15 x 21¾ in.)
Signed lower left: *Vincent*
Van Gogh Museum, Amsterdam (Vincent van Gogh Foundation) (d 361 V/1962)
F1230, JH770
Letters 408, 410

Amsterdam only

Provenance: Sent by the artist to Theo van Gogh (d. 1891), 1885 [410]; by inheritance to his son, Vincent Willem van Gogh (1890–1978), as part of his collection, administered by his widow, Johanna van Gogh-Bonger (d. 1925), 1891; placed on loan at the Stedelijk Museum, Amsterdam, 1931–73; ownership transferred to the Vincent van Gogh Foundation, 1962; placed on permanent loan at the Van Gogh Museum, Amsterdam, 1973.

Selected exhibitions: Amsterdam 1905, no. 334; Amsterdam 1914–15, no. 44; Utrecht 1923, no. 3; Rotterdam 1923; Berlin 1927–28, no. 27; Paris–Albi 1966, no. 20; London 1968–69, no. 40; 's Hertogenbosch 1987–88, no. 45; Otterlo 1990, no. 104; Amsterdam 1997; Tokyo 2000, no. 14.

Summary of the literature: Bremmer 1924, vol. 4, no. 25. De la Faille (1928, no. 1230) dated the sheet to May 1885—a date that has remained unchallenged—and referred to it as "La vente des croix sur le cimetière de Nuenen," the title given it by Jo van Gogh-Bonger at the time of its exhibition in Amsterdam in 1905, and adopted by many subsequent authors. Vanbeselaere 1937, pp. 269, 412; Leurs and Tralbaut 1957, p. 57. De la Faille 1970 (no. 1230) called attention to the related drawings F1112r and v and F1231r and v. Hulsker 1980/1996, no. 770. Van Uitert and Hoyle (1987, pp. 126, 127, 418, no. 2.304) cited the date of the public sale, May 11, 1885, and suggested that while Van Gogh may have made a sketch on the spot, the drawing itself was done in the studio. Trappeniers (in 's Hertogenbosch 1987–88, pp. 178, 179) noted that in letter 410 Van Gogh referred to the sheet under a French title, "Vente pour cause de demolition," indicating that it may have been intended for the French art market; she offered no opinion on whether it was made on location or in the studio. Heenk (1995, pp. 106, 109, 122) called the work a studio piece, intended for sale. Van Heugten (1997, pp. 185–91) noted that the mistaken title originated with Jo van Gogh-Bonger; recorded that the sale was of building scrap, particularly from the demolished roof, hence the title "Sale of Building Scrap"; discussed the sale document, which summarizes the items sold and identifies the burgomaster and the police officer; and wrote that the drawing was done in the studio, based on sketches made on the spot. De Brouwer (2000, pp. 79–83, 97) dated the sheet to May 11, 1885, the day of the sale.

The old tower that so often appears in Van Gogh's Nuenen work was located in the fields behind the vicarage; it was the last remnant of a medieval church possibly dating back to the end of the fifteenth century. During Van Gogh's time in Nuenen, the massive structure was slowly dismantled and finally razed in 1885. A print of 1880 shows the tower in better days (fig. 101).

The scene at the left has led some authors to view the subject as a sale of cemetery crosses. What we see, however, is the large-scale disposal of building scrap, in particular sections of the recently demolished roof of the tower. The sale, which took place on May 11, 1885, was supervised by the burgomaster, Jan van Hombergh (at the right of the open door, holding a piece of paper), with village policeman Johannes Biemans standing on a platform, watching over the proceedings.

SvH

Letter to Theo van Gogh, ca. May 22, 1885 [408]: These last days I have been working hard on drawings. They are busy pulling down the old tower in the fields. So there was an auction of lumber and slates and old iron, including the cross. I have finished a watercolor of it, in the style of the lumber auction, but better I think; I also had another large watercolor of the churchyard, but so far it has been a failure. Yet I have it well in my head, i.e. what I want to express—and perhaps I shall get what I mean onto the third sheet of paper. And if not, then not. I have just sponged out the two failures, but I am going to try again. If you like, you can have the one of the auction.

Letter to Theo van Gogh, ca. June 2, 1885 [410]: I hope to send you this week a small box marked V2, containing:
1 picture la Chaumière
1 watercolor id.
1 " " vente pour cause de démolition
12 etudes peintes.

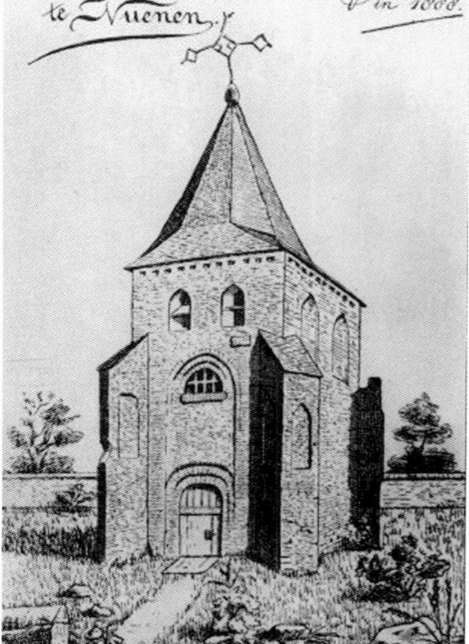

Fig. 101. August Sassen, *The Old Church Tower at Nuenen*, 1880. Etching (photo: Van Gogh Museum, Amsterdam)

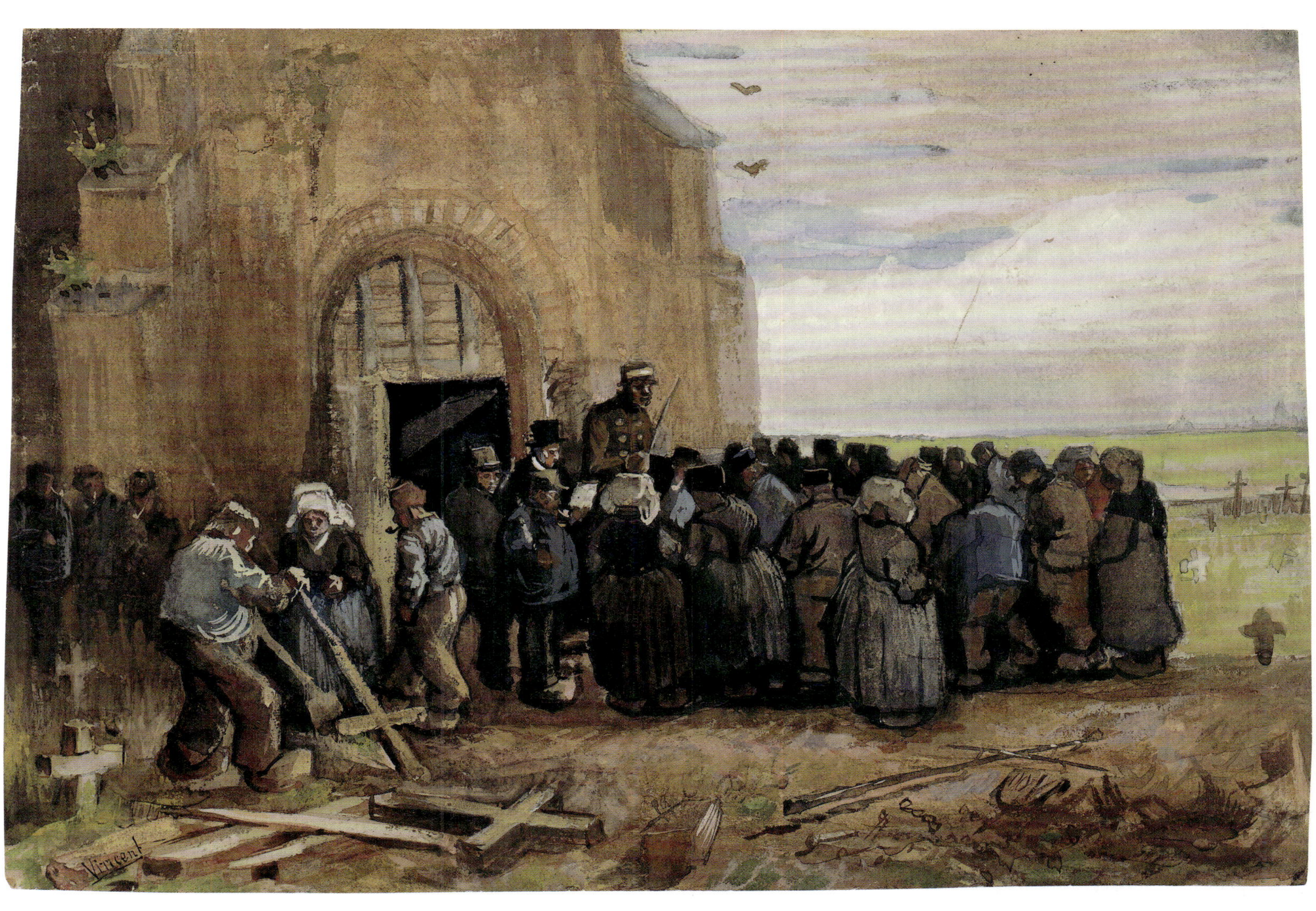
Vincent

29. *Peasant Woman Gleaning*

July–September 1885
Black chalk on wove paper watermarked TS & Z
51.5 x 41.5 cm (20¼ x 16⅜ in.)
Museum Folkwang, Essen
F1279, JH836

Provenance: Acquired by Karl Ernst Osthaus (d. 1921), founder of the Museum Folkwang, Hagen, 1910; transferred with the rest of his collection to the new Museum Folkwang, Essen, 1922.

Selected exhibitions: Hagen 1912, no. 302; Essen 1957, no. 201; 's Hertogenbosch 1987–88, no. 53; Otterlo 1990, no. 116; Vienna 1996, no. 73; Paris 1998–99, no. 12.

Summary of the literature: De la Faille (1928, no. 1279) saw the woman's activity as pulling grass; he dated the sheet to August 1885. In Museum Folkwang 1929 (no. 439) the activity depicted was referred to as gleaning, an interpretation upheld by all subsequent authors. Vanbeselaere 1937, pp. 273, 412. Hulsker (1980, no. 836) dated the work to July 1885. Wadley 1991, p. 57; Heenk 1995, pp. 124, 126. Druick and Zegers (in Chicago–Amsterdam 2001–2, pp. 195, 204) noted that Van Gogh, inspired by Paul Gauguin to work from memory, added a similar bending figure (plucking flowers) to his *Memory of the Garden in Etten* (F496).

Upon completion of *The Potato Eaters* (F82, fig. 88) in April 1885, Van Gogh realized that he still needed practice in depicting the human figure (see "The Dutch Years, 1880–85"). This led to a series of large drawings of agricultural laborers of a monumentality thus far not seen in his work. This quality and the size of the sheets themselves notwithstanding, these drawings were not designed as autonomous works of art; they were studies, which Van Gogh intended to use in a painting [417]. He may have been thinking of a harvest scene, which, in the event, he never carried out. The woman shown here is gleaning, that is, gathering the ears of wheat left over after the reaping. The subject was most famously depicted by Jean-François Millet (fig. 102).

SvH

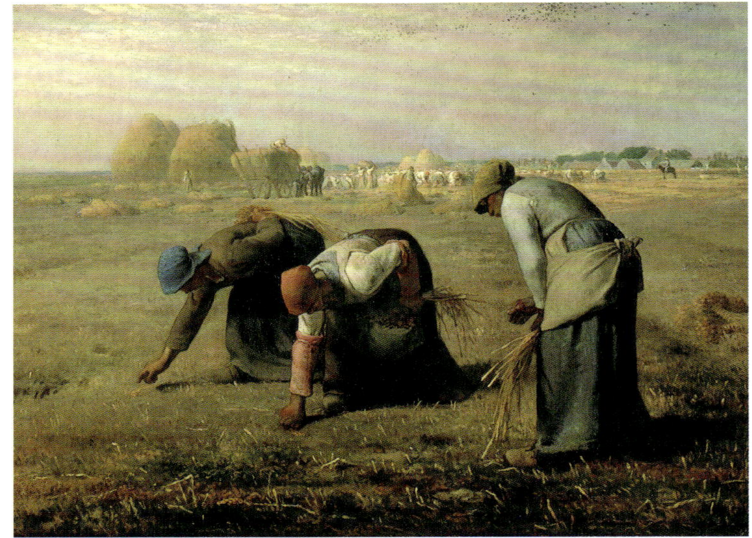

Fig. 102. Jean-François Millet, *The Gleaners*, 1857. Oil on canvas, 83.5 x 111 cm (32⅞ x 43¾ in.). Musée d'Orsay, Paris (photo: Jean Schormans—RMN/Art Resource, NY)

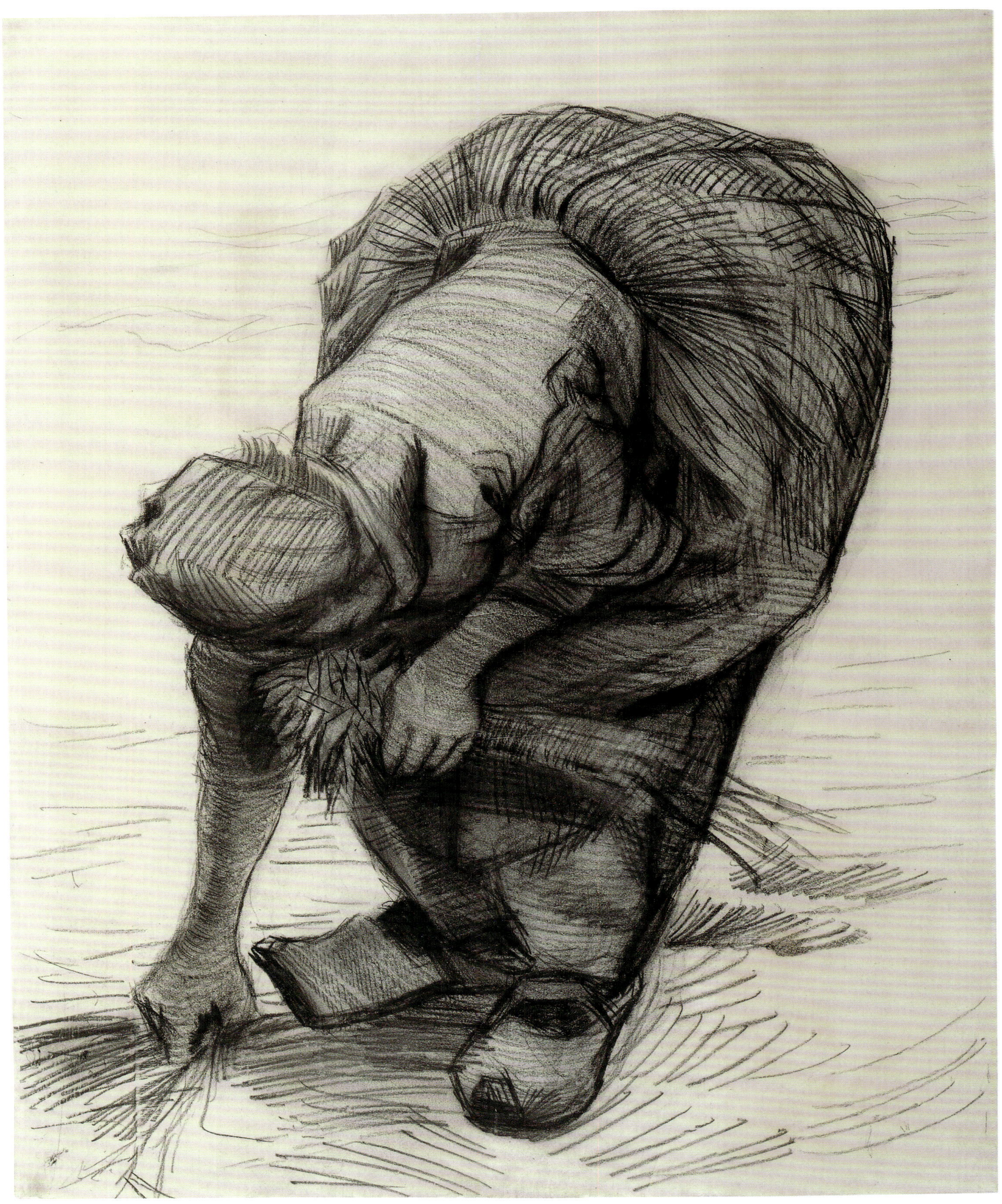

30. *Man with a Hoe*

August 1885
Black chalk on wove paper watermarked TS & Z
43 x 32 cm (16⅞ x 12⅝ in.)
Signed lower right: *Vincent*
Kröller-Müller Museum, Otterlo (KM 122.652)
F1326, JH904
Letter 422

Provenance: Sent by the artist to Theo van Gogh (d. 1891), late August 1885 [422]; by inheritance to his son, Vincent Willem van Gogh, as part of his collection, administered by his widow, Johanna van Gogh-Bonger, 1891; acquired by J. Hidde Nijland, Dordrecht and The Hague, before 1918; sold to Helene Kröller-Müller, The Hague, 1928; Kröller-Müller Foundation, 1932; Kröller-Müller Museum, Otterlo, 1937.

Selected exhibitions: The Hague 1918; Amsterdam 1924, no. 113.

Summary of the literature: De la Faille (1928, no. 1326) dated the drawing to December 1883–November 1885 and characterized the man's activity as "remuant du fumier." Vanbeselaere (1937, pp. 276, 413) interpreted the man's tool as a rake, and he dated the sheet rather later, to September–October 1885. In De la Faille 1970 (no. 1326) it was suggested that the sheet was executed in the autumn of 1885. Hulsker (1980, no. 904) identified the man's activity as hoeing, and he dated the drawing to the second half of August 1885. Kröller-Müller Museum 1980, pp. 54, 55. In De la Faille 1992 (no. 1326) the date was given as autumn 1885. Heenk (1995, p. 124) pointed out that Van Gogh was probably inspired by a similar work by Millet.

Among the drawings in the series of laboring peasants from the summer of 1885 are six somewhat smaller sheets in which the figures are shown in more detailed surroundings. A letter Van Gogh wrote to Theo at the end of August [422] indicates that these works represent Van Gogh's reaction to his brother's earlier observations that detailed drawings were potentially more salable than the rather bare, large studies he had seen so far. Vincent thus sent him "drawings of figures with entourage" [422], of which this sheet is one. The man, working the ground with his hoe, was captured just at the moment he pulls his tool from the earthen mound. He appears in another drawing in the Kröller-Müller Museum (F1325, fig. 103).

Letter 422 allows us to date all six worked-up sheets to August 1885.

SvH

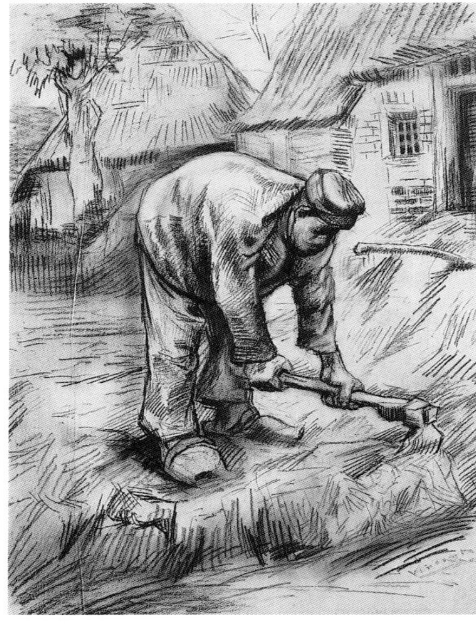

Fig. 103. *Man with a Hoe* (F1325), August 1885. Black chalk on wove paper, 44 x 33.5 cm (17⅜ x 13¼ in.). Kröller-Müller Museum, Otterlo

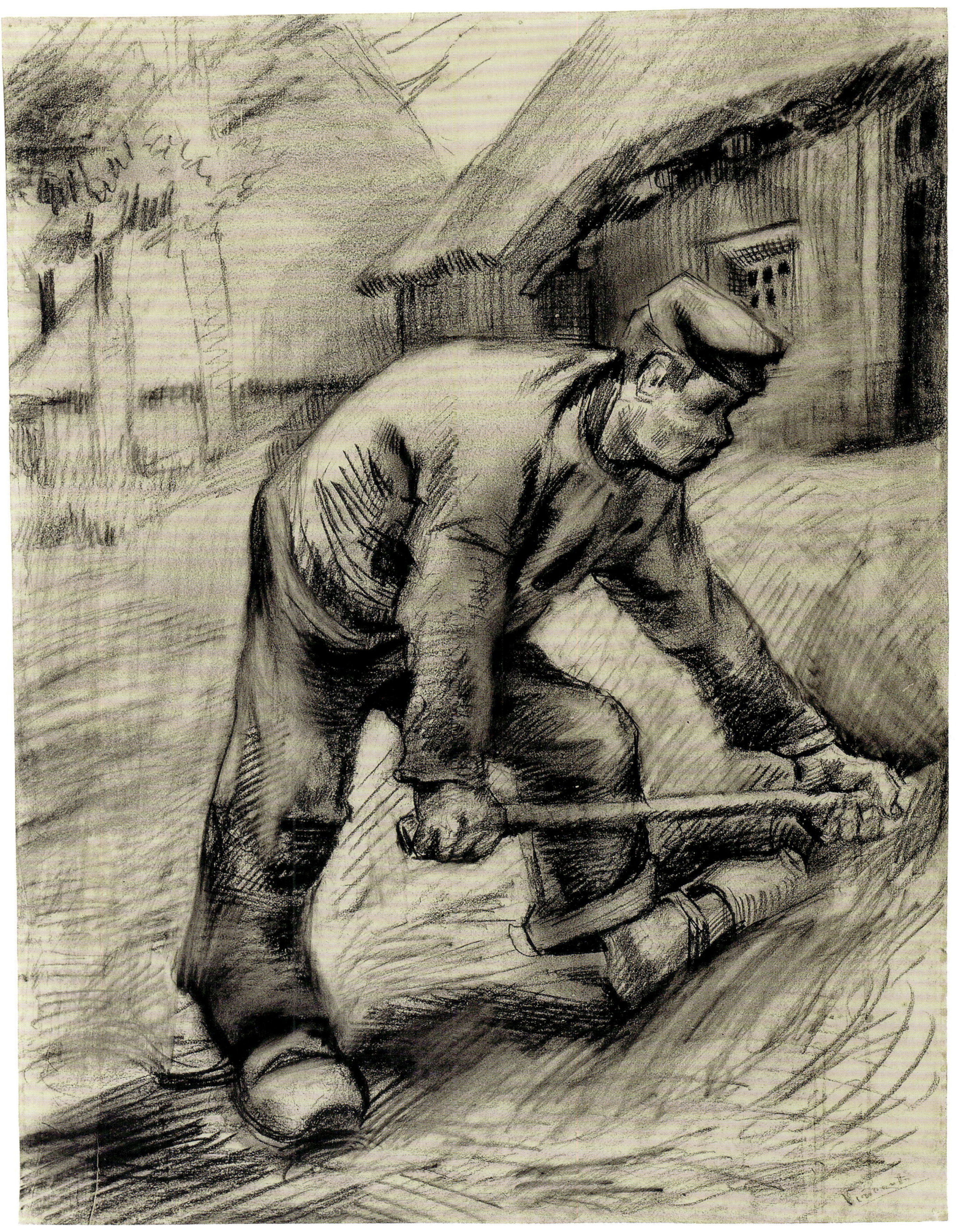

31. *Woodcutter*

July–September 1885
Black chalk and wash on laid paper watermarked with a shield with fleur-de-lis and HFDC
45 x 55.5 cm (17¾ x 21⅞ in.)
Van Gogh Museum, Amsterdam (Vincent van Gogh Foundation) (d 81 V/1962)
F1327, JH902

Provenance: Theo van Gogh (d. 1891); by inheritance to his son, Vincent Willem van Gogh (1890–1978), as part of his collection, administered by his widow, Johanna van Gogh-Bonger (d. 1925), 1891; placed on loan at the Stedelijk Museum, Amsterdam, 1931–73; ownership transferred to the Vincent van Gogh Foundation, 1962; placed on permanent loan at the Van Gogh Museum, Amsterdam, 1973.

Selected exhibitions: Paris 1896–97; Amsterdam 1905, no. 288; Berlin 1906, no. 61; Hamburg 1911–12; Dresden–Breslau 1912, no. 24; Amsterdam 1914–15, no. 106; Basel 1924, no. 84; Zürich 1924, no. 84; Stuttgart 1924, no. 2; Paris 1925, unnumbered; The Hague 1925; London–Birmingham–Glasgow 1947–48, no. 127; London 1968–69, no. 42; Amsterdam 1980–81, no. 157; Otterlo 1990, no. 106; Amsterdam 1997; Paris 1998–99, no. 8.

Summary of the literature: Van Meurs 1910, no. 11; *Lettres* 1911, pl. XIV. De la Faille (1928, no. 1327) gave the title "Le bûcheron" and situated the sheet in Nuenen, without giving a more precise date. Meier-Graefe 1928a, pl. 6. Vanbeselaere (1937, pp. 392, 413) referred to the work as "Houthakker vóór den gevelden boom" (these titles have remained more or less unchanged) and dated it to the summer of 1885. De Gruyter (1961, p. 101) dated the drawing to autumn 1885. De la Faille 1970 (no. 1327) accepted De Gruyter's dating. Chetham (1976, pp. 33, 34) saw the sheet as proof of Van Gogh's progress in drawing the human figure. Hulsker (1980, no. 902) situated the work among the drawings of the summer of 1885, more specifically to August. Van Uitert and Hoyle (1987, p. 426, no. 2.350) followed Hulsker. Feilchenfeldt and Veenenbos 1988, p. 130. De la Faille 1992 (no. 1327) also dated the work to August. Heenk 1995, p. 125. Hulsker (1996, no. 902) narrowed the date to the second half of August. Van Heugten (1997, pp. 244, 245) dated the drawing more broadly to July–September 1885 and pointed out that it is one of the few sheets that shows a worker not in the fields; he linked it to Lhermitte's *The Woodcutters.*

Of the large-scale laboring figures that Van Gogh drew in the summer of 1885, this is the only one not actually working the land. The artist perfectly captured the physical strain the woodcutter's work entails and paid equally careful attention to the other parts of the composition. He may have been encouraged to give his drawing such polish by his wish to emulate Léon Lhermitte, whose work he admired. In March of that year Van Gogh saw a print by Lhermitte, *The Woodcutters,* in *Le monde illustré* and was deeply impressed [395, 396] (fig. 104). Van Gogh's own *Woodcutter* is more or less a mirror image of the man standing on a tree trunk in the print, his ax raised into the air.

The lines above Van Gogh's subject's head suggest that he originally considered showing the entire ax in a more horizontal position. As in the large drawings of agricultural laborers, he stumped the chalk in several places and moistened it (probably with water) to create a kind of gray wash. Once the sheet dried, he used an eraser to achieve the lighter areas. Most of the figure studies from the summer of 1885 were done on wove paper watermarked TS & Z; the *Woodcutter,* however, was done on laid paper.

SvH

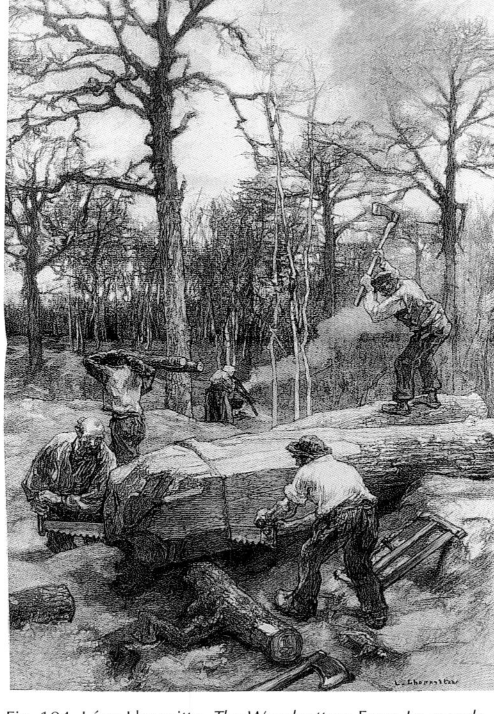

Fig. 104. Léon Lhermitte, *The Woodcutters.* From *Le monde illustré,* no. 1457 (1885)

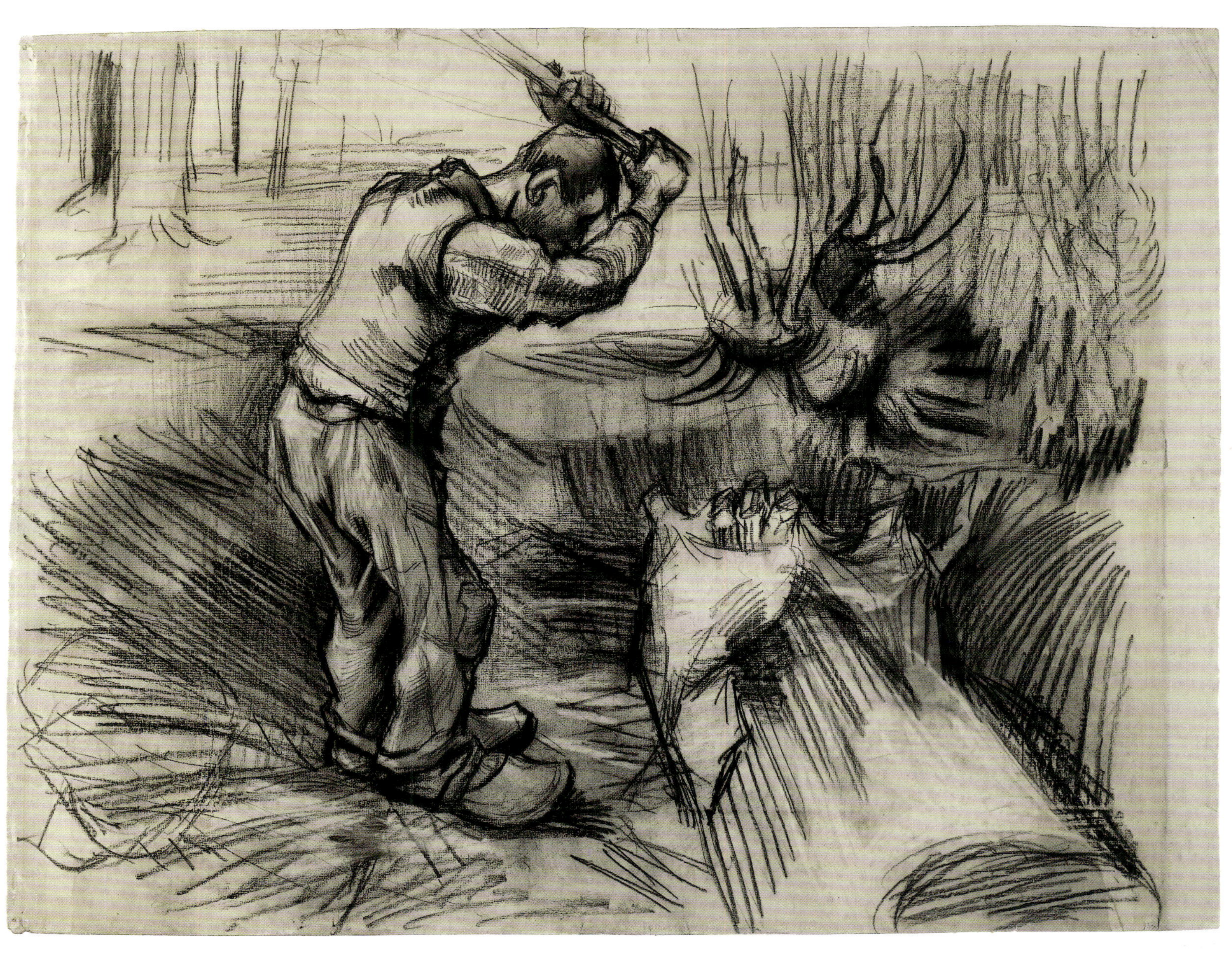

Antwerp and Paris, 1885–88: The Academy and the Avant-Garde

In late November 1885 Van Gogh left Nuenen and settled in Antwerp. In December he spent most of his time exploring the city: he visited the museums and made contact with dealers in order to gain insight into the local art market. He hoped to earn some money with city views, but he made no more than a few halfhearted attempts in this direction. At the end of December he began to concentrate once again on heads and the figure, and in the first half of January 1886 he registered at the Koninklijke Academie voor Schone Kunsten (Royal Academy of Fine Arts). With his usual enthusiasm he began to draw plaster casts, but he found that he was unable to accept the theories of his teachers, who, in drawing live models, placed considerable emphasis on the contours. Van Gogh had learned in Nuenen, however, that he achieved the best results by building up his figures through volume. Since these principles were diametrically opposite, Van Gogh's period at the academy was bound to be unsuccessful. Only one of the numerous drawings he made of plaster casts has been preserved, *The Discus Thrower* (F1364e, cat. 33), and it is not surprising that this study is unpolished in a way strongly reminiscent of the Nuenen peasant drawings from the summer of 1885.

As a newcomer to the academy, Van Gogh was not permitted to draw from the live model there, so he joined two drawing clubs, where in the evenings he would draw both the nude and the clothed model. No teachers were present at these sessions, and the studies Van Gogh made once again exhibit his typical powerful, angular modeling (see F1699, cat. 32).

Van Gogh worked long and exhausting hours: during the day and early evening at the academy, followed by time at the drawing clubs. He remained dissatisfied with the academic program and eventually decided to move on to Paris, where there were far better opportunities for continuing his artistic training.

Van Gogh's arrival in Paris initiated a period of relatively little development in terms of his drawn oeuvre. At the studio of Fernand Cormon he drew both nude models and plaster casts and continued to study the plasters at home as well. These works, however, generally demonstrated little ambition. A single sheet stands out because it shows a plaster cast and a nude in a way that inadvertently forms a striking whole (F1366v, cat. 34).

In Paris, Van Gogh discovered that the painting style he had developed in Nuenen was hopelessly dark and old-fashioned and felt that changing this should be his priority. He did not begin working on more ambitious drawings until February–March 1887, when his experiments with an updated manner of painting had begun to bear fruit and he no longer had to concentrate exclusively on this technique. Strikingly, color played a central role in many of the drawings executed in 1887. In cases in which Van Gogh worked in pen, without color, his style was much looser than it was in the elaborate pen-and-ink drawings of Nuenen (see F1407, cat. 37). Several drawings in color from the early months of 1887 were done primarily in chalk; Van Gogh also experimented with a combination of chalk and ink, although these efforts were not terribly successful.

In the summer of 1887, Van Gogh worked on two series of cityscapes in watercolor which reveal a whole new side of the artist as draftsman, both technically and stylistically (F1401, cat. 38; F1406, cat. 39; F1411, cat. 40; F1410, cat. 41). One must admit, however, that in this period Van Gogh did not evolve as much in his drawings as in his paintings, in which he needed to throw off the burden of the past. Nonetheless, there are substantial differences between the watercolors of the Dutch period and those of 1887: the former are mainly subdued and somewhat muddy in color, while the Paris sheets are transparent and bright. This resulted not just from a more widely varied palette but from a technical shift as well. In the Netherlands Van Gogh worked almost exclusively with opaque watercolor, sometimes highly thinned. In Paris he began working like a traditional watercolorist, with transparent instead of opaque watercolors, which strengthened the clarity of his works. In their compositions, bright colors, and small figures, these cityscapes owed their inspiration to ukiyo-e prints, and Van Gogh consciously followed in the footsteps of the great Japanese masters he so admired and whose works he collected avidly.

Van Gogh's artistic possibilities increased enormously in Paris, and he was well aware of it. Filled with confidence in his abilities, he left in February 1888 for Arles, where he would realize his full potential as a draftsman.

SvH

32. *Standing Female Nude Seen from the Side*

Late January–late February 1886
Graphite on wove paper watermarked J WHATMAN 1884
50.9 x 39.2 cm (20 x 15$^{3}/_{8}$ in.)
Van Gogh Museum, Amsterdam (Vincent van Gogh Foundation) (d 22 V/1962)
F1699, JH1013

Provenance: Theo van Gogh (d. 1891); by inheritance to his son, Vincent Willem van Gogh (1890–1978), as part of his collection, administered by his widow, Johanna van Gogh-Bonger (d. 1925), 1891; ownership transferred to the Vincent van Gogh Foundation, 1962; placed on permanent loan at the Van Gogh Museum, Amsterdam, 1973.

Selected exhibitions: London 1962, no. 31 (as part of F1363); Amsterdam 2001–2; Hamburg 2002, no. 14.

Summary of the literature: Not listed in De la Faille 1928. Hammacher (in London 1962, p. 50) included the drawing among the fifteen cited as F1363; he regarded it as a highly personal interpretation of the Venus de Milo and dated it to February 1886. In De la Faille 1970 (no. 1699) the work was titled "Study after Living Model" and dated to winter 1885–86; the medium was given as carpenter's pencil. Hulsker (1980, no. 1013) also saw the drawing as a study from life, made at a drawing club, and dated it to February 1886. Van Uitert and Hoyle (1987, p. 431, no. 2.381) followed Hulsker. Heenk 1995, p. 138. Vellekoop and Van Heugten (2001, pp. 71–82) erroneously claimed that Hulsker had believed it a work done at the academy. They narrowed the dating to late January–late February 1886, the period when Van Gogh often worked at the drawing clubs, and wrote that the figure is anatomically incorrect but has the expressivity of the large peasant studies from Nuenen. The same model is seen in F1696.

A number of nude studies have been attributed to Van Gogh's period at the Antwerp academy. There is no evidence, however, that he ever drew from the live model at the academy itself, and all the works in this genre, including this sheet, were undoubtedly executed during his evening sessions at one of the drawing clubs he attended. This is also indicated by the style of the drawings, which makes no concessions to the expectations of the academy, for there were no teachers present during these exercises. *Standing Female Nude Seen from the Side* resembles the drawings from Nuenen: realistic expression prevails over anatomical correctness, as, for example, the somewhat unfortunate right leg demonstrates.

SvH

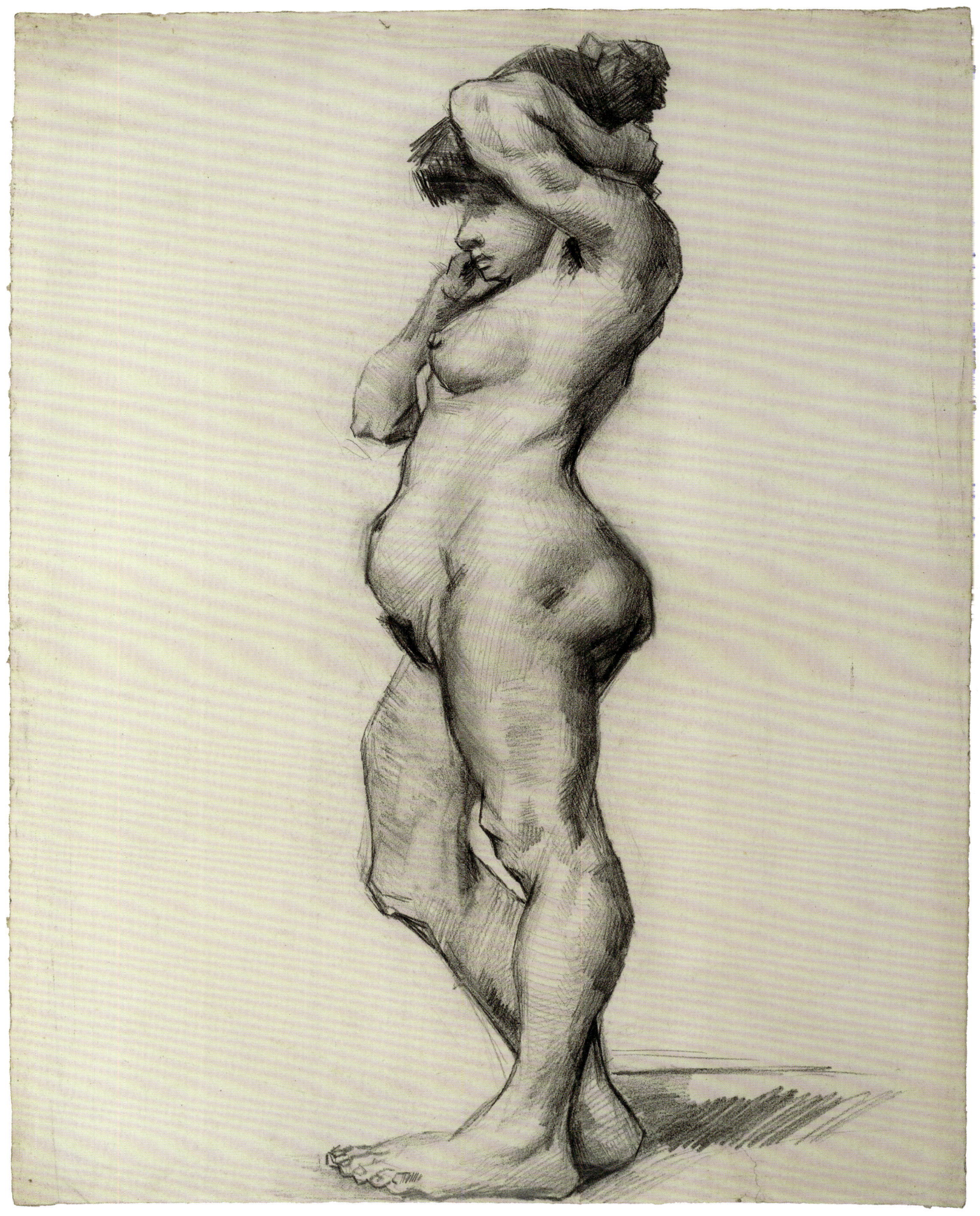

33. *The Discus Thrower*

First half of February 1886
Black chalks on wove paper watermarked TS & Z
56.1 x 44.5 cm (22 1/8 x 17 1/2 in.)
Van Gogh Museum, Amsterdam (Vincent van Gogh Foundation) (d 398 V/1962)
F1364e, JH1080

Provenance: Theo van Gogh (d. 1891); by inheritance to his son, Vincent Willem van Gogh (1890–1978), as part of his collection, administered by his widow, Johanna van Gogh-Bonger (d. 1925), 1891; ownership transferred to the Vincent van Gogh Foundation, 1962; placed on permanent loan at the Van Gogh Museum, Amsterdam, 1973.

Selected exhibitions: Otterlo 1990, no. 138; Amsterdam 2001–2; Hamburg 2002, no. 12.

Summary of the literature: Not in De la Faille 1928, although possibly among two groups of fifteen studies each (nos. 1363, 1364). Bern 1954–55 (no. 120) was the first publication of the drawing (as F1364), with the title "Studie nach männlichem Akt." De la Faille 1970 (no. 1364e) listed the title as "Study after Plaster Statuette: the Discus Thrower" and dated the sheet to Paris 1886. Hulsker (1980, no. 1080) adopted that title and narrowed the date to April–June 1886. Van Uitert and Hoyle 1987, p. 437, no. 2.419. Van der Wolk (1987, pp. 270–71) noted the strong similarities to a figure in the sketchbook published as SB 2, and in Otterlo 1990 (pp. 179, 191) was the first to situate the sheet in Antwerp in early 1886 on the evidence of the watermark, TS & Z, on paper that Van Gogh must have taken with him from Nuenen. Heenk (1995, pp. 135, 136, 270) followed Van der Wolk and referred to the sheet as the only academic study from Antwerp; she gave charcoal as one of the drawing materials. Hulsker (1996, no. 1080) stood by the dating to Paris, spring 1886. Vellekoop and Van Heugten (2001, pp. 63–70) accepted Van der Wolk's arguments for Antwerp and discussed in detail academic practice as well as Van Gogh's own theoretical premises. They wrote that the drawing is a copy after a cast of Myron's *Discus Thrower*, and they based the date—first half of February—on the fact that at this time Van Gogh began practicing drawing sculptures against a dark background, referring to his works from this period as "brusque" [436].

Despite his earlier aversion to drawing plaster casts, in Antwerp Van Gogh took to the discipline with relish, realizing that it would help him improve his understanding of human anatomy. Students at the Antwerp academy were expected to work three or four days on a single drawing, so that during his six-week stay Van Gogh probably executed about a dozen sheets. We know both from his letters and from eyewitness accounts that he copied several different sculptures, but this study from a cast of the *Discus Thrower* (ca. 450 B.C.) by Myron of Eleutherai is the only example to have survived. The drawing follows the academic method in its emphasis on contour but is otherwise marked by the angular expressivity so typical of Van Gogh's style.

Van Gogh here employed two types of chalk, a soft one and a harder variety with a hint of brown. As in the large peasant studies from the summer of 1885, he applied water over the chalk, probably with a brush, creating a grayish wash. Once the sheet dried he used an eraser to produce the lighter areas.

SvH

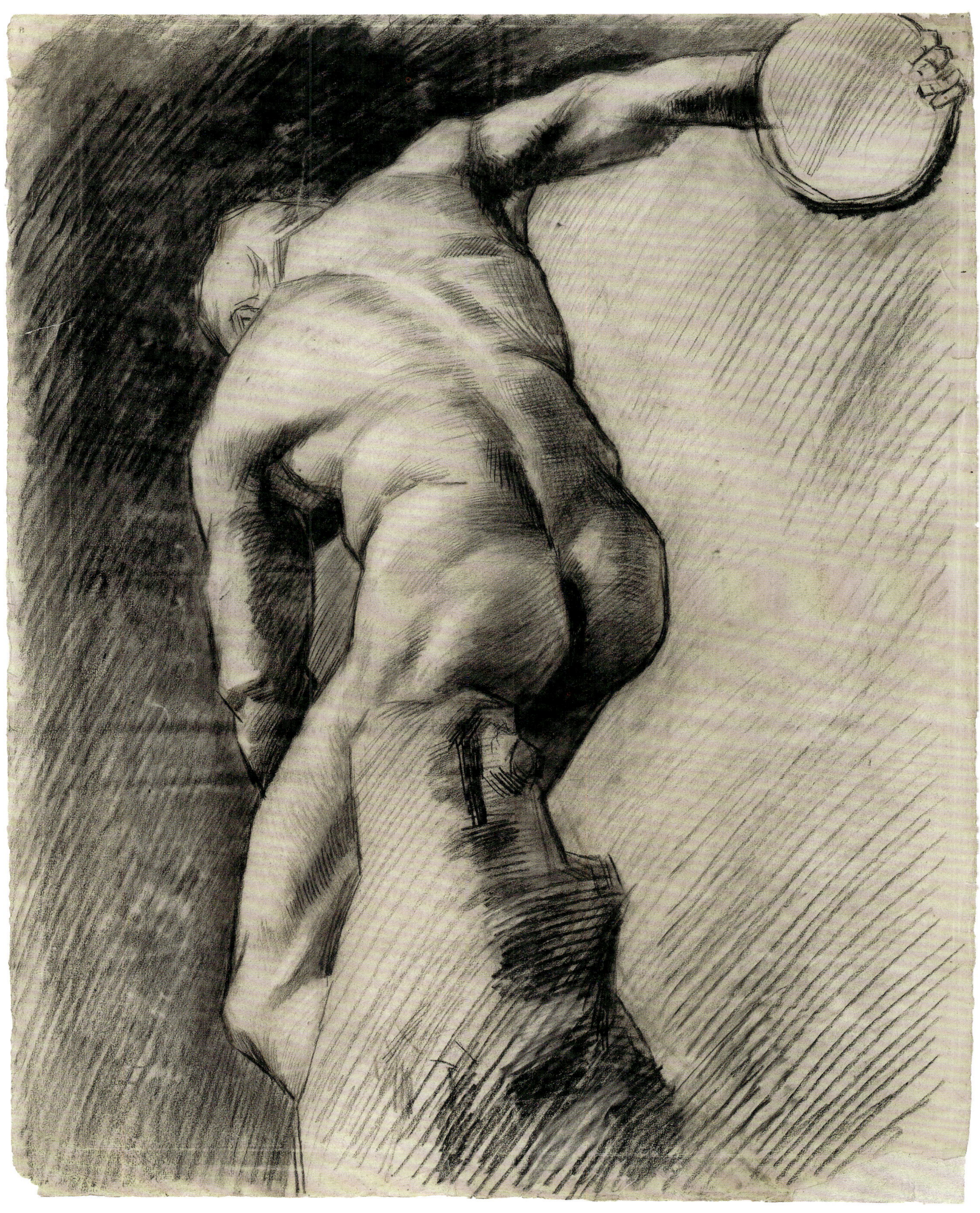

34. *Seated Girl and Venus*

October 1886–January 1887
Black chalk on laid paper watermarked MICHALLET
47.5 x 62 cm (18¾ x 24⅜ in.)
Van Gogh Museum, Amsterdam (Vincent van Gogh Foundation) (d 12 V/1962)
F1366v, JH1044

Amsterdam only

Provenance: Theo van Gogh (d. 1891); by inheritance to his son, Vincent Willem van Gogh (1890–1978), as part of his collection, administered by his widow, Johanna van Gogh-Bonger (d. 1925), 1891; ownership transferred to the Vincent van Gogh Foundation, 1962; placed on permanent loan at the Van Gogh Museum, Amsterdam, 1973.

Selected exhibitions: Amsterdam 2001–2; Hamburg 2002, no. 42.

Summary of the literature: De la Faille (1928, no. 1366) gave the title "Études pour un enfant nu assis," dated the work to the Paris period, and described it as "une feuille avec cinq croquis divers de la tête et de la fillette assise." He described one side of the sheet (recto) as having four studies of the girl, which actually also has a fifth very sketchy one (bringing the total of sketches of her on recto and verso to six, not five), in a separate entry and illustrated that side under F1363. Bowness (in London 1968–69, p. 59), referring to F1367 in which the same girl is depicted, identified the girl as a model in the studio of Fernand Cormon and noted that naked children also feature in Cormon's work. De la Faille 1970 (no. 1366) published the verso of the sheet as F1366v, provided a very detailed, descriptive title—all later publications use similar titles, although some are less elaborate—and dated the sheet to early 1886. It was noted that the girl appears in a number of works and reference was also made to Bowness's remark about the girl depicted on F1367. Hulsker (1980, no. 1044) dated the work to April–June 1886, the period he believed Van Gogh worked with Cormon. Van Uitert and Hoyle (1987, p. 436, no. 2.415) followed Hulsker with a date of spring 1886. De la Faille 1992 (no. 1366) dated the sheet to early 1886. Heenk (1995, pp. 139, 144, 146) noted that the small study of a boxer on F1366v illustrates Van Gogh's notion that knowledge of the art of antiquity is not a hindrance to realism but rather a help [451]. She regarded the studies as independent works rather than as preparatory sketches for paintings. Vellekoop and Van Heugten (2001, pp. 112–37) identified the statuette as a Venus and suggested the sheet was executed in Cormon's studio. They judged Van Gogh to have worked there from October 1886 to January 1887, and they referred to a study of a nude girl by Cormon. They also noted that in the studies done at Cormon's, both Van Gogh and Toulouse-Lautrec used laid paper with the watermark MICHALLET, as in this sheet, which may have been purchased at the studio or nearby.

Van Gogh drew from both live models and plaster casts at the studio of Fernand Cormon. This large sheet combines the two disciplines. One half is taken up with a study of a little girl, while the other shows a sculpted Venus standing on one leg. These figures appear repeatedly in drawings from this period, and there is even a small painting of the little girl (F215, fig. 105). Van Gogh used these studies to practice the techniques of *dessin au trait* and *dessin ombré*, that is, drawing in which the modeling is achieved through contour and line, or by shading, respectively. In some of the sheets, one or the other method predominates; in others, like this one, they are successfully combined.

SvH

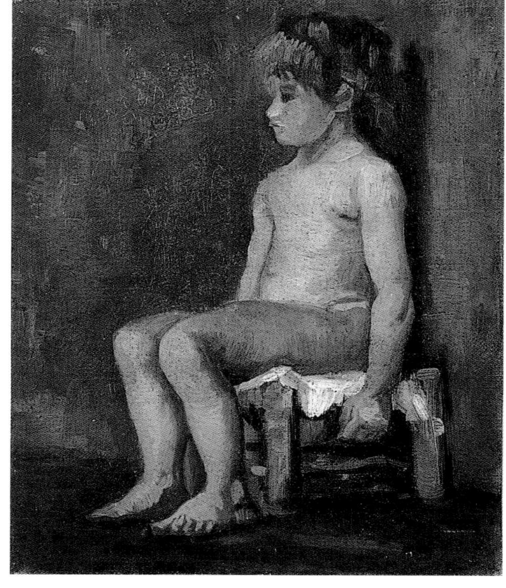

Fig. 105. *Nude Girl, Seated* (F215), October 1886–January 1887. Oil on canvas, 27 x 22.5 cm (10⅝ x 8⅞ in.). Van Gogh Museum, Amsterdam (Vincent van Gogh Foundation)

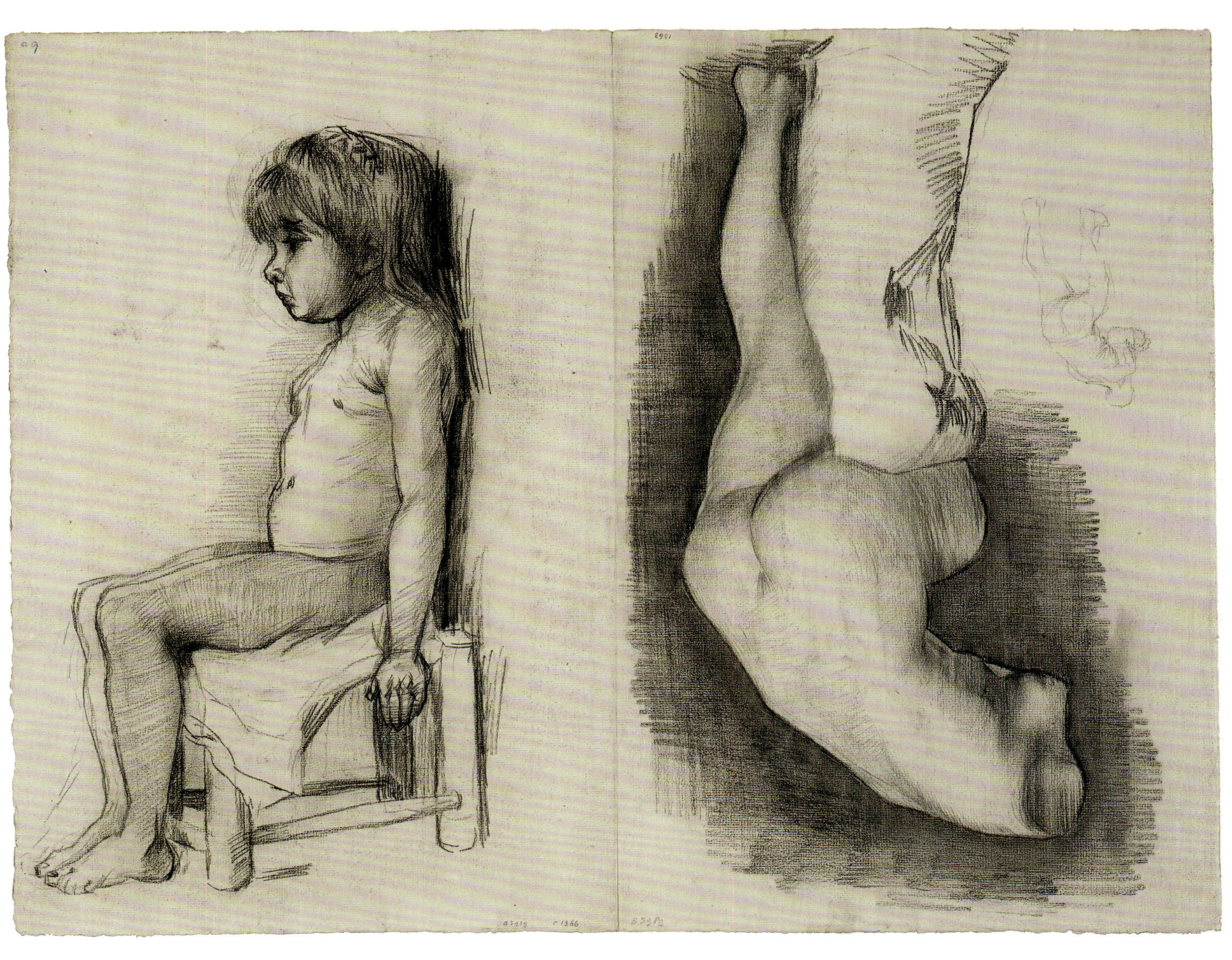

35. *Self-Portraits*

January–June 1887
Pen and ink, graphite on wove paper blind embossed
VIDALON-LES-ANNONAY; ANCNE MANUFRE CANSON & MONTGOLFIER
31.1 x 24.4 cm (12¼ x 9⅝ in.)
Van Gogh Museum, Amsterdam (Vincent van Gogh Foundation) (d 432 V/1962)
F1378r, JH1197

Provenance: Theo van Gogh (d. 1891); by inheritance to his son, Vincent Willem van Gogh (1890–1978), as part of his collection, administered by his widow, Johanna van Gogh-Bonger (d. 1925), 1891; ownership transferred to the Vincent van Gogh Foundation, 1962; placed on permanent loan at the Van Gogh Museum, Amsterdam, 1973.

Selected exhibitions: London 1968–69, no. 92; Tokyo–Kyōto–Nagoya 1976–77, no. 48; Paris 1988, no. 36; Otterlo 1990, no. 164; Hamburg 1995, unnumbered; Amsterdam 2001–2; Hamburg 2002, no. 84.

Summary of the literature: De la Faille (1928) published the drawing as no. 1378, with no differentiation between recto and verso, under the title "Feuille d'étude avec trois croquis de son portrait"—the titles used in subsequent publications are all variants—and dated it to the Paris period. Bromig-Kolleritz (1954, p. 101) saw the sheet as a preliminary study for F345 and dated it equally broadly: March 1886–February 1888. De Gruyter (1961, pp. 102, 103) dated it to Paris 1886. Erpel (1964, p. 74) followed Bromig-Kolleritz. Bowness (in London 1968–69, p. 69) gave the date September–December 1887 and regarded the drawing as an "expressive development" from the other drawn self-portrait, F1379. In De la Faille 1970, this side of the sheet was numbered 1378r, dated to the summer of 1887, and compared to F380. Hulsker (1980, no. 1197) dated the work to October–December 1886 and regarded it as a preliminary study for a painted self-portrait. He rejected the earlier suggestions of its relation to F345 or F380, proposing instead that it was a study for F528. Van Uitert and Hoyle (1987, p. 446, no. 2.471) dated the sheet to winter 1886–87. Welsh-Ovcharov (in Paris 1988, pp. 110, 111) dated it to early 1887, regarded it as a study for F345, and remarked on its stylistic similarities to F1404. Van der Wolk (in Otterlo 1990, pp. 193, 216) pointed out that the paper is identical to that used for F1401, F1411, and F1406. Heenk (1995, p. 154) referred only to F1401 as on identical paper. Vellekoop and Van Heugten (2001, pp. 249, 255–59, 303) dated the sheet to January–June 1887 and noted the (Neo-Impressionist) style, similar to F1404 and F1718. They felt the large head might have been a study for F345, and they wrote that the sheet was once part of a larger piece of paper to which F1404 and F1718 also belonged.

These studies are in marked contrast to Van Gogh's thirty-five painted self-portraits. In addition to the sheet included here, which shows two complete likenesses and several details of the face, there is also a pencil study of the artist's features (F1379, fig. 106). The larger of the two heads was laid down with a pencil and worked up in pen and ink; the detail to the right—the nose and one eye—was done directly in ink. This carefully executed work may well have been a preparatory study for the self-portrait in the Art Institute of Chicago (F345, fig. 107), but we cannot be certain since Van Gogh often depicted himself from this angle. The second head is far too sketchy to have been anything more than a simple exercise.

A rectangular piece is missing from the sheet at the upper left (restored). On the verso is a sketch of a sorrowing nude woman (F1378v).

SvH

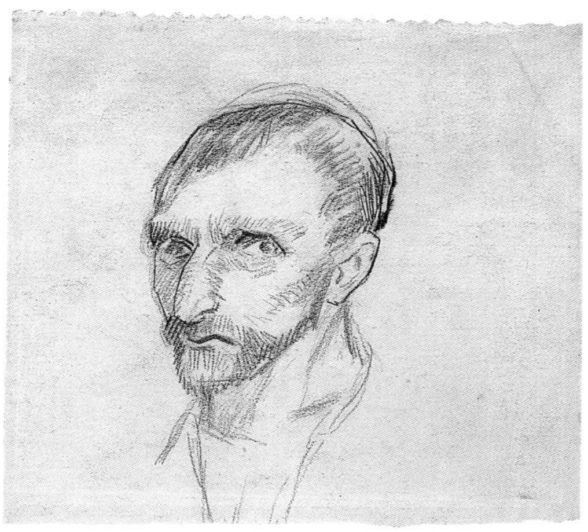

Fig. 106. *Self-Portrait* (F1379), January–June 1887. Graphite on wove paper, 19.2 x 21.1 cm (7½ x 8¼ in.). Van Gogh Museum, Amsterdam (Vincent van Gogh Foundation)

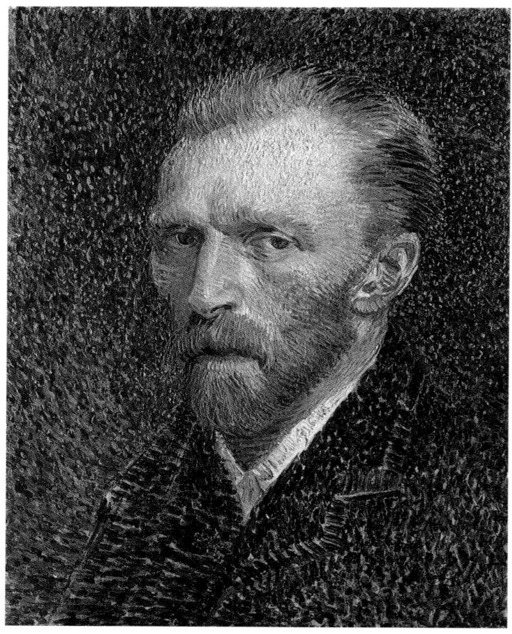

Fig. 107. *Self-Portrait* (F345), 1887. Oil on artist's board mounted on cradled panel, 41 x 32.5 cm (16⅛ x 12¾ in.). The Art Institute of Chicago, Joseph Winterbotham Collection

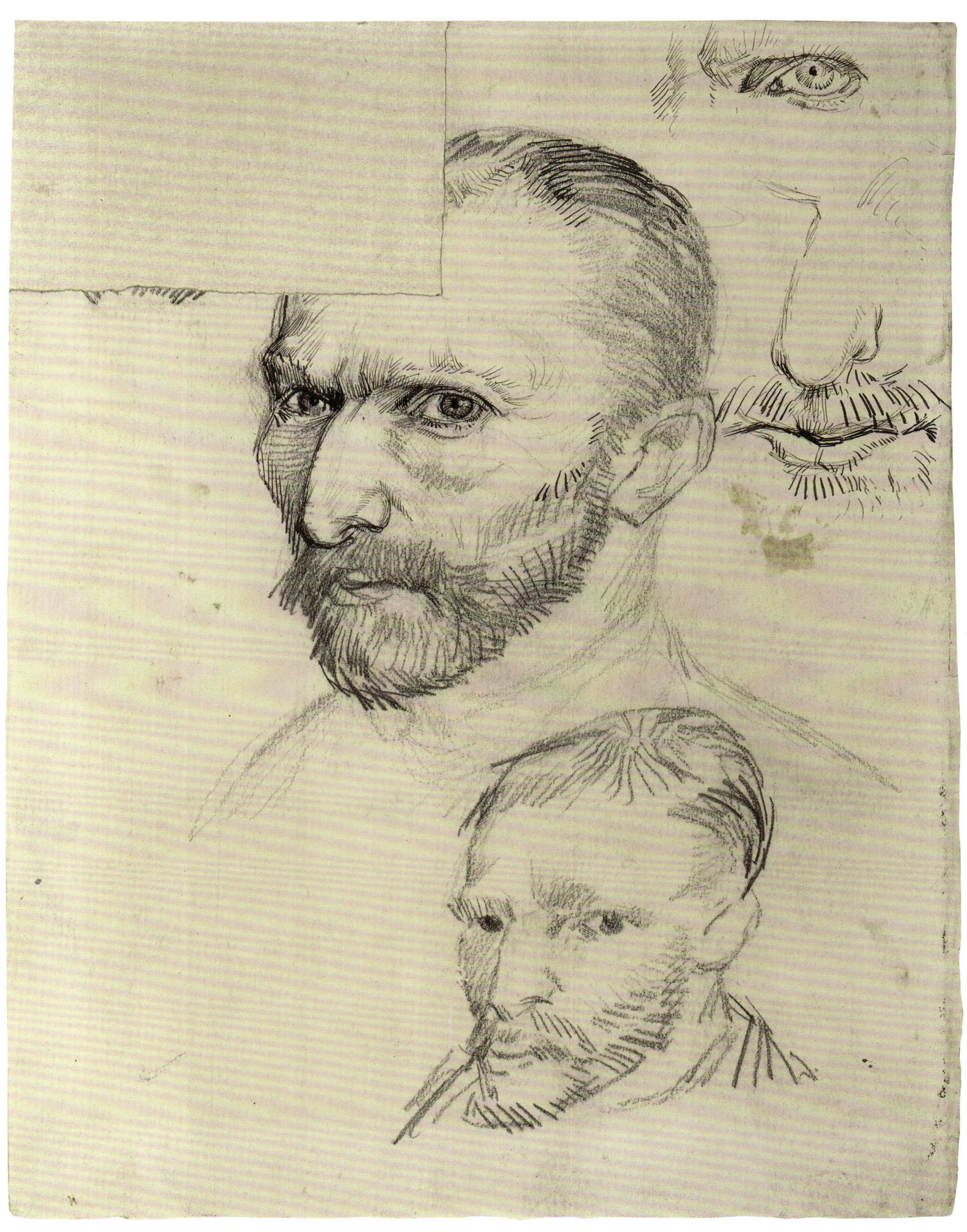

36. *The Blute-Fin Mill*

February–March 1887
Pen and ink, graphite on laid paper
42.5 x 56.5 cm (16¾ x 22¼ in.)
The Phillips Collection, Washington, acquired 1953 (0798)
F1396a, JH1185

Provenance: Theo van Gogh (d. 1891); by inheritance to his son, Vincent Willem van Gogh, as part of his collection, administered by his widow, Johanna van Gogh-Bonger, 1891; sold by her to Artz en De Bois, Haarlem (for 1,000 gulden), 1912; H. Stinnes, Cologne, 1917; bought back by Kunsthandel J. H. de Bois, Haarlem, 1917; Elizabeth Hudson, Syracuse, 1934–53; sold by her to The Phillips Collection, Washington, 1953.

Selected exhibitions: Amsterdam 1905, no. 354; Cologne–Frankfurt 1910; Berlin 1910, no. 66; Amsterdam 1917, no. 6; Otterlo 1990, no. 152.

Summary of the literature: Not in De la Faille 1928; De la Faille 1970 (no. 1396a) referred to the mill as the Moulin de la Galette, dated the sheet to the winter of 1886–87, and linked the drawing to a very similar view of the same mill by Hendrik Koning (now in the Van Gogh Museum). Hulsker (1980, no. 1185) called the mill the Blute-Fin, but he dated the drawing to the autumn of 1886; he also mentioned the Koning painting and suggested that the artists worked together from the same spot. Passantino 1985, p. 93; Feilchenfeldt and Veenenbos 1988, p. 130. Van der Wolk (in Otterlo 1990, p. 204) again wrote of the Moulin de la Galette, and he dated the work to early 1887. Heijbroek and Wouthuysen (1993, p. 203) noted the provenance with reference to Artz en De Bois. Heenk 1994, p. 37. Heenk (1995, p. 243) related the sheet loosely to F348a.

The windmills on Montmartre had been a popular motif for artists since the beginning of the nineteenth century. Three of them were still standing in Van Gogh's time, and he often took them as his subject. The mill in this drawing is the Moulin Blute-Fin (built in 1622), often mistakenly referred to as the Moulin de la Galette. In fact, none of the mills bore that particular name, which instead applied to the whole entertainment district of which the Blute-Fin was part (see also F1406, cat. 39). The terrace on top of the mill, a popular place, afforded a panoramic view of Paris. In making his drawing, Van Gogh sat looking in a northwesterly direction, probably with the Moulin Radet behind him. The small tavern there may have been where Van Gogh took up his position.

Given the medium (graphite and ink on laid paper) this drawing was likely part of the group of works executed in February–March 1887 to which *A Guinguette* (F1407, cat. 37) also belongs. The bare trees at the left confirm a dating to the late winter.

SvH

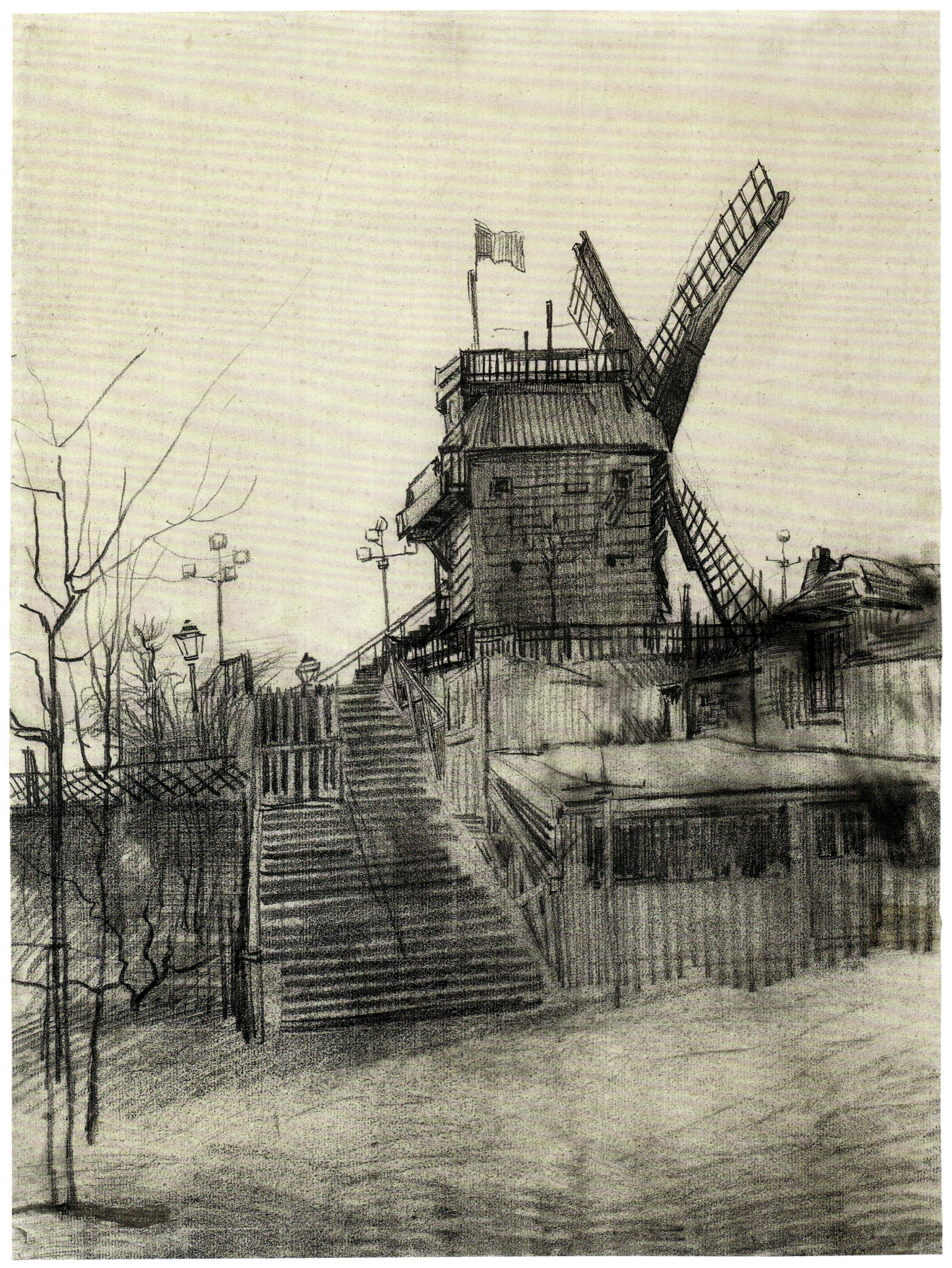

37. *A Guinguette*

February–March 1887
Pen, brush, and ink, white chalk, graphite on laid paper
38.7 x 52.5 cm (15¼ x 20⅝ in.)
Van Gogh Museum, Amsterdam (Vincent van Gogh Foundation) (d 351 V/1962)
F1407, JH1034

Provenance: Theo van Gogh (d. 1891); by inheritance to his son, Vincent Willem van Gogh (1890–1978), as part of his collection, administered by his widow, Johanna van Gogh-Bonger (d. 1925), 1891; placed on loan at the Stedelijk Museum, Amsterdam, 1931–73; ownership transferred to the Vincent van Gogh Foundation, 1962; placed on permanent loan at the Van Gogh Museum, Amsterdam, 1973.

Selected exhibitions: Groningen 1897; Amsterdam 1905, no. 355; Berlin 1906, no. 56; Amsterdam 1914–15, no. 130; London–Birmingham–Glasgow 1947–48, no. 137; New York–Chicago 1949–50, no. 65; London 1968–69, no. 59; Tokyo–Kyōto–Nagoya 1976–77, no. 54; Paris 1988, no. 10; Otterlo 1990, no. 151; Tokyo 2000, no. 17; Amsterdam 2001–2; Hamburg 2002, no. 69.

Summary of the literature: Meier-Graefe 1928a, pl. 15. De la Faille (1928, no. 1407) called the sheet "La guinguette," a title followed with little variation by all later authors, but gave no date. De Gruyter (1961, p. 103) dated the work to March 1886 and regarded it as a predecessor to the painting F238. Bowness (in London 1968–69, p. 58) followed De Gruyter. De la Faille 1970 (no. 1407) gave a date of October 1886 and also made a connection to F238. Leprohon 1972, pp. 349, 350. Hulsker (1980, no. 1034) gave April–June 1886, followed by F238, executed in the autumn. Van Uitert and Hoyle 1987, p. 434, no. 2.402; Feilchenfeldt and Veenenbos 1988, p. 130. Welsh-Ovcharov (in Paris 1988, pp. 58, 59) suggested the locale might be the Guinguette du Moulin Radet, drawn ca. November 1886. Richard (1988, pp. 20, 21) suggested the venue might be the café Au Franc Buveur, drawn in April 1886. Van der Wolk (in Otterlo 1990, p. 203) dated the work later than had previously been the case, to early 1887. Heenk 1994, p. 37. Heenk (1995, pp. 152, 243) also saw the drawing as a preliminary study for the painting. Vellekoop and Van Heugten (2001, pp. 216–20) proposed a date of February–March 1887 on the basis of the technique, which resembles that of a group of works of this period, among them F1393 and F1394, as well as F1392, dated 1887, and said it is impossible to identify the location with any certainty.

With this drawing of a *guinguette*, a kind of working-class café and dance site, Van Gogh added the theme of Paris nightlife to his repertoire. Avant-garde painters, with their love of all aspects of modern life, had long found such themes of interest, but apart from a small sketch of a dance hall made in Antwerp (F1350a, fig. 108), Van Gogh had not tackled the subject. The exact location of the café can no longer be determined (see Summary of the literature); the structure also appears in a small painting executed in the autumn of 1886 (F238, fig. 109). The drawing belongs to a group of six or seven sheets depicting views of the city. *A Guinguette* and two other works from this series were done on a type of blue paper that has faded over time (see "Metamorphoses: Van Gogh's Drawings Then and Now").

The edges reveal that the paper was once blue-gray. Moreover, in addition to having lost its original color, the paper has yellowed considerably because it contains wood pulp.

SvH

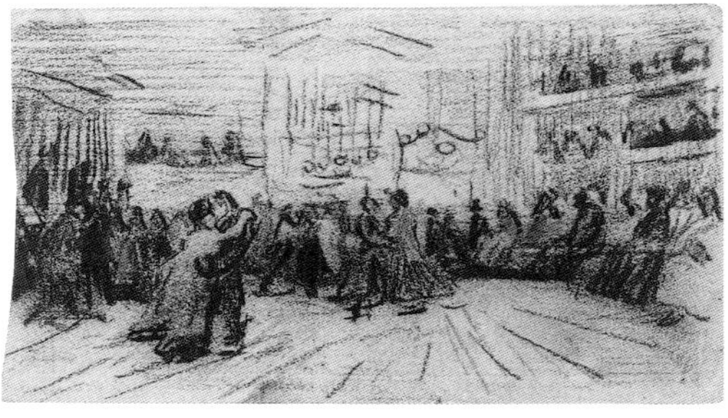

Fig. 108. *Dance Hall* (F1350a), December 1885. Colored chalks on wove paper, 9.2 x 16.3 cm (3⅝ x 6⅜ in.). Van Gogh Museum, Amsterdam (Vincent van Gogh Foundation)

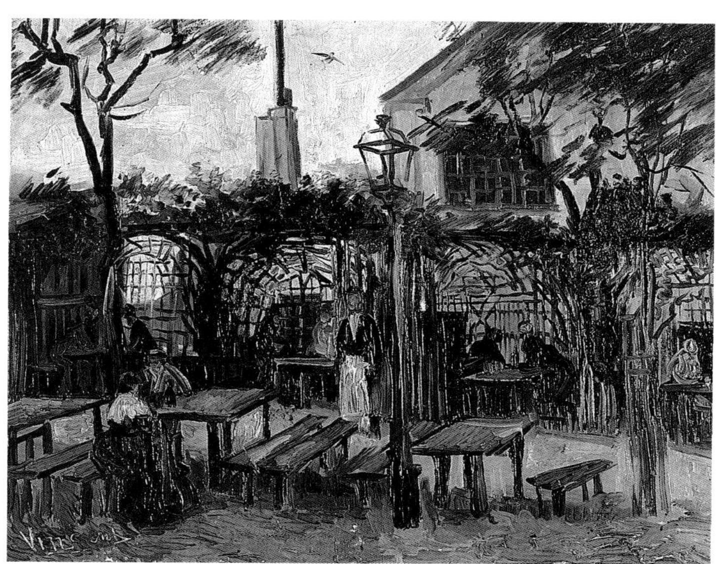

Fig. 109. *Café Terrace (La Guinguette)* (F238), autumn 1886. Oil on canvas, 49 x 64 cm (19¼ x 25¼ in.). Musée d'Orsay, Paris (photo: Gérard Blot—RMN/Art Resource, NY)

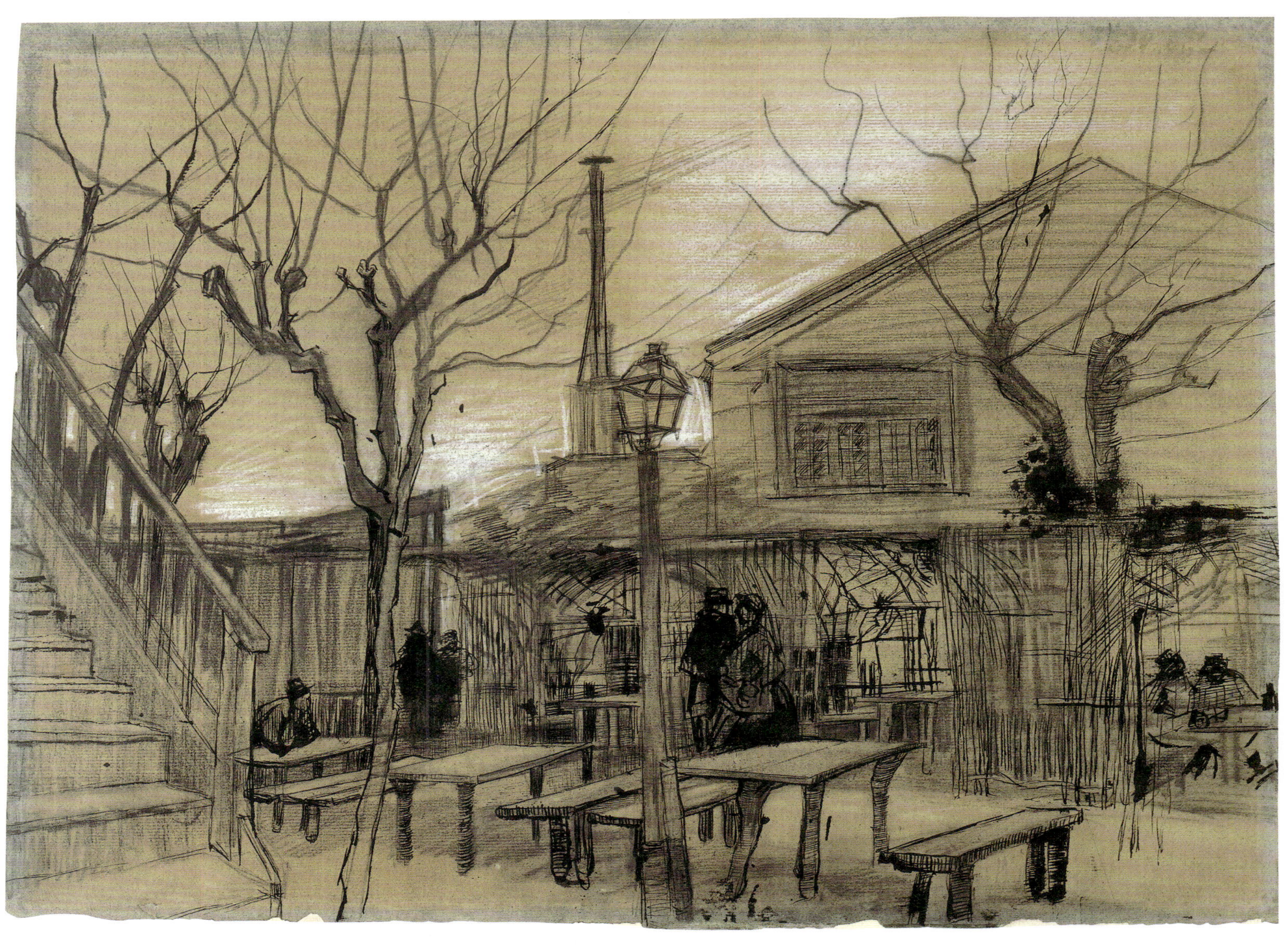

38. *Gate in the Paris Ramparts*

June–September 1887
Transparent and opaque watercolor, pen and ink, graphite on wove paper
24.1 x 31.6 cm (9½ x 12½ in.)
Traces of perspective guidelines
Van Gogh Museum, Amsterdam (Vincent van Gogh Foundation) (d 420 V/1962)
F1401, JH1284

Provenance: Theo van Gogh (d. 1891); by inheritance to his son, Vincent Willem van Gogh (1890–1978), as part of his collection, administered by his widow, Johanna van Gogh-Bonger (d. 1925), 1891; placed on loan at the Stedelijk Museum, Amsterdam, 1931–73; ownership transferred to the Vincent van Gogh Foundation, 1962; placed on permanent loan at the Van Gogh Museum, Amsterdam, 1973.

Selected exhibitions: Paris 1896–97 (or possibly F1400); Amsterdam 1914–15, no. 127; Utrecht 1923, no. 28; Rotterdam 1923; Berlin 1927–28, no. 47; London–Birmingham–Glasgow 1947–48, no. 135; London 1968–69, no. 85; Toronto–Amsterdam 1981, no. 6; Paris 1988, no. 48; Otterlo 1990, no. 161; Amsterdam 2001–2; Hamburg 2002, no. 98.

Summary of the literature: De la Faille (1928, no. 1401) gave the title "Entre les fortifications" and dated the sheet to Paris. Cooper (1955, p. 56) related it to F1400, F1402, and F1403, and dated it to the summer of 1887—a date followed by all later authors. He noted Van Gogh's remarkable development. De la Faille 1970 (no. 1401) called the sheet "La barrière with horse-tramway"—few subsequent authors have deviated from this—and suggested the location is the same as that seen in F1400 and F1719. Hulsker (1980, no. 1284) noted the influence of Japanese woodcuts and saw F1719v as a possible preliminary study. Welsh-Ovcharov (in Toronto–Amsterdam 1981, p. 105) regarded the Porte de Clichy or the Porte de Saint-Ouen as possible locations, noted the similarities in theme to Seurat's *Sunday Afternoon on the Island of La Grande Jatte*, and suggested Van Gogh may have been inspired by the Goncourt brothers' *Germinie Lacerteux*. Van Uitert and Hoyle 1987, p. 448, no. 2.486. Thomson (1987, pp. 18, 20, 21, 23) pointed out this work's technical dissimilarity to Van Gogh's other depictions of the Paris ramparts. He regarded the gate as the Porte de Clichy. Welsh-Ovcharov (in Paris 1988, pp. 134, 135) further specified the topography. Heenk (1995, pp. 151, 152, 154) called attention to the color annotations and noted that the work was probably finished in the studio. Vellekoop and Van Heugten (2001, pp. 300–303) gave the title as "Gate in the Paris ramparts," since the identification of the subject as the Porte de Clichy is probable but not entirely certain; they also provided a detailed description of the technique.

In Van Gogh's time, Paris was still encircled by a thirty-kilometer defensive wall and ramparts (now destroyed). This watercolor depicts one of the fifty-two gates that gave entrance to the city, perhaps the Porte de Clichy. The ramparts are also the subject of three larger watercolors. In contrast to those, the smaller work shown here—like catalogue entries 39 (F1406) and 40 (F1411)—was inspired by Japanese ukiyo-e prints (see fig. 110). This is evidenced not only by the brilliant coloration and the composition, but also by the numerous little figures populating the scene. The measurements of the sheets are also more or less identical with the classic ōban format (ca. 34 x 22.5 cm)—although most ōban woodcuts are vertical.

This sheet probably comes from the same sketch pad as catalogue entries 39 (F1406) and 40 (F1411) and exhibits the same traces of squaring in pencil, indicating the use of the perspective frame. Van Gogh also made notes on the coloration: "violet" on the wall at the left, "jaune" on the grass at the right, and "rose" at the lower left, suggesting that he finished the drawing in the studio.

SvH

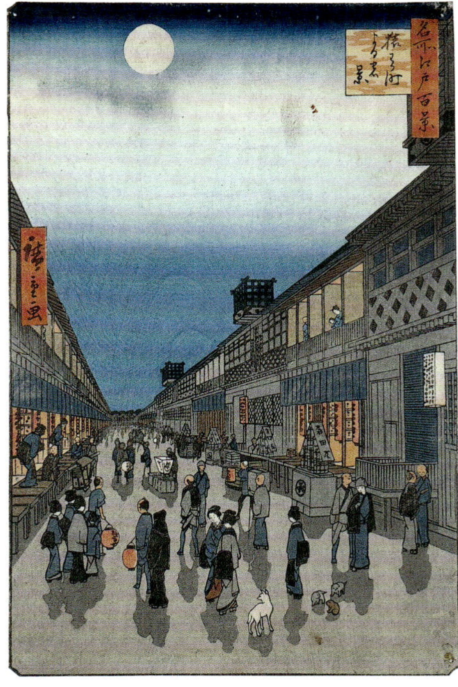

Fig. 110. Utagawa Hiroshige, *View of the Saruwakacho Theater Street by Night*, from the series *A Hundred Views of Famous Places in Edo*, 1856–59. Woodcut, 34 x 22.5 cm (13⅜ x 8⅞ in.). Van Gogh Museum, Amsterdam (Vincent van Gogh Foundation)

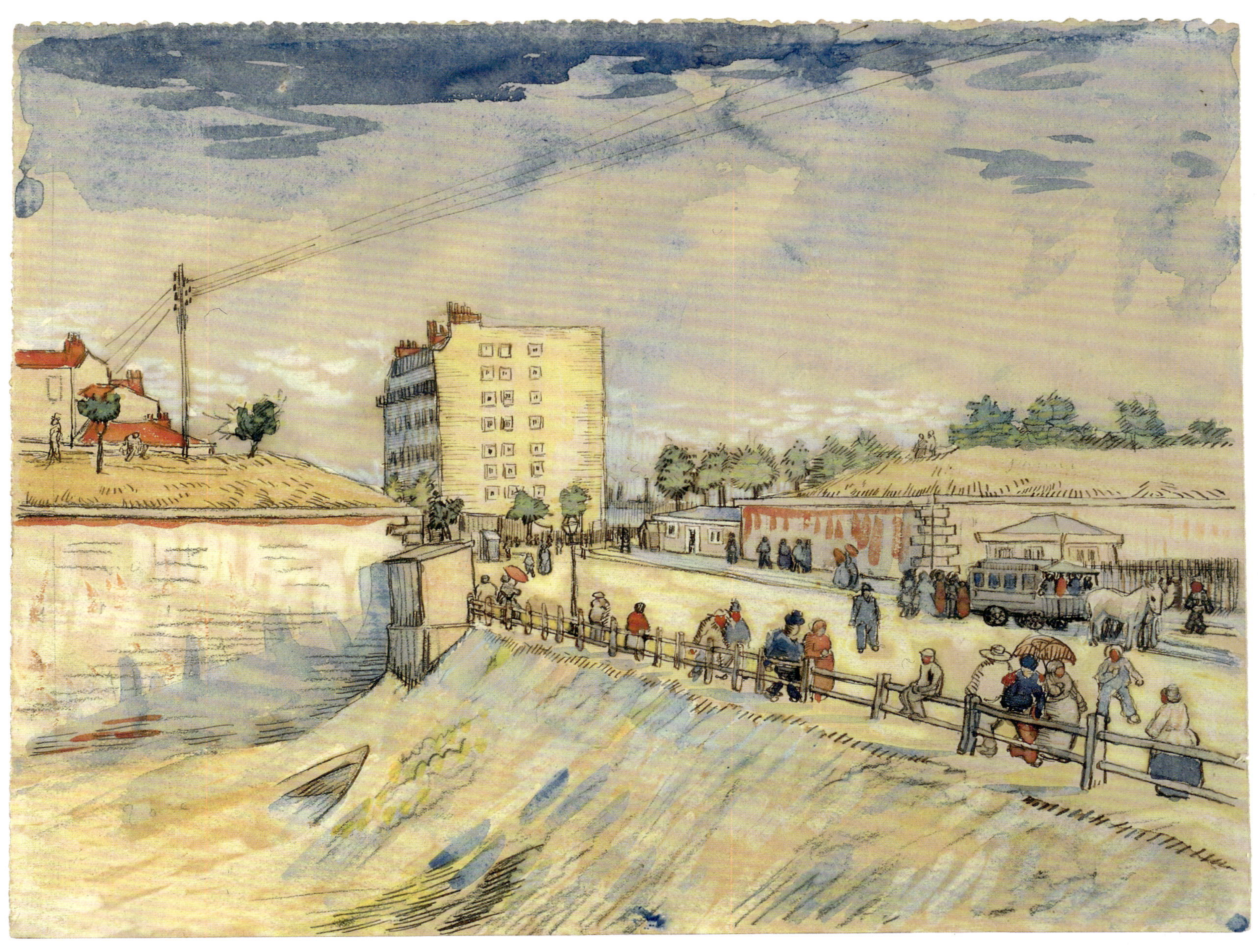

39. *Entrance to the Moulin de la Galette*

June–September 1887
Transparent and opaque watercolor, pen and ink, graphite on wove paper blind embossed VIDALON-LES-ANNONAY ♠ ANCNE MANUFRE CANSON & MONTGOLFIER (truncated at the top and bottom edges)
31.6 x 24 cm (12½ x 9½ in.)
Traces of perspective guidelines
Van Gogh Museum, Amsterdam (Vincent van Gogh Foundation) (d 148 V/1962)
F1406, JH1277

Provenance: Theo van Gogh (d. 1891); by inheritance to his son, Vincent Willem van Gogh (1890–1978), as part of his collection, administered by his widow, Johanna van Gogh-Bonger (d. 1925), 1891; placed on loan at the Stedelijk Museum, Amsterdam, 1931–73; ownership transferred to the Vincent van Gogh Foundation, 1962; placed on permanent loan at the Van Gogh Museum, Amsterdam, 1973.

Selected exhibitions: Amsterdam 1905, no. 364; Berlin 1927–28, no. 50; London–Birmingham–Glasgow 1947–48, no. 136; London 1968–69, no. 84; Tokyo–Kyōto–Nagoya 1976–77, no. 46; Otterlo 1990, no. 163; Amsterdam 2001–2; Hamburg 2002, no. 99.

Summary of the literature: Meier-Graefe 1928a, pl. 17. De la Faille (1928, no. 1406) gave the title "Jour ensoleillé (14 juillet)" but no exact date. Bowness (in London 1968–69, p. 67) maintained the connection to July 14 on the basis of the flag. De la Faille 1970 (no. 1406) entitled the sheet "Garden Entrance on a Sunny Day" but rejected the association with July 14 since the flag is Dutch; the dating to the summer of 1887 was adopted by most later authors. Hulsker (1980, no. 1277) called the work "Path to the Entrance of a Belvedere," dated it to April–June 1887, and refuted the link to July 14 by comparing it with other works. Van Uitert and Hoyle 1987, p. 448, no. 2.482. Richard (1988, pp. 19, 20) provided detailed topographical information and an old photograph of the location (fig. 111). In Otterlo 1990 (pp. 193, 215, 228) it was suggested that the sheet was once part of a sketchbook. Heenk (1995, pp. 153, 154) questioned the sketchbook connection. Vellekoop and Van Heugten (2001, pp. 304–7) gave the location proposed here and followed Richard in his interpretation of the topography; the sheet was probably once part of a sketch pad that was also used for cats. 38 (F1401) and 40 (F1411).

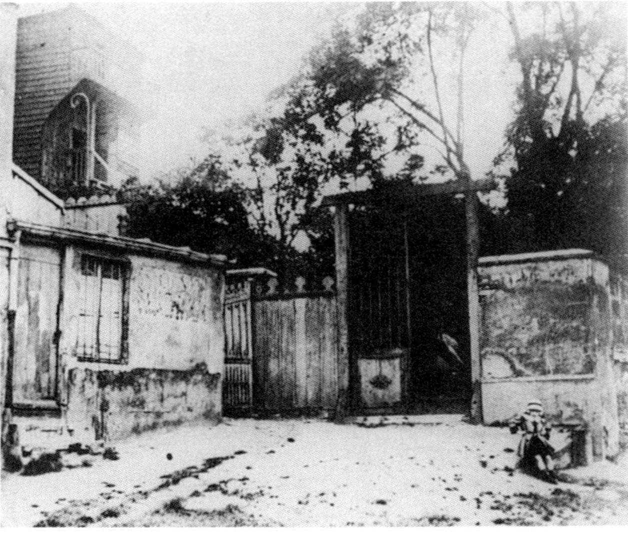

Fig. 111. Photograph of the entrance to the Moulin de la Galette, ca. 1908. From Pierre Richard, "Vincent van Gogh's Montmartre," *Jong Holland* 4, no. 1 (1988), p. 20

Van Gogh drew this view of the entrance to the famous Moulin de la Galette, an area of working mills and places of popular entertainment on Montmartre, from the chemin des Deux Frères, a location that can be identified from a photograph of about 1908 (fig. 111); in 1912 the chemin des Deux Frères was destroyed to make way for the avenue Junot. Van Gogh and many other artists of his generation were greatly inspired by Montmartre, a working-class district with numerous picturesque places. Like this example, a number of Van Gogh's Paris works were executed close to the apartment he and Theo shared at 54 rue Lepic.

SvH

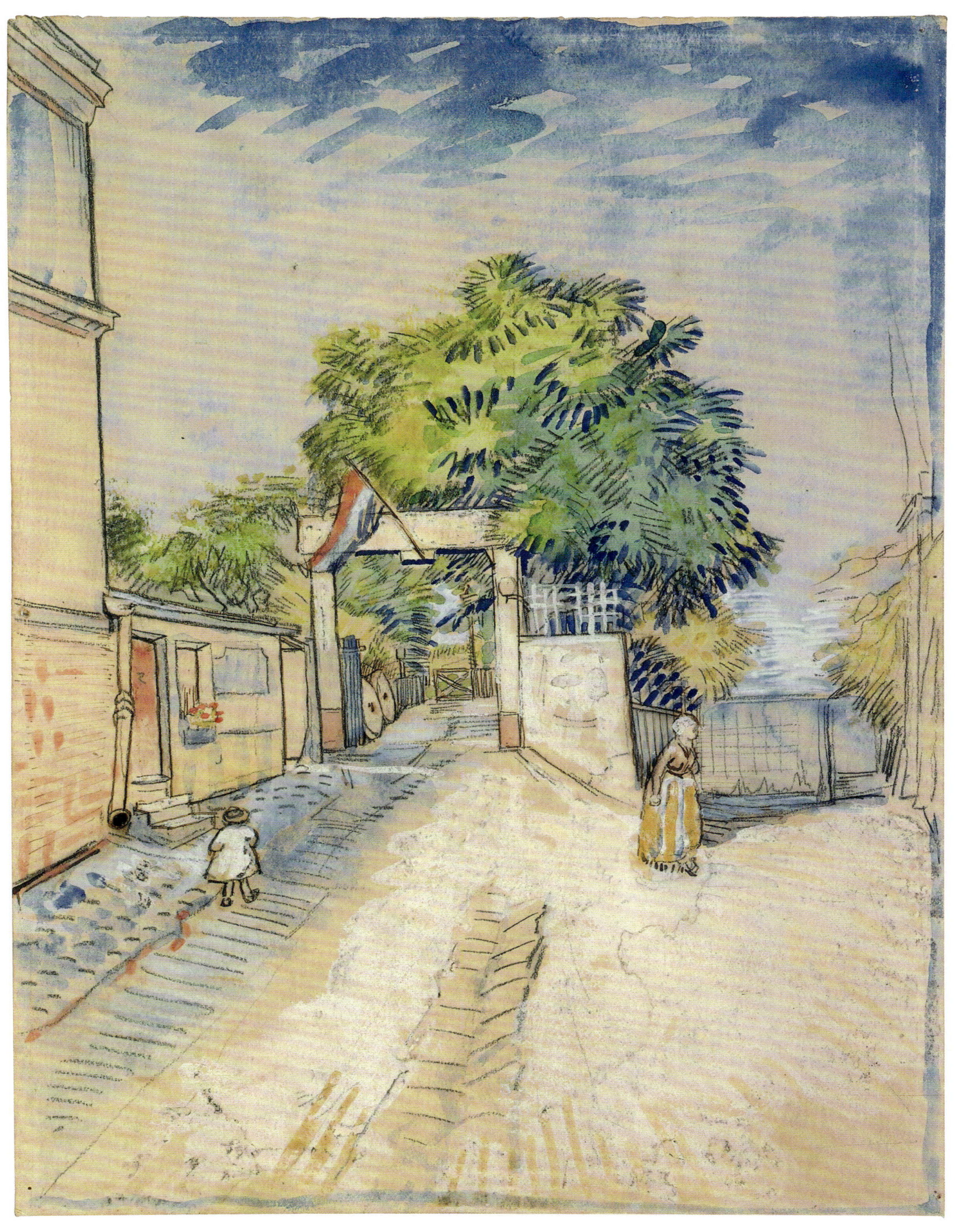

40. *Shed with Sunflowers*

August–September 1887
Transparent and opaque watercolor, pen and ink, graphite on wove paper blind embossed VIDALON-LES ANNONAY ANCNE MANUFRE CANSON & MONTGOLFIER, truncated at the top and bottom edges
31.6 x 24.1 cm (12½ x 9½ in.)
Traces of perspective guidelines
Van Gogh Museum, Amsterdam (Vincent van Gogh Foundation) (d 352 V/1962)
F1411, JH1305

Provenance: Theo van Gogh (d. 1891); by inheritance to his son, Vincent Willem van Gogh (1890–1978), as part of his collection, administered by his widow, Johanna van Gogh-Bonger (d. 1925), 1891; ownership transferred to the Vincent van Gogh Foundation, 1962; placed on permanent loan at the Van Gogh Museum, Amsterdam, 1973.

Selected exhibitions: Paris 1896–97; Amsterdam 1905, no. 353; Amsterdam 1914–15, no. 153; Utrecht 1923, no. 24; Rotterdam 1923; Paris 1937, no. 66; London–Birmingham–Glasgow 1947–48, no. 138; London 1968–69, no. 86; Tokyo–Kyōto–Nagoya 1976–77, no. 55; Otterlo 1990, no. 162; Amsterdam 2001–2; Hamburg 2002, no. 100.

Summary of the literature: De la Faille (1928, no. 1411) situated the drawing in the Paris period and entitled it "Aux environs de Paris." Cooper (1955, p. 58) also saw it as a view of the environs of Paris and dated it to the summer of 1887; this date has been accepted by most later authors. Bowness (in London 1968–69, p. 67) saw the composition as a pendant to F1406 and also compared it to F264a. De la Faille 1970 (no. 1411) gave it the title "Shelter on Montmartre, with Sunflowers," and referred to the similarities to F264a, but dated the canvas to a year earlier. Hulsker (1980, no. 1305) called the drawing "Path in Montmartre with Sunflowers" and regarded the city in the background the same as in cat. 41 (F1410), viewed from more or less the same standpoint on Montmartre. New York 1984, p. 36. Van Uitert and Hoyle (1987, p. 449, no. 2.488) followed De la Faille 1970. Van der Wolk (in Otterlo 1990, pp. 193, 228) remarked that the sheet was originally part of a sketchbook. Heenk (1995, pp. 153, 154) did not believe it was once part of a sketchbook. Hulsker (1996, no. 1305) regarded it as a preliminary study for F264a. Vellekoop and Van Heugten (2001, pp. 308–10) gave a detailed description of the work's genesis and assumed the sheet itself was once part of the same sketch pad as cats. 38 (F1401) and 39 (F1406).

This drawing shows how easy it was for Van Gogh to find picturesque motifs on Montmartre, an area undergoing rapid urbanization but which still retained something of its original rustic character. In the background at the left is the modern city and its factories—a view of Clichy or Saint-Ouen. An almost rural scene dominates the foreground, however. Van Gogh also made a painting of the same spot (F264a, fig. 112), although he must have stood somewhat closer to the shed and viewed it from a slightly different angle. The drawing is not a preliminary study for the canvas, however, but an independent work.

As in the other watercolors of this period, Van Gogh first sketched the scene in pencil. He made use of his perspective frame, as evidenced by the various graphite lines: a horizontal one along the bottom edge, a vertical one along the left side, and a vertical one in the center of the foreground. Another such line can be seen near the vanishing point. The graphite pencil sketch was then worked up in pen and ink, with the watercolor added last. Oxidation of the lead white used in the sky is the cause of the black patches.

SvH

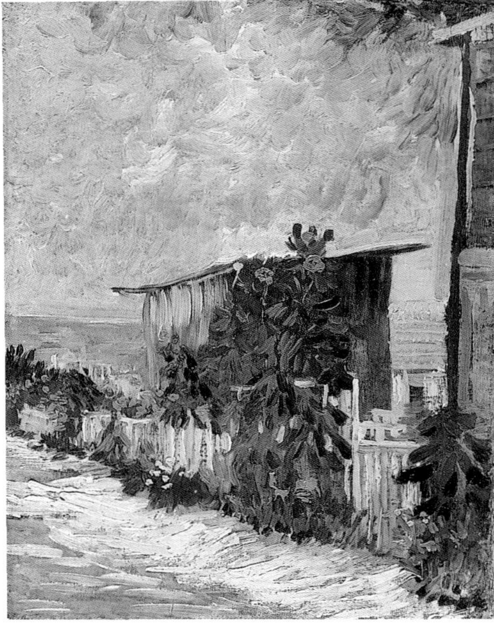

Fig. 112. *Shed with Sunflowers* (F264a), summer 1887. Oil on canvas, 35.5 x 27 cm (14 x 10⅝ in.). Fine Arts Museums of San Francisco, Bequest of Frederick J. Hellman

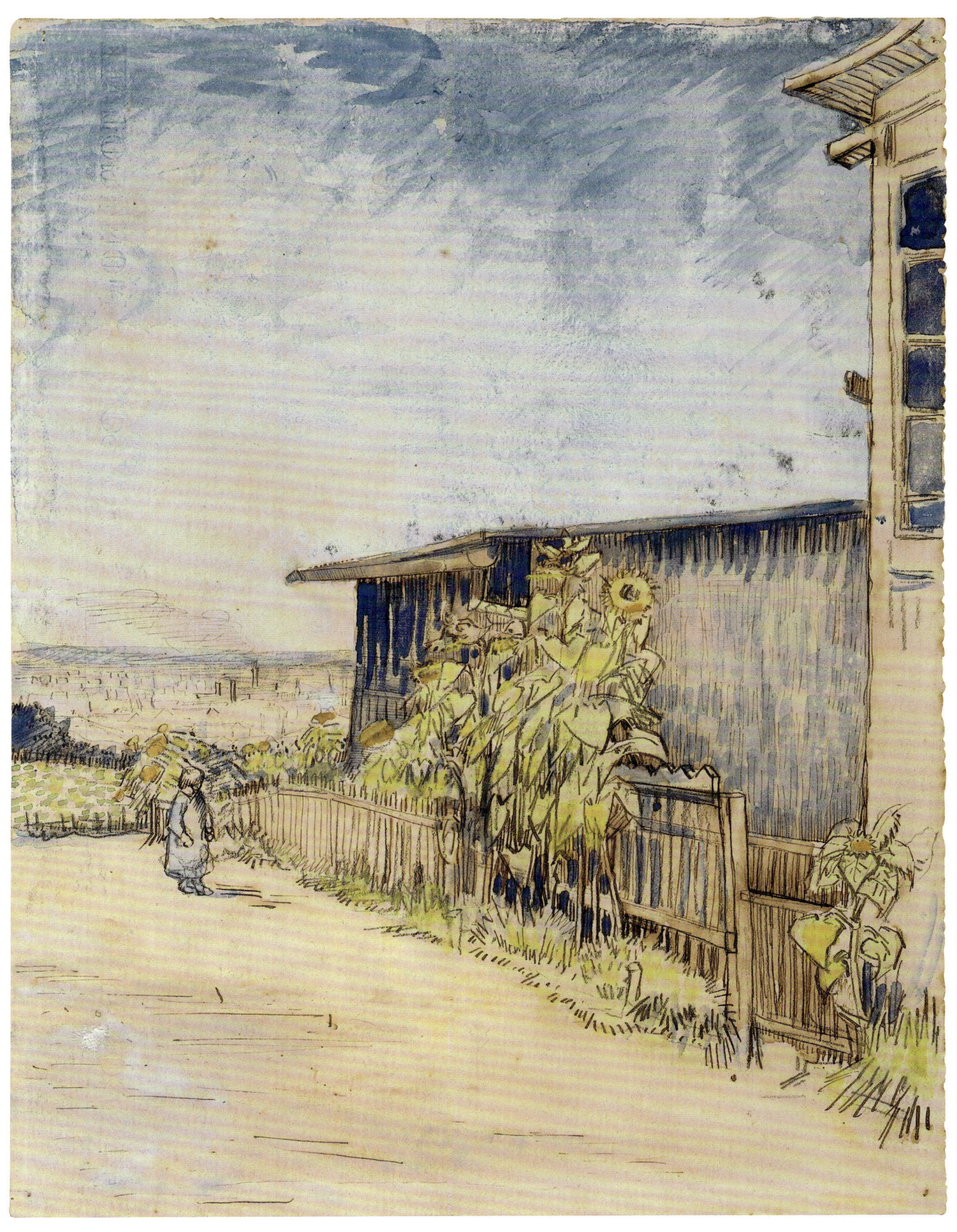

41. *View from Montmartre*

June–September 1887
Opaque watercolor, colored chalk, pen and ink, oil paint, graphite on laid paper
39.5 x 53.5 cm (15½ x 21 in.)
Stedelijk Museum, Amsterdam (A2236)
F1410, JH1286

Provenance: Theo van Gogh (d. 1891); by inheritance to his son, Vincent Willem van Gogh, as part of his collection, administered by his widow, Johanna van Gogh-Bonger, 1891; sold by her, through Artz en De Bois (for 2,000 gulden), to the Vereeniging tot het Vormen van een Openbare Verzameling van Hedendaagsche Kunst, Amsterdam, 1912; given by the association to the Stedelijk Museum, Amsterdam, 1912.

Selected exhibitions: The Hague–Amsterdam 1912, no. 13; Paris 1937, no. 65; Frankfurt 1970, no. 43; Paris 1988, no. 50; Otterlo 1990, no. 159; Florence 1996, no. 76; Martigny 2000, no. 26; Saint Louis–Frankfurt 2001, unnumbered.

Summary of the literature: Stedelijk Museum 1914 (pl. 39) published the first reproduction of the drawing as "Fabriekswijk," a watercolor. De la Faille (1928, no. 1410) dated the sheet to the Paris period and titled it "Vue d'une ville industrielle." Cooper (1955, pp. 54, 55) dated the sheet to the spring of 1887 and suggested it is a view of Asnières. Van Gelder 1958, pp. 25a, 25b. De Gruyter (1961, p. 90) dated it to the summer of 1887. De la Faille 1970 (no. 1410) also dated it to the summer of 1887 but titled the work a more general "Outskirts of Paris." Hulsker (1980, no. 1286) maintained the same date but suggested the town in the distance is Asnières. Thomson (1987, pp. 17, 18, 20) linked the motif to the Paris ramparts. Welsh-Ovcharov (in Paris 1988, pp. 138, 139) saw the jumble of buildings as Saint-Denis/Saint-Ouen and pointed out the similarities between Van Gogh's view and a print by Raffaëlli that Van Gogh owned (*La Bièvre*, 1880). Heijbroek and Wouthuysen (1993, pp. 39, 165, 204) published information on the role of De Bois in the sale by Jo van Gogh-Bonger. Heenk (1995, pp. 150, 243) dated the sheet to spring–summer 1887. Amsterdam–Boston 2000, pp. 29, 30. Pickvance (in Martigny 2000, pp. 176, 263, 293) interpreted the town as Saint-Denis/Saint-Ouen and the foreground area as an abandoned quarry. See Vellekoop and Van Heugten (2001, pp. 304, 306) for the connection to the other three watercolors, and Stolwijk and Veenenbos (2002, pp. 54, 151, 152, 131, 163, 194) on Jo van Gogh-Bonger's sale of the sheet. Ten Berge (in Kröller-Müller Museum 2003, p. 149) linked the work with *Still Life with Herring* (F203), underneath which an X-ray revealed a similar view.

This sheet belongs to the group of large watercolors Van Gogh executed in the summer of 1887. It is the only one of the series that does not show the Paris ramparts but instead a panoramic view of the city from Montmartre. It is known neither where Van Gogh stood nor which suburban agglomeration of buildings is depicted in the distance. The modern buildings and factories could have been located in the adjoining towns of Saint-Denis and Saint-Ouen, although Asnières has also been suggested. In the foreground is a pit, convincingly identified by Pickvance (in Martigny 2000) as one of the quarries in which Montmartre was once rich.

The drawing is highly worked up, and Van Gogh even provided it with a painted frame in blue, indicating that he viewed it as potentially salable.

SvH

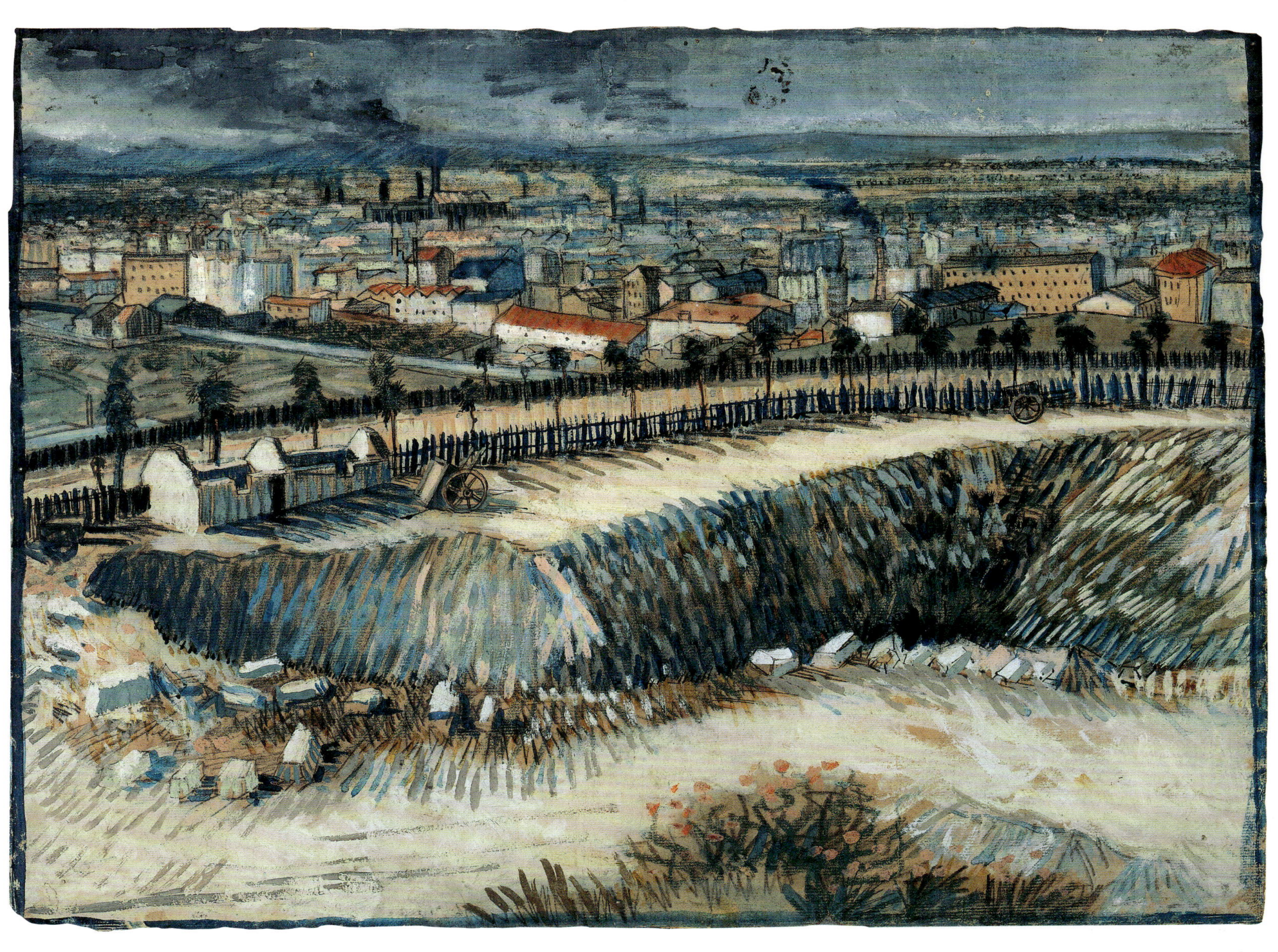

Arles, 1888–89: The Synthesis

After spending two years in Paris, Van Gogh had found it "almost impossible to work" and longed for "some place of retreat where one can recuperate and get one's tranquility and poise back" [463]. On February 19, 1888, he left for Arles, a Provençal town in the south of France, where he lived until his departure on May 8, 1889, for the nearby asylum in Saint-Rémy. For much of this period he worked alone, depending on correspondence with his brother Theo and such artist-friends as Émile Bernard and John Russell for feedback and dialogue (his share amounting to some two hundred letters). He enjoyed occasional outings with the Danish artist Christian Mourier-Petersen, who was in town in the spring of 1888, and day trips to see the American Dodge MacKnight and the Belgian Eugène Boch in the neighboring village of Fontvieille. For a time, he gave drawing lessons to Milliet, a second lieutenant in the French Zouave regiment. Van Gogh had hoped, however, to establish an artists' community in the south of France and thought this dream would be realized when Paul Gauguin agreed to join him in Arles and Theo agreed to finance their joint venture. But the fateful nine weeks the two men spent together, painting side by side and sharing quarters in the Yellow House (October 23–December 23, 1888) ended abruptly when Van Gogh became mentally unhinged, eclipsing his vision of a "Studio of the South" and the promise of fellowship he craved.

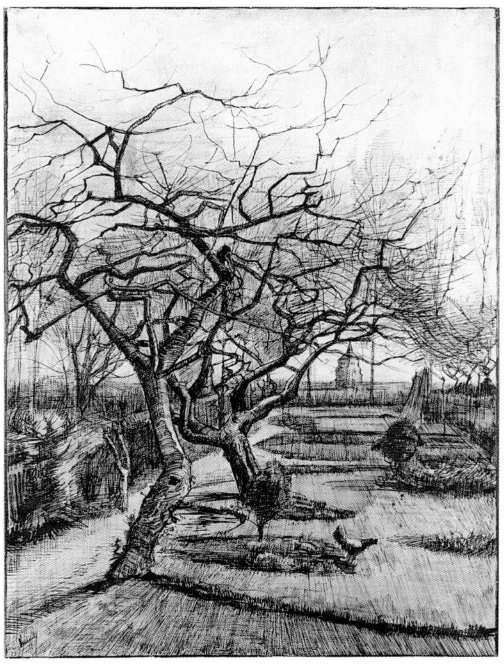

Fig. 113. *Winter Garden,* March 1884 (F1130, cat. 22)

Although Van Gogh's artistic contacts were limited in Provence, the outpost he chose seems to have afforded him the distance necessary for his art to come fully into its own. In this "land of blue tones and gay colors" [459a] past experience gelled. And in the process of sifting and editing what he had learned in Paris against the lessons that had anchored his Dutch art and given it its distinctive character and momentum, he succeeded in creating a "new art of color and design" [469] of great originality and integrity. As he later wrote to Theo, "I came to the South and threw myself into my work for a thousand reasons. Wishing to see a different light, thinking that looking at nature under a bright sky might give us a better idea of the Japanese way of feeling and drawing . . . and because one feels that the colors of the prism are veiled in the mist of the North" [605]. His prolific output of over two hundred paintings and one hundred drawings and watercolors in the space of fifteen months is as striking for its continuities as for its innovations.

In Arles, drawing regained the significance it had had for Van Gogh earlier in the Netherlands

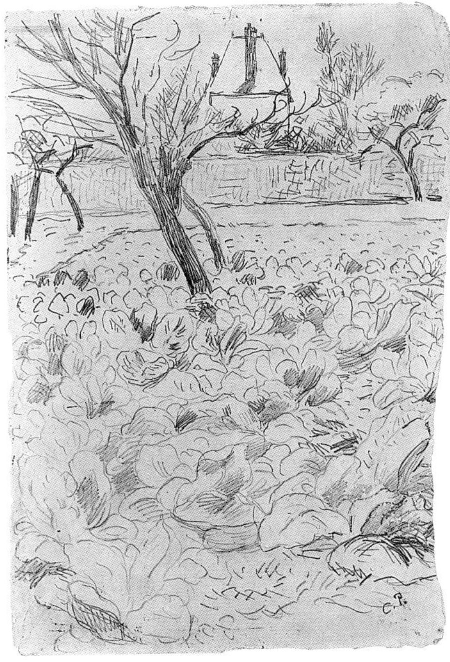

Fig. 114. Camille Pissarro, *The Cabbage Field*, ca. 1880. Graphite on paper, 25 x 17 cm ($9^{7}/_{8}$ x $6^{3}/_{4}$ in.). National Gallery of Art, Washington, Rosenwald Collection

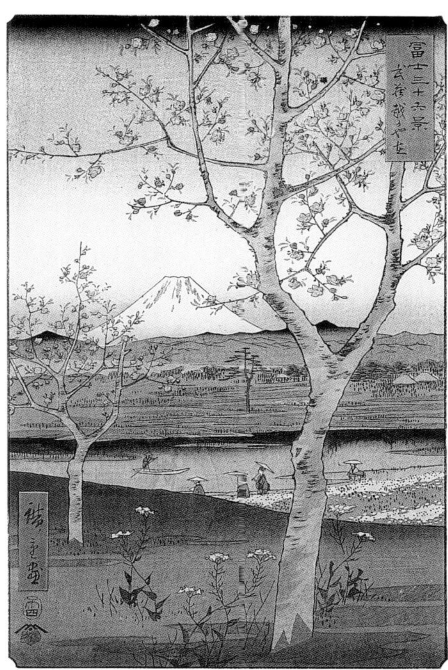

Fig. 115. Utagawa Hiroshige, *Fuji Seen from the Outskirts of Koshigaya in Musashi Province*, 1858. Color woodcut on paper, 34 x 22 cm ($13^{3}/_{8}$ x $8^{5}/_{8}$ in.). Van Gogh Museum, Amsterdam (Vincent van Gogh Foundation)

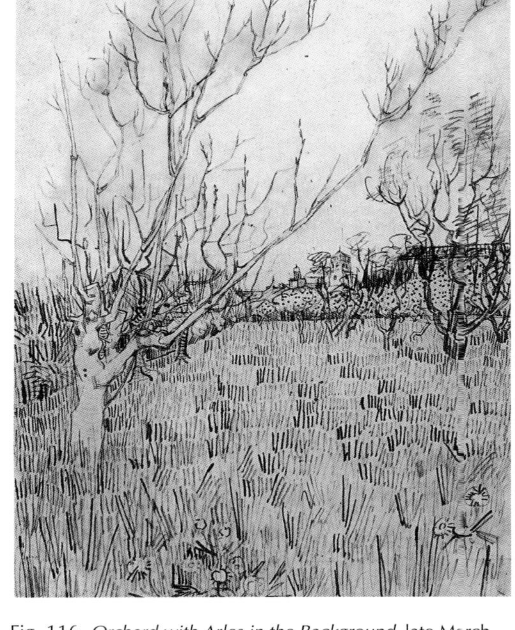

Fig. 116. *Orchard with Arles in the Background*, late March 1888 (F1516, cat. 44)

and, like writing, once again became a staple of his routine and working practice. He felt encouraged to "draw a great deal" [495] for a variety of reasons, some practical. "Canvases and paint simply swallow up our money while they are waiting to be sold. Drawings, on the other hand, don't cost a lot" [B7]. "I wish paint was as little of a worry to work with as pen and paper. I often pass up a painted study for fear of wasting the color. With paper, whether it's a letter I'm writing or a drawing I'm working on, there's never a misfire" [502]. Since he acquired his paper, ink, and pens locally, he was able to create artworks at his leisure. He could draw when he was "cleaned out of colors" on order from Paris [532], for example, or when the fierce mistral winds interfered with painting subjects *en plein air*: "That is the maddening thing here, no matter where you set up the easel. And that is why the painted studies are not so finished as the drawings; the canvas is shaking all the time. It does not bother me when I'm drawing" [509].

Van Gogh depended on his skill as a draftsman to complement and extend his work as a painter. He developed a "more spontaneous, more exaggerated" method of drawing in which line, like color, was also used "more arbitrarily, to express [himself] forcibly" [495, 520]. With remarkable versatility, he freely alternated between his pen and his brush to create images that lost none of their intensity in translation from one form of expression to the other. Not unlike the sketches in his letters that introduced or punctuated a thought or that were sometimes on a separate enclosed sheet, drawings intervened at various stages in his artistic conception from the first to the final statement, and they also stood on their own. He turned to pen and paper not only to arrest an "on the spot" impression, but also to record one he had already captured in paint. In keeping with conventional practice, he relied on drawing to explore a subject of interest, to tackle a motif before venturing it on canvas, and to prepare a composition for completion in the studio. Yet more often than not, he reversed the process: many of his drawings were made *after* his paintings, to be sent to Theo or artist-friends to give them a sense of his recent work. In Provence Van Gogh exploited old strategies in original ways, engaging drawing and painting in a rich dialectic that cast aside traditional roles to fully realize the creative potential of both means of expression.

Drawing in Arles: Reed Pen in Hand

Van Gogh seems to have taken up drawing about a month after his arrival in Arles. He had settled in, met local amateur artists, and shopped for art supplies in town [467]. Theo's letters had just brought news about the atelier sale of a draftsman he admired, Auguste André Lançon, and about the new addition to their collection of a drawing by Seurat [468]. The ice and bitter cold had relented, enabling him to work out-of-doors. And he embarked on his first major series, devoted to the Langlois Bridge, sketching the subject in his first illustrated letter from Arles [B2] and painting a view of it with women washing linens amid the tall reedy grasses of the riverbank (F397). This was prime territory in which to scout out motifs and, moreover, homegrown drawing tools, namely, the reed pen. If the confluence of these factors led to Van Gogh's renewed interest in drawing in mid- to late March 1888—reed pen in hand—his discovery of this providential tool also depended on past experience.

Seven years earlier, the fledgling artist had been encouraged to explore the virtues of the reed pen, "which has a broader stroke," as he reported in an 1881 letter to Theo [146]. While he did not mention what prompted him to try this pen, his discussion is framed by several references to drawing manuals by Armand Cassagne. Van Gogh credited Cassagne's books as key to his understanding of perspective and noted his recent purchase of Cassagne's *Traité d'aquarelle*. For a self-taught artist who had "drawn exclusively in pencil accented and worked up by the pen, sometimes a reed pen," a treatise on watercolor, in which he might "find many things, for instance about sepia and ink," would have been the natural supplement to Cassagne's *Guide pratique pour les différents genres de dessin*. In that drawing manual, which Van Gogh must surely have owned (and followed to a tee, for example, in terms of its paper recommendations), he would have found a chapter on pen and ink, replete with a sketch of the reed pen, directions on how to cut the bamboolike reed with a penknife, and the highest praise: Cassagne called it "the best pen" to use for drawing. Highlighting its facility to "glide" over the surface of the paper and its superiority to the "weak and puny" nibs of other pens, Van Gogh's de facto teacher advocated the reed as a vehicle for realizing a "bold and firm" manner of expression.[1] This was surely inspiration enough to venture Rembrandt's favorite tool.

Yet these experiments were short-lived, probably because the reeds of Van Gogh's homeland proved a disappointment. Cassagne had specified, however, that the best reeds, those that were "fine, elegant and firm," could be "found in the Midi, in the area of Cannes and Nice."[2] And Cassagne's advice was borne out when, in the early spring of 1888, Van Gogh discovered the pliant Midi-grown reed and duly noted, apropos of his first drawings, that it was "a method I already tried in Holland some time ago, but I hadn't such good reeds there as here" [478]. Van Gogh had not forgotten the value of Cassagne's books. Indeed, that summer when he took on the Zouave Milliet as his drawing pupil, he badgered Theo on half a dozen occasions to send him Cassagne's *Abécédaire du dessin*, calling it "the *only* really practical book I know" and adding "I know pretty well from experience how useful it is" [519, and see also 502, 505, 510, 522].

Whatever chain of events led Van Gogh to adopt the flexible reeds indigenous to the Midi as his drawing tool, his discovery proved auspicious—and, one might say, a long time in coming. Finally he found an implement that met his artistic aims and his natural abilities. For Van Gogh, an inveterate letter writer, drawing in pen and ink seems to have come most easily to his untutored hand. This is betrayed quite clearly in the extent to which so many of his early successes depend on pen and ink and the rapidity and ease (given the absence of complaint in his letters and his abundant output) with which he adapted himself to the reed pen in Arles.

If drawing landscapes with a quill or reed presented relatively little difficulty for Van Gogh, this was hardly the case with other subjects (such as figures or interior views in chiaroscuro) and most other drawing tools. Van Gogh's early correspondence provides a running account of his tribulations. He found conté crayon "indifferent and unwilling" [272], and watercolor repeatedly trying, if not downright "exasperating" [173] (unlike the respective preferences of the two other great innovators of drawing in the 1880s, Seurat and Cézanne); he complained that charcoal, because it "gets effaced so easily," required him to be too careful [R36], and he doused drawings with milk to temper the sheen of graphite. His inclination to experiment with untraditional media (for example, lithographer's crayon) in novel combinations was dictated as much by his skill, which he compensated for with his inventive approaches, as by an abiding sense of the qualities he sought, and thus fought, to obtain in black and white. He once confessed, "I *see* things like pen drawings," to which an artist-friend replied, "Then you must draw with the pen" [195]. But other priorities beckoned. His curiosity, his ambition, especially the premium he placed on the figure, and the well-meaning advice of those he relied on for guidance encouraged him to broaden his technique and range and forecast the detours that inevitably placed seven years between his prescient 1881 views of marshlands in Etten and his 1888 reed-pen landscapes in Arles.

SAS

1. Cassagne 1873, pp. 55–56.
2. Ibid., p. 55.

First Encounters

First Encounters and First Glimpses: Vincent to Theo

Van Gogh's correspondence provides few clues as to when he first began to draw in Arles or what prompted him to use the reed pen at this time. Not until April 9, 1888, seven weeks after his arrival, did Van Gogh broach the subject. But if he failed to provide a written account of his earliest efforts as a draftsman in Arles, he did not neglect to leave behind a paper trail—in the form of his drawings—that allows us to track his development prior to the point at which he disclosed to Theo: "I must do a *tremendous* lot of drawing, because I want to make some drawings in the manner of Japanese prints. . . . If there should happen to be a month or a fortnight when you were hard pressed, let me know, and I will set to work on some drawings, which will cost us less" [474].

By this date, Van Gogh clearly knew he was onto something. However, it would be another week before he was ready to send two examples [478], and yet a few more until Theo, who was finally sent a dozen smaller sheets in early May [480], would fully appreciate the potential Van Gogh envisioned and the time he was eager to set aside to do a "*tremendous* lot of drawing." All that he needed, it would seem, was an excuse or the license to draw, and perhaps to garner that support or to assuage his own doubts, he did not fail to mention its practicality—that it "will cost us less."

Van Gogh had already introduced the economy card, and later that April he succeeded in playing out this hand, albeit without revealing all his cards. After learning of a financial upset at Theo's gallery over the sale of Impressionist pictures, Van Gogh wrote, "As far as I'm concerned, I stopped painting at once, and went on with a series of pen drawings, of which you have the first two but this time in a smaller size. . . . [S]ince it's possible to produce a work of art at less cost than one must spend on a painting, I've begun the series of pen-and-ink drawings. . . . I'll send you pen drawings in a little while; I've done four already" [479]. Van Gogh had, in fact, "already" completed this group in "March 88," the date he inscribed on one of the four drawings. He could well have used them to document the step-by-step strides he had recently made as a draftsman. However, an artist who preferred hyperbole in general and dramatic contrast in particular advocated his cause more simply: he sent Theo a pair of large drawings of orchards, comparable in subject and scale but differing in format and, more consequentially, in date. Along with this compelling demonstration of the gains he had made in a relatively short time, he properly introduced the subject: "These drawings were made with a reed sharpened the way you would a goose quill; I intend to make a series of them, and hope to do better ones than the first two. It is a method I already tried in Holland some time ago, but I hadn't such good reeds there as here" [478]. His Midi reed pen in hand and the novelty of the landscape as further incentive, Van Gogh broke new ground as a draftsman, completing four "large" and some seventeen "small" drawings by early May.

Keenly invested in forging ahead, Van Gogh allowed generic descriptions—the number he had made and their relative size, "small" versus "large," to suffice—and did not dwell on the obvious when he introduced his first reed-pen drawings to Theo. He did not comment on how far he had come between his March *Orchard with Arles in the Background* (F1516, fig. 117) and his April *Provençal Orchard* (F1414, fig. 118). The differences in handling were blatant enough, and the two or three weeks that had guaranteed the broader, looser fluency of his pen had guaranteed a change in season as well: the end of winter that clung to the spiky branches of a barren tree standing guard in a March field like the ghosts of Nuenen winter gardens past (see F1128, cat. 21; F1130, cat. 22) had given way to spring, abloom in the flurry of dots and whiplash lines that animate the trees of his April orchard.

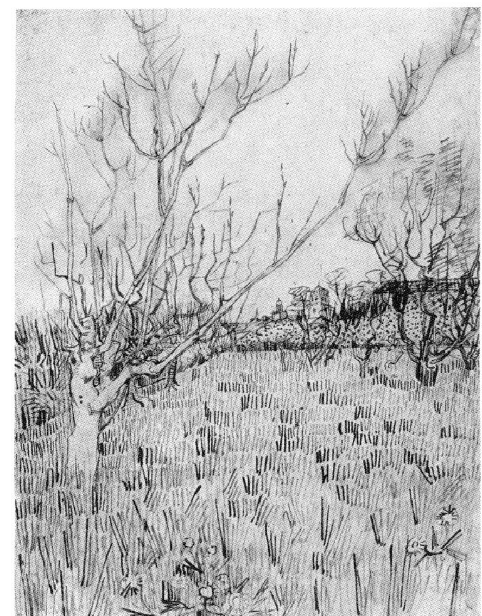

Fig. 117. *Orchard with Arles in the Background,* late March 1888 (F1516, cat. 44)

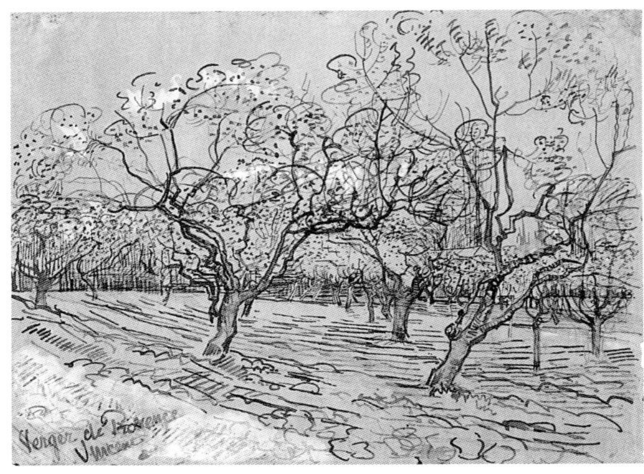

Fig. 118. *Provençal Orchard* (F1414), April 1888. Reed pen, ink, and graphite heightened with white and pink on laid paper, 39.5 x 54 cm (15½ x 21¼ in.). Van Gogh Museum, Amsterdam (Vincent van Gogh Foundation)

First Encounters in Focus: A Fuller Account

The evidence at hand suggests that Van Gogh began drawing in mid- to late March 1888 and continued to explore the merits of the reed pen, in earnest and with new confidence, from mid-April through early May. The inscription on one drawing, *Arles Mars 88* (F1499, fig. 119), is as unequivocal as the state of foliage on barren trees in others that must predate the onset of spring by month's end. However, the value of these sheets toward establishing a chronology for Van Gogh's development as a draftsman in Arles has yet to be fully appreciated in the literature, which has always relied on the artist's correspondence for dating his works, hence the tendency to advance most of his early drawings to April or May to accord with the written account. Indeed, the March date on *Path through a Field with Pollard Willows* has even been "put into question" because Van Gogh's activity is not documented in the letters until a month later. Nor has the significance of this singular inscription, as a kind of marker or record of achievement, invited any particular consideration. The drawing itself, which depends on his perspective frame and much graphite preparation, reflects a deliberateness in technique, with passages considered and reconsidered in the process of working them over in graphite and pen, and back again. The insistency and the hesitancy of his approach betray the ambition of the sheet as a proving ground, or rather as laying the groundwork, for further experiments along these lines vis-à-vis the drawings that followed.

Three related drawings show the artist's progressive development. Though he continued to rely on a perspective frame (his early insecurity about drawing landscapes in correct spatial depth and proportion having followed him to Arles), he became increasingly confident in his use of the reed pen, eventually allowing it to play the principal rather than the supporting role accorded to it in both *Path through a Field with Pollard Willows* and its immediate successor, *Meadow with Flowers* (F1474, fig. 120). Whereas here, too, he seems to have begun and largely worked the drawing in quill, accentuating the forms with the reed pen, the equation is reversed in *Farmhouse in a Wheat Field* (F1415, fig. 121). In this work, the reed pen dominates, and appears to have come first, in broader, freer, more unguarded strokes; then he added finishing touches in quill, as would be his habit. The same procedure was adopted in *Public Garden in the Place Lamartine* (F1421, fig. 122), which, however, stands apart for the compositional finesse that he achieved directly—and in one go—with the benefit of almost no preparatory graphite. Instead, he

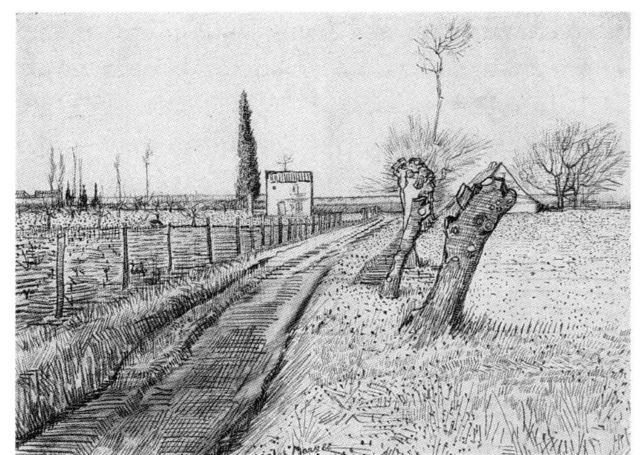

Fig. 119. *Path through a Field with Pollard Willows,* mid- to late March 1888 (F1499, cat. 42)

allowed the constituent parts of the whole to fall into line, using quick, staccato strokes and curlicues for the dandelion-covered grass; adding a lively mix of diagonal and arced lines, ranging from spiky to feathered for the bushes, treetops, and hedges along the road; and pushing his prowess to overreach somewhat in venturing a broader, more sinuous approach to the tree branch, which is a pastiche of shorter, angular, and tubular lines, worked first in reed and then with finer, darker strokes in quill. Insofar as Van Gogh would exploit this divide-and-conquer strategy to its full potential in his summer series of drawings after paintings (see "*Répétitions*: Drawings after Paintings"), the drawing looks ahead, but its backward glance is no less compelling. The foreground treatment of grass may be traced to the marshy swamplands in 1881 Etten drawings (F846, cat. 1; F845, fig. 89), and the branch, beyond its nod to any number of ukiyo-e prints in Van Gogh's collection, to his pen-and-ink Nuenen winter gardens of 1884 (F1128, cat. 21; F1130, cat. 22). The barren branch, as close examination of the drawing reveals, was integral to the composition from the start, while pencil lines indicating his use of the perspective frame confirm that it was made out-of-doors—and thus evidently before March 25, when the blossoming trees began to engage the artist's brush. Before he painted this series, however, he allowed his pen first crack at the motif in a large-scale demonstration piece, *Orchard with Arles in the Background* (F1516, fig. 117).

The quartet of landscapes, which cohere as a stylistic group and which Van Gogh reckoned were a fine start to a series—as his April letter [479] reflects—were succeeded by drawings that exhibit in their bolder and more confident handling his continued exploration of the expressive potential of the reed pen. He seems to have proceeded in a rather methodical fashion, for the drawings that are the closest heirs to his breakthrough *Provençal Orchard* (F1414, fig. 118) tend to divide into pairs in the following sequence: two views of trees along the road, one a strident frontal view of a tree trunk and its lower branches (F1509) and the other composed along a diagonal thrust (F1502, cat. 45); two river views, one a dramatic, expansive view of the Rhône, the other a more prosaic, tapered vista of a canal (F1472, F1473); and two public gardens, one vertical and one horizontal (F1476, F1487) (made at the same time as a third [F1513], which he distinguished, perhaps for this reason, as a "hasty sketch" [480]). Not unlike the orchards he sent to Theo in mid-April, these drawings took up the challenges of tackling frontal and oblique views as well as varying formats.

In terms of style, one is apt to see *View of Rooftops* (F1480a) and *Workers in a Field* (F1090) as immediate precursors of the more open, looser handling of *Provençal Orchard* (its ground patterned after the furrowed field) and *The Road to Tarascon with a Man Walking* (F1502, cat. 45) as its most direct and inspired successor. Spirited trees composed of restless lines and an unhesitant flourish of short stubby strokes (courtesy of the blunt nib of the reed) frame a road within an ambitious composition in which Van Gogh ventured further challenges, from that of vistas receding into depth and extending to the Alpilles in the distance to that of an ambulatory figure, albeit with difficulty, as the telltale marks of an eraser's rubbing and pentimenti record.

No doubt the group of a dozen "small" drawings that Theo was sent on May 1 [480] included most of the works described above and was retrospective in scope, extending from Van Gogh's first to his most recent successes as a draftsman. From this consignment, Theo could trace Van Gogh's increased versatility through a succession of images, related in pairs or groups and intimately linked to one another, owing to his progressive devel-

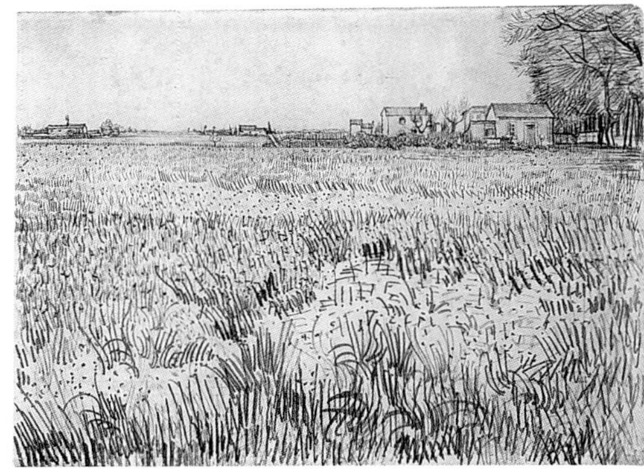

Fig. 120. *Meadow with Flowers* (F1474), late March 1888. Pen, reed pen, ink, and graphite on wove paper, 25.5 x 34.5 cm (10 x 13⅝ in.). Van Gogh Museum, Amsterdam (Vincent van Gogh Foundation)

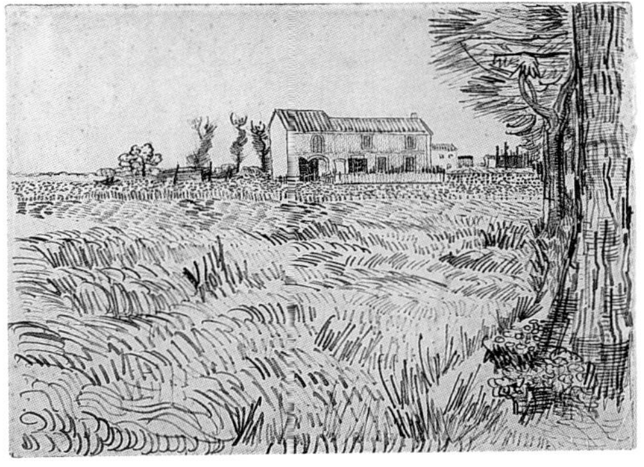

Fig. 121. *Farmhouse in a Wheat Field* (F1415), late March 1888. Reed pen, pen, ink, and graphite on wove paper, 25.5 x 34.5 cm (10 x 13⅝ in.). Van Gogh Museum, Amsterdam (Vincent van Gogh Foundation)

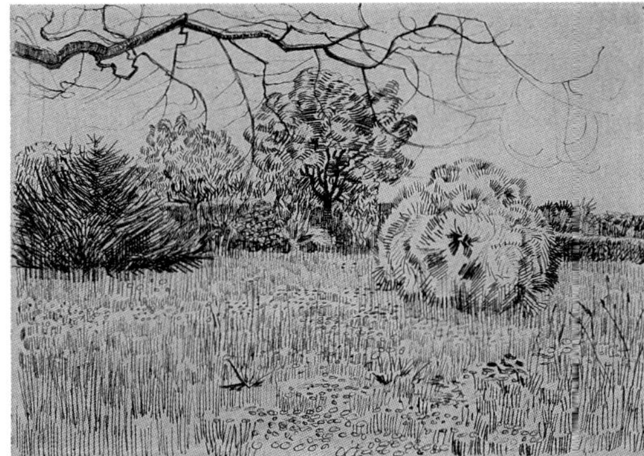

Fig. 122. *Public Garden in the Place Lamartine*, late March 1888 (F1421, cat. 43)

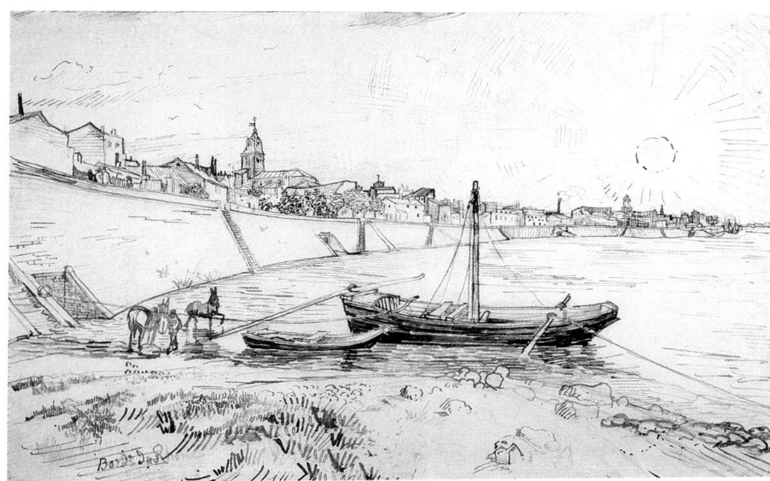

Fig. 123. *Bank of the Rhône* (F1472a), first week of May 1888. Reed pen, pen, graphite, and ink on paper watermarked AL PL BAS, 38.5 x 60.5 cm (15 1/8 x 23 7/8 in.). Museum Boijmans Van Beuningen, Rotterdam

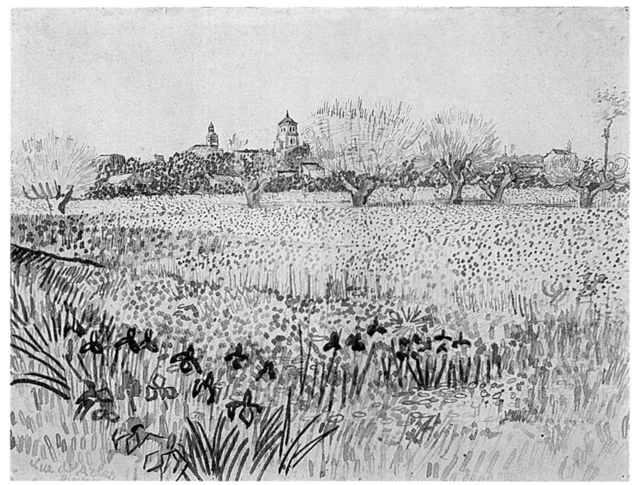

Fig. 124. *View of Arles with Irises in the Foreground,* first week of May 1888 (F1416r, cat. 46)

opment of a graphic vocabulary for landscape motifs that built upon the lessons gained along the way.

That same week Van Gogh continued to draw, and by May 7 he had completed five additional landscapes of this scale and two on "large" sheets of paper [483]. The "small" drawings presumably included a pair of breezy studies of trees along the road (F1518, F1518a) and a trio of fields with Provençal buildings that are distinctive for their concession to architectural and incidental detail (F1500, F1506, F1517).[1] These more modest efforts give way to two large-scale drawings inscribed with titles, *Bank of the Rhône* (F1472a, fig. 123) and *View of Arles with Irises in the Foreground* (F1416r, fig. 124). Both present panoramic vistas of Arles, one along the riverbanks of the Rhône, the other across flowering meadows. The former, a rather picturesque if somewhat conventional view of the Rhône, experiments with a more refined linear style and defers to anecdotal details that echo the horse and carriage in one of the fields and the plowman in the other (F1500, F1517), while incorporating the schematic sun of the third (F1506). *View of Arles with Irises in the Foreground* gives almost encyclopedic currency to the rich vocabulary of dynamic line that Van Gogh had developed to date within a composition no less calculated or carefully composed for all its bravura. The strategies of both drawings were exploited in his first Montmajour series and presage his continued explorations, in Sainte-Maries, of the expressive potential of "delicate" versus "harsh" lines.

Montmajour: The First Series

Van Gogh, who employed discretion until circumstance was on his side, seems to have made a persuasive case for devoting time and effort to drawing. In his protracted correspondence with Theo, he advocated the pragmatic merits of the activity, and in the works he sent he laid bare their artistic virtues. In late May, Theo proposed that Vincent submit a group of drawings to an upcoming exhibition of the Dutch Etching Society [489].

With this incentive, Van Gogh set to work. During the week of May 20–26, he completed a series of seven drawings devoted to Montmajour, a rocky hillock crowned with an abbey in ruins, which afforded views of the countryside extending from the flat plain of La Crau to the towns of Arles and Fontvieille in the distance a few miles away. Unified by subject, made on sheets of the same type and size (half-sheets of paper watermarked AL PL BAS) and with an aniline ink so fugitive that the images are barely visible today, the group represents the artist's most ambitious undertaking as a draftsman since the winter gardens of 1884. Six of the seven sheets are inscribed with a title, and one is signed. Van Gogh varied the views and their format: he dedicated five to vistas of La Crau and two to the abbey itself; five are horizontal and two are upright compositions. Having demonstrated his versatility with the reed pen in views of similar breadth, those of the Rhône (F1472a, fig. 123) and of Arles (F1416r, fig. 124), he had at his disposal the means and the graphic vocabulary to meet the challenges of the site. The stylistic tendencies that he had explored in these two works find counterparts within the Montmajour series, which waver between architectonic drawings, somewhat static and tightly composed (F1423, fig. 67; F1417, fig. 69; F1419, fig. 71), and others of a spirited kind (F1418; F1475; F1448; F1493, fig. 72).

The expressive potential of contrast was fundamental to Van Gogh's artistic thinking in general and uppermost in his mind during the week of May 20, when he took a break from landscape painting to immerse himself in the carefully orchestrated play of complementary colors in *Still Life with Coffee Pot* (F410) and conceived the Montmajour series with its pairing of vertical and horizontal works, which presented vistas near and far, depicting nature unbridled and tamed and drawn in lines that arguably sought to evoke the same qualities. Describing the views to Theo, Vincent wrote, "The contrast between the wild and the romantic foreground, and the distant perspective, wide and still, with horizontal lines sloping into the chain of the Alpilles . . . is very striking" [490]. Not long after, in a letter to Bernard (illustrated with a sketch of the still life [B6]), he expounded at length on the subject of contrast, comparing the striking "simultaneous contrast" of black and white to color.

It is difficult to judge the merits of these drawings, which, owing to fading, are mere ghosts of their former selves, but apparently fellow artist Mourier-Petersen was unimpressed [B10] and Van Gogh himself was clearly dissatisfied. Not only did he feel it was not worth the bother of framing them for exhibition [490], but within the next couple of days, he returned to Montmajour to tackle the subject anew and with confident determination to get it right, given the full-size sheet of Whatman paper he took with him. This time he was not disappointed in the result, *View of Arles from Montmajour* (F1452, cat. 47). He immediately announced the motif and the technique that had assured his success to a Dutch artist-friend, Arnold Hendrik Koning [498a; quoted under cat. 47], and rushed to post it to Theo in the hope that it would arrive by the weekend, as he "would very much like the Pissarros to see [it] if they come on Sunday" [495].

While the drawing may be seen as an epic coda to Van Gogh's first period of activity as a draftsman, he was quick to disengage it from his past efforts and to see it instead as a touchstone for the future; he referred to his next major drawing, done the following week at Saintes-Maries (F1439, fig. 130), as its "pendant" [499]. And in July, persuaded to take up the Montmajour project again (see "The Heights of Montmajour" and cats. 82–86), Van Gogh considered his campaign complete, by co-opting this May drawing as the "sixth of that series" [509].

First Encounters, Some Last Remarks

Sensing that he could command the reed pen as effectively as the brush, Van Gogh pursued drawing as a viable alternative to painting in the early spring of 1888. His investigations of the evocative nature of line paralleled those of color and with a like insistence on distilling the vital character of a motif in a decisive manner. No more than a handful of Van Gogh's earliest works on paper are related to paintings, and not only is there often a lag between the two, but sometimes, having already sent the sheet to Theo, he no longer had the model when he took up the motif in paint. He drew for drawing's sake—or for the sake of having a means readily at hand, without waiting for costly materials on order from Paris or for the mistral to die down, that would enable him to create works of art in black and white that were as compelling as those in color. He seems to have recognized almost immediately the potential of drawing to make compositions or an ensemble of significance, and once he gained facility and confidence, whatever vague ideas about grand schemes that were imparted by large sheets inscribed with titles or smaller works thematically paired began to surface in the correspondence.

The strides he had made by early May 1888 led him to consider how he could further exploit his skill in practical and creative ways. He ventured more demanding, even commercially appealing, compositions (like F1472a) and experiments using drawn motifs as models for studio compositions, noting to Theo, "this will show you that, if you like, I can make little pictures like the Japanese prints of all these drawings" [484]. Perhaps mindful of the market appeal of color (which, after all, had been a primary impetus for his earlier efforts at watercolor), at the end of the month he "asked for some watercolors . . . to make some pen drawings, to be washed afterward in flat tints like the Japanese prints" [491]. And thinking expansively on the heels of his Montmajour series, he put forth yet another idea: "You know what you must do with these drawings—make sketchbooks with 6 or 10 or 12 like those books of original Japanese drawings. *I very much want* to make such a book for Gauguin, and one for Bernard. For the drawings are going to be better than these" [492]. In June, when Van Gogh incorporated color studies in his working process and prepared "cartoons" for his oils, and in July, when he produced suites of drawings after his paintings for artist-friends, he succeeded, in a fashion, in carrying out these projected schemes. Before he left for Saintes-Maries, Van Gogh was convinced of the value of drawing. He went on to realize fully its rich potential.

SAS

1. Presumably, on the basis of its style and subject, the landscape with Daudet's Mill (F1496) was made on his day trip to see friends in Fontvieille about May 3 [481] and remarked upon the following day, when he noted making "another drawing" [482].

42. *Path through a Field with Pollard Willows*

Mid- to late March 1888
Pen and ink, graphite, with touches of reed pen on wove paper
25.8 x 34.7 cm (10⅛ x 13⅝ in.)
Inscribed, lower center: *Arles Mars 88*
Inscribed on verso, in another hand: *173*
Van Gogh Museum, Amsterdam (Vincent van Gogh Foundation) (d 168 V/1962)
F1499, JH1372
Letters 479, 480, 483, 484

Provenance: Sent by the artist to Theo van Gogh (d. 1891), Paris, May 1, 1888 [480, 484]; by inheritance to his son, Vincent Willem van Gogh (1890–1978), as part of his collection, administered by his widow, Johanna van Gogh-Bonger (d. 1925), 1891; placed on loan at the Stedelijk Museum, Amsterdam, 1931–73; ownership transferred to the Vincent van Gogh Foundation, 1962; placed on permanent loan at the Van Gogh Museum, Amsterdam, 1973.

Selected exhibitions: Leiden 1893; Groningen 1897; Amsterdam 1905, no. 404; Cologne–Frankfurt 1910; Amsterdam 1914–15, no. 165; Utrecht 1923, no. 51; Rotterdam 1923; Berlin 1927–28, no. 62; London–Birmingham–Glasgow 1947–48, no. 139; New York–Chicago 1949–50, no. 95; London 1968–69, no. 102; Amsterdam 1980–81, no. 174; New York 1984, no. 15; Otterlo 1990, no. 165; Kyōto–Tokyo 1992, no. 20; Martigny 2000, no. 43.

Summary of the literature: Catalogued by De la Faille (1928, no. 1499) among works "not mentioned in the letters," this drawing has since been associated with several letter references: letter 484 (as noted in De la Faille 1970, no. 1499, and earlier by Bowness in London 1968–69, no. 102) and letters 480 and 483, as Roskill (1971, p. 166) first proposed. Pickvance (in New York 1984, no. 15; in Otterlo 1990, no. 165; and in Martigny 2000, no. 43) also connected the sheet with the "four drawings" mentioned in letter 479, recognizing it as part of a stylistically coherent group that includes F1415, F1474, and F1421. However, whereas in New York 1984, Pickvance flagged the value of the inscribed date "as evidence that Van Gogh had already begun to draw well before April," in Otterlo 1990, he contended that since Van Gogh's letters indicate that he did not begin this group until mid-April, this "put into question" the March date on the "only drawing inscribed from Arles." He maintained that "if we accept that date . . . we then have to admit that four drawings already existed in March" but hypothesized that Van Gogh may have "executed them all painstakingly in quill alone in March . . . and then reworked them with reed pen in mid-April." Pickvance dated the three other drawings to

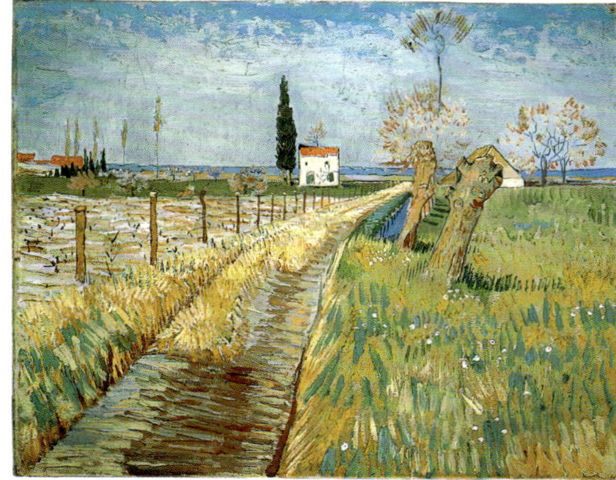

Fig. 125. *Path through a Field with Pollard Willows* (F407), April 1888. Oil on canvas, 31.5 x 38.5 cm (12¼ x 15⅛ in.). Private collection, courtesy Pierre Gianadda Foundation, Switzerland

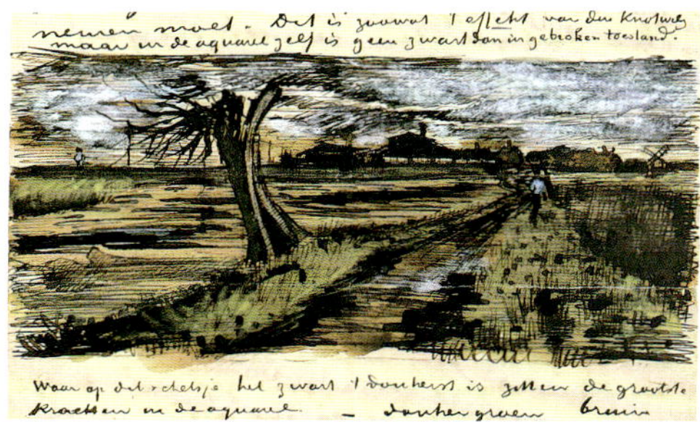

Fig. 126. Letter sketch of *Landscape with Path and Pollard Willow* (F1762), between July 29 and August 1, 1882 [221]. Watercolor and ink on paper, sketch 6.6 x 13.4 cm (2⅝ x 5¼ in.), sheet 14 x 13.5 cm (5½ x 5¼ in.). Van Gogh Museum, Amsterdam (Vincent van Gogh Foundation)

April. Heenk (1995, p. 165) described this drawing as a "prototype" for the oil (F407), observing the close proportions between the two (see also Pickvance in Martigny 2000), but argued that "its elaboration and annotations suggest that the artist saw it as an independent drawing and an end in itself." Hulsker (1980/1996, no. 1372) relied on the inscribed date as a basis for assigning other drawings to March that relate to this "minutely executed, somewhat delicate pen-and-ink drawing with its wide perspective," yet without making a persuasive case for those named (i.e., F1500, F1506, F1517). Several scholars have pointed to this drawing's relationship to Van Gogh's earlier Dutch works in terms of style (as Millard 1974, p. 157, and pl. 23, who traced the "angular and somewhat reticent style" back to the Nuenen period) or of motif (as Pickvance in Otterlo 1990, who compared such prosaic views as this "humble mas in a field" to those Van Gogh did in The Hague for C. M. van Gogh). For early history, see Feilchenfeldt and Veenenbos 1988, p. 135.

This drawing is unique for its inscribed date, which provides a terminus a quo for Van Gogh's activity as a draftsman in Arles. It is one of three drawings of March 1888 (with F1474, fig. 120; F1415, fig. 121) that the artist adapted for paintings later that spring. Given the close correspondence between the contours of the main elements, he presumably transferred the design from paper to canvas (F407, fig. 125) by tracing. His technique, in particular the use of graphite not only for the preliminary sketch but to further articulate landscape forms rendered in ink, and the motif of a path lined with pollard willows invite association with his earlier Dutch works (see F1762, fig. 126). Van Gogh seems to have relied on the reed pen very minimally, for accents (like the broad ink dots) applied last.

SAS

Letter to Theo van Gogh, ca. April 25, 1888 [479]: [S]ince I believe that it's possible to produce a work of art at less cost than one must spend on a painting, I've begun the series of pen-and-ink drawings. . . . I'll send you pen drawings in a little while; I've done four already [F1499, F1474, F1415, F1421].

Letter to Theo van Gogh, May 1, 1888 [480]: I have just sent you a roll of small pen-and-ink drawings, a dozen I think. By which you will see that if I have stopped painting, I haven't stopped working.

Letter to Theo van Gogh, May 7, 1888 [483]: There has been a good deal of mistral here, so I did the dozen little drawings which I have sent you.

Letter to Theo van Gogh, May 7, 1888 [484]: There is a little landscape with a hovel, white, red, and green, and a cypress beside it [F407, fig. 125]; you have a drawing of it, and I did the whole painting of it in the house. This will show you that, if you like, I can make little pictures like the Japanese prints of all these drawings.

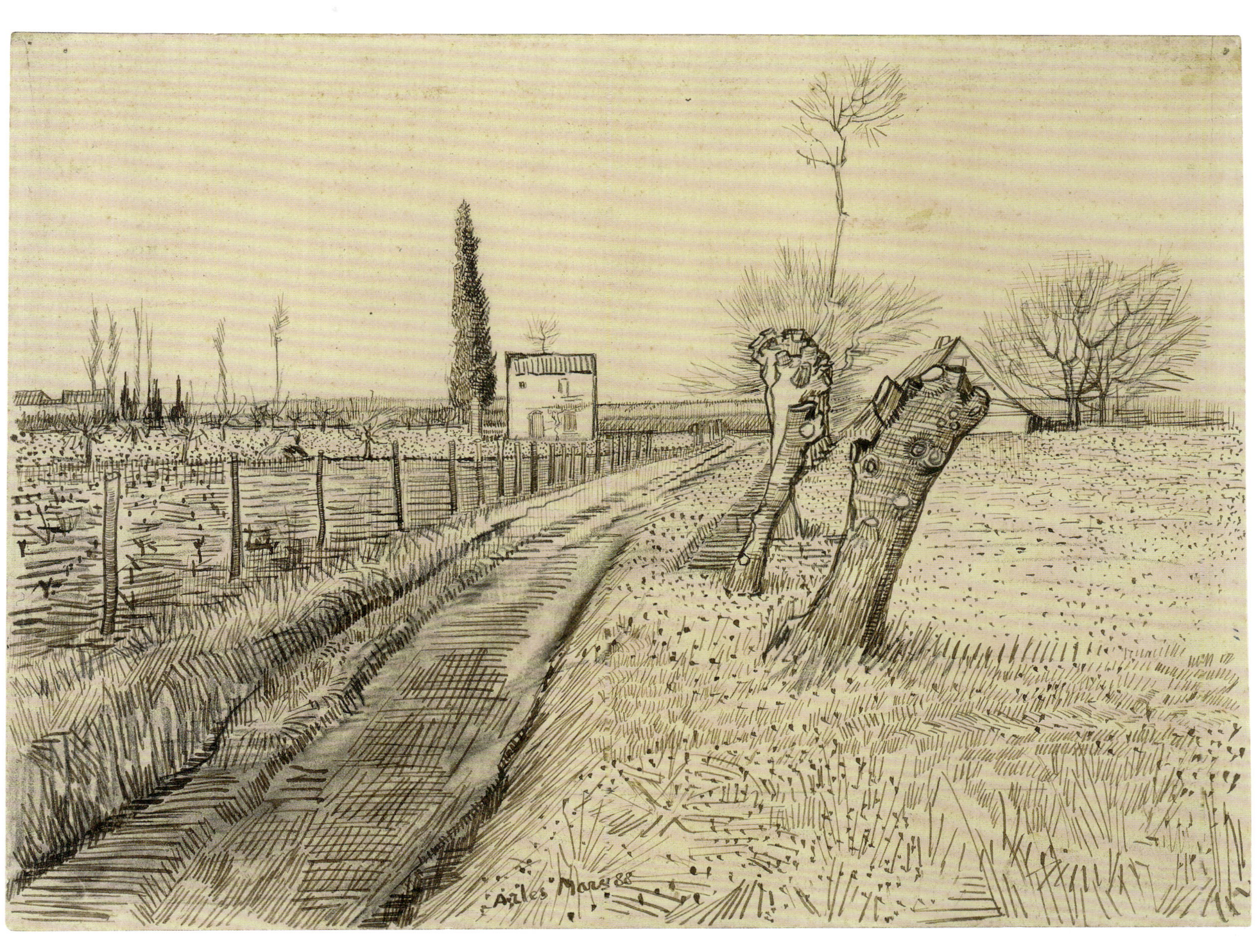
Arles Mars 88

43. *Public Garden in the Place Lamartine*

Late March 1888
Reed pen, pen and ink, over faint graphite on wove paper
25.8 x 34.6 cm (10 1/8 x 13 5/8 in.)
Inscribed in ink on verso, in another hand: *186*
Van Gogh Museum, Amsterdam (Vincent van Gogh Foundation) (d 343 V/1962)
F1421, JH1414
Letters 479, 480, 483

Provenance: Sent by the artist to Theo van Gogh (d. 1891), presumably on May 1, 1888 [480]; by inheritance to his son, Vincent Willem van Gogh (1890–1978), as part of his collection, administered by his widow, Johanna van Gogh-Bonger (d. 1925), 1891; placed on loan at the Stedelijk Museum, Amsterdam, 1931–73; ownership transferred to the Vincent van Gogh Foundation, 1962; placed on permanent loan at the Van Gogh Museum, Amsterdam, 1973.

Selected exhibitions: Leiden 1893; Groningen 1897; Amsterdam 1905, no. 400; Munich and other cities 1909–10; Cologne–Frankfurt 1910; The Hague–Amsterdam 1912, no. 3; Amsterdam 1914–15, no. 158; Utrecht 1923, no. 50; Rotterdam 1923; Berlin 1927–28, no. 77; London–Birmingham–Glasgow 1947–48, no. 143; London 1968–69, no. 128; Tokyo–Kyōto–Nagoya 1976–77, no. 62; New York 1984, no. 23; Arles 1989, no. 18; Otterlo 1990, no. 168; Martigny 2000, no. 46.

Summary of the literature: Originally dated to May–June 1888 in De la Faille 1928 (no. 1421) and considered the depiction of the motif described to Bernard [B19], this drawing was later associated with the artist's public garden pictures of July in De la Faille 1970 (no. 1421) and by Bowness in London 1968–69 (no. 128). However, it has since been recognized as one of the earliest Arles drawings, and among the seventeen sent to Theo in early May [480, 483]: first by Roskill (1971, p. 166 and n. 134), "especially in view of the bare trees," and by Millard (1974, pp. 157–58, 162), given its similarity in technique to F1499 and other drawings made before mid-May that betray Van Gogh's use of the perspective frame and "continue the angular and somewhat reticent style," which "goes back [to his] Nuenen period." Hulsker (1980, no. 1414) initially associated it with the public gardens described in letter 480 (as had Millard) but in 1996 simply dated it to May. In De la Faille 1992 (no. 1421), it is dated to April. For early history, see Feilchenfeldt and Veenenbos 1988, p. 131.

The drawing has been extensively published by Pickvance (in New York 1984, no. 23; in Arles 1989, no. 18; in Otterlo 1990, no. 168; and in Martigny 2000, no. 46), who proposed that it was one of the "four drawings" mentioned to Theo [479], the others being F1415, F1474, and F1499, to which it is related in style, quill base, and traces of the artist's use of perspective frame. Noting the complete absence of a preliminary pencil sketch and declaring the stylized branch at the top of the sheet a later, studio addition (as Heenk 1995, p. 170, subsequently contended), Pickvance recognized the "feathery round bush" of the Place Lamartine garden as the landscape motif that most attracted Van Gogh in Arles; it figures in ten works. While he has consistently advanced these views, Pickvance has variously dated the work: to April 1888 (in Otterlo 1990) and, more recently, to May (in Martigny 2000). Closer inspection of the drawing challenges several of his technical observations (as noted in "First Encounters"). For early history, see Feilchenfeldt and Veenenbos 1988, p. 131.

From late March 1888—as this drawing records—until the eve of his departure for Saint-Rémy in May 1889 (see F1468, cat. 100), the public gardens opposite Van Gogh's Yellow House in Arles engaged his artistic interest and his draftsman's skill. For his successive drawings of the subject, see "Gardens, Parks, and Byways" (and F1449, cat. 89; F1450, cat. 88; F1451, cat. 90; F1477, cat. 94; F1468, cat. 100).

SAS

Letters to Theo van Gogh, ca. April 25, 1888 [479], May 1, 1888 [480], and May 7, 1888 [483]: See cat. 42 (F1499).

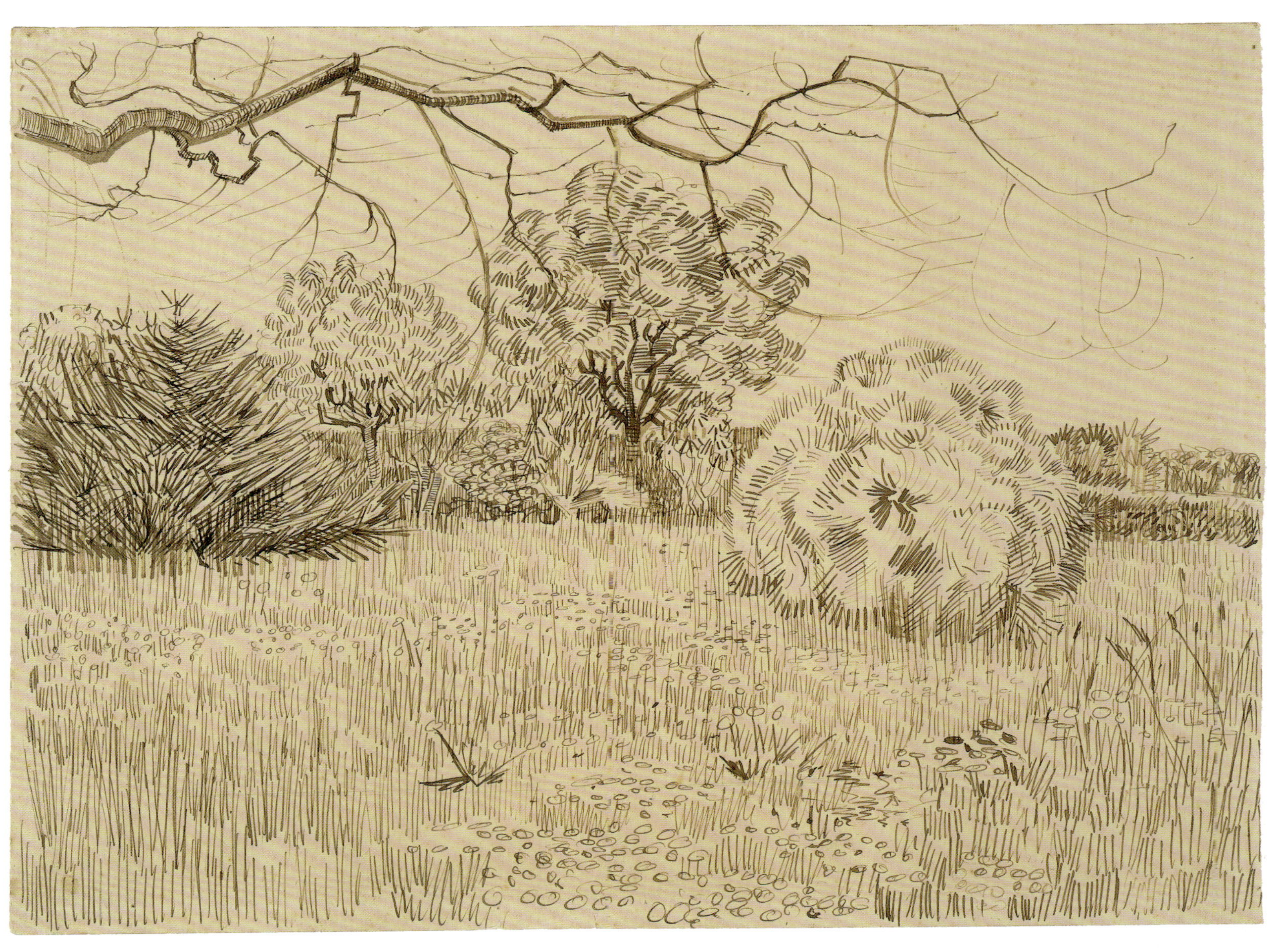

44. *Orchard with Arles in the Background*

Late March 1888
Reed pen, pen, ink, and graphite on laid paper
53.2 x 38.8 cm (21 x 15¼ in.)
Inscribed in ink on verso, in another hand: *138*
The Hyde Collection, Glens Falls, New York (1971.81)
F1516, JH1376
Letters 478, 479

New York only

Provenance: Sent by the artist to Theo van Gogh (d. 1891), presumably ca. April 17, 1888 [478]; by inheritance to his son, Vincent Willem van Gogh, as part of his collection, administered by his widow, Johanna van Gogh-Bonger, 1891; sold by her to Ernest Brown & Phillips (Leicester Galleries), London, for Sir Michael E. Sadler, Oxford, January 1924; Mrs. Cornelius J. Sullivan, New York, by 1935; her sale, Parke-Bernet, New York, December 6–7, 1939, no. 157; purchased at this sale by Charlotte Pruyn Hyde (1867–1963), Glens Falls, N.Y., 1939, until 1952, when she founded the public collection that bears her name.

Selected exhibitions: Leiden 1893; Groningen 1897; Amsterdam 1905, no. 397; Cologne–Frankfurt 1910; Utrecht 1923, no. 65; Rotterdam 1923; London 1923–24, no. 10; New York and other cities 1935–36, no. 117; New York 1984, no. 19; Otterlo 1990, no. 175.

Summary of the literature: Although originally placed among the artist's last Arles drawings in De la Faille 1928, no. 1516 (where its media were described as "China ink, pencil and violet ink"), this work has since been recognized as one of the artist's earliest efforts as a draftsman in Arles: De la Faille 1970, no. 1516, as March 1888; Roskill 1971, p. 165, as presumably a March drawing given its leafless trees and one of the first two sent to Theo (with F1468) [478, 479]; Hulsker (1980, no. 1376) assigned it to March-April 1888. Pickvance (in New York 1984, no. 19) distinguished it as the earliest Arles orchard, its "spiky and leafless trees" suggesting a date prior to the first oil mentioned on March 24 [471], noted its uniqueness in presenting a view of the town, and pinpointed its locale to the south. However, in Otterlo 1990 (no. 175, pp. 219, 221), where Pickvance argued that it was one of the first two drawings sent to Theo [478], along with F1414, he dated it to April, presumably on this basis, and flagged Van Gogh's use of the perspective frame and violet ink. Heenk (1995, p. 176) considered it the earliest drawing from Arles (prior to March 24) and noted that it was "made on 'Glaslan' paper which Van Gogh probably brought from Paris" using violet ink as well as some black ink "on top of it." She pointed to the visible aiding lines of the perspective frame and agreed that it was sent with F1414 to Theo [478]. Hulsker in 1996 (no. 1376) dated it to the first half of April 1888 and also said it was sent to Theo with F1414 [478]. For early history, see Feilchenfeldt and Veenenbos 1988, p. 136; Stolwijk and Veenenbos 2002, pp. 136, 164–65, 197.

In mid-April, Van Gogh introduced his brother to his first efforts as a draftsman in Arles by sending him two large-scale drawings of orchards [478]: this one, of March vintage, before the trees had blossomed, and another he had made more recently (F1414, fig. 118). He allowed the decisive differences between the two images, in date and style, to suffice as a visual progress report and did not elaborate further. The present drawing provides a singularly compelling introduction to his work in Arles in terms of the way its approach and composition reflect the filtering of past experience—the heritage of both his Dutch graphic oeuvre and his Parisian sojourn—through his vision of Provence or, as he put it, through "an eye more Japanese" [500].

Van Gogh's use of the perspective frame is betrayed by the telltale vertical, horizontal, and intersecting diagonal graphite lines visible on the sheet (though largely lost on the right side, where the paper has been trimmed). The artist left little to chance: virtually every element was first sketched out, with the exception of the thin, spindly branches, which were done freehand in ink. In certain places Van Gogh did not bother to articulate details with his pen, for example, the tall vertical branch at left. Nor did he slavishly follow the underdrawing; indeed, much of the graphite (as in the adjacent lines of graphite and ink that create the grassy foreground) stands on its own as a compositional element, not unlike various Hague drawings (e.g., see F930, cat. 8). The ink (which has bled through to the verso) is most trenchant in passages that have been heavily worked with graphite, such as the tree at right. Given the different kinds of inking and widths of pen marks, it is clear that Van Gogh used at least two, and possibly three, different pens: reed, quill, and perhaps even an ordinary writing pen.[1] There is no violet ink or watermark visible, contrary to previous descriptions.

SAS

1. Christian Mourier-Petersen, who spent time with Van Gogh between March and May, before he left Arles for Paris, recalled that Van Gogh always carried two reed pens. Noted by Kirsten Olesen in Copenhagen 1984–85, p. 108, and documented in privately held correspondence, as Håkan Larsson was kind enough to confirm.

Letter to Theo van Gogh, ca. April 20, 1888 [478]: I got [your earlier letter] too, and I wrote you about it the day, or two days, before I sent the two drawings [F1516, F1414]. These drawings were made with a reed sharpened the way you would a goose quill; I intend to make a series of them, and hope to do better ones than the first two. It is a method I already tried in Holland some time ago, but I hadn't such good reeds there as here.

I have had a letter from [Dutch artist-friend] Koning, please thank him for it; I shall be very pleased to exchange the two drawings for one of his studies, which you must choose and keep in your collection. I will write him to explain the method and send him some sharpened reeds so that he can try it too.

Letter to Theo van Gogh, ca. April 25, 1888 [479]: You see, I dare not go on in a line of things which are going to cost you more than they will bring in at present. . . . As far as I'm concerned, I stopped painting at once, and went on with a series of pen drawings, of which you have had the first two [F1516, F1414] but this time in a smaller size.

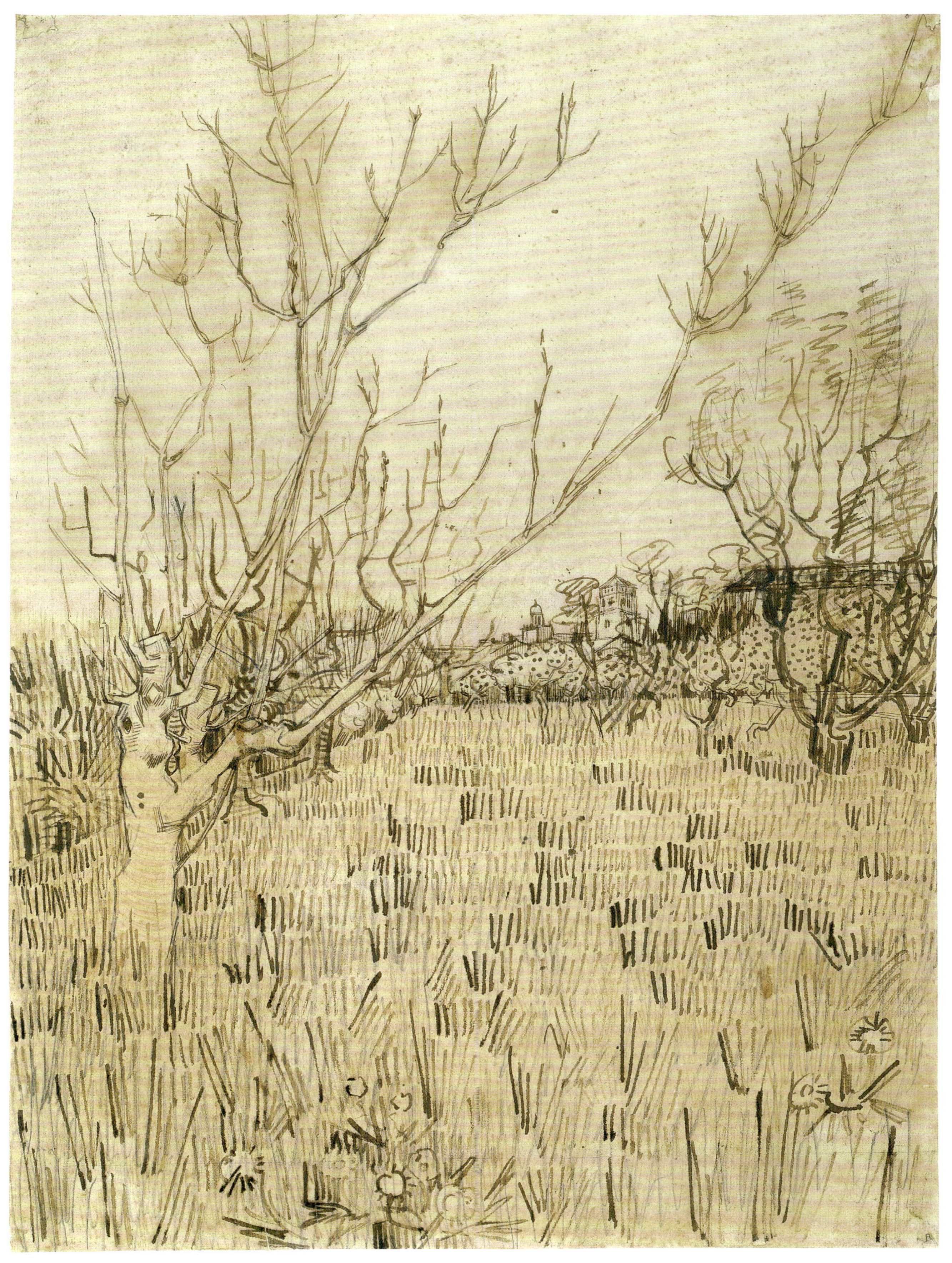

45. *The Road to Tarascon with a Man Walking*

April 1888
Reed pen and ink, graphite on wove paper
25.8 x 35 cm (10⅛ x 13¾ in.)
Kunsthaus Zürich, Graphische Sammlung (1940/1)
F1502, JH1492
Letters 480, 483

Provenance: Sent by the artist to Theo van Gogh (d. 1891), Paris, presumably on May 1, 1888 [480]; by inheritance to his son, Vincent Willem van Gogh, as part of his collection, administered by his widow, Johanna van Gogh-Bonger, 1891; sold to Artz en De Bois, The Hague, July/August 1912; with J. H. de Bois, Haarlem, summer 1913; offered to Felix Graefe, Wenen, September 1917, and to R. E. Buhler, Winterthur, January 1918; still with De Bois, 1926; private collection, England; Otto Wacker Art Gallery, Berlin, 1926; Galerie Aktuaryus, Zürich, until 1940; sold to the museum, 1940.

Selected exhibitions: Amsterdam 1905, no. 370; Berlin 1909–10, no. 207; London 1926–27, no. 28; Berlin 1927–28, no. 63; Milan 1952, no. 102; Munich 1956, no. 118; Munich 1961, no. 66; Frankfurt 1970, no. 56; New York 1984, no. 18; Otterlo 1990, no. 170; Martigny 2000, no. 47; Arles 2003, pp. 34–35.

Summary of the literature: Because the motif relates to Van Gogh's summer 1888 oil *The Artist on the Road to Tarascon* (F448, fig. 173), some scholars have dated the drawing to August 1888 (De la Faille 1970/1992, no. 1502) or July 1888 (Millard 1974, p. 159; Hulsker 1980/1996, no. 1492, with stylistically similar drawings of tree-lined roads "which cannot be accurately dated," i.e., F1509, F1518, F1518a). Its rightful place among the artist's earlier efforts in Arles was first suggested by Roskill (1971, p. 167) and subsequently supported by Pickvance (in New York 1984, no. 18), who recognized it as one of several works of late April–early May that depict the same stretch of road (F1415, F1474, F1509, F1518, F1518a, F567). Pickvance further proposed that the mistral winds may have affected the work's "agitated touches and angular forms" and that the "resolute and briskly walking figure," which was realized in the studio after scraping off an initial attempt, is possibly a self-portrait. In Otterlo 1990 (no. 170), Pickvance considered it an April drawing that demonstrates greater confidence and "more open articulation" in the use of the reed pen (like F1473 and F1476), and in Martigny 2000 (no. 47), he assigned it to April–May 1888, noting the artist's "increased freedom" in touch and reiterating that the figure, added in the studio, may be a "symbolic self-portrait." For early history, see Feilchenfeldt and Veenenbos 1988, p. 135; Heijbroek and Wouthuysen 1993, p. 205.

See "First Encounters."

SAS

Letters to Theo van Gogh, May 1, 1888 [480], and May 7, 1888 [483]: See cat. 42 (F1499).

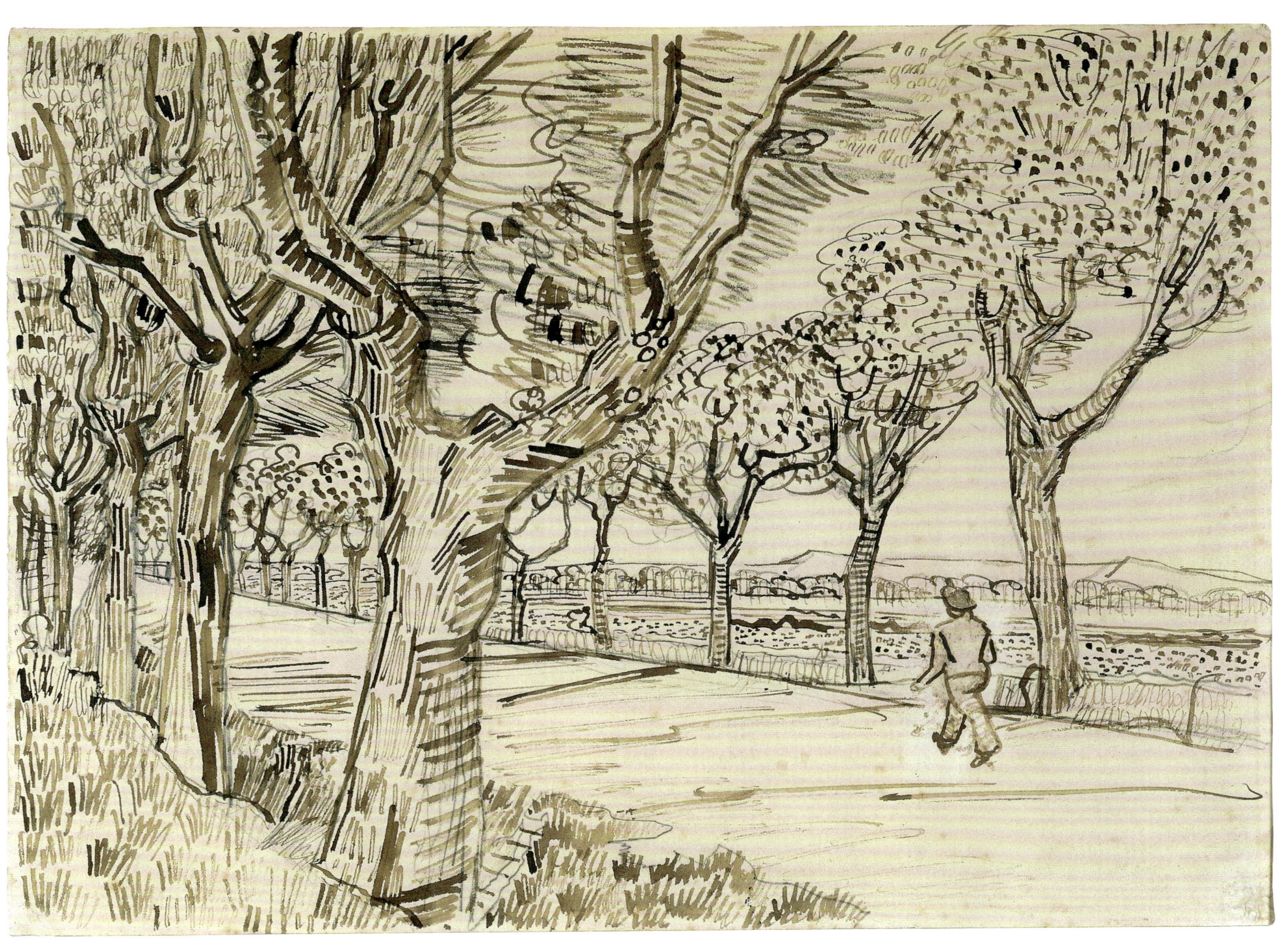

46. *View of Arles with Irises in the Foreground*

First week of May 1888
Reed pen, pen, ink, and wash over graphite on wove paper watermarked J. WHATMAN (partial)
43.5 x 55.5 cm (17⅛ x 21⅞ in.)
Inscribed and signed, lower left: *Vue d'Arles / Vincent*
Verso: graphite sketch of a drawbridge at Arles (fig. 127)
Inscribed in ink on verso, upper left, in another hand: *151*
Museum of Art, Rhode Island School of Design, Providence, Gift of Mrs. Murray S. Danforth (42.212A)
F1416r, JH1415
Letter 483

New York only

Provenance: Sent by the artist to Theo van Gogh (d. 1891), Paris, at an unrecorded date in 1888–89; by inheritance to his son, Vincent Willem van Gogh, as part of his collection, administered by his widow, Johanna van Gogh-Bonger, 1891; sold by her to Paul Cassirer, Berlin, December 1906; sold to Hermann Freudenberg, Berlin, December 1906, until at least 1921; Mrs. Murray S. Danforth, Providence, R.I., by 1934; her gift to the museum, 1942.

Selected exhibitions: Amsterdam 1905, no. 386; Berlin 1906, no. 77; Berlin 1921; Berlin 1927–28, hors cat.; New York 1955, no. 97; New York 1984, no. 26.

Summary of the literature: Because the related painting (F409, fig. 129) is documented in a letter of May 12, 1888 [487], this drawing has always been dated to May, and it has invariably been thought to have preceded the oil. The sketch on the verso was not recorded in De la Faille 1928, no. 1416, but was added to the 1970/1992 editions as F1416v. Several scholars have discussed Van Gogh's use of the perspective frame, in particular, Wylie (1970, p. 220) and Komanecky (1975, pp. 83–87), who provided a diagram of the pencil grid and a thorough formal analysis; see also Pickvance (in New York 1984, no. 26; and in Otterlo 1990, pp. 219–20) and Hansen (in Bremen 2002–3, p. 110; and in Toledo 2003, p. 56) for the artist's reliance on this device as a way of addressing the "compositional difficulties" he admitted to having with the motif [487]. Roskill (1971, pp. 167–68, 172) was the first to propose this work as one of the two "large drawings" mentioned in letter 483. This view was shared by Millard (1974, p. 148, pairing it with F1516, cat. 44), by Hulsker (1980, no. 1415, pairing it with F1513), and by Pickvance (in Otterlo 1990, pp. 219–20), who recognized F1472a as the other large drawing, having earlier refuted its mention in the correspondence. The question of dating and the drawing's relationship to the painting have invited some refinements: Pickvance in New York 1984 (and Heenk 1995, p. 177, in virtually identical terms) argued for its independent status and its earlier date, noting that the spring season and the cutting of the grass are slightly less advanced; Pickvance in Otterlo 1990 dated the drawing to May 1–7, 1888; Hulsker 1996, no. 1415, to ca. May 9–10; and Hansen in Bremen 2002–3 observed that the oil composition is simpler and more clearly defined, which may be attributed to the grass having been mowed or to artistic considerations that "may have prompted him to construct a clear line out of the irregularly mowed strips as parallel to the line of irises along the ditch." For early history, see Feilchenfeldt and Veenenbos 1988, p. 130; Stolwijk and Veenenbos 2002, pp. 51, 126, 147, 194.

Letter to Theo van Gogh, May 7, 1888 [483]: There has been a good deal of mistral here, so I did the dozen little drawings which I have sent you. Now the weather is splendid, I have already done another two large drawings [F1416r, F1472a] and five small ones. I have found a case to send my things in, and I hope they'll leave tomorrow. I am sending the five small drawings to you in Brussels today.

Letter to Theo van Gogh, May 12, 1888 [487]: Just now I have done two new [oil] studies. . . . A meadow full of very yellow buttercups, a ditch with irises, green leaves and purple flowers, the town in the background, some gray willows—a strip of blue sky. If the meadow does not get mowed, I'd like to do this study again, for the subject was very beautiful, and I had some trouble getting the composition. A little town surrounded by fields all covered with yellow and purple flowers; exactly—can't you see it?—like a Japanese dream.

Undoubtedly one of the two "large" drawings that Van Gogh noted in a letter to Theo in early May ([483], along with F1472a, fig. 123), this impressive sheet showcases the strides Van Gogh had made since March in his command of the reed pen. He met the demands of his most ambitious composition to date by depending on his perspective frame[1] and on various graphic strategies he had used to good effect in smaller works, from staccato lines and curlicue ciphers to articulate patchy areas of grass dotted with flowers (as in F1421, cat. 43) to short, emphatic dashes and feathered

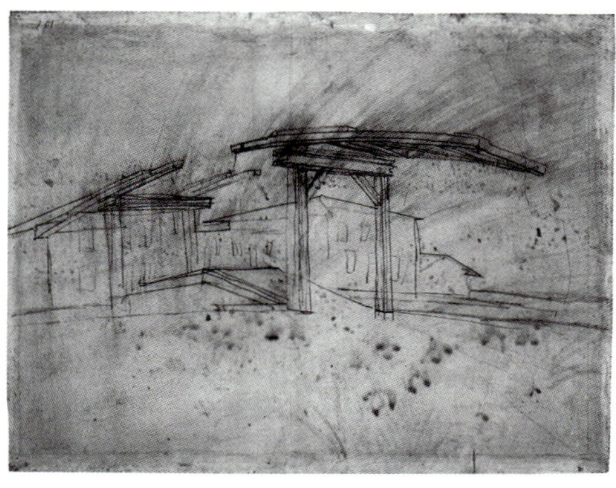

Fig. 127. *Drawbridge at Arles* (F1416v), sketch on verso of F1416r, cat. 46. Graphite, 43.5 x 55.5 cm (17⅛ x 21⅞ in.). Museum of Art, Rhode Island School of Design, Providence, Gift of Mrs. Murray S. Danforth

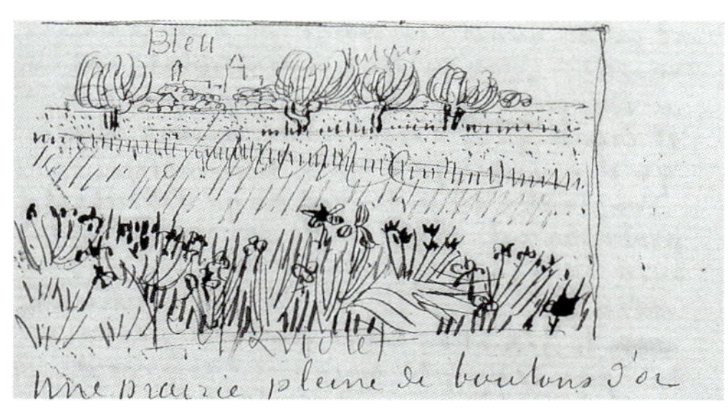

Fig. 128. Letter sketch of *View of Arles with Irises in the Foreground* (F1833), May 12, 1888 [487]. Ink on paper, image 6 x 10.5 cm (2⅜ x 4⅛ in.). Van Gogh Museum, Amsterdam (Vincent van Gogh Foundation)

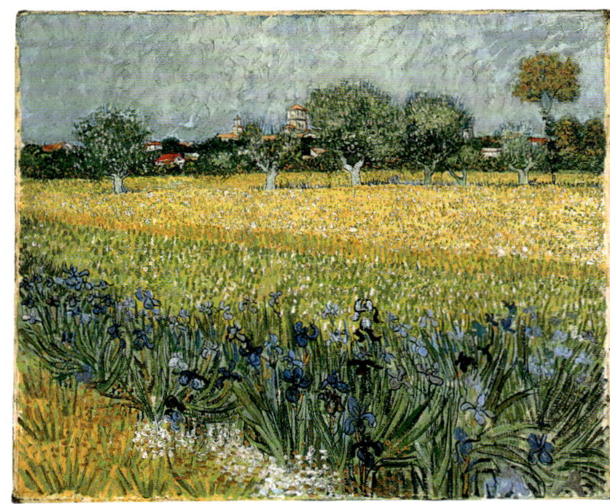

Fig. 129. *View of Arles with Irises in the Foreground* (F409), early May 1888. Oil on canvas, 54 x 65 cm (21¼ x 25⅝ in.). Van Gogh Museum, Amsterdam (Vincent van Gogh Foundation)

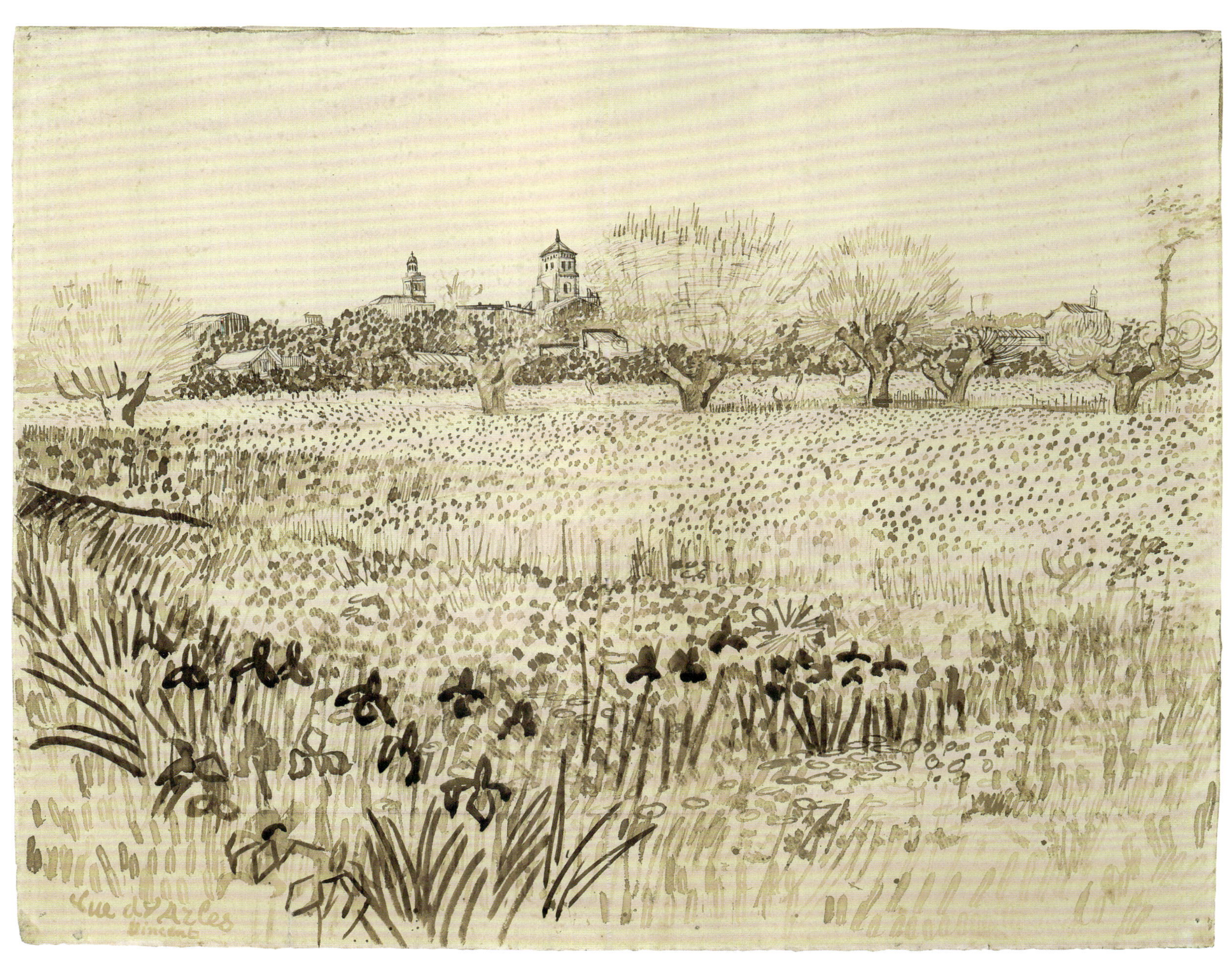
Vue d'Arles
Vincent

strokes to fashion dense foliage and sunburst-like trees (as anticipated by F1502, cat. 45). His conception of an expansive, variegated field receding into the distance, engaged his pen to solve the problems of filling space in new ways. He relied on dots that decrease in size as they near the townscape to suggest distance and dappled sunlight, and on a full-barreled pen stroke to create irises that accentuate the dynamic thrust of the foreground.

Van Gogh's efforts to produce a harmonious and balanced composition extend to trimming the paper along the top and right side, where his pen guidelines are still visible, and the deckled edges are lost. Slightly smaller than most drawings made on full sheets of Whatman stock (by approximately 4.5 centimeters in height and width), the squarer format anticipates the canvas he chose for the oil version. His intervention succeeded in reducing the sky, which was left bare as an effective foil for the play of line, and in focusing visual interest toward the center.

Making use of the lessons gained in working out the composition in pen and ink, Van Gogh simplified the design when he put his brush to the task (F409, fig. 129). In the painting, the flower beds, field, and sky are essentially reduced to three parallel bands (or, as his letter sketch, fig. 128, suggests, color zones: violet, yellow, blue). This solution eliminated the pitfall he had encountered in his initial, more daring conception of the transition at left, one of the drawing's least successful passages, where he resorted to a series of up-and-down pen strokes, as one writer observed "almost as if he were trying to fence off the irises from the field of yellow buttercups behind them."[2]

SAS

1. The artist's graphic framing lines are plainly visible in the infrared reflectogram (fig. 241).
2. Komanecky 1975, p. 84.

47. *View of Arles from Montmajour*

ca. May 27–29, 1888
Reed and quill pen and ink over graphite on paper watermarked J. WHATMAN TURKEY MILL 1879
48.6 x 60 cm (19⅛ x 23⅝ in.)
Signed lower left: *Vincent*
Nasjonalmuseet/Nasjonalgalleriet, Oslo (NG.K&H.00068)
F1452, JH1437
Letters 495, 498a, 499, 509

Provenance: Sent by the artist to Theo van Gogh (d. 1891), Paris, May 29 or 30, 1888 [495]; by inheritance to his son, Vincent Willem van Gogh, as part of his collection, administered by his widow, Johanna van Gogh-Bonger, 1891; sold by her to Hans Christian Christensen, Copenhagen, July 1893; sold by him to the museum, 1905.

Selected exhibitions: Copenhagen 1893, no. 193; Munich 1961, no. 59; Frankfurt 1970, no. 47; New York 1984, no. 33; Copenhagen 1984–85, no. 58; Otterlo 1990, no. 183.

Summary of the literature: The dating of this drawing to ca. May 27–29, 1888, and its distinctive intermediary role of succeeding the first series of Montmajour drawings and prefiguring the second were put forth by Pickvance (in New York 1984, no. 33; and in Otterlo 1990, no. 183). His view has since held sway in the literature (see Heenk 1995, p. 175; Hulsker 1996, no. 1437), which had earlier depended on the pioneering observations of Tellegen-Hoogendoorn (1967). Tellegen essentially established the drawings that made up each of the two Montmajour campaigns and distinguished this work in terms of its size and finish, but she failed to recognize completely its pivotal role. In her study, the drawing is dated to June and associated with the second series of drawings, which were likewise made on full sheets of Whatman paper, but in July. In De la Faille 1970 (no. 1452, which includes a recap of Tellegen's discussion), the drawing is dated to June and associated with letters 495 and 498a, as it is in Roskill 1971, p. 168; Millard 1974, pp. 158–60, 163 n. 29; Hulsker 1980, no. 1437. For Johanna's 1893 sale, see Stolwijk and Veenenbos 2002, pp. 46, 94, 141, 195.

See "Montmajour: The First Series" under "First Encounters."

SAS

Letter to Theo van Gogh, May 29 or 30, 1888 [495]: If the roll is not too big to be accepted by the post office, you will receive another big pen drawing, which I would very much like the Pissarros to see if they come on Sunday.

Letter to Arnold Hendrik Koning, a Dutch artist staying with Theo in Paris, May 29 or 30, 1888 [498a]: I have just finished a drawing, even larger than the first two, of a cluster of straight pines on a rock, seen from the top of a hill. Behind this foreground a perspective of meadows, a road with poplars, and in the far distance the town. The trees very dark against the sunlit meadow; perhaps you will get an opportunity to see this drawing.

I did it with very thick reeds on thin Whatman paper, and in the background I worked with a quill for the finer strokes.

I can recommend this method to you, for the quill strokes are more in character than those of the reed.

Letter to Theo van Gogh, ca. June 3, 1888 [499]: Besides half-page drawings I have a big drawing [F1439, fig. 130], the pendant of the last [big] one.

Letter to Theo van Gogh, ca. July 13, 1888 [509]: I have just sent off to you by post a roll containing five big pen drawings. You have a sixth of that series from Mont Majour—a group of very dark pines and the town of Arles in the background.

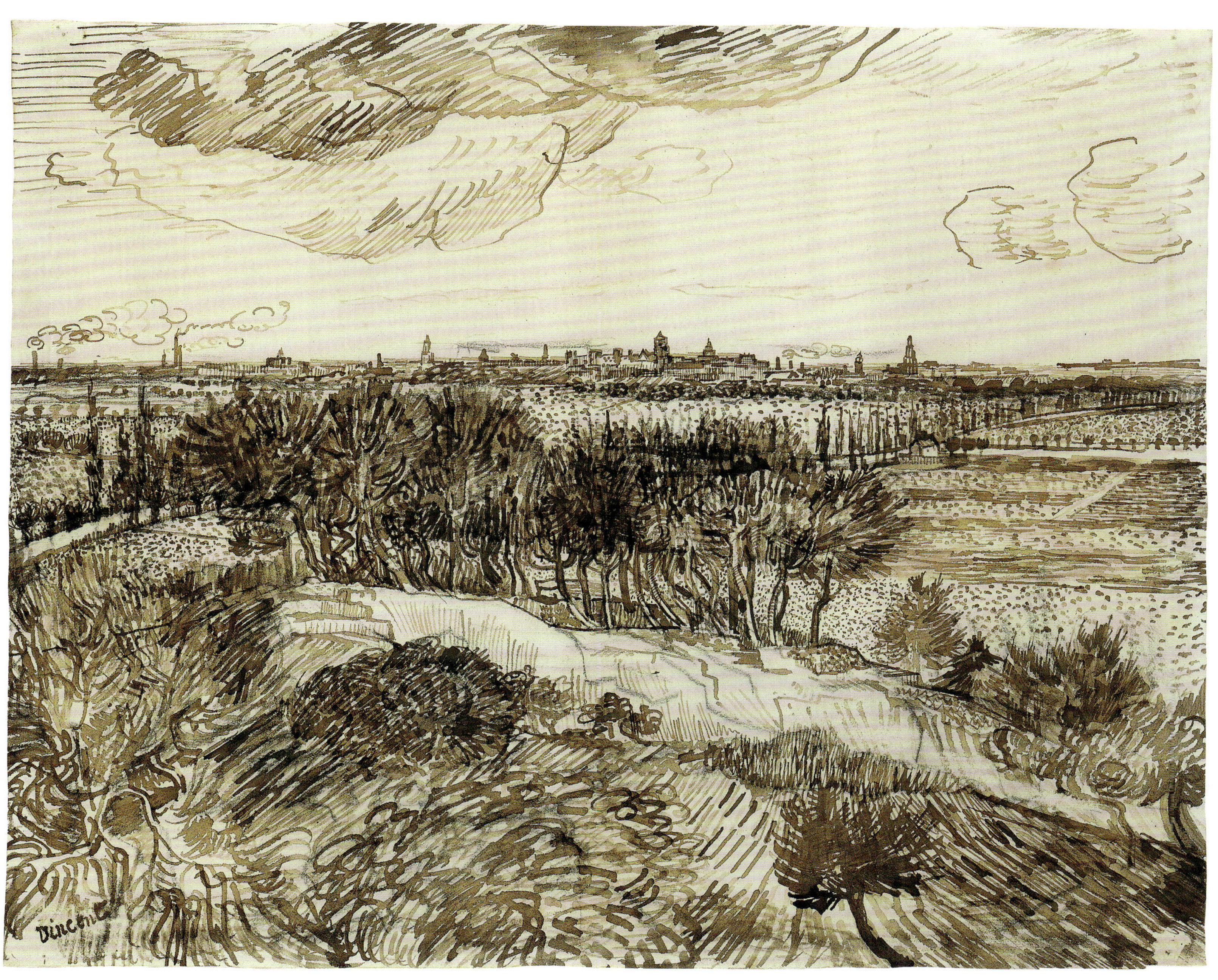
Vincent

A Visit to the Sea

Van Gogh's visit to Saintes-Maries-de-la-Mer was brief (ca. May 30–June 5, 1888), but its impact was profound.[1] In about a week's time, the artist discovered that drawing was an activity comfortably within his grasp. Under vast blue skies, a dazzling sun, and the reflected light of the Mediterranean, the artist relaxed his grip on the rule books and set his hand free.

The sea always held an attraction for Van Gogh. "Sand, sea and sky—is something I certainly hope to express sometime" [222], he said in 1882, while sketching beaches at Scheveningen, near The Hague. Six years later, during his first three months in Provence, he spoke intermittently of making a trip to the Mediterranean and painting seascapes in Marseille or Martigues. But it was not until the end of May, just after the annual Gypsy pilgrimage took place at a nearby coastal town renowned as the seaport of the three sainted Marys, that he defined a plan: "I expect to make an excursion to Saintes-Maries, and see the Mediterranean at last" [492]. A short time later he left Arles by morning coach to arrive midday at the fishing village some twenty-four miles distant, there to salute the sea in two oil studies and at least an equal number of pen-and-ink drawings.

Perhaps to his own surprise, Van Gogh became enchanted by the town itself, drawing and painting a view of its clustered buildings from the lavender fields on its outskirts (F1439, fig. 130; F416, fig. 131) and tramping its dirt paths to admire the local gabled cottages (*cabanes*). In six extraordinary pen-and-ink studies, each a foot tall, he detailed the townspeople's "nests," with their steep, thatched roofs that were made from cut grasses, just like his own reed pens (see F1440, cat. 48; F1438, cat. 49; F1434, cat. 50; F1437, cat. 54). Some of these drawings, Van Gogh admitted, were "rather harsh," others "more carefully drawn" [500]. All are spare, focused designs, boldly delineated.

As a whole, this group signals the breakthrough the artist had hoped for and anticipated when relating his departure plans to his brother: "I am taking especially whatever I need for drawing. I must draw a great deal. . . . Things here have so much line. And I want to get my drawing more spontaneous, more

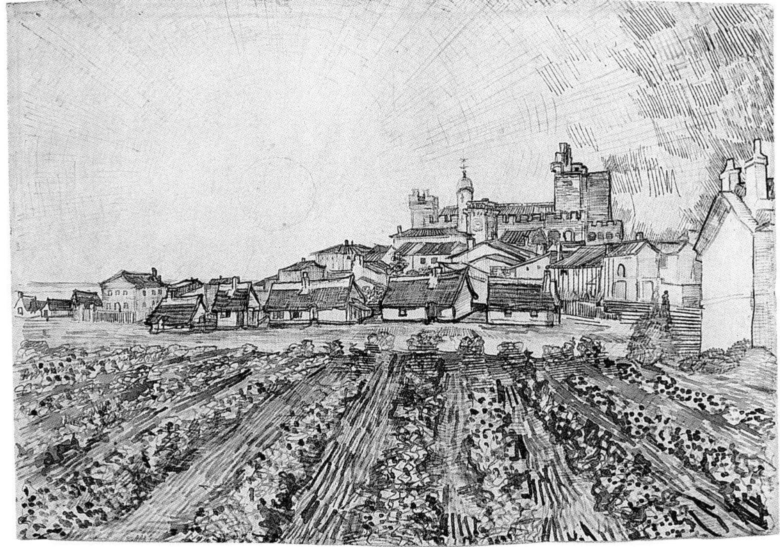

Fig. 130. *View of Saintes-Maries* (F1439), ca. May 30–June 3, 1888. Reed pen and ink, 43 x 60 cm (17 x 23⅝ in.). Sammlung Oskar Reinhart "Am Römerholz," Winterthur

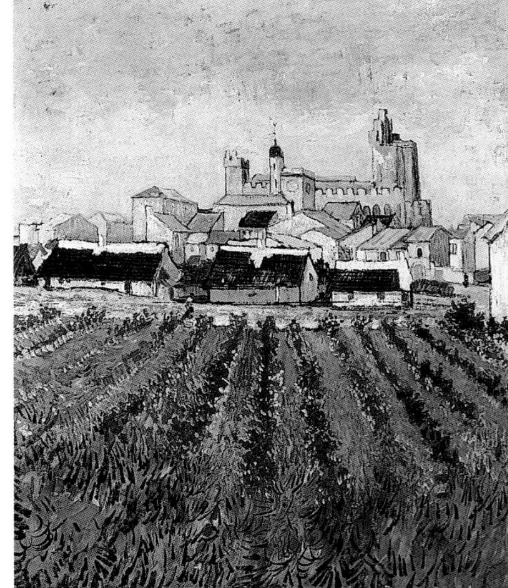

Fig. 131. *View of Saintes-Maries* (F416), ca. May 30–June 3, 1888. Oil on canvas, 64 x 53 cm (25¼ x 20⅞ in.). Kröller-Müller Museum, Otterlo

exaggerated" [495]. Indeed, Van Gogh could report to Theo, upon his return to Arles, the gratifying liberation of his pen in Saintes-Maries and his pride in producing a finished drawing there, just before he left, "*in an hour* . . . [not] even with the perspective frame . . . without measuring, just by letting my pen go" [500] (see F1428, cat. 60).

The emphatic new way of drawing that Van Gogh now found possible must be owed in no small part to his ever-deepening appreciation of the principles underlying Japanese woodcuts, which, for the past three years, he had been enthusiastically collecting and even copying (figs. 132, 133). Indeed, reporting to Theo the successes of this excursion to Saintes-Maries, Vincent framed his experience in terms of ukiyo-e: "I wish you could spend some time here, you would feel it after a while, one's sight changes: you see things with an eye more Japanese, you feel color differently. The Japanese draw quickly, very quickly, like a lightning flash, because their nerves are finer, their feeling simpler. I am convinced that I shall set my individuality free simply by staying on here . . . you must boldly exaggerate the effects of either harmony or discord which colors produce. It is the same as in drawing—accurate drawing, accurate color, is perhaps not the essential thing to aim at" [500].

The quirky calligraphy that Van Gogh was now emboldened to practice featured chopped-up lines, scattered dots, and squiggles organized into an agitated surface balanced between black and white. This graphic approach allowed him to work in a less hidebound, more personal style—one distinct from Impressionism or Pointillism and yet grounded in a genuine artistic tradition. Ukiyo-e's principles, furthermore, extolled spontaneity, exaggeration, and striking contrasts in the

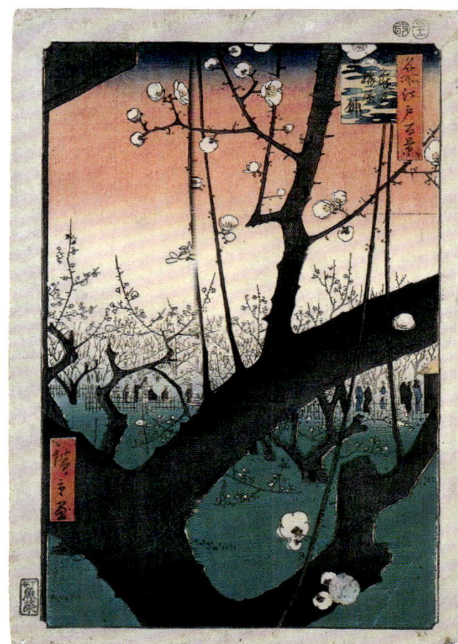

Fig. 132. Utagawa Hiroshige, *The Plum Tree Teahouse at Kameidō*, 1857. Color woodcut, 35.5 x 23.2 cm (14 x 9⅛ in.). Van Gogh Museum, Amsterdam (Vincent van Gogh Foundation)

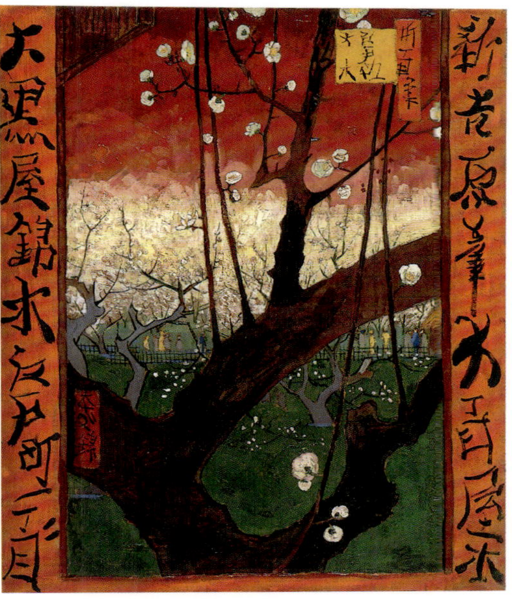

Fig. 133. *The Flowering Tree* (after Hiroshige) (F371), 1887. Oil on canvas, 55 x 46 cm (21⅝ x 18⅛ in.). Van Gogh Museum, Amsterdam (Vincent van Gogh Foundation)

application of color as well as line. Thus, Van Gogh revealed his new plans to fellow artist Émile Bernard: "I am going to put the *black* and the *white*, just as the color merchant sells them to us, boldly on my palette and use them just as they are . . . observe that I am speaking of the simplification of color in the Japanese manner. . . . The Japanese artist ignores reflected colors, and puts the flat tones side by side, with characteristic lines marking off the movements and the forms" [B6].

Almost immediately upon his return to Arles from Saintes-Maries, Van Gogh sent sketches of pictures made there to his brother and to Bernard. The following month he sent to them and to the painter John Russell more finely penned descriptions (see F1430, cat. 57; F1430a, cat. 58; F1430b, cat. 59; F1435, cat. 53). He further set about translating three of the Saintes-Maries drawings into oil paintings forcefully brushed and brightly colored—celebrations of the epiphanies of his pilgrimage (F413, fig. 136; F419, fig. 134; F420, cat. 51). "Now that I have seen the sea here," he wrote Theo, "I am absolutely convinced of the importance of staying in the Midi, and of positively piling it on" [500].

CI

1. Van Gogh's visit to Saintes-Maries was dated June 17–23, 1888, in the literature until Ronald Pickvance (in New York 1984, pp. 83–84, 260–62) redated the sojourn May 30–June 3, 1888, on the basis of the artist's letters and corresponding weather reports. Pickvance's dates have been embraced in subsequent literature, notably in the revised edition of Hulsker (1996), although Roland Dorn (1997–98) argued that the trip to the sea took place between June 10 and 16. The chronology Dorn proposed was based on his redating of some of Van Gogh's letters and also on his understanding of the artist's progressive explorations of the role of drawing. However, his insights into the decisive impact of Van Gogh's experiences at Saintes-Maries, the artist's experimentation and discovery of his own personal graphic language or "style," can be seen unfolding more logically within the chronology proposed by Pickvance. More recently, in their ongoing study and examination of Van Gogh's letters, Leo Jansen and Hans Luijten have found it reasonable to assume that the artist departed for Saintes-Maries on May 30 or 31 and returned to Arles about June 5. Their conclusions are based on the texts of letter 495, written May 29 or 30, and letters 494 and 500, written no earlier than June 4 and no later than June 6.

48. *Two Cottages, Saintes-Maries-de-la-Mer*

ca. May 30–June 5, 1888
Reed pen and ink over graphite on laid paper watermarked PL BAS
31.5 x 47.4 cm (12 3/8 x 18 3/4 in.)
Numbered in pen and ink on verso, upper left, in another hand: *132*
Pinholes in corners
Thaw Collection, The Pierpont Morgan Library, New York
F1440, JH1451
Letters 499, 500

Provenance: Sent by the artist at an unrecorded date to Theo van Gogh (d. 1891), Paris; by inheritance to his son, Vincent Willem van Gogh, as part of his collection, administered by his widow, Johanna van Gogh-Bonger, 1891; Elizabeth Bonger (d. 1944), Amsterdam, by 1905; Professor Dr. J. Willem Mengelberg, Amsterdam; his sale, Mak van Waay, Amsterdam, March 25, 1952, no. 78; Mr. and Mrs. Louis Ritter, Scarsdale, N.Y., by 1955; Ritter Foundation Inc., Scarsdale, N.Y., by 1959, until at least 1966; Eli and Edythe L. Broad, Los Angeles; Acquavella Galleries, New York, by 1983; Mr. and Mrs. Eugene Thaw, New York, 1983.

Selected exhibitions: Paris 1902 (no. 13 on Johanna's list of loans); Amsterdam 1905, no. 382; New York 1955, no. 100; New York 1984, no. 35; Otterlo 1990, no. 181.

Summary of the literature: Scholars, beginning with De la Faille (1928, no. 1440), have associated this drawing with Van Gogh's trip to Saintes-Maries and have dated it June 1888 (De la Faille 1970/1992, no. 1440; and Hulsker 1980/1996, no. 1451). Roskill (1971, p. 169 n. 148; later joined by Pickvance in Otterlo 1990, no. 181) recognized this drawing as "probably the third held back" in the group of Saintes-Maries studies Van Gogh retained for use in the preparation of paintings. Pickvance (in New York 1984, p. 85) noted (in contrast to F1438, cat. 49) "the mood of this drawing, more soigné . . . almost tender" and "a rare instance of human presence in the Saintes-Maries drawings—and the distant view of the Mediterranean." Heenk (1995, p. 165) inferred from the "rapid pen marks" that the drawing was "executed on the spot." See also New York–Richmond 1985–86, no. 53; New York 1994–95, no. 92.

During his short visit to Saintes-Maries, Van Gogh produced at least five ink drawings of *cabanes*, the distinctive thatched cottages of the Camargue. The artist apparently retained this particular drawing (rather than sending it on immediately to Theo) with some thought to re-creating it in oils. However, it was a much more stylized sketch of the subject (F1438, cat. 49) that became the springboard for his vividly painted abstraction of the same cottages (F419, fig. 134). This more delicate and lyrical interpretation of the clustered shelters, undoubtedly among those Van Gogh described as "carefully drawn ones," was sidestepped in favor of a more daring experiment in the style Van Gogh characterized as "harsh" [500].

CI

Letter to Theo van Gogh, ca. June 3–4, 1888 [499]: I do not think there are 100 houses in the village, or town. . . . And the houses—like the ones on our heaths and peat bogs in Drenthe; you will see some specimens of them in the drawings [see F1104, cat. 14].

Letter to Theo van Gogh, ca. June 5, 1888 [500]: I am sending you by the same post the drawings of Stes.-Maries. . . . I have three more drawings of cottages which I still need, and which will follow these: they are rather harsh, but I have some more carefully drawn ones.

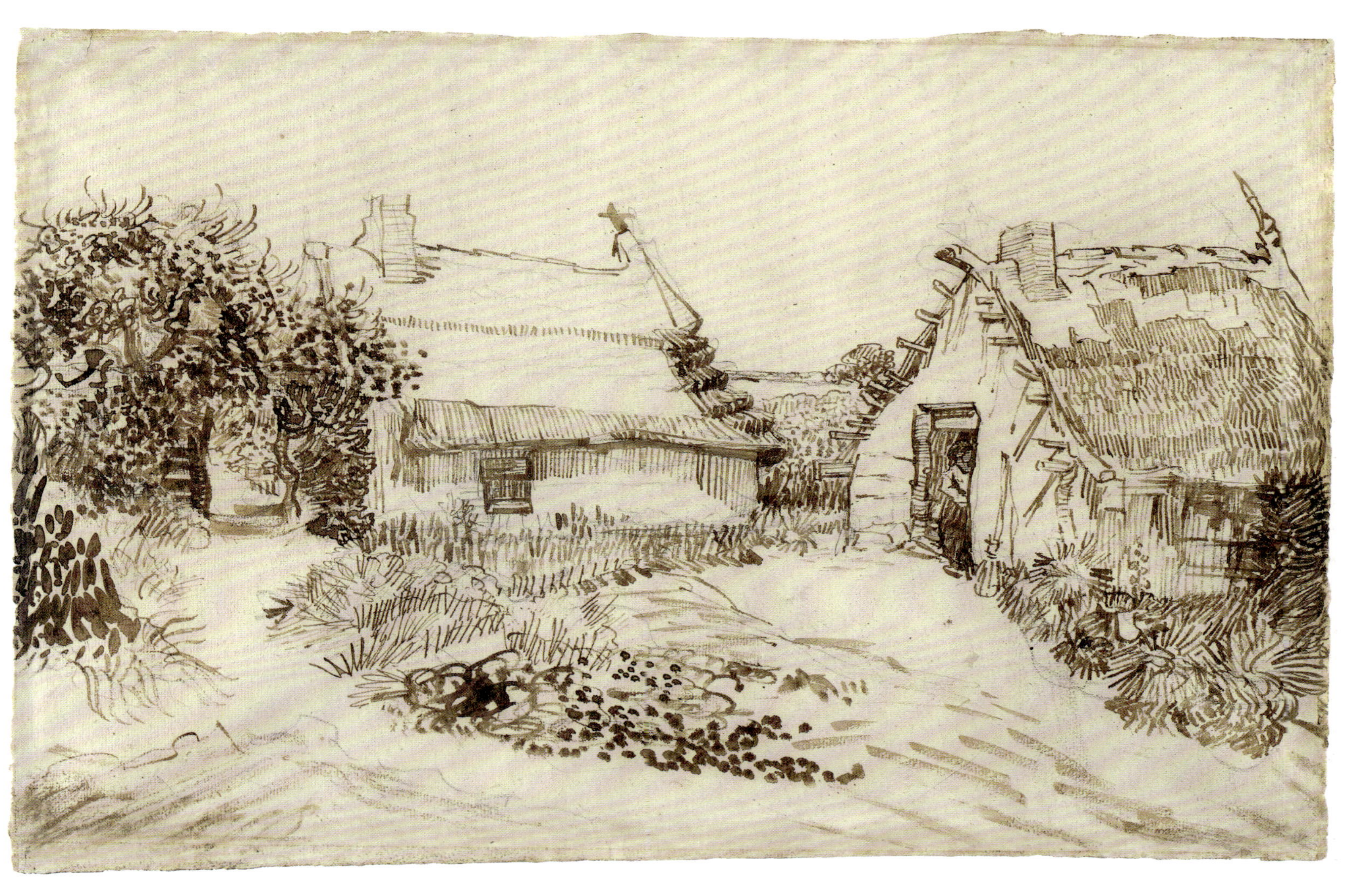

49. *Three Cottages, Saintes-Maries-de-la-Mer*

ca. May 30–June 5, 1888
Reed pen, brush, and ink over graphite on laid paper watermarked AL
30.2 x 47.4 cm (11 7/8 x 18 5/8 in.)
Inscribed on verso, in another hand: *134*
Van Gogh Museum, Amsterdam (Vincent van Gogh Foundation) (d 161 V/1962)
F1438, JH1448
Letters 499, 500

Provenance: Sent by the artist at an unrecorded date to Theo van Gogh (d. 1891), Paris; by inheritance to his son, Vincent Willem van Gogh (1890–1978), as part of his collection, administered by his widow, Johanna van Gogh-Bonger (d. 1925), 1891; placed on loan at the Stedelijk Museum, Amsterdam, 1931–73; ownership transferred to the Vincent van Gogh Foundation, 1962; placed on permanent loan at the Van Gogh Museum, Amsterdam, 1973.

Selected exhibitions: Leiden 1893; Groningen 1897; Amsterdam 1905, no. 380; Cologne–Frankfurt 1910; Amsterdam 1914–15, no. 142; Utrecht 1923, no. 52; Rotterdam 1923; Berlin 1927–28, no. 66; London–Birmingham–Glasgow 1947–48, no. 145; New York–Chicago 1949–50, no. 100; Aix-en-Provence 1959, no. 29; Tokyo–Kyōto–Nagoya 1976–77, no. 64; New York 1984, no. 36; Otterlo 1990, no. 182; Martigny 2000, no. 56.

Summary of the literature: Scholars, beginning with De la Faille (1928, no. 1438), have associated this drawing with Van Gogh's trip to Saintes-Maries and have dated it June 1888 (De la Faille 1970/1992, no. 1438; and Hulsker 1980/1996, no. 1448). Roskill (1971, p. 169) identified the work as one of three Sainte-Maries drawings Vincent refrained from sending immediately to Theo but "held back for further use" along with F1434 and "probably" F1440, in preparation for painting (F419). Pickvance (in New York 1984, no. 36) placed the "almost brutal" drawing among the group Van Gogh referred to as "harsh" [500]. He dated the sheet "late May–early June 1888" (in Otterlo 1990, no. 182), connecting it to one of "three clearly documented instances of Van Gogh's direct use of a drawing in making a painting." For early history, see Feilchenfeldt and Veenenbos 1988, p. 132.

Instead of sending this drawing to Theo along with others he made in Saintes-Maries, Van Gogh held the sheet back, as he had two similar views of cottages (F1434, cat. 50; F1440, cat. 48), so that he might picture in paintings the thatched huts fishermen built close together to withstand the mistral. Like the fishing boats he drew tied up side by side on the beach (F1428, cat. 60) and the small one-man vessels he showed sailing together at sea (F417, cat. 55), the clustered *cabanes* stirred Van Gogh's thoughts of a community of artists he hoped would gather in the south of France for mutual support.

It could not have been more than a day or two after Van Gogh returned to Arles from Saintes-Maries before he began to paint this same subject (F419, fig. 134). He evidently used tracing to transfer his pen-and-ink composition to a canvas that was somewhat taller and narrower than his drawing paper. The painting's squarer format necessitated some changes to the roof and doorway of the left-most building in the drawing; at the same time, it allowed for expansions of land and sky. Judging from the vigor of his brushwork, Van Gogh seems to have proceeded to painting with considerable enthusiasm and the same sense of freedom he had felt "letting his pen go" at Saintes-Maries. The energy that charged his pen strokes was now channeled in blunt swipes of the brush; the bold contrasts of black and white re-created in clashing hues: the color-wheel opposites orange and blue, yellow and violet. CI

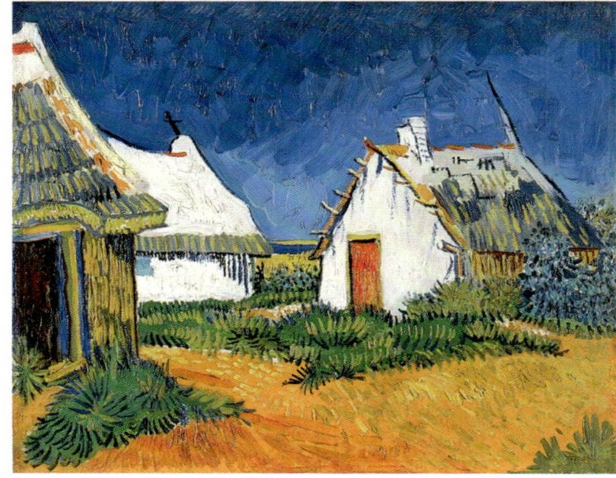

Fig. 134. *Three White Cottages in Saintes-Maries-de-la-Mer* (F419), June 1888. Oil on canvas, 33.5 x 41.5 cm (13 1/4 x 16 3/8 in.). Walter Haefner Schenkung, Kunsthaus Zürich

Letter to Theo van Gogh, ca. June 3, 1888 [499]: I do not think there are 100 houses in the village. . . . [They are] like the ones on our heaths and peat bogs in Drenthe. . . .

Letter to Theo van Gogh, ca. June 5, 1888 [500]: I am sending you . . . drawings of Stes.-Maries. . . . I have three more drawings of cottages which I still need, and which will follow these: they are rather harsh. . . .

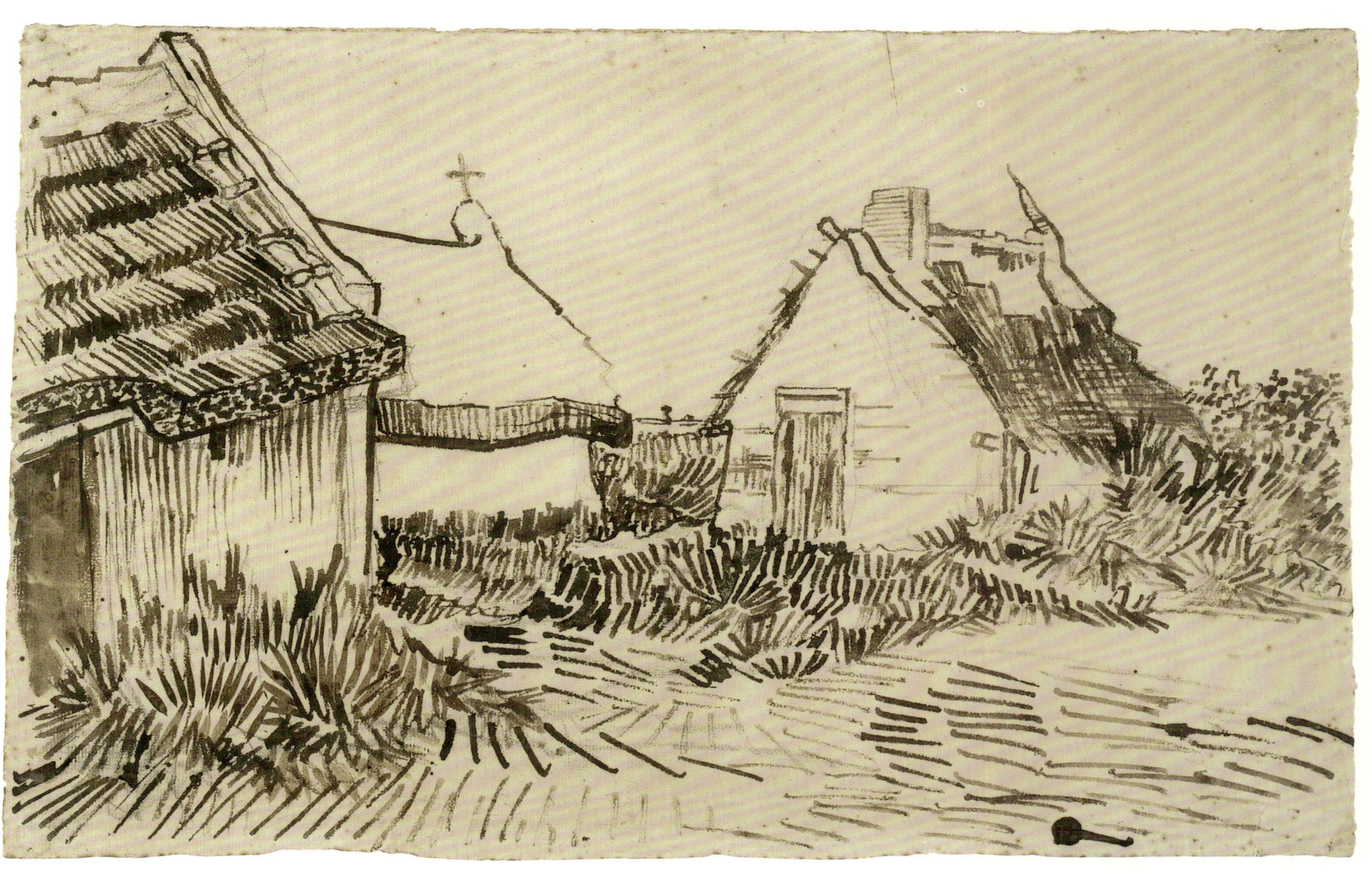

50. *Street in Saintes-Maries-de-la-Mer*

ca. May 30–June 5, 1888
Reed pen and ink over graphite on laid paper watermarked AL in double oval
30.5 x 47 cm (12 x 18½ in.)
Numbered and inscribed in faint (erased?) graphite, upper center: *320 / + / Pour* [?] *Vendredi 20* [or *27*] *Juillet*
Numbered in pen and ink on verso, upper left: *136*; in graphite, center: *150*
Tack holes in all corners
Private collection, on deposit at The Pierpont Morgan Library, New York
F1434, JH1449
Letters 499, 500

Provenance: Sent by the artist at an unrecorded date to Theo van Gogh (d. 1891), Paris; by inheritance to his son, Vincent Willem van Gogh, as part of his collection, administered by his widow, Johanna van Gogh-Bonger, 1891; sold by her to Paul Cassirer, Berlin, November 1907; sold to Johannes Guthmann, Berlin, November 1907; Dr. Joachim Zimmermann, Berlin and Mittelschreiberhau; Neumann, Wannsee; Fritz Nathan, Zürich; Robert von Hirsch, Basel, by ca. 1970; his sale, Sotheby's, London, June 27, 1978, no. 844; purchased by the British Rail Pension Fund; its sale, Sotheby's, London, April 4, 1989, no. 20, to present owner.

Selected exhibitions: Amsterdam 1905, no. 379; Berlin 1906, no. 70; Berlin 1907; Berlin 1908; Berlin 1914, no. 97; Berlin 1927–28, no. 104; Paris 1960, no. 93; New York 1984, no. 38; Tokyo–Nagoya 1985–86, no. 74; Otterlo 1990, no. 180.

Summary of the literature: After De la Faille (1928, no. 1434) and Hulsker (1980, no. 1449) identified this drawing as one Van Gogh made in Saintes-Maries, the principal question regarding it became its relationship to other versions of the same subject, particularly to the Metropolitan Museum's drawing (F1435, cat. 53). Novotny (1936, pp. 370–80) determined that this was the first-drawn of the two; Roskill (1966, p. 13 n. 32) clarified the place of each by maintaining that this earlier one "was surely done at Saintes-Maries [500] and was the basis for the corresponding canvas painted in Arles [F420] and the later drawing F1435." Pickvance (in New York 1984, no. 38) described the draftsmanship as "a powerful tour de force," later noting (in Otterlo 1990, no. 180) that the work presented one of only three documented instances in which Van Gogh relied so directly upon a drawing in preparation for a painting. Heenk (1995, p. 169) observed the previously overlooked pencil inscription near the top center of the drawing sheet but found it too faint to read except for one word: "vendredi" (Friday). For early history, see Feilchenfeldt and Veenenbos 1988, p. 131.

Van Gogh's excited discovery of a pathway to the sea is conveyed in this pointed composition, lined on one side with a row of thatched cottages and on the other with tangled vegetation. The motifs are ones Van Gogh favored in Holland; he must have been delighted to find them reiterated in southern climes. His organization of the view along lines of a sharply receding single-point perspective was evidently accomplished swiftly, on the spot, and is remarkably unlabored. Strokes of the pliant reed pen follow cues from a skeletal underdrawing and then speed off on their own. All that Vincent might have hoped to realize on his excursion to Saintes-Maries—a conception "manly" and "free" [429]—seems to have been achieved in this composition that almost immediately upon his return to Arles was turned into a painting (F420, cat. 51).

CI

Letters to Theo van Gogh, ca. June 3, 1888 [499], and ca. June 5, [500]: See F1440, cat. 48.

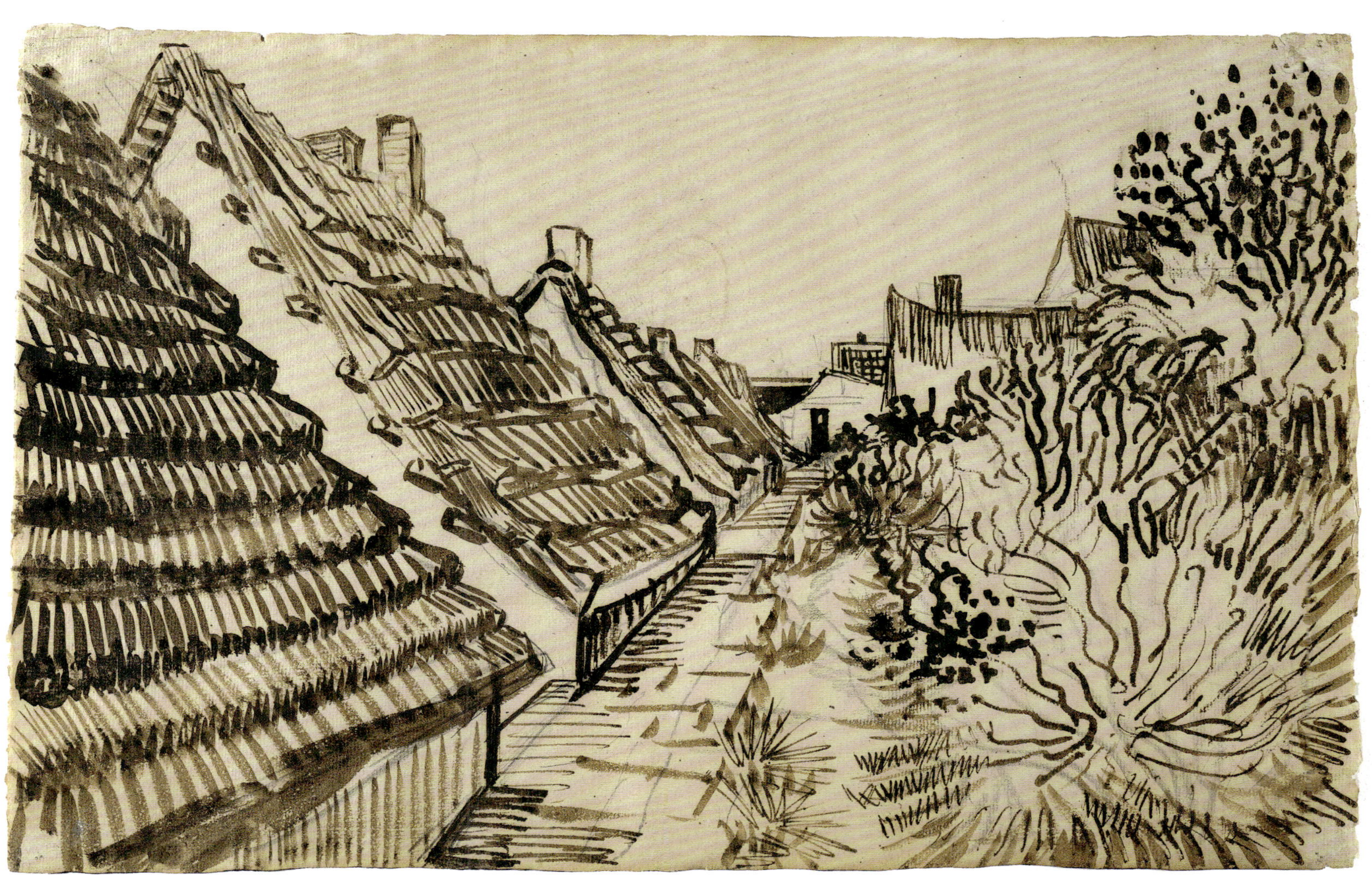

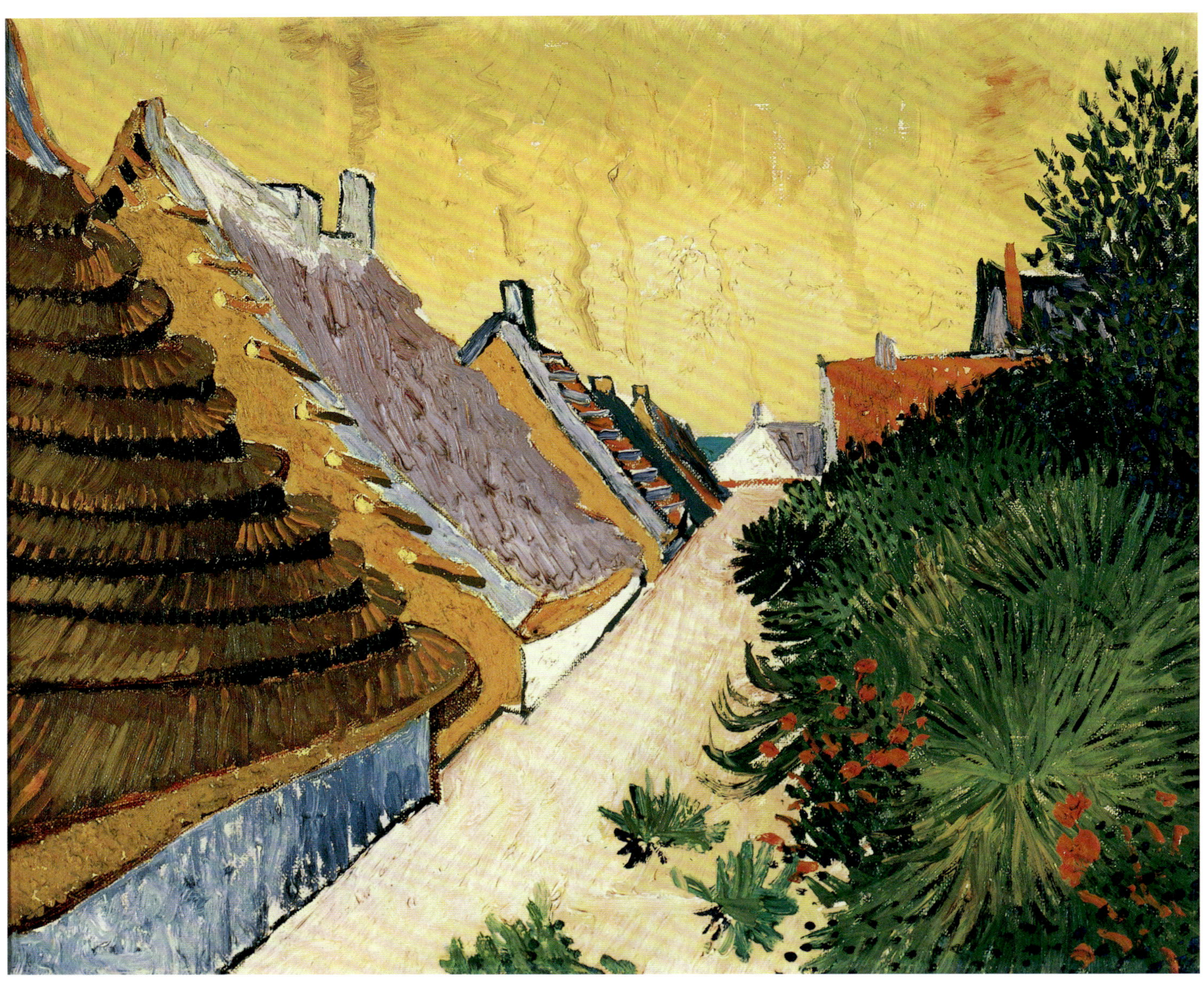

51. *Street in Saintes-Maries-de-la-Mer*

ca. June 6, 1888
Oil on canvas
38 x 46 cm (15 x 18⅛ in.)
Private collection
F420, JH1462
Letter B6

New York only

Van Gogh was remarkably faithful to the drawing he had made looking down a dirt path leading to the sea. When he returned to his studio in Arles he traced the composition in order to transfer it for painting, adding more sky at the top and more pathway at the bottom to fill the squarer format of his canvas. Vibrant complementary colors—yellow and violet, red and green, orange and blue—took the place of graphic exuberance, in an eye-tingling demonstration of the laws of simultaneous contrast. It is astounding that the artist was able to shift completely from defining a subject in line to defining it in full-blown color. At the time, Vincent wrote to Theo of his great satisfaction with this experience: "Now that I have seen the sea here, I am absolutely convinced of the importance of staying in the Midi, and of positively piling it on, exaggerating the color—Africa not so far away" [500]. Days earlier, he had reminded Theo of Corot's reported dream of "landscapes with skies all pink." "Well," he wrote, "haven't they come, those pink skies, and yellow and green into the bargain, in the impressionist landscapes?" [489].

CI

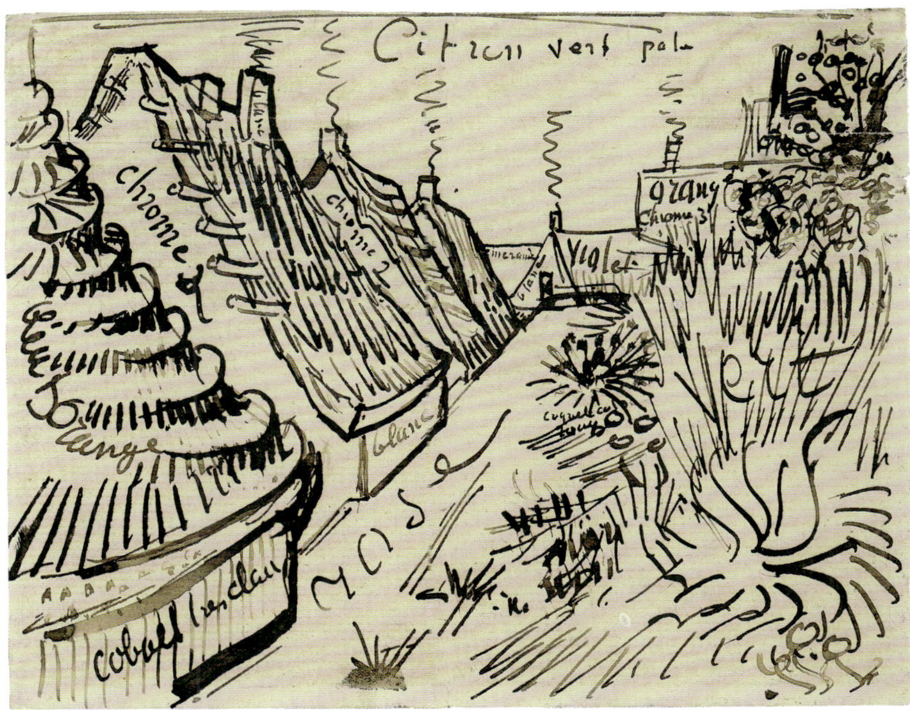

52. *Street in Saintes-Maries-de-la-Mer*

Sketch included in a letter to Émile Bernard, ca. June 7, 1888 [B6] (see also F1839, cat. 56; F1837, cat. 61)
Reed pen and ink on wove paper watermarked with an indecipherable design (crown with hunting horns?)
14.3 x 17.9 cm (5⅝ x 7 1/16 in.)
Inscribed in pen and ink, left to right: *bleu / orange / cobalt tres clair / chrome 2 / blanc / violet / blanc / chrome 2 / rose / citron vert pale / emeraude / blanc / coquelicot rouge / violet / orange / chrome 3 / vert*
Verso: *Boats at Sea, Saintes-Maries-de-la-Mer; Two Landscapes* (F1839, cat. 56)
Thaw Collection, The Pierpont Morgan Library, New York
F1838, JH1463
Letter B6

Provenance: Sent by the artist to Émile Bernard (d. 1941), Saint-Briac, ca. June 7, 1888 [B6]; Baroness Goldschmidt-Rothschild (d. 1965), Paris; private collection, New York; Eugene V. and Clare E. Thaw, New York and Santa Fe, N.M.

Summary of the literature: Scholars generally agree that Van Gogh's letter to Bernard [B6] and the sketches of paintings enclosed with it were sent sometime between June 6 and 11, 1888, and that this drawing represents the painting the artist made upon his return from Saintes-Maries to Arles (F420, cat. 51).

Van Gogh's copious color notes—seventeen—on his sketched copy of a painting (F420, cat. 51) only recently finished and hung up to dry suggest his pride in the achievement. Clearly, he was eager to demonstrate to his friend Bernard the success of the picture as an exercise in pairing complementary colors. In the letter attached he spoke at length and intently about the effects of color (see excerpt at right) and its use by him, by Japanese artists, and by contemporary painters like Eugène Fromentin and Jean-Léon Gérôme who, he noted with dismay, could only "see the soil of the South as colorless" [B6].

The precision of Van Gogh's color choices is documented in this breezy souvenir, as is the artist's confident familiarity with the composition he now rendered for the third time.

CI

Letter to Émile Bernard, ca. June 7, 1888 [B6]: [W]hen for instance one composes a motif of colors representing a yellow sky, then the fierce hard white of a white wall against this sky may be expressed if necessary—and this in a strange way—by raw white, softened by a neutral tone, for the sky itself colors it with a delicate lilac hue. . . . Suffice it to say that black and white are also colors, for in many cases they can be looked upon as colors, for their simultaneous contrast is as striking as that of green and red, for instance.

53. *Street in Saintes-Maries-de-la-Mer*

(for Émile Bernard)

Mid-July 1888
Reed pen, quill, and ink over graphite on wove paper (laid down on wove paper; tack holes in all corners); later additions (by a restorer?) in black chalk, lower and upper right
24.3 x 31.7 cm (9⅝ x 12½ in.)
Signed in pen and ink, lower left: *Vincent*
Inscribed in graphite on verso, lower right: *24 . . .* (obscured)
The Metropolitan Museum of Art, New York, Bequest of Abby Aldrich Rockefeller, 1948 (48.190.1)
F1435, JH1506
Letters B10, 511

Provenance: Sent by the artist to Émile Bernard, Saint-Briac, July 15, 1888 [B10, 511]; probably sold to Ambroise Vollard, Paris, between 1899 and 1904; Galerie d'Art Druet, Paris; Galerie Thannhauser, Munich; Galerie Marcel Goldschmidt, Frankfurt; A. Ronde, Mainz; Abby Aldrich Rockefeller, New York, by 1935; her bequest to the Metropolitan Museum, 1948 (subject to possession by the Museum of Modern Art for fifty years following her death).

Selected exhibitions: New York and other cities 1935–36, no. 110; Munich 1956, no. 113; New York 1984, no. 64.

Summary of the literature: In all editions of De la Faille (no. 1435), this work is catalogued as one drawn in Saintes-Maries in June 1888. Novotny (1953) provided formal analyses of this drawing and another of the same motif (F1434, cat. 50). The relationship between these two works was clarified by Roskill (1966, p. 13 n. 32). Roskill (1971, p. 152), Hulsker (1980/1996, no. 1506), and Pickvance (in New York 1984, no. 64) recognized the drawing as one based on the painting (F420) and sent by Van Gogh to Bernard in mid-July 1888. Pickvance clarified its relationship to earlier depictions, seeing it as "stage four" in an "elaborate work sequence."

Van Gogh's pen-and-ink copy of the painting (F420, cat. 51) he had completed more than a month earlier is a striking surrogate for the canvas, designed both to inform and to delight its recipient, Émile Bernard. The artist had drawn the subject twice before (see F1434, cat. 50; F1838, cat. 52), and thus, not surprisingly, his final version is the most decided and refined in composition and graphic expression. Surfaces are now defined in patterns of parallel lines and dots, while the tangle of plant life across the road from the cottages enjoys something of the dynamic fluidity with which it was first rendered. Ever, and perhaps excessively, conscious of the rules of perspective, Van Gogh here adjusted sight lines to converge exactly at the triangle of distant sea and, in this version alone, added a tiny sailboat to the horizon. His alterations, both playful and plotted, concentrate and focus all the drawing's elements.

See "*Répétitions:* Drawings after Paintings."

CI

Letter to Émile Bernard, July 15, 1888 [B10]: Perhaps you will be inclined to forgive me for not replying to your letter immediately, when you see that I am sending you a little batch of sketches along with this letter. . . . Now I should like to have some things of yours too—without spoiling your chances of making a sale in Paris, however. At any rate I don't think you will lose by it, if I can persuade you to make a mutual exchange of sketches after painted studies.

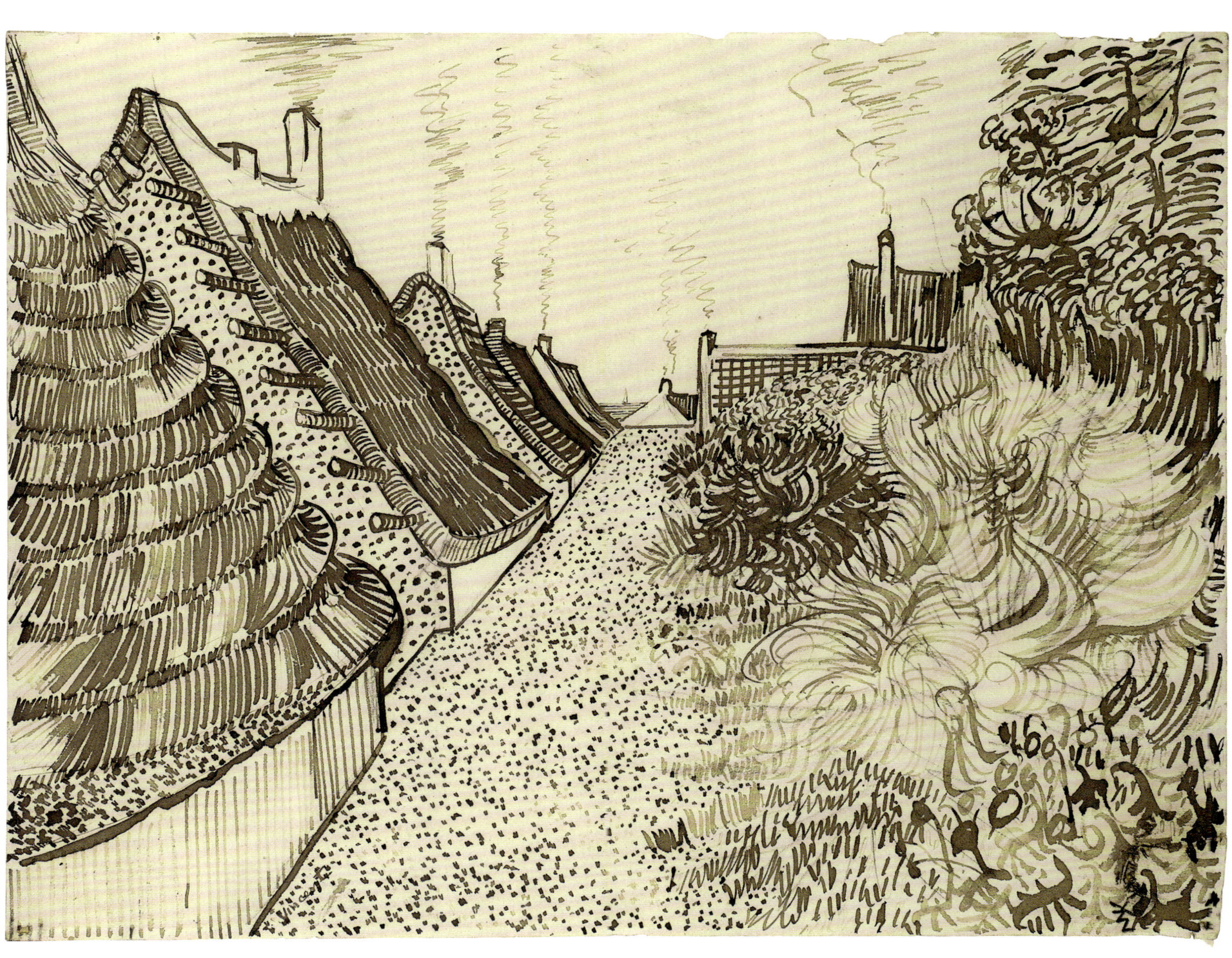

54. *Cottages, Saintes-Maries-de-la-Mer*

ca. May 30–June 5, 1888
Reed pen, quill, and ink over graphite on laid paper watermarked PL BAS
30.5 x 47.2 cm (12 x 18⅝ in.)
Inscribed on verso: *135*
Tack holes in corners
Van Gogh Museum, Amsterdam (Vincent van Gogh Foundation) (d 426 V/1962)
F1437, JH1450
Letters 499, 500

Provenance: Sent by the artist to Theo van Gogh (d. 1891), Paris, ca. June 5, 1888 [500]; by inheritance to his son, Vincent Willem van Gogh (1890–1978), as part of his collection, administered by his widow, Johanna van Gogh-Bonger (d. 1925), 1891; placed on loan at the Stedelijk Museum, Amsterdam, 1925–73; ownership transferred to the Vincent van Gogh Foundation, 1962; placed on permanent loan at the Van Gogh Museum, Amsterdam, 1973.

Selected exhibitions: Leiden 1893; Groningen 1897; Amsterdam 1905, no. 381; Berlin 1908 (no. 22 on Johanna's list of loans); Amsterdam 1914–15, no. 141; New York 1920, no. 13; The Hague 1925; Berlin 1927–28, no. 64; London–Birmingham–Glasgow 1947–48, no. 144; New York–Chicago 1949–50, no. 101; Paris–Albi 1966, no. 47; London 1968–69, no. 121; Paris 1977.

Summary of the literature: Both De la Faille (1928, no. 1437) and Hulsker (1980, no. 1450) placed this drawing among those Van Gogh made in Saintes-Maries in June 1888. Pickvance (in New York 1984, no. 34) referred to this work as "a companion view" to F1436, "one of the seven half-page drawings done on the spot in Saintes-Maries," and among those "that Van Gogh described as 'harsh.'" Later, Pickvance (in Otterlo 1990, p. 224) described the same two street scenes as "almost savagely executed in their elisions of form and short-hand attack." For early history, see Feilchenfeldt and Veenenbos 1988, p. 132.

Among the drawings Vincent made in the village of Saintes-Maries, this must be one he called "rather harsh" [500]. Here, he brandished the reed pen in an extraordinarily vigorous way, rapidly sketching thatch-roofed cottages, rutted road, and a blazing sun that seems to bleach out everything but his blunt ink marks. Just a few days later, Van Gogh called his brother's attention to "the harsh side of Provence . . . very different from what it was in spring, and yet I have certainly no less love for this countryside, scorched as it begins to be from now on. Everywhere now there is old gold, bronze, copper . . . the sky blanched with heat . . ." [497].

The daring of Van Gogh's draftsmanship is reinforced here by a perspective exaggerated to thrust the ground forward and open a field for the artist to plow up with reed pen and ink.

CI

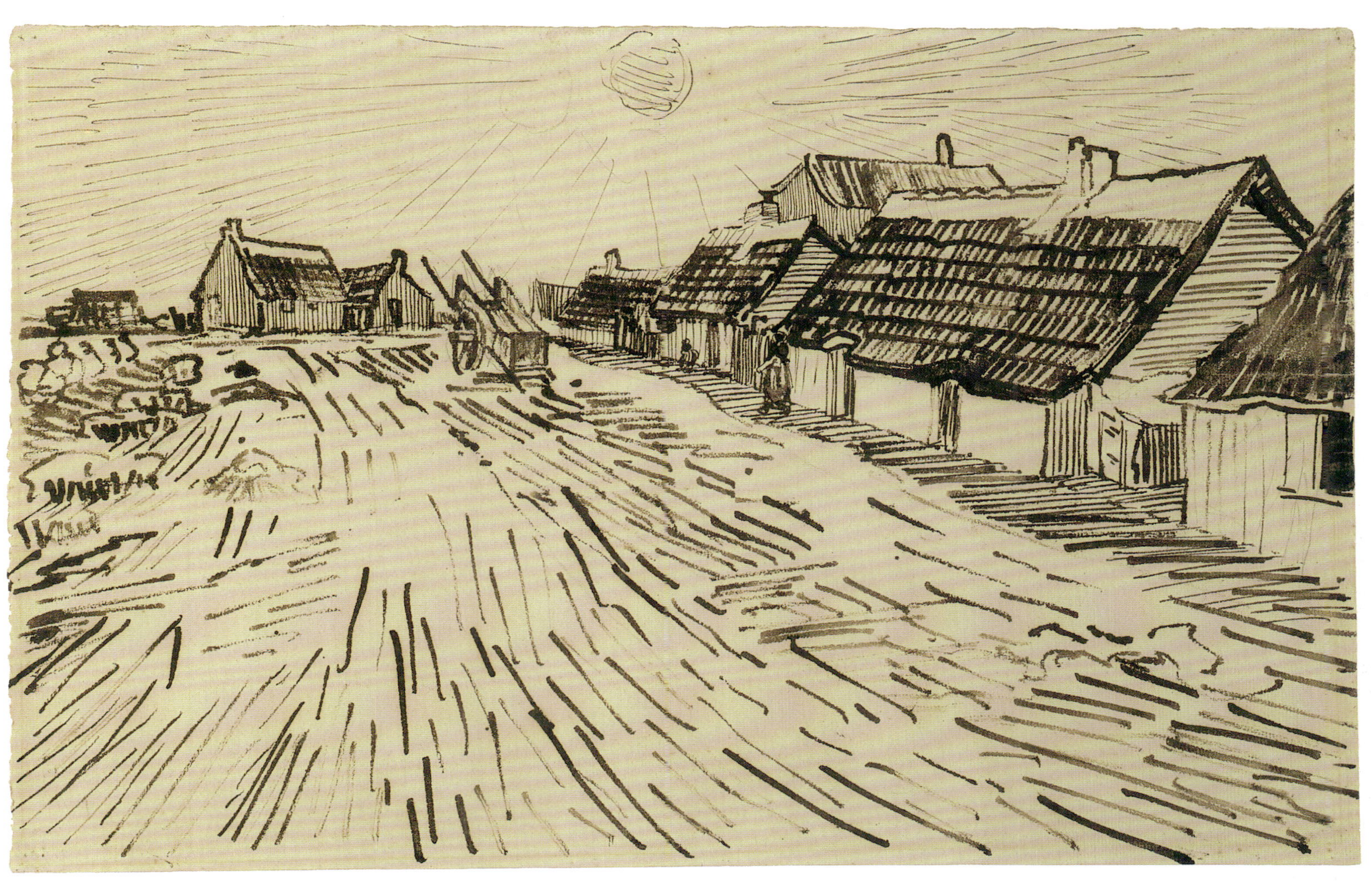

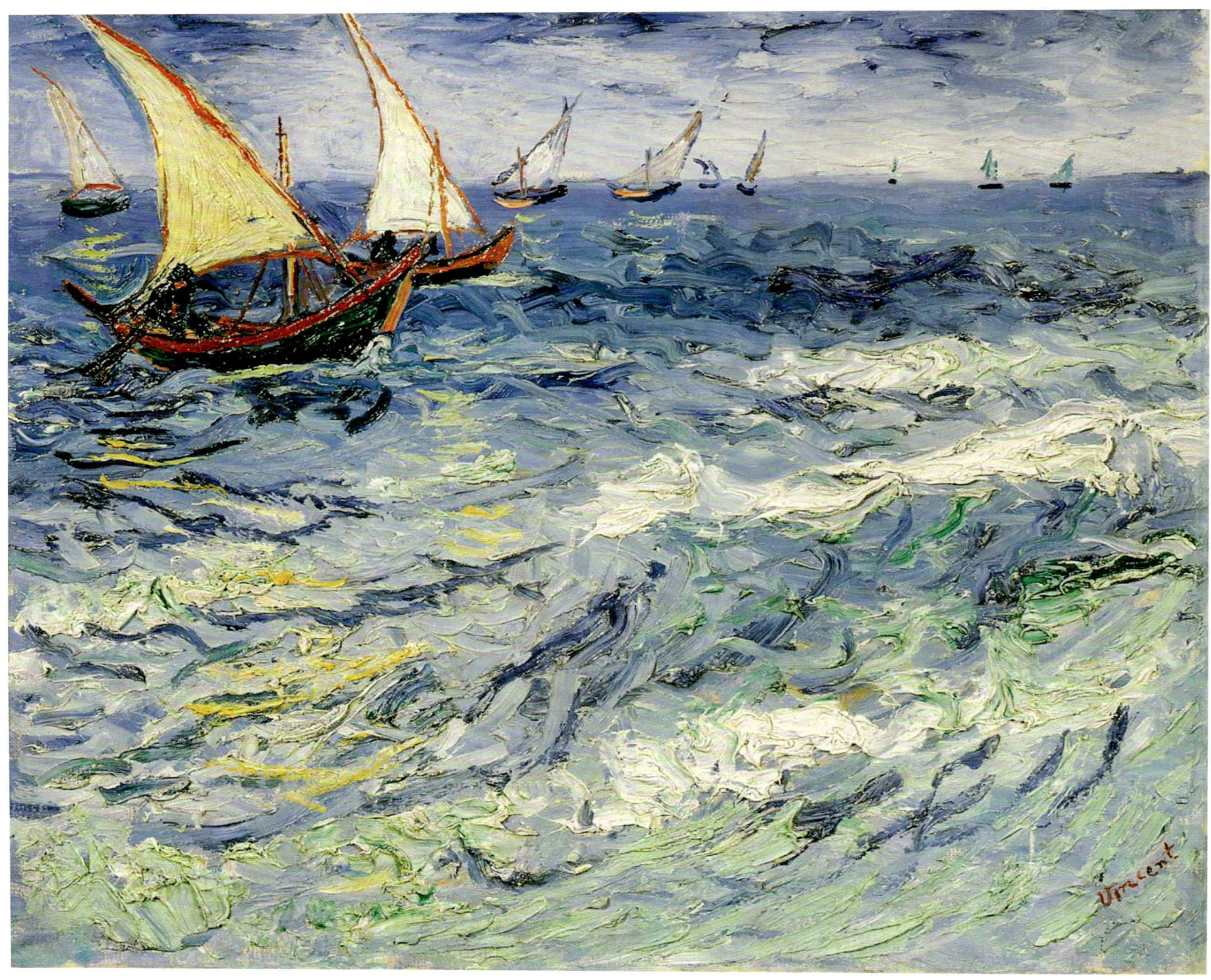

55. *Boats at Sea, Saintes-Maries-de-la-Mer*

ca. May 30–June 5, 1888
Oil on canvas
44 x 53 cm (17 3/8 x 20 7/8 in.)
Signed in red oil paint, lower right: *Vincent*
Pushkin State Museum of Fine Arts, Moscow (3438)
F417, JH1453
Letters 499, 524, 531

New York only

Van Gogh had taken three canvases to Saintes-Maries and while there painted a view of the village (F416, fig. 131) and two small seascapes that pictured the local single-skipper fishing boats at sea (F415, F417). This one, the more briskly worked painting of the latter two, evidently became a favored souvenir of the artist's first visit to the Mediterranean. It was one of four paintings Van Gogh advised Theo to mount on stretchers upon their delivery to Paris in mid-August. "I am rather keen on them," he told his brother. "You will easily see from the drawing of the little seascape that it is the most thought-out piece" [531]. Van Gogh sent a sketch of his oil right away to Émile Bernard (F1839, cat. 56) and weeks later produced three careful repetitions of the painting in pen and ink, for Bernard, John Russell, and Theo (F1430, cat. 57; F1430a, cat. 58; F1430b, cat. 59).

CI

Letter to Theo van Gogh, ca. June 3–4, 1888 [499]: I brought three canvases and have covered them—two marines, a view of the village. . . . The Mediterranean has the colors of mackerel, changeable I mean. You don't always know if it is green or violet, you can't even say it's blue, because the next moment the changing light has taken on a tinge of pink or gray.

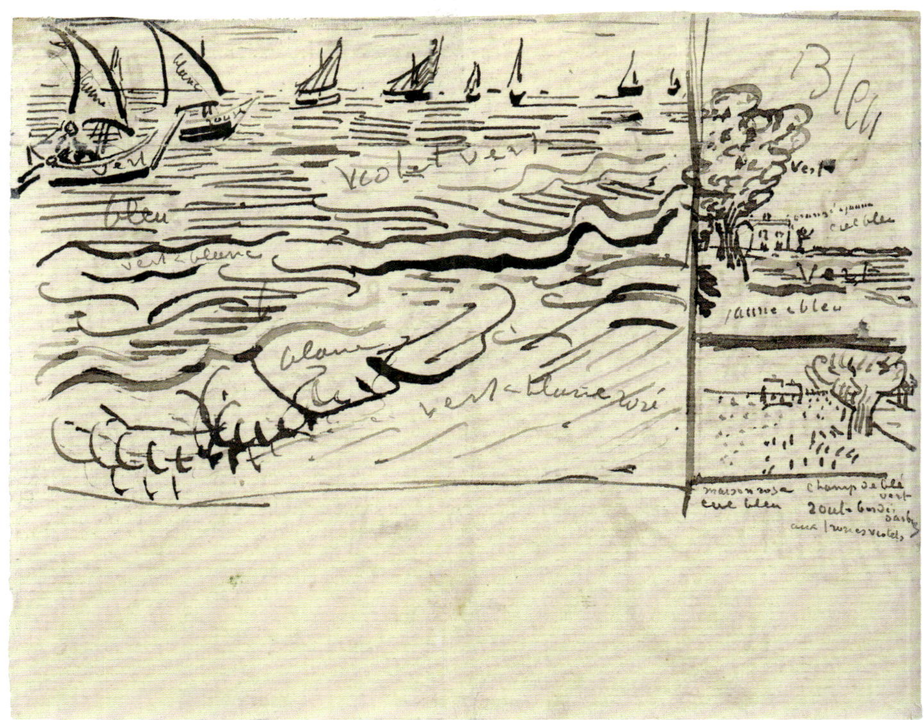

56. *Boats at Sea, Saintes-Maries-de-la-Mer; Two Landscapes*

Sketch sent with a letter to Émile Bernard, ca. June 7, 1888 [B6] (see also F1838, cat. 52; F1837, cat. 61)
Reed pen and ink on wove paper watermarked with an indecipherable design (crown with hunting horns?)
14.3 x 17.9 cm (5⅝ x 7¹⁄₁₆ in.)
Inscribed in pen and ink, left to right: *blanc / vert / bleu / blanc / vert-blanc / violet vert / vert-blanc-rosé / bleu / vert / [illegible] / vert / jaune-bleu / maison rose / ciel bleu / champ sable / vert / [illegible] / rue es[t] violet*
Recto: *Street in Saintes-Maries-de-la-Mer* (F1838, cat. 52)
Thaw Collection, The Pierpont Morgan Library, New York
F1839, JH1464
Letter B6

Provenance: Sent by the artist to Émile Bernard (d. 1941), Saint-Briac, ca. June 7, 1888 [B6]; Baroness Goldschmidt-Rothschild (d. 1965), Paris; private collection, New York; Eugene V. and Clare E. Thaw, New York and Santa Fe, N.M.

Summary of the literature: Scholars generally agree that Van Gogh's letter [B6] and the four drawings enclosed with it were sent to Bernard between June 6 and 11, 1888, and that this drawing represents the seascape painted in Saintes-Maries-de-la-Mer (F417, cat. 55).

Soon after returning to Arles from his brief visit to the Mediterranean, Van Gogh sent to Émile Bernard this sketch of a seascape he had painted while in Saintes-Maries. On the same sheet, two other recently completed oils are pictured: *A Walk near Arles* (F567) and *Farmhouse in a Wheat Field* (F408). Three other paintings were also illustrated in this same letter written about June 7 (F1835; F1837, cat. 61; F1838, cat. 52).

Van Gogh included detailed color notes to spark his friend's appreciation of his efforts and hastily scrawled the rolling waves that churned up most of his canvas. Some five weeks later, Vincent sent Bernard a more formal and faithfully detailed description of the painting (see F1430, cat. 57). CI

Letter to Émile Bernard, ca. June 7, 1888 [B6]: At last I have seen the Mediterranean. . . . I spent a week at Saintes-Maries. . . . On the perfectly flat, sandy beach little green, red, blue boats, so pretty in shape and color that they made one think of flowers. A single man is their whole crew, for these boats hardly venture on the high seas. They are off when there is no wind, and make for the shore when there is too much of it. . . . I myself am still doing nothing but landscapes—enclosed a sketch.

57. *Boats at Sea, Saintes-Maries-de-la-Mer*

(for Émile Bernard)

Mid-July 1888
Reed pen and ink over graphite on wove paper
24 x 32 cm (9½ x 12½ in.)
Kupferstichkabinett, Staatliche Museen zu Berlin (SZ 2)
F1430, JH1505
Letter B10

New York only

Provenance: Sent by the artist to Émile Bernard, Saint-Briac, July 15, 1888 [B10, 511], until 1904; sold to Hugo von Tschudi, Berlin, by October 11, 1904 (for 100 marks); his anonymous gift to the Nationalgalerie Berlin, December 1906.

Selected exhibitions: Stuttgart 1924; Munich 1961, no. 55; New York 1984, no. 63; Arles 2003, pp. 36–37.

Summary of the literature: In all editions of De la Faille (no. 1430), this work is associated with drawings Van Gogh made in Saintes-Maries in June 1888; however, the relationship between them is not addressed and Bernard's ownership is unrecognized. Roskill (1971, p. 152), Hulsker (1980/1996, no. 1505), and Pickvance (in New York 1984, no. 63) identified the drawing as a translation of a painting (F417, cat. 55) and one of the suite of drawings Van Gogh sent to Bernard in mid-July 1888. Pickvance enumerated four drawn versions of this subject, all reproducing Van Gogh's painting: two sent to Bernard, one to Russell, and one to Theo van Gogh. For early history, see Feilchenfeldt and Veenenbos 1988, p. 131; Paul 1993, p. 388.

While Van Gogh's painting of fishing boats at Saintes-Maries (F417, cat. 55) was tacked up to dry on his studio wall, he copied it in three pen-and-ink drawings: this one sent to Émile Bernard, another to John Russell (F1430a, cat. 58), and the last, for Theo (F1430b, cat. 59). The seascape was decidedly important to him; we know of only one other painting he bothered to copy three times in this way: *Arles: View from the Wheat Fields* (F545, cat. 69; see F1491, cat. 70; F1490, cat. 71; F1492, cat. 72).

Each pen-and-ink replica Van Gogh made differs from the painting in various ways, but in every case the draftsman sought to clarify and strengthen his vision of scattered fishermen in one-man boats, steering through choppy waters. In a letter that followed his posting of the drawing to Bernard, he wrote of his concern for "the material difficulties of the painter's life [that] make collaboration, the uniting of painters, desirable." And in words that might have been written to describe the pictured scene, he regretted "that life drags us along so fast that we haven't time both to argue and to act . . . we are at present sailing the high seas in our wretched little boats, all alone on the great waves of our time" [B11].

See "*Répétitions*: Drawings after Paintings."

CI

Letter to Émile Bernard, July 15, 1888 [B10]: Perhaps you will be inclined to forgive me for not replying to your letter immediately, when you see that I am sending you a little batch of sketches along with this letter.

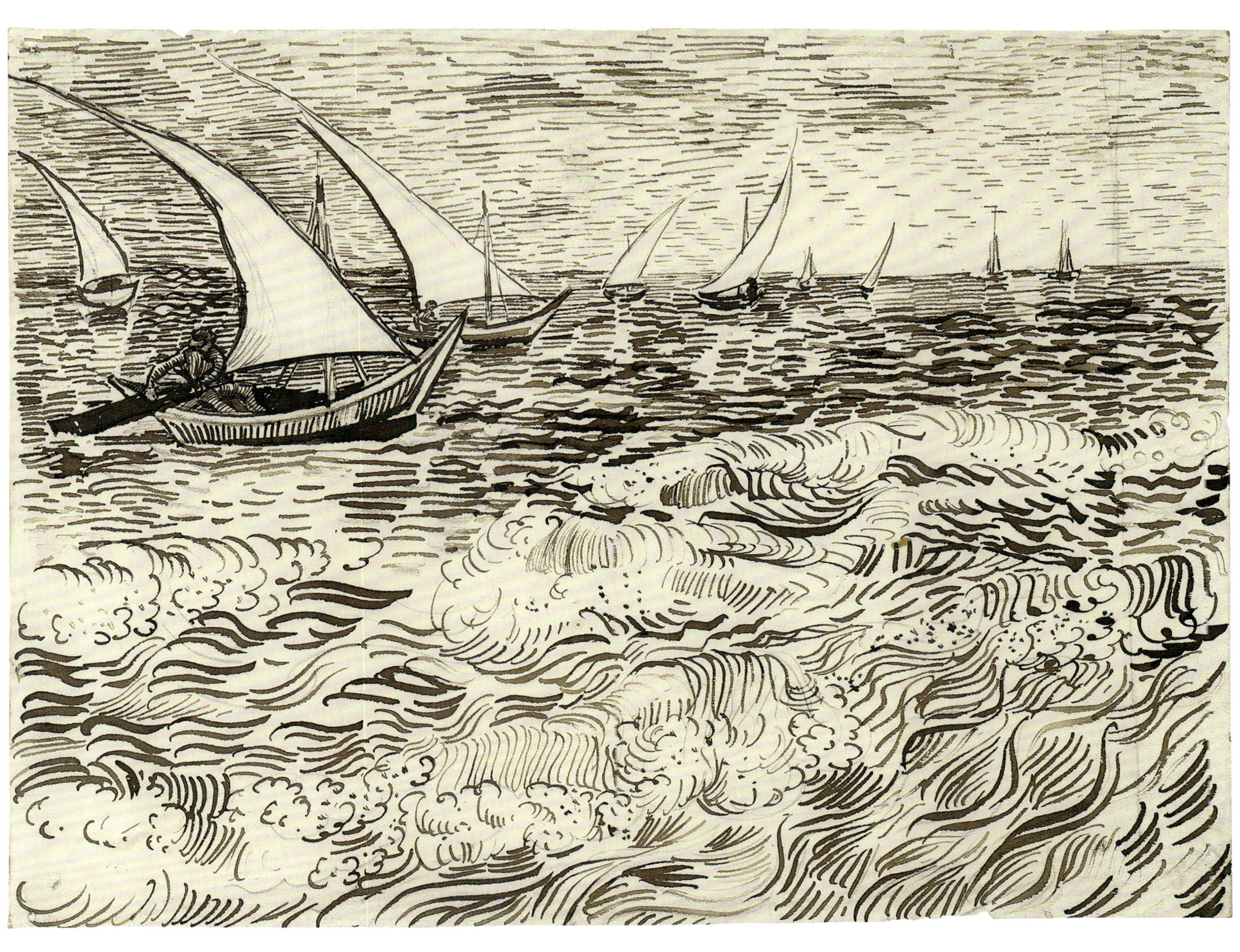

58. *Boats at Sea, Saintes-Maries-de-la-Mer*

(for John Russell)

ca. July 31–August 3, 1888
Reed pen and ink over graphite on wove paper
24.3 x 31.9 cm (9⅝ x 12½ in.)
Solomon R. Guggenheim Museum, New York, Thannhauser Collection, Gift, Justin K. Thannhauser, 1978 (78.2514.21)
F1430a, JH1526
Letters 516, 517

New York only

Provenance: Sent by the artist to John Russell (d. 1930), Belle-Île, ca. August 3, 1888 [517], until his death; to his daughter, Jeanne Jouve, Paris, probably 1930–31; purchased from her by Justin K. Thannhauser, Paris, probably 1938–39; his bequest to the Guggenheim Museum, 1978.

Selected exhibitions: New York 1984, no. 73; Arles 2003, pp. 38–39.

Summary of the literature: First published in Thannhauser 1938 as one of three previously "unknown" drawings among the dozen that Van Gogh sent to John Russell in 1888, this work was added to the 1970/1992 editions of the De la Faille catalogue raisonné as no. 1430a, but was misplaced and misdated there to Saintes-Maries in June 1888. Roskill (1971, p. 152), Hulsker (1980/1996, no. 1526), and Pickvance (in New York 1984, no. 73) all clarified that the drawing, done after the painting (F417), was made later in the summer as part of the suite of *répétitions* for Russell. Pickvance further observed that Van Gogh "filled the sky with dots," as he had done "with all but one of the landscape drawings for Russell."

Only about two weeks after sending an ink sketch of one of his Saintes-Maries seascapes to Émile Bernard (see F417, cat. 55; F1430, cat. 57), Van Gogh sent another *répétition* of the same painting to the artist John Russell. It was one of a group of twelve drawings after his paintings that he sent to Russell in early August 1888, two of which were boating scenes he might have expected would appeal to his friend, a sailor, then living seaside in Brittany.

Remembering their shared fondness for Japanese woodcut prints, Van Gogh seems to have taken special pains to translate his compositions for Russell into the language of ukiyo-e, covering them with calligraphic patterns of rippling pen strokes, linear curls, and dots. Each element of the picture was assigned its own distinct graphic identity, whether sea, boat, or sky, and yet was inextricably enmeshed in the fabric of the whole. The careful and rather witty formality of this approach lent the drawings sent to Russell an air of sophistication, which Van Gogh may have hoped would help to convince the wealthy Australian to lend him and Gauguin support.

See "*Répétitions:* Drawings after Paintings."

CI

Letter to Theo van Gogh, July 31, 1888 [516]: I am working hard for Russell; I thought that I would do him a series of drawings after my painted studies; I believe that he will look upon them kindly, and that, at least I hope so, will help to bring him to make a deal. . . . If we prod Russell, perhaps he will take the Gauguin that you bought. . . . When I write him, sending the drawings, it will of course be to urge him to make up his mind. . . . Anyway, let's finish the drawings—I have 8 and shall do 12—and let's wait to hear what he says.

Letter to Theo van Gogh, ca. August 3, 1888 [517]: I have sent Russell 12 drawings after painted studies, and so I had an opportunity to speak to him about it again [i.e., Russell's purchase of a painting by Gauguin, which would provide Gauguin with money to visit Vincent in Arles].

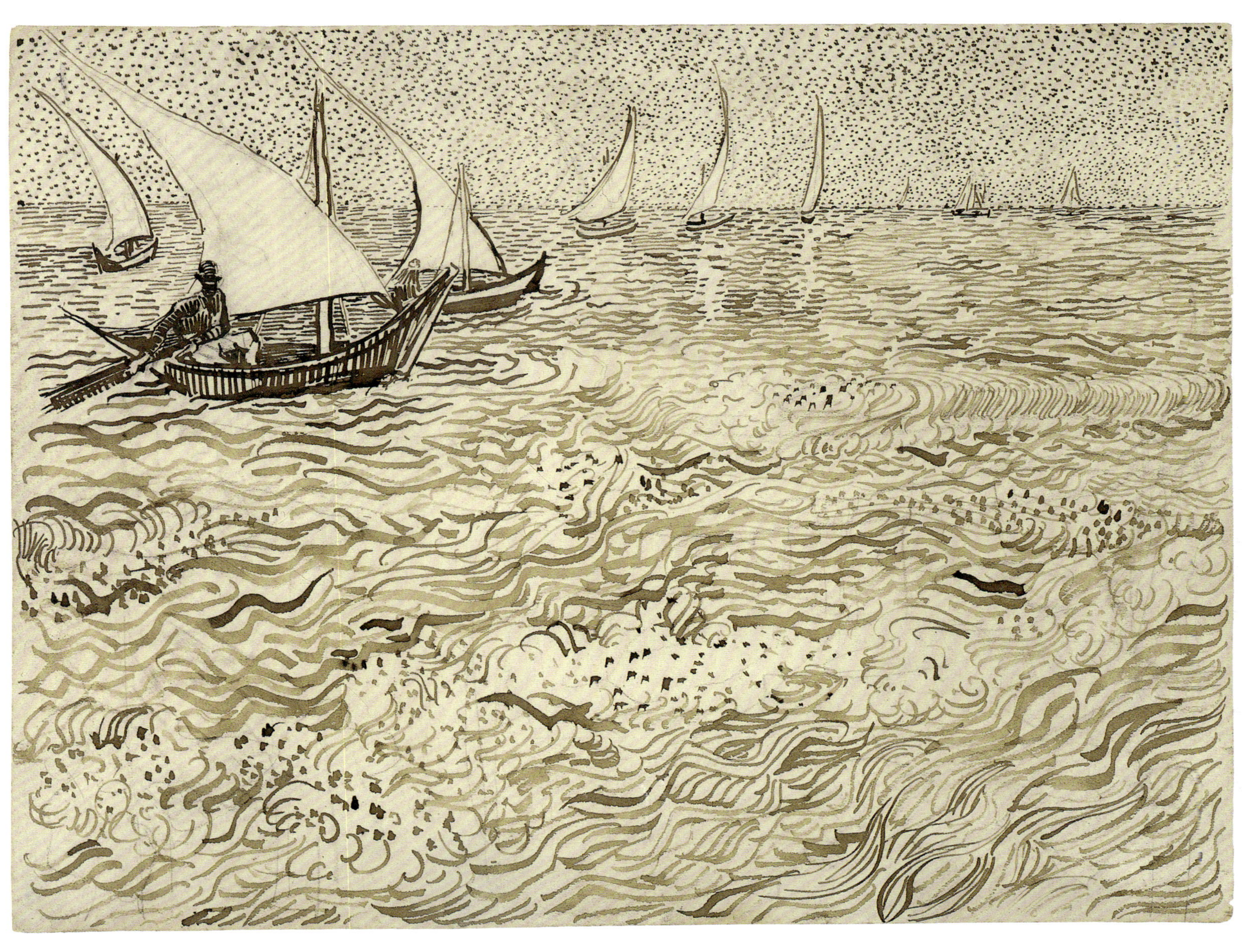

59. *Boats at Sea, Saintes-Maries-de-la-Mer*

(for Theo van Gogh)

ca. August 6–8, 1888
Reed pen, quill, and pen and ink over graphite on wove paper
24 x 31.5 cm (9½ x 12⅜ in.)
Signed in pen and ink, lower right: *Vincent*
Inscribed in pen and ink on verso, upper right: *n° 10*
Musées Royaux des Beaux-Arts de Belgique—Koninklijke Musea voor Schone Kunsten van België, Brussels (6743)
F1430b, JH1541
Letters 516, 518, 519, 531

Provenance: Sent by the artist to Theo van Gogh (d. 1891), Paris, August 8, 1888 [519]; by inheritance to his son, Vincent Willem van Gogh, as part of his collection, administered by his widow, Johanna van Gogh-Bonger, 1891; her gift to Octave Maus (d. 1919), Brussels, 1891; his widow, Mrs. Madeleine Octave Maus, Brussels; Charles Leirens (d. 1963), Paris; acquired from him by the Musée d'Art Moderne, Brussels, 1955.

Selected exhibitions: Brussels 1891, no. 10; Essen 1957, no. 284; Paris 1960, no. 104; Munich 1961, no. 56; Frankfurt 1970, no. 50; Otterlo 1990, no. 201; Martigny 2000, no. 55.

Summary of the literature: Unlisted in De la Faille's catalogue of 1928, this drawing was added to revised editions of 1970 and 1992 (no. 1430b) but was misdated to Van Gogh's sojourn in Saintes-Maries in June 1888. Roskill (1971, pp. 152, 171), Hulsker (1980/1996, no. 1541), and Pickvance (in New York 1984, p. 138) cited the work as a *répétition* of the painting (F417, cat. 55) sent by Vincent to Theo in early August 1888 [519].

Although Van Gogh had promised his brother a suite of penned reproductions of his paintings, he never completed the intended dozen and sent only five such sketches to Theo on August 8, 1888. The mailing included three large drawings of garden subjects, which perhaps had distracted him from completing his initial task (see F1455, fig. 163; F1456, cat. 91; F1457, cat. 92).

For the third time, Van Gogh repeated his favorite seascape painting from Saintes-Maries (F417, cat. 55) in a carefully elaborated drawing. As he had in copies made for Émile Bernard (F1430, cat. 57) and John Russell (F1430a, cat. 58), he continued to tighten his picture with compositional alterations and a unifying system of marks. In this final version of the subject, he pulled the two principal boats closer to the middle of the picture and stretched their sails in exaggerated arcs. Boats, sea, and sky are made to coalesce in decorative harmony.

See "*Répétitions:* Drawings after Paintings."

CI

Letter to Theo van Gogh, July 31, 1888 [516]: I hope to do these sketches after the studies for you as well. You will see that they have something of a Japanese air.

Letter to Theo van Gogh, August 6, 1888 [518]: Did I tell you that I had sent the drawings to friend Russell? At the moment I am doing practically the same ones over again for you, there will likewise be twelve. You will then see better what there is in the painted studies in the way of drawing.

Letter to Theo van Gogh, August 8, 1888 [519]: [T]he two marines [F1430b, F1431] are sketches after painted studies. I think all these ideas are good, but the painted studies lack clearness of touch. That is another reason why I felt it necessary to draw them.

Letter to Theo van Gogh, September 3, 1888 [531]: You will easily see from the drawing of the little seascape that it is the most thought-out piece.

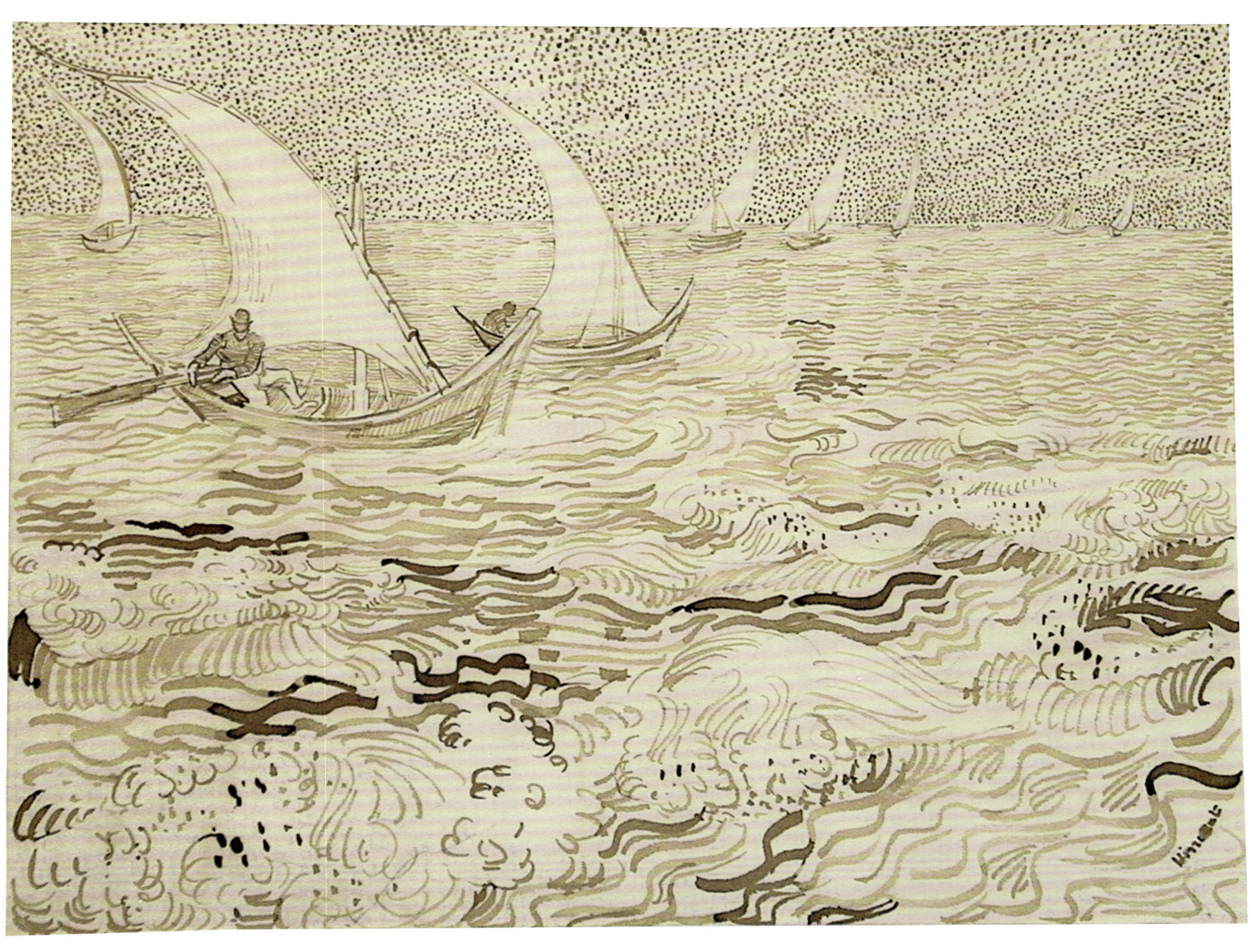

60. *Souvenir of Saintes-Maries on the Mediterranean; Boats on the Beach, Saintes-Maries-de-la-Mer*

ca. June 4, 1888
Reed pen and ink over graphite on wove paper
39.5 x 53.3 cm (15½ x 21 in.)
Signed in pen and ink, lower left: *Vincent;* inscribed in pen and ink, upper left: *Souvenir de St. Maries Méditerranée;* middle right, on a boat: *AMITIE*; color notes: *blanc / rouge / vert / bleu / bleu pale, etc.*
Private collection
F1428, JH1458
Letter 500

Provenance: Sent by the artist to Theo van Gogh (d. 1891), Paris, ca. June 5, 1888 [500]; by inheritance to his son, Vincent Willem van Gogh, as part of his collection, administered by his widow, Johanna van Gogh-Bonger, 1891; sold to Paul Cassirer, Berlin, December 1906; sold to Hugo von Tschudi, Berlin, December 1906, until his death in 1911; his widow, Angela von Tschudi, who sold it on the art market; Dr. Peter Nathan, Zürich; sold, Christie's, New York, May 5, 1998, no. 14.

Selected exhibitions: Paris 1902 (no. 7 on Johanna's list of loans); Amsterdam 1905, no. 376; Berlin 1906, no. 72; New York 1984, no. 37.

Summary of the literature: Both De la Faille (1928, no. 1428) and Hulsker (1980/1996, no. 1458) connected this drawing to Van Gogh's visit to Saintes-Maries and dated it to the month of June. Roskill (1966, p. 5) noted it was one of twelve drawings done in 1888 to which Van Gogh added similar inscriptions. Pickvance (in New York 1984, no. 37) suggested a date of Sunday, June 3, for this "working drawing" done by Van Gogh "to prove to his brother that without the crutch of the perspective frame he could quickly produce a large and intricate drawing." Heenk (1995, p. 168) observed that the work was "a drawing in its own right" and "significantly different" from the painting modeled on it. She noted further that the watercolor of the same subject (F1429) was likely based on this drawing rather than on Van Gogh's painting (F413) because it preserved the same "composition and mise-en-page of the boats." For early history, see Feilchenfeldt and Veenenbos 1988, p. 131; Paul 1993, pp. 392–93; Stolwijk and Veenenbos 2002, pp. 51, 126, 147, 194.

When Van Gogh sent this drawing to Theo upon returning from his visit to the sea, he was jubilant at having made the picture "in an hour," "[n]ot even with the perspective frame . . . without measuring." The work was a breakthrough for the artist, who had discovered he could compose a credible picture without crutches, "just by letting [his] pen go" [500].

There is indeed a decisive boldness in this drawing, made the morning of his departure, which sets a cap on Van Gogh's energetic production of land- and seascapes at Saintes-Maries. His pleasure in meeting the Mediterranean Sea there and his satisfaction in painting and drawing the local scenery evidently put the artist in an expansive frame of mind. His hopes for a fellowship of artists, all working together harmoniously, seem to be reflected in the cluster of beached fishing boats, one with the name *Amitie* (friendship). The work also echoes subjects Van Gogh had pictured in Holland in 1882, while strolling the beach at Scheveningen.

Once back in Arles, Van Gogh traced the outlines of this composition onto another sheet and, following notes he had made on the spot, applied splashes of color with the new set of watercolors he had asked Theo to send him in order to "make some pen drawings, to be washed afterward in flat tints like the Japanese prints" [491] (F1429, fig. 135). He also added, to the well of the foremost boat, a second fishing rod propped up by the mast. Both bamboo rods rise high into the sky in the painting that Van Gogh then made (F413, fig. 136).

CI

Letter to Theo van Gogh, ca. June 5, 1888 [500]: I am sending you by the same post the drawings of Stes.-Maries. I made the drawing of the boats just before I was going to leave, very early in the morning, and I am working on a picture after it, a size 30 canvas with more sea and sky on the right. It was before the boats cleared off; I had watched it all the other mornings, but as they leave very early, I didn't have time to do it. . . . I have only been here a few months, but tell me this—could I, in Paris, have done the drawing of the boats* in an hour*? Not even with the perspective frame, and this one is done without measuring, just by letting my pen go.

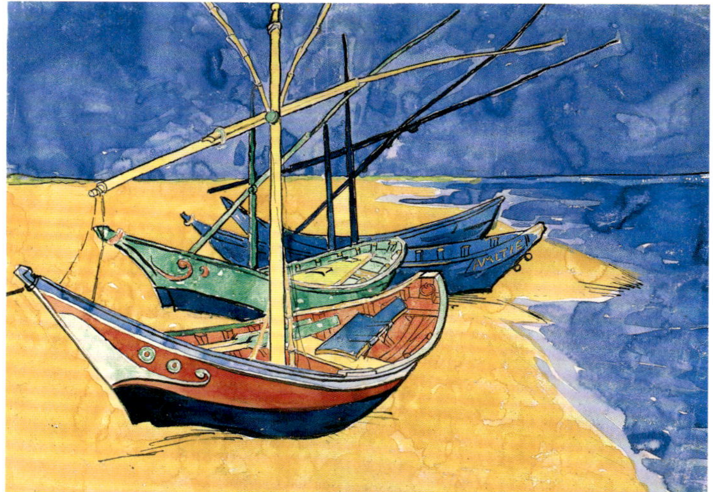

Fig. 135. *Boats on the Beach, Saintes-Maries-de-la-Mer* (F1429), between June 3 and 5, 1888. Watercolor, pen, and ink over graphite, 40.4 x 55.5 cm (15⅞ x 21⅞ in.). State Hermitage Museum, Saint Petersburg

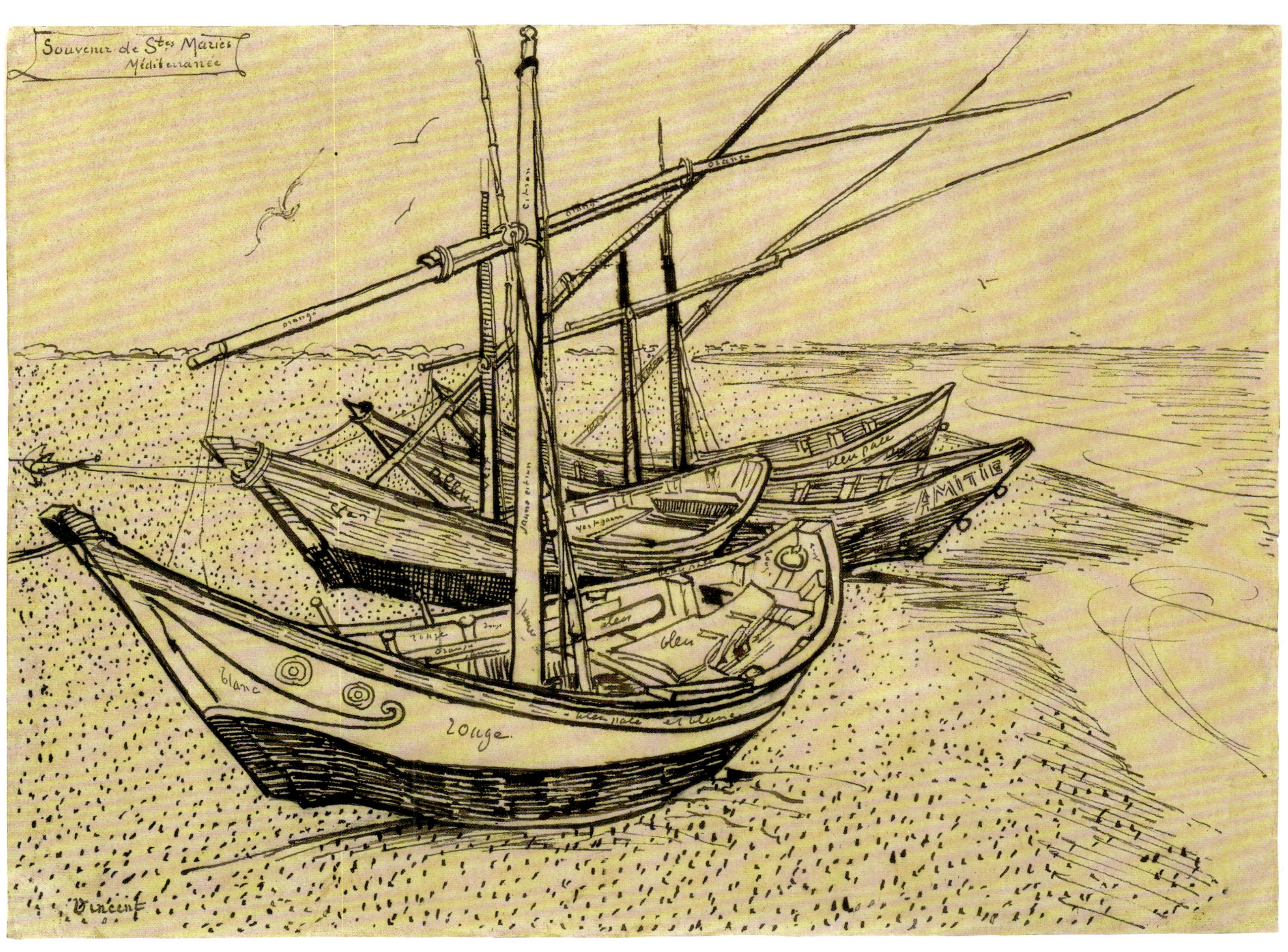
Souvenir de Stes Maries
Méditerranée
AMITIE
blanc
rouge
Vincent

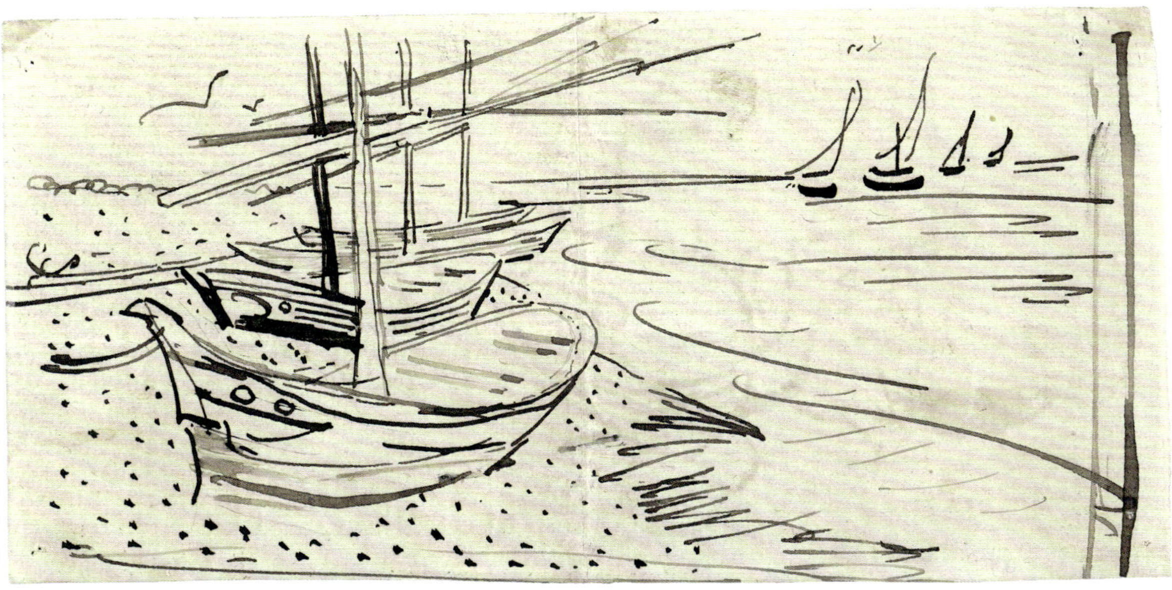

61. *Boats on the Beach, Saintes-Maries-de-la-Mer*

Sketch included in a letter to Émile Bernard, ca. June 7, 1888 [B6] (see also F1838, cat. 52; F1839, cat. 56)
Pen and ink on wove paper watermarked ORIGINAL PALET MILL
9 x 17.8 cm (3 9/16 x 7 in.)
Verso: *Still Life with Coffee Pot* (F1835)
Pen and ink
Thaw Collection, The Pierpont Morgan Library, New York
F1837, JH1461
Letter B6

Provenance: Sent by the artist to Émile Bernard (d. 1941), Saint-Briac, ca. June 7, 1888 [B6]; Baroness Goldschmidt-Rothschild (d. 1965), Paris; private collection, New York; Eugene V. and Clare E. Thaw, New York and Santa Fe, N.M.

Summary of the literature: Scholars generally agree that Van Gogh's letter [B6] and the four drawings enclosed with it (see also F1838, cat. 52; F1839, cat. 56) were sent to Bernard between June 6 and 11, 1888, and that this drawing represents the painting of beached boats executed by Van Gogh on his return to Arles from Saintes-Maries-de-la-Mer (F413, fig. 136).

In a letter posted to Émile Bernard in Brittany, Van Gogh enclosed this sketch and others to show his young friend his latest paintings. This small reproduction of a seascape (F413, fig. 136) based on both a drawing made at Saintes-Maries-de-la-Mer (F1428, cat. 60) and a subsequent watercolor (F1429, fig. 135) demonstrates how, in the painted version, Van Gogh expanded his picture of four fishing boats on the beach (probably traced from the watercolor onto his canvas) to embrace four more boats in full sail at sea. The letter sketch fails to show, however, the extent to which the painter had enlarged stretches of sand and sky, providing headroom for rigging and poles, also ground space for anchor lines and cargo. These scenic additions altered radically the initial overall decorative design and introduced a sharp contrast between boats and background: the stark outlines and flat, bright colors of the wooden vessels now surrounded by vague atmospheric elements, which Van Gogh described like an Impressionist.

CI

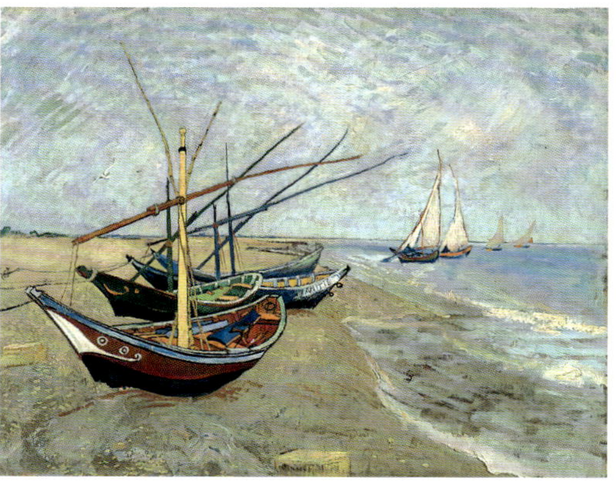

Fig. 136. *Boats on the Beach, Saintes-Maries-de-la-Mer* (F413), ca. June 5, 1888. Oil on canvas, 65 x 81.5 cm (25 5/8 x 32 1/8 in.). Van Gogh Museum, Amsterdam (Vincent van Gogh Foundation)

Letter to Émile Bernard, ca. June 7, 1888 [B6]: At last I have seen the Mediterranean. . . . I spent a week at Saintes-Maries. . . . On the perfectly flat, sandy beach little green, red, blue boats, so pretty in shape and color that they made one think of flowers. A single man is their whole crew, for these boats hardly venture on the high seas. They are off when there is no wind, and make for the shore when there is too much of it.

Summer Harvest

Surveying the broad landscape of Van Gogh's work, we find everywhere an expression of the artist's profound faith—not so much in specific religious tenets, but in the laws of nature. The revolving seasons, the rising and setting of the sun and moon, even the perpetual tasks of nature's ally, the farmer, in his rounds from plowing, to planting, to harvest, and the laying in of food—until seeding could commence again—all these recurring cycles gave reassuring order and meaning to the artist's life, as they do to all human existence.

From the very inception of his artistic career, Van Gogh portrayed the land and its laborers with a sincere and single-minded devotion, often harkening to the pictures of Millet, champion of the French peasant. Millet's iconic *Sower,* which Van Gogh copied in the spring of 1881 (F830, fig. 137) periodically inspired him to picture in new ways this hero of the landscape, life-giver to the harvest (F865, fig. 138; F451, fig. 140).

It is significant that, in one of his few paid commissions as an artist, Van Gogh created for an Eindhoven goldsmith a series of compositions symbolizing the seasons (F41–43, F172). Illustrating one of these for his brother Theo in a letter from Nuenen in August 1884 (F1812, fig. 139), Vincent reported preparing for the task: "Last week I was in the fields every day during the harvest . . ." [374]. Although at first his patron had been determined to decorate his dining room with pictures of "various saints," Van Gogh had dissuaded him, reasoning that "the appetite of the worthy people who would have to sit down at that table would . . . be more stimulated by six illustrations taken from peasant life . . . than by . . . mystical personages." Signing off the same letter, the artist warmed to his brother's approaching visit with news of the local farming scene: "When you come here, you will find all the farmers plowing and sowing. . . . I have seen splendid sunsets over the fields of stubble" [374].

It is not surprising, therefore, that in Provence, after completing views of the village and sea at Saintes-Maries, Van Gogh turned wholehearted attention to the activity of harvest time in Arles, declaring, "I am still charmed by . . . a longing for the infinite, of which the sower, the sheaf are the symbols" [B7]. After less than two weeks of "hard, close work among the wheat fields in the full sun," he could boast, "The result is some [ten] studies of wheat fields, landscapes, and—a sketch of a sower" [501].

Dazzled by the color and light of southern France and alive to the prospect of envisioning a familiar, seasonal rite in fresh surroundings, the artist was exhilarated. "I feel much better here than I did in the North," he wrote

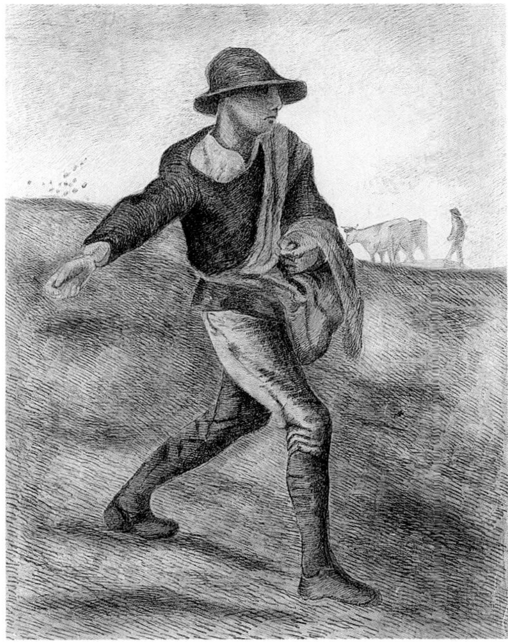

Fig. 137. *The Sower,* after Millet (F830), April 1881. Pen and ink, watercolor, and wash over graphite, 48.1 x 36.7 cm (19 x 14½ in.). Van Gogh Museum, Amsterdam (Vincent van Gogh Foundation)

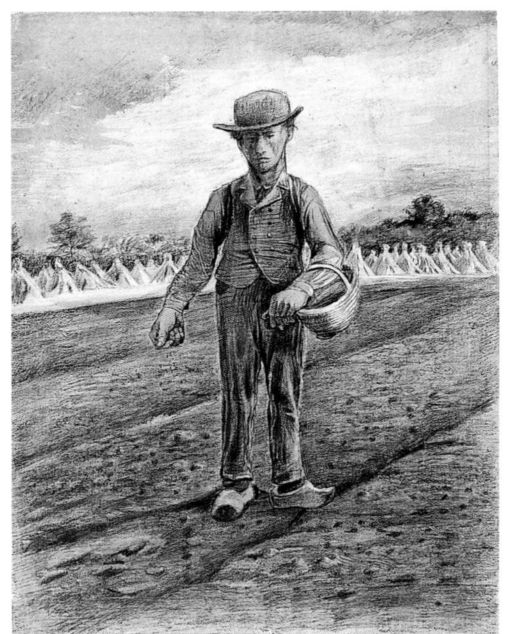

Fig. 138. *Sower with a Basket* (F865), Etten, September 1881. Black chalk, wash, and watercolor, heightened with white, 62 x 47.5 cm (24½ x 18¾ in.). Kröller-Müller Museum, Otterlo

Bernard about June 19. "I work even in the middle of the day, in the full sunshine, without any shadow at all, in the wheat fields, and I enjoy it like a cicada" [B7]. He confessed to being utterly exhausted by a morning in the fields, but reasoned to his brother Theo that "during the harvest my work was not any easier than what the peasants who were actually harvesting were doing." However, "far from complaining of it," he rejoiced, "it is just at these times in artistic life . . . that I feel almost as happy as I could be in the ideal . . . real life" [507]. Thus, gratified to be working in the fields just as hard as a peasant, and productively so, Van Gogh devoted himself to the toil he loved best, all the while remembering the Dutch landscape, Christian parables of the sower, and the stirring examples of Delacroix, Millet, and especially Cézanne, "because he has rendered so forcibly—as in the 'Harvest' we saw at Portier's [fig. 142]—the harsh side of Provence" [497].

Only the earliest and largest paintings Van Gogh made while focused on the harvest, in mid-June, seem to have benefited from the artist's preparation of preliminary drawings. In two of these (F412, cat. 63; F425, fig. 144), Van Gogh made use of the new box of watercolors he had requested in May from Theo [491], which allowed him to add color between the black ink lines of his drawings and thereby produce imitations of Japanese woodcuts that might serve also as cartoons for paintings. Two of the preliminary drawings he made (F1478, cat. 66; F1425) are so close in detail and scale to paintings of the same subjects that their compositions must have been traced or in some other way directly transferred to the canvases.

Most of the drawings Van Gogh produced in connection with his harvest paintings of the summer of 1888 are those he made a month or so later to demonstrate the success of his campaign to Émile Bernard, John Russell, and brother Theo. Beyond simple copies, the drawings, or *croquis,* as Vincent liked to call them, allowed him to tinker with his pictures anew, to replay them in pen and ink, in line, rather than color.

In the meantime, he had felt a need to modify his paintings "to make the touch harmonious" [507], knowing his oils would be criticized for looking hasty. He admitted that he had been compelled to work "quickly, quickly, quickly and in a hurry, just like the harvester . . . silent under the blazing sun, intent . . . on his reaping" [B9]. And besides the heat, he had had to contend with mistral winds that sometimes forced him to fasten the legs of his easel to iron pegs he forced into the earth. Van Gogh wished his brother, in particular, to understand that the landscapes, despite their "haggard look," represented "sheer work and calculation with one's mind strained to the utmost" [507]. His *répétitions* would reveal the reasoned structure underlying the compositions of his paintings and what he believed to be "the root of everything" [290], their drawing.

Demonstrating satisfaction in his efforts and an enduring interest in the themes, Van Gogh produced pen-and-ink copies of seven of the ten harvest paintings he had made in June, each of them one-half or one-third the canvases' size. The process of translation presented new but clearly not unwelcome challenges, necessitating the invention of marks and then their organization into patterns that would convey the color and texture of his richly impastoed oils. Van Gogh refined the shorthand he had been developing during the spring months in Arles and Saintes-Maries with stunning ingenuity—and the results are brilliant.

CI

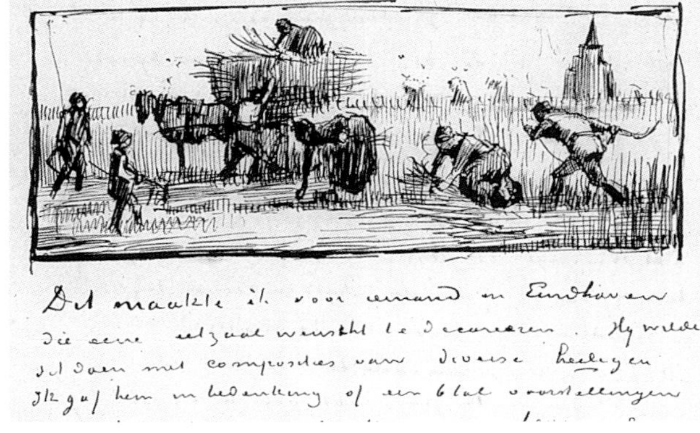

Fig. 139. *Wheat Harvest* (F1812), sketch in letter 374, early August 1884. Pen and ink. Van Gogh Museum, Amsterdam (Vincent van Gogh Foundation)

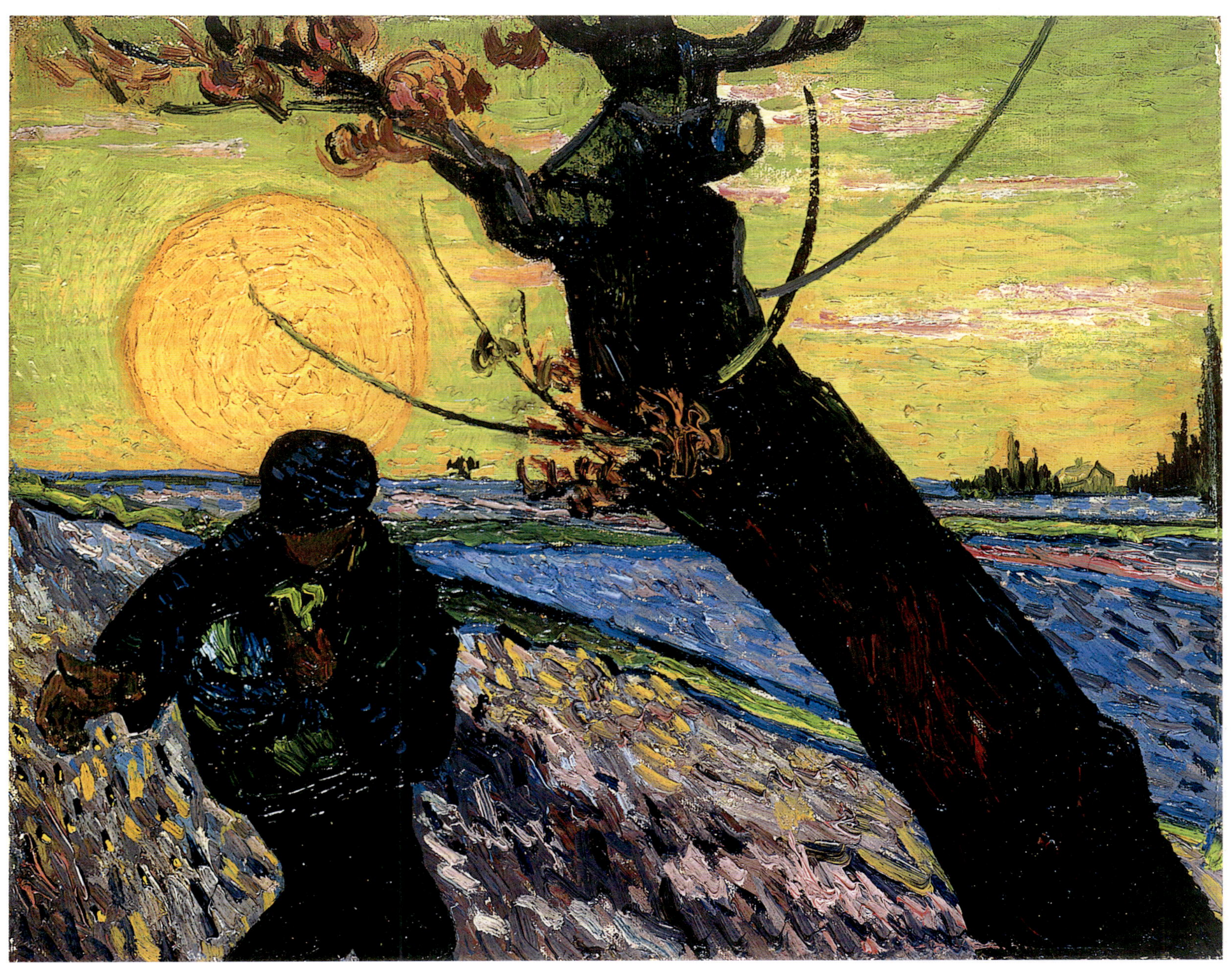

Fig. 140. *The Sower* (F451), November 1888. Oil on canvas, 32 x 40 cm (12⅝ x 15¾ in.). Van Gogh Museum, Amsterdam (Vincent van Gogh Foundation)

62. *Harvest in Provence*

ca. June 12, 1888
Reed and quill pens and ink with watercolor, wax crayon, and gouache over charcoal on wove paper laid down on millboard
50.5 x 61 cm (19⅞ x 24 in.)
Signed in pen and black ink, lower right: *Vincent*
Inscribed in pen and brown ink, lower left: *La moisson en Provence*
Tack holes in corners
Private collection
F1483, JH1439
Letters 496, 498

Provenance: Probably sent by the artist to Theo van Gogh (d. 1891), Paris, ca. June 15 or 16, 1888 [498]; by inheritance to his son, Vincent Willem van Gogh, as part of his collection, administered by his widow, Johanna van Gogh-Bonger, 1891, presumably until 1897, when it was probably sold to Ambroise Vollard, Paris; Julius Meier-Graefe, Berlin, probably by 1899; Jos Hessel Art Gallery, Paris, by 1901, until 1914; Paul Cassirer, Berlin, placed on consignment with Galerie Georges Bernheim, Paris, 1914–18; Galerie Flechtheim, Düsseldorf; F. Haniel, Wistinghausen; Galerie Paul Rosenberg, Paris; Lefevre Gallery (Alex Reid and Lefevre Ltd.), London; Mrs. J. B. A. Kessler, London, by 1930; her sale, Sotheby's, London, June 24, 1997, no. 7; purchased by a private collector; sold, Sotheby's, New York, November 5, 2003, no. 6; to present owner.

Selected exhibitions: Paris 1896–97 (no. 49 on Johanna's list of loans); Paris 1901, no. 66; Paris 1909, no. 23; Berlin 1914, no. 76a.

Summary of the literature: First catalogued by De la Faille (1928, no. 1483), this drawing is dated June 1888 in subsequent catalogues raisonnés, including that of Hulsker (1980/1996, no. 1439). Roskill (1966, pp. 3–7; 1971, pp. 155, 168–69) recognized the work as the immediate model for Van Gogh's painting of the same subject (F412) rather than an earlier drawing of the same motif (F1484). Pickvance (in New York 1984, p. 131) observed that each of the two preliminary drawings "was an independent confrontation with the motif," a conclusion reached also by Heenk (1995, pp. 166, 173–74), who suggested that, since Van Gogh considered his paintings *Haystacks* (F425) and *The Harvest* (F412) pendants, he "may have tried to make the drawings [F1425, F1483] look like pendants, too." For early history, see Feilchenfeldt and Veenenbos 1988, p. 135.

As haying season began in Provence, Van Gogh walked some three miles to the northeast of Arles, there to survey the plains of La Crau that reminded him so much "of the Holland of Ruysdael or Hobbema" [502]. Looking toward the old abbey atop Montmajour, the Mont des Cordes, and the distant peaks of the Alpilles, he drew the intervening fields and farms where there were signs of the harvest under way. After drawing the vista with eyes scanning the distance (F1484, fig. 141), he soon returned to the edge of the fields, shifting his station somewhat to the left, to focus his gaze on the blue wagon awaiting its cargo of hay.

The expanse of open terrain and clustered buildings recalls Van Gogh's watercolor views of the outskirts of The Hague (see F916) and of Paris (see F1410, cat. 41). But there was now a livelier touch to the artist's pen work and a brisk sense of atmosphere conveyed in scattered accents. Although the drawing was soon to serve as the model for one of Van Gogh's most prized paintings (F412, cat. 63), it was treated as a finished work in itself, embellished with watercolors the artist had recently requested from Theo: "I have asked for some watercolors because I would like to make some pen drawings, to be washed afterward in flat tints like the Japanese prints" [491].

CI

Letter to Theo van Gogh, June 12, 1888 [496]: I am working on a new subject, fields green and yellow as far as the eye can reach. I have already drawn it twice, and I am starting it again as a painting. . . .

Letter to Theo van Gogh, ca. June 15 or 16, 1888 [498]: [Y]ou will think the [drawing] . . . with the haystacks in a farmyard too bizarre. . . . The Harvest is rather more serious.

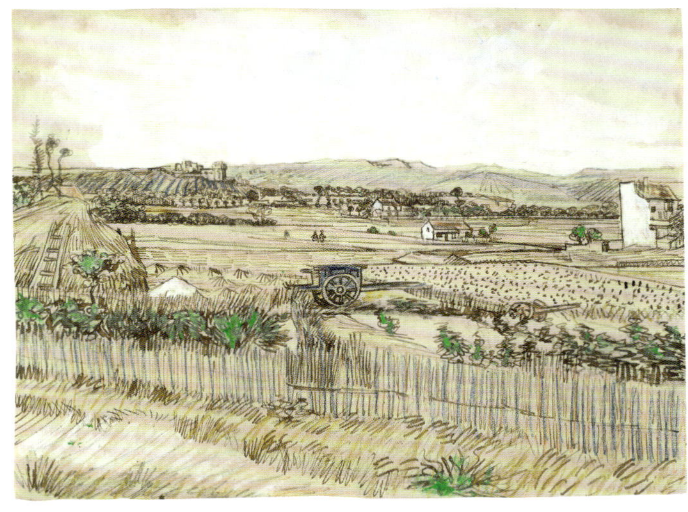

Fig. 141. *Harvest in Provence* (F1484), June 1888. Graphite, black chalk, wax crayon, ink, watercolor, and gouache on tan laid paper, 39.4 x 52.3 cm (15½ x 20⅝ in.). Fogg Art Museum, Harvard University Art Museums, Cambridge, Mass., Bequest of Grenville L. Winthrop (photo: Katya Kallsen)

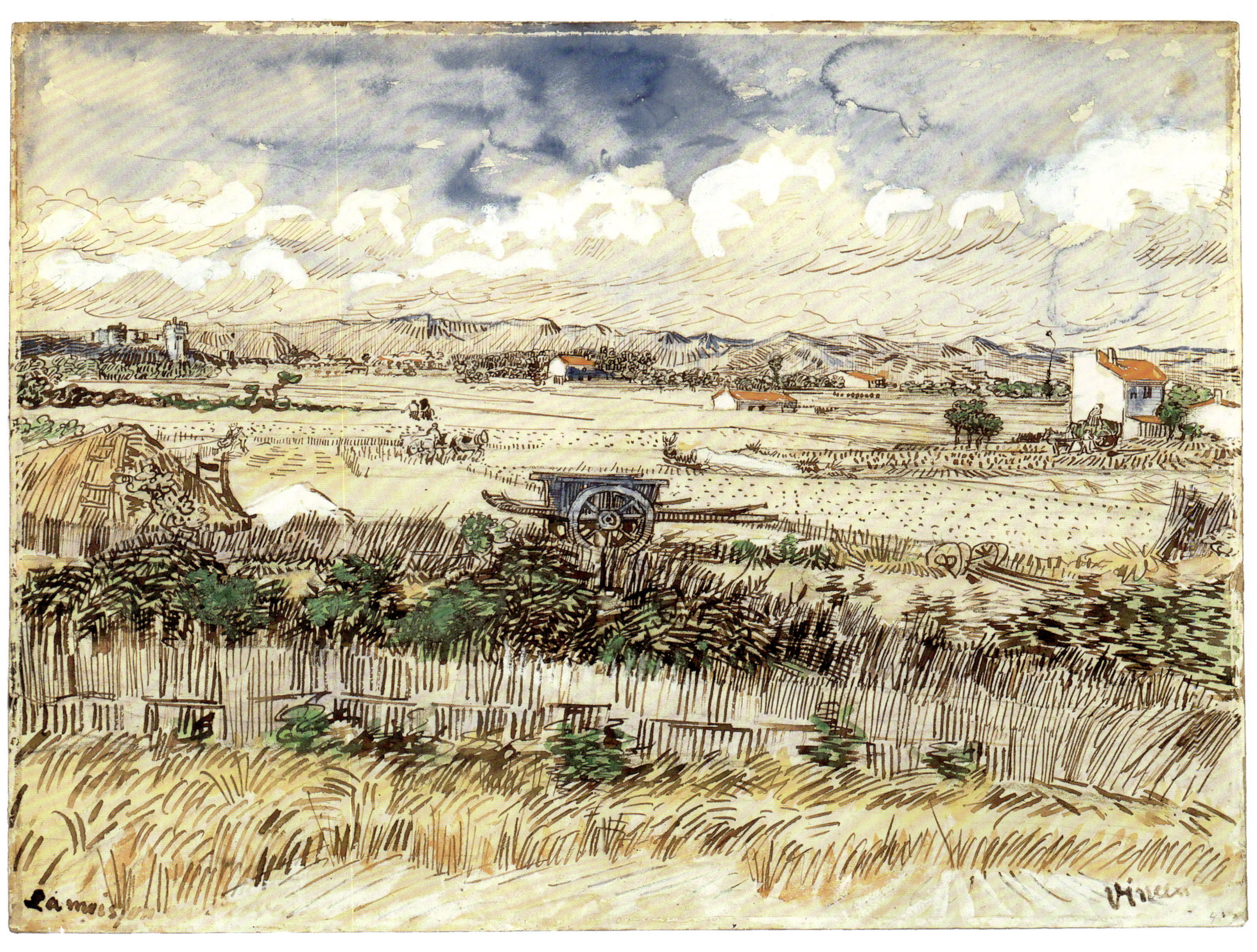

63. *Harvest in Provence*

ca. June 12, 1888
Oil on canvas
73 x 92 cm (28¾ x 36¼ in.)
Signed, lower left: *Vincent*
Van Gogh Museum, Amsterdam (Vincent van Gogh Foundation) (s 30 V/1962)
F412, JH1440
Letters 496, 497, 507, 531

Letter to Theo van Gogh, June 12, 1888 [496]: I am working on a new subject, fields green and yellow as far as the eye can reach. I have already drawn it twice, and I am starting it again as a painting; it is exactly like a Salomon Konink [sic]***—you know, the pupil of Rembrandt who painted vast level plains.***

Letter to Theo van Gogh, June 12 or 13, 1888 [497]: I am working on a landscape with wheat fields. . . . I think I am going to take a larger sized canvas and launch out boldly into the 30 square. . . . I keep remembering what I have seen of Cézanne's because he has rendered so forcibly—as in the "Harvest" we saw at Portier's—the harsh side of Provence [fig. 142]. . . .

It has become very different from what it was in spring, and yet I have certainly no less love for this countryside, scorched as it begins to be from now on. Everywhere now there is old gold, bronze, copper, and this with the green azure of the sky blanched with heat: a delicious color, exceptionally harmonious, with the blended tones of Delacroix.

Letter to Theo van Gogh, ca. July 1, 1888 [507]: As for landscapes, I begin to find that some done more rapidly than ever are the best of what I do. For instance, the one I sent you the cartoon of, the harvest. . . . It is true that I have to retouch the whole ***to rearrange the composition a bit, and to make the touch harmonious, but all the essential work was done in a single long sitting. . . .***

Letter to Theo van Gogh, September 3, 1888 [531]: The Harvest (a wide landscape with the ruin in the background and the line of the Alps), . . . it would be a good thing if you could put [it] . . . on stretchers. I am rather keen on [it]. . . .

CI

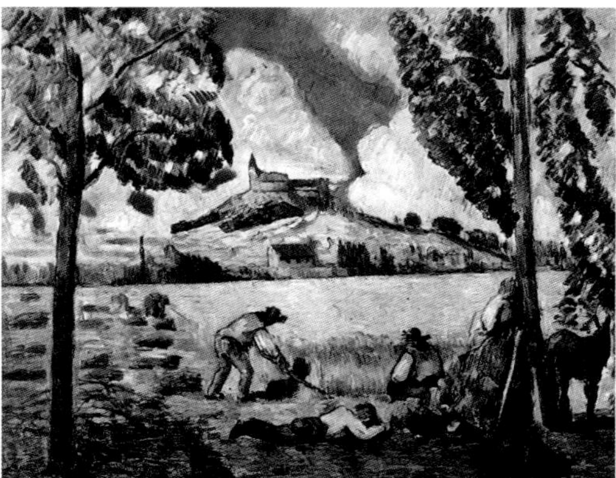

Fig. 142. Paul Cézanne, *The Harvest*, ca. 1877. Oil on canvas, 45.7 x 55.2 cm (18 x 21¾ in.). Private collection

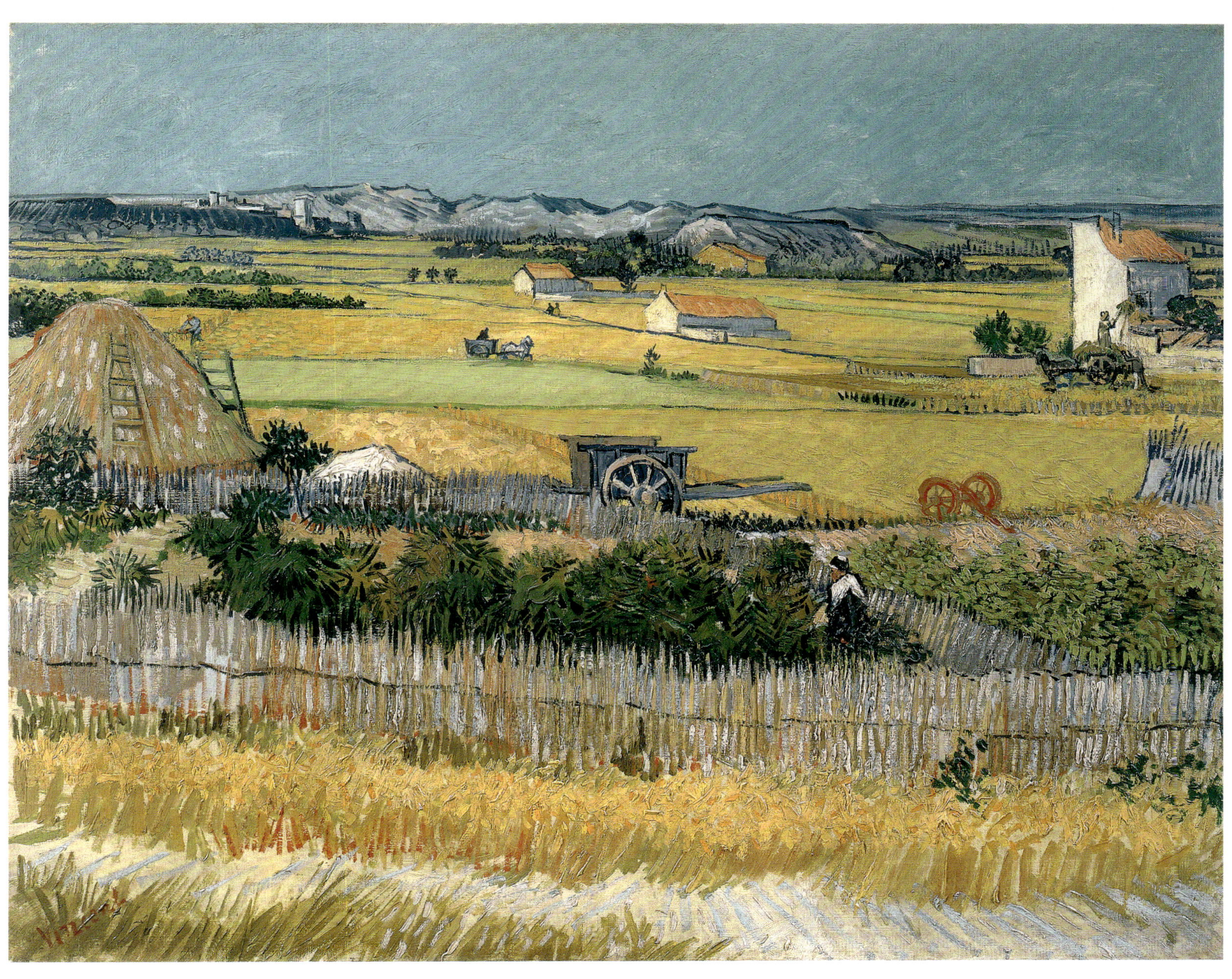

64. *Harvest in Provence*

(for Émile Bernard)

Mid-July 1888
Reed pen, quill, and ink over graphite on wove paper
24 x 32 cm (9½ x 12⅝ in.)
Kupferstichkabinett, Staatliche Museen zu Berlin (SZ 1)
F1485, JH1540
Letter B11

Amsterdam only

Provenance: Sent by the artist to Émile Bernard, Saint-Briac, between July 17 and 20, 1888 [B11], until 1904; sold to Hugo von Tschudi, Berlin, by October 11, 1904 (for 100 marks); his anonymous gift to the Nationalgalerie Berlin, December 1906.

Selected exhibitions: Stuttgart 1924; Munich 1961, no. 63; New York 1984, no. 65; Otterlo 1990, no. 194; Bremen 2002–3, no. 37.

Summary of the literature: De la Faille (1928) catalogued the four drawings Van Gogh devoted to this subject (nos. 1483–86) without dating them or establishing their relationship to the painting *Harvest in Provence* (F412). In his article on the *Harvest*, Roskill (1966, pp. 3–7) distinguished the two preliminary drawings (F1483, F1484) from those drawn after the oil but assumed, incorrectly, that this version had been sent to Theo. He later (1971, pp. 155–56) revised his opinion, noting that the drawing was sent to Bernard, but his earlier contention held sway in the catalogues raisonnés by De la Faille (1970/1992, no. 1485, where the drawing is dated June 1888) and Hulsker (1980/1996, no. 1540, where it is dated August). Pickvance (in New York 1984, no. 65) provided a clear summary of Roskill's definitive observations that Van Gogh made two drawings (F1483, F1484) before his *Harvest* painting (F412) and two afterward: this version for Bernard and another for Russell (F1486). For early history, see Feilchenfeldt and Veenenbos 1988, p. 135; Paul 1993, p. 388.

This *répétition* Van Gogh sent in a second batch of sketches to Bernard differs liberally and good-naturedly from the painting three times its size that he had tacked up recently to dry (F412, cat. 63). Like others of the fifteen copy drawings made to show Bernard his work and invite exchange, it is a brisk, enthusiastic souvenir penned in the kind of blunt black-ink notation both artists favored (see fig. 25). Entirely familiar now with the subject he had worked on intermittently for well over a month, Van Gogh put down only a few penciled guidelines before plunging into his fourth rendition of the *Harvest in Provence*.

Broadening the foreground of his picture and narrowing the band of sky, Van Gogh rolled out his landscape in regiments of straw-chopped lines for fences and grass and other foliage, followed by a field of dots marking the stubble of wheat. The artist's decorative shorthand carpets the drawing, overwhelming the cart that appears at the center of his painting, now diminished in importance to share attention with seasonal activities.

See "*Répétitions*: Drawings after Paintings."

CI

Letter to Émile Bernard, between July 17 and 20, 1888 [B11]: I have just sent you—today—nine more sketches after painted studies . . . subjects taken from the sort of scenery that inspires "father" Cézanne, for the Crau near Aix is pretty similar to the country surrounding Tarascon or the Crau here. . . . As I know how much you like Cézanne, I thought these sketches of Provence might please you; not that there is much resemblance between a drawing of mine and one by Cézanne.

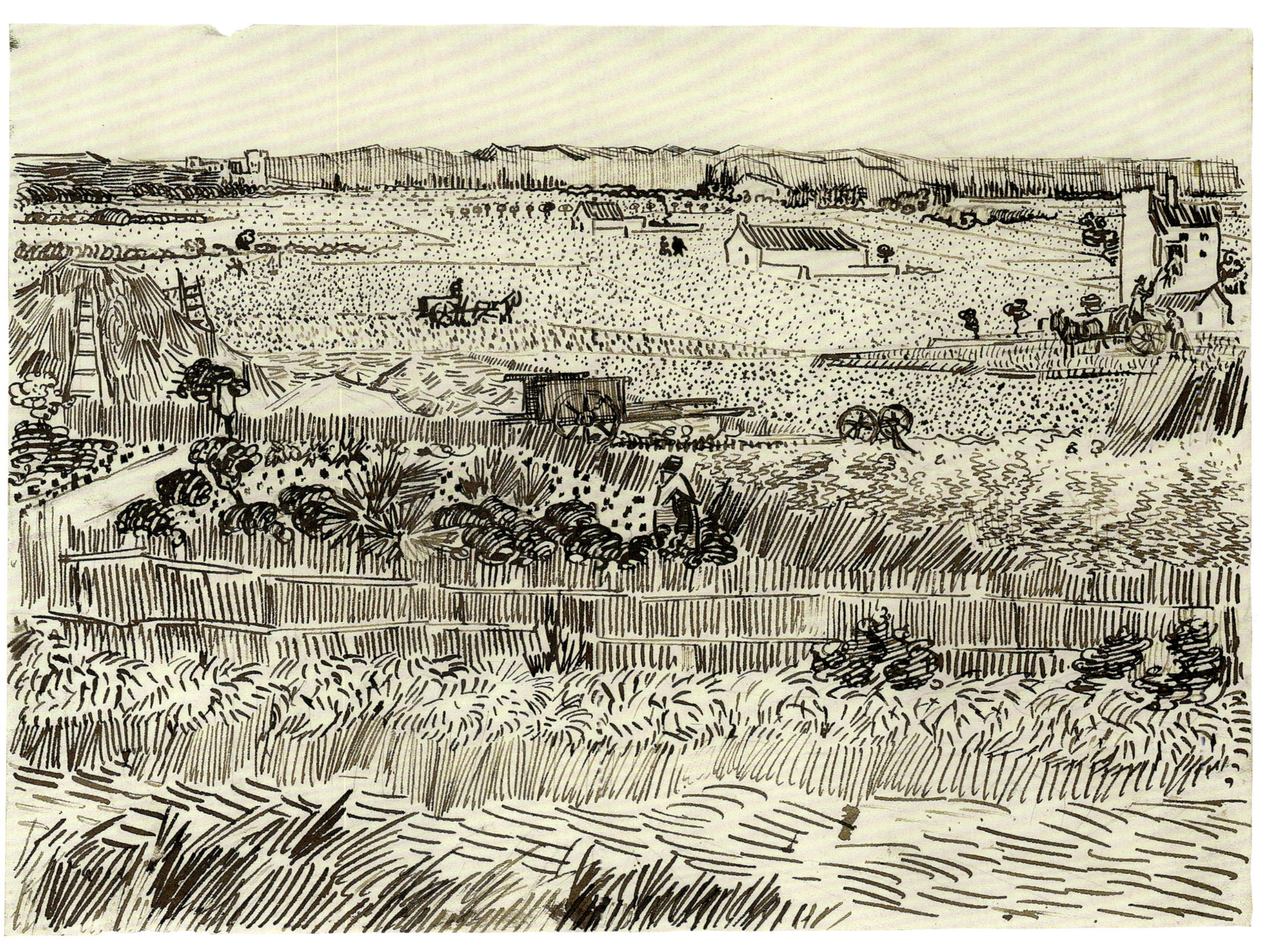

65. *Harvest in Provence*

(for John Russell)

ca. July 31–August 3, 1888
Reed pen, quill, and ink over graphite on wove paper
24 x 32 cm ($9\frac{1}{2}$ x $12\frac{1}{2}$ in.)
Signed, lower left: *Vincent*
National Gallery of Art, Washington, Collection of Mr. and Mrs. Paul Mellon (1985.64.91)
F1486, JH1527
Letters 516, 517

Provenance: Sent by the artist to John Russell, Belle-Île, Brittany, ca. August 3, 1888 [517], until 1920; sold, [Anon.], Hôtel Drouot, Paris, March 31, 1920, no. 63; purchased by Georges Bernheim, Paris; Kunstzalen d'Audretsch, The Hague; Galerie Lutz, Berlin; Dr. George Hirschland, Werden an der Ruhr; to his son, Richard S. Hirschland, Englewood, N.J., by 1943; Hector Brame, Paris, by 1965; Mr. and Mrs. Paul Mellon, Upperville, Va., 1965; their gift to the National Gallery of Art, 1992.

Selected exhibitions: New York 1943, no. 75; New York 1955, no. 102; Los Angeles 1957, no. 35.

Summary of the literature: Included in De la Faille's catalogue of 1928 (no. 1486), this sheet was recognized by Henry Thannhauser (1938) as one of the twelve drawings sent by Van Gogh to John Russell in early August 1888. Confirmed as such in subsequent catalogues, including that of Hulsker (1980/1996, no. 1527), the work is nonetheless incorrectly dated June 1888 in later editions of De la Faille's catalogue and, in the editors' notes to the 1970 revision, is confused (as to its inscription) with F1483.

The drawing Van Gogh made for John Russell of his oil *Harvest in Provence* (F412, cat. 63) is a much closer copy of the painting than the one he sent to Émile Bernard about two weeks earlier (F1485, cat. 64). The hay cart sits at the picture's center, and all other elements of the composition radiate out from it in more or less proper alignment with the painting, even to the row of three trees in the center distance.

While he had achieved in his *répétition* for Bernard a unified surface of marks, Vincent now varied his touch to transmit a sense of atmosphere: the dazzling summer light, the vibrant heat of July's sun, and perhaps, too, the incessant thrumming of cicadas. There is greater liveliness in the pen work, in the variety of marks and in their varying weights. In his delicate distribution of dots and tonal accents throughout the composition, Van Gogh achieved a shimmering effect quite different from the static decorative design of his drawing for Bernard.

See "*Répétitions*: Drawings after Paintings."

CI

Letter to Theo van Gogh, July 31, 1888 [516]: I am working hard for Russell; I thought that I would do him a series of drawings after my painted studies; I believe that he will look upon them kindly, and that, at least I hope so, will help to bring him to make a deal. . . . Anyway, let's finish the drawings—I have 8 and shall do 12—and let's wait to hear what he says.

Letter to Theo van Gogh, ca. August 3, 1888 [517]: I have sent Russell 12 drawings after painted studies. . . .

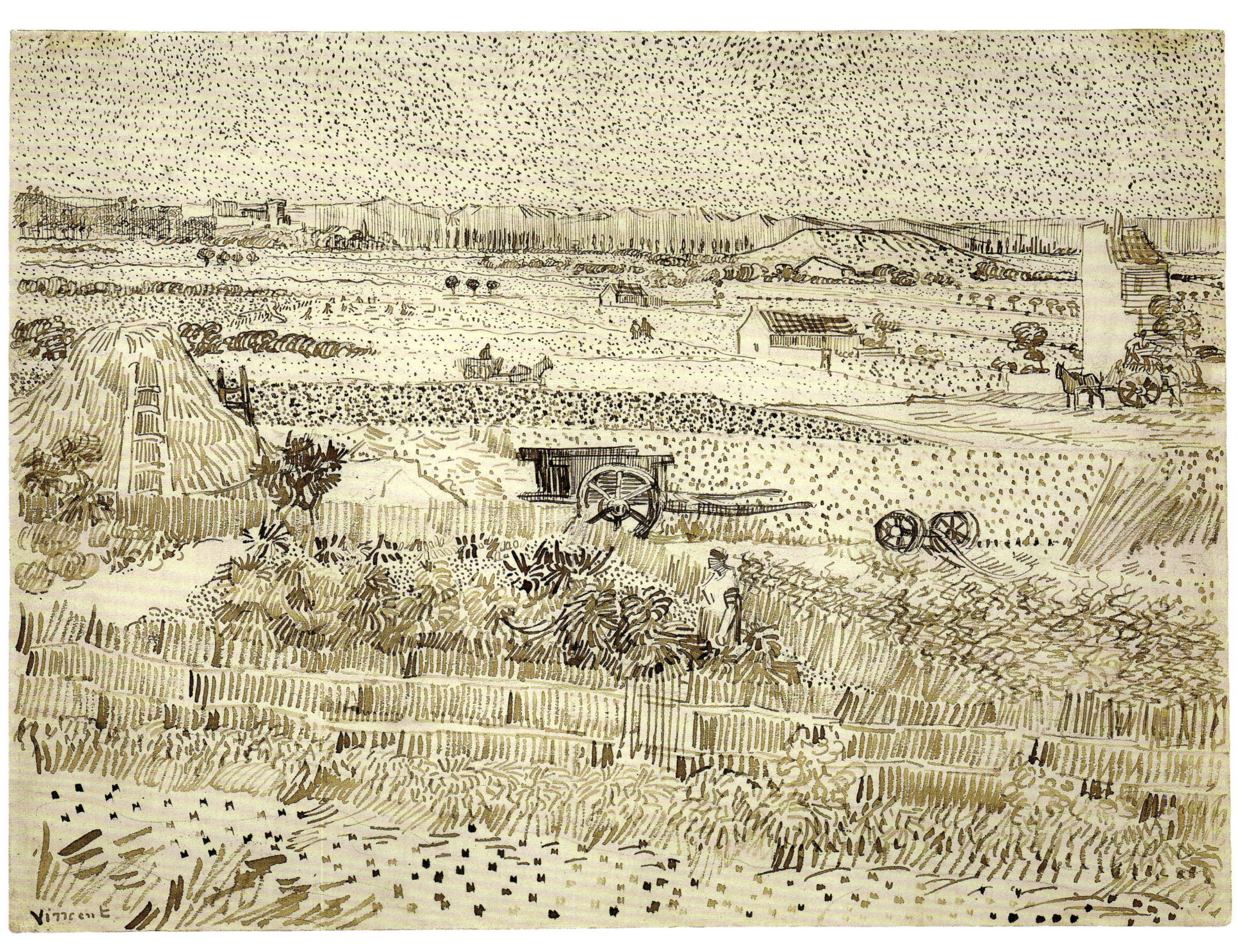
Vincent

66. *A Farmhouse in Provence*

Early June 1888
Reed pen and ink over graphite on laid paper
39 x 53.3 cm (15³⁄₈ x 21 in.)
Signed and inscribed in pen and ink, lower right: *un mas de Provence / Vincent*
Inscribed on verso, in another hand: *155*
Rijksmuseum, Amsterdam (SK-A-2226)
F1478, JH1444

Provenance: Sent by the artist to Theo van Gogh (d. 1891), Paris, probably ca. June 15–16, 1888 [498]; by inheritance to his son, Vincent Willem van Gogh, as part of his collection, administered by his widow, Johanna van Gogh-Bonger, 1891; her gift to the Rijksmuseum, Amsterdam, 1905.

Selected exhibitions: Paris 1902 (no. 24 on Johanna's list of loans); Amsterdam 1905, no. 385; Paris 1937, no. 71; Milan 1952, no. 101; Munich 1956, no. 117; Essen 1957, no. 293; Paris 1960, no. 103; Munich 1961, no. 62; Frankfurt 1970, no. 51; New York 1984, no. 43; Otterlo 1990, no. 204.

Summary of the literature: Although undated in De la Faille's first catalogue (1928, no. 1478), this drawing and the painting of the same motif (F565) are more recently dated by most scholars to early June 1888. Opinions differ, however, regarding the relationship between the ink study and the oil: Roskill (1971, p. 170) saw the drawing as preliminary to the painting and as perhaps sent to Theo in mid-July [509]; Hulsker (1980/1996, no. 1444) believed the drawing a "copy" of the oil; Pickvance (in New York 1984, no. 43), dating the work June 8–12 [496] and possibly sent to Theo about June 15 [498], considered the drawing an "on-the-spot confrontation with the motif" "separate" from the painting. He later (in Otterlo 1990, no. 204) reconsidered this view and defined the drawing as a "working document" for "the subsequent studio-made painting" and "almost certainly the first drawing Van Gogh made in Arles after his return from Saintes-Maries on 3 June." Heenk (1995, p. 65) dated the work June 8 or 9, in relation to another drawing (F1425), and noted an inexplicable faint inscription in graphite at the drawing's upper right: *f . . . Samedi 8 Juillet.* Dorn (1997–98, p. 20) dated the drawing to the week of June 3–10 (which he believed *preceded* the artist's trip to Saintes-Maries) and saw it as one of three drawings sent to Theo about June 15 or 16, 1888 [498]. Hansen (in Bremen 2002–3, no. 39) regarded the work as a separate study of the subject, previous to the painting dated in her catalogue entry May–June 1888.

Only about a dozen of the drawings Van Gogh made during his first months in Arles are inscribed with descriptive titles; among them are *Verger de Provence* (F1414, fig. 118), *Vue d'Arles* (F1416r, cat. 46), and *Bords du Rhône* (1472a, fig. 123). Each of these pen-and-ink landscapes presents some aspect typical of the region, as might photographs taken on holiday. This one, inscribed *mas de Provence*, is a souvenir of the artist's introduction to Mediterranean farm life, which he encountered in a flat, open terrain somewhat reminiscent of the Dutch lowlands: a remarkably complete rendering of a Provençal homestead with stuccoed house, outbuilding, and wall surrounding fruit trees and piles of hay; beyond the pillared gateway stretch cultivated fields and native grasses.

Quite a large and finished drawing, this detailed view, complete in itself, nonetheless was re-created as a painting (F565, fig. 143). The artist evidently traced the composition to transfer it to a canvas very nearly the same size.

Vincent revealed an enduring interest in this "mas de Provence" in his letter to Theo of June 12 or 13, 1888. After speaking enthusiastically of his monumental canvas of *Harvest in Provence* (F412, cat. 63), he added, "And I have another subject, a farm and some haystacks, which will probably be a pendant" [497]. He seems to have been envisioning his large painting of the three tall haystacks just inside the farmyard walls (F425, fig. 144).

CI

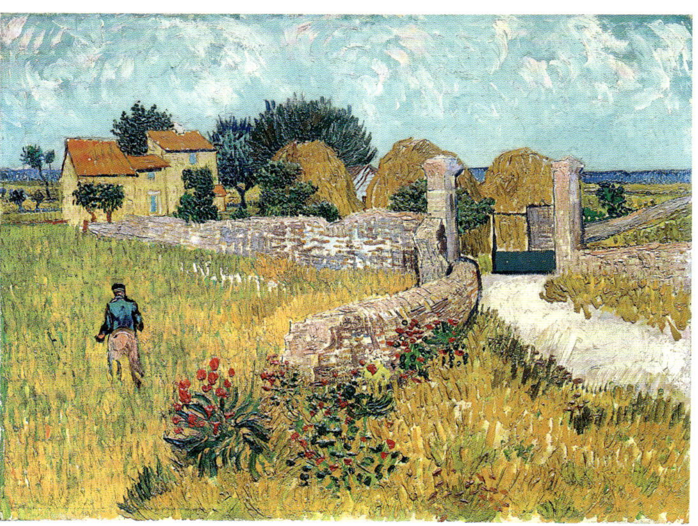

Fig. 143. *Farmhouse in Provence* (F565), June 1888. Oil on canvas, 46.1 x 60.9 cm (18¹⁄₈ x 24 in.). National Gallery of Art, Washington, Ailsa Mellon Bruce Collection

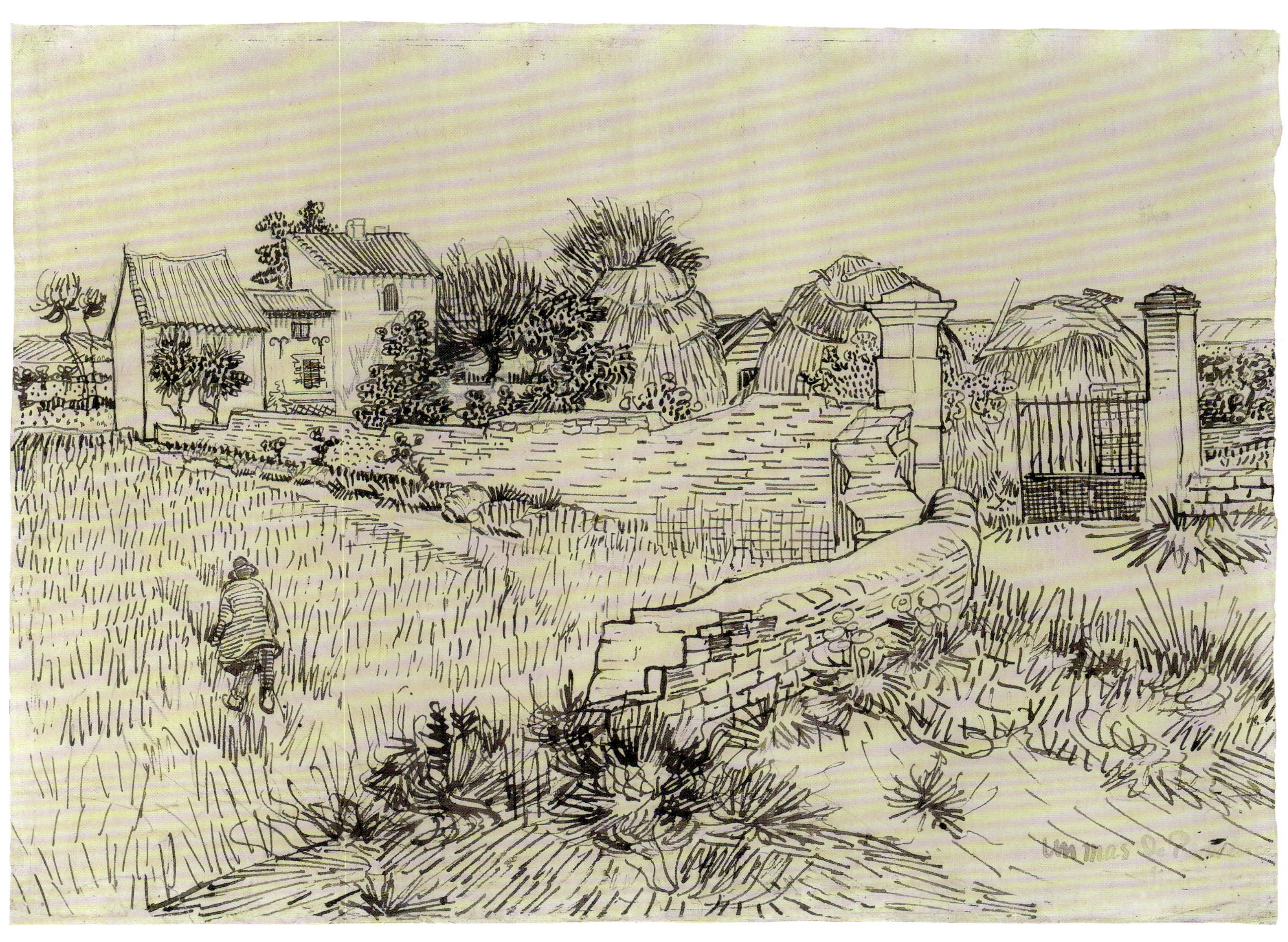

67. *Haystacks*

(for John Russell)

ca. July 31–August 3, 1888
Reed pen, quill, and ink over graphite on wove paper
24 x 31 cm ($9^{1}/_{2}$ x $12^{1}/_{4}$ in.)
Signed in pen and ink, lower left: *Vincent*
Philadelphia Museum of Art, The Samuel S. White 3rd and Vera White Collection, 1962 (1962-229-1)
F1427, JH1525
Letters 516, 517

Provenance: Sent by the artist to John Russell, Belle-Île, Brittany, ca. August 3, 1888 [517]; his gift to Henri Matisse, 1897, until at least 1905; Pierre Matisse Art Gallery, New York, by 1935, until 1944; purchased by Samuel S. White 3rd and Vera White, Ardmore, Pa., 1944; their gift to the Philadelphia Museum of Art, 1962.

Selected exhibitions: Paris 1905, no. 31; New York and other cities 1935–36, no. 105; New York 1943, no. 71; New York 1984, no. 75; Otterlo 1990, no. 197; Arles 2003, pp. 42–43.

Summary of the literature: De la Faille (1928, no. 1427) recognized Russell as the drawing's first recipient but mistakenly dated the work to June (rather than late July or early August) and confused its place in Van Gogh's work by describing it as "a copy" of the drawing sent to Bernard (F1426), the latter work erroneously deemed "the study for the painting" of the same motif (F425). Roskill (1966, p. 5 n. 20; 1971, p. 171) correctly understood the drawing to be a *répétition* of the painting, as did Hulsker (1980/1996, no. 1525), and Pickvance (in New York 1984, no. 75; in Otterlo 1990, p. 232), who noted distinct differences between this version of the haystacks painting and the one sent earlier to Émile Bernard (F1426). Thannhauser (1938) provided documentation on the work's early provenance.

After completing his canvas *Harvest in Provence* (F412, cat. 63), Van Gogh began a second painting of the same large size (F425, fig. 144) depicting "a farm and some haystacks, which will probably be a pendant" [497]. In realizing this subject, striking evidence of the harvest's results, the artist apparently stepped inside the farmyard pictured in a small oil a short time earlier (F565, fig. 143) and focused his gaze on three tall stacks of hay standing guard before the farmer's house. He sent a watercolored study of the scene (F1425) to Theo about June 15 or 16, with the warning, "You will think the one with the haystacks in a farmyard too bizarre, but it was done in a great hurry as a cartoon for a picture and it is to show you the idea" [498]. A month later, having completed his painting, Van Gogh sent a copy drawing of it to Émile Bernard (F1426, fig. 185), and about two weeks after that he sent this *répétition* to John Russell. Through these four stages, the design evolved from relatively rough to polished, from fragmented to seamless. Remarkably, this final drawing, caricatural in its fussiness of pin dots and needles, fairly vibrates with the thrum of summer farm life, its haystacks tended like idols by peasants and chickens. John Russell placed the drawing in Matisse's welcoming hands in 1897.

See "*Répétitions*: Drawings after Paintings."

CI

Letter to Theo van Gogh, July 31, 1888 [516]: I am working hard for Russell; I thought that I would do him a series of drawings after my painted studies; I believe that he will look upon them kindly. . . . I have 8 and shall do 12. . . .

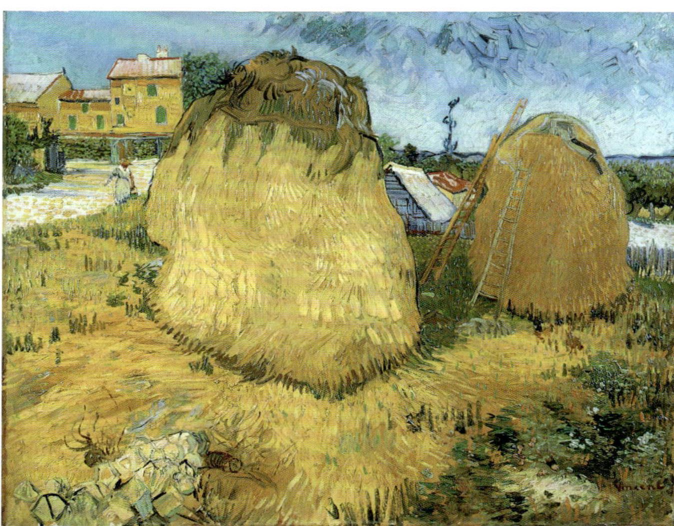

Fig. 144. *Haystacks* (F425), June 1888. Oil on canvas, 73 x 92.5 cm ($28^{3}/_{4}$ x $36^{3}/_{8}$ in.). Kröller-Müller Museum, Otterlo

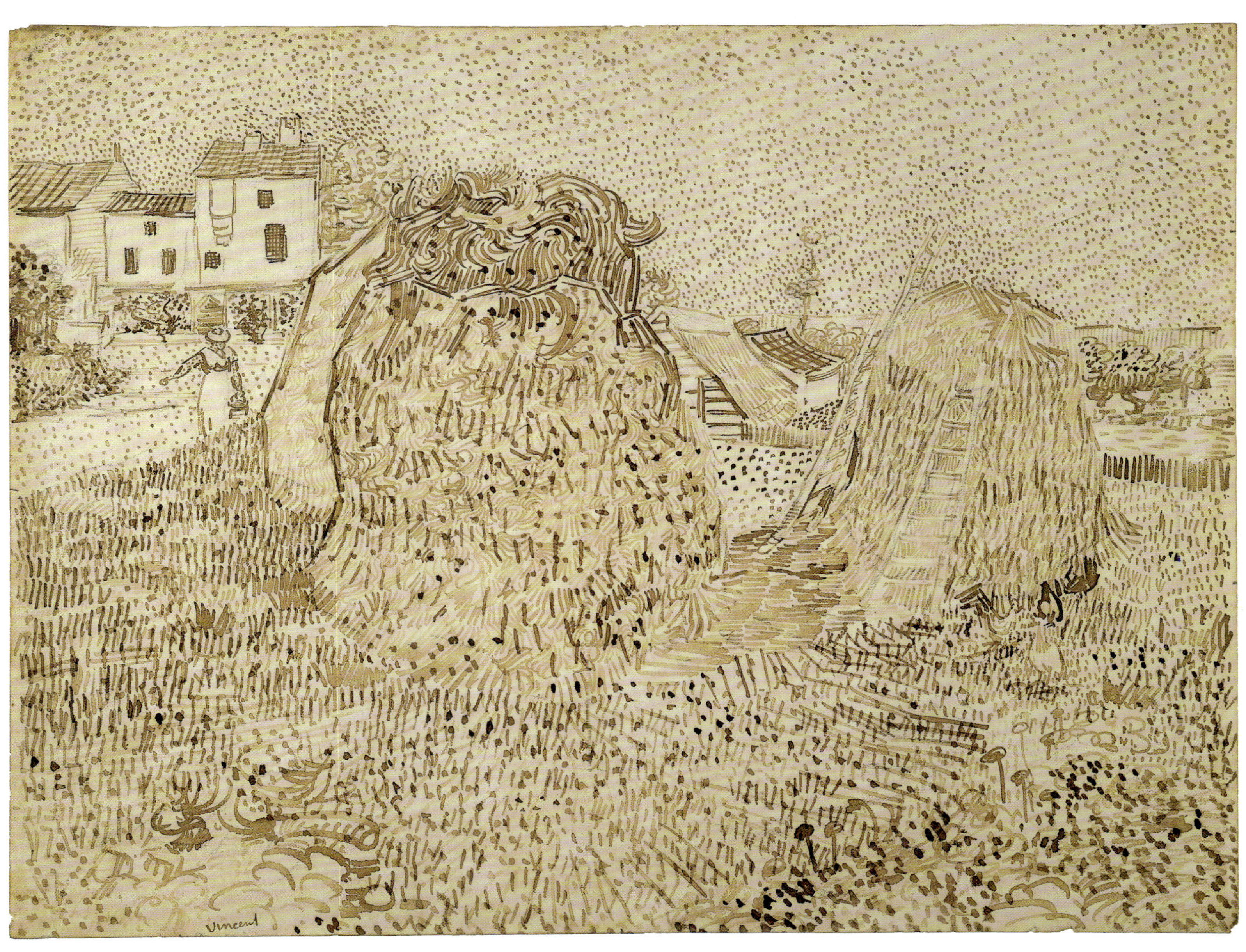
Vincent

68. *A Summer Evening*

(for Émile Bernard)

Mid-July 1888
Reed pen, quill, and ink over graphite on wove paper
24 x 31.5 cm (9½ x 12⅜ in.)
Kunstmuseum Winterthur, Donated by Dr. Emil Hahnloser, 1928
F1514, JH1546
Letter B11

Provenance: Sent by the artist to Émile Bernard, Saint-Briac, between July 17 and 20, 1888 [B11], until it was sold to Ambroise Vollard, Paris, probably between 1899 and 1904; purchased by Pál Majovszky, Budapest, from Vollard in 1911 (or through Simon Meller, Vienna, between 1911 and 1914), until mid-1920s; Hans Robert Hahnloser, Vienna, mid-1920s; Emil Hahnloser, Zürich, until 1928; his gift to the Kunstmuseum Winterthur, March 8, 1928.

Selected exhibitions: Paris 1937, no. 172; Milan 1952, no. 104; Munich 1956, no. 114; Munich 1961, no. 57; Frankfurt 1970, no. 52; New York 1984, no. 69; Otterlo 1990, no. 195.

Summary of the literature: Following the lead of De la Faille (1928, no. 1514), who listed Theo's wife, Johanna van Gogh-Bonger, in this drawing's early provenance, both Roskill (1971, pp. 155, 171) and Hulsker (1980/1996, no. 1546) assumed it a work sent by Vincent to his brother [519]. However, Millard (1974, p. 160) identified the drawing as one of the *répétitions* Van Gogh mailed to Bernard in July 1888, and this was confirmed by Welsh-Ovcharov (in Toronto–Amsterdam 1981, p. 128) and Pickvance (in New York 1984, no. 69), who observed that the sheet illustrated the painting of the subject (F465) in a state before it was "extensively reworked" in September. Dorn (1999, pp. 11–42) discussed both painting and drawing at length and established the drawing's line of descent from Bernard to Vollard to Majovszky.

Although only one-third the size of his painting *Summer Evening* (F465, fig. 145), the *répétition* Van Gogh sent to Bernard is a jauntier, rather more pulled-together version of the same composition. The oil was one of the four ambitiously large (size 30) canvases Van Gogh produced during the haying in June. When he first described it to Bernard in a letter that included a small sketch of the work (F1842, fig. 146), he admitted the view might be inaccurate ("Sunset? Rising moon?"), acknowledging the fact that, from where he had stood in the windblown wheat field, the sun could not possibly have been seen setting behind the spires and Roman ruins of Arles. About a week later, he further disparaged the work, wondering if he ought to "destroy it?" [B9], since it had been dashed off during a mistral so fierce that he had been forced to tie down the legs of his easel.

By the time Van Gogh sent this more finished pen-and-ink copy of the painted landscape, he seems, temporarily, to have made his peace with it. He tinkered about with the townscape and other details of the composition and gave the great orb a halo of wheeling lines.

See "*Répétitions*: Drawings after Paintings."

CI

Letter to Émile Bernard, between July 17 and 20, 1888 [B11]: I have just sent you—today—nine more sketches after painted studies. In this way you will see subjects taken from the sort of scenery that inspires "father" Cézanne. . . .

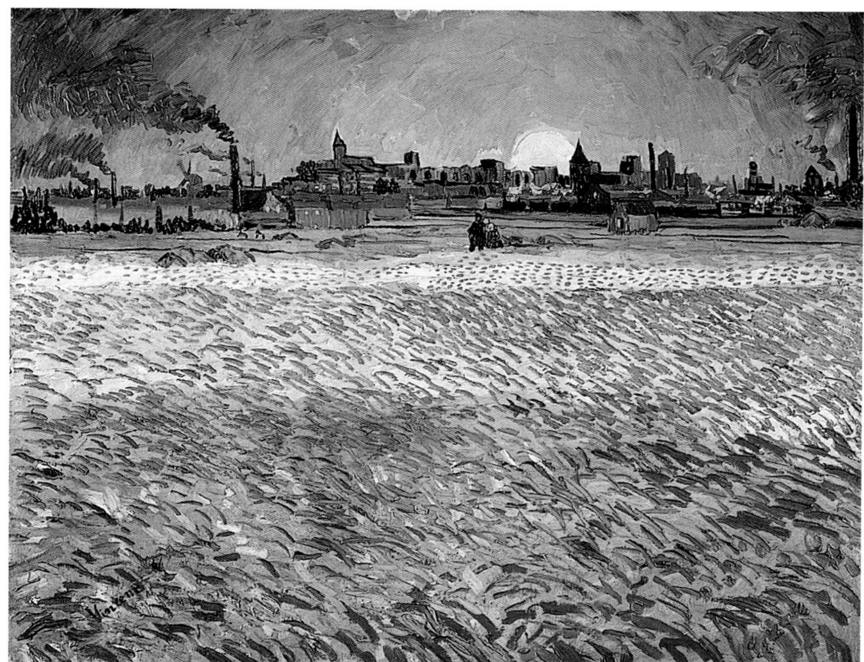

Fig. 145. *Summer Evening* (F465), mid-June and September, 1888. Oil on canvas, 74 x 91 cm (29⅛ x 35⅞ in.). Kunstmuseum Winterthur, donated by Dr. Emil Hahnloser, 1922

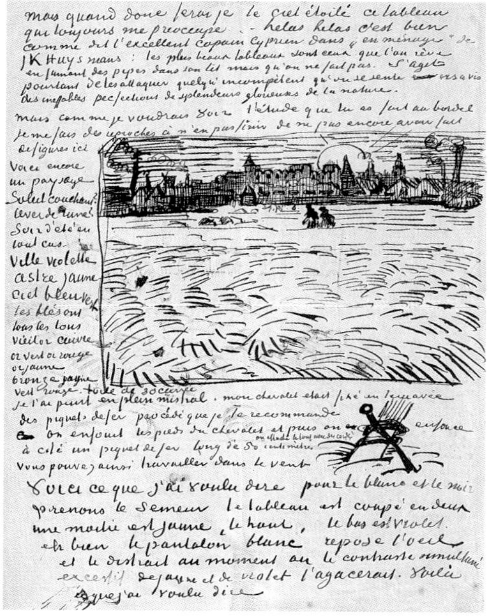

mais quand donc ferai je le ciel étoilé ce tableau
qui toujours me preoccupe. – helas helas c'est bien
comme dit l'excellent copain Cyprien dans « en ménage » de
JK Huysmans : les plus beaux tableaux sont ceux que l'on rêve
en fumant des pipes dans son lit mais qu'on ne fait pas. S'agit
pourtant de les attaquer quelqu'incompétent qu'on se sente vis à vis
des ineffables perfections de splendeurs glorieuses de la nature.
mais comme je voudrais voir l'étude que tu as fait au bordel
je me fais des reproches à n'en pas finir de ne pas encore avoir fait
de figures ici
Voici encore
un paysage
Soleil couchant?
lever de lune?
Soir d'été en
tout cas
Ville violette
astre jaune
ciel bleu vert
les blés ont
tous les tons
vieil or cuivre
or vert or rouge
or jaune
bronze jaune
vert rouge. toile de 30 carrée
je l'ai peint en plein mistral. mon chevalet était fixé en terre avec
des piquets de fer procédé que je te recommande
on enfonce les pieds du chevalet et puis on enfonce
à côté un piquet de fer long de 50 centimètres
vous pouvez ainsi travailler dans le vent
Voici ce que j'ai voulu dire pour le blanc et le noir
prenons le Semeur le tableau est coupé en deux
une moitié est jaune, le haut, le bas est violet.
eh bien le pantalon blanc repose l'oeil
et le distrait au moment où le contraste simultané
excessif de jaune et de violet l'agacerait. Voilà
ce que j'ai voulu dire

Fig. 146. *Summer Evening* (F1842), sketch in a letter to Émile Bernard, ca. June 19, 1888 [B7]. Pen and ink on wove paper, 11 x 16.5 cm (4⅜ x 6½ in.). The Pierpont Morgan Library, New York (photo: Joseph Zahavi)

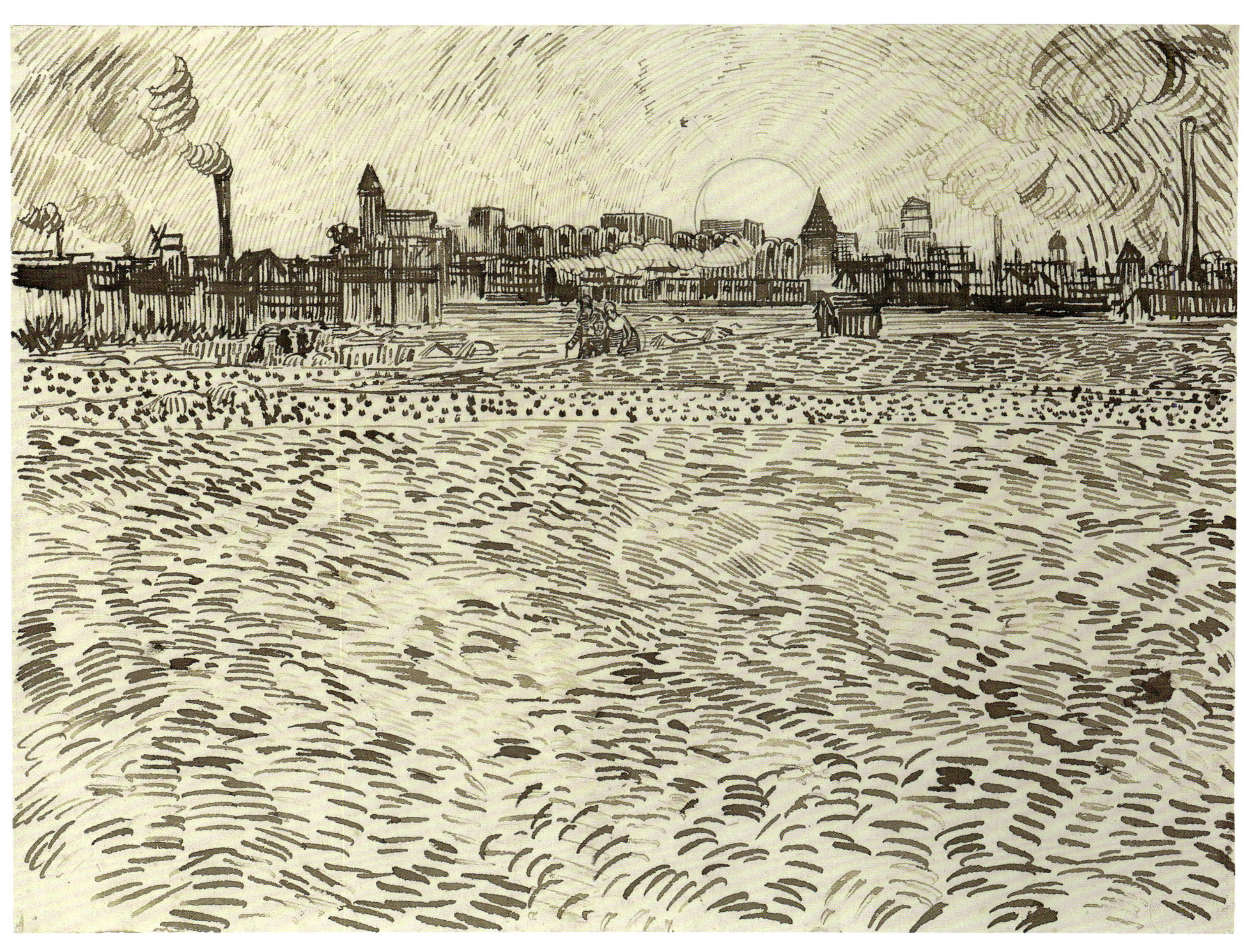

69. Arles: View from the Wheat Fields

Between June 10 and 21, 1888
Oil on canvas
73 x 54 cm (28¾ x 21¼ in.)
Musée Rodin, Paris (P.7304)
F545, JH1477
Letters 501, B9

New York only

The wind-whipped wheat field of *Summer Evening* (F465, fig. 145) appears almost fully mown in this view of the harvest. Once again Van Gogh set before himself the task of defining a deep space in a uniformly textured surface, however this time in a vertical format. His composition seizes the central section of *Summer Evening*, with the silhouetted town of Arles, its chimneys and the passing locomotive still billowing smoke. (But now, more convincingly, all are blowing in the same direction.)

This charmingly conceived hymn to industry and the cycles of the seasons arises out of Van Gogh's love of metaphor and his admiration for Millet, Japanese artists, and other canny masters of simplicity. "I would much rather make naïve pictures out of old almanacs, those old 'farmer's almanacs' in which hail, snow, rain, fair weather are depicted in a wholly primitive manner," Van Gogh explained to Bernard, while noting particularly "the one Anquetin has hit on so well in his 'Harvest'" [B7] (fig. 147).

CI

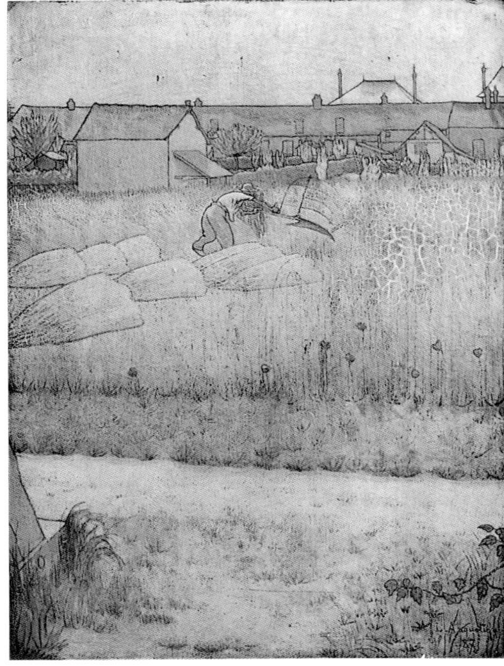

Fig. 147. Louis Anquetin, *The Mower at Noon: Summer,* 1887. Oil on canvas, 69.2 x 52.7 cm (27¼ x 20¾ in.). Private collection

Letter to Theo van Gogh, June 21, 1888 [501]: I have had a week's hard, close work among the wheat fields in the full sun.

Letter to Émile Bernard, June 27, 1888 [B9]: I have seven studies of wheat fields. . . . The landscapes yellow—old gold—done quickly, quickly, quickly and in a hurry, just like the harvester who is silent under the blazing sun, intent only on his reaping.

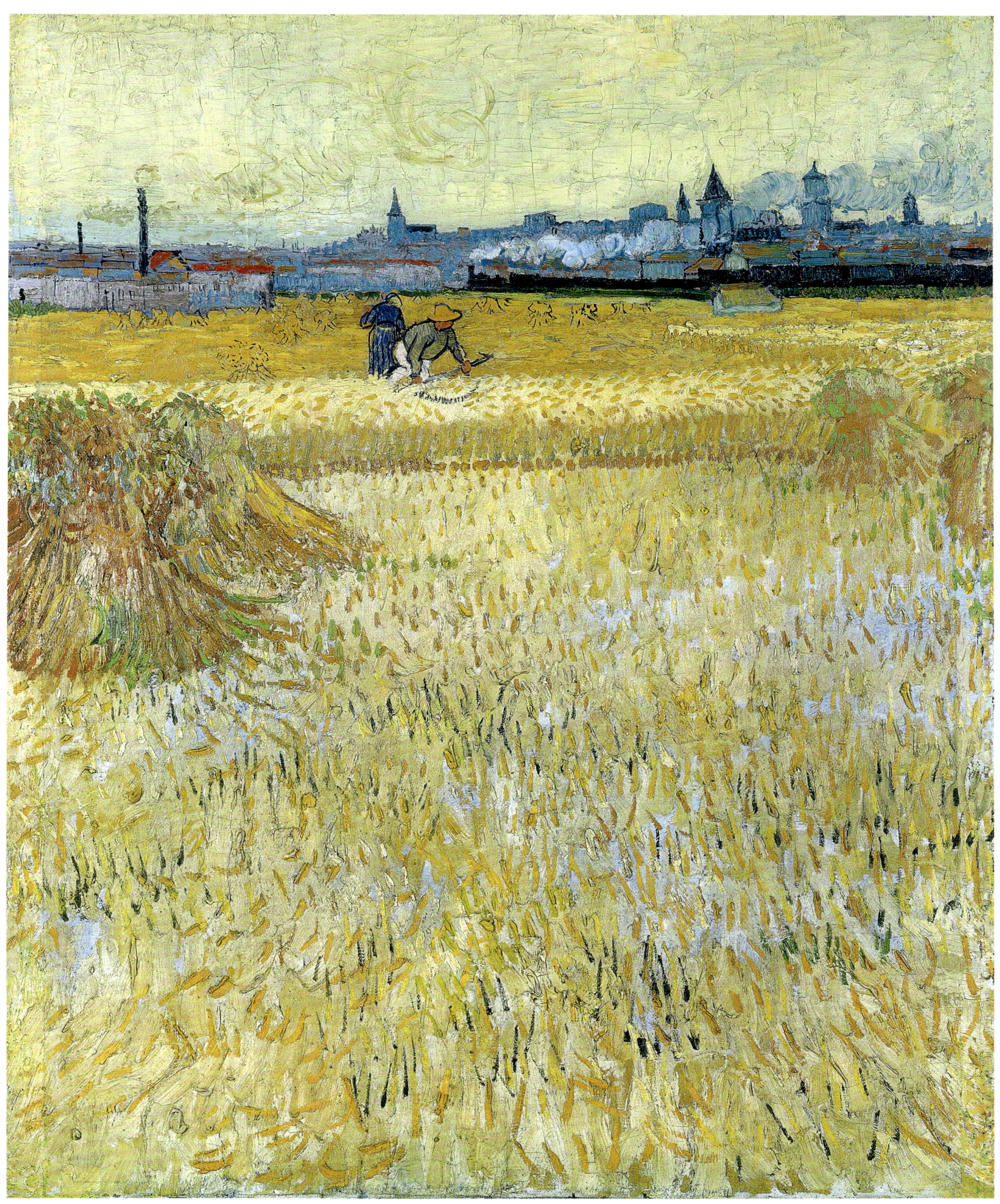

70. *Arles: View from the Wheat Fields*

(for Émile Bernard)

Mid-July 1888
Reed pen and ink over graphite on wove paper
31.9 x 24.2 cm ($12\frac{1}{2}$ x $9\frac{1}{2}$ in.)
National Gallery of Art, Washington, Collection of Mr. and Mrs. Paul Mellon, in Honor of the 50th Anniversary of the National Gallery of Art, 1992 (1992.51.10)
F1491, JH1516
Letter B11

New York only

Provenance: Sent by the artist to Émile Bernard, Saint-Briac, between July 17 and 20, 1888 [B11], until it was sold to Ambroise Vollard, Paris, probably between 1899 and 1904; Henri Matisse, Paris, by 1905; Pierre Matisse, New York, 1941–47; sold to Charles Boyer, Beverly Hills; E. Coe Kerr Gallery, New York; purchased by Mr. and Mrs. Paul Mellon, Upperville, Va., April 1969; their gift to the National Gallery of Art, 1985.

Exhibition: Paris 1905, no. 30.

Summary of the literature: De la Faille (1928, no. 1491) catalogued this drawing and two others of the same motif but did not date them or address their relationship to one another or to the related painting (F545, cat. 69). In later editions of his catalogue (1970/1992, no. 1491), these works are dated to summer 1888, and the editors contended that this drawing "must have been made on the spot." Roskill (1971, p. 152), Hulsker (1980/1996, no. 1516), and Pickvance (in New York 1984, p. 146) all recognized this as the *répétition* sent to Bernard in mid-July 1888.

Arles: View from the Wheat Fields (F545, cat. 69) must have been one of Van Gogh's favorite paintings for it was the only one of his harvest canvases that he copied three times in drawings he sent to Émile Bernard, John Russell, and Theo van Gogh in late July and early August of 1888. Like the other eight *répétitions* in the second batch of copy drawings Van Gogh mailed to Bernard, this one too is marked by a rhythmic play of dots and dashes, here describing chopped wheat stubble and gathered sheaves. Arles' buildings are defined more distinctly by sharp, ruler-straight lines, while clouds of smoke are lazily penned in loops.

It is perhaps easier to see in Van Gogh's drawings than in his paintings the high degree of his indebtedness to the idiosyncrasies of Japanese woodcut prints like those that were in his and Theo's collection (see fig. 26), with their scattered ciphers, uptilted aerial perspective, and clear respect for the paper ground as a source of light. "I hope to do these sketches after the [painted] studies for you as well," Van Gogh wrote to Theo a fortnight after having completed this drawing for Bernard. "You will see that they have something of a Japanese air" [516].

See "*Répétitions*: Drawings after Paintings."

CI

Letter to Émile Bernard, between July 17 and 20, 1888 [B11]: I have just sent you—today—nine more sketches after painted studies. In this way you will see subjects taken from the sort of scenery that inspires "father" Cézanne. . . .

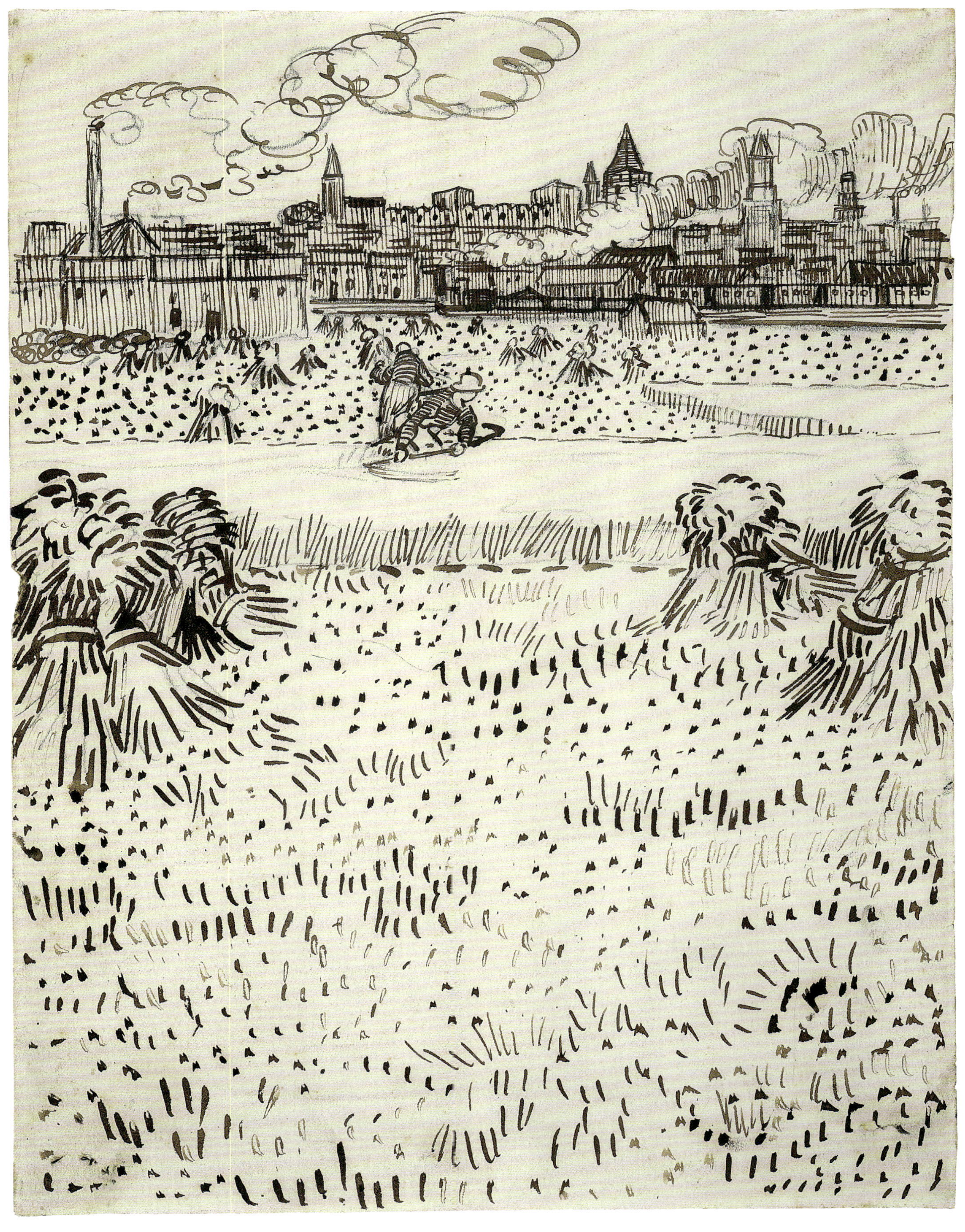

71. *Arles: View from the Wheat Fields*

(for John Russell)

ca. July 31–August 3, 1888
Reed pen, quill, and ink over graphite on wove paper
31.5 x 23.5 cm ($12\frac{1}{2}$ x $9\frac{1}{4}$ in.)
Signed in pen and ink, lower left: *Vincent*
Private collection
F1490, JH1529
Letters 516, 517

New York only

Provenance: Sent by the artist to John Russell, Belle-Île, Brittany, ca. August 3, 1888 [517], until 1920; sold, [Anon.], Hôtel Drouot, Paris, March 31, 1920, no. 64; purchased by Jos Hessel, Paris; H. J. Laroche, Paris; Wildenstein and Co., New York, by 1935, until at least 1949; Mr. and Mrs. Leigh B. Block, Chicago, by 1967; Richard Nagy, Dover Street Gallery, London, ca. 2000; private collection.

Selected exhibitions: New York and other cities 1935–36, no. 116; Martigny 2000, no. 62.

Summary of the literature: De la Faille (1928, no. 1490) catalogued this drawing among works "not mentioned in the letters." Taking into account documentation furnished by Thannhauser (1938), the revised edition of De la Faille (1970/1992, no. 1490) added Russell's name to the provenance, associating the drawing with those Van Gogh sent him in August [517], but dated it June 1888 (the date of the related painting). In accordance with Roskill (1966, p. 5 n. 17; 1971, p. 171), Hulsker (1980/1996, no. 1529) dated the drawing to the time of its dispatch to Russell. Pickvance (in New York 1984, p. 82) distinguished this drawing from the other two *répétitions*: F1491, sent to Bernard, and F1492, sent to Theo.

To his second pen-and-ink copy of his painting *Arles: View from the Wheat Fields* (F545, cat. 69), Van Gogh brought greater detail and tonal variation that make the landscape more realistic, spatially. Like the other eleven *répétitions* he prepared for the Australian painter John Russell, whom he made efforts to cajole and impress, this drawing too wears a deferential cloak of formality in its precision and delicacy.

Compared to the rather summary version of the picture sent some two weeks earlier to Bernard (F1491, cat. 70), this interpretation is filled to brimming with graphic elaboration: dabs and strokes of the reed pen, tonal additions in quill, the orderly regiments of lines emphasizing the composition's verticality. Increased attention given to the couple haying perhaps signals Van Gogh's wish to renew study of the human figure.

See "*Répétitions*: Drawings after Paintings."

CI

Letter to Theo van Gogh, July 31, 1888 [516]: I am working hard for Russell; I thought that I would do him a series of drawings after my painted studies; I believe that he will look upon them kindly. . . . Anyway, let's finish the drawings—I have 8 and shall do 12. . . .

Letter to Theo van Gogh, ca. August 3, 1888 [517]: I have sent Russell 12 drawings after painted studies. . . .

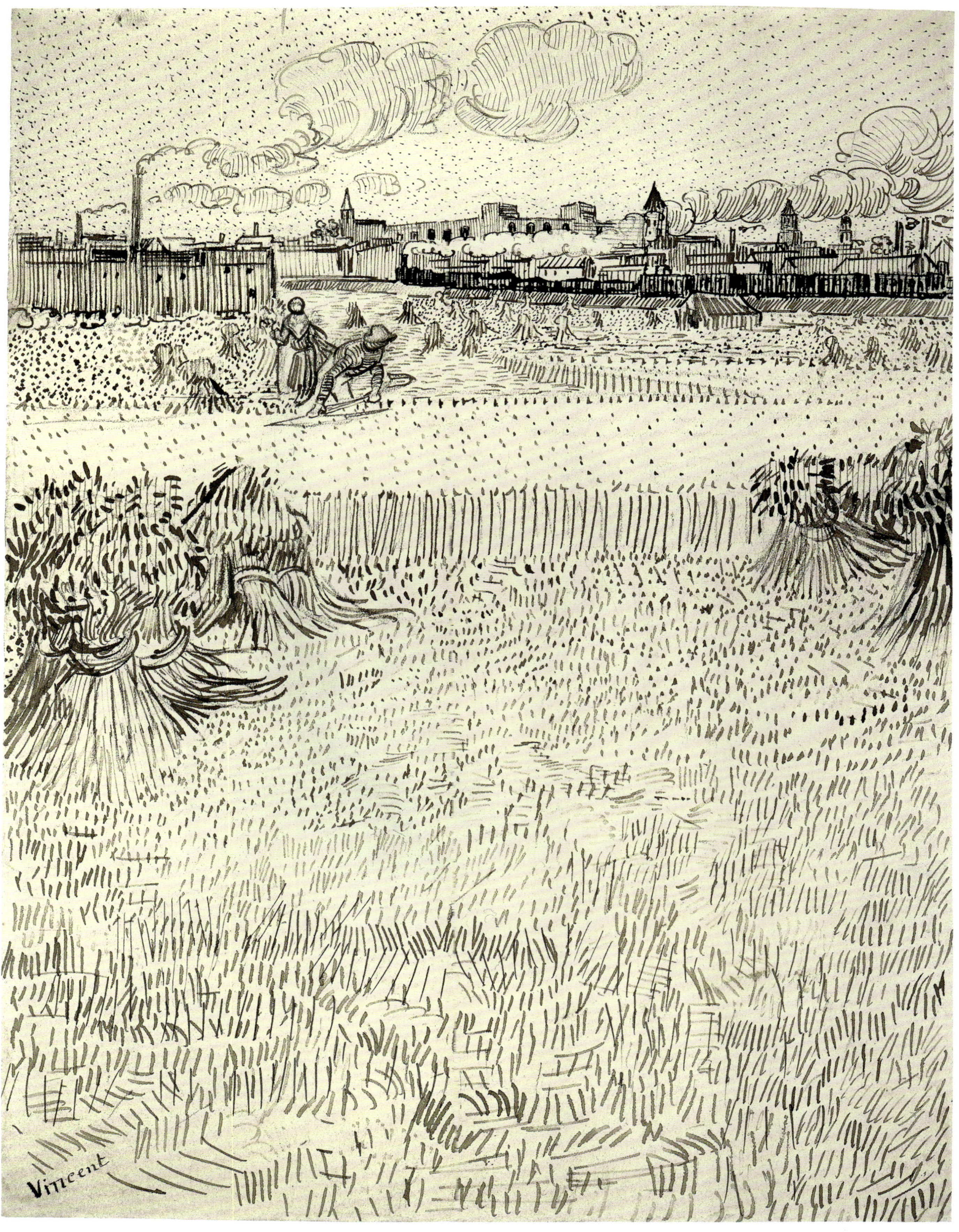
Vincent

72. *Arles: View from the Wheat Fields*

(for Theo van Gogh)

ca. August 6–8, 1888
Reed pen, quill, and ink over graphite on wove paper
31.2 x 24.2 cm (12 1/4 x 9 1/2 in.)
Signed in pen and ink, lower right: *Vincent*
Stamped, lower right, with the mark of Gustav Engelbrecht (Lugt 1148)
The J. Paul Getty Museum, Los Angeles (2001.25)
F1492, JH1544
Letters 518, 519

Provenance: Sent by the artist to Theo van Gogh (d. 1891), Paris, August 8, 1888 [519]; by inheritance to his son, Vincent Willem van Gogh, as part of his collection, administered by his widow, Johanna van Gogh-Bonger, 1891, until 1907; sold to Paul Cassirer, Berlin, November 1907; sold to Gustav Engelbrecht, Hamburg, December 1907; Julius Freund, Berlin, 1928; Robert von Hirsch, Basel, presumably by 1943; his estate sale, Sotheby's, London, June 27, 1978, no. 843; acquired by J. B. Goulandris, London; Thomas Gibson Fine Art, London; Heinz Berggruen, by 1991; his sale, Phillips, New York, May 7, 2001, no. 6; purchased by the Getty Museum.

Selected exhibitions: Amsterdam 1905, no. 374; Berlin 1907, no. 123; Berlin 1914, no. 87a; Berlin 1927–28, hors cat.; New York 1984, no. 82; Bremen 2002–3, no. 42.

Summary of the literature: This drawing was catalogued by De la Faille (1928, no. 1492) among works "not mentioned in the letters." In revised editions of his catalogue (1970/1992, no. 1492), it is dated to summer 1888, considered "close in style to F1490 which apparently preceded it," and counted among drawings Van Gogh mentioned sending to Theo in early August [519]. Roskill (1971, p. 153), Hulsker (1980/1996, no. 1544), and Pickvance (in New York 1984, no. 82) identified the work likewise. For early history, see Feilchenfeldt and Veenenbos 1988, p. 135.

When Vincent sent this drawing to Theo in early August, the painting he reproduced in pen and ink was close to two months old and already had been copied by him twice, once for Émile Bernard (F1491, cat. 70) and again for John Russell (F1490, cat. 71). This unusual production of three *répétitions* after one painting would appear to signal the artist's satisfaction with the picture. (He distinguished only one other painting in this way, *Boats at Sea, Saintes-Maries-de-la Mer* [F417, cat. 55].) However, he complained that his painted study "lack[ed] clearness of touch" and that it was therefore "necessary to draw [it]" [519].

In all three of his graphic revisions of *Arles: View from the Wheat Fields*, Van Gogh labored to bring "a livelier touch" to "the 'haggard' look" of his canvas, which he blamed on his disruptive "fight against the mistral" [518]. And in this instance, he seems to have been successful. Neither so summary as the drawing for Bernard, nor as emphatically decorative as the one sent to Russell, Theo's version is a relaxed and confident synthesis of the previous efforts, rich in variations and selective accents.

See "*Répétitions*: Drawings after Paintings."

CI

Letter to Theo van Gogh, August 6, 1888 [518]: Did I tell you that I had sent the drawings to friend Russell? At the moment I am doing practically the same ones over again for you, there will likewise be twelve. You will then see better what there is in the painted studies in the way of drawing.

Letter to Theo van Gogh, August 8, 1888 [519]: Now the Harvest, the Garden, the Sower, and the two marines are sketches after painted studies. I think all these ideas are good, but the painted studies lack clearness of touch. That is another reason why I felt it necessary to draw them.

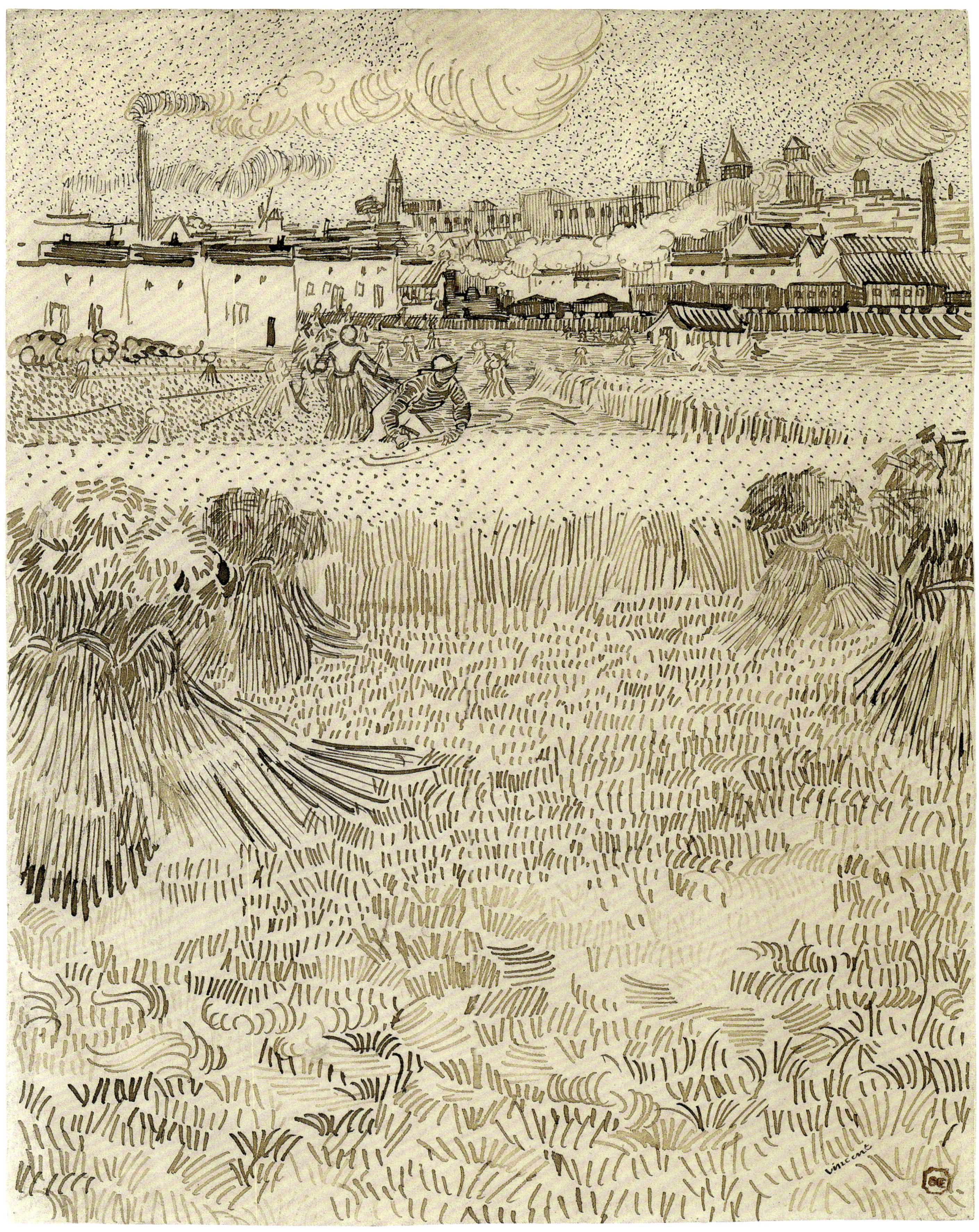

73. *Wheat Field with Sheaves*

(for Émile Bernard)

Mid-July 1888
Reed pen and ink over graphite on wove paper
24.5 x 32 cm (9⅝ x 12⅝ in.)
Signed in pen and ink, lower right: *Vincent*
Kupferstichkabinett, Staatliche Museen zu Berlin (SZ 3)
F1488, JH1517
Letter B11

New York only

Provenance: Sent by the artist to Émile Bernard, Saint-Briac, between July 17 and 20, 1888 [B11], until 1904; sold to Hugo von Tschudi, Berlin, by October 11, 1904 (for 100 marks); his anonymous gift to the Nationalgalerie Berlin, December 1906.

Selected exhibitions: Paris 1892 (per Francis 1892); Stuttgart 1924, no. 20; Munich 1961, no. 64; New York 1984, no. 67; Bremen 2002–3, no. 41.

Summary of the literature: Catalogued among works "not mentioned in the letters" by De la Faille (1928, no. 1488), this drawing was dated to summer 1888 in revised editions of his catalogue (1970/1992, no. 1488) and described as one that "must have been executed on the spot." Roskill (1971, pp. 156 n. 56, 170), Hulsker (1980/1996, no. 1517), and Pickvance (in New York 1984, no. 67) recognized the work as a *répétition* of a painting (F561) and as one of the drawings sent to Bernard in mid-July 1888.

In several studies focused on sheaves of wheat standing in the fields of Provence, Van Gogh returned to a subject that had attracted him in Holland (see F193). However, his art had changed dramatically in only three years. The penned *répétition* of his painting of 1888 (F561, fig. 148) highlights the artist's stunning break with traditions of pictorial realism. It is a daring summary of the canvas, drawn systematically and rapidly, with little preparation in pencil. Like so many of the fifteen copy drawings Van Gogh sent to Bernard, it is caricatural in its exaggerated, seemingly naive simplicity—rather like the Japanese woodcut prints both artists admired.

See "*Répétitions*: Drawings after Paintings."

CI

Letter to Émile Bernard, between July 17 and 20, 1888 [B11]: I have just sent you—today—nine more sketches after painted studies. In this way you will see subjects taken from the sort of scenery that inspires "father" Cézanne. . . .

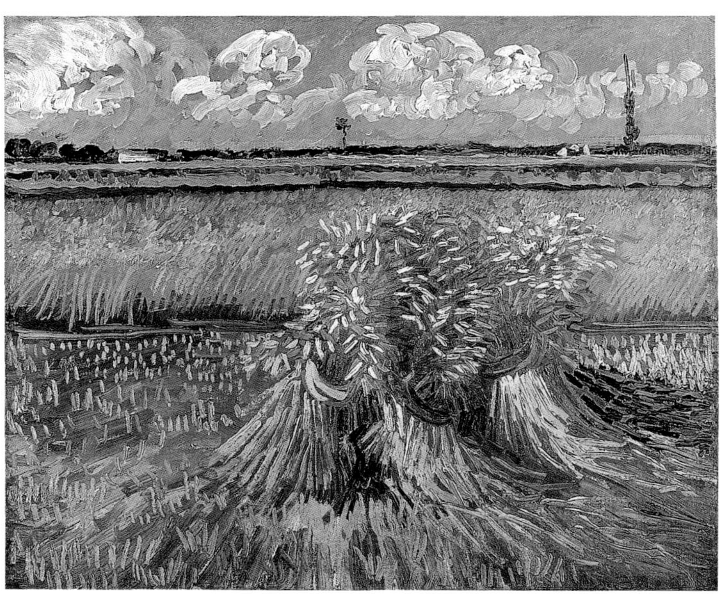

Fig. 148. *Wheat Field with Sheaves* (F561), ca. June 17–23, 1888. Oil on canvas, 55.2 x 66.6 cm (21¾ x 26¼ in.). Honolulu Academy of Arts, Gift of Mrs. Richard A. Cooke and Family in memory of Richard A. Cooke, 1946

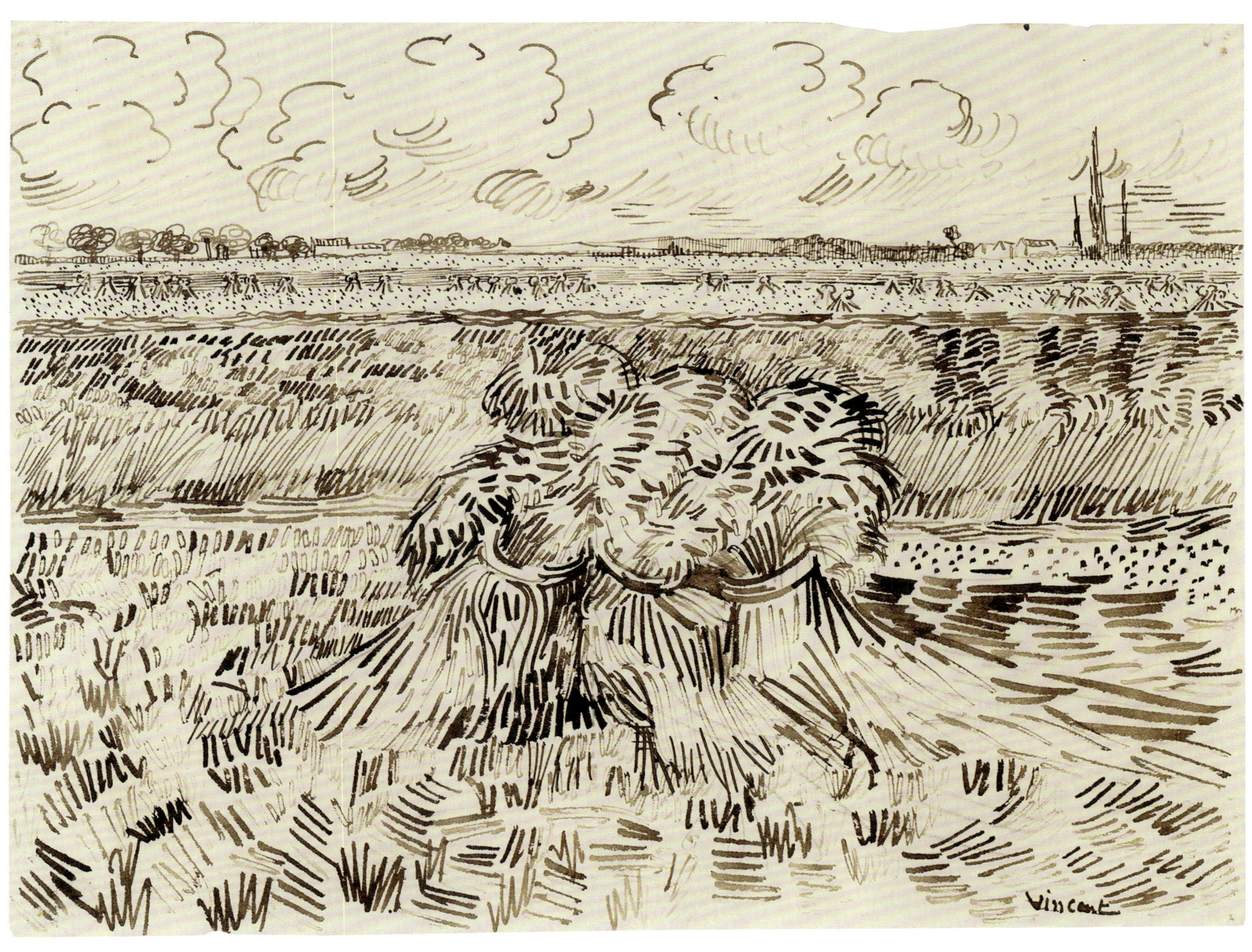
Vincent

74. *Wheat Field with Sheaves*

(for John Russell)

ca. July 31–August 3, 1888
Reed pen, quill, and ink over graphite on wove paper
24.2 x 31.7 cm (9½ x 12½ in.)
Signed in pen and ink, lower left: *Vincent*
Private collection
F1489, JH1530
Letters 516, 517

New York only

Provenance: Sent by the artist to John Russell, Belle-Île, Brittany, ca. August 3, 1888 [517], until 1920; sold, [Anon.], Hôtel Drouot, Paris, March 31, 1920, no. 68; Gallery Le Garrec, Paris; Arthur Hahnloser (d. 1936), Winterthur, by 1927 (and probably by 1922); his son, Hans R. Hahnloser, Bern, by 1970; by descent to a private Swiss collector, by 1984; sold, Sotheby's, New York, November 8, 1994, no. 11, to present owner.

Selected exhibitions: Zürich 1924, no. 77; Berlin 1927–28, no. 107; Munich 1961, no. 65; Frankfurt 1970, no. 53; New York 1984, no. 76.

Summary of the literature: Russell's ownership of this drawing was not recorded by De la Faille (1928, no. 1489) but was noted in subsequent editions of the catalogue raisonné in keeping with documentation cited by Thannhauser (1938). In De la Faille 1970/1992 (no. 1489), the work is dated to the summer of 1888, associated with the twelve drawings Van Gogh sent to Russell that August [517], and considered, relative to F1488, "the more elaborated version done after the picture [F561]." Roskill (1971, pp. 156, 171), Hulsker (1980/1996, no. 1530), and Pickvance (in New York 1984, no. 76) also identified the drawing as one sent to Russell. Hansen (in Toledo 2003, p. 62) noticed how "Van Gogh 'translated' the color nuances of the oil study to the drawing by means of heavier or more delicate dabs and dots" and "supplemented a reed pen with a fine drawing pen."

When Van Gogh copied his oil study of wheat sheaves for Émile Bernard, he used pen strokes just as blunt as the brushstrokes he had used in his painting (see F1488, cat. 73). But when he redrew the composition for John Russell some two weeks later, he varied the weight and direction of his touch and laced, among the broad tracks of the reed pen, finer lines and dots, applied with a quill. His meticulous and varied detailing of nearly every centimeter of space on the sheet resulted in a much more atmospheric landscape that, simply by means of tiny, clustered marks in black ink, suggested all the richness and tonal variations of his painting.

See "*Répétitions*: Drawings after Paintings."

CI

Letter to Theo van Gogh, July 31, 1888 [516]: I am working hard for Russell; I thought that I would do him a series of drawings after my painted studies; I believe that he will look upon them kindly. . . . I have 8 and shall do 12 . . . they have something of a Japanese air.

Letter to Theo van Gogh, ca. August 3, 1888 [517]: I have sent Russell 12 drawings after painted studies. . . .

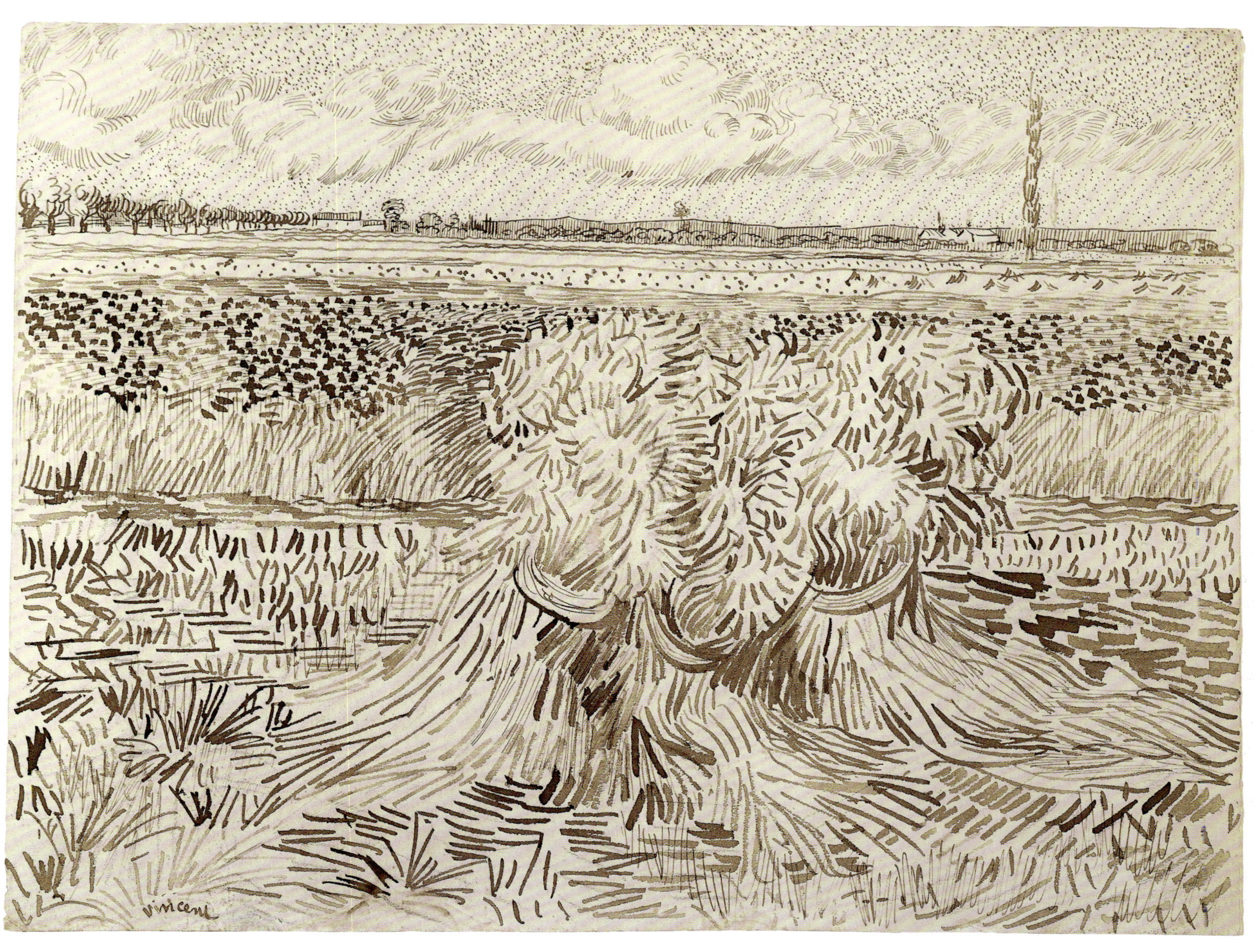
Vincent

75. *The Sower*

Sketch in a letter to John Russell, ca. June 17, 1888
Pen and ink on wove paper watermarked L-J D L&C°
20.3 x 26.3 cm (8 x 10 3/8 in.)
Solomon R. Guggenheim Museum, New York, Thannhauser Collection, Gift, Justin K. Thannhauser, 1978
F1840, JH1471
Letter 501a

New York only

Provenance: Sent by the artist to John Russell, Belle-Île, Brittany, ca. June 17, 1888 [501a], until his death in 1930; to his daughter, Jeanne Jouve, Paris, probably in 1930–31; acquired from her by Justin K. Thannhauser, Paris, probably in 1938–39; his bequest to the Guggenheim Museum, 1978.

Selected exhibitions: New York 1955, no. 110; New York 1984, no. 151.

Summary of the literature: This letter remained generally unknown until Thannhauser (1938, pp. 97–98) reproduced it and published its full text, dating it to the end of June or the beginning of July 1888 and noting "its amazing variety of handwritings . . . [that] should also be of very special interest to the graphologist." Pickvance (in New York 1984, no. 49) and Hulsker (1993, p. 32) suggested the letter be dated on or around June 17, 1888. The most complete analysis of the contents is provided by Barnett (1978, no. 19). In even the most recent edition of De la Faille (1992, no. 1840), the letter remains miscatalogued as one sent to Theo.

The fabled sower, striding across open fields with outflung arm, appears in at least thirty of Van Gogh's works, dating from the start of his career in 1880 to the end in 1890. Symbol of the renewal of life, the planter of grain naturally follows the reaper—to generate the growth cycle all over again. To Van Gogh, the heroic subject offered an opportunity to refocus his art on the study of the human figure.

Around the middle of June as the harvest in Arles continued, he began a painting of a sower at work in the fields in late day, just as the sun sank behind still-standing stalks of grain (F422, fig. 150). He presented four verbal descriptions of the painting in his letters, along with two sketches of the work in progress: this one for John Russell and another for Émile Bernard (F1841, fig. 149). He later made two *répétitions* of the completed painting for Bernard (F1442, fig. 189) and his brother Theo (F1441, cat. 76).

In this letter sent to John Russell, Van Gogh mentioned his painting only briefly as "a hard subject to treat," noting the complementary hues of its palette: "the great field *all violet*, the sky & sun very yellow" [501a]. A day or two later, when he sketched the composition for Émile Bernard (F1841, fig. 149), he elaborated on its colors: "There are many hints of yellow in the soil, neutral tones resulting from mixing violet with yellow; but I have played hell somewhat with the truthfulness of the colors. . . . The white trousers [of the sower] allow the eye to rest and distract it at the moment when the excessive simultaneous contrast of yellow and violet irritate it" [B7].

CI

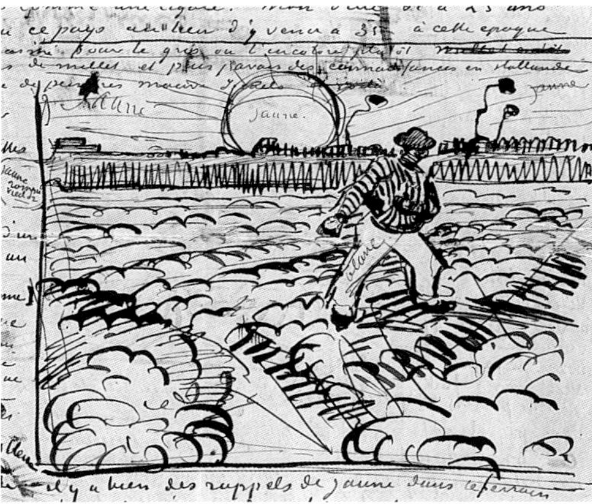

Fig. 149. *The Sower* (F1841), sketch in a letter to Émile Bernard, ca. June 19, 1888 [B7]. Pen and ink, 11.4 x 14.4 cm (4 1/2 x 5 5/8 in.). The Pierpont Morgan Library, New York

Letter to John Russell, ca. June 17, 1888 [501a]:
My dear Russell for ever so long I have been wanting to write to you—but then the work has so taken me up. We have harvest time here at present and I am always in the fields.

And when I sit down to write I am so abstracted by recollections of what I have seen that I leave the letter. . . .

My brother has an exhibition of 10 new pictures by Claude Monet, his latest works, for instance a landscape with red sun set and a group of dark fir trees by the seaside. The red sun casts an orange or blood red reflection on the blue green trees and the ground. . . . I wished I could see them. . . .

I must hurry off this letter for I feel some more abstractions coming on and if I did not quickly fill up my paper I would again set to drawing and you would not have your letter. . . .

Am working at a Sower. [sketch inserted] the great field **all violet*****, the sky & sun very yellow. It is a hard subject to treat.***

I heard Rodin had a beautiful
head at the Salon.
I have been to the seaside for a
week and very likely am going thither
again soon. – Flat shore [illegible]
sands – fine figures there
like Cimabue – straight stylish
Am working at a Sower.

the great field all violet the sky & sun very
yellow. it is a hard subject to treat.
Please remember me very kindly to
Mrs Russell – and in thought I heartily
shake hands.
Yours very truly
Vincent

My dear [illegible] for ever so long I have
been wanting to write to you – but then
the work has so taken me up. We have
harvest time here at present and I am
always in the fields.
And when I sit down to write I
am so abstracted by recollections of
what I have seen that I leave the
letter. For instance at the present
occasion I was writing to you and
going to say something about Arles
as it is – and as it was in the
old days of Boccaccio. –
Well instead of continuing the letter
I began to draw on the very paper
the head of a dirty little girl I saw
this afternoon whilst I was painting
a view of the river with a greenish yellow
sky.
This dirty 'mudlark' I thought
yet had a vague florentine sort of figure
like the heads in the Monticelli
pictures. and reasoning and drawing
this wise I worked on the letter

76. *The Sower*

(for Theo van Gogh)

ca. August 5–8, 1888
Reed pen, quill, and ink over graphite on wove paper
24.4 x 32 cm (9⅝ x 12⅝ in.)
Inscribed on verso, upper left, in another hand: *175*
Van Gogh Museum, Amsterdam (Vincent van Gogh Foundation) (d 441 V/1962)
F1441, JH1543
Letters 518, 519

Provenance: Sent by the artist to Theo van Gogh (d. 1891), Paris, August 8, 1888 [519]; by inheritance to his son, Vincent Willem van Gogh (1890–1978), as part of his collection, administered by his widow, Johanna van Gogh-Bonger (d. 1925), 1891; placed on loan at the Stedelijk Museum, Amsterdam, 1931–73; ownership transferred to the Vincent van Gogh Foundation, 1962; placed on permanent loan at the Van Gogh Museum, Amsterdam, 1973.

Selected exhibitions: Amsterdam 1905, no. 384; Berlin 1906, no. 69; Munich 1908, no. 74; Dresden 1908, no. 78; Frankfurt 1908, no. 85; Berlin 1909–10, no. 206; New York 1920, no. 34; Paris 1937, no. 173; London–Birmingham–Glasgow 1947–48, no. 147; New York 1984, no. 83; Otterlo 1990, no. 199; Tokyo 2000, no. 22.

Summary of the literature: In all editions of De la Faille's catalogue this drawing (no. 1441) is dated June 1888 and associated with the "sketch of a sower" mentioned in letter 501; in revised editions (1970/1992, no. 1441) it is connected also to letters 501a and B7. Roskill (1971, pp. 152–53), Hulsker (1980/1996, no. 1543), and Pickvance (in New York 1984, no. 83) established the work as a drawing made after the painting (F422), sent by Vincent to Theo in early August 1888 [519]. Pickvance noted further that "Van Gogh used pencil rapidly to establish the layout of both figure and landscape. . . . [T]he sower's stride is made wider and more purposeful than in the painting itself, or in the copy for Émile Bernard. . . . Bernard's copy is much closer to the painting than Theo's. . . . [V]an Gogh eliminated the house and tree at left, increased the height of the uncut wheat, and considerably enlarged the sun. The composition becomes simpler, grander, more elemental." For early history, see Feilchenfeldt and Veenenbos 1988, p. 132.

In numerous compositions dating between 1881 and 1889 (see F830, fig. 137; F865, fig. 138; F451, fig. 140), Van Gogh evidenced his intense regard for Millet's *Sower*. During the final days of the harvest in Arles in 1888, he was inspired to envision the subject in novel terms, with emphasis on a resounding clash of colors: yellow and violet.

Alterations Van Gogh made to the painting he began in mid-June (F422, fig. 150) can be tracked from one drawing to another made to report his progress (see also F1840, cat. 75; F1842, fig. 146; F1442, fig. 189). Narrative details (buildings and birds) that appeared here and there at various stages were swept entirely away in this drawing sent to Theo, which concentrated decorative effects in a picture pared down to just three elements: sun, field, and sower. This fourth and final drawing based upon the painting is the most abstract version of the composition, peppier in many ways than the oil—so certain was Van Gogh's pen at this time of making graphic magic.

Initially, the artist had judged his painting "a failure" [522], but he sent it on to Theo in mid-August, soon to confess, "The idea of the 'Sower' continues to haunt me" [535]. By December, he had produced four more versions of the subject (see F451, fig. 140), and in February, reconsidering the earlier, summer canvas, he suggested to Theo it might be shown at the annual Paris exhibit of the Indépendants [576].

See "*Répétitions*: Drawings after Paintings."

CI

Letter to Theo van Gogh, August 6, 1888 [518]: Did I tell you that I had sent the drawings to friend Russell? At the moment I am doing practically the same ones over again for you, there will likewise be twelve.

Letter to Theo van Gogh, August 8, 1888 [519]: Now the Harvest, the Garden, the Sower, and the two marines are sketches after painted studies. I think all these ideas are good, but the painted studies lack clearness of touch. That is another reason why I felt it necessary to draw them.

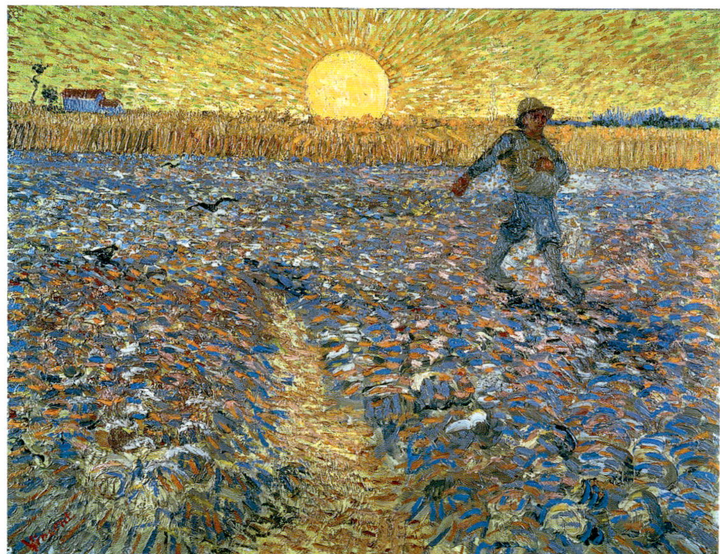

Fig. 150. *The Sower* (F422), ca. June 17, 1888. Oil on canvas, 64 x 80.5 cm (25¼ x 31¾ in.). Kröller-Müller Museum, Otterlo

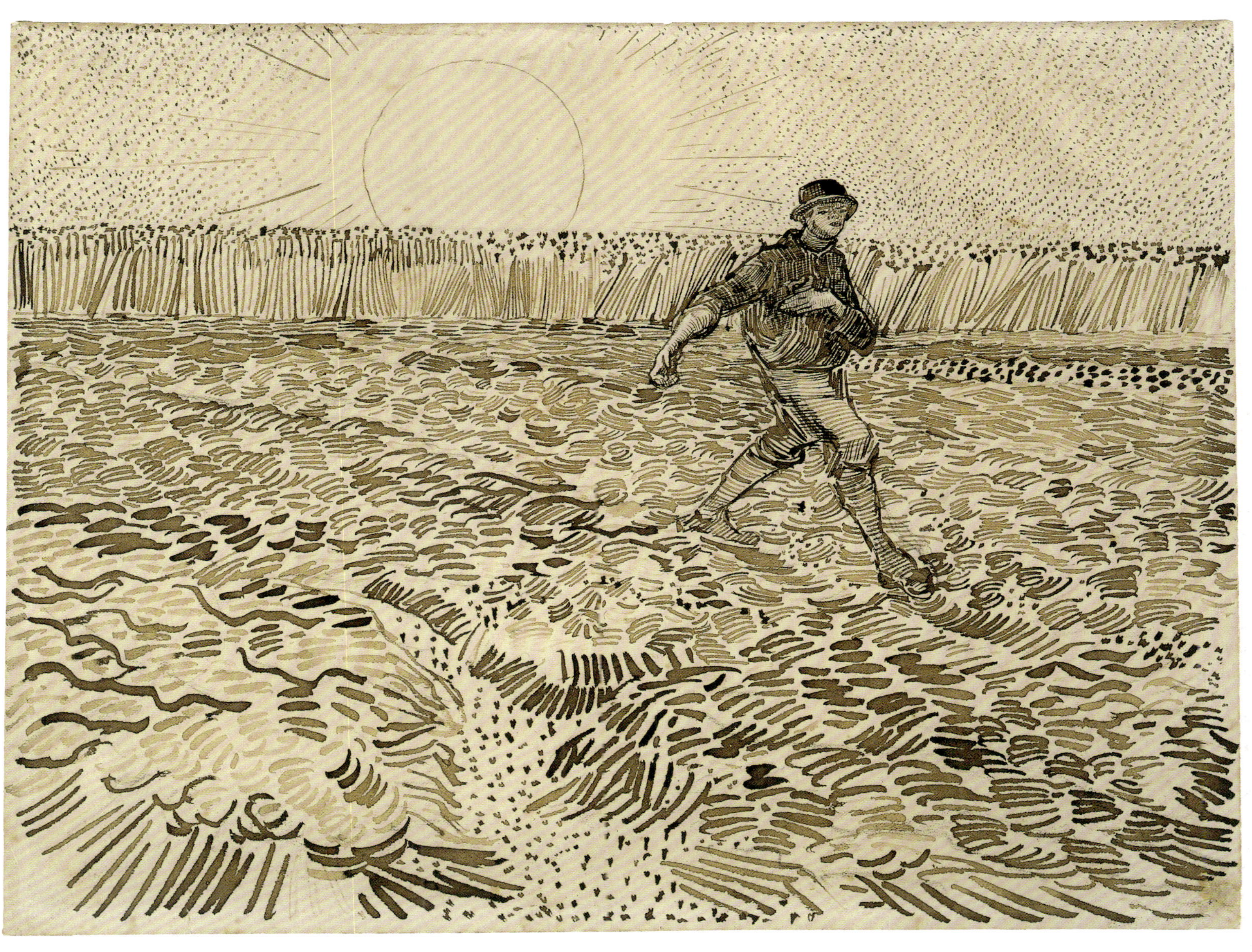

Figure and Portrait Drawings

Despite Van Gogh's professed ambition during his Arles sojourn to "do figures, figures and more figures" [B15], there are a mere dozen drawings that record his interest in arresting a characteristic likeness on paper. These works, all made during the summer of 1888, range from modest off-the-cuff sketches to commanding large-scale portraits framed in line and include drawings done from memory, from the sitter, and from paintings. Van Gogh sent his three most ambitious pen-and-ink portraits on full sheets of Whatman paper to Theo; the rest were dispersed among artist-friends: four to Russell, three plus an inscribed watercolor to Bernard, and a single example to Gauguin. Evidence suggests that from mid-June to late August 1888 Van Gogh explored drawing figures with the reed pen, trying out different approaches of varying ambition, and then did not venture, or did not venture to save, further experiments.[1] Thereafter the figure, which moved him to the "depths of [his] soul" [516], became the exclusive domain of his brush.

Van Gogh seems to have been in no particular hurry to test the reed pen on figures. An early effort to draw a man walking on the Tarascon road, in April 1888 (F1502, cat. 45), gave him a bit of trouble, and he did not attempt another of prominence until his harvest scenes in early June. In the interim, he inserted staffage folk in landscapes and thought about making portraits, but not until the very end of May did he confide any real plans to "make a serious assault on the figure" [498a]. The idea soon took hold of his pen, and while composing a letter to Russell in mid-June [501a], he succumbed to the urge to sketch a head of a "dirty little girl" (F1507a). Within a few days, he had found "a model at last" [501], and during a spell of torrential rain, June 20–24, which interrupted his harvest series, he made his first full-fledged "assault" on the subject.

The model, a young Zouave soldier—who had conveniently shown up at Van Gogh's door at an opportune time and indulged him with multiple sittings—might well have been arranged through his new acquaintance and soon-to-be art student Milliet, a second lieutenant in the same branch of the French army. Making the most of this opportunity, Van Gogh seems to have produced a drawing, a watercolor, and two oil portraits over the five-day period, apparently adopting the procedure he had successfully employed for his last two series, namely, engaging preparatory drawings and color studies toward the realization of paintings, as he had done upon his return from Saintes-Maries the first week in June and again, the following week, when he began the harvest pictures. Beyond the context, which might advocate for his continued reliance on the same strategy, it would seem reasonable to assume that, during the third week in June, Van Gogh would have taken advantage of having a captive sitter (who came back at least twice, having changed from slacks to pantaloons between sessions, as the full-length drawing and oil reveal) to familiarize himself with his model and to flesh out ideas for the portraits on paper before tackling the subject on canvas. No such sequence has been proposed in the literature. Because Van Gogh did not mention the reed-pen seated Zouave (F1443, fig. 151) until two days after he told Theo about his "half-length" oil (F423, cat. 78) and his plans for a "second portrait . . . full length, seated against a white wall" (F424, fig. 155) [501], and because he made no reference at all to the watercolor (F1482, cat. 77), scholars have tended to regard the drawing as an "independent" afterthought and the watercolor as a later *répétition* made in either June or July.

For all their ambition, the drawing and the watercolor are more exploratory in conception than they are resolved. The drawing of the seated figure, placed front and center on a rush chair in a barely defined setting, makes little use of the large sheet of Whatman paper, which Van Gogh generally reserved, as he did adding his signature, for works of importance. The confidence he had gained as a draftsman perhaps recommended the choice of paper but did not carry over completely to the drawing itself; the ungainly figure with knotty and awkward limbs was, however, an accomplishment just the same. It had been two years since Van Gogh's life-model drawings at Cormon's studio in Paris, and he had finally made his first stab at a figure in Arles. Doubtless this was reason enough to sign the sheet (without further elaboration, as he may have intended originally when he added touches of white to the background). The drawing seems to have served not only as testing ground for the reed pen but to acclimate the sitter and artist to their respective roles. The Zouave, presumably told to take a seat on a chair too small for his build and to strike a comfortable pose, clutches his thighs to hold himself still and upright and looks faintly amused, even somewhat relaxed, perhaps thanks to the pipe. That this drawing came first and the watercolor second may be signaled by one clue: the inch-long stroke that begins at the Zouave's lips and extends to one side of his mouth in the watercolor could well be the start of a pipe—an attribute that stops here.

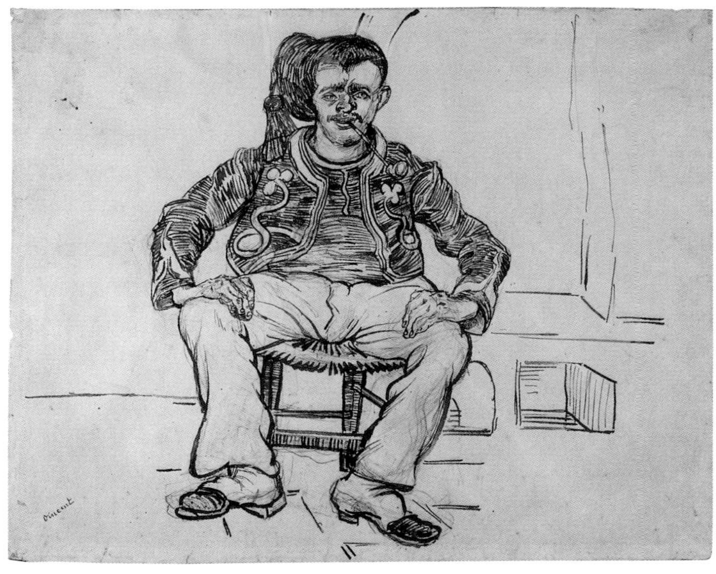

Fig. 151. *The Seated Zouave* (F1443), late June 1888. Reed pen and ink over graphite heightened with white on Whatman paper, 52 x 66 cm (20½ x 26 in.). Van Gogh Museum, Amsterdam (Vincent van Gogh Foundation)

The watercolor manifests similar qualities in its hesitant and irresolute modeling of the figure, as is particularly evident in the graphite sketch (detectable under infrared reflectography; see fig. 250), which lacks the ease that is the hallmark of drawings based on familiar motifs. Likewise, contrary to Van Gogh's tendency in grafting features from canvas to paper, there are no decisive markers present in the underdrawing for passages that required shading or highlights along the chin, nose, or brow (seen, for example, in the infrared reflectograph of F1482a, fig. 251); in fact, various facial features are unarticulated in graphite. Moreover, if Van Gogh had fine-tuned the composition and resolved the setting—the geometry of brickwork, an effective foil to the arabesque design of the embroidered jacket—why would he have resorted to a nondescript background? The role of the watercolor seems self-evident: it establishes the fundamental head-and-shoulders likeness and the color relationships of the oil, no more. Owing partly to the blonder tones of watercolor and to fading, the original intensity of color is mitigated, softening the "savage combination of incongruous tones" still intact in the oil [501]. In terms of its presumed function and its media, the watercolor closely relates to other colored drawings Van Gogh made as "cartoons" for major paintings earlier in June; the blue and pink waxy crayons, for example, are the same material and color as in *Harvest in Provence* (F1483, cat. 62; F1484, fig. 141). Notwithstanding the effort Van Gogh expended on the making of this mixed-media watercolor, the work has none of the forcefulness of the oil, nor does the technique show the same degree of command. It was the last color study Van Gogh made for a painting and his last figure study from the model in Arles. Having served one purpose in June, it presumably served another in July, when he added an inscription to Bernard and sent it as the "face image" for the second set of drawings he made after paintings (see "*Répétitions*: Drawings after Paintings Sent to Bernard").

By early July, having learned that Gauguin was planning to join him in Arles, Van Gogh became increasingly eager to expand his repertoire of figure paintings, even trying a

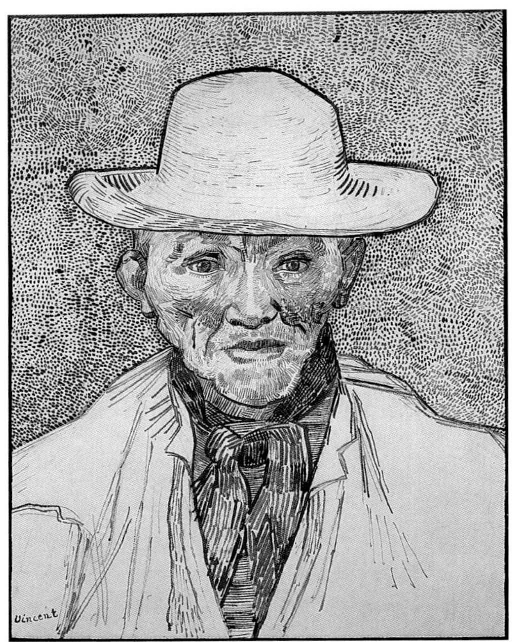

Fig. 152. *Portrait of Patience Escalier* (F1460), early August 1888. Reed pen and ink over graphite on wove paper, 49.4 x 38 cm (19½ x 15 in.). Fogg Art Museum, Harvard University Art Museums, Cambridge, Mass., Bequest of Grenville L. Winthrop (photo: Katya Kallsen)

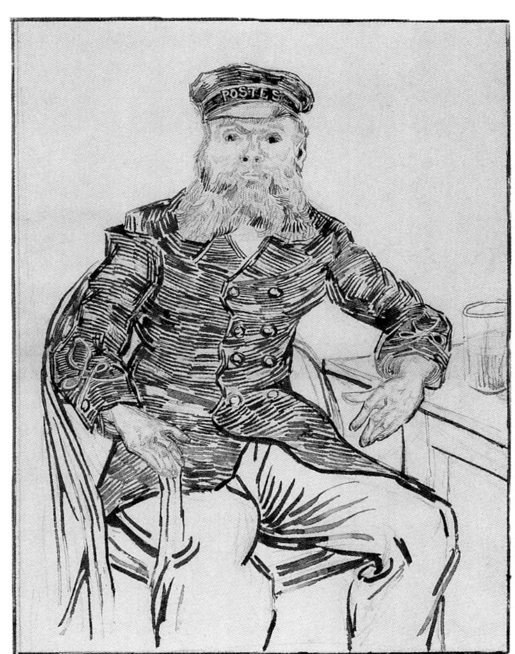

Fig. 153. *Portrait of Joseph Roulin* (F1459), early August 1888. Reed pen and ink over graphite on Whatman paper, sheet 51.4 x 42.2 cm (20¼ x 16⅝ in.). Los Angeles County Museum of Art, Mr. and Mrs. George Gard De Sylva Collection

biblical subject in keeping with the efforts of his Pont-Aven cronies, "a figure of Christ in blue and orange, and an angel in yellow." Scraped off and discarded, this exercise convinced Van Gogh that he "must not do figures of that importance without models" [505]. Yet he made a second, equally futile attempt in September, only to admit that he "mercilessly destroyed . . . a 'Christ with the Angel in Gethsemane,' and another one representing the 'Poet against a Starry Sky' . . . because the form had not been studied beforehand from the model, which is necessary in such cases" [B19]. Van Gogh may have been persuaded to try again since he had dedicated himself to working in a more improvisatory fashion in his summer suites of drawings after paintings, with particular success at figure drawing one step removed from the model.

The bust-length pen-and-ink renditions of oil portraits that Van Gogh made in early August 1888 number among his very finest achievements as a draftsman. Whatever difficulties he had in drawing figures from memory or life were countered when he exploited his paintings as models for ink portraits. Armed with an intimate knowledge of the sitter preserved in the effigy at hand and with just a few guidelines in graphite, he was able to compose figures with remarkable facility and command. He used this approach for three drawings he sent to Russell about August 3 (F1482a, cat. 79; F1503, cat. 80; F1458, cat. 81) and applied it to two large-format ink portraits he sent to Theo the following week (F1460, fig. 152; F1459, fig. 153). These five sheets were predicated on the figures he had painted to date: the half-length Zouave of June (F423, cat. 78) and its more recent successors of late July and early August—a young Provençal girl whom he invested with the persona of the character in Pierre Loti's *Madame Chrysanthème* and called *La Mousmé* (F431, fig. 157); two portraits of the "postman" Joseph Roulin in keeping with the spirit of Daumier (F432, fig. 158; F433, fig. 159); and a portrait of the peasant Patience Escalier, a kind of homage to Millet's *Man with a Hoe* (F443).

This distinctive group of drawings may be seen as a triumph over adversity. Making *répétitions* of this sort allowed Van Gogh to extend his repertoire of "characteristic types" without the attendant foibles of his sitters or the shortcomings of his hand. But it was not a practice he chose to exploit further. In fact, he seems to have rejected the sophistication, refinement, and linear stylization that are the hallmark of these works in favor of a simpler, looser, and more forthright approach in the last drawings after paintings that he made in August 1888. These efforts, forecast by the broader pen work exhibited in his three-quarter-length seated *Roulin* (F1459, fig. 153), include two drawings with marginal color notes (F1723, F1504) and two small sketches (F1461, fig. 154; F1722). The decisive shift in his drawing style from the magisterial grandeur of his pen-and-ink *Patience Escalier* (F1460, fig. 152) to the unpretentious works that followed, highlighted by the uncompromisingly unrefined sketch of Escalier (F1461, fig. 154), seems to reflect his artistic thinking at the time.

Having addressed the question of style in relation to prevailing views—using sheets of paper as a vehicle for reassessment—Van Gogh emerged committed to artistic aims that he recognized stood at odds with the imperatives of his avant-garde friends. Lamenting the fact that Parisians had yet to acquire a taste for crude things, he confessed to Theo on August 18, "what I learned in Paris is leaving me, and I am returning to the ideas I had in the country before I met the impressionists. And I should not be surprised if the impressionists soon find fault with my way of working, for it has been fertilized by Delacroix's ideas rather than by theirs. Because instead of trying to reproduce exactly what I have before my eyes, I use color more arbitrarily, in order to express myself forcibly" [520].

The premium that Van Gogh was determined to place on direct, undiluted expression through color had an immediate and lasting effect on his drawing. Ultimately it challenged the role of drawing both as an intermediary step in creating or refining a composition and as a means to represent works that were all about color. That August, he simply adopted a rather straightforward manner in the sketch he made after the *Mousmé* for Gauguin (F1722) and in two drawings for Bernard, one after the *Mousmé* (F1504) and the other after the large-format *Roulin* (F1723), to which he added color notes. He seems to have opted for this solution as more efficacious than making colored drawings, having debated and dismissed the virtues of watercolor for seizing a characteristic likeness [525]. At the same time, however, when he set out to illustrate his peasant portrait for Bernard, he was stymied, since "it was a study in which color plays a part such as the black and white of drawing could not possibly reproduce." Hence, while he wanted to send "a very large and very careful drawing," the one he sent—undoubtedly the small, brash, yet forceful sketch of Escalier (F1461, fig. 154)—"turned out quite different, though it is still correct" [B15]. What made this drawing "correct" was that it not only gave currency to the sensibility evoked by harsh color in the portrait of a peasant reminiscent of a "wild beast" [B15], who bore a kinship to Millet's *Man with a Hoe,* but also spoke to the artist's original conception of a coarse likeness "bordering on caricature" [519]. There were no successors to this portrait sketch; in effect, it was the artist's final statement, a defining moment in his activity as a draftsman; and indeed owing to its ownership by Matisse, who ensured its early fame, it became the image that defined for the next generation something of Van Gogh's struggle to get it "right" or rather "correct" in his own terms, and as circumstances—ranging from unwilling sitters to his unobliging hand—allowed.

SAS

1. In a letter of September 23 or 24, 1888 [542], to Theo, Van Gogh confided plans to devote time that winter to drawing "figures from memory," in order to "do a figure in a few strokes . . . with a head, body, legs and arms that all fit together," and reported that while writing, he had "already drawn a dozen." These sketches are unknown, and there is no evidence to show whether he made further progress or reached a dead end.

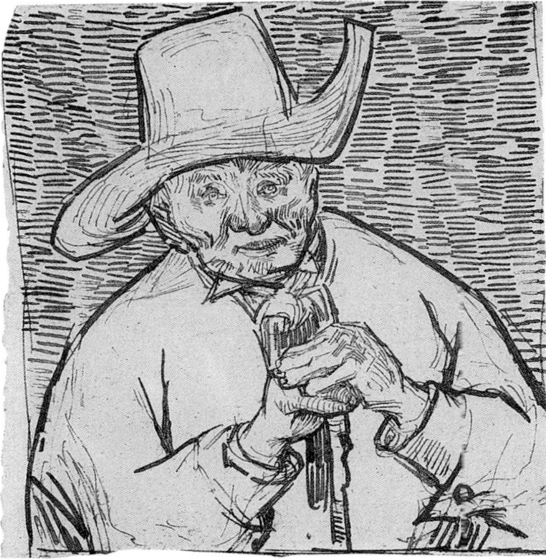

Fig. 154. *Portrait of Patience Escalier* (F1461), late August 1888. Pen and ink on paper, 13.5 x 13 cm (5⅜ x 5⅛ in.). Private collection

77. *The Zouave*

ca. June 20, 1888
Watercolor, reed pen and ink, wax crayon, over graphite on wove paper
31.5 x 23.6 cm (12⅜ x 9¼ in.)
Inscribed and signed, upper right: *à mon cher copain / Emile Bernard / Vincent*
The Metropolitan Museum of Art, New York, Gift of Emanie Philips, 1962 (62.151)
F1482, JH1487

New York only

Provenance: Sent by the artist to Émile Bernard, Saint-Briac, presumably between July 17 and 20, 1888 [B11], until at least 1892; probably sold to Ambroise Vollard, Paris, between 1899 and 1904; Émile Druet, Paris, by 1913 (Druet photo no. 42159); Raoul de Gunzbourg, Geneva; C. Moos Art Gallery, Geneva; Paul A. Adamide Bey, Geneva; Walter E. Sachs, New York, by 1929; to his former wife, Mrs. Emanie Nahm Arling Philips, New York, 1939; her gift to the Metropolitan Museum, 1962.

Selected exhibitions: Paris 1892, hors cat. (per Saunier 1892); New York 1913, no. 426; New York 1943, no. 74; New York 1984, no. 62; Otterlo 1990, no. 193; Detroit–Boston–Philadelphia 2000–2001 (Philadelphia only), no. 114.

Summary of the literature: Scholars generally contend that this Zouave was made after the half-length portrait (F423; cat. 78) in keeping with other "drawings after paintings" that Van Gogh sent to Bernard in mid-July 1888. There is some variance in conviction and dating. Roskill (1971, pp. 151–52) introduced this view, dating the watercolor to late June or "probably July," and proposing that it was probably sent in the first consignment [511]. Hulsker (1980/1996, no. 1487) and Welsh-Ovcharov (in Toronto–Amsterdam 1981, p. 122) dated it to June in accordance with its original assignation in De la Faille (which recorded the dedicatory inscription but neglected Bernard in the provenance). Pickvance (in New York 1984, no. 62; in Otterlo 1990, no. 193) advocated that it was made in mid-July and that it may have served as a kind of "cover illustration" for the first group of six drawings.

Additional notes: The present study proposes that this watercolor was sent in the second shipment to Bernard [B11] and challenges current thinking about when and for what purpose it was made. Technical findings refute Pickvance's observation (in New York 1984, no. 62; repeated in Heenk 1995, p. 172) that it represents the artist's "unique use in Arles of wax crayon." The blue and pink waxy crayons are, in fact, the same material and color as in *The Langlois Bridge* (F1480, fig. 63) and *Harvest in Provence* (F1483, cat. 62; F1484, fig. 141) (see "Technical Studies: Observations on the Drawing Materials Used by Van Gogh in Provence").

Infrared reflectography (see fig. 250), which provides a relatively unobstructed view of the artist's original graphite sketch, reveals telling differences between Van Gogh's approach to this drawing of the Zouave and the version made for Russell (F1482a, cat. 79; and see fig. 251). His sketch has none of the ease or shorthand fluency based on familiarity with the motif that is apparent in the Russell "copy" or in other contemporary drawings made after paintings.

In this watercolor, Van Gogh set down his initial conception for a half-length portrait of a young Zouave soldier. He succeeded in oil (F423, cat. 78) to heighten the "savage combination of incongruous tones" [501], to flesh out the character's likeness, and to place him in a convincing setting. Six weeks later, Van Gogh produced a confident pen-and-ink rendition of the oil portrait for John Russell (F1482a, cat. 79), having sent the watercolor, to which he added a dedicatory inscription, to Émile Bernard in mid-July.

See "Figure and Portrait Drawings" and "*Répétitions*: Drawings after Paintings."

SAS

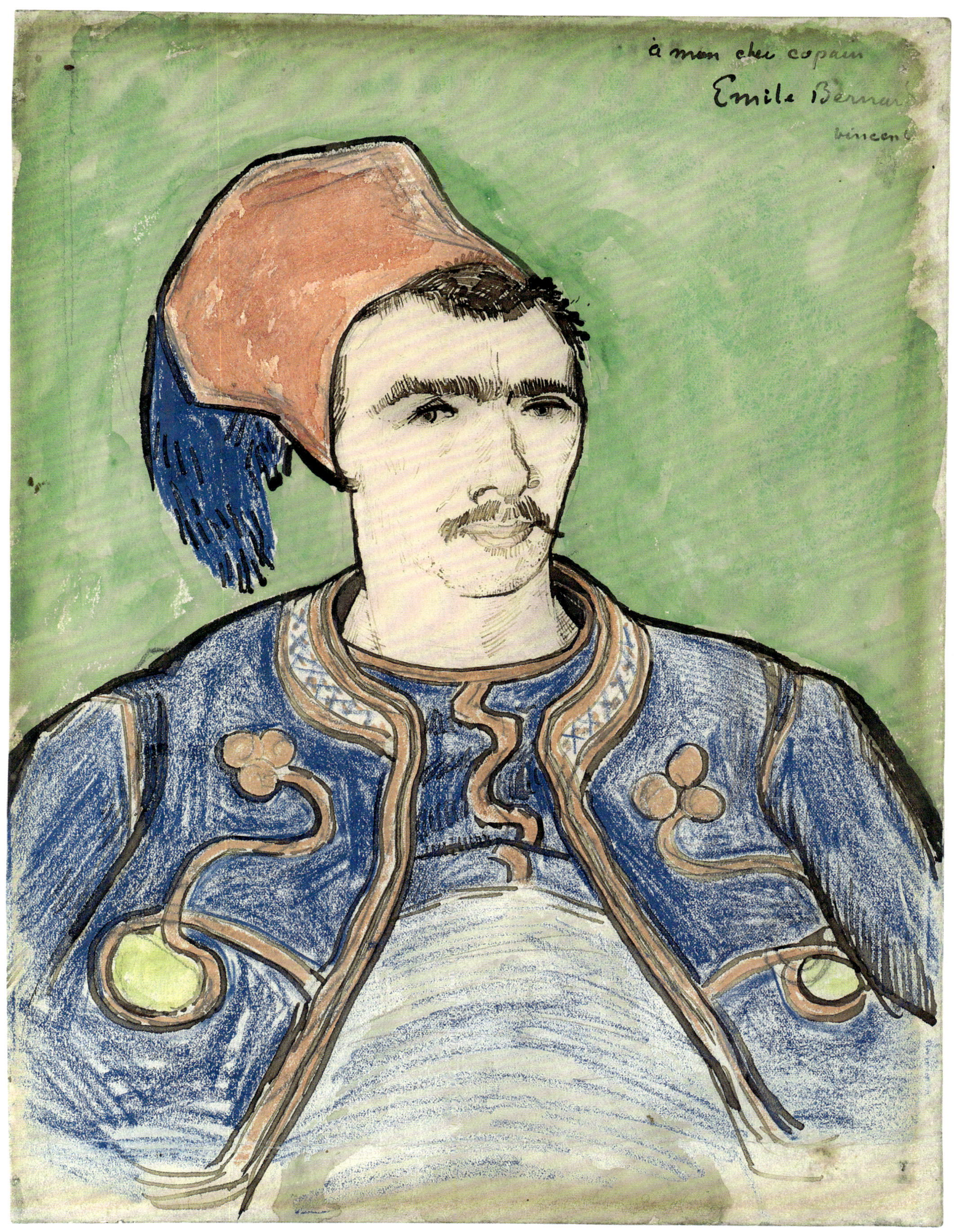
à mon cher copain
Emile Bernard
Vincent

78. *The Zouave*

ca. June 21, 1888
Oil on canvas
65 x 54 cm (25⅝ x 21¼ in.)
Van Gogh Museum, Amsterdam (Vincent van Gogh Foundation) (s 67 V/1962)
F423, JH1486
Letters 501, 502, B8, W5

Letter to Theo van Gogh, June 21, 1888 [501]: I have a model at last—a Zouave—a boy with a small face, a bull neck, and the eye of a tiger, and I began with one portrait, and began again with another; the half-length I did of him was horribly harsh, in a blue uniform, the blue of enamel saucepans, with braids of a faded reddish-orange, and two yellow stars on his breast, an ordinary blue, and very hard to do. That bronzed, feline head of his with a red cap, I placed it against a green door and the orange bricks of a wall. So it's a savage combination of incongruous tones, not easy to manage. The study I made of it seems to me very harsh, but all the same I'd like always to be working on vulgar, even loud portraits like this. It teaches me something, and above all that is what I want of my work. The second portrait [F424, fig. 155] will be full length, seated against a white wall.

Letter to Theo van Gogh, June 23, 1888 [502]: I am very dissatisfied with what I have been doing lately, because it is very ugly. But all the same, figure is interesting me more than landscape.

Anyway, I shall send you a drawing of the Zouave today [F1443, fig. 151]. In the end making studies of figures so as to experiment and to learn will be the shortest way for me to do something worth while.

Letter to Émile Bernard, June 27, 1888 [B9]: If you like I would set aside for an exchange with you the head of the Zouave which I have painted.

SAS

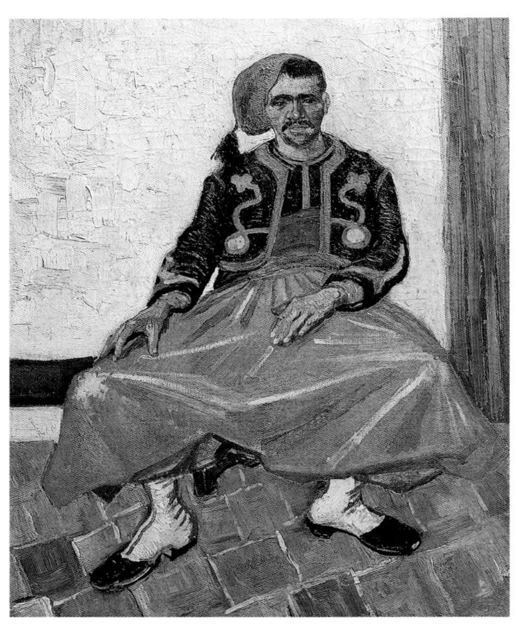

Fig. 155. *The Zouave* (F424), late June 1888. Oil on canvas, 81 x 65 cm (31⅞ x 25⅝ in.). Private collection

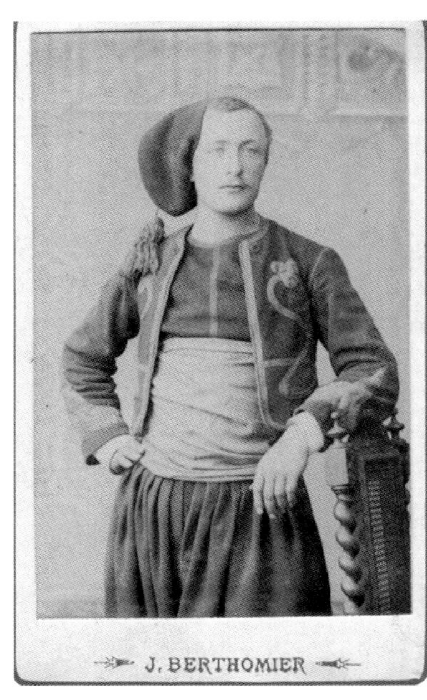

Fig. 156. J. Berthomier, *French Zouave*, ca. 1880. Carte de visite, 10 x 5 cm (4 x 2 in.). Collection Jerome Discours—www.military-photos.com/zouave1.htm

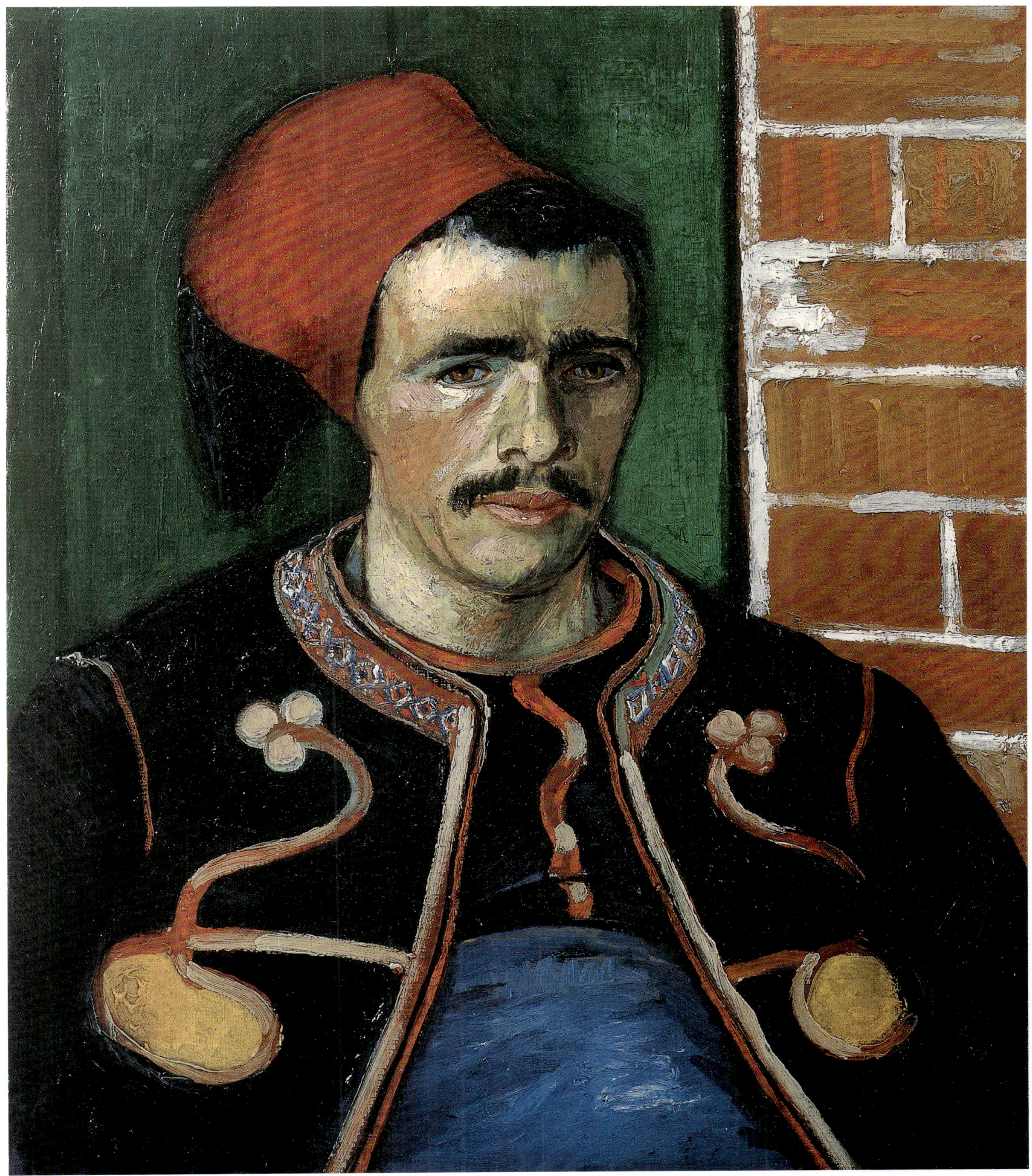

79. *The Zouave*

(for John Russell)

ca. July 31–August 3, 1888
Reed pen, pen, and ink over graphite on wove paper
31.9 x 24.3 cm (12½ x 9⅝ in.)
Signed, lower left: *Vincent*
Solomon R. Guggenheim Museum, New York, Thannhauser Collection, Gift, Justin K. Thannhauser, 1978 (78.2514.23)
F1482a, JH1535
Letters 516, 517

Provenance: Sent by the artist to John Russell (d. 1930), Belle-Île, Brittany, ca. August 3, 1888 [517], until his death; to his daughter, Jeanne Jouve, Paris, probably 1930–31; acquired from her by Justin K. Thannhauser, Paris, probably 1938–39; his bequest to the Guggenheim Museum, 1978.

Selected exhibitions: New York 1984, no. 77; Detroit–Boston–Philadelphia 2000–2001, no. 113.

Summary of the literature: This drawing was first published in Thannhauser 1938 as one of three "unknown" drawings that Russell received from Van Gogh in 1888 and kept until his death in 1931. It is catalogued in the revised editions of De la Faille (1970/1992, no. 1482a) as having belonged to Russell and associated with the group of drawings Van Gogh sent to him in early August 1888, but it was dated to June 1888 in keeping with other portraits of the sitter (F423, F424, F1443, F1482). Roskill (1971, p. 171), Barnett (1978, p. 80, no. 23), Hulsker (1980/1996, no. 1535), and Pickvance (in New York 1984, no. 77) clarified that it was made later that summer, after *The Zouave* (F423, cat. 78), and was among the dozen drawings sent to Russell in early August [516, 517]. Pickvance compared it to the more "picturesque" rendition of the Zouave in the watercolor Van Gogh sent to Bernard (F1482, cat. 77), noting in the present work the artist's "increasing concentration on the Zouave's squat and powerful head."

Examination of this work by infrared reflectography affords a clear sense of the artist's original graphite underdrawing (fig. 251). Van Gogh outlined the figure broadly, establishing his pose and principal details of his costume and, with a single vertical line, at right, the setting. Clearly the sitter's features and expression were of primary importance: Van Gogh devoted almost finicky attention to the facial hair and, more significantly, to modeling the head and neck. Having carefully defined the tunic's neckline and yoke in graphite, he only roughed out the embroidered jacket. The penciled guidelines that Van Gogh exploited to realize the drawing were given added emphasis in ink, applied with the incisiveness of a steel pen.[1]

See "*Répétitions*: Drawings after Paintings."

SAS

1. See Marjorie Shelley, "Technical Studies: Observations on the Drawing Materials Used by Van Gogh in Provence," note 2.

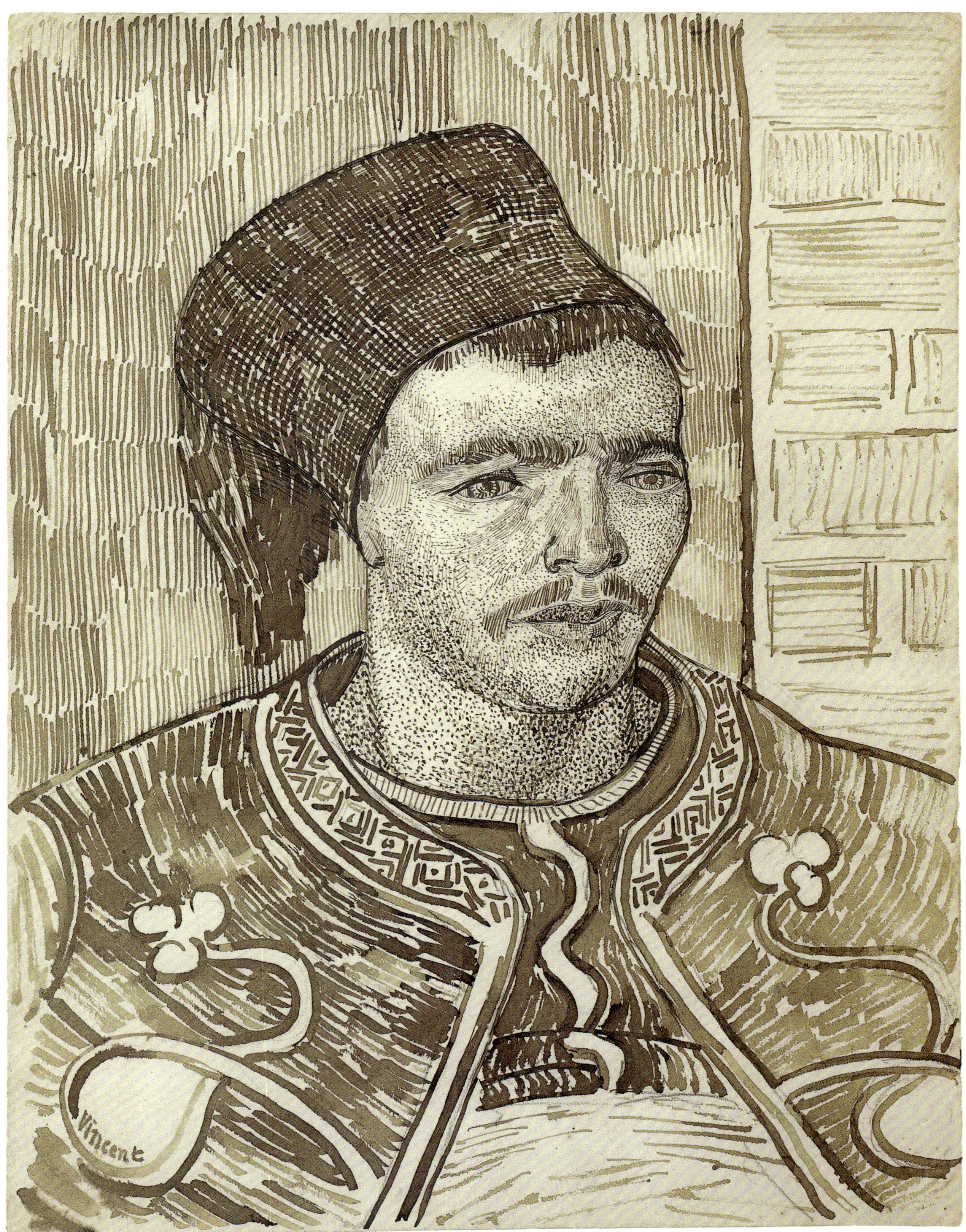
Vincent

80. *La Mousmé*

(for John Russell)

ca. July 31–August 3, 1888
Reed pen, pen, and ink over graphite on wove paper
31.5 x 24 cm (12⅜ x 9½ in.)
Signed, lower left: *Vincent*
Private collection, courtesy of Thomas Gibson Fine Art Ltd.
F1503, JH1533
Letters 516, 517

New York only

Provenance: Sent by the artist to John Russell, Belle-Île, Brittany, ca. August 3, 1888 [517], until 1920; sold, [Anon.], Hôtel Drouot, Paris, March 31, 1920, no. 69; acquired at that sale by Galerie Le Garrec, Paris; Kunstzalen d'Audretsch, The Hague; Galerie Lutz, Berlin; Dr. Kurt Hirschland (d. 1956), Essen and New York, by 1928, until his death (with the Stedelijk Museum, Amsterdam, ca. 1947–53); to his widow, Mrs. K. Hirschland, New York, until at least 1965; by descent to Mr. and Mrs. Paul M. Hirschland, New York, by 1970, until 1983; sold to present owner.

Selected exhibitions: Milan 1952, no. 100; New York 1984, no. 81.

Summary of the literature: Apropos of the documentation furnished in Thannhauser 1938, Russell's ownership of this drawing is recorded in the revised editions of De la Faille (1970/1992, no. 1503), where it is dated to July 1888 and associated with the dozen drawings Van Gogh sent to him in early August [517]. It is recognized as part of the Russell campaign in Roskill (1966, p. 5, and 1971, p. 171); in Hulsker (1980/1996, no. 1533), who described this mousmé drawing (relative to F1504 and F1722) as the "most carefully executed and most beautiful version (but only of the head and upper part of the body)"; and in Pickvance (in New York 1984, no. 81), who observed that it was drawn shortly after the oil (F431) and that Van Gogh concentrated on the head and shoulders, accentuated the "Oriental look" of the sitter's eyes, and "allowed both the deliberate and the accidental to play their roles."

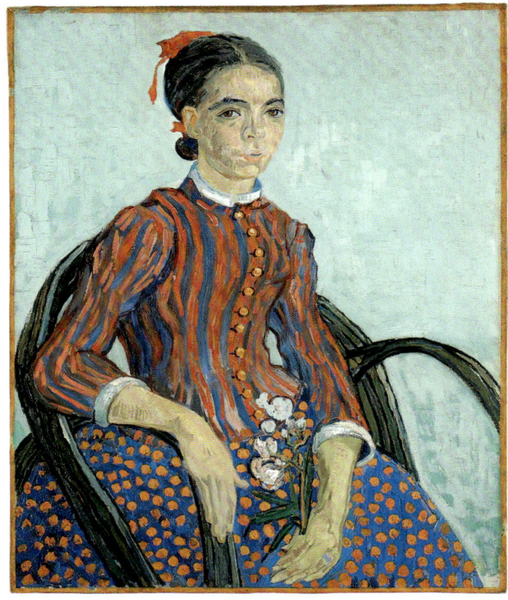

Fig. 157. *La Mousmé* (F431), July 1888. Oil on canvas, 73.3 x 60.3 cm (28⅞ x 23¾ in.). National Gallery of Art, Washington, Chester Dale Collection

If the hale and hearty Joseph Roulin was Van Gogh's answer to Daumier and his Patience Escalier to Millet's "Man with a Hoe," other figure studies took for their inspiration literary rather than visual images. Van Gogh's summer reading of Pierre Loti's novel *Madame Chrysanthème,* with its "interesting details about Japan" [B7], gave rise to his weeklong effort in late July 1888 to create a characteristic likeness of a mousmé, or rather a figure-type invested with the spirit of a character that had captivated him in prose (F431, fig. 157). Having found as a suitable model a local Provençal adolescent who may have sat for his friend Mourier-Petersen that spring and possessed such qualities as "slimness" and a "quaint little head," Van Gogh created an image in keeping with the fictional protagonist's initial encounter with a "perfectly exquisite mousmé," "charmingly dressed," who stood out like "a fresh touch of color against the sombre background." Through his palette, the semicircular flounce of her skirt, and the oleander placed in her hand, Van Gogh met Loti's description: "Over her quaint little head, her round umbrella with its thousand ribs threw a great halo of blue and red, edged with black, and an oleander-tree full of flowers . . . spread its glory beside her, bathed, like herself, in the sunshine." A few days later, Van Gogh put his pen to the same task. The delicate, almost ethereal quality of the doll-like visage that emerges from the dotted backdrop of his drawing is no less evocative of the protagonist's first sense of the "little mousmé" in Loti's novel, who suddenly "appeared . . . in full sunshine, and stood out in brilliant clearness like a fairy vision," or of his characterization of the figure as "a doll like the rest, evidently, an ornament for a china shelf." One might even argue that in his bold departure from the painted composition Van Gogh came closer to the literary source, producing (to quote Loti) a similarly "delightful effect."[1]

See "*Répétitions*: Drawings after Paintings."

SAS

1. Pierre Loti [Julien Viaud], *Madame Chrysanthème* (Paris, 1888), chap. 42, "An Oriental Vision: September 4." http://www.literaturepost.com/chapter/15646.html.

Letter to Theo van Gogh, July 29, 1888 [514]: Now if you know what a "mousmé" is (you will know when you have read Loti's* Madame Chrysanthème*), I have just painted one. It took me a whole week, and I haven't been able to do anything else, not having been very well either. . . . A mousmé is a Japanese girl—Provençal in this case—12 to 14 years old. That makes two portraits now, the Zouave and her. . . .

The portrait of the girl is against a background of white strongly tinged with malachite green, her bodice is striped blood red and violet, the skirt is royal blue, with large yellow-orange dots. The mat flesh tones are yellowish-gray; the hair tinged with violet; the eyebrows and the eyelashes are black; the eyes, orange with Prussian blue. A branch of oleander in her fingers, for the two hands are showing.

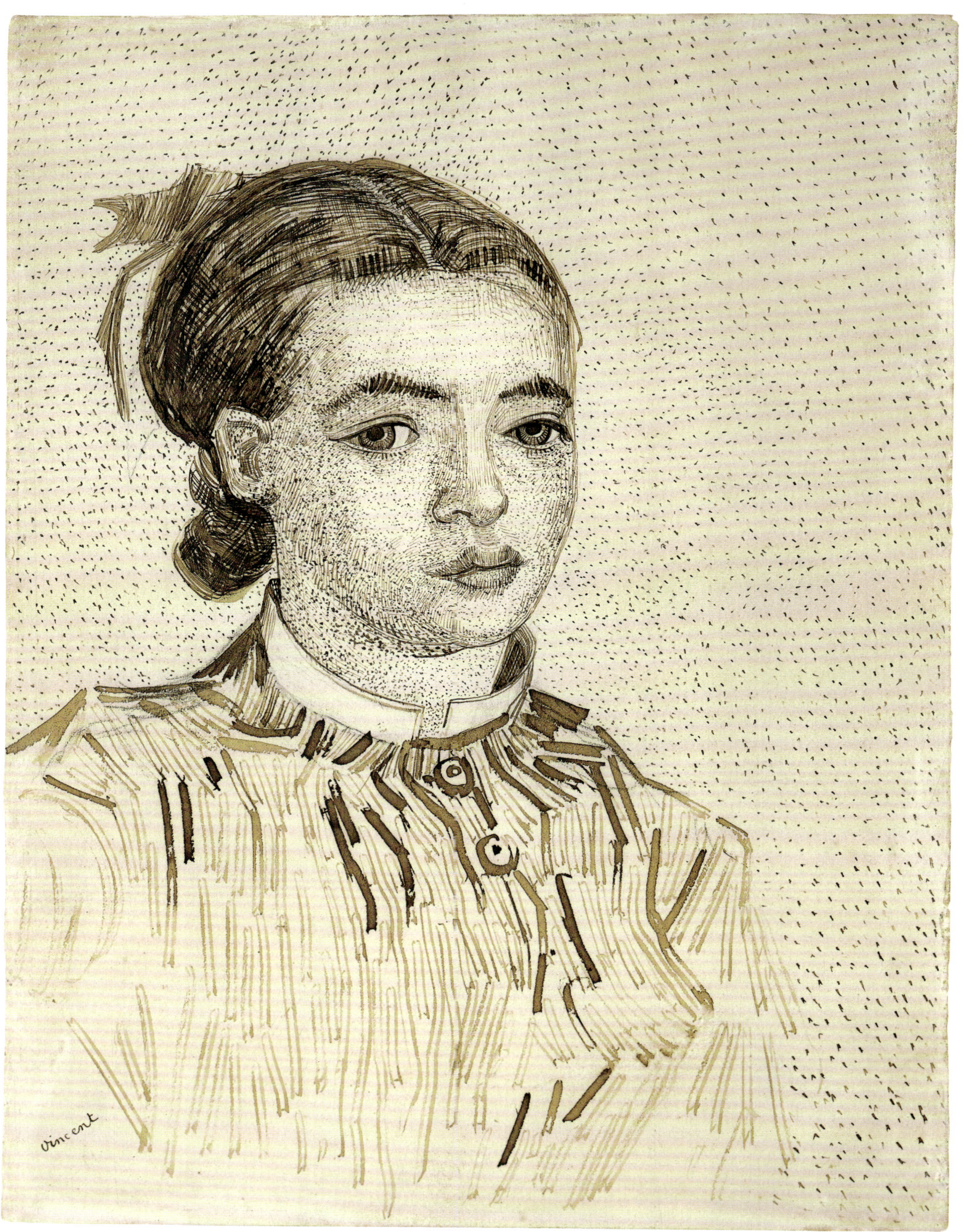
Vincent

81. *Portrait of Joseph Roulin*

(for John Russell)

ca. July 31–August 3, 1888
Reed pen, pen, and ink over graphite on wove paper
31.8 x 24.3 cm (12½ x 9⅝ in.)
The J. Paul Getty Museum, Los Angeles (85.GA.299)
F1458, JH1536
Letters 516, 517

Provenance: Sent by the artist to John Russell, Belle-Île, Brittany, ca. August 3, 1888 [517], until 1920; sold, [Anon.], Hôtel Drouot, Paris, March 31, 1920, no. 70; Dr. Arthur Hahnloser (d. 1936), Winterthur, by 1922; to his widow, Mrs. Hedy Hahnloser-Bühler, Winterthur, until at least 1952; to her son Dr. Hans R. Hahnloser, by 1970; by descent, private collection, Switzerland, until 1985; purchased by the Getty Museum, 1985.

Selected exhibitions: Zürich 1924, no. 79; Berlin 1927–28, no. 101; Milan 1952, no. 99; Frankfurt 1970, no. 55; New York 1984, no. 89; Otterlo 1990, no. 198; Detroit–Boston–Philadelphia 2000–2001 (Detroit only), no. 100.

Summary of the literature: In De la Faille 1928 (no. 1458) this drawing was dated August 1888 but was identified erroneously with letter 520, neglecting Russell's ownership. Apropos of the documentation furnished in Thannhauser 1938, the revised editions of De la Faille (1970/1992, no. 1458) associated the drawing with the Russell campaign [517] and listed his name in the provenance. Roskill (1971, p. 171), Hulsker (1980/1996, no. 1536), and Pickvance (in New York 1984, no. 89; in Otterlo 1990, no. 198) recorded that it was made after the bust-length *Portrait of Joseph Roulin* (F433) and was among the dozen drawings sent to Russell in early August 1888 [516, 517]. Pickvance (in New York 1984) proposed that the drawing was done the same day as the oil portrait (F433)—August 1 or 2, 1888, and likened the "fine web of quill strokes" in the background to that of *The Zouave* (F1482a) and the "basket-weave effect" of the painted studies of these sitters; and noted that Van Gogh improvised and changed certain details (e.g., the buttons and lapel).

Letter to Wilhelmina van Gogh, July 31, 1888 [W5]: I am now engaged on a portrait of a postman in his dark-blue uniform with yellow [F432, fig. 158]. A head somewhat like Socrates, hardly any nose at all, a high forehead, bald crown, little gray eyes, bright red chubby cheeks, a big pepper-and-salt beard, large ears. The man is an ardent republican and socialist, reasons quite well, and knows a lot of things. His wife was delivered of a child today, and he is consequently feeling as proud as a peacock, and is all aglow with satisfaction.

Letter to Émile Bernard, ca. August 5, 1888 [B14]: I have just done a portrait of a postman, or rather even two portraits. . . . He kept himself too stiff when posing, which is why I painted him twice, the second time at a single sitting [F433, fig. 159].

Van Gogh's friend and neighbor Joseph Roulin was not, strictly speaking, a postman, but an *entreposeur des postes* who handled the mail at the railroad station. The present drawing was made in the wake of Roulin's first sittings for the artist, begun by July 31, 1888, when he posed too stiffly for a three-quarter-length seated portrait (F432, fig. 158). Van Gogh then painted a "head, life-size" in a single session (F433, fig. 159)—ostensibly, the basis for this *répétition.* The drawing, however, shares little more than the format of the bust-length oil. For its expressive character and for any number of details, from the cross-hatching of the background to the curve of the lapel, the sheet depends on the three-quarter-length. It is either a composite image of the two portrayals, or instead enjoys the same relationship with its model as that of the ink rendition of *La Mousmé* (F1503, cat. 80; F431, fig. 157). The facial features closely follow those of the larger canvas, indeed line for line in passages that required shading or highlighting. Van Gogh seems to have relied on such markers as the double lines at the side of Roulin's temple at left and the single line at the side of his nose to graft the expression of one to the other, adopting the same strategy that he used in translating the Zouave to paper (see infrared reflectogram, fig. 251, of F1482a, cat. 79). Van Gogh's decision to change Roulin's uniform from a double- to a single-breasted coat was doubtless dictated by the truncated composition—although perhaps not all trace of the second button was eliminated given the darker hatching in that very spot.

As the presumptive model for this drawing, which was sent to Russell about August 3, the half-length portrait has been dated to August 1 or 2, but it may have been made afterward.

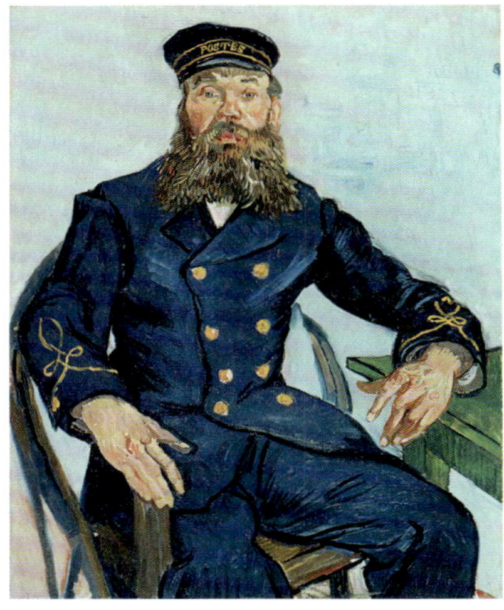

Fig. 158. *Portrait of Joseph Roulin* (F432), ca. July 31–August 3, 1888. Oil on canvas, 81.2 x 65.3 cm (32 x 25¼ in.). Museum of Fine Arts, Boston, Gift of Robert Treat Paine II

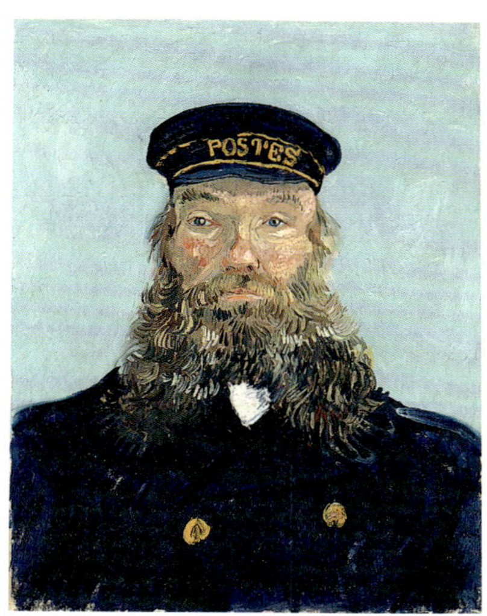

Fig. 159. *Portrait of Joseph Roulin* (F433), ca. August 3, 1888. Oil on canvas, 64.1 x 47.9 cm (25¼ x 18⅞ in.). The Detroit Institute of Arts, Gift of Mr. and Mrs. Walter Buhl Ford II

Van Gogh's letters report that he was working on both portraits on August 3 and was "done" two days later [517, B14]. He sent the "head" to Theo in mid-August but held onto the "big portrait of the postman" seated, which was the basis for two other drawings (F1723; F1459, fig. 153).

See "*Répétitions*: Drawings after Paintings."

SAS

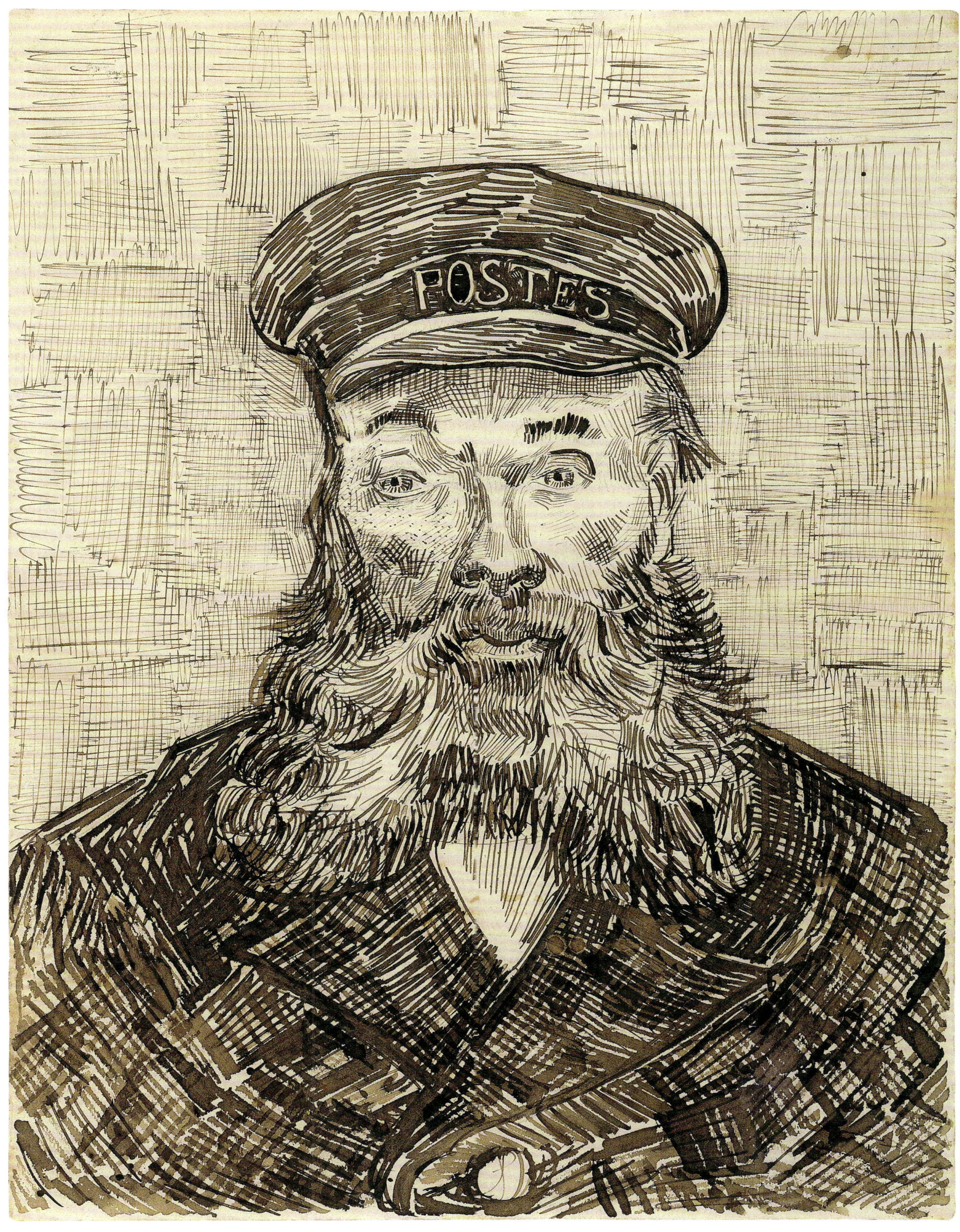
POSTES

The Heights of Montmajour

Soon after he arrived in Provence in February of 1888, Van Gogh must have spied, off in the distance, the old abbey atop Montmajour. Remains of the medieval buildings lured the occasional tourist up the rocky hill, and Van Gogh too was attracted to the site just three miles northeast of Arles. He wrote Theo early in March to say that he had "been for several walks in the country" and "seen lots of beautiful things," among them "a ruined abbey on a hill covered with holly, pines, and gray olives." And he supposed, "we'll have a try at that soon, I hope" [467]. But the artist seems not to have ventured a trip there until the weather warmed and the orchards released their spring flowers and consequently their hold on his attention.

In his first joyously painted response to the harvest in June (F412, cat. 63), Van Gogh included a glimpse of Montmajour's old walls and fortified tower on the far horizon. By that time he had made a pilgrimage to the site and produced a suite of seven drawings: two of the ruins (see F1423, fig. 67) and five looking out from the hill toward the flat plain of La Crau (see F1419, fig. 71). He sent these to Theo on May 26 as entries to an exhibition of the Dutch Etching Society in Amsterdam, but later, considering the cost of framing them for the show, thought better of it. Instead, he wrote Theo two days later, "You know what you must do with these drawings—make sketchbooks . . . like those books of original Japanese drawings. *I very much want* to make such a book for Gauguin, and one for Bernard. For the drawings are going to be better than these" [492]. He included an illustration of the kind of folded-paper Japanese book he and Theo had in their collection (fig. 160). He probably also had in mind the serial landscapes ukiyo-e printmakers produced, such as Hiroshige's *Fifty-three Stations along the Tōkaidō Road* or Hokusai's *Thirty-six Views of Mount Fuji,* examples of which the brothers owned.

Promising "drawings . . . better than these" in his letter to Theo, Vincent returned to Montmajour in order to make another series of views, but this time on full (rather than half-size) sheets of Whatman paper, and in inks that were more stable than the fugitive anilines he had used earlier. The first of a new, grander suite of landscapes (F1452, fig. 161) was sent off to Theo almost immediately, but the five other views that completed the ensemble were not produced until July, after the artist had visited the sea at Saintes-Maries and exhausted the possibilities of the harvest.

It may have been the news that Gauguin would be coming to join him in Arles that sent Van Gogh back up the mountain. He wanted to raise money to finance the meeting and perhaps thought he could find a buyer most readily for a group of big Barbizon-style landscapes such as Millet, Rousseau, and Daubigny had drawn. Furthermore, as he told Theo, "I think it right to work especially at drawing just now, and to arrange to have paints and canvas in reserve for when Gauguin comes" [506].

That he was wandering in the vicinity of Montmajour in the early days of July is evidenced by an oil study he painted of a windswept tree struggling to maintain a hold in rocky ground (F466, fig. 162). "Yesterday at sunset," he reported to Theo, "I was on a stony heath where some very small and twisted oaks grow; in the background, a ruin on the hill . . . the sun was pouring bright yellow rays on the bushes and the ground, a perfect shower of gold . . . all the lines were lovely, the whole thing nobly beautiful. . . . I brought

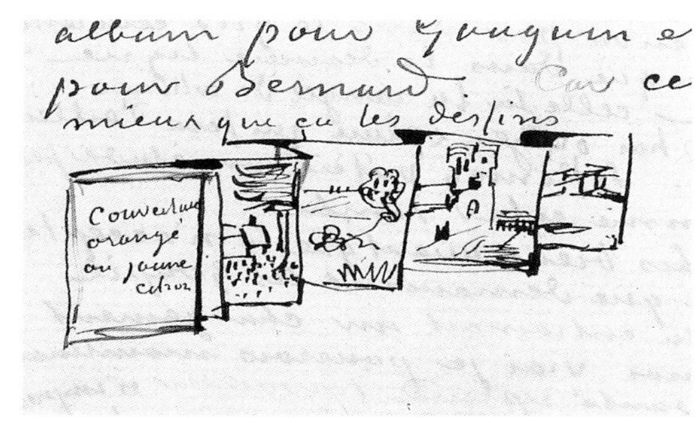
album pour Gauguin e
pour Bernard. Car ce
mieux que ces les dessins

Fig. 160. Design for a folded paper album of drawings, included in a letter to Theo van Gogh, May 28, 1888 [492]. Pen and ink, 3.5 x 8.5 cm (1⅜ x 3⅜ in.). Van Gogh Museum, Amsterdam (Vincent van Gogh Foundation)

back a study, but," he concluded, "it is very far below what I tried to do" [508].

The oft-cursed mistral was to be blamed again for the artist's failure to paint what, when, where, or how he wished. Indeed, his only effort to produce an oil painting from the heights of Montmajour seems to have been foiled by "this damn wind. That is the maddening thing here, no matter where you set up your easel. And that is largely why the painted studies are not so finished as the drawings; the canvas is shaking all the time." That the artist quickly added, "It does not bother me when I am drawing," helps to explain why he could create five large drawings (JH Add. 3, cat. 82; F1447, cat. 83; F1446, cat. 84; F1420, cat. 85; F1424, cat. 86) on paper securely tacked to board in less than a week and under inhospitable conditions.

"Not everyone would have the patience to get themselves devoured by mosquitoes and to struggle against the nagging malice of this constant mistral," Van Gogh bragged, explaining that his fortitude depended on the fact that "[t]he fascination that these huge plains have for me is very strong, so that I felt no *weariness,* in spite of the really wearisome circumstances" [509].

The five monumental views of Montmajour's slopes and outstretched plains sent to Theo about July 13, 1888, share with the "sixth," drawn some six weeks before (F1452, fig. 161) an expansive vision, clearly inspired by the heights from which they were observed. Van Gogh, we recall, was a native of flatlands and seldom found himself far above sea level. However, in the tradition of Dutch masters, he was gratified by deep spaces and open skies. In Paris he was attracted to vistas he surveyed from Montmartre and from the elevated outskirts of the city (see F1410, cat. 41). At Montmajour he found "the contrast between the wild and romantic foreground, and the distant perspective, wide and still . . . very striking" [490]. "It remind[s] me of the old Holland of Ruysdael's time" [509].

Perhaps most astounding are the final views of this group, two obsessively detailed panoramas. In an unusual expression of satisfaction, Van Gogh told Theo, "the two views of the Crau and of the country on the banks of the Rhône [F1420, cat. 85; F1424, cat. 86] are the best things I have done in pen and ink" [509]. And soon after, he described them delightedly to Bernard as "an immense stretch of flat country, a bird's-eye view of it seen from the top of a hill—vineyards and fields of newly reaped wheat . . . multiplied in endless repetitions, stretching away toward the horizon like the surface of a sea . . . really the most Japanese thing I have done" [B10]. Alluding to ukiyo-e woodcuts again, in connection with the second group of Montmajour views, as he had in speaking of the first, Van Gogh insisted to Theo that although the drawings *"do not look Japanese* . . . [they] really are, perhaps more so than some others." And he urged his brother to "[l]ook at them in some café where it's clear and blue and nothing else in the way, or else outside . . . to [obtain] . . . *a true idea* of the simplicity of nature [in Provence]" [509].

It must be reckoned a measure of Van Gogh's singular pleasure in his achievement that he compared his own landscapes to the exported woodcuts he collected and admired. So confident was he that his absorption of an oriental sensibility was complete and that Eastern modes of graphic expression were fully in his command, he expected even fellow champions of ukiyo-e might not recognize the affinities. Indeed there is an uncanny integration of Dutch realism and Japanese abstraction in Van Gogh's panoramic views of July that supersedes his earlier attempts to encompass sweeping vistas (F1419, fig. 71).

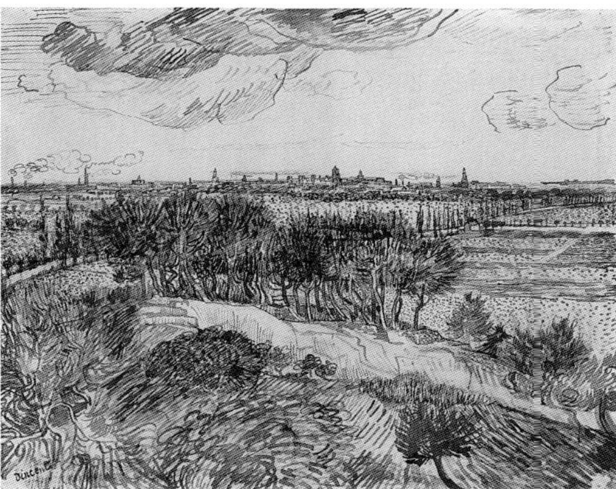

Fig. 161. *View of Arles from Montmajour* (F1452, cat. 47)

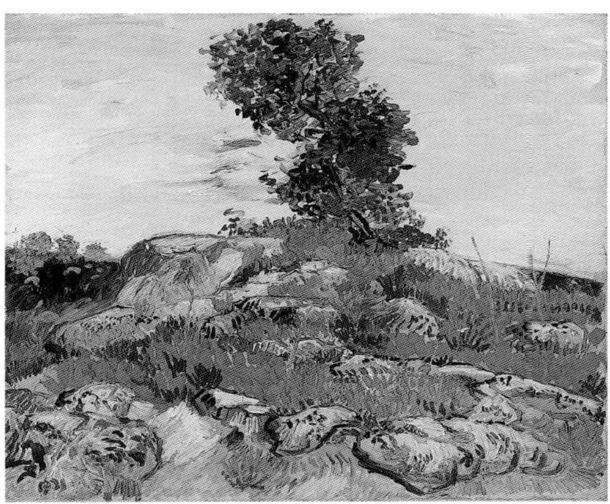

Fig. 162. *Rocks with Oak Tree* (F466), probably July 4, 1888. Oil on canvas, 54.6 x 65 cm (21½ x 25⅝ in.). Museum of Fine Arts, Houston, John A. and Audrey Jones Beck Collection

Literally and figuratively, Van Gogh seems to have had the larger picture in mind when he pulled the viewer into an endless terrain of shrinking dots and lines leading, step by step, toward the infinite. "Looking at the stars always makes me dream," he said, "as simply as I dream over the black dots representing towns and villages on a map" [506]. CI

82. *Olive Trees, Montmajour*

July 6–12, 1888
Reed pen and ink on wove paper watermarked J. WHATMAN TURKEY MILL 1879
48 x 60 cm (18⅞ x 23⅝ in.)
Signed in pen and ink, lower left: *Vincent*
Musée des Beaux-Arts, Tournai
F unlisted, JH Add. 3
Letters 505, 509

Provenance: Sent by the artist to Theo van Gogh (d. 1891), Paris, ca. July 13, 1888 [509]; by inheritance to his son, Vincent Willem van Gogh, as part of his collection, administered by his widow, Johanna van Gogh-Bonger, 1891; sold by her to Octave Maus for Henri van Cutsem (d. 1904), Brussels, March 21, 1891; his bequest to the city of Tournai, 1904; transferred to the newly built Musée des Beaux-Arts, Tournai, 1928.

Selected exhibitions: Brussels 1891, no. 9; New York 1984, no. 55; Otterlo 1990, no. 185; Martigny 2000, no. 68.

Summary of the literature: This drawing was included in an exhibition of drawings and prints from the Van Cutsem Collection in Tournai in 1957 (no. 96) and illustrated in a collection catalogue of the Musée des Beaux-Arts (Pion 1971, pl. 27). Pickvance discovered the generally unnoticed work and included it in the 1984 New York exhibition and catalogue (no. 55), providing information on its provenance and exhibition history. It thus made its first appearance in the Van Gogh literature. By identifying this as the first of two drawings the artist reported having finished by July 8 or 9, 1888 [505], Pickvance put an end to years of speculation regarding the unaccounted-for "fifth" drawing Van Gogh mentioned making at Montmajour. The drawing was catalogued by Hulsker (1996, no. Add. 3). For early history, see Stolwijk and Veenenbos 2002, pp. 18, 46, 80, 193.

This drawing of rocks and olive trees and the one that follows (F1447, cat. 83) are probably the "two new big ones" Van Gogh declared having finished on July 8 or 9 [505]. Alike in subject, size, and medium, these form an impressive, monumental pair, conveying the rough textures of Provençal vegetation, the region's bright light, and skies empty of all but wheeling birds. The landscapes quite possibly were designed to be hung side by side (cat. 82 at left, cat. 83 at right), so that their sloping compositions might seem to meet in a shared peak, with the fields and plains of La Crau seen to be rolling into the distance at either side.

Although Pickvance (in New York 1984, no. 55) thought this drawing the later of the two, it may well be the earlier, done while Van Gogh's reed pens still held narrow points and he had the morning's energy to fuss with a greater variety of marks and lines.

CI

Letter to Theo van Gogh, July 8 or 9, 1888 [505]: They made trouble at the post office, saying that the drawings which I was sending you were too big to be forwarded that way. I have two new big ones. When there are six of them I will send them in a roll by rail. . . . If the four other drawings that I have in mind are like the first two I have done, then you will have an epitome of a very beautiful corner of Provence.

Letter to Theo van Gogh, ca. July 13, 1888 [509]: I have just sent off to you by post a roll containing five big pen drawings.

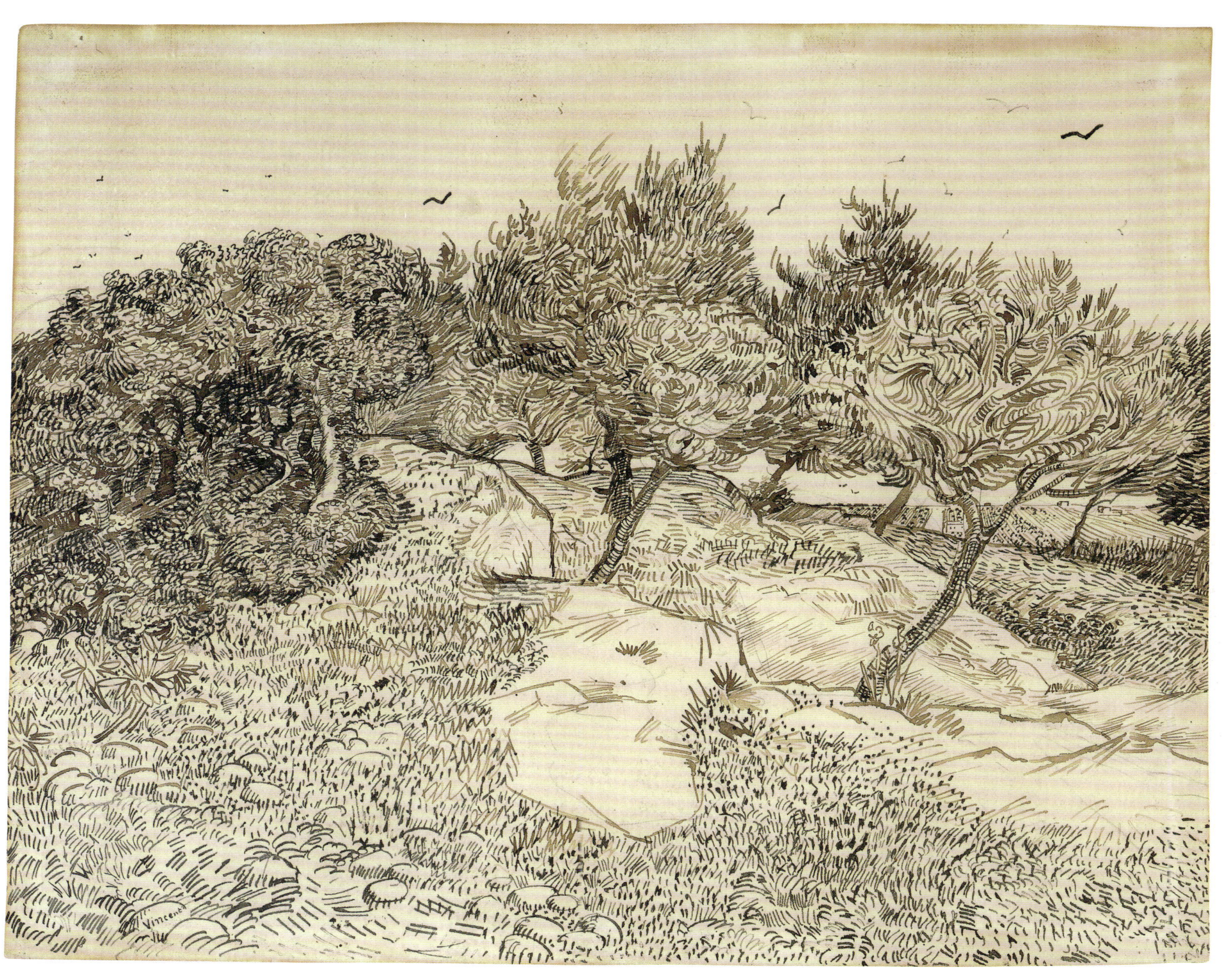

83. *Rocks and Trees, Montmajour*

July 6–12, 1888
Reed pen and ink over graphite on wove paper
49.1 x 61 cm (19⅜ x 24 in.)
Signed in pen and ink, lower right: *Vincent*
Inscribed on verso, in another hand: *157*
Tack holes in corners
Van Gogh Museum, Amsterdam (Vincent van Gogh Foundation) (d 344 V/1962)
F1447, JH1503
Letters 505, 509

Provenance: Sent by the artist to Theo van Gogh (d. 1891), Paris, ca. July 13, 1888 [509]; by inheritance to his son, Vincent Willem van Gogh (1890–1978), as part of his collection, administered by his widow, Johanna van Gogh-Bonger (d. 1925), 1891; placed on loan at the Stedelijk Museum, Amsterdam, 1931–73; ownership transferred to the Vincent van Gogh Foundation, 1962; placed on permanent loan at the Van Gogh Museum, Amsterdam, 1973.

Selected exhibitions: The Hague 1891; Leiden 1893; Paris 1896–97; Paris 1902 (no. 26 on Johanna's list of loans); Amsterdam 1905, no. 396; Berlin 1906, no. 54; Berlin 1914, no. 56; Amsterdam 1914–15, no. 175; Amsterdam 1915, no. 27; New York 1920, no. 5; London 1926–27, no. 20; Berlin 1927–28, no. 61; New York and other cities 1935–36, no. 108; Paris 1937, no. 75; London–Birmingham–Glasgow 1947–48, no. 148; New York–Chicago 1949–50, no. 103; Aix-en-Provence 1959, no. 30; London 1968–69, no. 129; New York 1984, no. 54; Otterlo 1990, no. 186; Tokyo 2000, no. 21.

Summary of the literature: In all editions of the catalogues raisonnés, De la Faille (no. 1447) and Hulsker (no. 1503) put this drawing with others of Montmajour done in July 1888. Tralbaut (1958) provided a photograph of the exact site, and Tellegen-Hoogendoorn (1967, pp. 18 n. 3, 26, 27), who established the sequence and sites of all Vincent's Montmajour drawings, placed this one among those completed within about a week in the middle of July. Having initially thought the drawing one sent to Russell, Roskill (1966, p. 5; 1971, p. 170) later corrected himself and dated the work mid-July 1888. Walker (1982, p. 382) maintained that "Van Gogh's intention was certainly to provide a systematic documentation of La Crau in approximate concordance with the four main points of the compass." Pickvance (in New York 1984, no. 54) thought this "most likely one of the first two drawings of the second Montmajour series, reported as finished on Sunday 8 July [505]." In Otterlo 1990 (no. 186), he identified the medium as "Indian ink" over graphite, a view shared by Heenk (1995, p. 175). For early history, see Feilchenfeldt and Veenenbos 1988, p. 132.

Of the two large drawings Van Gogh made in July of Montmajour's rocky slopes and trees, this one comes closer in its handling to the "harsh" style the artist developed in views of Saintes-Maries-de-la-Mer. With broad strokes of ink and sharp contrasts of dark and light, the artist conveyed the roughness of the terrain, wrought by the wear and tear of hot, dry mistral winds. In a rare dependence on the age-old drawing device cross-hatching, he attempted to describe the shattered edges and sides of broken rock. (See also JH Add. 3, cat. 82.) CI

Letter to Theo van Gogh, July 8 or 9, 1888 [505]: They made trouble at the post office, saying that the drawings which I was sending you were too big to be forwarded that way. I have two new big ones. When there are six of them I will send them in a roll by rail. . . . If the four other drawings that I have in mind are like the first two I have done, then you will have an epitome of a very beautiful corner of Provence.

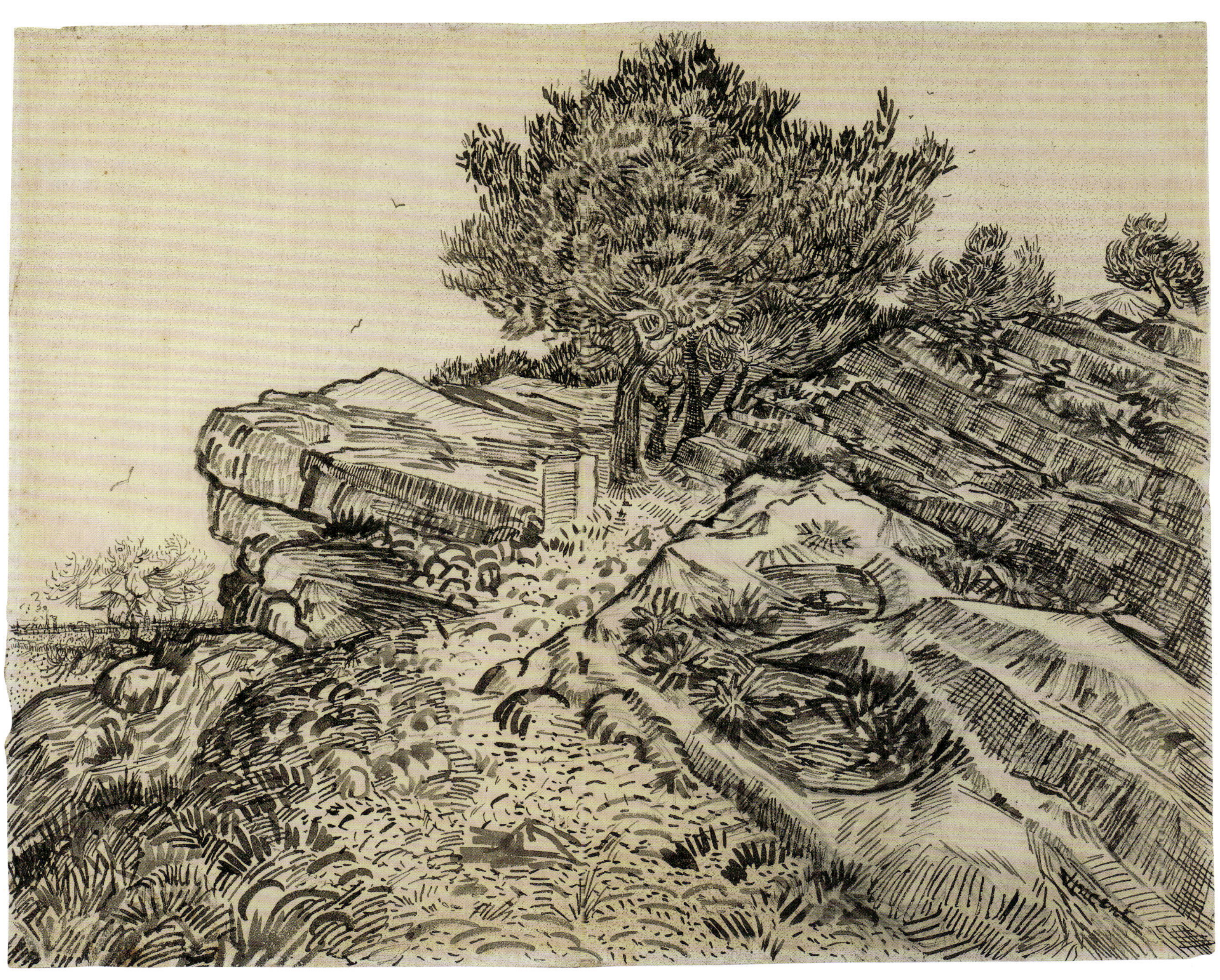

84. *Rock and Ruins, Montmajour*

July 6–12, 1888
Reed pen, quill, and ink over graphite on wove paper watermarked J. WHATMAN TURKEY MILL 1879
47.5 x 59 cm (18¾ x 23¼ in.)
Signed in pen and ink, lower right: *Vincent*
Inscribed on verso, upper left, in another hand: *141*
Rijksmuseum, Amsterdam (RP-T-1962-65)
F1446, JH1504
Letters 506, 509

Provenance: Sent by the artist to Theo van Gogh (d. 1891), Paris, ca. July 13, 1883 [509]; by inheritance to his son, Vincent Willem van Gogh, as part of his collection, administered by his widow, Johanna van Gogh-Bonger, 1891; her gift to her brother Willem Adriaan Bonger (d. 1940), Amsterdam, 1905; to his wife, Maria Hendrika Bonger-van Heteren (d. 1961), Haarlem; acquired from her heirs by the Rijksmuseum, Amsterdam, 1962.

Selected exhibitions: The Hague 1891; Amsterdam 1905, no. 406; Amsterdam 1914–15, no. 172; New York 1920, no. 5; New York 1984, no. 56; Otterlo 1990, no. 184.

Summary of the literature: De la Faille (1928/1970/1992, no. 1446) consistently catalogued this drawing as one executed in July 1888, as did Hulsker, who in his latest edition (1996, no. 1504) dated it July 13, 1888, in accord with the date of the letter Vincent sent to Theo reporting shipment of the work. While establishing the sequence and specific sites of Van Gogh's Montmajour drawings, Tellegen-Hoogendoorn (1967) placed this landscape among those completed within about a week's time during the middle of July. She published a photograph of the ruins Van Gogh pictured, as had Carroy (1962), who suggested that this drawing and another (F1420, cat. 85) could be joined to form a continuous panorama. Pickvance (in New York 1984, p. 110) dated the work as "finished by 10 July," later (in Otterlo 1990, no. 184) estimating it was "most probably completed on 9 July." Heenk (1995) observed that "the second type of ink" used on this drawing, as well as on JH Add. 3 (cat. 82) and F1420, "may have been applied later."

Although Van Gogh had studied the ruined architecture of Montmajour in at least two drawings made in late May (see F1423, fig. 67), he pictured the abbey's crumbling walls and fortified tower in only one of the five landscapes he drew there in early July. Perhaps remembering the rustic nature studies of Barbizon artists like Corot and Rousseau, he now chose to set aside the imposing buildings to focus on more humble, native features of the site. The huge stone boulder he positioned in the center of this drawing sheet dominates the view, but it visually connects the rugged hilltop to the orderly fields seen below. Behind the big rock, under a medieval archway, two figures holding parasols stand as surrogates for the artist and his unofficial student, Lieutenant Milliet, with whom he explored the region.

CI

Letter to Theo van Gogh, July 9 or 10, 1888 [506]: I have come back from a day at Montmajour, and my friend the second lieutenant was with me. We explored . . . ogive windows in ruins, blocks of white rock covered with lichen, . . . crumbling walls here and there among the green. I brought back another big drawing. . . . That makes three drawings. When I have half a dozen I shall send them along.

Letter to Theo van Gogh, ca. July 13, 1888 [509]: I have just sent off to you by post a roll containing five big pen drawings.

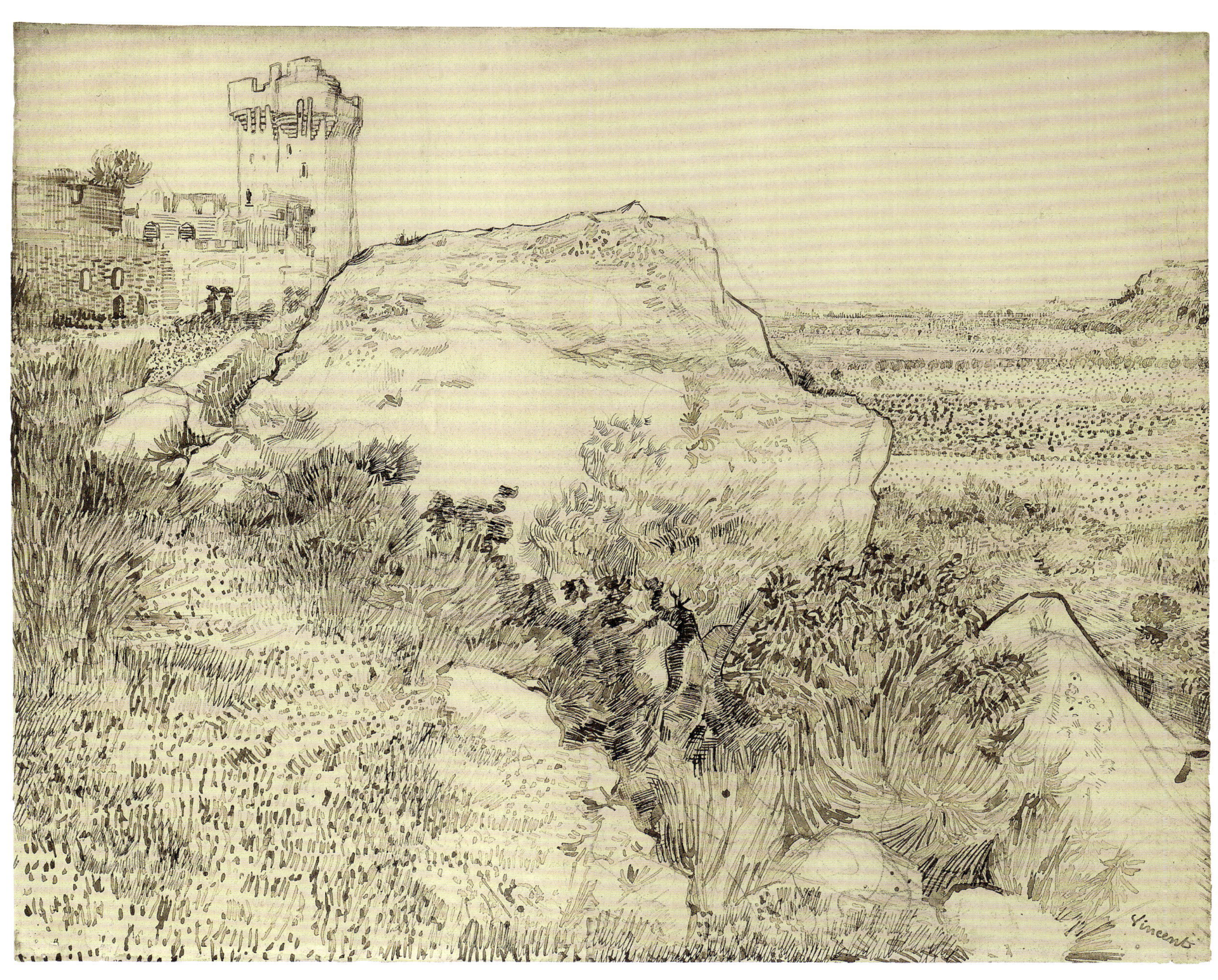
Vincent

85. *La Crau: The View from Montmajour*

July 6–12, 1888
Reed pen, pen, and ink over graphite on wove paper watermarked J. WHATMAN TURKEY MILL 1879
49 x 61 cm (19¼ x 24 in.)
Signed and inscribed in pen and ink, lower left: *Vincent / LaCrau / Vue prise à Mont Major*
Inscribed on verso, in another hand: *143*
Van Gogh Museum, Amsterdam (Vincent van Gogh Foundation) (d 349 V/1962)
F1420, JH1501
Letters B10, 509

Provenance: Sent by the artist to Theo van Gogh (d. 1891), Paris, ca. July 13, 1888 [509]; by inheritance to his son, Vincent Willem van Gogh (1890–1978), as part of his collection, administered by his widow, Johanna van Gogh-Bonger (d. 1925), 1891; placed on loan at the Stedelijk Museum, Amsterdam, 1931–73; ownership transferred to the Vincent van Gogh Foundation, 1962; placed on permanent loan at the Van Gogh Museum, Amsterdam, 1973.

Selected exhibitions: Groningen 1897; The Hague 1898, hors cat.; Amsterdam 1905, no. 413; Berlin 1906, no. 60; Amsterdam 1915, no. 26; Basel 1924, no. 88; Zürich 1924, no. 88; Stuttgart 1924, no. 12; The Hague 1925; London 1926–27, no. 22; Berlin 1927–28, no. 60; Paris 1937, no. 72; London–Birmingham–Glasgow 1947–48, no. 142; New York–Chicago 1949–50, no. 96; Aix-en-Provence 1959, no. 26; Paris–Albi 1966, no. 44; London 1968–69, no. 115; New York 1984, no. 57; Otterlo 1990, no. 187.

Summary of the literature: At first, De la Faille (1928, no. 1420) thought this a drawing of May 1888, but later (1970/1992, no. 1420), after connecting it to letters B10 and 509, dated it mid-July, as did Hulsker (1980/1996, no. 1501). Based on Van Gogh's letters, Tellegen-Hoogendoorn (1967) established the sequence and sites of Van Gogh's Montmajour drawings and placed his panoramas (F1420, cat. 85; F1424, cat. 86) among the group completed in about a week's time, around the middle of July. Walker (1982) analyzed the technique and structure of the pair, relating them to sixteenth- and seventeenth-century Flemish and Dutch landscapes and speculating as to the special appeal of the vantage point chosen by Van Gogh. Pickvance (in New York 1984, no. 57; in Otterlo 1990, no. 187) placed the two drawings between July 10 and 13, 1888, and pointed out that their completion occasioned one of Van Gogh's rare statements evaluating his own work. Like Pickvance, Silverman (2001, pp. 55–57) compared the Montmajour landscapes executed in May with those done in July, seeing in the first group "a pattern of inattention to the complex of sacred buildings that provided the major attraction for other visitors to the site," and in the second group a tendency to minimize the Alpilles mountain range. Heenk (1995, p. 175) observed that "the second type of ink" Van Gogh used on three of the July drawings, F1420 (cat. 85), F1446 (cat. 84), and JH Add. 3 (cat. 82), "may have been applied later."

See "The Heights of Montmajour."

CI

Letter to Émile Bernard, July 15, 1888 [B10]: I have done some large pen-and-ink drawings. Two: an immense stretch of flat country, a bird's-eye view of it seen from the top of a hill—vineyards and fields of newly reaped wheat. All this multiplied in endless repetitions, stretching away toward the horizon like the surface of a sea, bordered by the little hills of La Crau. It does not have a Japanese look, and yet it is really the most Japanese thing I have done; a microscopic figure of a ploughman, a little train running across the wheat field—this is all the animation there is in it.

Letter to Theo van Gogh, ca. July 13, 1888 [509]: I have just sent off to you by post a roll containing five big pen drawings. . . . In my opinion the two views of the Crau and of the country on the banks of the Rhône are the best things I have done in pen and ink . . . the flat countryside covered with vines and stubble fields, seen from a height. . . . You will see . . . that there is no attempt at effect. At first sight it is like a map, a strategic plan. . . . Would you like to experiment with these two drawings of the Crau and the banks of the Rhône, **which do not look Japanese,** ***but which really are, perhaps more so than some others? Look at them in some café where it's clear and blue and nothing else in the way, or else outside. Perhaps they need a reed frame, like a thin stick. . . . If I urge you to look at these two drawings in this way, it is because I so much want to give you a*** **true idea** ***of the simplicity of nature here.***

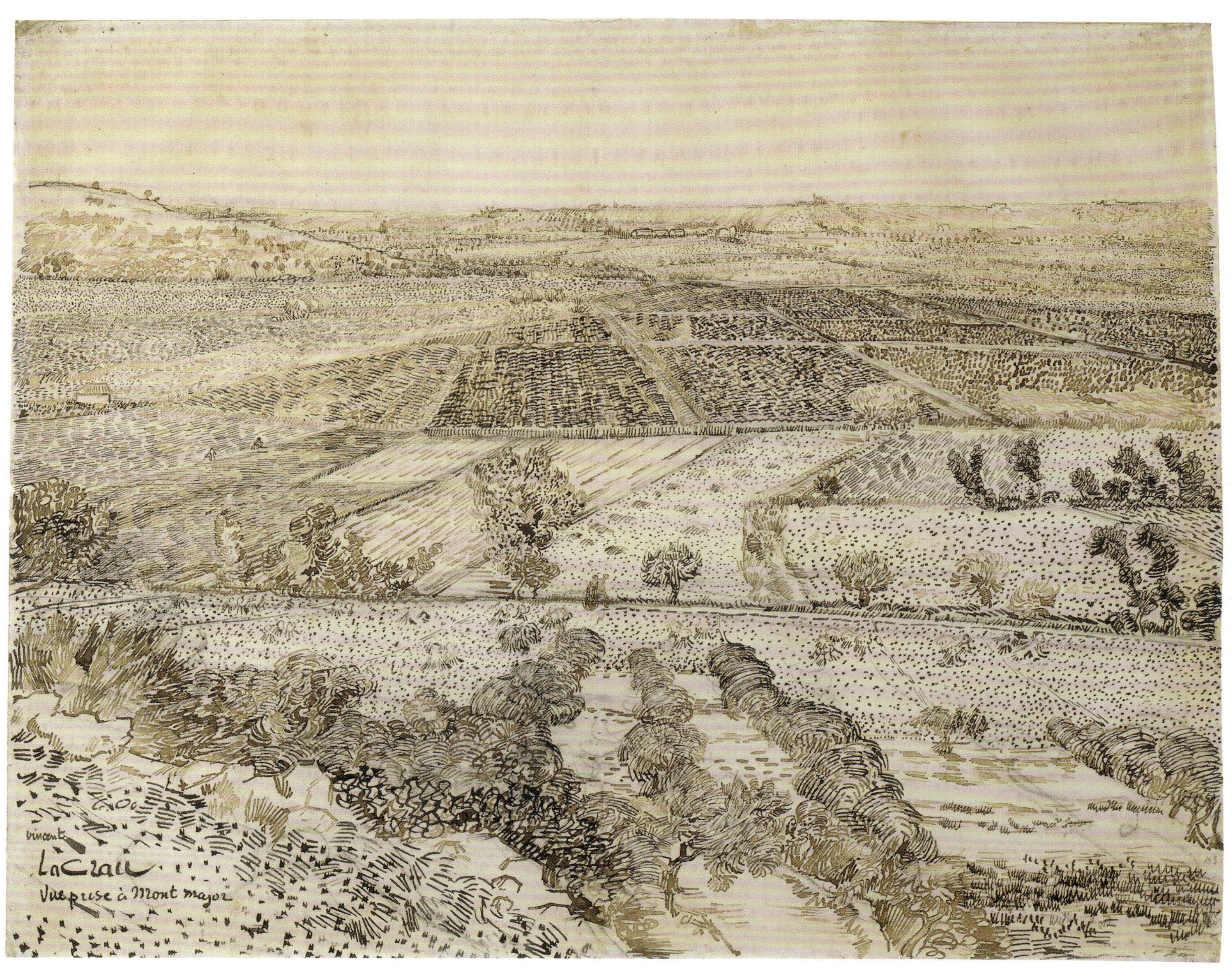
Vincent
La Crau
Vue prise à Mont major

86. *The Country on the Banks of the Rhône Viewed from Montmajour*

July 6–12, 1888
Reed pen, quill, and ink over black chalk and graphite on wove paper watermarked J. WHATMAN TURKEY MILL 1879
48.7 x 60.7 cm ($19^{1}/_{8}$ x $23^{7}/_{8}$ in.)
Signed in pen and ink, lower right: *Vincent*
Inscribed in pen and ink inside a cartouche, lower right: *La campagne du côté des bords / du Rhône vue de / Mon[t] Majour*
Tack holes in corners
Trustees of the British Museum, London (1968-2-10-20)
F1424, JH1502
Letters B10, 509

Provenance: Sent by the artist to Theo van Gogh (d. 1891), Paris, ca. July 13, 1888 [509]; by inheritance to his son, Vincent Willem van Gogh, as part of his collection, administered by his widow, Johanna van Gogh-Bonger, 1891, until at least 1898; presumably her gift to Mrs. H. Mauve-Carbentus; by descent to Rudolf Mauve, Scheveningen; Kunstzalen d'Audretsch, The Hague; Anthony van Hoboken, Vienna, Lausanne, and Ascona, by 1928, until at least 1945; Matthiesen Gallery, London; César Mange de Hauke, Paris and New York, by 1948; his bequest to the British Museum, 1968.

Selected exhibitions: Paris 1896–97 (no. 13 on Johanna's list of loans); The Hague 1898, hors cat.; New York 1984, no. 58; Otterlo 1990, no. 188; Bremen 2002–3, no. 36.

Summary of the literature: See cat. 85 (F1420).

Letters to Émile Bernard, July 15, 1888 [B10], and to Theo van Gogh, ca. July 13, 1888 [509]: See cat. 85 (F1420).

See "The Heights of Montmajour."

CI

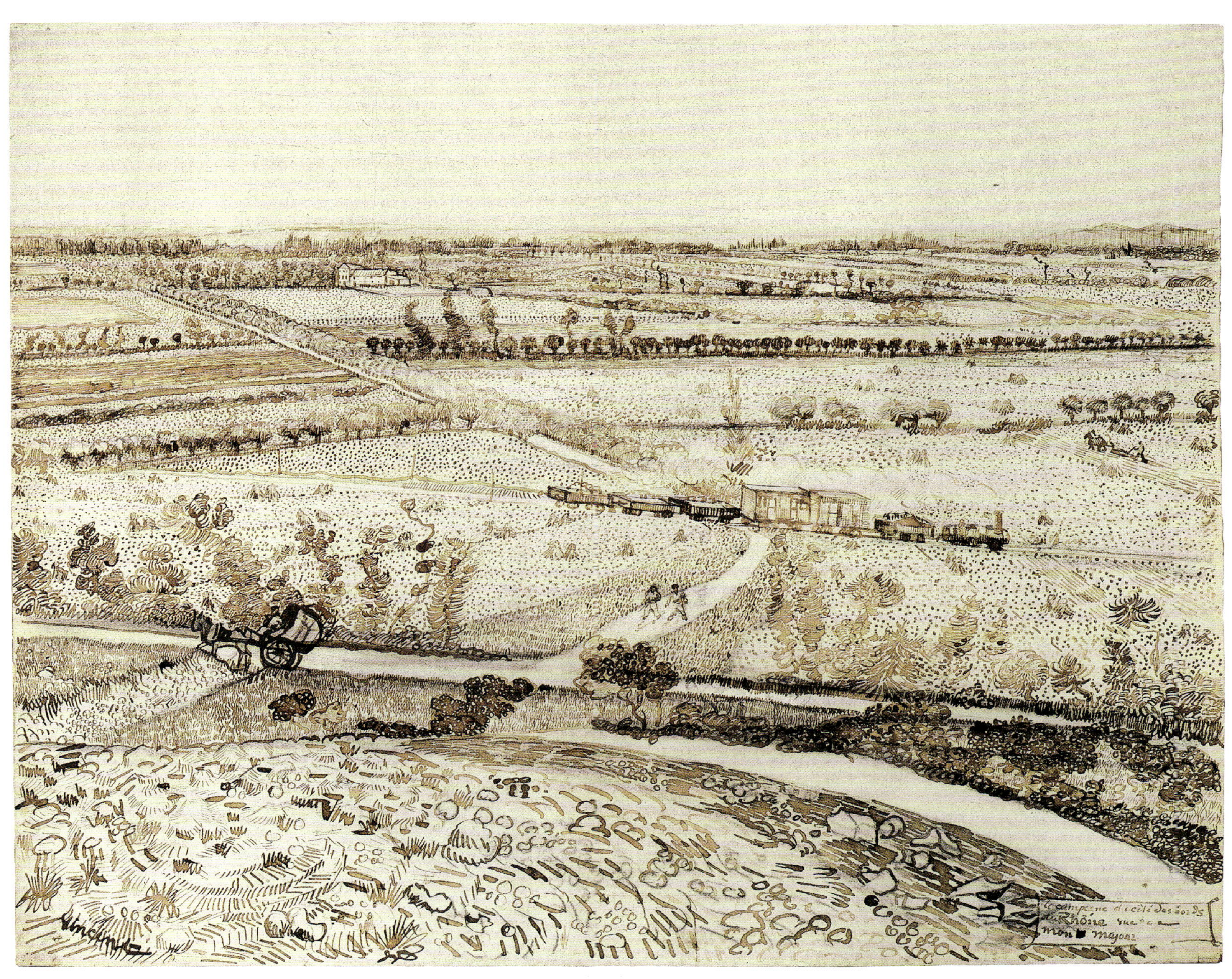
campagne du côté des bords
du Rhône
mont majour

Gardens, Parks, and Byways

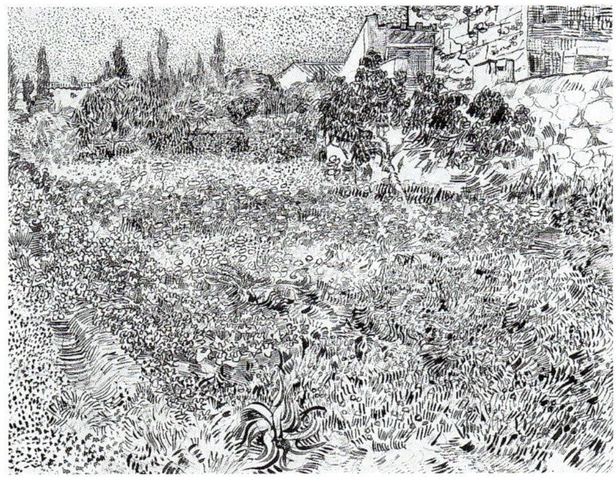

Fig. 163. *Garden with Flowers* (F1455), by July 19, 1888. Reed pen and ink on paper, 49.5 x 61 cm (19½ x 24 in.). Sammlung Oskar Reinhart "Am Römerholz," Winterthur

When Van Gogh arrived in Arles in February of 1888, he was attracted first to sites that either reminded him of his former home in Holland or recalled landscapes he had come across in Japanese prints. In consequence he recorded familiar-looking bridges and waterways, orchards, and flatlands divided by channels and roads. It was not long, however, before his eyes wandered out into the surrounding fields and plains of La Crau and up the rocky heights of Montmajour. There, expansive vistas commanded his sights, seeming to symbolize nature's grandest schemes: the cycle of life; the infinity of space; the eternity of time.

In June, Vincent focused on the harvest. But before the month was over, he felt compelled to contemplate "the next campaign." In the process, he reminded Theo of the progress he had made since his arrival: "The orchards meant pink and white; the wheatfields, yellow; and the marines, blue. Perhaps now I shall begin to look around a bit for greens" [504]. By July 5, the artist had rediscovered an oasis that first caught his eye in March: the public gardens that bordered the Place Lamartine across the way from his lodgings. The grass, shrubs, and trees there offered an infinite variety of greens, only occasionally interrupted by the pink and red blooms of oleanders. Here, as refreshing counterparts to the grand, sweeping views of Provence he had already embraced, were smaller, more circumspect corners of the landscape, intimate sites that pulled Van Gogh into close focus and, conveniently, while he readied the Yellow House for Gauguin's approaching visit, lay only a few footsteps from home.

As he had become consistently inclined to cover a canvas or drawing sheet with a field full of marks, Van Gogh now discovered delight in the park's newly mown lawn, embroidered with cuttings. He made a small patch of grass the stage for intense studies of aerial perspective, color, light, and shadow

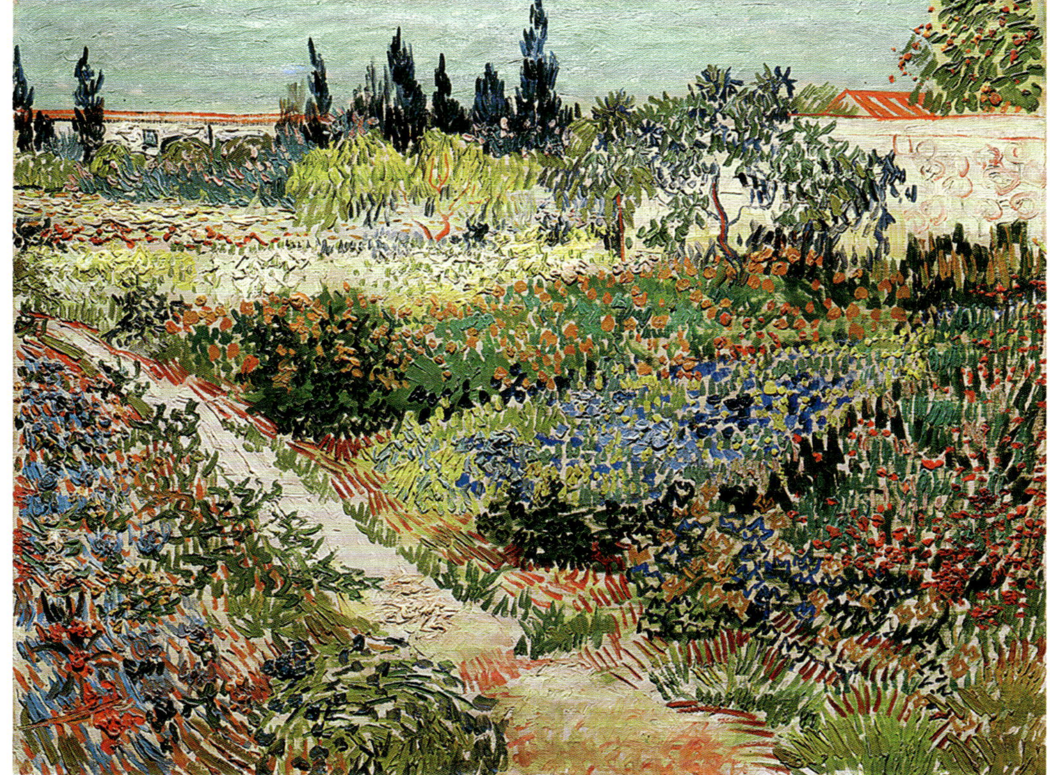

Fig. 164. *Garden with Flowers* (F429), ca. July 19, 1888. Oil on canvas, 72 x 91 cm (28⅜ x 35⅞ in.). Rijksdienst Beeldende Kunst, The Hague, on loan to the Haags Gemeentemuseum

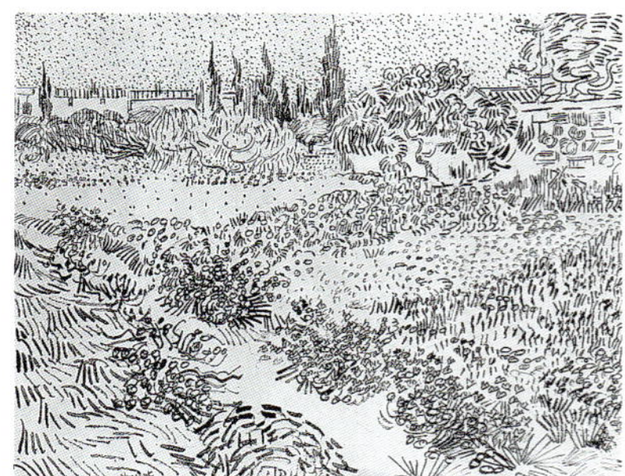

Fig. 165. *Garden with Flowers* (for John Russell) (F1454), ca. July 31–August 3, 1888. Reed pen and ink, 24 x 31.5 cm (9½ x 12⅜ in.). Private collection

(F428, fig. 170; F1450, cat. 88; F1449, cat. 89; F1451, cat. 90) and then addressed the woody plants that stood around it, particularly the odd couple on opposite sides of the clearing: a clipped cedar bush and a weeping beech. The round bush (or another like it) figured in one of Van Gogh's first drawings of Arles in March (F1421, cat. 43); by late September, it came to occupy the foreground of a painting (F1465, F1847).

Both weeping tree and bush appear in a painting of mid-September (F468) distinguished by the fact that Van Gogh declared it the first scene in a series called "the Poet's garden," which he designed to decorate Gauguin's room in the Yellow House. To his eagerly awaited guest, Van Gogh introduced the four pictures in the ensemble as "the essence of . . . the immutable character of this country [Provence] . . . [captured] in such a way that one is put in mind of the old poet from these parts . . . , Petrarch, and of the new poet from these parts—Paul Gauguin—" [544a]. Thus, in Arles, Gauguin would be welcomed into a personal bower reminiscent of the idyllic spots lauded in verse and troubadours' songs. Thereby refreshed, he would be prepared to create his own modern poetry.

The path of drawings leading up to the four paintings of *The Poet's Garden* and related pictures of the public park was typically a winding one, extending over time from March of one year to May of the next. Within this period, drawing became increasingly an intrinsic part of Van Gogh's creative progress and positively essential to its forward dynamic. Morever, the artist discovered he could shift his weight gracefully between the two media, bringing to painting from the practice of drawing greater clarity of design and precision in his touch, carrying over to drawing from painting more "colorful" tonal variation and new tactile excitement.

The brilliant group of garden pictures Van Gogh produced at the height of summer provides similar revelations of the artist's agile maneuvers through a progression of varying media and techniques, sizes and formats. Essential information-gathering might commence with a thorough study in pen and ink (F1455, fig. 163), progress to a painting twice its size (F429, fig. 164), only to be followed by a concise summary of the composition, drawn on a much smaller scale (F1454, fig. 165). Concurrently, Van Gogh painted the same flowering garden in a vertical format (F430, fig. 166). This activity furthermore inspired the production of two large reed-pen drawings, equally flamboyant and densely textured (F1456, cat. 91; F1457, cat. 92), from which yet another painting was spun (F578, fig. 172). By switching back and forth between his blunt-tipped reed pen and a paint-loaded brush, Van Gogh saw his views of flowering gardens extravagantly enriched. For the moment, color and line appeared to be nearly interchangeable. His paintings were drawn with a brush; his drawings were painted with a pen.

CI

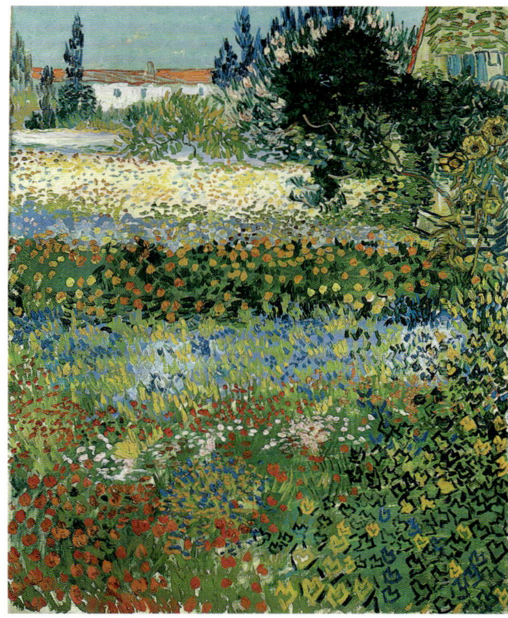

Fig. 166. *Garden with Flowers* (F430), ca. July 19, 1888. Oil on canvas, 92 x 73 cm (36¼ x 28¾ in.). Private collection

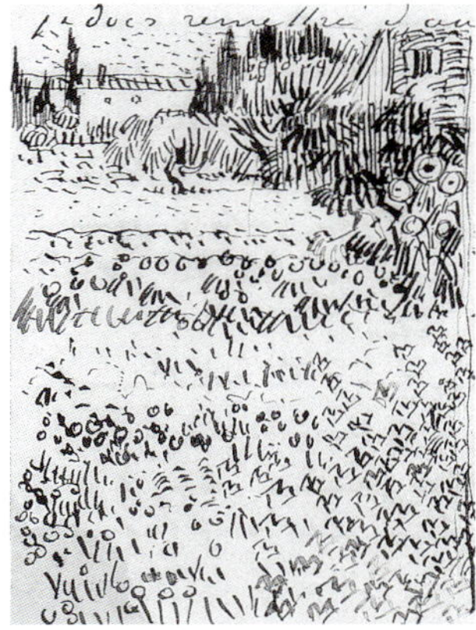

Fig. 167. *Garden with Flowers* (F1844), sketch in letter 512, between July 17 and 20, 1888. Pen and ink, 9.2 x 7 cm (3⅝ x 2¾ in.). Van Gogh Museum, Amsterdam (Vincent van Gogh Foundation)

87. *The Langlois Bridge*

(for Émile Bernard)

Mid-July 1888
Reed pen and ink over graphite on wove paper
24.2 x 31.8 cm (9½ x 12½ in.)
Inscribed on verso, upper right, in another hand: *Dessin à la plume a Vincent van Gogh / Reunis par Émile Bernard / sur Biographie aout 91*
Los Angeles County Museum of Art, Mr. and Mrs. George Gard De Sylva Collection (M.49.17.2)
F1471, JH1420
Letters B10, 511

Provenance: Sent by the artist to Émile Bernard, Saint-Briac, presumably July 15, 1888 [B10, 511], until sold to Ambroise Vollard, Paris, probably between 1899 and 1904; Bernheim-Jeune, Paris, by 1910; acquired by Tilla Durieux-Cassirer, Berlin, 1910, until the death of her husband, Paul Cassirer, 1926; his daughter, Suse Cassirer-Paret, Berlin and Meudon, 1926–29; Paul Cassirer Art Gallery, Amsterdam, 1929; Jacques Seligmann and Co., New York and Paris, 1929, until at least 1935; acquired by George Gard De Sylva, Los Angeles, 1938; acquired as part of the George Gard De Sylva collection by the Los Angeles County Museum, 1949.[1]

Selected exhibitions: Berlin 1910, no. 64; Berlin 1914, no. 72; New York and other cities 1935–36, no. 115; Frankfurt 1970, no. 46; New York 1984, no. 24.

Summary of the literature: Until recently, this drawing was routinely catalogued as one of the earliest made in Arles in keeping with other depictions of the subject that are documented in letters Van Gogh wrote between March and May 1888. Yet varying dates within these brackets were proposed. De la Faille (1928, no. 1471) assigned it to May, but the editors of De la Faille 1970, to March. Roskill (1971, p. 166) regarded it as a study for the painting (F570), which was probably sent to Theo in early May [483], observing that it was sketched in a later letter [492] in connection with an album of drawings "already sent." Hulsker (1980/1996, no. 1420) dated it to mid-May. Pickvance (in New York 1984, no. 24), supporting his view with Roskill's observations, argued that it was a "rapid, on-the-spot" sketch "from late April" that "announced the motif" of the mid-May oil (F570); however, in Martigny 2000 (p. 300, under no. 53), he referred to it as a mid-July drawing made after the painting for Bernard, as Dorn (in Essen–Amsterdam 1990–91, p. 93) and Davis (1997, no. 59) contended. To date, no rationale or compelling evidence has been furnished to establish that this drawing was indeed part of the Bernard campaign.

Additional comments: Scholars might earlier have recognized the drawing as a *répétition* for Bernard had they given more weight to their observations regarding the artist's deft command of the reed pen and less to the drawing's presumed provenance, which had been traced in error to Theo's widow in De la Faille (1928/1970/1992, no. 1471) and in Feilchenfeldt and Veenenbos (1988, pp. 133–34), who confused its history of ownership with the other pen-and-ink version (F1470). Both drawings, as the latter source recorded, were shown by Cassirer in 1910 and 1914: one was acquired from Bernheim-Jeune in 1910 and the other from Jo van Gogh-Bonger in 1911, having previously been lent to an exhibition in Berlin in 1909 as "Street with Bridge." This title aptly describes only F1470, thus distinguishing it as the drawing that was once part of the Van Gogh family collection, as recently documented by Stolwijk and Veenenbos (2002, p. 196) and confirmed by the presence of Jo's inked inventory number (*171*) on the reverse, upper left. Alternately, the present drawing came from the Paris art market, as is characteristic of works formerly owned by Émile Bernard. Inscriptions on the reverse of the drawing add further credence to its Bernard ownership.

The elegant ease of this drawing is as much a reflection of Van Gogh's familiarity with the reed pen by mid-July 1888 as with the subject, for between mid-March and late May he had devoted eight works to the Langlois Bridge: a letter sketch [B2], an earlier drawing (F1470, fig. 169), a watercolor (F1480, fig. 63), and five oils (F397, F544 [now a fragment], F400, F571, and F570, fig. 168), the last of which served as the model for the present sheet. In these variations on a theme, he gave currency to his sense of Provence being "like Holland in character" yet "as beautiful as Japan for the limpidity of the atmosphere and gay color effects" [488, B2]. The motif of the bridge has a long lineage in his oeuvre that may be traced from an 1883 watercolor of a drawbridge in Nieuw-Amsterdam (F1098) to the 1887 *Japonaiserie: The Bridge in the Rain* (after Hiroshige) (F372).

Prepared with minimal graphite and striking for its economy and fluency of line, Van Gogh's swan song to the Langlois Bridge was doubtless one of the first pen-and-ink drawings after paintings he made for Émile Bernard in July 1888 (see "*Répétitions*: Drawings after Paintings"). It stands apart from the labored, anecdotal rendering of the subject in an earlier sheet (F1470, fig. 169), probably made about the same time as a related letter sketch of mid-March 1888 [B2].[2]

The bridge, erected by a Dutch engineer and nicknamed for its keeper, Langlois, crossed the Arles-Bouc canal on the southwestern side of town, some distance from the artist's lodgings at the northernmost edge.

SAS

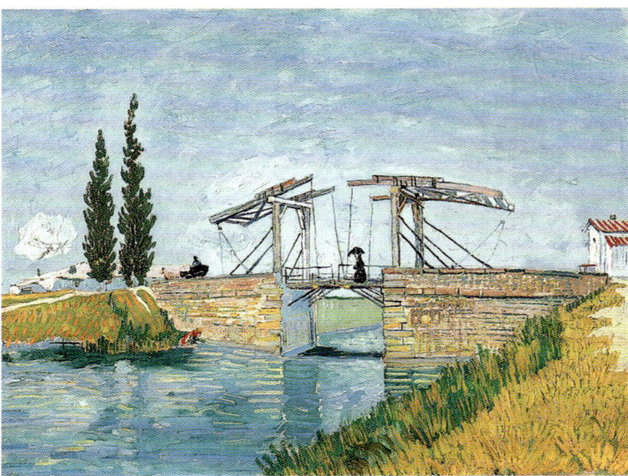

Fig. 168. *The Langlois Bridge* (F570), mid–late May 1888. Oil on canvas, 49.5 x 64 cm (19½ x 25¼ in.). Wallraf-Richartz-Museum, Cologne (photo: Rheinisches Bildarchiv, Cologne)

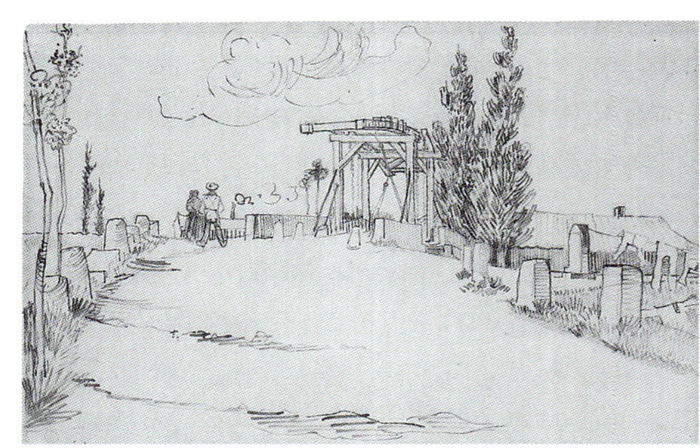

Fig. 169. *The Langlois Bridge with Road* (F1470), March 1888. Pen, reed pen, ink, and graphite on paper, 30.5 x 47.5 cm (12 x 18¾ in.). Graphische Sammlung, Staatsgalerie Stuttgart

1. New information concerning the provenance of this work from 1910 to 1929 was generously furnished by Walter Feilchenfeldt.
2. Though generally dated to April 1888, this drawing, dutifully worked out with pencil and ruler, presents an early conception of the motif dependent on a strolling couple, as in the March 18 letter sketch [B2] and an oil fragment (F544) preserved from a study Van Gogh "ruined" about March 25 [471].

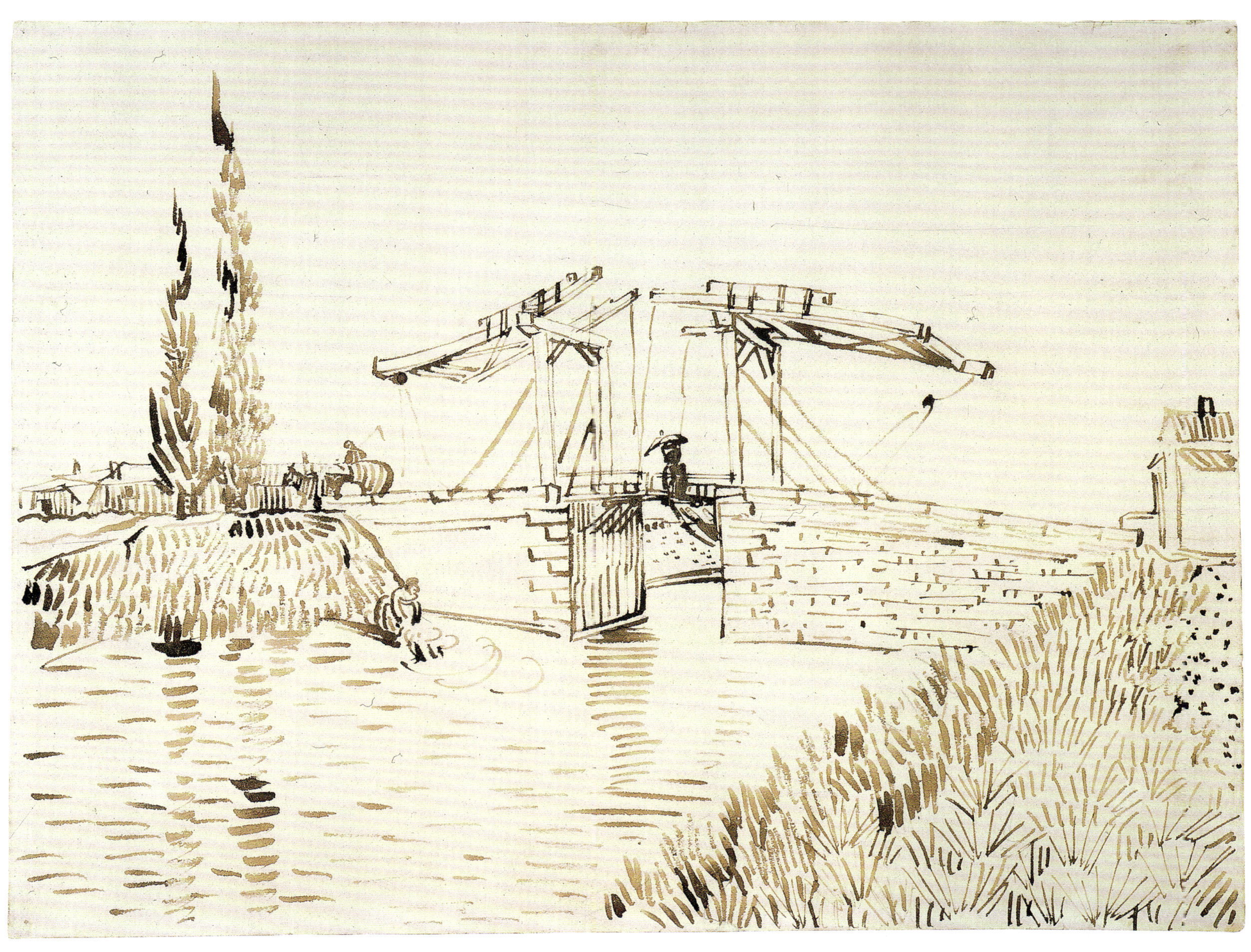

88. *The Garden; A Corner of a Garden in the Place Lamartine*

(for Émile Bernard)

Mid-July 1888
Reed pen and ink over graphite on wove paper watermarked AL (in an oval), surrounded by narrow strips of marbled paper
24.2 x 31.6 cm ($9\frac{1}{2}$ x $12\frac{1}{2}$ in.)
Signed in pen and ink, lower left: *Vincent*
Private collection, courtesy of Wildenstein & Co., Inc.
F1450, JH1509
Letter B10

New York only

Provenance: Sent by the artist to Émile Bernard, Saint-Briac, July 15, 1888 [B10, 511], until ca. 1892; acquired from Bernard's exhibition at Le Barc de Boutteville (or else from Julien Tanguy), Paris, 1892, by Johan Rohde, Copenhagen, until his death in 1935; by descent to Mrs. Asa Johan Rohde, Copenhagen; her estate sale, Sotheby's, London, July 6, 1960, no. 160; purchased by M. Knoedler and Co., New York and London; M. F. Feheley, Toronto, 1970; sold, Sotheby's, London, June 28, 1972, no. 5, to J. S. Lewis, New York; to private collection.

Selected exhibitions: Paris 1892 (?); Copenhagen 1893, no. 197; New York 1984, no. 72; Copenhagen 1984–85, no. 64; Martigny 2000, no. 65.

Summary of the literature: This drawing was dated to July 1888 and associated with letter 508 in De la Faille 1928 (no. 1450), which records that it was acquired in 1892 from Père Tanguy by the artist Johan Rohde. It was redated to September 1888 and associated with Van Gogh's Poet's Garden series in the 1970 and 1992 editions of the catalogue raisonné. Roskill (1971, p. 156), Hulsker (1980/1996, no. 1509), and Pickvance (in New York 1984, no. 72) recognized that it was one of the *répétitions* sent to Bernard in mid-July 1888. Pickvance noted that this is "the only one of the set of fifteen drawings destined for Bernard that is actually referred to in the letters."

"The Garden" was the only one of the fifteen *répétitions* Van Gogh sent to Bernard in mid-July that he singled out for mention. Quoting two lines of verse that Bernard had sent to him earlier, Van Gogh suggested his study of new-mown grass fit the poetic description "shaggy carpets woven of flowers and greenery." "I wanted to answer your quotations with the pen, but not by writing down words," he explained [B10]. His pen-and-ink drawing repeats the oil study Van Gogh had painted about ten days earlier showing a corner of the public garden in the Place Lamartine.

See "*Répétitions*: Drawings after Paintings."

CI

Fig. 170. *Sunny Lawn in a Public Park* (F428), by July 8, 1888. Oil on canvas, 60.5 x 73.5 cm ($23\frac{7}{8}$ x 29 in.). Private collection, Switzerland

Letter to Theo van Gogh, July 5, 1888 [508]: Here is a new subject. A corner of a garden with clipped shrubs and a weeping tree, and in the background some clumps of oleanders. And the lawn just cut with long trails of hay drying in the sun, and a little corner of blue sky at the top [see F1843, fig. 171].

Letter to Émile Bernard, July 15, 1888 [B10]: Perhaps you will be inclined to forgive me for not replying to your letter immediately, when you see that I am sending you a little batch of sketches along with this letter.

In the sketch "The Garden" maybe there is something like "Des tapis velus / De fleurs et de verdures tissues" [Shaggy carpets woven of flowers and greenery].

Letter to Wilhelmina van Gogh, July 31, 1888 [W5]: I have also got a garden [painting] without flowers, that is to say a lawn, newly mown, bright green with the gray hay spread in long streaks. A weeping ash and a number of cedars and cypresses, the cedars yellowish and spherical in form. . . . At the back, oleander and a patch of green-blue sky. The blue shadows of the shrubs on the grass.

Letter to Paul Gauguin, October 3, 1888 [553a/544a]: I have expressly made a decoration for the room you will be staying in, a poet's garden (among the sketches Bernard has there is a first rough draft of it, later simplified).

Letter to Émile Bernard, October 3, 1888 [B18]: . . . I myself have the "Poet's Garden" (2 canvases; among the sketches you have there is the first conception of it, done after a smaller study that is already at my brother's).

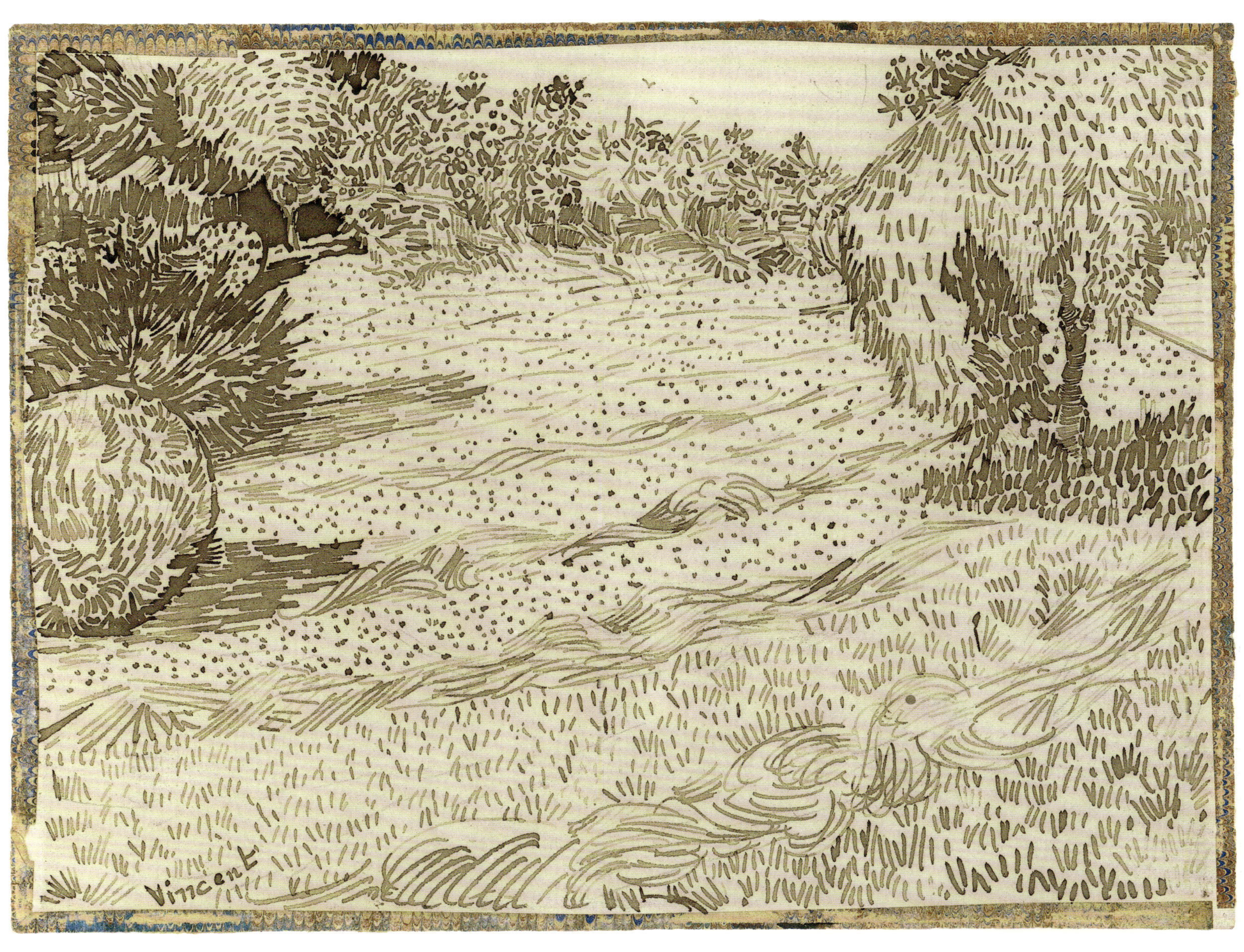
Vincent

89. *A Corner of a Garden in the Place Lamartine*

(for John Russell)

ca. July 31–August 3, 1888
Reed pen and ink over graphite on wove paper
31.5 x 24.5 cm (12⅜ x 9⅝ in.)
Signed in pen and ink, lower left: *Vincent*
Miles, Sebastian, and Hugh Gibson
F1449, JH1534
Letters 516, 517

New York only

Provenance: Sent by the artist to John Russell, Belle-Île, Brittany, ca. August 3, 1888 [517], until 1920; sold, [Anon.], Hôtel Drouot, Paris, March 31, 1920, no. 65; purchased by Galerie Le Garrec, Paris; Kunstzalen d'Audretsch, The Hague; Galerie Lutz, Berlin; David Leder, Berlin; his sale, Amsler & Ruthardt, Berlin, October 29, 1925, no. 247; purchased by Galerie Van Diemen, Berlin; Galerie Thannhauser, Berlin, Paris, and New York; Josef von Sternberg, Hollywood, by 1935; his sale, Parke-Bernet, New York, November 22, 1949, no. 28; Wildenstein & Co., New York; Audrey Sheldon (d. 1978), New York; her estate sale, Christie's, New York, October 22, 1980, no. 328; purchased by David K. R. Thomson, Toronto, 1980; sold, Sotheby's, London, November 6, 1991, no. 12; private collection; sold, Sotheby's, London, June 27, 1995, no. 10; Thomas Gibson, London; to Miles, Sebastian, and Hugh Gibson

Selected exhibitions: New York 1984, no. 79; Martigny 2000, no. 67.

Summary of the literature: Associating it with Van Gogh's letter [508], De la Faille (1928, no. 1449) dated this drawing July 1888. But after it was firmly identified by Thannhauser (1938) as one of the twelve sheets sent to Russell about August 3, 1888, De la Faille's entry was revised (1970/1992, no. 1449). Hulsker (1980/1996, no. 1534) and Pickvance (in New York 1984, no. 79) understood the work as one made for Russell, but both presumed it illustrated a painting, now lost. Hulsker suggested that it was probably made from a variant of a similar painting (F428), no longer known, and Pickvance was of the same opinion although he granted that in Van Gogh's work "the same motif in both vertical and horizontal versions is by no means unknown."

After copying his painting of this same patch of lawn for Émile Bernard (F1450, cat. 88), Van Gogh gave his drawing paper a quarter-turn and stretched the horizontal scene into a vertical view. Although it has been suggested that the upright composition depends on a now-lost painting, it is more likely that Van Gogh simply tried out a new format, as he had times before. Among the twelve drawings he made for Russell, not only this one but also *The Road to Tarascon* (F1502a, cat. 93) and *La Mousmé* (F1503, cat. 80) departed significantly from their parent paintings.

Van Gogh told Theo his sketches for Russell had "something of a Japanese air" [516], and indeed this lawn-scape seems to owe its tilted perspective, its graphic shorthand, and its elegant emptiness to ukiyo-e. In this revised "Corner of the Garden," aside from its redirecton to a vertical view several changes were made. The grass now appears raked; time has shifted from midday to late afternoon; the foliage of shrubs and trees appears very dense, and dark shadows lie long on the grass.

See "*Répétitions*: Drawings after Paintings."

CI

Letter to Theo van Gogh, July 5, 1888 [508], describing the oil: Here is a new subject. A corner of a garden with clipped shrubs and a weeping tree, and in the background some clumps of oleanders.

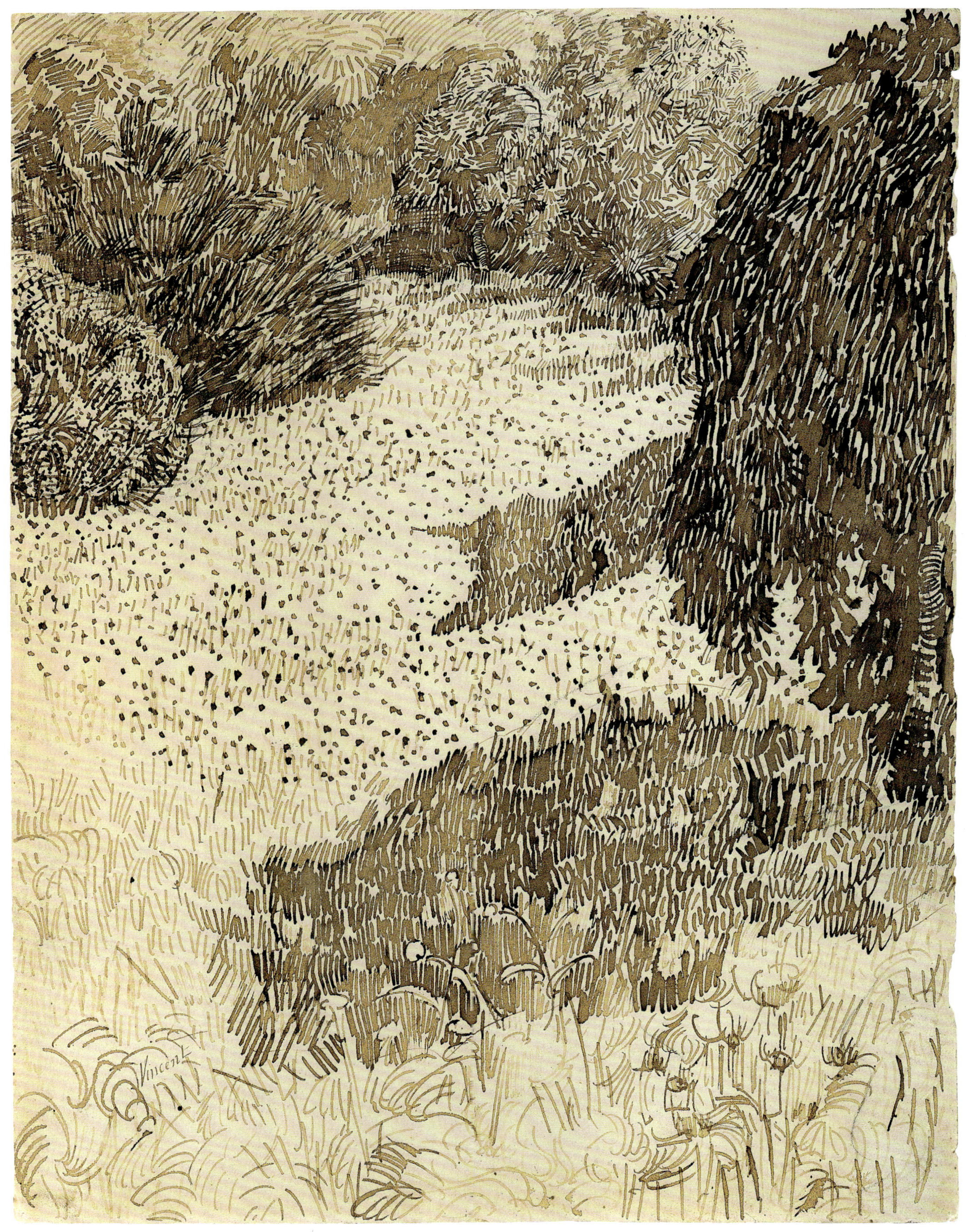
Vincent

90. *A Corner of a Garden in the Place Lamartine*

(for Theo van Gogh)

ca. August 6–8, 1888
Reed pen, quill, and ink over graphite on wove paper
24.1 x 31.5 cm (9½ x 12⅜ in.)
Inscribed in pen and ink on verso, upper left, in another hand: *187*
The Menil Collection, Houston (78-172 E)
F1451, JH1545
Letter 519

Provenance: Sent by the artist to Theo van Gogh (d. 1891), Paris, August 8, 1888 [519]; by inheritance to his son, Vincent Willem van Gogh, as part of his collection, administered by his widow, Johanna van Gogh-Bonger, 1891; sold by her to J. H. de Bois, The Hague, 1912; private collection, Paris; Galerie Thannhauser, Berlin; Fairbairn Collection, Australia; Galerie Thannhauser, New York; Vladimir Golschmann, Saint Louis, Mo.; Galerie Thannhauser, New York; purchased by John and Dominique de Menil, 1951; Menil Foundation, Inc., Houston, 1978; The Menil Collection, Houston.

Selected exhibitions: Amsterdam 1905, no. 412; Cologne–Frankfurt 1910; Berlin 1910, no. 61; Frankfurt 1970, no. 54; New York 1984, no. 84; Otterlo 1990, no. 200; Martigny 2000, no. 66; Saint Louis–Frankfurt 2001, unnumbered; Arles 2003, pp. 40–41.

Summary of the literature: At first dated July 1888 by De la Faille (1928, no. 1451), this drawing was listed in revised editions of his catalogue (1970/1992, no. 1451) as part of the Poet's Garden series of September 1888. It was recognized by Roskill (1971, p. 151), Hulsker (1980/1996, no. 1545), and Pickvance (in New York 1984, no. 84) as Van Gogh's *répétition* of his painting (F428) made for Theo at the beginning of August 1888 [519]. For early history, see Feilchenfeldt and Veenenbos 1988, p. 132; Heijbroek and Wouthuysen 1993, p. 204.

While his painting of a corner of the neighborhood park (F428, fig. 170) continued to dry, Van Gogh interpreted it in pen and ink for his brother. He had sent Theo a rough sketch right after finishing the picture just one month before (F1843, fig. 171) but now re-created it, as he had in drawings for Émile Bernard (F1450, cat. 88) and John Russell (F1449, cat. 89). Benefiting from experience, this fourth drawn *répétition* is the most uniformly confident and tightly knit of all. Each form of vegetation is assigned its own graphic pattern to clarify the composition. Van Gogh added quill lines to the "long trails of hay" and the weeping beech tree at right, intensifying their tonal distinction. And, in this version alone, he gave the "little corner of blue sky at the top" its proper due with a sprinkling of dots [508].

See "*Répétitions*: Drawings after Paintings."

CI

Letter to Theo van Gogh, July 5, 1888 [508], describing the oil: Here is a new subject. A corner of a garden with clipped shrubs and a weeping tree, and in the background some clumps of oleanders. And the lawn just cut with long trails of hay drying in the sun, and a little corner of blue sky at the top.

Letter to Wilhelmina van Gogh, July 31, 1888 [W5]: I have also got a garden [painting] without flowers, that is to say a lawn, newly mown, bright green with the gray hay spread in long streaks. A weeping ash and a number of cedars and cypresses. . . . At the back, oleander and a patch of green-blue sky. The blue shadows of the shrubs on the grass.

Letter to Theo van Gogh, August 8, 1888 [519]: I have just sent off three large drawings, as well as some other ones. . . . Now the Harvest, the Garden . . . are sketches after painted studies. I think that all these ideas are good, but the painted studies lack clearness of touch. That is another reason why I felt it necessary to draw them.

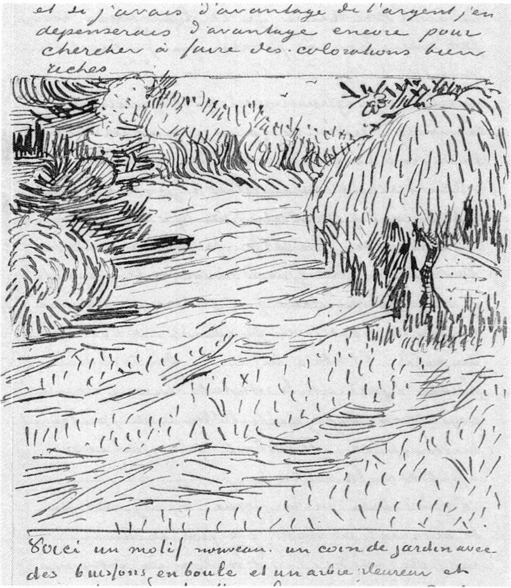

Fig. 171. *The [Poet's] Garden* (F1843), sketch in letter 508 to Theo, Paris, July 5, 1888. Pen and ink. Van Gogh Museum, Amsterdam (Vincent van Gogh Foundation)

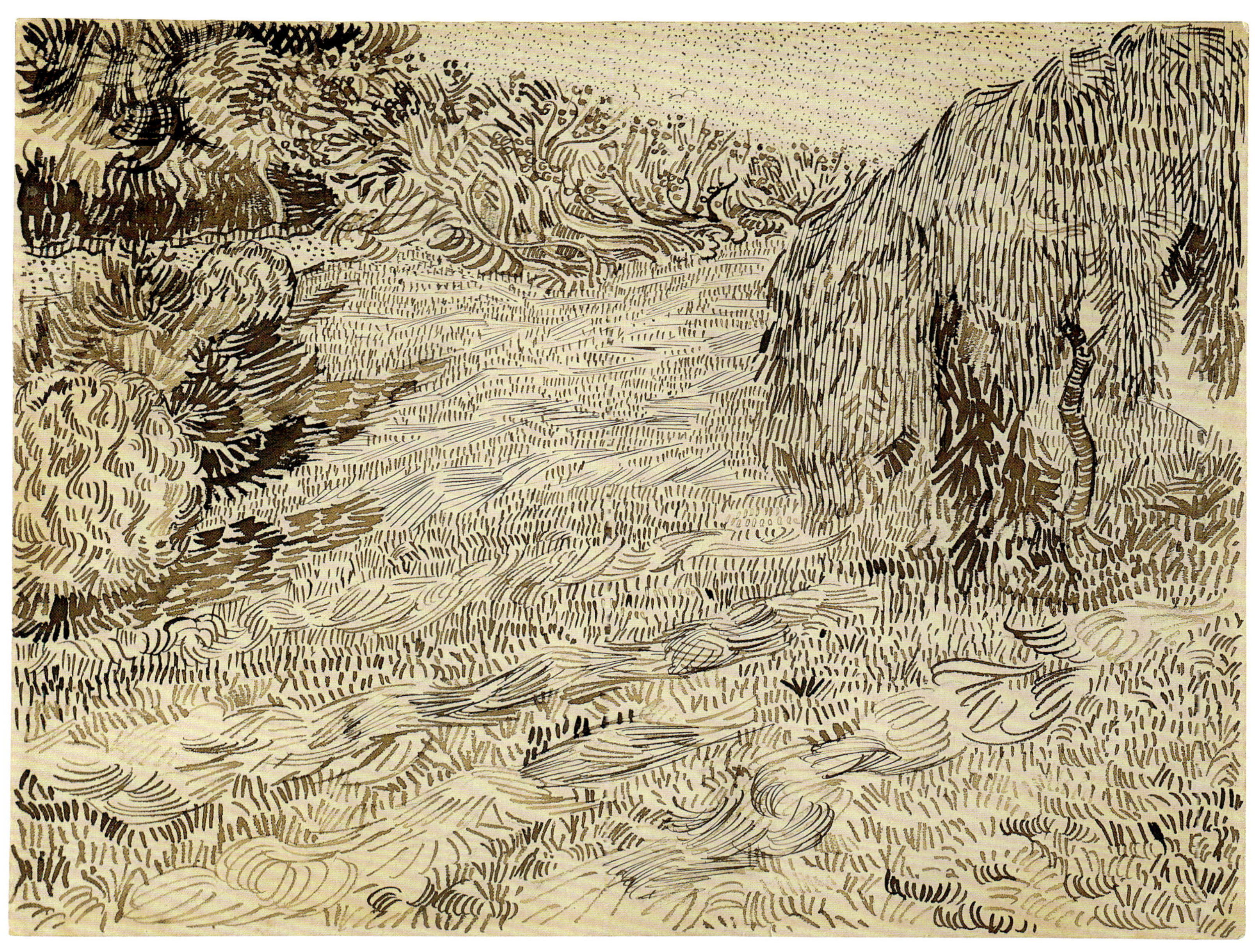

91. *Cottage Garden*

By August 8, 1888
Reed pen, quill, and ink over graphite on wove paper watermarked J. WHATMAN TURKEY MILL 1879
61 x 49 cm (24 x 19¼ in.)
Signed in pen and ink, lower left: *Vincent*
Inscribed in pen and ink on verso, in another hand: *[1]69*
Tack holes in corners
Private collection
F1456, JH1537
Letters 519, 521

Provenance: Sent by the artist to Theo van Gogh (d. 1891), Paris, August 8, 1888 [519]; by inheritance to his son, Vincent Willem van Gogh, as part of his collection, administered by his widow, Johanna van Gogh-Bonger, 1891; sold by her to Paul Cassirer, Berlin, December 1906; sold to Hugo von Tschudi (d. 1911), Berlin, December 1906; to his widow, Angela von Tschudi, Munich; sold by her family to Dr. Fritz Nathan, Zürich, ca. 1960; by descent to Elisabeth Sigrist-Nathan, Zürich, until 1990; her sale, Christie's, New York, November 14, 1990, no. 14; purchased by Theodore Forstmann; offered for sale at Christie's, New York, May 14, 1997, no. 25, bought in; subsequently purchased through Christie's by present owner.

Selected exhibitions: Amsterdam 1905, no. 395; Berlin 1906, no. 78; Otterlo 1990, no. 207.

Summary of the literature: Beginning with De la Faille (1928, no. 1456), scholars have associated this drawing with a work the artist described in his letter of August 8, 1888 [519], and have dated it accordingly. Roskill (1971, p. 160 n. 92) thought it the first of the three large drawings described in that letter. While Hulsker (1980/1996, no. 1537) dated the work August 6–8, Pickvance (in Otterlo 1990, p. 236) suggested August 5–6, and preliminary to the related painting (F578), which "must have been realized soon afterwards, but without the benefit of the drawing at his side." He also observed that the drawing had inspired one of "two instances" in which Van Gogh "expressed a value judgment on his drawings," declaring it "the best" of his three large Provençal gardens. Heenk (1995, p. 177) held to a broader dating, "between mid July and about 8 August 1888." For early history, see Feilchenfeldt and Veenenbos 1988, p. 133; Paul 1993, p. 393; and Stolwijk and Veenenbos 2002, pp. 51, 126, 147, 195.

Having posted this drawing to his brother on August 8, Van Gogh returned to the "little cottage garden" a short time later to paint the same view ostensibly from a pace or two more to the left (F578, fig. 172). He seems to have had this plan in mind early on, for he advised Theo, "If the drawings I send you are too hard, it is because I have done them in such a way as to be able later on, if they're still around, to use them as guides for painting" [519].

Very close in size to this drawing and probably roughed in by means of tracing, Van Gogh's painting is, however, a looser, more summary depiction of the subject, relying on swipes of color to differentiate forms and textures, in the place of a multiplicity of graphic ciphers. Although Vincent presented a vivid verbal description of the scene in his letter, the garden painting intentionally slurred "somber purple . . . pink . . . white . . . and red" to emphasize complementary colors: orange and green; yellow and violet.

CI

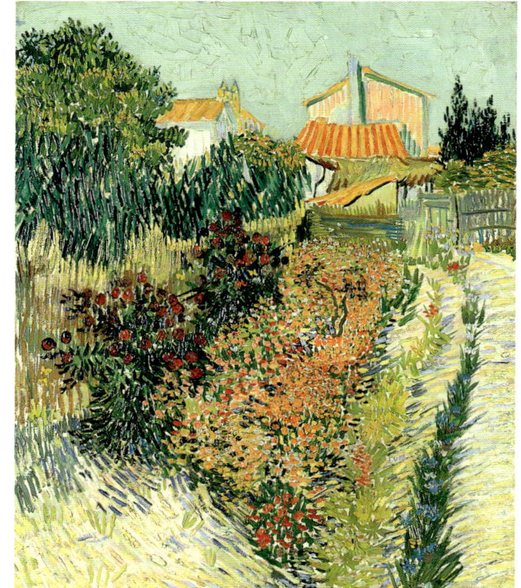

Fig. 172. *Garden with Flowers* (F578), ca. August 15, 1888. Oil on canvas, 63.5 x 52.5 cm (25 x 20⅝ in.). Private collection

Letter to Theo van Gogh, August 8, 1888 [519]: I have just sent off three large drawings. . . . The little cottage garden done vertically is, I think, the best of the three big ones [F1455, F1456, F1457]. . . . [It] has in itself amazing colors: the dahlias are a rich and somber purple; the double row of flowers is pink and green on one side, and orange with hardly any leaves on the other. In the midst a white dwarf dahlia, and a little pomegranate with flowers of the most vivid reddish-orange, with yellowish-green fruits. The ground gray, the tall reeds, "canes," blue-green, the fig trees emerald, the sky blue, the houses white with green windows and red roofs, in the morning full in the sunshine, in the evening drowned in the shadows thrown by the fig trees and the reeds.

Letter to Theo van Gogh, August 9, 1888 [521]: I think it is likely that we are going to have a great heat now without wind. . . . If so, it is a very good thing that I have a supply of paints and canvas, because I already have my eye on half a dozen subjects, especially that little cottage garden I sent you the drawing of yesterday.

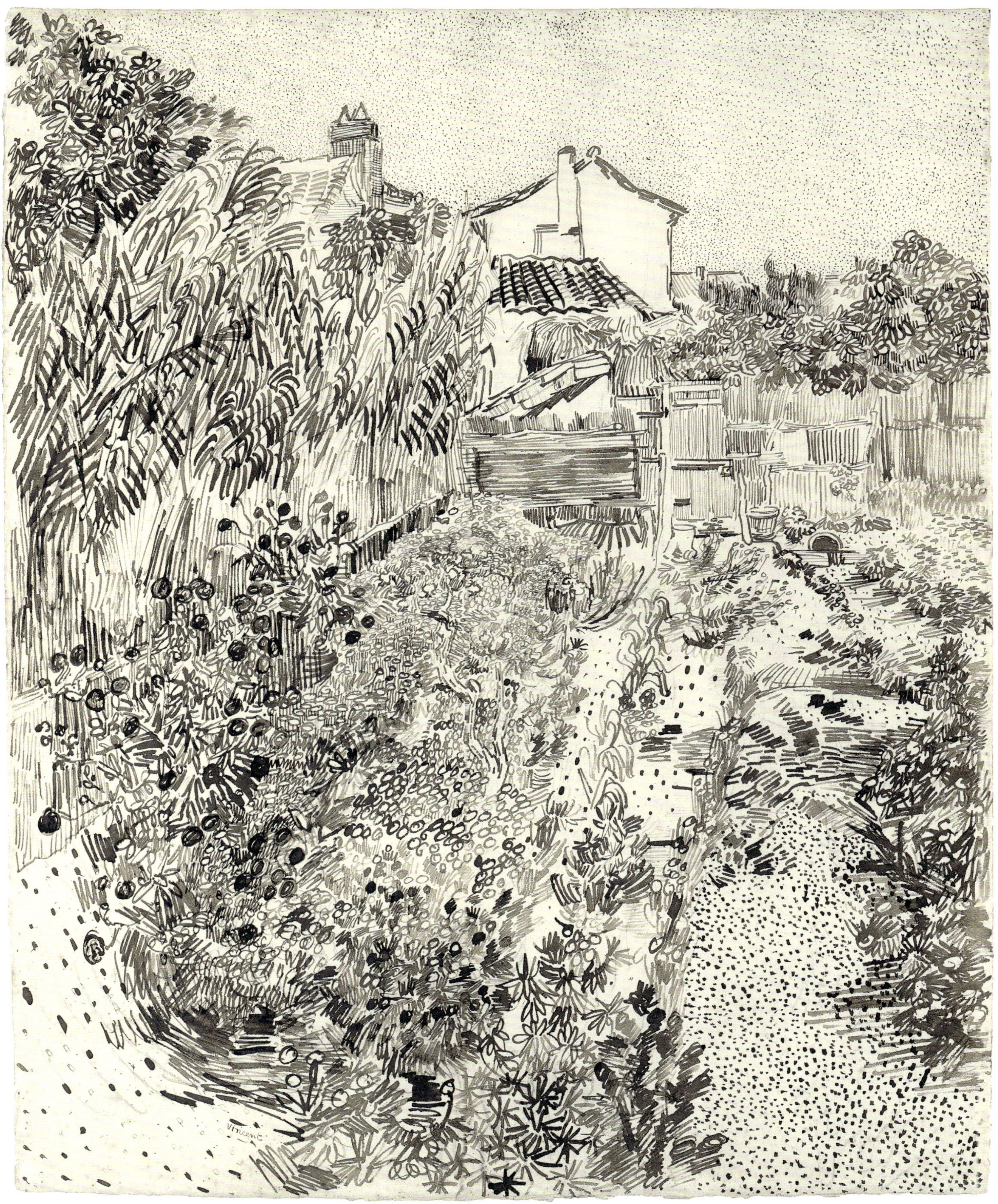

92. *Garden with Sunflowers*

By August 8, 1888
Reed pen, pen, brush, and ink over graphite on wove paper watermarked J. WHATMAN TURKEY MILL 1879
60.7 x 49.2 cm (23⅞ x 19⅜ in.)
Signed in pen and ink, lower right: *Vincent*
Inscribed on verso, in another hand: *168*
Van Gogh Museum, Amsterdam (Vincent van Gogh Foundation) (d 175 V/1962)
F1457, JH1539
Letter 519

Provenance: Sent by the artist to Theo van Gogh (d. 1891), Paris, August 8, 1888 [519]; by inheritance to his son, Vincent Willem van Gogh (1890–1978), as part of his collection, administered by his widow, Johanna van Gogh-Bonger (d. 1925), 1891; placed on loan at the Stedelijk Museum, Amsterdam, 1931–73; ownership transferred to the Vincent van Gogh Foundation, 1962; placed on permanent loan at the Van Gogh Museum, Amsterdam, 1973.

Selected exhibitions: Paris 1902 (no. 29 on Johanna's list of loans); Amsterdam 1905, no. 390; Cologne–Frankfurt 1910; Berlin 1910, no. 72; Utrecht 1923, no. 47; Rotterdam 1923; Basel 1924, no. 97; Zürich 1924, no. 97; Stuttgart 1924, no. 16; The Hague 1925, no. 70; Berlin 1927–28, no. 68; London–Birmingham–Glasgow 1947–48, no. 149; New York–Chicago 1949–50, no. 104; London 1962, no. 55; London 1968–69, no. 130; Tokyo–Kyōto–Nagoya 1976–77, no. 66; Toronto–Amsterdam 1981, no. 20; New York 1984, no. 85; Otterlo 1990, no. 206; Kyōto–Tokyo 1992, no. 21.

Summary of the literature: Beginning with De la Faille (1928, no. 1457), scholars have always associated this garden drawing with "the one with the sunflowers" Vincent mentioned having sent to Theo in his letter of August 8, 1888 [519], and have dated it accordingly. Pickvance (in Otterlo 1990, p. 236) surmised that both vertical garden drawings mentioned in the letter were made about August 5 or 6, unlike the horizontal garden design sent with them, which he believed was an earlier work, done about July 19. For early history, see Feilchenfeldt and Veenenbos 1988, p. 133.

Vincent told Theo that his drawing "with the sunflowers" represented the "garden of a bathing establishment" [519]. It therefore seems likely that the water bucket standing in the foreground of the picture, bearing the artist's signature, alludes to activities within the buildings in the background. The little cat seated in the pathway contributes another anecdotal element to this unusually whimsical tableau. More still life than landscape, the scene presents at center a massive, riotous bouquet, stubbornly rooted in its flower bed.

The mood of the artist at this moment may be guessed from the nature of his subject and the lighthearted mode of description—a jumble of loops, pinwheels, and hearts. "Oh, that beautiful midsummer sun here," Van Gogh exclaimed to Bernard less than two weeks later, as he voiced plans for an entirely new campaign, probably fueled in the heat of this very garden. "I am thinking of decorating my studio with half a dozen pictures of 'Sunflowers,' a decoration in which . . . yellows will blaze forth" [B15].

CI

Letter to Theo van Gogh, August 8, 1888 [519]: I have just sent off three large drawings. . . . The one with the sunflowers is a little garden of a bathing establishment. . . . Under the blue sky the orange, yellow, red splashes of the flowers take on an amazing brilliance, and in the limpid air there is something or other happier, more lovely than in the North.

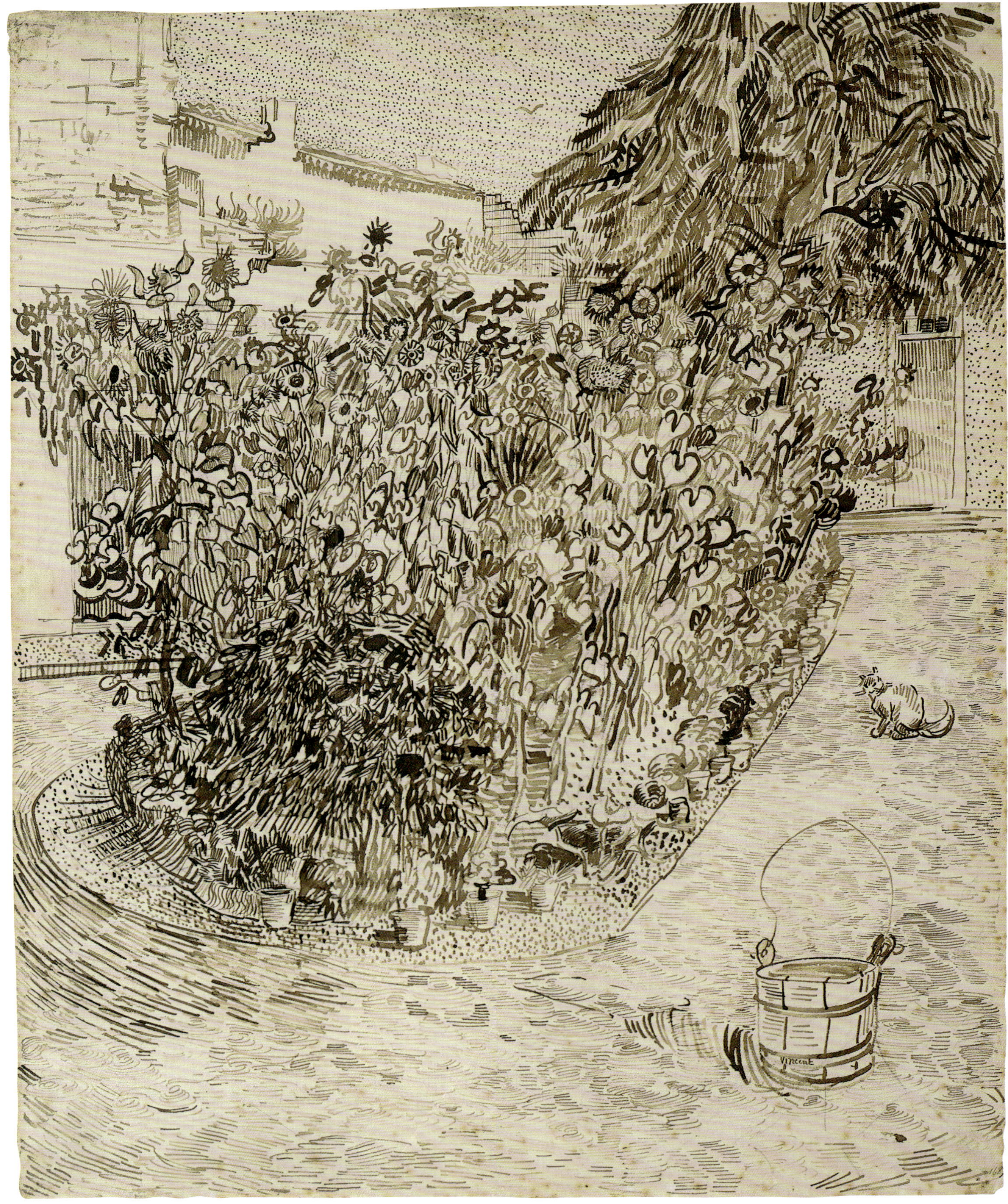

93. *The Road to Tarascon*

(for John Russell)

ca. July 31–August 3, 1888
Reed pen, pen, and ink, over graphite on wove paper
23.2 x 31.9 cm (9⅛ x 12½ in.)
Signed, lower right: *Vincent*
Solomon R. Guggenheim Museum, New York, Thannhauser Collection, Gift, Justin K. Thannhauser, 1978 (78.2514.22)
F1502a, JH1531
Letters 516, 517

Provenance: Sent by the artist to John Russell (d. 1930), Belle-Île, Brittany, ca. August 3, 1888 [517], until his death; to his daughter, Jeanne Jouve, Paris, probably 1930–31; sold to Justin K. Thannhauser, Paris, probably 1938–39; his bequest to the Guggenheim Museum, 1978.

Exhibition: New York 1984, no. 78.

Summary of the literature: First published in Thannhauser 1938 as one of three "unknown" drawings of the dozen that Van Gogh sent to John Russell in 1888, this drawing was added to the revised editions of De la Faille (1970/1992, no. 1502a), where it was dated August 1888; compared to F448, F1502, F1518; and associated with the Russell campaign [517]. Though consistently ascribed to this series of drawings by other scholars (e.g., Roskill 1971, p. 171), the parentage of the motif has been questioned. Barnett (1978, no. 22, p. 78) observed its close resemblance to the oil F448 in the "general disposition of road, trees, and field" and its notable substitution of the figure for a blazing sun and suggested that the differences may stem from Van Gogh's having continued to work on the canvas, between August 3 and 14, after he sent the drawing to Russell. Hulsker (1980, no. 1531) accepted it as a drawing based on painting F448, albeit "without the figure." Pickvance (in New York 1984, no. 78) argued that that the "radical change in format" and "many differences in composition" suggest it is after a lost painting, a view he restated unequivocally in Otterlo 1990 (p. 252).

In the spring of 1888 Van Gogh devoted several drawings to this tree-lined stretch of road, including one with a strolling figure (F1502, cat. 45) that anticipates the motif of a July painting (F448, fig. 173) in which the artist depicted himself "laden with boxes, props and canvas on the sunny road to Tarascon" [524]. Van Gogh appropriated the basic compositional scheme of the painting for the present drawing, but he adjusted it to the rectangular format of his sheet of paper, eliminated his effigy, and then freely improvised. Neither the prominent sun, encircled with striated lines that are echoed in the modeling of the tree trunks, nor the incidental additions to the background, such as the screen of cypresses, affects the integrity of the fundamental conception. He retained his tripartite division of vertical and horizontal space, the use of pillarlike trees to frame the vista, and even the triangular wedges of fields. In the drawing, each area becomes an arena for the inventive play of line.

Before Van Gogh set his pen to paper, he roughed out the composition in graphite (see infrared reflectogram, fig. 254). The sketch shows that he grafted the main zones of landscape from canvas to paper, including one that would be overtaken by cypresses, and that the sun was integral from the start, though he had considered its being smaller and placed leftward and lower in the sky; in addition, he shifted his initial placement of the trees (halfheartedly erasing his first go at the sapling at right), undoubtedly to open up the composition to use more of the sheet, if not also to accommodate a dominant sun. No less revealing, given his cursory sketch, is the extent to which the improvisatory nature of the drawing was determined from the outset.

See "*Répétitions*: Drawings after Paintings."

SAS

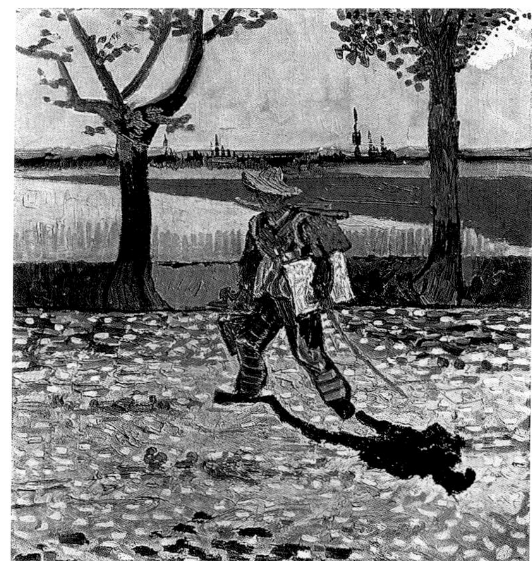

Fig. 173. *The Artist on the Road to Tarascon* (F448), July 1888. Oil on canvas, 48 x 44 cm (18⅞ x 17⅜ in.). Formerly Kaiser Friedrich Museum, Magdeburg (destroyed during World War II)

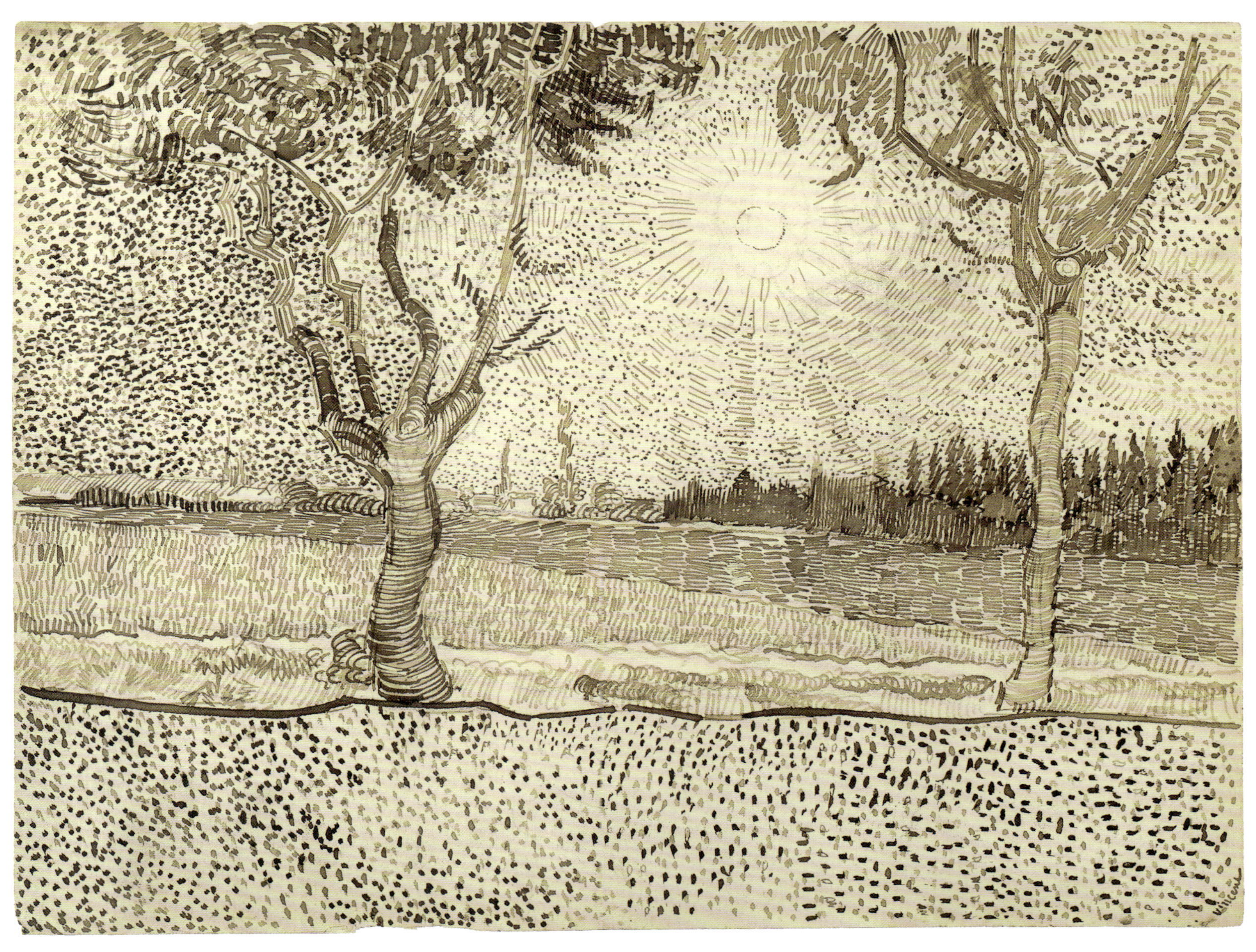

94. *Public Garden in the Place Lamartine; Park with Fence*

Mid-August 1888
Reed pen, pen, and ink over graphite on wove paper
31.9 x 24.4 cm (12½ x 9⅝ in.)
Inscribed on verso, in another hand: *185*
Van Gogh Museum, Amsterdam (Vincent van Gogh Foundation) (d 346 V/1962)
F1477, JH1411

Provenance: Sent by the artist at an unrecorded date to Theo van Gogh (d. 1891), Paris; by inheritance to his son, Vincent Willem van Gogh (1890–1978), as part of his collection, administered by his widow, Johanna van Gogh-Bonger (d. 1925), 1891; placed on loan at the Stedelijk Museum, Amsterdam, 1931–73; ownership transferred to the Vincent van Gogh Foundation, 1962; placed on permanent loan at the Van Gogh Museum, Amsterdam, 1973.

Selected exhibitions: Leiden 1893; Paris 1902 (no. 21 on Johanna's list of loans); Amsterdam 1905, no. 402; Cologne–Frankfurt 1910; Utrecht 1923, no. 53; Rotterdam 1923; Berlin 1927–28, no. 76; London–Birmingham–Glasgow 1947–48, no. 153; London 1968–69, no. 135; New York 1984, no. 106; Otterlo 1990, no. 173.

Summary of the literature: Although Roskill (1971, p. 166) and Hulsker (1980/1996, no. 1411) associated this drawing with Van Gogh's pen-and-ink views of the Place Lamartine gardens made in late April or early May 1888, most scholars have dated the work to August or September. De la Faille's catalogue raisonné (1928, no. 1477) initially gave no date for the work, but in revised editions (1970/1992, no. 1477) "19 September or shortly thereafter" was suggested. More convincingly, Millard (1974, p. 161) suggested a date of mid-August, generally agreed to by Pickvance (in New York 1984, no. 106; in Otterlo 1990, no. 173), who pointed out that the style of the drawing "continues the more deliberate and stylized treatment that can be seen in the drawings after paintings done for Theo [between ca. August 5 and 8]." For early history, see Feilchenfeldt and Veenenbos 1988, p. 134.

This view of the fence and trees bordering the Place Lamartine is close in size and style to drawings of a grassy corner of the park that Van Gogh sent to John Russell and Theo in early August (F1449, cat. 89; F1451, cat. 90). But, since it is not mentioned specifically in any of the artist's letters and appears unrelated to any one painting, it stands as a distinctive coda to the artist's last flurry of drawing activity. With the waning of summer Van Gogh turned his attention to painting "pictures of the gardens opposite the [Yellow] house . . . ordinary plane trees, pines in stiff clumps, a weeping tree, and the green grass" [539]. CI

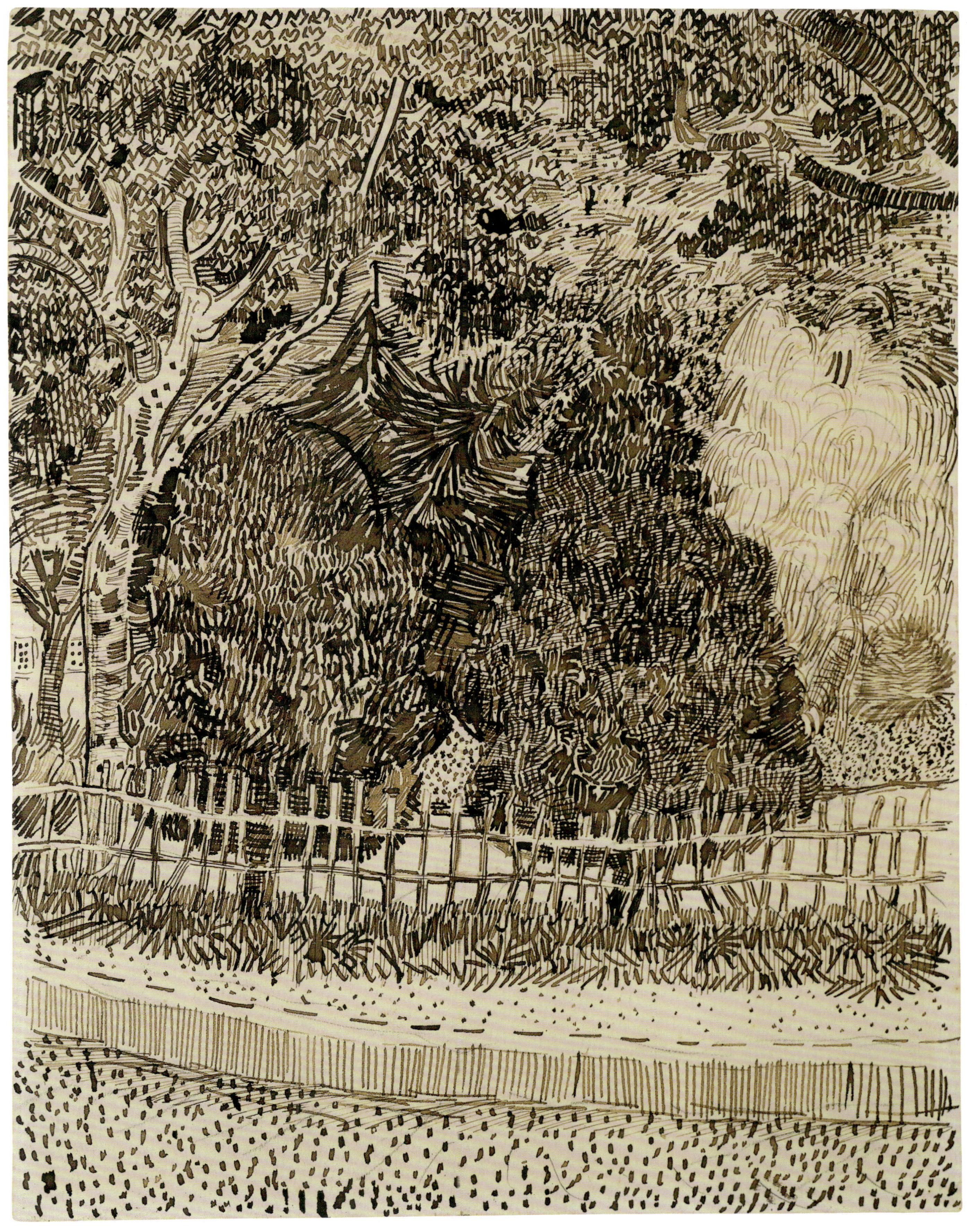

Répétitions: Drawings after Paintings

On the heels of his triumphant Montmajour series, Van Gogh undertook another drawing campaign. He was inspired to take stock of his recent canvases and to rely on sheets of paper as a forum for reconsideration and dialogue. Over a three-week period between mid-July and early August 1888, Van Gogh made thirty-two drawings after his paintings, which he sent to two artist friends, Émile Bernard and John Russell, and to his brother Theo. The activity of making these *répétitions* was fueled along the way by the fresh impetus that Van Gogh found for producing the successive suites of drawings. He selected each set of images with the recipient and a set agenda in mind: to elicit an exchange from Bernard, to win over the recalcitrant Russell as a prospective patron for Gauguin, and to report his progress to Theo.

Yet, beyond the practical reasons that Van Gogh gave for continuing on this tack—or the purposefulness he gave to what otherwise might have been considered a self-indulgent dalliance—there were, as one can glean between the lines of his letters or the linear invention of the works themselves, real gains to be had in revisiting, reassessing, and reinvigorating painted motifs in graphic form. The news that Gauguin would join him in Arles was a primary catalyst. Knowing that his friend would soon cast his eyes, if not look askance, on his artistic endeavors, Van Gogh was quite naturally prompted to reconsider aspects of his work that might be lacking, perhaps even out of step with current thinking. He had not, as he confessed, always been master of his brush; the elements—nature, if not his own—had militated against technical finesse. And yet, this had not previously been of much concern. He made no apologies to Bernard that April that his "brush stroke has no system at all." To the contrary, he touted the result as "a godsend to those people who have fixed preconceived ideas about technique." And while he may have toyed with the idea of working "at home and extempore" and even conceded that there might be something to be said for working from the "imagination" in order to create works of a "more exalting and consoling nature," he had not really ventured in Arles to follow the Synthetist aesthetic as it was defined in Pont-Aven in 1888 or, for that matter, the directives of other Parisian friends with their "preconceived ideas about technique," such as Seurat [B3]. But learning of Gauguin's impending visit, he made a hapless attempt at a biblically inspired "abstraction" and shortly after was compelled to reconsider his recent work in the quiet of his studio relying on his pen to explore the virtues of a more conscientious and creative approach. In the process, as we witness in the increasingly stylized and improvisatory reinterpretation of motifs, Van Gogh allowed himself to indulge in a more abstract mode of expression that closely paralleled the artful manipulations of his friends.

Gauguin, Bernard, and their cohorts in Pont-Aven championed artworks that were a synthesis between impressions of nature and abstract form. Their practice depended on the firsthand study of nature but insisted, in order to distill the essence of things observed, on composing works in the studio, where, free from the distractions and incidental details of sensate impressions, memory and imagination would play a guiding role. Did Van Gogh, intrigued if wary of the merits of such an approach, turn to sheets of paper as a pragmatic vehicle for like-minded experiments? Conveniently he had the raw material in some thirty plein air studies to serve as the basis for pen-and-ink improvisations, and he ensured the creative potential for linear invention by depending on only a summary graphite sketch. Adopting virtually the same method as his Pont-Aven friends and cognizant of their fascination with the abstract properties of line [B4], Van Gogh in his progressive suites of drawings ultimately arrived at remarkably similar ends, especially considering the premium Synthetist aesthetic placed on the harmonious integration of the whole, surface rhythms, patterns created by repetition of form, arabesques, and undulating line.

No less intriguing is the relationship between Van Gogh's *répétitions* and the investigations of his Neo-Impressionist colleagues. He had enjoyed close relationships with Signac and Pissarro at precisely the time they were experimenting with dotted drawings as an innovative vehicle for magazine illustration. No doubt he had seen, for example, Signac's *Passage du Puits-Bertin, Clichy* (fig. 174) published in *La vie moderne* of February 12, 1887. The following spring Seurat flirted with Pointillist pen work to depict the central nude in his celebrated canvas *Les poseuses* for an April 15, 1888, piece in the same magazine (fig. 175). His elegant confection of dots and lines joined stippled landscape drawings by Signac and Dubois-Pillet, which were also predicated on recent paintings, as their captions—"d'après son tableau"—made clear. These provocative pen-and-ink images, featured in a magazine that Van Gogh had followed for several years and that Theo routinely sent him, may well have reached Arles at a providential time.[1]

Nonpartisan in his friendships and in his artistic borrowings, Van Gogh exploited dotting in his own *répétitions* and to an ever increasing extent, apparently disregarding the fact that neither Bernard nor Russell—who mocked the "darn fools spotting canvas with points of pure colour" as being as "fashionable as gull's wings for hats"[2]—was a fan of Pointillism. Van Gogh seemed to gravitate to this stylistic vehicle as a way of meeting the essential task at hand: making *répétitions* presented him with the challenge of translating the bold color and loaded brushwork of his canvases into black and white. His search for an evocative graphic equivalent may have led him to adopt the method of "modeling with dots," the virtues of which were extolled in Charles Blanc's *Grammaire des arts du dessin* (1867), a treatise Van Gogh knew as intimately as Seurat, who had faithfully transcribed the passages on "pointillism." Blanc advised that "Pointillism is perfectly suitable when it is a question of reproducing a heavy, suave, and well-loaded brush like Correggio's" and, tracing its use by engravers since the Renaissance, noted that a "Paduan artist had interpreted in this technique the generous and savory paintings of Giorgione," adding "this procedure admirably suits the interpretation of light and

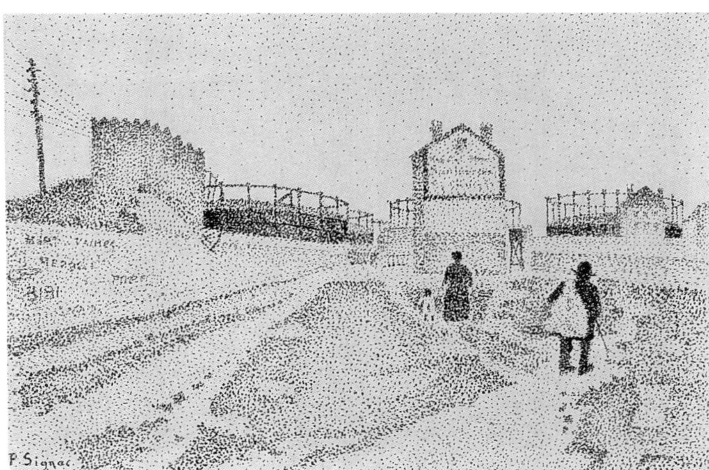

Fig. 174. Paul Signac, *Passage du Puits-Bertin, Clichy*, 1886 or 1887. Ink and graphite on paper, 16.3 x 24.8 cm (6⅜ x 9¾ in.), image framed in graphite 12.4 x 18.3 cm (4⅞ x 7¼ in.). Musée du Louvre, Département des Arts Graphiques, Fonds du Musée d'Orsay, Paris, Gift of Françoise Cachin in memory of her mother, Ginette Signac, 1996 (photo: RMN—M. Bellot)

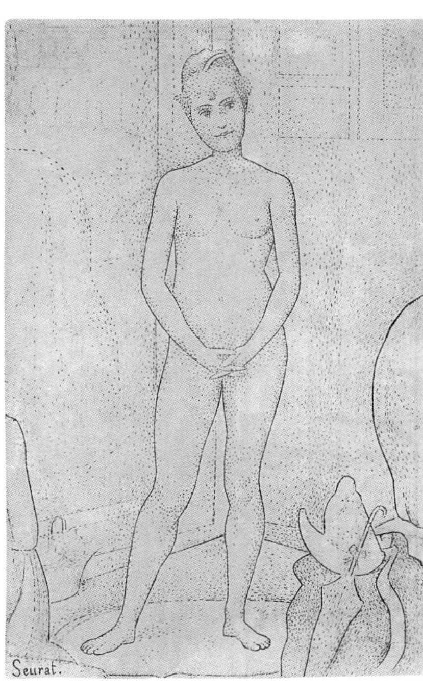

Fig. 175. Georges Seurat, *Poseuse debout (Model Standing)*, 1888. Pen and ink over graphite on wove paper, 26.4 x 16.1 cm (10⅜ x 6¼ in.). National Gallery of Art, Washington, The Armand Hammer Collection

color of a Giorgione."[3] And no less admirably a Van Gogh, as his *répétitions* suggest.

On each occasion that Van Gogh revisited a motif on one of the thirty-two sheets, he took the opportunity to make some improvement to his original conception or to interject something new. All of the sheets manifest compositional changes, ranging from subtle tweaks in placement to completely upending a motif, as we see quite literally, for example, in his rethinking of a horizontal garden in vertical format (F1449, cat. 89). With each successive series, as is particularly evident in the triplicate versions of two motifs—*Boats at Sea, Saintes-Maries-de-la-Mer* (F1430, cat. 57; 1430a, cat. 58; 1430b, cat. 59) and *Arles: View from the Wheat Fields* (F1491, cat. 70; F1490, cat. 71; F1492, cat. 72)—Van Gogh further indulged the spirit of invention. Not only did he engage line in an increasingly nonreferential fashion, but he did not always feel compelled to depend too closely on the painted motif. Witness three drawings he made for Russell: *La Mousmé* (F1503, cat. 80), *A Corner of a Garden in the Place Lamartine* (F1449, cat. 89), and *The Road to Tarascon* (F1502a, cat. 93). Though scholars have accepted the spirited half-length portrait drawing as a deft shorthand take on his labored full-length oil, they have been reluctant to accept the two landscapes as variants on known prototypes because of the seemingly "too radical" changes introduced to format and design. Here one may argue that the impulse toward reorchestrating or redesigning compositions was an extension or even a natural outgrowth of the tendency toward improvisation.

These three motifs that Van Gogh chose to reinvent in graphic form may have suggested themselves in light of the challenges each presented to him. For example, he had not painted both a full-length and a bust-length version of *La Mousmé* as he had for the *Zouave* and *Roulin,* and in the event, his adroit head-and-shoulders drawing sufficed admirably for a second take on the portrait, without the difficulties he had confronted when tackling the figure in full (betrayed in his sketch of the entire seated figure, F1504). In his pen-and-ink rendition of *The Road to Tarascon,* he did not draw himself "laden with boxes, props and canvas" [524] as in the painted motif. His introduction of the sun as the main protagonist in the drawing may have been dictated as much by previous struggles (for example, in rendering the walker in his related spring drawing, F1502, cat. 45) as by new concerns. The dominant sun in this work and Van Gogh's exploration of the abstract quality of cast shadow in his upright garden seem prescient of his evolving interest in representing time of day. Whereas Van Gogh, in describing a wheat field in mid-June, was happy to leave the question of whether it represented a "Setting sun? Rising Moon?" [B7] playfully unresolved, as summer gave way to early fall, he was bent on capturing the particular effects of daytime and nighttime, indoors and out, under gaslight and under star-filled skies. His improvisatory approach to the garden in relation to its format anticipates the trio of large-scale garden drawings, in contrasting formats—two vertical, one horizontal—that capped the consignment of drawings he sent to Theo the following week (F1455, fig. 163; F1456, cat. 91; F1457, cat. 92). In these drawings, the spirit of invention ultimately prevailed. No longer satisfied with reinterpretation of already realized motifs on a small scale, he created large-scale original drawings in a similar stylistic vein.

Repetition was fundamental to Van Gogh's working practice, as it was for so many artists from Ingres to Monet, whether for the insights and improvements that came from these "lazy labors" (as Ingres termed his indulgence in favorite themes) or to fuel the marketplace's demand for signature pieces. In this drawing campaign, Van Gogh exploited old strategies with his newfound facility as a draftsman. By mid-July, having set aside his perspective frame in Saintes-Maries and having drawn with great bravura and confidence without it at Montmajour, he had succeeded in realizing his often expressed wish of being able to "draw as easily as writing" [see, e.g., 232, 449]. In the process of undertaking a drawing campaign devoted to translating painted motifs in a graphic form, he also invented a whole new vocabulary to go with his "writing tool."

If Van Gogh began this campaign of *répétitions* largely to coax Bernard to send him comparable works, he seems to have recognized the creative potential the process offered and flexed the possibilities of line to the fullest. He engaged his brush in a similar fashion a year later. During his yearlong confinement at the asylum in Saint-Rémy, Van Gogh made some thirty oil copies after works by other artists because, as he explained, it satisfied various aims, from enhancing his repertoire of motifs to offering him consolation and pleasure. He considered his copies "translations" or "improvisations," likening them to a musician's interpretation of Beethoven. "I let the black and white by Delacroix or Millet or something made after their work pose for me as a subject. And then I improvise color," keeping in mind their pictures, and the "vague consonance of colors which are least right in feeling" [607]. This was much the same approach that he had explored in the summer of 1888—only the models and the manner of improvisation (line versus color) were different. His later candor offers illuminating insights into the earlier campaign.

SAS

1. On this subject, see Françoise Cachin's observations in Paris–New York 1991–92, no. 192, p. 294, and Stein 2001.
2. Letter from John Russell to Tom Roberts, October 5, 1887, quoted in Galbally 1977, p. 90.
3. Blanc's treatise is quoted in the context of passages transcribed by Seurat, under Appendix G, in Paris–New York 1991–92, p. 384.

Drawings after Paintings Sent to Bernard

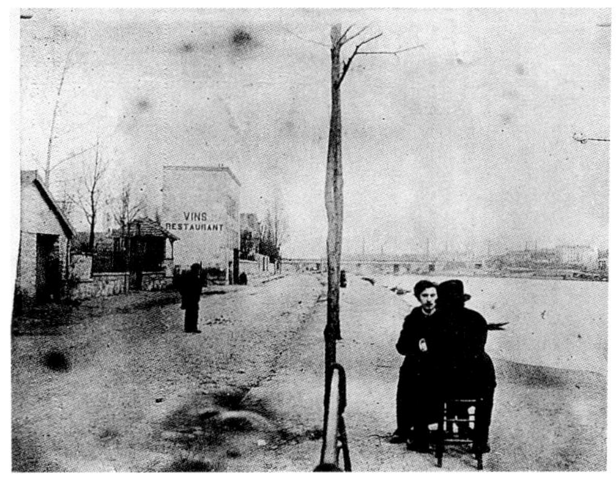

Fig. 176. Photograph of Vincent van Gogh and Émile Bernard at Asnières, 1886. Van Gogh Museum, Amsterdam (Vincent van Gogh Foundation)

In letters dated to mid-July 1888, Van Gogh recorded that he sent fifteen drawings after paintings to Émile Bernard: six on July 15, 1888 [B10, 511] (F1450, fig. 177; and see F1471, fig. 178; F1430, fig. 179; F1435, fig. 180; F1444, fig. 181; F1507, fig. 182), and another nine between July 17 and 20, 1888 [B11] (see F1482, fig. 183; F1485, fig. 184; F1426, fig. 185; F1481, fig. 186; F1491, fig. 187; F1488, fig. 188; F1442, fig. 189; F1514, fig. 190; F1554, fig. 191).

Summary of the literature: None of the drawings catalogued in De la Faille 1928/1970/1992 list Bernard as a former owner and no mention is made of this distinctive group of fifteen. Essentially starting from scratch, Roskill (1971, pp. 152–56) reconstructed the campaign, distinguishing this group of drawings from those identical in scale and similar in subject and technique that had been documented as having belonged to Russell or to Theo. Roskill's discerning study succeeded in establishing fourteen candidates, thirteen of which are now accepted as constituting the Bernard group. Hulsker (1980, p. 340), acknowledging his "almost complete agreement" with the drawings identified by Roskill, provided a partial list of the group, keying ten drawings to the painted studies on which they were based (F1426, F1430, F1435, F1442, F1444, F1450, F1481, F1488, F1491, F1554); he dated the campaign to July 22–24, 1888. These ten, along with the three not listed by Hulsker (F1482, F1485, F1507), were described by Pickvance (in New York 1984, pp. 124–25 and nos. 62–72) as among the group of fifteen drawings Van Gogh sent to Bernard between July 15 and 17, 1888. Pickvance added to the core group established by Roskill one drawing that "hitherto" was thought to have been sent to Theo, namely F1514 (New York 1984, no. 69), but subtracted a figure drawing (F1504), which he proposed was sent to Bernard at a later date (along with F1723; see ibid., nos. 91, 90). Pickvance did not acknowledge that documentation existed (courtesy of Roskill's reasoned proposals) to support the identifications that he presented as unequivocal fact; he skirted the fundamental issue of how we know these drawings were sent to Bernard by simply stating that they were.

Pickvance refined the assignments and dating of the campaign—to mid-July—while contributing the benefit of his insights on the nature of particular works and the dispatches in general. In turn, Hulsker (1996, pp. 334–36) revised his dating and extended credit for the identification of these works to "research by Mark Roskill and other scholars" (but unfortunately he dropped his helpful citation to Roskill 1971). Hulsker did not weigh in on the recasting of the group by Pickvance (who excluded one and added one, bringing the tally again to fourteen), instead republishing the same partial list of ten drawings. In the present study, fifteen are accounted for and documentation is furnished to support the idea that *The Langlois Bridge* (F1471) must also belong to the group of drawings after paintings Van Gogh sent to Bernard.

Recent scholarship has added little to the sketchy provenance of these works provided in De la Faille; the subject has not attracted much interest since 1971, when Roskill recognized the lack of early documentation as a distinguishing feature of the Bernard-owned drawings. A few observations can be made. By 1892, Bernard relinquished one drawing, *A Corner of a Garden in the Place Lamartine* (F1450), for it was acquired that year either from the exhibition held at Le Barc de Boutteville or from Julien Tanguy in Paris by the Danish artist Johan Rohde. Between 1899 and 1904 Bernard disposed of a large number of Van Gogh drawings through the Parisian dealer Ambroise Vollard. The dealer, whose shrewdness is as legendary as his opaque record keeping, seems to have paid the meager sum of 50 francs for each of the some twenty unnamed drawings he purchased from Bernard or from Bernard's mother.[1] The vast majority were sold in November 1904, a month after Bernard privately sold three drawings (F1430, F1485, F1488, for 100 marks apiece) to Hugo von Tschudi, director of the Nationalgalerie Berlin, who donated them anonymously to the Nationalgalerie in 1906.[2] The subsequent history of individual drawings may be found in the catalogue entries; and other observations may be found in "The Paper Trail: From Portfolios to Posterity."

Van Gogh befriended the precocious artist Émile Bernard (1868–1941) during his sojourn in Paris in 1886–87. Their relationship, cemented by such activities as outings painting in Asnières or studying Japanese prints at the shop of Siegfried Bing, was extended by the lively correspondence they maintained after Bernard left for Brittany and Van Gogh for Provence. The exchange of ideas gave way to the exchange of artworks, with Bernard playing the initiating role: in April and in late June 1888, he sent Van Gogh a group of pen-and-ink sketches. Then, after receiving fifteen drawings from Van Gogh in mid-July, Bernard promptly responded with ten more sketches, then another nineteen, including a dozen brothel studies, early that fall.[3] Van Gogh's reaction to Bernard's drawings was mixed, and Bernard's reaction, in the absence of letters from his side, is not entirely clear. Yet, in this regard, perhaps Bernard's actions speak louder than words: not only did he make an album of Van Gogh's drawings to show to Gauguin and other colleagues in Pont-Aven, but he later ensured that they would become known and appreciated by a wider audience by exhibiting and publishing several in the early 1890s.

For all their charms, Bernard's unassuming little sketches were something of a disappointment to Van Gogh because of what they may have lacked not in artistic but in documentary value. Van Gogh, in sending Bernard a suite of drawings based on his recent paintings, hoped to receive in return similar (reproductive) drawings that he could forward to Theo in order to encourage him to buy one of Bernard's oils for their collection. Van Gogh's letters make his intentions clear. The first half-dozen drawings that he sent to Bernard on July 15 came with the following request: "Let me know whether you will consent to make some sketches after your Breton studies for me." As added inducement, Van Gogh also promised to send "at

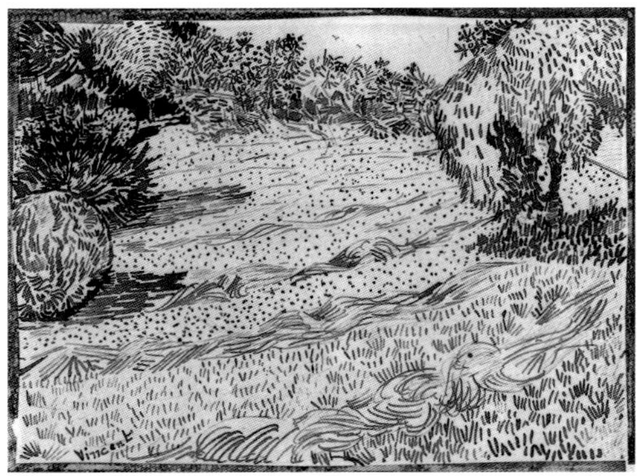

Fig. 177. *A Corner of a Garden in the Place Lamartine* (F1450, cat. 88)

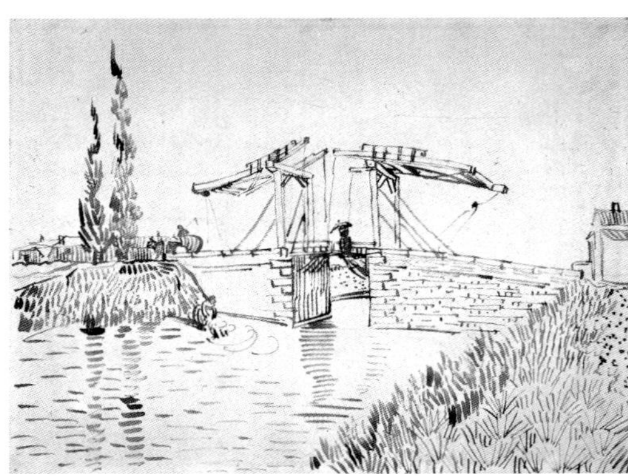

Fig. 178. *The Langlois Bridge* (F1471, cat. 87)

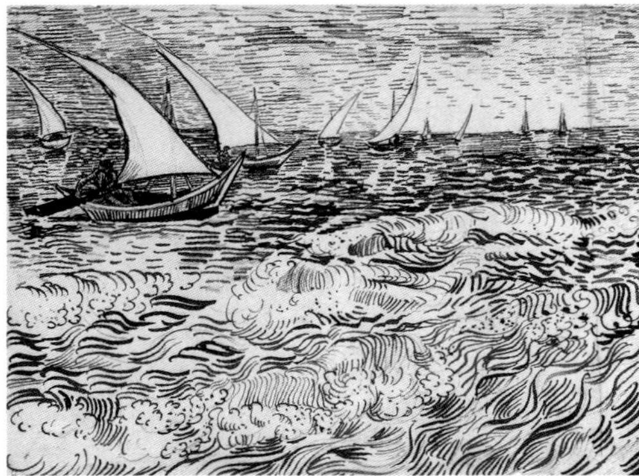

Fig. 179. *Boats at Sea, Saintes-Maries-de-la-Mer* (F1430, cat. 57)

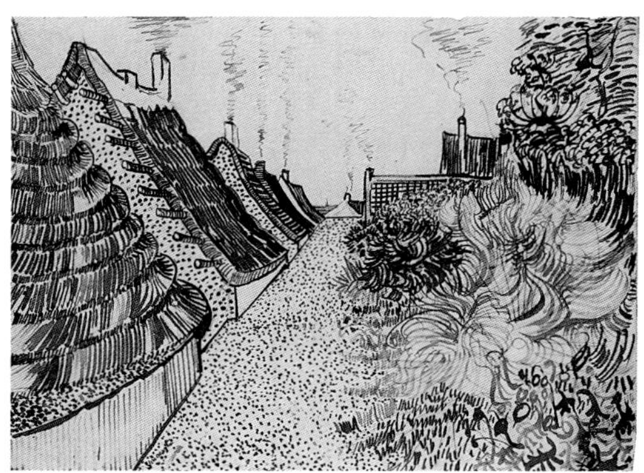

Fig. 180. *Street in Saintes-Maries-de-la-Mer* (F1435, cat. 53)

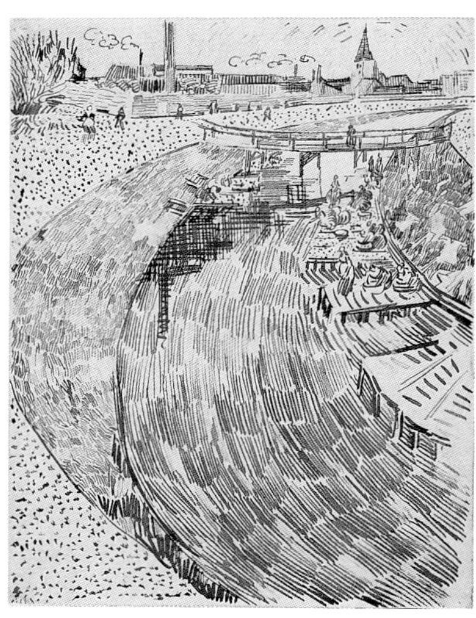

Fig. 181. *La Roubine du Roi with Washerwomen* (F1444), mid-July 1888. Reed pen and ink over graphite on wove paper, 31.5 x 24 cm (12³⁄₈ x 9¹⁄₂ in.). Kröller-Müller Museum, Otterlo

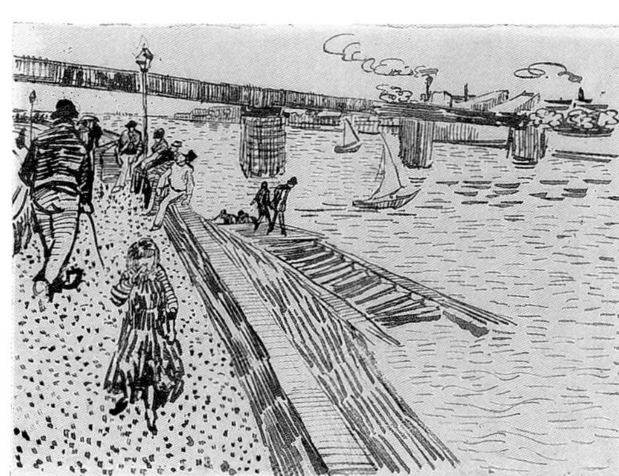

Fig. 182. *The Trinquetaille Bridge* (F1507), mid-July 1888. Reed pen and ink over graphite on wove paper, 24.3 x 31.6 cm (9⁵⁄₈ x 12¹⁄₂ in.). Private collection

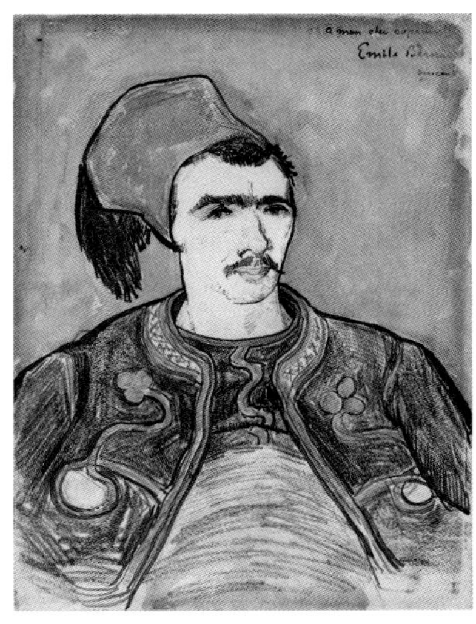

Fig. 183. *The Zouave* (F1482, cat. 77)

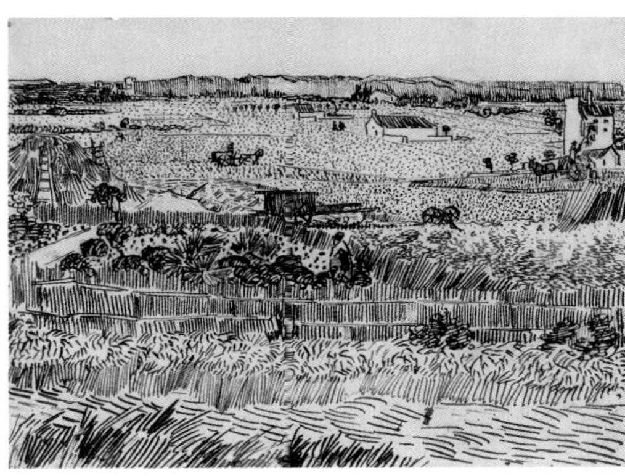

Fig. 184. *Harvest in Provence* (F1485, cat. 64)

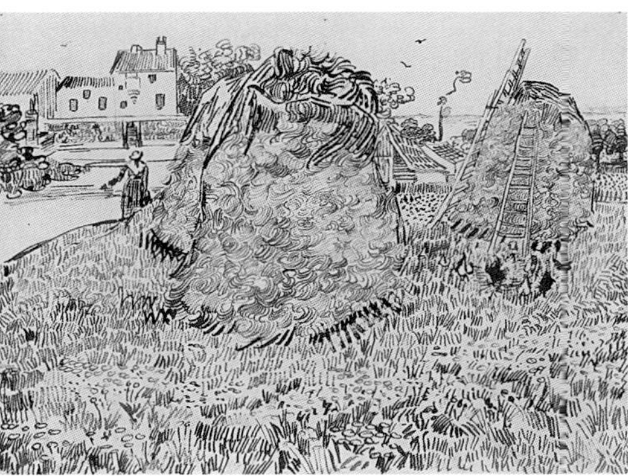

Fig. 185. *Haystacks* (F1426), ca. July 15, 1888. Reed pen and ink, 24 x 31.5 cm (9½ x 12⅜ in.). Szépművészeti Múzeum, Budapest (photo: András Rázsó)

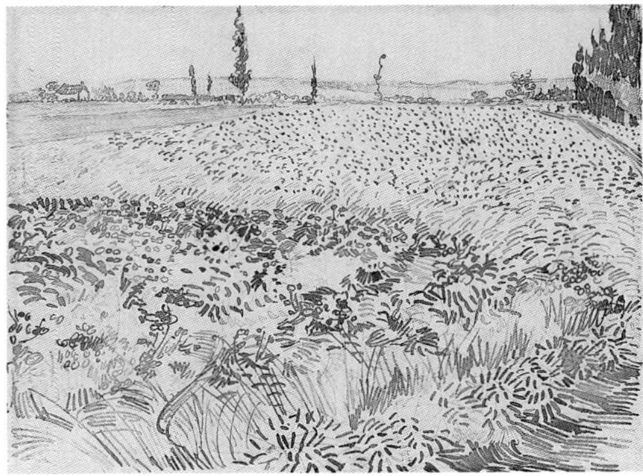

Fig. 186. *Wheat Field* (F1481), mid-July 1888. Reed pen and pen and ink over graphite, 24.1 x 31.7 cm (9½ x 12½ in.). The Metropolitan Museum of Art, New York, Gift of Mrs. Max J. H. Rossbach, 1964 (64.125.3)

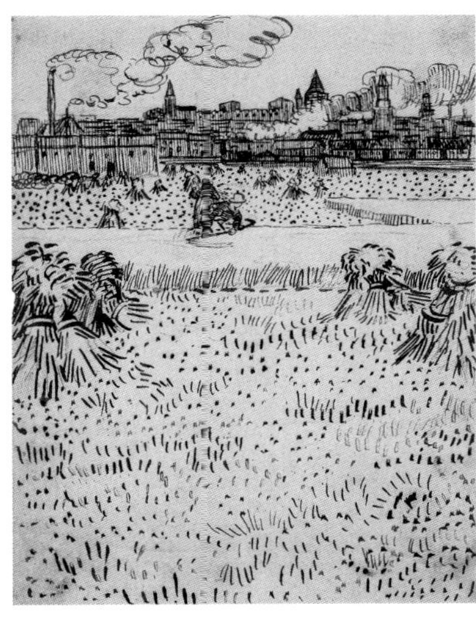

Fig 187. *Arles: View from the Wheat Fields* (F1491, cat. 70)

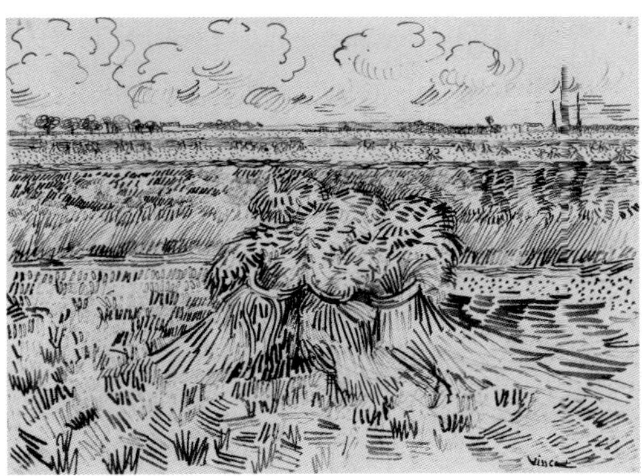

Fig. 188. *Wheat Field with Sheaves* (F1488, cat. 73)

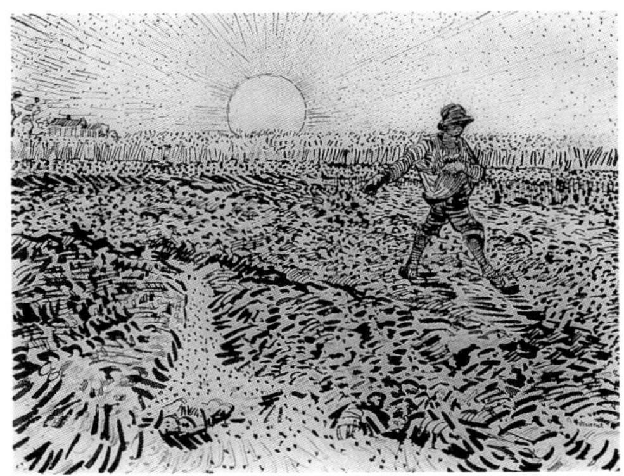

Fig. 189. *The Sower* (F1442), mid-July 1888. Reed pen and ink over graphite on wove paper, 24.5 x 31.7 cm (9⅝ x 12½ in.). Private collection

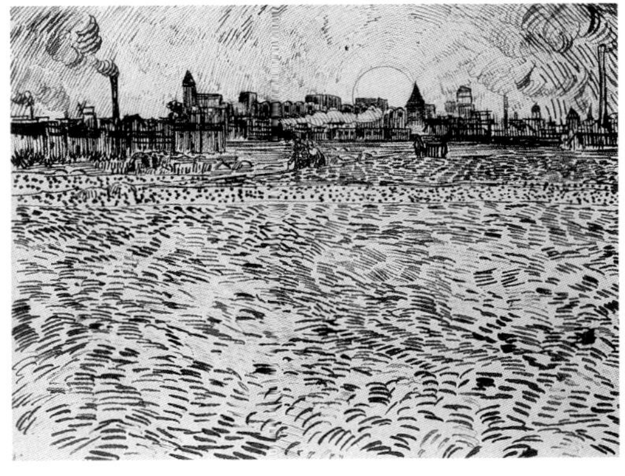

Fig. 190. *A Summer Evening* (F1514, cat. 68)

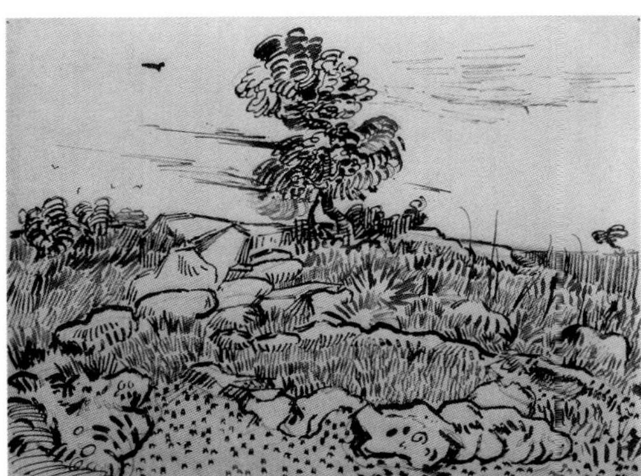

Fig. 191. *Rocks with Tree* (F1554), mid-July 1888. Reed pen and ink over graphite on wove paper, 24 x 31 cm (9½ x 12¼ in.). Private collection

least half a dozen new subjects for you, pen-and-ink sketches" [B10]; a few days later, he sent nine [B11]. The following week Bernard reciprocated with ten pen-and-ink drawings, but these incidental sketches gave little sense of his more serious efforts as a painter. Van Gogh sent them on to Theo anyway, despite Bernard's express wishes to the contrary.

Van Gogh, in undertaking this drawing campaign for Bernard, put his pen to the task of giving his friend an idea of his recent work, that is, a fuller idea than he had in the descriptions and marginal sketches he had already sent in letters. Van Gogh quite naturally continued to share those aspects of his work that he thought Bernard would most appreciate. With his recipient in mind, Van Gogh chose to reproduce about half of the canvases he had on hand.

The first group of six drawings seems to have required little introduction, for with the exception of "The Garden" (F1450, fig. 177), a recent motif that he specially highlighted [B10], Van Gogh provided none. Chances are he had already introduced three of the other subjects to Bernard in previous letters, namely, *The Langlois Bridge* (F1471, fig. 178), which he had sketched in its earliest conception in a letter of mid-March [B2], and the seascape and street scene from Saintes-Maries (F1430, fig. 179; F1435, fig. 180), illustrated in a letter of early June [B6] (cat. 52). Nor would it have been necessary to remark on two other drawings—views of the Rhône (F1444, fig. 181; F1507, fig. 182) close in spirit to those they had painted along the Seine in Paris.

For Bernard, many of the images in the second batch covered new ground. In these nine works, Van Gogh was keen to highlight that "you will see subjects taken from the sort of scenery that inspires 'father' Cézanne, for the Crau near Aix is pretty similar to the country surrounding Tarascon or the Crau here. . . . As I know how much you like Cézanne, I thought these sketches of Provence might please you; not that there is much resemblance between a drawing of mine and one by Cézanne" [B11]. The majority were based on Van Gogh's June Harvest series, and only two of the subjects (F1442, fig. 189; F1514, fig. 190) were featured in letter sketches made at the time [B7]. However, Bernard would have found another vaguely familiar, *Arles: View from the Wheat Fields* (F1491, fig. 187), since the motif had taken as its point of departure paintings known to him by Cézanne and Anquetin.

Van Gogh, who often gave thought to the presentation of his works—even those being shown informally to friends or family, as we witness in his enclosing gray mounting board with drawings sent to Van Rappard or his asking Theo to frame paintings in white for his sister's viewing benefit—seems to have provided each group of drawings he sent to Bernard with its own cover image. Presumably he recruited the watercolor of a Zouave inscribed to his "cher copain" (F1482, fig. 183) in this capacity, as has been suggested, not for the first but rather for the second consignment of drawings; here it served to introduce color to the equation and as a kind of recompense for never sending Bernard the painted portrait he had made a month earlier "in response to his sketch of a brothel" [B9]. For the first group of six drawings, Van Gogh designed a special front page. To his drawing *A Corner of a Garden* (F1450, fig. 177), he affixed a marbleized-paper border, giving the motif—which he had already singled out by mentioning it in his cover letter—the distinction of having a frame, albeit a makeshift one, apparently cobbled together from bits of book endpapers, portfolio, or wrapping paper.[4] Because the artist's pen strokes cross over from the drawing to the border in certain places, there can be no doubt that the border was part of Van Gogh's original conception. And because the motif so captured Van Gogh's imagination, the choice of paper is especially intriguing: did he intend to bring in the rich associations with Renaissance poets, primitive Italian painters, or tapestry designs, garnered by a motif he dubbed the "poet's garden"? Or did he wish to evoke association with Persian miniatures or with Japanese prints that had contrasting decorative borders of the type he had in his own collection? It is tantalizing to wonder whether Van Gogh was familiar with the vogue, which lasted from the sixteenth to the eighteenth century, for using marbleized papers in an *album amicorum*,[5] since he had essentially put together a kind of "friendship album" for Bernard. Whatever his reason, the idea seems to have had a certain appeal: Gauguin in his Volpini suite of 1889, undertaken at Theo's instigation, adapted not only the strategy of making graphic images to commend his painted endeavors, but used a marbleized frame around the motif Leda and the Swan, which served as the cover image for this series of zincographs.

SAS

1. The following purchases are recorded in Vollard's account books (Archives Vollard, Musée d'Orsay, Paris): from Mme Bernard, "five Van Gogh drawings," December 27, 1899; from Bernard, an unspecified number of "Van Gogh Gau[guin] drawings," April 5, 1900, for 1,000 francs (MS 421, 4.3); from Mme Bernard, "Van Gogh pen landscape, 24 x 31," for 50 francs (as no. 3450 in Register of Works acquired and sold between June 1904 and December 1907 [MS 421, 4.5]); from Bernard, "17 drawings by Van Gogh," November 1904 (MS 421, 4.10). I am grateful to Chris Stolwijk of the Van Gogh Museum for kindly making available to me his documentation from the Archives Vollard.
2. The transaction is recorded in correspondence of October 11 and 14, 1904, and the donation in the Central Archive of the Nationalgalerie, Berlin; for full documentation, see Paul 1993, pp. 388–89. Tschudi paid approximately two and a half times the price that Vollard paid per drawing (or roughly $25, as opposed to $10, equivalent to about $500 and $200 today).
3. As documented in letters B3, 480, B8, 502, B10, B12, 511, 514, B17, B18, B19, 545; see also Roskill 1971, p. 143. Bernard's drawings are preserved in the Van Gogh Museum, Amsterdam.
4. Though no sketchbook is known from the period Van Gogh worked in Arles, those he routinely used had marbled covers; see Van der Wolk 1987. The two from Saint-Rémy, which are no longer intact, contained sheets of the same size paper as the thirty-two *répétitions*, but the pattern of the extant blue-marbled covers (Van Gogh Museum, Amsterdam) is quite different.
5. See Richard J. Wolfe, *Marbled Paper: Its History, Techniques, and Patterns* (Philadelphia, 1990), p. 3 and pl. XXIII, nos. 10 and 11, illustrating similar "wide-comb" and "Dutch" pattern marbled papers.

Drawings after Paintings Sent to Russell

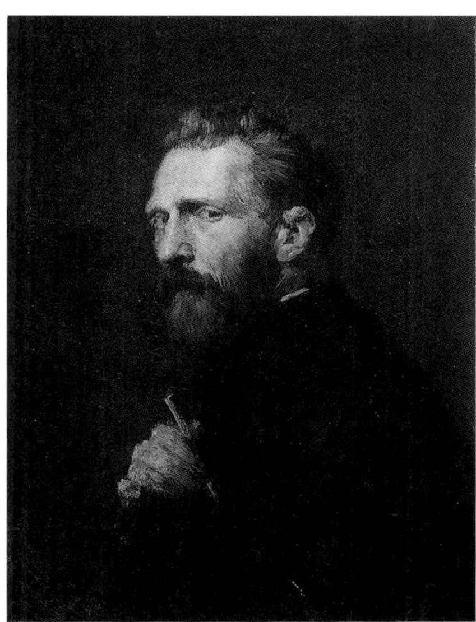

Fig. 192. John Russell, *Portrait of Vincent van Gogh*, 1886. Oil on canvas, 60 x 45 cm (23⅝ x 17¾ in.). Van Gogh Museum, Amsterdam (Vincent van Gogh Foundation)

Van Gogh's correspondence records that between July 31 and ca. August 3, 1888, he made and sent a dozen drawings after recent paintings to the Australian artist John Russell, in Belle-Île-en-Mer, Brittany [516, 517] (see F1430a, fig. 193; F1427, fig. 194; F1449, fig. 195; F1433, fig. 196; F1454, fig. 197; F1486, fig. 198; F1489, fig. 199; F1490, fig. 200; F1502a, fig. 201; F1482a, fig. 202; F1503, fig. 203; F1458, fig. 204).

Summary of the literature: Nine of the twelve drawings were catalogued in De la Faille 1928, but only one with Russell as a former owner (F1427). The provenance for these nine works and the three formerly "unknown" drawings is revealed in Thannhauser 1938. This article established that Russell gave one drawing (F1427) to the young Matisse, whom he had befriended during summer visits to Belle-Île in 1896 and 1897; and that Russell, insisting on anonymity and leaving the details to his son-in-law, sold eight drawings in 1920 at an auction (recorded in De la Faille) held at the Hôtel Drouot, Paris, March 31, 1920, as nos. 63–70 (respectively F1486, F1490, F1449, F1433, F1454, F1489, F1503, F1458).[1] The three other drawings, brought to light in Thannhauser 1938, Russell regarded as the "best" and kept until his death in 1930 (F1430a, F1482a, F1502a). They were inherited by his daughter, Jeanne Jouve, and acquired from her, along with a sketch of "a mudlark" (F1507a) and an illustrated letter [501a], probably in 1938–39 by Justin K. Thannhauser, who forty years later bequeathed them to the Guggenheim Museum (as recorded in Barnett 1978, pp. 64–81).

All twelve drawings are catalogued in De la Faille 1970 as having belonged to Russell but only some are redated to reflect this specific drawing campaign, which is briefly alluded to: a note appended to entry F1427 indicates that the dozen drawings listed "seem to fit the description in letter 517." (Though Thannhauser 1938 is consistently cited as a reference, the corresponding letter reference is not.) Roskill (1971, p. 171) noted that the execution and dispatch of these drawings are referred to in letters 516 and 517 and that the dozen drawings, which he listed, "have been firmly identified" in Thannhauser 1938. Roskill recognized the value of this study toward distinguishing the three sets of drawings, and he dated the Russell campaign to ca. July 31–August 3, 1888. Hulsker (1980, pp. 344–46; 1996, p. 344), noting that the drawings "can be identified with relative certainty because they were in Russell's possession and acquired from him by subsequent owners," muddled the provenance somewhat but clarified the Russell campaign in relation to the artist's letters [516, 517] and its chronology vis-à-vis the sets made for Bernard and Theo, and he provided a list of the twelve drawings keyed to the paintings on which they were based (in 1980 Hulsker dated the series to ca. August 1–6, 1888; in 1996, to ca. July 31–August 6, 1888). Pickvance (in New York 1984, pp. 125–26, and nos. 73–81), dating the campaign to July 31–August 3, 1888, succeeded in characterizing the dozen Russell drawings in terms of style, choice, and treatment of motifs, and he discussed nine works in full. He ignored the question of supporting documentation that confirmed Russell's ownership.

Relatively little is known about Van Gogh's relationship with the Australian artist John Russell (1858–1930), in part because Russell seems to have wanted it that way. Unlike Bernard, Gauguin, Signac, and others, Russell had no interest in confiding his reminiscences about Van Gogh to paper, even in a letter. Indeed, he kept all souvenirs of their friendship—a print, a painting, letters, a figure sketch, and the dozen drawings discussed below—a fairly well-kept secret, insisting on anonymity when he sold most of these works at auction in 1920. In fact, when the auction house requested proof of authenticity, an autograph letter was submitted with the proviso that Russell's name was crossed out in Van Gogh's salutation "Dear Russell" [501a] (F1840, cat. 75). Nor have scholars been particularly diligent in their efforts to flesh out the details: overlooked, for example, is Russell's ownership of Van Gogh's painting *Shoes* (F332) and lithograph *At Eternity's Gate* (F1662) though they were likely Van Gogh's half of an 1886–87 exchange that included Russell's well-known portrait of him (fig. 192).

No doubt the Australian and the Dutchman were among the only foreign students enrolled in Cormon's studio where they met in 1886–87, both newcomers to the Paris art scene. Van Gogh's command of English invited ready dialogue with this solid, well-heeled chap, who counted Claude Monet and Auguste Rodin as friends, patronized Émile Bernard and Armand Guillaumin, and, among other mutual admirations, shared Van Gogh's abiding interest in portraiture. Van Gogh respected Russell's efforts in this genre and found merit enough in one of his friend's unexceptional landscape studies to recall it, some three years later, in his Saint-Rémy *Blossoming Almond Branch* (F671).[2] Russell might well have directed Van Gogh to Arles; he put him in touch with the American painter Dodge MacKnight, who lived in nearby Fontvieille.

Van Gogh's Arles correspondence with Russell was as much an interchange of ideas, goings-on, and plans for future exchanges (which never materialized) as it was a dance that circled around Gauguin's dire straits and Van Gogh's sense of powerlessness to help him unless he could interest Russell in patronage. Van Gogh's campaign to persuade Russell began in early March, continued through the spring, and, when it came to funding Gauguin's move to Arles that summer, became a fixation for Van Gogh. The set of a dozen drawings he sent to Russell in early August was his last and most memorable overture—a carefully orchestrated symphony of lines in twelve-part harmony.

Van Gogh provided Russell with a representative sampling of motifs (two seascapes, four harvest scenes, two gardens, and three portraits) seemingly tailored to Russell's sensibilities, namely his respect for artists who were "full of courage in attacking difficult problems" and his efforts in Belle-Île to "try all things, figures, landscape, sea, cattle, etc." [501b]. Van Gogh repeated only five of the compositions he sent to Bernard, and, assuming that he began to sign the works subsequent to the first few, apparently he planned a unique selection from the start, when he chose to reproduce not one but two marines (F1430a, fig. 193; F1433, fig. 196) and a new garden view (F1454, fig. 197). Though he used the diminutive term "croquis" (sketch) to describe these highly refined drawings, it is telling that he signed all the rest—another mark of their finish—except for *Joseph Roulin* (F1458, fig. 204); made in virtually the same breath as the oil portrait in order to post it with the group, he may have neglected to add the *Vincent* in haste.

As his correspondence betrays, Van Gogh could hardly think of Russell without dwelling on Gauguin's financial predicament on the one hand and on portraiture on the other. Such was his mind-set that while writing to Russell in mid-June, the irrepressible urge to draw a head of a young girl simply took hold of his pen, transforming a page of a letter [501a] into a sketch of "a mudlark" (F1507a). It was the first figure that Van Gogh set to paper in Provence, and those of the Zouave (F1482a, fig. 202), the mousmé (F1503, fig. 203), and Roulin were among his last and finest. Russell, in fact, was the inspiration behind one-third of Van Gogh's small output of figure drawings in Arles.

Though Van Gogh's professed mission in sending these drawings to Russell was to advance Gauguin's cause, he may also have had his own in mind. Among the qualities that Van Gogh valued in this sound "good fellow" was his frankness [498]. Might not Van Gogh have hoped for a candid appraisal of his recent work from an artist he respected, and one, as he later confessed, who reminded him of Gauguin? Both friends possessed a certain "innate sweetness of far off fields" [625], a somewhat cryptic description of them that seems so relevant to the idyllic drawings.

Van Gogh's rich investigations of line and design challenge the single-mindedness of his campaign. While immersed in making these drawings, he was brooding over future projects. In fact, before he began his pen-and-ink *Boats at Sea, Saintes-Maries-de-la-Mer* (F1430a, fig. 193), as infrared reflectography shows (see figs. 246–49), he used the sheet, upright, to make a few figure sketches that would soon evolve into paintings. Two are clearly related to his portraits of Patience Escalier (figs. 247, 248), given the sitter's wide-brimmed hats and the ungainliness of the half-length figure that is repeated in a drawing (F1461, fig. 154). The third sketch (fig. 249), of a standing man, arm akimbo, was perhaps an initial thought for the pose for the similarly attired Joseph Ginoux of *The Night Café* (F463; and see F1463, fig. 217).[3] Discovering these underlying sketches on one of the first sheets he made for Russell seems fitting and ironic in light of the mutual interests on which their relationship was predicated.

While Russell declined to purchase a painting by Gauguin or pursue any number of invitations to exchange works with Van Gogh, he seems to have been very sympathetic to his Dutch friend's aims. Indeed, Russell parted with only one drawing early on—a gift to the fledgling artist Henri Matisse (F1427, fig. 194). In the three drawings he kept until his death—a landscape, a marine, and a figure—he acknowledged the selection Van Gogh had made for him, if not his appreciation of Van Gogh's multisided genius or, as Russell once put it, "courage in attacking difficult problems."

SAS

1. This sale also included Van Gogh's Paris still life *Shoes* (F332), no. 62, and an impression of the lithograph *At Eternity's Gate* (F1662; Amsterdam 1995, p. 93, no. 5.7), no. 71, but the fact that Russell had owned these works has escaped notice in the literature.
2. For Russell's painting *Amandiers en fleurs* of 1887, see Galbally 1977, pl. 13.
3. Van Gogh first told Theo of his plans for a peasant portrait in letters of August 8 and 18 [519, 520] and of his idea for the "café de nuit" on August 6 [518]—a few days after sending Russell's drawings—but, in the event, did not undertake the café painting until a month later.

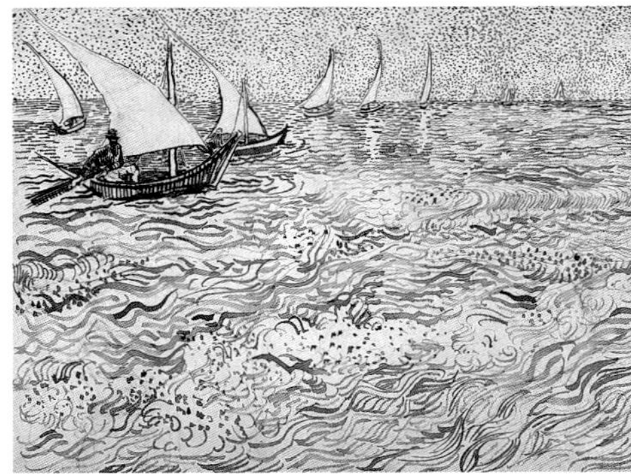

Fig. 193. *Boats at Sea, Saintes-Maries-de-la-Mer* (F1430a, cat. 58)

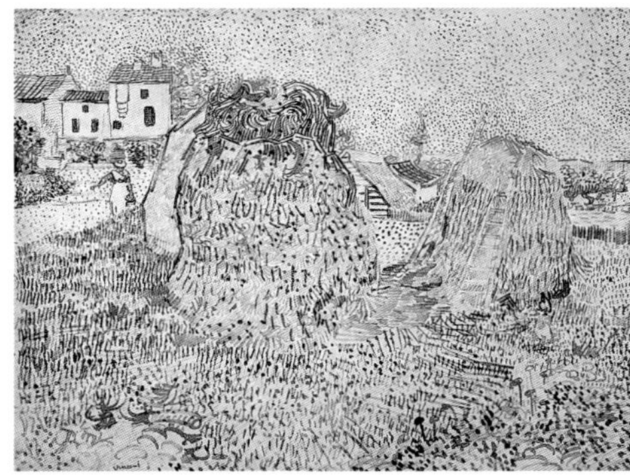

Fig. 194. *Haystacks* (F1427, cat. 67)

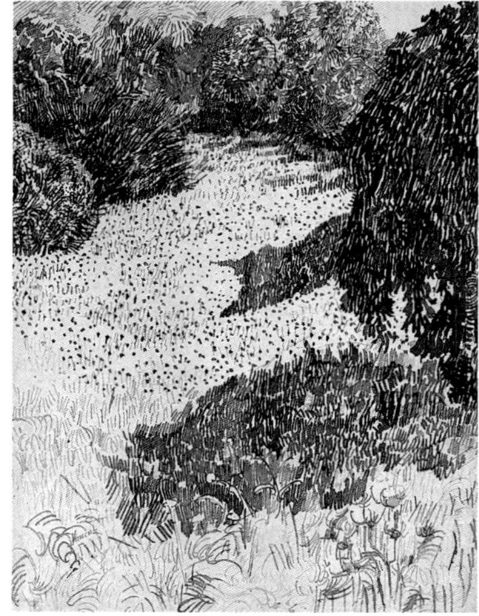

Fig. 195. *A Corner of a Garden in the Place Lamartine* (F1449, cat. 89)

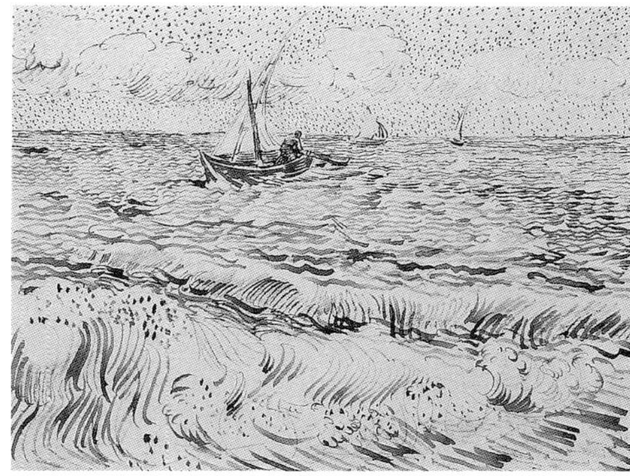

Fig. 196. *Boats at Sea, Saintes-Maries-de-la-Mer* (F1433), ca. July 31–August 3, 1888. Reed pen and ink over graphite on wove paper, 24.4 x 31.9 cm (9⅝ x 12½ in.). The Saint Louis Art Museum, Gift of Mr. and Mrs. Joseph Pulitzer Jr.

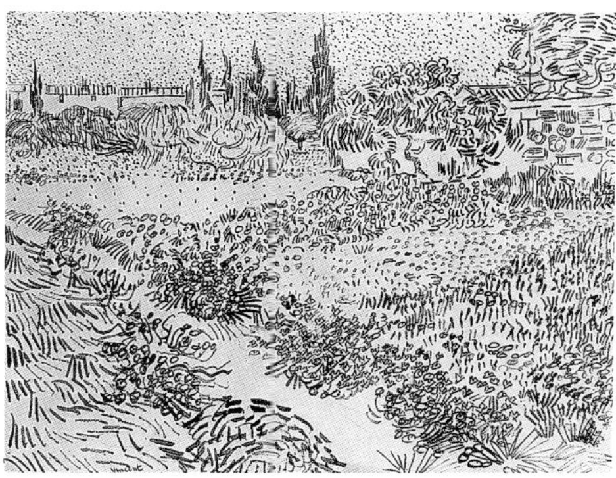

Fig. 197. *Garden with Flowers* (F1454), ca. July 1–August 3, 1888. Reed pen and ink, 24 x 31.5 cm (9½ x 12⅜ in.). Private collection

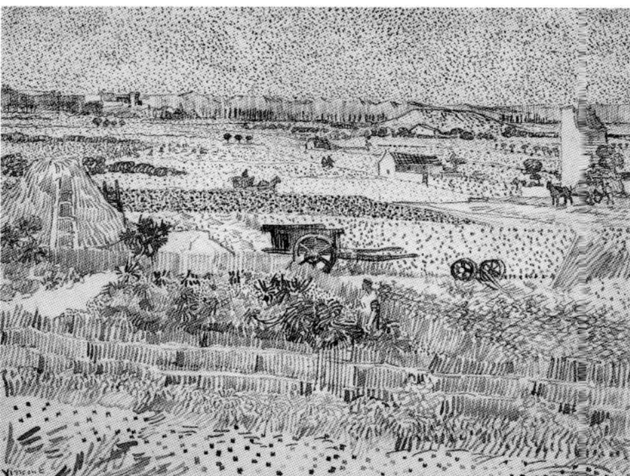

Fig. 198. *Harvest in Provence* (F1486, cat. 65)

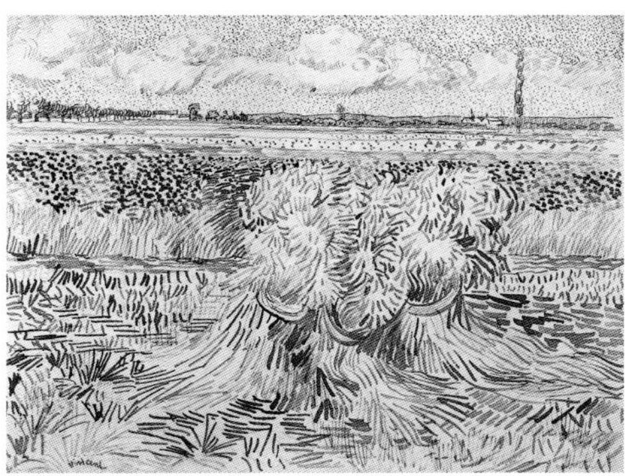

Fig. 199. *Wheat Field with Sheaves* (F1489, cat. 74)

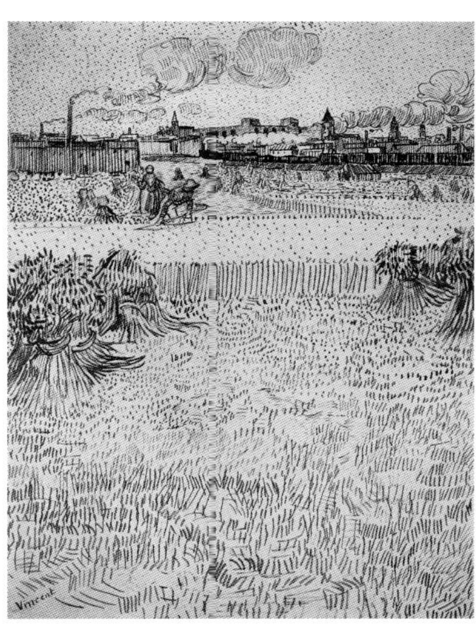

Fig. 200. *Arles: View from the Wheat Fields* (F1490, cat. 71)

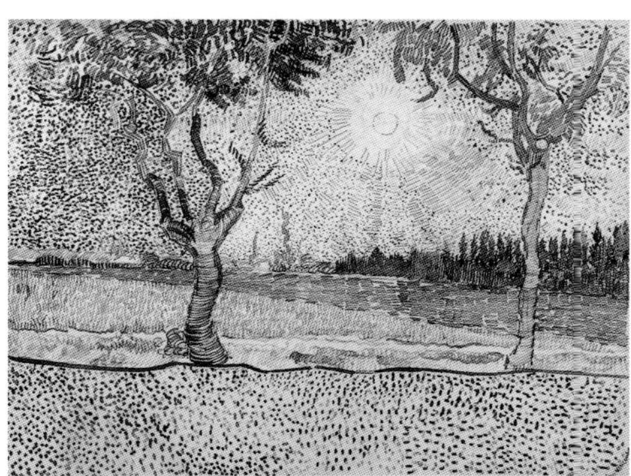

Fig. 201. *The Road to Tarascon* (F1502a, cat. 93)

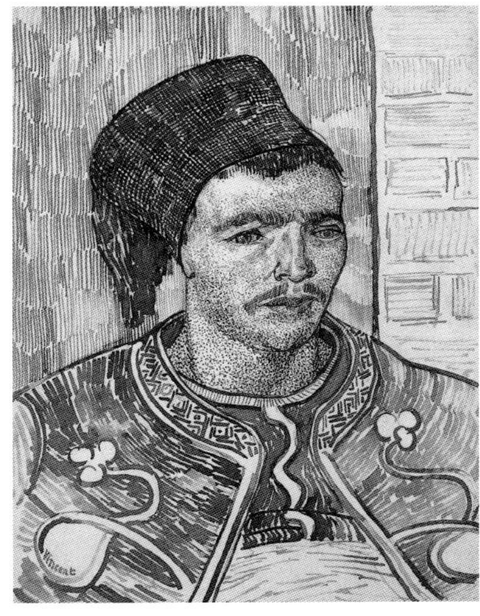

Fig. 202. *The Zouave* (F1482a, cat. 79)

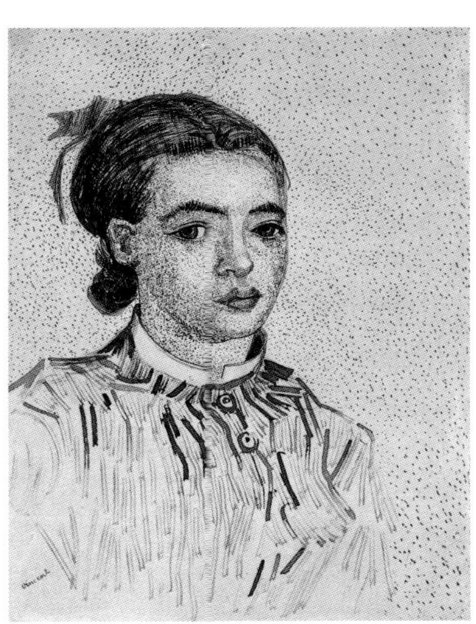

Fig. 203. *La Mousmé* (F1503, cat. 80)

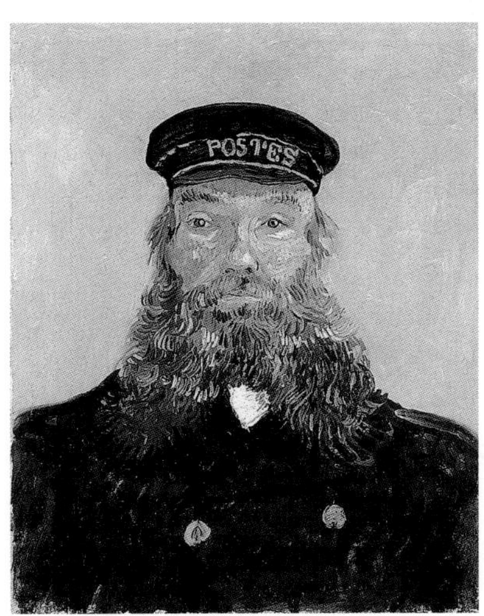

Fig. 204. *Portrait of Joseph Roulin* (F1458, cat. 81)

Drawings after Paintings Sent to Theo

Van Gogh's correspondence does not specify the precise number of drawings after paintings that he sent to his brother Theo in early August 1888, but five are described by subject. These five drawings have since been identified and may be taken as a full count (F1430b, fig. 205; F1431, fig. 206; F1441, fig. 207; F1492, fig. 208; F1451, fig. 209). On August 6, 1888, Van Gogh wrote Theo that he intended to send him twelve drawings in keeping with the ones he made for Russell [518]; two days later, he sent Theo "three large drawings, as well as some other ones" [519]. Having noted that the large ones represented gardens, Van Gogh wrote, "Now the Harvest, the Garden, the Sower, and the two marines are sketches after painted studies."

Summary of the literature: De la Faille 1928/1970/1992 identified the three gardens (F1455, F1456, F1457) but did not propose candidates for the "other ones." Roskill (1971, pp. 151–53, 170–71) observed that Van Gogh had mentioned the "subjects in five cases" of drawings after paintings [519] and argued that the "harvest" is most probably F1492 (with F1485 as a possible alternative); that the "garden" is likely F1451; the "sower," F1441; and the "two marines," F1430b and F1431. Roskill remarked that there is nothing to indicate that Van Gogh actually sent twelve drawings as intended. However, he entertained the idea that Van Gogh may have sent "further small drawings in the batch also"—possibly F1495, F1496, F1498r, F1514—and that "the addition of these four would give nine small drawings—making up, along with the three larger *Gardens*, twelve drawings in all." Hulsker (1980, p. 346) observed that Van Gogh "probably did fewer than twelve" drawings after paintings for Theo and listed seven as among those sent, noting that "since these drawings came from the collection of Theo van Gogh, it can almost certainly be assumed that this third group included at least the following." He then named three harvest scenes (F1485, F1492, F1514), a garden (F1451), a sower (F1441), and two marines (F1430b, F1431) but in an ad hoc order, without consideration of the artist's mention of these subjects in his letter. Pickvance (in New York 1984, pp. 126–27 and nos. 82–84) regarded Van Gogh's description of the "sketches after painted studies" as a complete list and stated that the artist sent five such drawings to Theo: "the Harvest" (F1492), "Garden" (F1451), "Sower" (F1441), and "two marines" (F1430b, F1431). Pickvance's reading of the letter seems irrefutable, especially since the two other harvest scenes included by Hulsker had belonged not to Theo but to Bernard (as Roskill originally suspected in the case of F1485, and Pickvance recognized in the case of F1514). Only Roskill provided supporting documentation for the drawings identified. Subsequent provenance research (Feilchenfeldt and Veenenbos 1988; Stolwijk and Veenenbos 2002) allows us to confirm that these five drawings originally belonged to Theo van Gogh.

Van Gogh had completed twenty-seven *répétitions*—fifteen for Bernard and twelve for Russell—before he embarked on a suite of a dozen drawings for Theo. However, midway through this effort, Van Gogh seems to have lost interest in continuing, at least in repeating motifs on sheets of this size, for he produced only five, supplementing the consignment with three garden scenes (F1455, fig. 163; F1456, cat. 91; F1457, cat. 92) that explore the virtues of a decorative calligraphic style on a grander scale and in compositions (two of them new) made from scratch. These landscapes would, within the week, find successors in large-format portrait drawings framed in line (F1459, fig. 153; F1460, fig. 29), which extend the strategy of studio reinterpretations beyond his prior, more modest efforts. The next step would have been to make the leap from paper to canvas, and indeed, even before he sent the group of five *répétitions* to Theo, he broached the subject: "You will tell me that instead of drawing them, I ought to paint them again on fresh canvases at home. I think so myself now and then, for it is not my fault in this case that the execution lacks a livelier touch. What would Gauguin say about it if he were here, would he advise seeking a more sheltered place?" [518].

Clearly the real question was whether Theo felt Vincent should adopt Gauguin's modus operandi as his own. Theo's response is not known, but he may have discouraged Vincent from further experiments along these (highly stylized) lines, for when the same tendencies surfaced in Van Gogh's Saint-Rémy paintings, his brother confided, "I feel that your search for style is at the expense of the true sentiment of things" [T19]. These *répétitions* would serve as a touchstone for later works that betray in whole or part something of Van Gogh's impulse toward a more abstract aesthetic, but they had no sequel in his Arles drawings. Van Gogh soon reigned in the impulse that had taken hold of his pen and ceased working in this vein. Later that fall, he suspended the activity of drawing altogether after flirting briefly with limiting his efforts to *ricordi* (in smaller format or in watercolor) and using full-size sheets more conventionally, as preparatory to studio paintings—not unlike Gauguin.

SAS

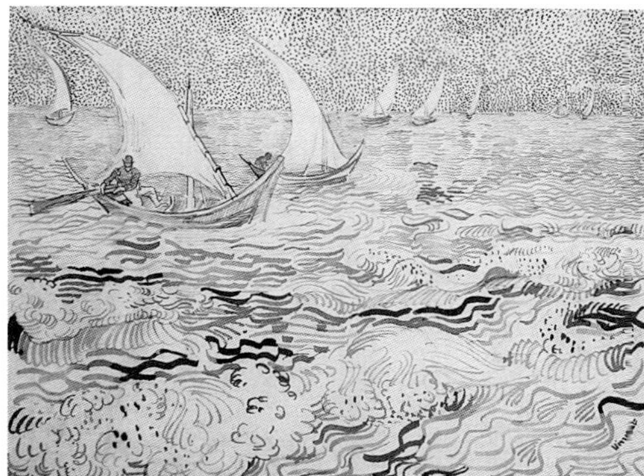

Fig. 205. *Boats at Sea, Saintes-Maries-de-la-Mer* (F1430b, cat. 59)

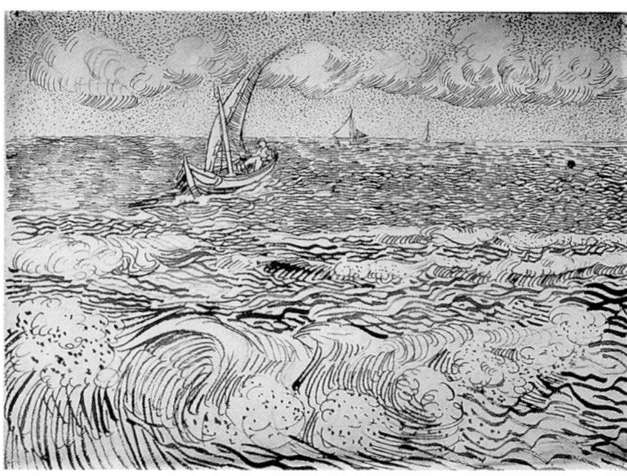

Fig. 206. *Boats at Sea, Saintes-Maries-de-la-Mer* (F1431), ca. August 6–8, 1888. Reed pen and ink over graphite on wove paper, 24 x 32 cm (9½ x 12⅝ in.). Location unknown (photo: Collection Rijksbureau voor Kunsthistorische Documentatie [RKD], The Hague)

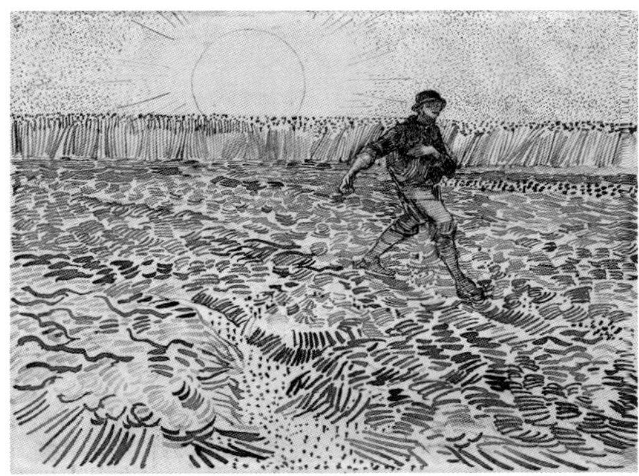

Fig. 207. *The Sower* (F1441, cat. 76)

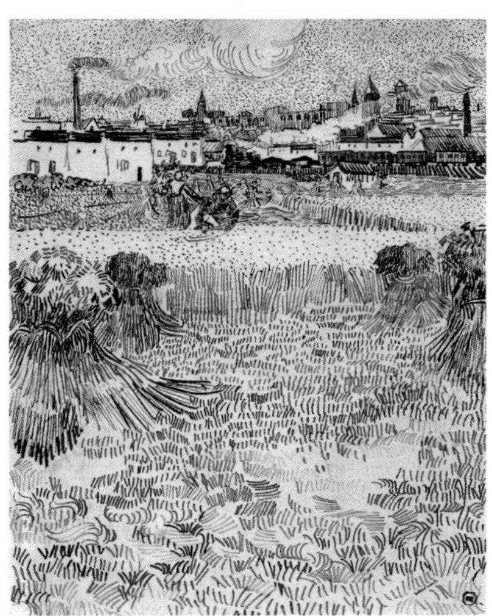

Fig. 208. *Arles: View from the Wheat Fields* (F1492, cat. 72)

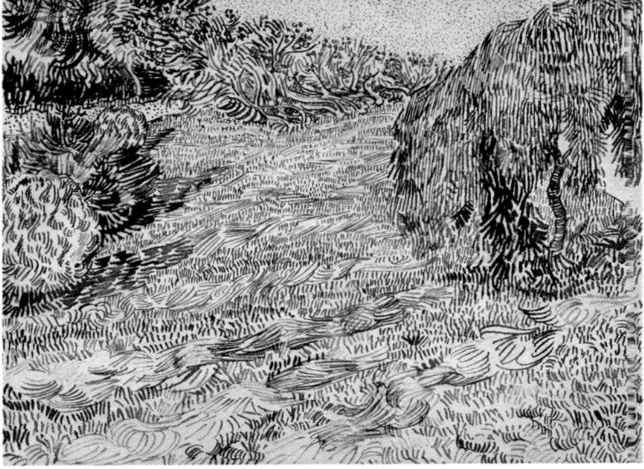

Fig. 209. *A Corner of a Garden in the Place Lamartine* (F1451 cat. 90)

Drawing to a Close

Between mid-August and Gauguin's arrival in Arles on October 23, 1888, as Van Gogh devoted his energies to preparing decorative schemes for the Yellow House and to fleshing out his repertoire, painting commanded his full, almost undivided attention. He made two large-scale drawings before tackling the subjects in paint; five smaller sheets after recently completed canvases (three in pen and two in watercolor); and a few landscapes while waiting in September for painting supplies to arrive. Drawing became a marginal activity and then ceased altogether, from early October 1888 until early May 1889, when he made two last works before his departure for Saint-Rémy.

Premières pensées and Second Thoughts

In the late summer of 1888, Van Gogh relied on his draftsman's skills to meet the challenges of two compositions that had engaged his imagination and artistic ambitions. The first, devoted to the subject of workers unloading cargo from a boat docked on the Rhône, had so captivated the artist one summer evening that he described the "magnificent and strange effect" as "pure Hokusai," challenging him "to give it a try" [516]. Some two weeks later, in mid-August 1888, he ventured the motif, starting out with a large-scale drawing (F1462, cat. 95), before giving "it a try" in paint (F449, fig. 214). From the start, as his underlying graphite sketch reveals (see infrared reflectogram, fig. 255), the artist brought his original sense of the scene's *japoniste* character into focus: he chose a bird's-eye vantage point and carefully plotted the emphatic diagonal of the quay, using it as a foil for the pair of boats; he was attentive to their alignment, shape, and pattern, in particular to the rhythmic play of crisscrossing lines. His initial conception in graphite may be seen as the blueprint for the oil painting. The canvas largely appropriates its simpler, pared-down form, allows the jutting bit of unarticulated landscape to suffice for background; and reverts, for example, to a lowered rectangular flag. From the finished drawing, he took only the dinghy at left, moving it closer to the stern of the boat, perhaps to fill in the space once enlivened at left by the charming detail of two men rescuing, or playing fetch with, a dog. In casting aside this bit of anecdotal, undoubtedly observed, incident and in adding workers to the boats, he kept the note of humanity more proletarian and, in their indifference and anonymity, more modern.

In effect, once Van Gogh had realized the basic composition, he produced a drawing and then a painting—two separate artworks: one that exploited the potential of line to animate the surface, from the rippling waves at low tide in the foreground to the panoramic townscape of Arles along the upper edge; the other, reining in extraneous detail, to heighten the bold play of color. And insofar as he had resolved the design in graphite, before pen and ink intervened to elaborate and invigorate the whole, he had no need to keep the drawing on hand to complete the painting and, in fact, sent it to Theo beforehand. Nor did he need to return to the site. Perhaps he did so in order to paint it *en plein air,* but the picture seems fundamentally a studio composition or hybrid (unless we can imagine that he found the boats and both wheelbarrows, along with the man pushing one across the plank, in virtually the same place). His essential design served him well; indeed, he appropriated it again later that month for his study *Shoes* aligned against the

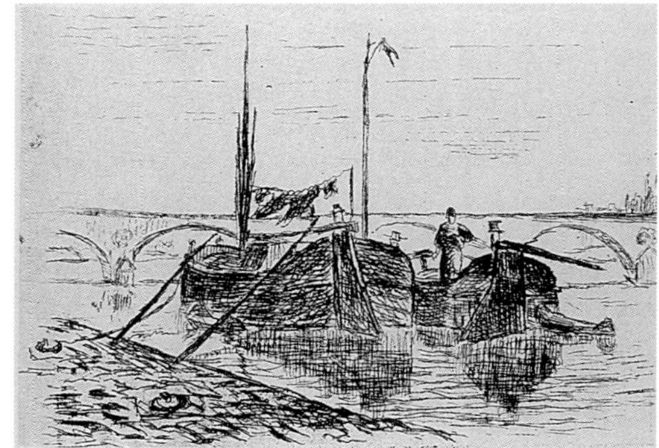

Fig. 210. Armand Guillaumin, *The Seine at Bercy*, ca. 1872. Etching, 6 x 8.6 cm (2³/₈ x 3³/₈ in.). Private collection

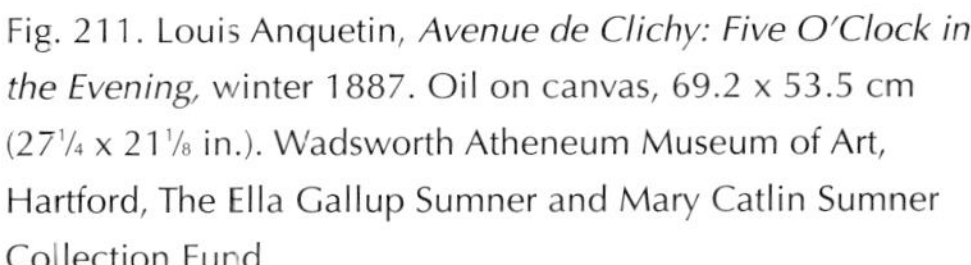

Fig. 211. Louis Anquetin, *Avenue de Clichy: Five O'Clock in the Evening*, winter 1887. Oil on canvas, 69.2 x 53.5 cm (27¼ x 21⅛ in.). Wadsworth Atheneum Museum of Art, Hartford, The Ella Gallup Sumner and Mary Catlin Sumner Collection Fund

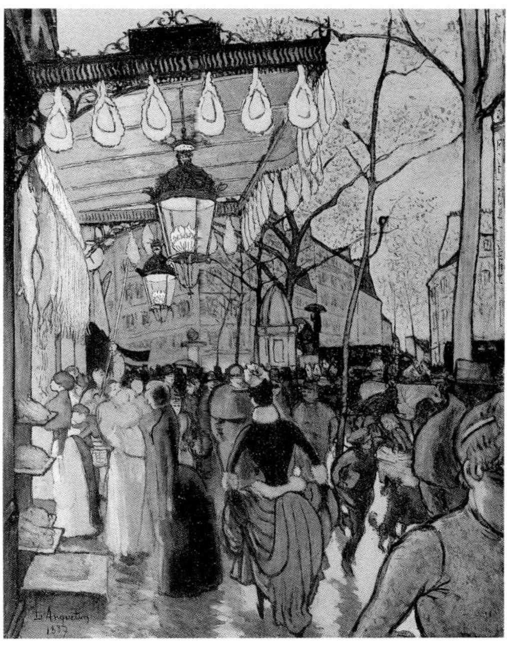

diagonal grid of the red-tiled floor of his Yellow House studio (F461, fig. 213).

No doubt the success of these works encouraged Van Gogh to again rely on his pen in advance of his brush for another composition that had been in his mind's eye for some time, namely, a café terrace at night (F1519, cat. 96; F467, fig. 215). Opening onto the Place du Forum in the center of town, the café, though some distance from his house, was one he had frequented with his artist-friend Eugène Boch and perhaps envisioned as a future haunt with Gauguin; but other associations prompted his trek, on two occasions it seems, to capture the character of the motif on paper and on canvas. Not unlike his view along the quay, with its clear ties to Guillaumin and other Impressionists (see fig. 210), his café scene was a quintessentially *vie moderne* subject, which took as its point of departure not only Louis Anquetin's 1887 *Avenue de Clichy* (fig. 211) but also Guy de Maupassant's description in *Bel-Ami* of a "starlit night in Paris with the brightly lighted cafés of the Boulevard" [W7].

Van Gogh's drawing of the Café du Forum functioned as a *première pensée* for the oil composition. It served to familiarize the artist with the motif and set the stage—tables and leading characters such as the waiter serving a top-hatted gent—for a scene he would largely recast (under proper lighting) on canvas, one in which the horse-drawn carriage makes an entrance through a widened road that accommodates more people strolling and in a setting that would include a tree at right, a loner lurking in the doorway at left, articulated facades, and, thanks to the truncated awning, a larger expanse of sky flecked with stars. Whatever he gained from his first draft, however, he also felt obliged to reject, indeed along with the very existence of such a drawing. The subject, as he reported to his sister Wil, demanded a direct, unmitigated approach: "It amuses me enormously to paint the night right on the spot. They used to draw and paint the picture in the daytime after the rough sketch. But I find satisfaction in painting things immediately." He insisted that "the only way to get rid of the conventional night scenes with their poor sallow whitish light" [W7] was to reject conventional practice; and in turn, he veritably disclaimed having made, let alone having relied on, a preparatory drawing, which would have robbed the painting of its authenticity as a nighttime effect studied in situ, under gaslight. The account is both telling and prescient. This was the last reed-pen drawing Van Gogh undertook of any ambition for the next seven months, and the last time he realized a motif on paper before setting his brush to the task in Arles.

Répétitions Redefined

Though in the fall of 1888 Van Gogh was disinclined to devote much time to drawing, he was persuaded on a handful of occasions to reproduce painted motifs for Theo's benefit. He confined his *ricordi* to pen-and-ink sketches on ordinary writing paper, or, instead, he relied on watercolor. At the end of September he made three small drawings after canvases of which he was particularly proud: *View of the Public Garden* (F1465), *Starry Night on the Rhône* (F1515), and *The Yellow House* (F1453, cat. 97). These extempore works are distinctive for their verve and degree of finish, which belie the modesty of their scale and ambition, or the fact that so compelling an image as *The Yellow House* was the flip side of a page given over to words. More than just a synoptic sketch of the ilk that intercepts or punctuates ideas in the body of a letter, this is a full-fledged drawing in compact form. Clearly the impulse to articulate details and give a sense of spirited expression to the composition took over, notwithstanding the modesty of intention, commanding the entire sheet, edge to edge and all the spaces in between. The lyrical quality of the penmanship is reflected in the sensibility of the watercolor of the Yellow House he sent soon after (F1413, cat. 98), having promised Theo a "better drawing" [543] and keen to give him "some idea of the color" [548].

While Van Gogh had imagined employing watercolor in various creative ways—for example, "to make some pen drawings, to be washed afterward in flat tints like Japanese prints" [491]—little came of these plans. After a few experiments in June, he made only a couple more watercolors in Arles, and not until the fall. Eager to give Theo a sense of two compositions that depended on the expressive use of color for their effect, he turned to making colored drawings after his paintings of *The Yellow House* (F1413, cat. 98), an outdoor scene in the full light of the Midi sun, which relied on the strong contrast of blue and yellow, and *The Night Café* (F1463, fig. 217), an indoor scene by gaslight in red and green. In style the works seem as temperamentally different as the paintings: the *Yellow House* watercolor, with its delicate and lighter approach, seems to take its cue from his Parisian townscapes of 1887 (F1401, cat. 38; F1406, cat. 39; F1411, cat. 40) while the more trenchant and painterly gouache of the *The Night Café* presages the interior views of the asylum of 1889 (F1528, cat. 114; F1529, cat. 113; F1530, cat. 115).

Final Statements

For some seven months, Van Gogh virtually quit drawing except for an occasional sketch in a letter. It was only on the eve of his departure for the asylum at Saint-Rémy in early May 1889, as he was packing up his belongings and had already bid adieu to Arles with his brush, that he picked up the reed pen in a parting gesture. Not unlike the subjects of his last Arles canvases, a path leading into the public garden and a road bordered by pollard trees leading out of town, those he chose for the last two drawings—a view of the cloistered garden of the Arles hospital (F1467, cat. 99) and a final reprise of the "poet's garden" he loved so well (F1468, cat. 100)—seem a fitting and poignant coda.

The drawing of the hospital garden is very much a summary piece. It is redolent with association to drawings he had considered earlier triumphs: the trees almost seem transplanted from the foreground of his breakthrough May 1888 view of Montmajour (F1452, cat. 47), while the signature on the watering can and exuberant flora in the flower beds recall his summer cottage gardens (F1456, cat. 91; F1457, cat. 92). For all the breathless, dynamic force of this drawing, the artist still found time to pause to add a few characteristic, indeed, inimitable details, such as the wheelbarrow slipped behind the pilaster, the men huddled in conversation above it, and to the right and below, a pair of nuns, tête-à-tête. The breadth of line and the bleeding of ink in certain passages are attributable to his use of a particularly soft and pliant reed pen, possibly one that was worn or else cut more broadly, which imparts a more fluid, brushlike character to the strokes. In this quality, the drawing anticipates various views of the asylum grounds that he did later that spring in Saint-Rémy. The unhesitant touch and liveliness of the drawing come in part from his familiarity with the subject, which he had explored, albeit from a different vantage point, in a recent painting (F519, fig. 218). In contrast, his final salute to the public garden seems at once more emphatic and less resolved in its heavier, inkier, harsher treatment of spiky grass, bulbous bushes, and the tentacled, restless boughs of the central tree. It is perhaps the artist's most impassioned drawing. Van Gogh saw both works as a continuation of those he devoted to Montmajour; but the Place Lamartine garden, notwithstanding the forceful vigor and virility of conception that would commend this association, looks back still further in form and spirit, it would seem, to his first reed-pen efforts in Arles. Van Gogh, in closing out this imposing chapter in his career as a draftsman, succeeded in bringing it full circle as well.

Postscript

The final drawings Van Gogh made in Arles in May 1889 may be seen as a reaffirmation of the qualities that he had consistently valued as a draftsman. To the extent that he had strayed from this mark (or this manner of mark-making) in summer feats of linear invention, he ultimately rebounded, albeit only after disengaging his draftsman's fist from pen and paper for an extended period of time. After mid-August, Van Gogh seems to have resolved, apropos of exploring a more decorative and abstract method of drawing in the *répétitions* he made for Bernard, Russell, and Theo, that this was not a tack he wished to pursue, and he recanted. In terms of style, he reined in the impulse toward a refined and stylized graphic idiom, implementing a broader, looser touch. At the same time, he confined the practice of making drawings after paintings to ink sketches on ordinary sheets of writing paper or to watercolors, seemingly determined to keep these efforts to a simple, direct, unpretentious affair or to ensure the integrity of his conception by relying on color. These tendencies are anticipated in the last figure drawings he made in August, with their deliberate lack of pretense in style and format and with the addition of color notes to two of them.

Van Gogh's artistic resolve to guarantee the authenticity of his vision through evocative color and forthright execution also challenged the intermediary role of drawing in the creative process. In the late summer of 1888, as he had in June, Van Gogh again turned to pen and paper before taking up motifs in paint (F1455, fig. 163; F1456, cat. 91; F1462, cat. 95; F1519, cat. 96), but on the last occasion, he virtually denied having even made the drawing when describing his approach to his sister Wil [W7]; instead he insisted that the effect he was after could not be achieved by relying on a preparatory study but only by seizing it directly and on the spot. Although later in Saint-Rémy, Van Gogh would again depend on his draftsman's skill to work out, for example, the "line and proportion" of the cypresses [596], in Arles he did not further exploit the practice, not even as an aid to making "abstractions" in Gauguin's company.

During their two-month interlude together, from late October to late December 1888, Van Gogh experimented with painting from memory, though he did not rely on preparatory sketches as did Gauguin. And yet he later used one such study, Gauguin's conté-crayon sketch of Mme Ginoux, as the basis for five Arlésienne paintings (F540–43). Nor does it appear that Van Gogh made drawings from memory, though he had intended to hone this skill over the winter, and as late as December he still imagined that he would spend the evening hours not only writing but drawing [506]. What became of these plans and of the "dozen" figures from memory that he made in September when he "felt he was on the track" of learning "to do a figure with a few strokes" of the pen [542]? Surely he must have experimented further with a skill that, beyond the aesthetic virtues touted by Gauguin, had its own seductions given his aims and legendary frustrations as a figure painter. Yet if the lack of drawings suggests an admission of defeat, it seems that Van Gogh never quite reconciled himself to giving up the idea of being able to capture a characteristic likeness on paper with the ease and confidence of a Hokusai or a Daumier (or, in Gauguin's terms, a Degas or a Raphael). In Auvers, just months before his death in 1890, Van Gogh began again to copy the pages from Charles Bargue's *Exercices au fusain* as he had done at the outset of his career in order to master the rudiments of figure drawing.

SAS

95. *Sand Barges on the Rhône*

ca. August 13, 1888
Reed pen, pen, ink, and graphite on wove paper watermarked J. WHATMAN TURKEY MILL 1879
48.9 x 59.4 cm (19¼ x 23⅜ in.)
Cooper-Hewitt, National Design Museum, Smithsonian Institution, New York, Gift of Miss Edith Wetmore (1960-232-1)
F1462, JH1556
Letters 524, 525

Provenance: Included in the consignment of works delivered by Paul-Eugène Milliet to Theo van Gogh (d. 1891), Paris, August 17, 1888 [525]; by inheritance to his son, Vincent Willem van Gogh, as part of his collection, administered by his widow, Johanna van Gogh-Bonger, 1891; sold by her to Klas Valter Fåhræus, Stockholm, December 1911, until at least 1917; Augst T. Levinson, Copenhagen; Hugo Perls Art Gallery, Berlin, 1927–28; Miss Edith Wetmore, New York, by 1935; her gift to Cooper-Hewitt, 1960.

Selected exhibitions: The Hague 1891 (per Anonymous 1891); Antwerp 1892; Amsterdam 1905, no. 417; Berlin 1906, no. 59; Berlin 1927–28, no. 106; New York and other cities 1935–36, no. 113; New York 1984, hors cat.; Otterlo 1990, no. 205; Tokyo–Nagoya 1985–86, no. 63; Martigny 2000, no. 69.

Summary of the literature: This drawing has always been dated to August 1888 on the basis of letters 524 and 525 and associated with the painting of the motif (F449, fig. 214). However, the relationship between the two has been variously interpreted, partly because of the artist's use of the phrase "dessin du tableau" (mistranslated, notably in the English edition of the letters, as "after" the painting rather than "of" the painting). De la Faille (1928/1970/1992, no. 1462) gave the date as August 1888; Tralbaut (in Essen 1957) as probably done before the painting; Roskill (1971, pp. 162, 172 and n. 165) as "most probably done from [the painting]." Millard (1974, pp. 161, 164 n. 61) considered it a mid-August 1888 drawing made "on the spot" that is more detailed and "apparently independent of the painting of the same subject," and argued that since Van Gogh mentioned the drawing while still working on the oil, "If anything the drawing served as a model for the painting." Hulsker (1980/1996, no. 1556) contended that the drawing "must have been made first," and that Van Gogh had already sent it off before completing the painting, which was significantly simplified and governed by a concern with the "forceful contrasts of color." In Amsterdam 1990 (p. 139), it was noted that Van Gogh executed the canvas F449 (ca. August 14) *en plein air,* after making a careful preliminary drawing. Pickvance (in Otterlo 1990, no. 205) determined that the August 1888 drawing was done "more or less contemporaneously with the painting" but enjoyed an "independent status," since "there are sufficient changes between the two media to suggest that each represents a separate recording." Heenk (1995, pp. 166–67) described this "complex, carefully constructed drawing" as done on the spot and preparatory to the painting (F449) but conceived as a work in its own right; she argued that the artist did not return to the site, as the painting contains no "extra information" or expected differences in the disposition of certain figures and felt its relative lack of detail and simplification could instead be attributed to the fact that the drawing, which had served "to some extent as a model," had been sent to Theo, while the painting was still in progress. Pickvance (in Martigny 2000, no. 69) saw it as an "independent drawing," completed before the painting, which betrays "too many differences" in viewpoint, time of day, and other details (e.g., shadows, boats, figures) to be thought a preparatory study. For early history, see Feilchenfeldt and Veenenbos 1988, p. 133; Stolwijk and Veenenbos 2002, pp. 54, 126, 151, 195.

Letter to Theo van Gogh, ca. August 13, 1888 [524]: Just now I am working on a study like this [fig. 212], of boats seen from the quay above, the two boats are pink tinged with violet, the water is bright green, no sky, a tricolor on the mast. A workman with a barrow is unloading sand. I have a drawing of it as well.

Letter to Theo van Gogh, August 15, 1888 [525]: I have put in this package a drawing of a picture which I am working on now—the boats with the man unloading sand.

See "Drawing to a Close" and, for the infrared reflectogram, see figure 255. SAS

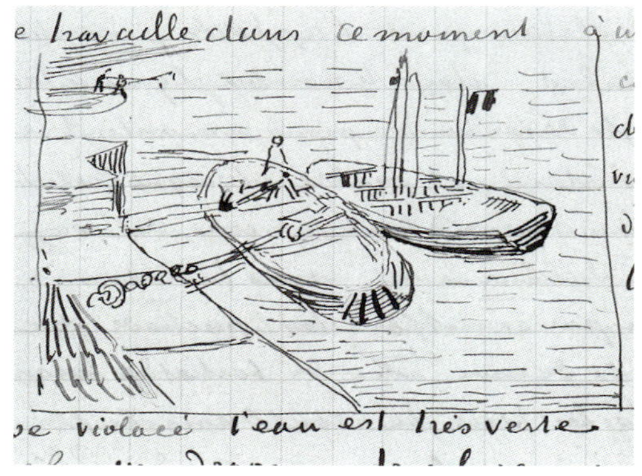

Fig. 212. Letter sketch of *Sand Barges on the Rhône* (F1845), ca. August 13, 1888 [524]. Ink on paper, image 6 x 9 cm (2⅜ x 3½ in.). Van Gogh Museum, Amsterdam (Vincent van Gogh Foundation)

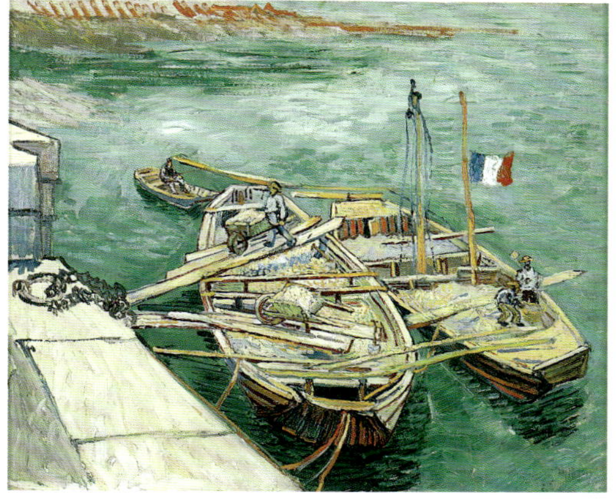

Fig. 214. *Sand Barges on the Rhône* (F449), mid-August 1888. Oil on canvas, 55 x 66 cm (21⅝ x 26 in.). Museum Folkwang, Essen

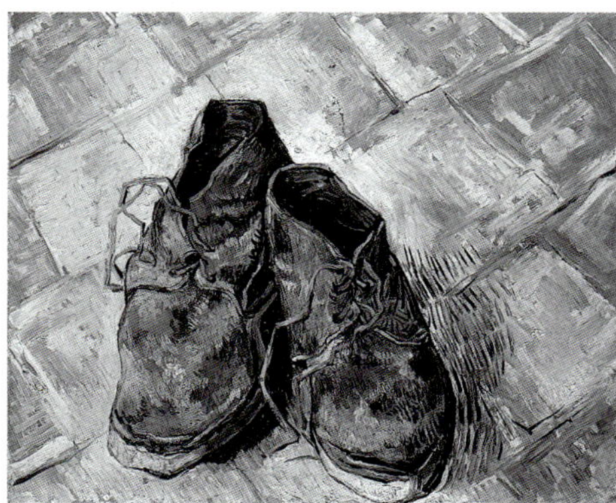

Fig. 213. *Shoes* (F461), late August 1888. Oil on canvas, 45.7 x 55.2 cm (18 x 21¾ in.). The Metropolitan Museum of Art, New York, Purchase, The Annenberg Foundation Gift, 1992 (1992.374)

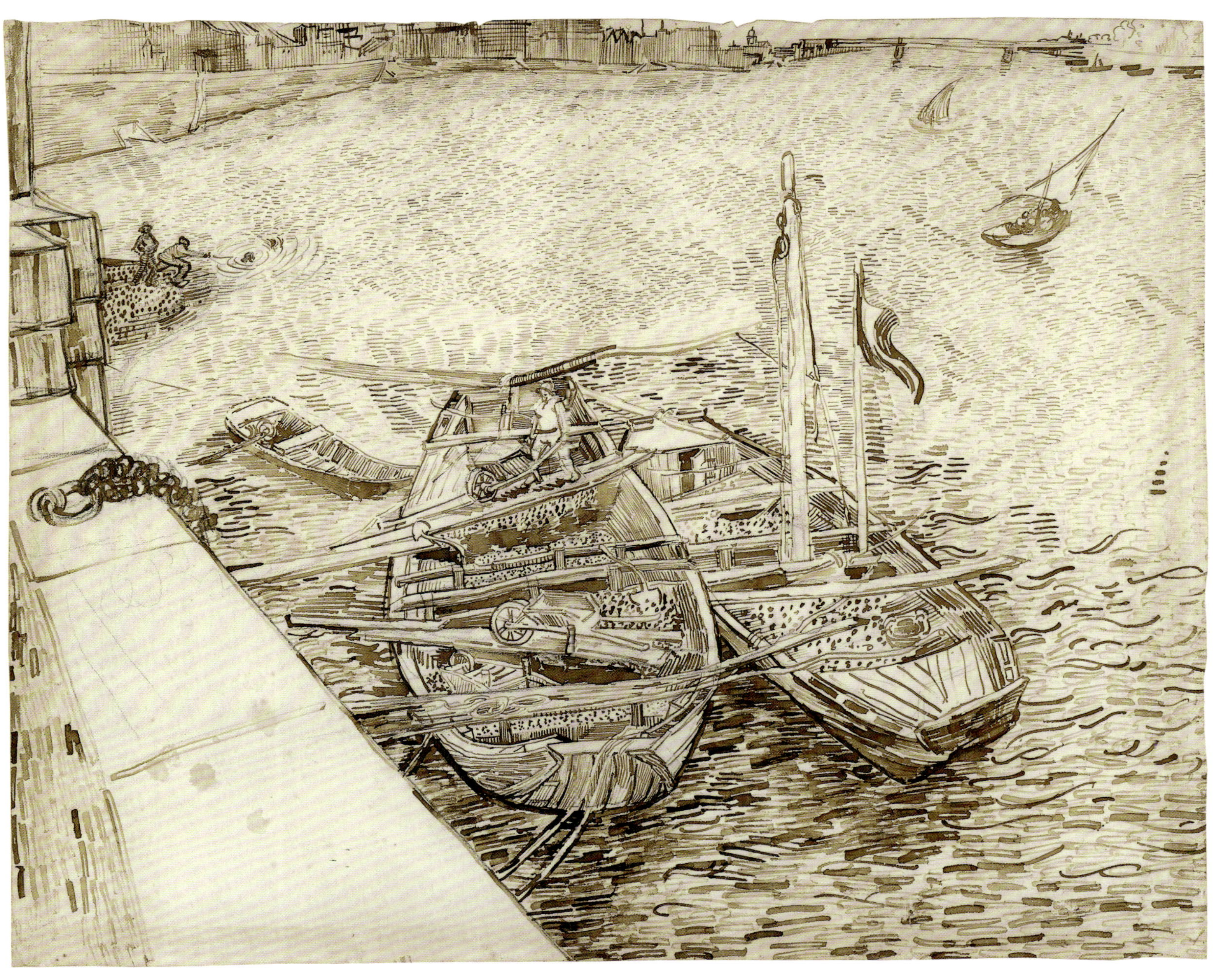

96. *Café Terrace on the Place du Forum*

Early September 1888
Reed pen, ink, and graphite on laid paper
62 x 47 cm (24⅞ x 18½ in.)
Inscribed in ink on verso, in another hand: *154*
Dallas Museum of Art, The Wendy and Emery Reves Collection (1985.R.79)
F1519, JH1579

New York only

Provenance: Sent by the artist to Theo van Gogh (d. 1891), Paris, on an unrecorded date in 1888–89; by inheritance to his son, Vincent Willem van Gogh, as part of his collection, administered by his widow, Johanna van Gogh-Bonger, 1891; sold by her to Paul Cassirer, Berlin, December 1906; sold to Hugo von Tschudi (d. 1911), Berlin, December 1906; to his widow, Angela von Tschudi, Munich (placed on loan at the museum in Breslau); sold by the von Tschudi family to the Fritz Nathan Art Gallery, Zürich, until 1960; sold to Emery Reves, Cabbe-Roquebrune, France, 1960; acquired as part of the Wendy and Emery Reves collection by the Dallas Museum of Art, 1985.

Selected exhibitions: Paris 1896–97 (no. 33 on Johanna's list of loans); Paris 1902 (no. 16 on Johanna's list of loans); Amsterdam 1905, no. 388; Berlin 1906, no. 71; Otterlo 1990, no. 208.

Summary of the literature: While this drawing was often featured in the early literature (as recorded in De la Faille 1928, no. 1519, which lists ten publications between 1910 and 1928), it has not attracted much scholarly attention, especially relative to the often-discussed painting of the motif (F467, fig. 215), which is firmly documented in the letters [537, 553b, W7]. The drawing's relationship to the painting has been variously assessed. De la Faille (1970, no. 1519) flagged differences in such details missing from the drawing as the stars and tree branches and suspected it was made slightly earlier than the painting of September. Roskill (1971, p. 173) similarly proposed that it was "most probably preliminary to" the mid-September painting, from which it differs in certain details. Hulsker (1980, no. 1579) described it simply as a large drawing of the motif dating to September (in 1996, more precisely as ca. September 16, 1888). Welsh-Ovcharov (in Toronto–Amsterdam 1981, p. 134) argued that the drawing "might well have recorded rather than preceded" the oil "since it scarcely seems an on-the-spot sketch, but rather an afterthought *résumé* of the painting," and that such a view is supported by Van Gogh's account of making the painting in situ [W7] and his primary interest in the subject's color. Pickvance (in Otterlo 1990, p. 237) highlighted the artist's silence about the drawing in his letters and contended that it was probably made on September 4, 1888, during the daytime (given the clarity of signage details, treatment of the sky, etc.) as an "independent drawing" that is "separate in view, disposition and above all opposition to day and night" from the oil. For early history, see Feilchenfeldt and Veenenbos 1988, p. 136; Paul 1993, p. 393; Stolwijk and Veenenbos 2002, pp. 51, 126, 197.

Before venturing the motif in paint, Van Gogh set down his initial conception in this remarkably unhesitant drawing. The café scene was broadly conceived in reed pen, commanded with great ease and spontaneity that impart to this large sheet something of the character of the artist's letter sketches. He relied on graphite, not for the preliminary sketch but only for shading and to further articulate details, such as the wood grain of the floor. Having resolved the basic composition, Van Gogh returned to the site to paint it in situ (F467, fig. 215), where he directed his attention to rendering the atmospheric effect of light and color of a nighttime scene bathed in gaslight under a star-filled sky.

See "Drawing to a Close." SAS

Fig. 215. *Café Terrace on the Place du Forum* (F467), September 1888. Oil on canvas, 80.7 x 65.3 cm (31¾ x 25¾ in.). Kröller-Müller Museum, Otterlo

Letter to Wilhelmina van Gogh, September 9 and ca. September 14, 1888 [W7]: It is already a few days since I started writing this letter, and now I will continue it. In point of fact I was interrupted these days by my toiling on a new picture of the outside of a café at night [F467, fig. 215]. On the terrace there are the tiny figures of people drinking. An enormous yellow lantern sheds its light on the terrace, the house front and the sidewalk, and even casts a certain brightness on the pavement of the streets, which takes a pinkish violet tone. The gabled-topped fronts of the houses in the street stretching away under a blue sky spangled with stars are dark blue or violet and there is a green tree. Here you have a night picture without any black in it, done with nothing but beautiful blue and violet and green, and citron-yellow color. It amuses me enormously to paint the night right on the spot. They used to draw and paint the picture in the daytime after the rough sketch. But I find satisfaction in painting things immediately.

Of course it's true that in the dark I may mistake a blue for a green, a blue-lilac for a pink-lilac, for you cannot rightly distinguish the quality of a hue. But it is the only way to get rid of the conventional night scenes with their poor sallow whitish light, whereas a simple candle already gives us the richest yellows and orange tints. . . .

So far you have not told me whether you have read **Bel Ami** ***by Guy de Maupassant, and what in general you think of his talent now. I say this because the beginning of*** **Bel Ami** ***happens to be a description of a starlight night in Paris with the brightly lighted cafés of the Boulevard, and this is approximately the same subject I just painted.***

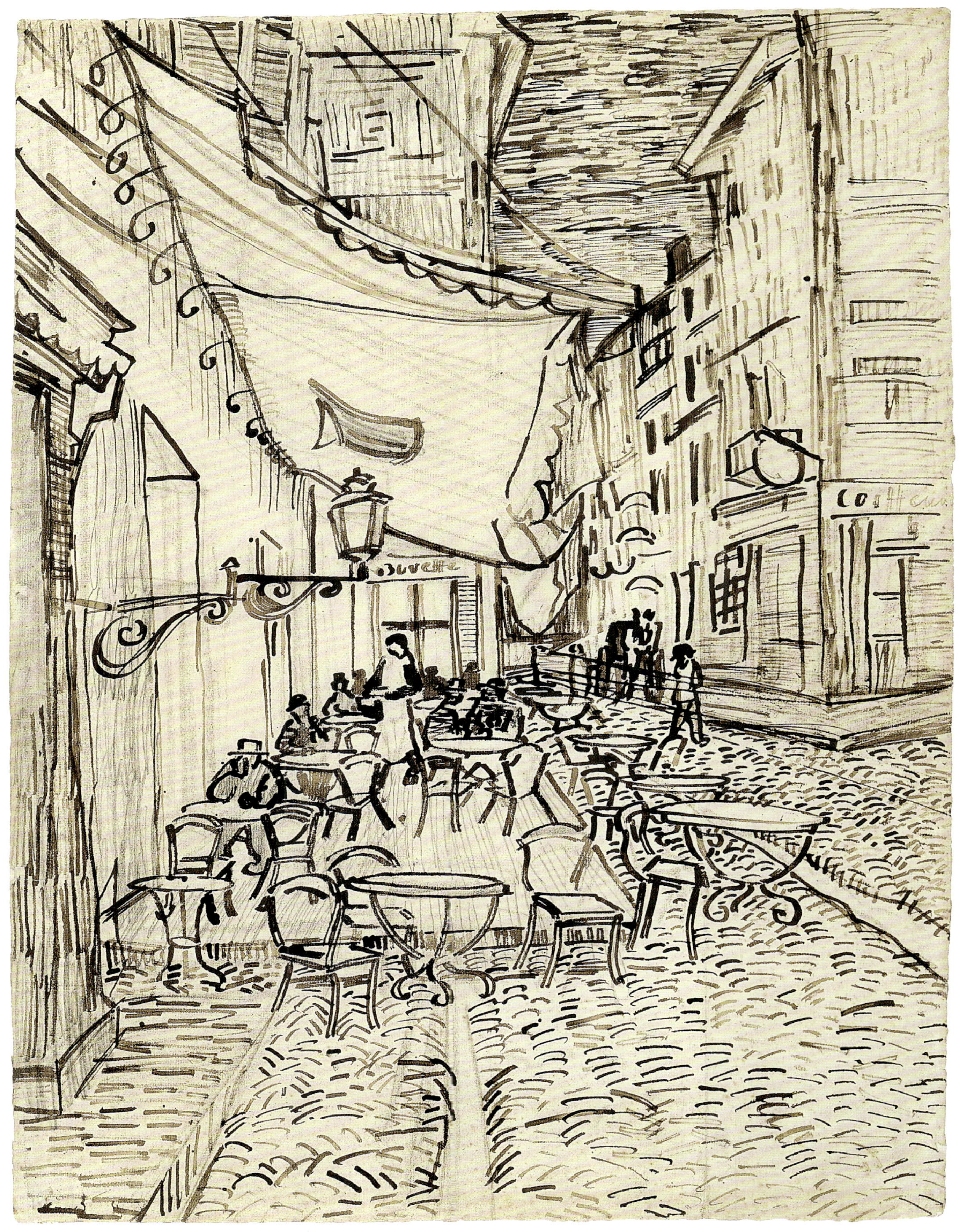

97. *The Yellow House*

ca. September 29, 1888
Pen and ink on graph paper
13.4 x 20.6 cm (5¼ x 8⅛ in.)
Verso: page of a letter to Theo van Gogh [543]
Signed on verso at end of letter: *Vincent*
Private collection, Minnesota
F1453, JH1590
Letter 543

Provenance: Sent by the artist to Theo van Gogh (d. 1891), Paris, ca. September 29, 1888 [543]; by inheritance to his son, Vincent Willem van Gogh, as part of his collection, administered by his widow, Johanna van Gogh-Bonger, 1891, until at least ca. 1893; sent by her to Émile Bernard, Paris, who reproduced it in 1893; perhaps sold by him, with other drawings, to Ambroise Vollard, Paris, between 1899 and 1904; Tanner Art Gallery, Zürich, 1918; R. Dreher, Brienz, Switzerland, 1918; by descent to a private European collector, until 2003; sold, Christie's, London, June 24, 2003, no. 52, to present owner.

Exhibition: Zürich 1924, no. 99.

Summary of the literature and additional observations: The reemergence of this drawing after nearly eighty years of obscurity has allowed for its place in Van Gogh's graphic oeuvre and his correspondence to be understood. Last exhibited in 1924, it is featured here in light of recent documentation furnished by Pickvance (in the catalogue of Christie's sale in London in 2003, no. 52) that resolves some riddles about this distinctive sheet. Apparently the artist ran short of paper while writing a letter to his brother Theo about September 29, 1888 [543], and used the back of this extempore sketch of his recent painting *The Yellow House* (F464, fig. 216) to complete it. Pickvance persuasively argued that, in terms of penmanship and content, this sheet was the fifth and final page of that letter, in which the "rough" sketch was described.

No scholar since De la Faille (1928, no. 1453) had had the opportunity to study firsthand this "croquis," which he described as "an illustration belonging to one of Vincent's letters" drawn on blue-lined graph paper; he noted that Van Gogh had "on verso, written the end of a letter in which he spoke, e.g., of a portrait which he had painted of Milliet." De la Faille gave a very accurate description of the sheet but made two errors that proved critical: he did not recognize which letter it belonged to, and he quoted only one sentence from it. Subsequent scholars assumed that this was all Van Gogh had written and regarded it as an "annotation" or "postscript" on the back of a small sketch, separately "enclosed" or "included" with the letter in which Van Gogh described sending it to Theo in late September 1888 [543]; see De la Faille 1970/1992, no. 1453; Roskill 1971, p. 172; Millard 1974, p. 161; Hulsker 1980/1996, no. 1590. Seeing the work as a letter sketch with a brief afterthought jotted on the back, a view that has held sway in the literature for thirty-odd years, was perhaps the only logical deduction to make, especially since the letter itself seemed not to be missing its last page in all the editions of the correspondence going back to the original volumes published by Johanna van Gogh-Bonger in 1914. Johanna, perhaps having "lost" the actual last page when she sent the sheet to Bernard, found a different ending to the letter in four pages that belonged to another one [541a]. Pickvance (in New York 1984, p. 260) recognized that the four pages were part of letter 541a, and with the emergence in 2003 of the sketch of the Yellow House, the last page of letter 543 was also found.

New documentation has clarified the history of the sheet from the time it was sent to Theo in 1888 and its purchase from a Swiss dealer in 1918 but not the thirty-year period in between. How did it find its way to the Swiss dealer? There is no record of its sale by Johanna van Gogh-Bonger. She did, however, respond to Émile Bernard's interest in publishing drawings in her possession, and this work appeared in the October 1893 issue of the *Mercure de France* (no. 45, p. 117). It was subsequently illustrated with captions that do not disclose its ownership in Meier-Graefe's 1910 monograph on Van Gogh (p. 67); Gauguin's "Vincent van Gogh," in *Kunst und Kunstler* 8 (1910), p. 581; and an edition of the *Lettres* edited by Bernard in 1911 (pl. XLV). Possibly it also found its way to the art marketplace through Bernard—among the some twenty-odd *dessins* that passed from him to the dealer Vollard between 1899 and 1904.[1]

Letter to Theo van Gogh, ca. September 29, 1888 [543]: Also [enclosed is] a sketch of a size 30 canvas representing the house and its surroundings in sulfur-colored sunshine, under a sky of pure cobalt [F464, fig. 216]. The subject is frightfully difficult; but that is just why I want to conquer it. It's terrific, these yellow houses in the sun, and the incomparable freshness of the blue. And everywhere the ground is yellow too. I shall send you a better drawing than this rough improvised sketch out of my head later on.

The house on the left is pink with green shutters, I mean the one in the shadow of the tree. That is the restaurant where I go for dinner every day. My friend the postman lives at the end of the street on the left, between the two railway bridges. The night cafe I painted is not in the picture, it is to the left of the restaurant.

Milliet thinks this horrible, but I need not tell you that when he says he cannot understand anyone amusing himself doing such a dull grocer's shop, and such stark, stiff houses with no grace whatever, remember that Zola did a certain boulevard at the beginning of L'Assommoir and Flaubert a corner of the Quai de la Villette in the midst of the dog days at the beginning of Bouvard et Pécuchet and neither of them is moldy yet.

In early May 1888, Van Gogh rented the Yellow House at 2 Place Lamartine and used it as his studio until he moved in that September. Consonant with making the house his home and preparing it for Gauguin's arrival, Van Gogh celebrated it in paint, completing the memorable canvas by September 29 (F464, fig. 216). He immediately sent Theo this spirited drawing of the subject (F1453, cat. 97) and within a week or so also a watercolor (F1413, cat. 98). Located at the edge of town, near the train station, the house was devastated by Allied bombing in June 1944 and was subsequently torn down.

SAS

1. The same scenario may resolve the early provenance for the other sketch sent in letter 543, F1515. It was not recorded in Johanna's account book but was similarly published by Bernard. For drawings reproduced by Bernard in the *Mercure de France* between 1892 and 1895, see "The Paper Trail," note 24; for his sales to Vollard, see "*Répétitions*: Drawings after Paintings Sent to Bernard."

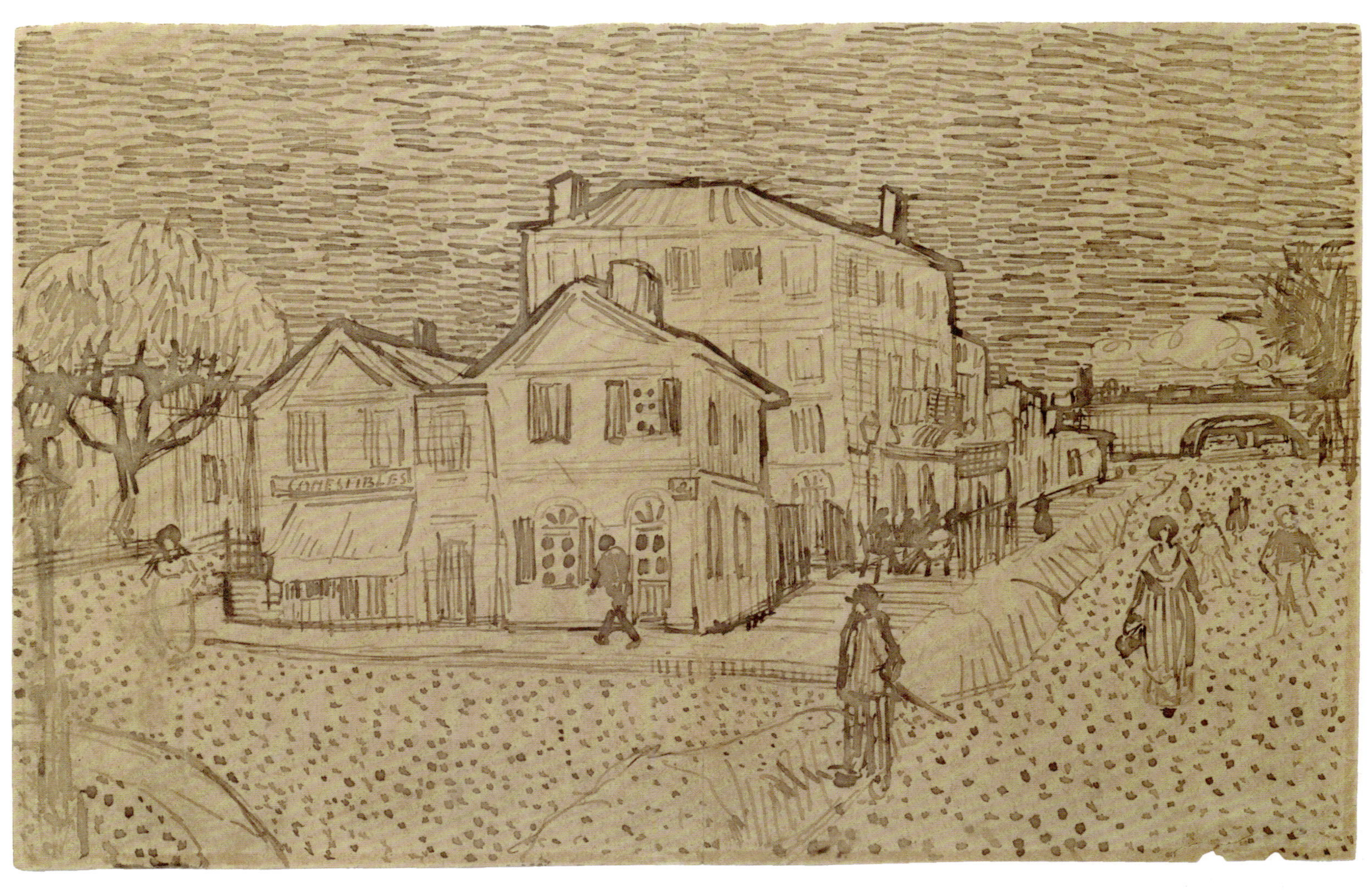
COMESTIBLES

98. *The Yellow House*

First week of October 1888
Opaque and transparent watercolor, pen, ink, and graphite on laid paper watermarked GLASLAN
Sheet 25.7 x 32 cm (10⅛ x 12⅝ in.), within drawn frame 24.8 x 31 cm (9¾ x 12¼ in.)
Van Gogh Museum, Amsterdam (Vincent van Gogh Foundation) (d 431 V/1962)
F1413, JH1591
Letter 548

Provenance: Sent by the artist to Theo van Gogh (d. 1891), Paris, by October 9 or 10, 1888 [548]; by inheritance to his son, Vincent Willem van Gogh (1890–1978), as part of his collection, administered by his widow, Johanna van Gogh-Bonger (d. 1925), 1891; placed on loan at the Stedelijk Museum, Amsterdam, 1931–73; ownership transferred to the Vincent van Gogh Foundation, 1962; placed on permanent loan at the Van Gogh Museum, Amsterdam, 1973.

Selected exhibitions: Amsterdam 1905, suppl. no. 474; Amsterdam 1914–15, no. 181; Paris 1937, no. 73; London–Birmingham–Glasgow 1947–48, no. 141; New York–Chicago 1949–50, no. 98; London 1962, no. 53; London 1968–69, no. 126; Tokyo–Kyōto–Nagoya 1976–77, no. 60; Paris 1977; Toronto–Amsterdam 1981, no. 25; New York 1984, no. 102; Arles 1989, no. 23; Otterlo 1990, no. 191; Tokyo 2000, no. 23.

Summary of the literature: Scholars long assumed that this watercolor was made before the oil painting (F464, fig. 216), though they disagreed on its date of execution. It was dated to May 1888 by De la Faille (1928, no. 1413) and Hammacher (in London 1962, no. 53); to the summer months by Cooper (1955, no. 23, within the context of a formidable discussion of the motif) and Bowness (in London 1968–69, no. 168); and to September by Millard (1974, p. 161), who considered it a "preparatory drawing." However, as the editors of De la Faille 1970 (no. 1413) first proposed and Hulsker (1980, no. 1591) contended, it was undoubtedly the "better drawing" made after the painted motif that Van Gogh promised to Theo [543] when sending him a smaller sketch (F1453, cat. 97) in late September. Welsh-Ovcharov (in Toronto–Amsterdam 1981, no. 24) cogently advanced this view, observing that the watercolor, which she dated to ca. October 1888, thus "served an analogous function to the wash drawing of *The Night Café*" (F1463). Her observations, including the essential differences between the oil and the watercolor that stem from technique, frame later discussions, in particular by Pickvance (in New York 1984, no. 102; in Otterlo 1990, no. 191), who did not neglect to mention letter 548, which confirms that the drawing served to give Theo an "idea of the color," as Roskill (1971, p. 173 and n. 173, equivocating on the watercolor's date but deciding that it preceded the September painting) first noted. Heenk (1995, p. 173) remarked that it was "probably done directly after the painting" and that the "similarities are more striking than the differences in detail." Hulsker (1996, no. 1591) changed his earlier dating of September to ca. October 9, 1888, to accord with the letter reference [548].

The first two watercolors Van Gogh made in Arles in the spring of 1888 (F1480, F1469) served the same function as the two he made that fall—*The Night Café* of early September 1888 (F1463, fig. 217) and this image of the Yellow House of early October: to give Theo "some idea of the color" of the oil paintings on which they were based [548]. The expressive use of color was fundamental to the artist's conception of these contrasting night and day scenes, which depend on the juxtapositions of red and green versus yellow and blue.

For all its dependence on the oil painting (F464, fig. 216), the present work has a distinctive charm of its own. The blonder tones and lighter touch of watercolor, as well as various subtractions and additions made in translation, contribute to its more lyrical quality. Streamlining the view by barely hinting at the unsightly mounds on the street (the likely consequence of road work), Van Gogh enhances it with descriptive detail of a more picturesque nature: in the signage and candy-cane awning of the food shop at left and the more legible local "types" like the costumed Arlésiennes at right.

SAS

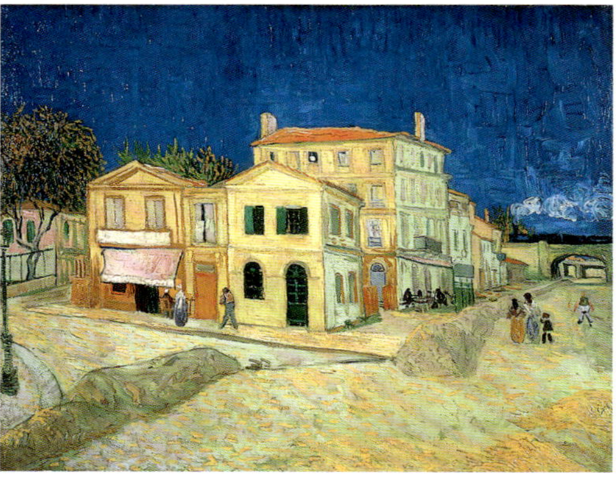

Fig. 216. *The Yellow House* (F464), September 1888. Oil on canvas, 72 x 91.5 cm (28⅜ x 36 in.). Van Gogh Museum, Amsterdam (Vincent van Gogh Foundation)

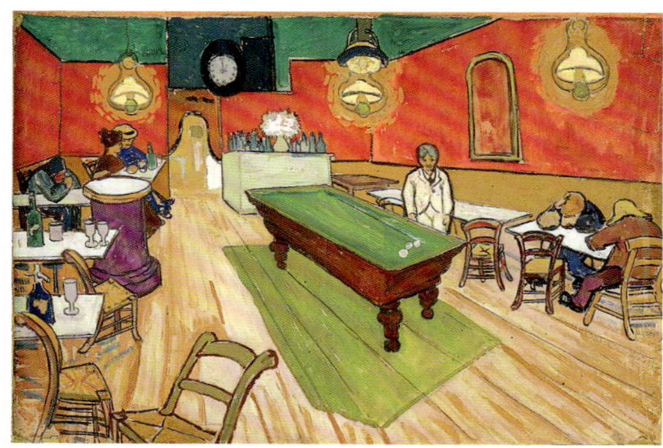

Fig. 217. *The Night Café* (F1463), September 8–9, 1888. Gouache, watercolor, ink and graphite on paper, 44.4 x 63.2 cm (17½ x 24⅞ in.). Private collection (photo: Gerhard Howald, Bern)

Letter to Theo van Gogh, October 9 or 10, 1888 [548]: Did you see that drawing of mine which I put in with Bernard's drawings, representing the house? You can get some idea of the color. I have a size 30 canvas [F464, fig. 216] of that drawing.

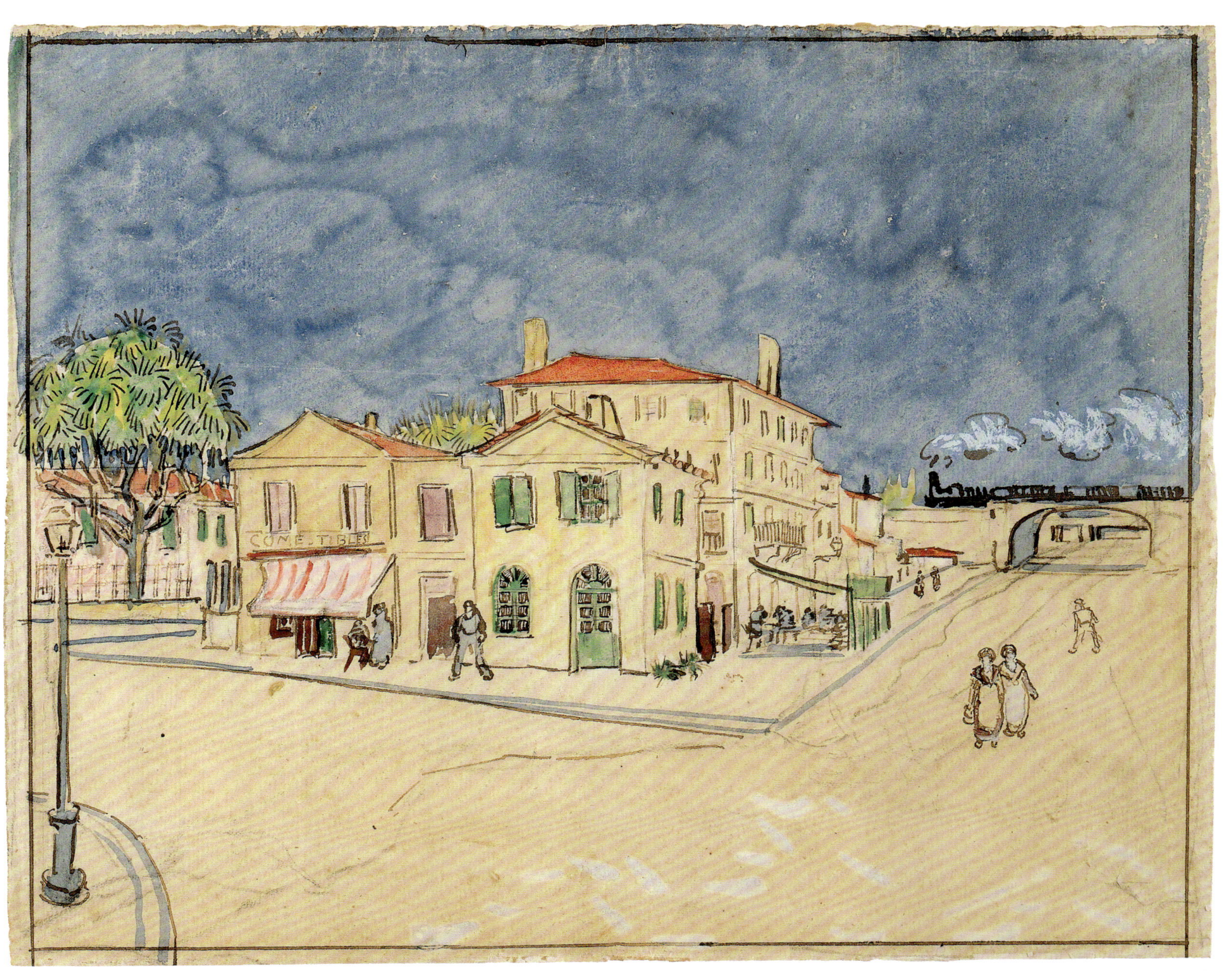
COMESTIBLES

99. *The Courtyard of the Hospital in Arles*

First week of May 1889
Reed pen, pen and ink, and graphite on laid paper watermarked AL PL BAS
46.6 x 59.9 cm (18⅜ x 23⅝ in.)
Signed on watering can, lower right: *Vincent*
Van Gogh Museum, Amsterdam (Vincent van Gogh Foundation) (d 222 V/1962)
F1467, JH1688
Letters 595, 597, T12

Provenance: Sent by the artist to Theo van Gogh (d. 1891), Paris, June 19, 1889 [595]; by inheritance to his son, Vincent Willem van Gogh (1890–1978), as part of his collection, administered by his widow, Johanna van Gogh-Bonger (d. 1925), 1891; placed on loan at the Stedelijk Museum, Amsterdam, 1931–73; ownership transferred to the Vincent van Gogh Foundation, 1962; placed on permanent loan at the Van Gogh Museum, Amsterdam, 1973.

Selected exhibitions: Brussels 1891, no. 12; Antwerp 1892; Copenhagen 1893, no. 194; Rotterdam 1900–1901, no. 12; Amsterdam 1905, no. 393; Berlin 1906, no. 53; Amsterdam 1914–15, no. 144; Amsterdam 1915, no. 25; Utrecht 1923, no. 35; Rotterdam 1923; The Hague 1925; London 1926–27, no. 27; Berlin 1927–28, no. 59; London–Birmingham–Glasgow 1947–48, no. 158; New York–Chicago 1949–50, no. 106; Aix-en-Provence 1959, no. 35; Paris–Albi 1966, no. 52; London 1968–69, no. 144a; Tokyo–Kyōto–Nagoya 1976–77, no. 67; Copenhagen 1984–85, no. 68; Arles 1989, no. 5; Otterlo 1990, no. 209; Tokyo 2000, no. 24.

Summary of the literature: This drawing, routinely dated to the end of April or early May 1889 and associated with the related painting (F519, fig. 218), has always been recognized as one of the last Van Gogh made in Arles and as the "hospital at Arles" referred to in letter 595 when it was sent to Theo from Saint-Rémy that June. De la Faille (1928, no. 1467) dated it to May 1889; De la Faille (1970/1992, no. 1467) to April–May 1889; Hulsker (1980, no. 1688) to April–May 1889, remarking that it "cannot be regarded as a preliminary study for the painting." Pickvance (in Arles 1989, no. 5) described the two-tiered, arcaded courtyard of the Hôtel-Dieu (founded in 1573); observed that the drawing differs from the painting in its vantage point and placement of potted plants; and proposed that it was made between May 3 and 8, 1889. Pickvance (in Otterlo 1990, no. 209) refined his dating, arguing that the work was probably "drawn a day or so later" than May 3 (the likely date of F1468) and "several days after the painting" (which is recorded in letter W11 of April 30), given the placement of the plants, and contending that "the changed viewpoint further emphasizes the drawing's independent qualities." He also remarked that in its "combination of loosely structured touches and rapid working," it presages the early Saint-Rémy drawings made on the same kind of paper. Heenk (1995, pp. 179, 184–85) dated it to early May and observed that it is drawn on the beige AL PL BAS paper Van Gogh used in Saint-Rémy. Hulsker (1996, no. 1688) specifies that it was an independent drawing of ca. April 30, 1889. For early history, see Feilchenfeldt and Veenenbos 1988, p. 133.

See "Drawing to a Close."

SAS

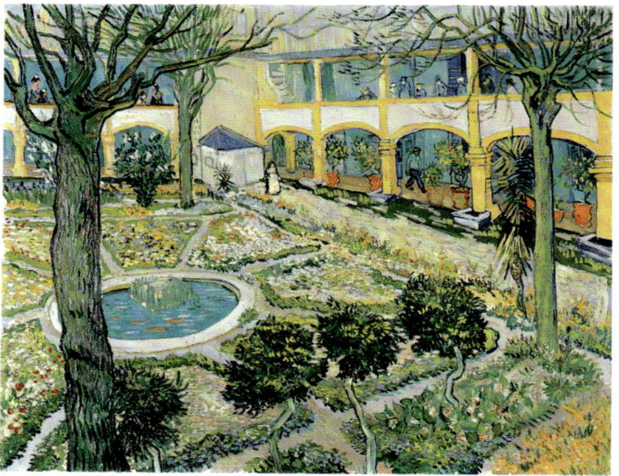

Fig. 218. *The Courtyard of the Hospital in Arles* (F519), ca. April 30, 1889. Oil on canvas, 73 x 92 cm (28¾ x 36¼ in.). Sammlung Oskar Reinhart "Am Römerholz," Winterthur

Letter to Wilhelmina van Gogh, ca. April 30, 1889 [W11]: [I] have just finished two pictures of the hospital, one of a ward [F646]. . . . And then, as a pendant, the inner court [F519, fig. 218]. It is an arcaded gallery like those one finds in Arab buildings, all white-washed. In front of those galleries an antique garden with a pond in the middle, and eight flower beds, forget-me-nots, Christmas roses, anemones, ranunculus, wallflowers, daisies, and so on. And under the gallery orange trees and oleander. So it is a picture quite full of flowers and vernal green. However, three gloomy black tree trunks pass through it like serpents, and in the foreground four big dismal clusters of somber box shrub. It is probable that people here won't see very much in it, but nevertheless it has always been my great desire to paint for those who do not know the artistic aspect of a picture.

Letter to Theo van Gogh, June 19, 1889 [595]: I am sending you a roll of drawings. . . . The drawings—hospital at Arles [F1467, cat. 99], the weeping tree in the grass [F1468, cat. 100], the fields and the olives are a continuation of those old ones of Montmajour, the others are hasty studies made in the garden.

Letter to Theo van Gogh, July 2, 1889 [597]: The drawings seem to me to have little color this time, and the too-smooth paper is a little responsible for that. Anyway, the weeping tree [F1468, cat. 100] and the courtyard of the hospital at Arles [F1467, cat. 99] have more color, but all the same this will give you an idea of what I am doing.

Letter to Vincent from Theo van Gogh, July 16, 1889 [T12]: I thank you for your letters and the fine drawings you sent me. The hospital at Arles is very remarkable. . . .

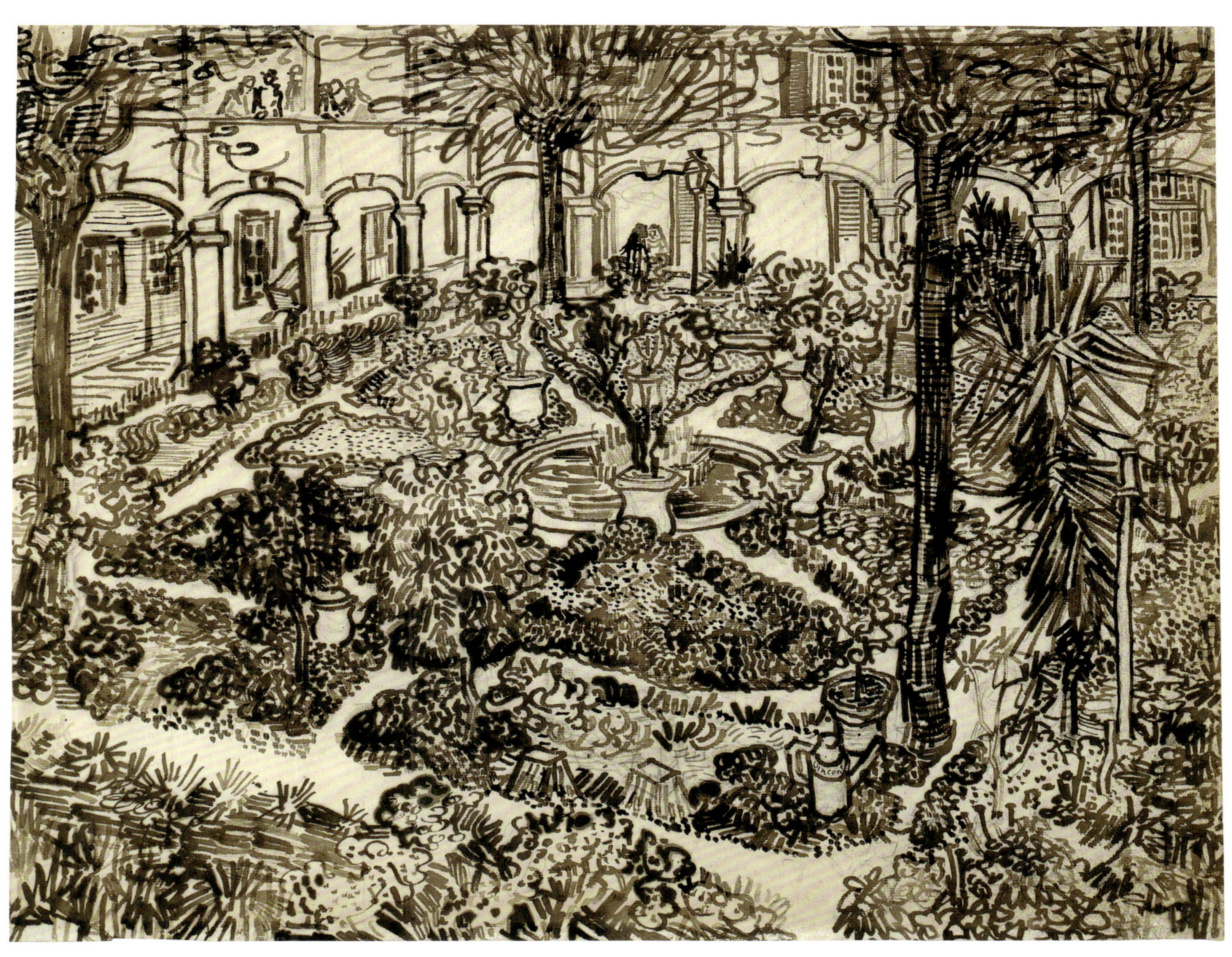

100. *A Garden in the Place Lamartine (Weeping Tree in the Grass)*

ca. May 3, 1889
Black chalk, reed pen, pen, and ink on paper watermarked J. WHATMAN MANUFACTURER 1888
48.9 x 61.5 cm (19¼ x 24¼ in.)
The Art Institute of Chicago, Gift of Tiffany and Margaret Blake (1945.31)
F1468, JH1498
Letters 590, 595, 597

Provenance: Sent by the artist to Theo van Gogh (d. 1891), Paris, June 19, 1889 [595]; by inheritance to his son, Vincent Willem van Gogh, as part of his collection, administered by his widow, Johanna van Gogh-Bonger, 1891; her gift to Dr. Jan Pieter Veth (d. 1925), Amsterdam; by descent to his daughter-in-law Mrs. Christine Veth, San Francisco, by 1935; consigned by her for sale to Wildenstein & Co., New York, 1945; acquired by the Art Institute of Chicago, 1945.

Selected exhibitions:[1] New York and other cities 1935–36, no. 114; New York 1984, no. 149; Otterlo 1990, no. 210; Chicago–Amsterdam 2001–2, no. 115.

Summary of the literature: This drawing arguably dates to early May 1889, as De la Faille (1928, no. 1468) originally contended and Pickvance (in New York 1984, no. 149; in Otterlo 1990, no. 210) persuasively established. Pickvance proposed that it was described in letter 590 of May 3, 1889, and sent to Theo in June from Saint-Rémy [595]; he referred to it as the last depiction of a "favored motif" from the Place Lamartine garden and (in Otterlo 1990) attributed its mood, "inhibited deliberateness," and "Gothic spikiness" to the artist's need to refamiliarize himself with the medium after a period of "long hibernation." His views are reflected in Heenk (1995, p. 195) and also in Druick and Zegers (in Chicago–Amsterdam 2001–2, no. 115, pp. 273–75, fig. 23), who, however, saw the image as intimately related to the Van Gogh–Gauguin dialogue. For other thoughts on the dating of this drawing, see De la Faille 1970, no. 1468, as part of the September 1888 Poet's Garden series; Roskill 1971, p. 165, as possibly one of the first Arles drawings, made in March 1888; Millard 1974, p. 158, as an early Arles drawing, perhaps reworked in September 1888; Hulsker 1974, p. 32, as one of five July 1888 drawings of the motif; Hulsker 1980/1996, no. 1498, as made prior to the oil of the Weeping Tree of July 12 (F428) "before the tall grass was mowed."

Letter to Theo van Gogh, May 3, 1889 [590]: I am also thinking again of beginning to draw more with a reed pen, which, like last year's views of Montmajour [F1420, cat. 85; F1424, cat. 86; F1446, cat. 84; F1447, cat. 83; JH Add. 3, cat. 82] for instance, costs less and distracts my mind just as much. Today I made a drawing of that sort, which has turned out very dark and rather melancholy for one of spring. . . .

Letters to Theo van Gogh, June 19 [595] and July 2, 1889 [597]: See cat. 99 (F1467).

See "Drawing to a Close." SAS

1. This drawing was misidentified by De la Faille (1928, no. 1468) as being the garden with weeping tree shown in Amsterdam 1905, as no. 412. The garden lent by Johanna, numbered 187 on her inventory list (and in ink on the reverse of the sheet), corresponds to a different drawing: see F1451, cat. 90. Johanna may have presented Jan Veth with the present work as a token of her appreciation for his role in helping to organize the large-scale Van Gogh retrospective held in Amsterdam in 1892–93; she seems to have presented a drawing to co-organizer Richard Roland-Holst (F1475).

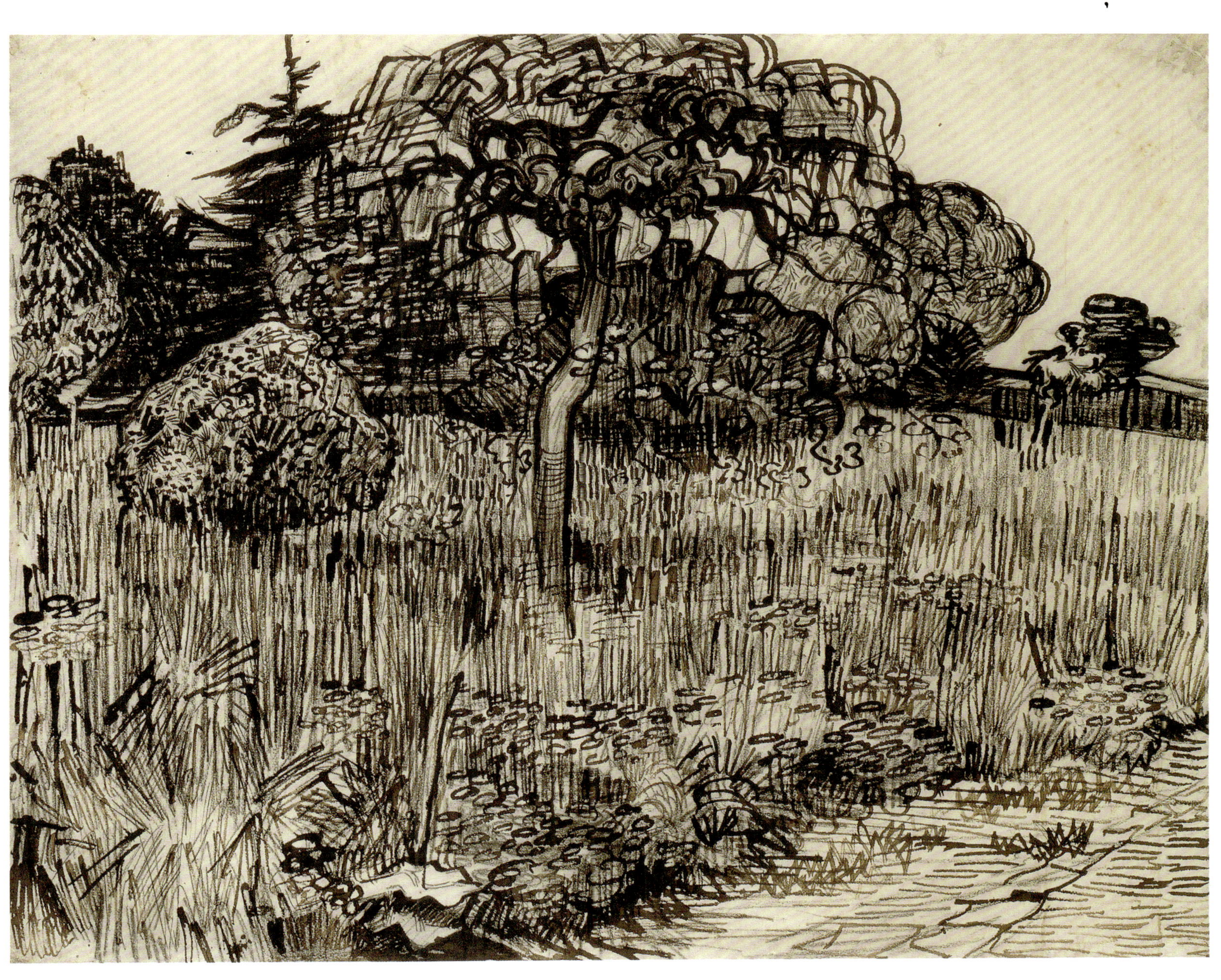

Saint-Rémy, 1889–90: Taking Asylum

On May 8, 1889, Van Gogh took the train from Arles to Saint-Rémy-de-Provence, having decided to commit himself to the psychiatric asylum Saint-Paul-de-Mausole, formerly a monastery. Although the two towns are only twenty-five kilometers apart, their surrounding landscapes differ enormously. Vast plains ring Arles, while Saint-Rémy lies at the foot of the low massifs of the Alpilles. At the asylum, Van Gogh was given two rooms, one for a bedroom and one to use as a studio. The former, located on the floor above the ground floor, had a view of a walled wheat field; the latter was probably also on the second floor, although in a different wing of the building, and it looked out over the garden of the extensive complex.

Van Gogh concentrated mainly on painting during the year he spent in Saint-Rémy. The drawings he did vary from quick sketches to large, autonomous works. All were executed during periods when he was unable to paint—when he ran out of oils or canvas or when, following one of his attacks, he was prevented from painting by the doctors, who were afraid he might poison himself by eating the paints. Van Gogh's letters from Saint-Rémy, therefore, contain only sporadic references to drawings. In contrast to his works on paper from Arles, which he often felt were good enough for exhibition, sale, exchange, or gifts, he made no mention of such intentions regarding the sheets done in Saint-Rémy. He neither signed nor annotated any of the drawings.

In the first month of his stay, Van Gogh was not allowed to go beyond the walls of the asylum. He was thus limited to the neglected monastery garden with its old trees, bushes, and flower beds, which nonetheless provided him with a variety of motifs. He spent his first two weeks in Saint-Rémy painting, soon exhausting the supply of oils and canvas he had taken with him from Arles, and then began exploring his new surroundings with drawing tools. During the next fourteen days, he made a number of drawings that are among the most beautiful of the Saint-Rémy period. He employed a highly graphic style with the lines covering most of the sheet, imbuing the works with a rhythmic, almost decorative quality. Large, worked-up drawings in pen and ink depict different aspects of the garden, such as the fountain (F1531, cat. 103), the trees in one corner (F1497, cat. 101), and a tree covered in ivy (F1532, cat. 102). In terms of style, technique, and medium, however, these do not form as cohesive a group as another seven drawings of the garden executed at the same time (F1526; F1527, fig. 219; F1533, cat. 104; F1534; F1535, cat. 105; F1536, fig. 227; F1537), which were done

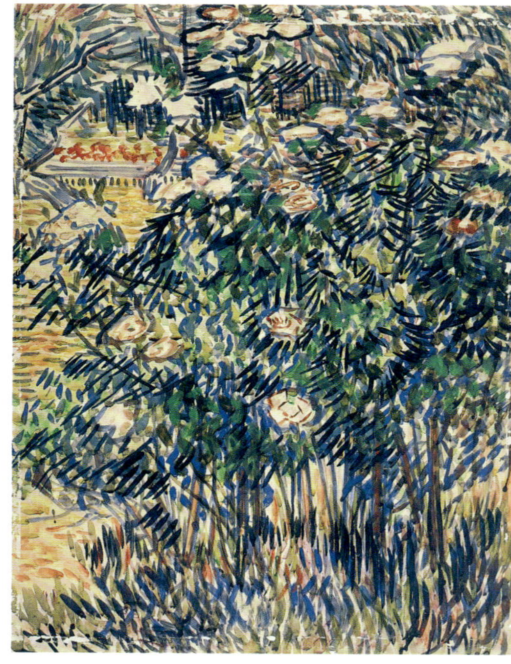

Fig. 219. *Flowering Shrubs* (F1527), late May–early June 1889. Oil paint and ink on paper, 61.4 x 46.7 cm (24¼ x 18⅜ in.). Kröller-Müller Museum, Otterlo

with brush and diluted oil paints (not transparent or opaque watercolor as has always been assumed).

For this group of brush drawings, Van Gogh probably used paint left over from supplies he had brought from Arles, and the colors are the same ones we find in the paintings from his first two weeks in Saint-Rémy, such as *Irises* (F608) and *The Garden of the Asylum at Saint-Rémy* (F734, fig. 220). His first request from Saint-Rémy to Theo for new supplies came after he finished these canvases. The shipment arrived about June 8, that is, after he had done the seven drawings. One is struck by the fact that these marvelous, colorful sheets, done moreover in a novel technique, are not mentioned in the surviving correspondence.

During the same two-week period, the artist made a pen-and-ink drawing of the view from his bedroom window: *Sun above the Walled Field* (F1728, cat. 106). The highly finished drawing style and the use of cross-hatching—unusual in the Saint-Rémy period—can also be seen in the sheet that features the fountain in the garden (F1531, cat. 103). Van Gogh regarded the fully worked pen drawings from the end of May and early June as a sequel to the extraordinarily successful sheets he had produced on Montmajour the previous summer (JH Add. 3, cat. 82; F1447, cat. 83; F1446, cat. 84; F1420, cat. 85; F1424, cat. 86).

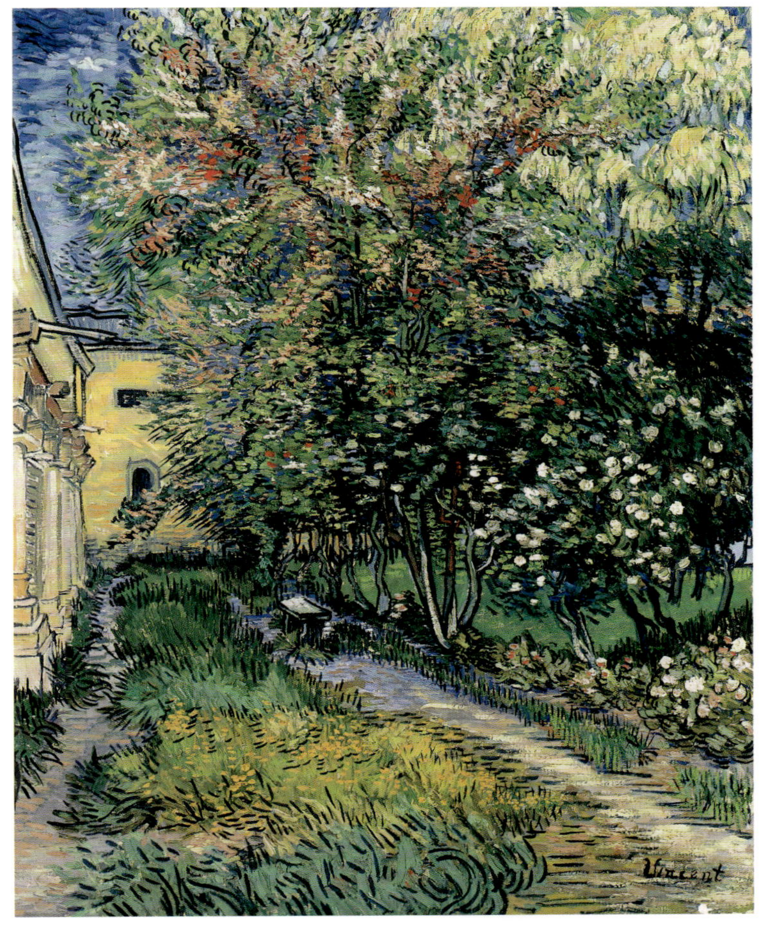

Fig. 220. *The Garden of the Asylum at Saint-Rémy* (F734), May 1889. Oil on canvas, 91.5 x 72 cm 36 x 28⅜ in.). Kröller-Müller Museum, Otterlo

The new paints and canvas arrived just as Van Gogh received permission to work outside the asylum walls, and he once again turned his full attention to painting the surrounding landscape: cypresses, wheat fields, olive groves, and mountain ridges. In order to give Theo an impression of these Provençal canvases, Van Gogh copied about ten of them in pen-and-ink drawings that he sent to his brother in early July (F1522, cat. 107; F1525, cat. 108; F1538, cat. 110; F1540, fig. 30; F1524; F1494; F1544; F1548; F1547; F1546; and perhaps F1542, cat. 112). These impressive works are executed on full sheets of a smooth wove paper not previously found in Van Gogh's oeuvre. The artist was not terribly pleased with this paper, feeling that the sleek surface detracted from the works' "color"—their variegations or strength—and he did not use it again. In these landscapes on paper, as in the ones on canvas, Van Gogh emphasized large forms achieved with dashing, wavy lines—mostly built up with short strokes—seeking to "bring things together through a drawing [style] that tries to show how the components are intertwined" [613]. Van Gogh hoped that the powerful linear style would connect to the work of Gauguin and Bernard. Theo was not particularly impressed with these stylized works: he felt they were too far removed from nature, that Van Gogh's "search for style is at the expense of the true sentiment of things" [T19].

In mid-July Van Gogh suffered an attack

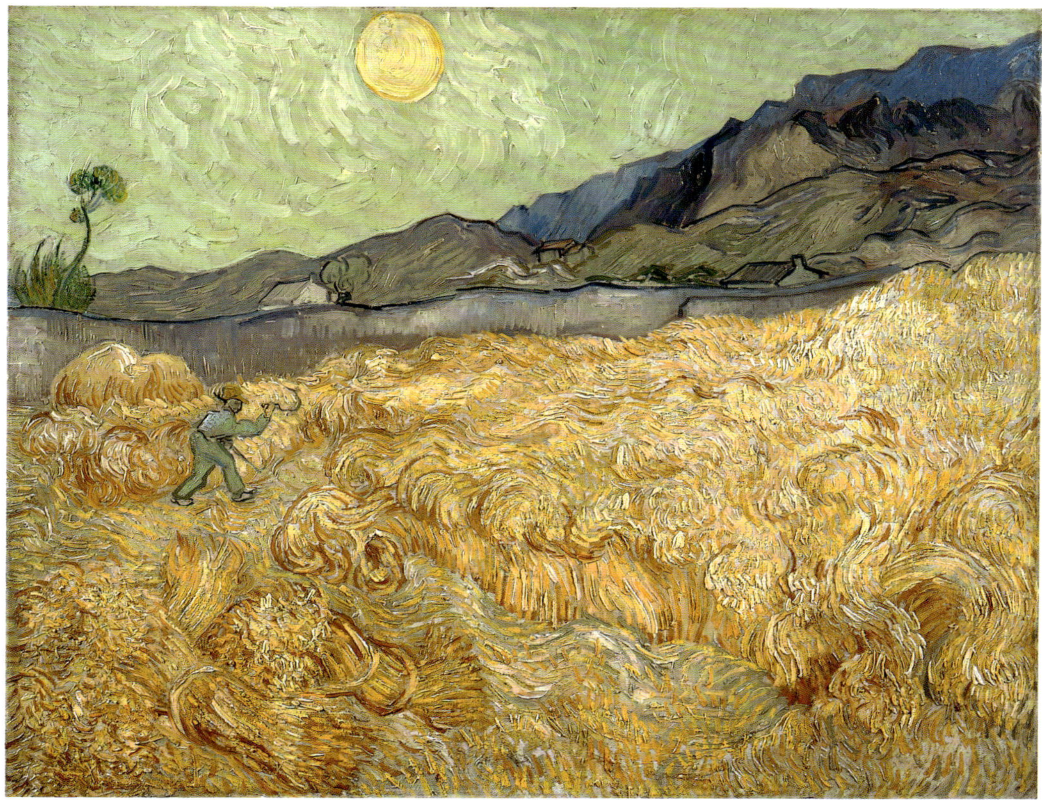

Fig. 221. *Wheat Field with Reaper* (F618), September 1889. Oil on canvas, 73 x 92 cm (28¾ x 36¼ in.). Van Gogh Museum, Amsterdam (Vincent van Gogh Foundation)

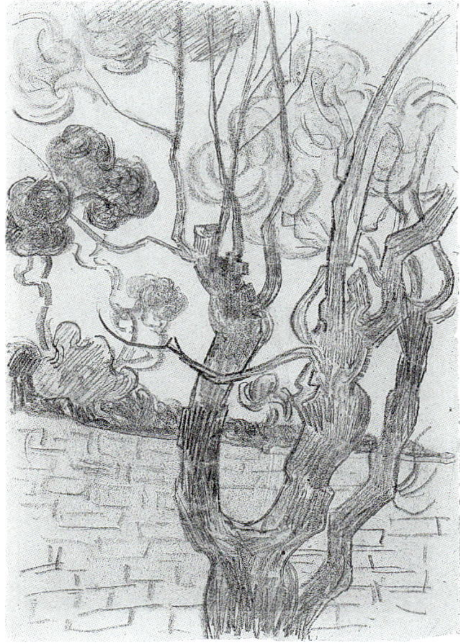

Fig. 222. *Tree near the Wall of the Asylum* (F1580), October 1889. Graphite on paper, 29.8 x 20.6 cm (11¾ x 8⅛ in.). Van Gogh Museum, Amsterdam (Vincent van Gogh Foundation)

and was unable to work for the next five weeks. When he picked up his brushes again in September, he did not feel strong enough to go outdoors, even into the garden. He began painting copies after black-and-white reproductions of works by his favorite artists—Millet, Rembrandt, and Delacroix. We have reason to believe that three monumental views of the interior of the asylum executed in diluted oils on paper (F1529, cat. 113; F1528, cat. 114; F1530, cat. 115) were also done at this time, although Van Gogh said nothing about drawings in his letters. These sheets, which have previously been dated to late May–early June or to October, depict his studio, an entranceway with a view of the fountain, and one of the many corridors in the former monastery. The colors are soberer than those in the garden scenes done in diluted oils in May–June. These tones—Van Gogh referred to them as "the palette of the North" [601]—correspond to those of the paintings from the period around his attack (see F618, fig. 221). These paints were part of the shipment he received in early July. Further, his emphasis in these paintings on large forms and masses is also seen in the three interior drawings.

It was only in late September or early October that Van Gogh resumed working outdoors. He began with painting but probably turned to drawing the trees in the garden when, in the first weeks of October, he once again ran out of paint (see F1580, fig. 222). About two weeks later, a new shipment arrived, and he returned to copying reproductions of works by Millet, pursuing this project into

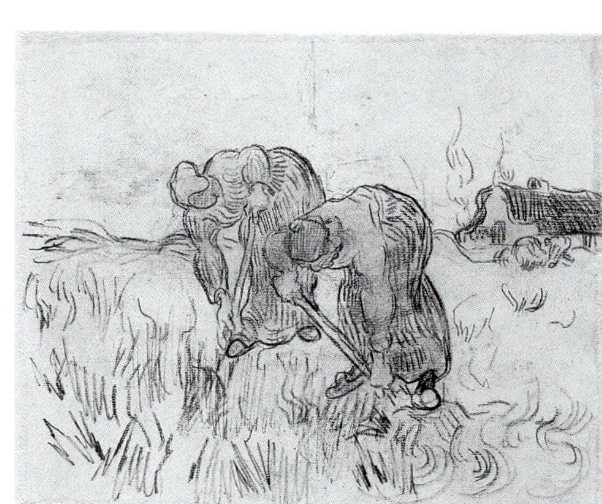

Fig. 223. *Two Women Digging* (F1586v), March–April 1890. Pen and ink on paper, 23.7 x 28.1 cm (9⅜ x 11 in.). Van Gogh Museum, Amsterdam (Vincent van Gogh Foundation)

November. In addition to these copies, he again depicted the view from his bedroom window, the walled field, on canvas and paper (F737, fig. 235; F1552, cat. 116). In the drawing, the short, powerful parallel lines that delineate the landscape are stylistically related to the paintings from this time.

From the end of December 1889 until his departure from Saint-Rémy in May 1890, Van Gogh suffered another three attacks. The last of these, which persisted from February 22 until the end of April, was particularly detrimental to his health and well-being. Even in this exhausting period, however, he managed to work, executing five paintings and approximately fifty sketches, all related to the theme "memories of the North" [629]. These revisited subjects were ones he had explored five years earlier in the Netherlands on both canvas and paper—peasants working the land, cottages with thatched roofs, and peasants enjoying a meal (see F1586v, fig. 223). Making these sketches, which he did not develop into fully worked drawings, helped him get through this difficult time.

MV

101. *Pine Trees in the Walled Garden of the Asylum*

Last week of May–first week of June 1889
Reed pen, pen, brush, and ink, graphite on pink laid paper watermarked AL (in banderole) PL BAS
62.3 x 48 cm (24¼ x 18⅞ in.)
Inscribed on verso, in another hand: *219* [crossed out], *502*
Traces of perspective frame guidelines
Tate, London, Bequeathed by C. Frank Stoop, 1933 (NO 4716)
F1497, JH1852

Provenance: Theo van Gogh (d. 1891); by inheritance to his son, Vincent Willem van Gogh, as part of his collection, administered by his widow, Johanna van Gogh-Bonger, 1891; sold by her (together with F1242, cat. 24; F1639, cat. 119) through Kunsthandel C. M. van Gogh to Dutch stockbroker and collector C. F. Stoop, London, 1911; bequeathed by him to the Tate Gallery, 1933.

Selected exhibitions: Amsterdam 1905, suppl. no. 470; Cologne–Frankfurt 1910; Berlin 1910, no. 54; London–Birmingham–Glasgow 1947–48, no. 169; Frankfurt 1970, no. 62; New York 1986–87, no. 4; Otterlo 1990, no. 212; Bremen 2002–3, no. 5.

Summary of the literature: Cohen-Gosschalk (1908, p. 235) was the first to publish a reproduction. De la Faille (1928, no. 1497) situated the drawing in the Arles period. Cooper (in London–Birmingham–Glasgow 1947–48, no. 169) was the first to date it to the Saint-Rémy period; he identified the locale as the walled field to the east of the asylum complex. The correct location and a more specific dating (June 1889) were first given in Frankfurt 1970 (no. 62); De la Faille 1970 (no. 1497) accepted this, as did Alley (1981, p. 293), who felt that the hypothesis was supported by the flowering irises in the foreground. The same flowers led Pickvance (in New York 1986–87, no. 4) to date the drawing to May 1889; in Otterlo 1990 (pp. 284–85, 290), he reiterated the date but now on the basis of the style and use of a perspective frame. Hulsker (1980/1996, no. 1852) was practically the only author to disagree: the autumnal mood and similarities to F1545 led him to date the sheet to November 1889. Heenk (1995, pp. 184, 185) and Hansen (in Bremen 2002–3, no. 5) gave the date maintained here: last week of May–first days of June. Pickvance (in Otterlo 1990, p. 284) and Heenk (1995) described the sheet in the context of other drawings of the asylum garden.

Pickvance (in New York 1986–87, p. 88) suggested that this was one of the "hasty studies made in the garden" [595] that Vincent sent to Theo ca. June 18, 1889, a date difficult to reconcile with the use of a perspective frame, on which Pickvance was the first to remark. He corrected his dating in Otterlo 1990, noting letter T12, which indicates that other drawings were sent with the ca. June 18 letter.

Feilchenfeldt and Veenenbos (1988, p. 135) published new information on the early exhibition history and provenance. Heijbroek and Wouthuysen (1993, pp. 32, 179, 205) and Stolwijk and Veenenbos (2002, pp. 53, 129, 151, 163, 197) further refined the provenance. All mistakenly stated that Johanna sold the drawing to C. M. van Gogh, but gallery correspondence indicates that the sheet was there on consignment.

This drawing shows the southwest corner of the walled garden of the asylum Saint-Paul-de-Mausole, where the entrance to the complex is situated. The porter's loge, which forms a break in the wall, can be seen in the left background. Van Gogh made a sketch of the same location in the fall of 1889 (F1581, fig. 224).

In *Pine Trees in the Walled Garden of the Asylum,* the artist used a pencil not only to sketch the initial composition but also to work up the drawing, for example, in the tonal rendering of the trees. The graphite plays an independent role and in several places was applied over the ink. The ink itself has faded considerably and is now a brownish green, which may indicate that the drawing was originally done in color. It has been suggested (New York 1986–87, no. 4; Bremen 2002–3, no. 5) that the bending figure in the middle of the field was added later, but graphite underdrawing indicates that the figure was part of the original composition.

Oddly, Van Gogh here made use of his perspective frame, a device he had abandoned after his visit to Saintes-Maries-de-la-Mer a year earlier. That he still had it on his mind in 1890 is demonstrated by a sheet from Auvers (F1637v, fig. 225).

MV

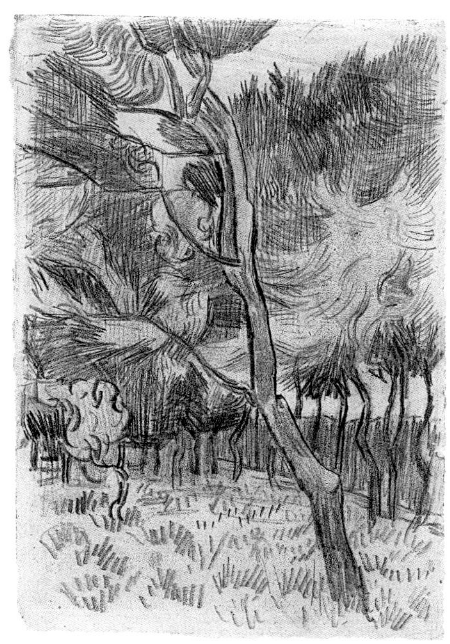

Fig. 224. *Pine Trees in the Walled Garden of the Asylum* (F1581), autumn 1889. Graphite on paper, 30.2 x 20.6 cm (11⅞ x 8⅛ in.). Van Gogh Museum, Amsterdam (Vincent van Gogh Foundation)

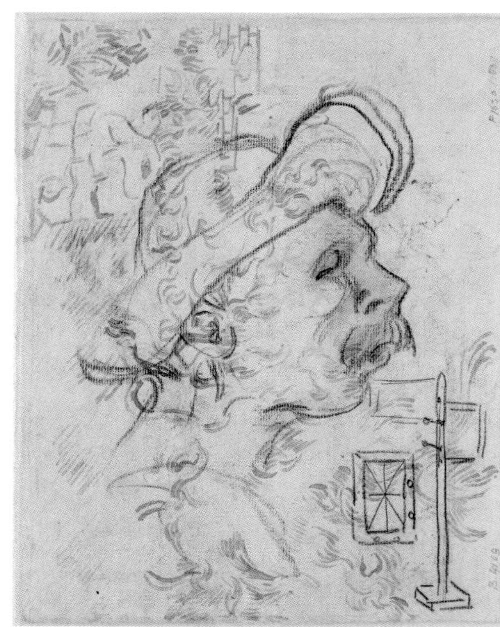

Fig. 225. *Head of a Man and Sketch of a Perspective Frame* (F1637v), May–July 1890. Blue and black chalk on laid paper, 48.2 x 31.2 cm (19 x 12¼ in.). Van Gogh Museum, Amsterdam (Vincent van Gogh Foundation)

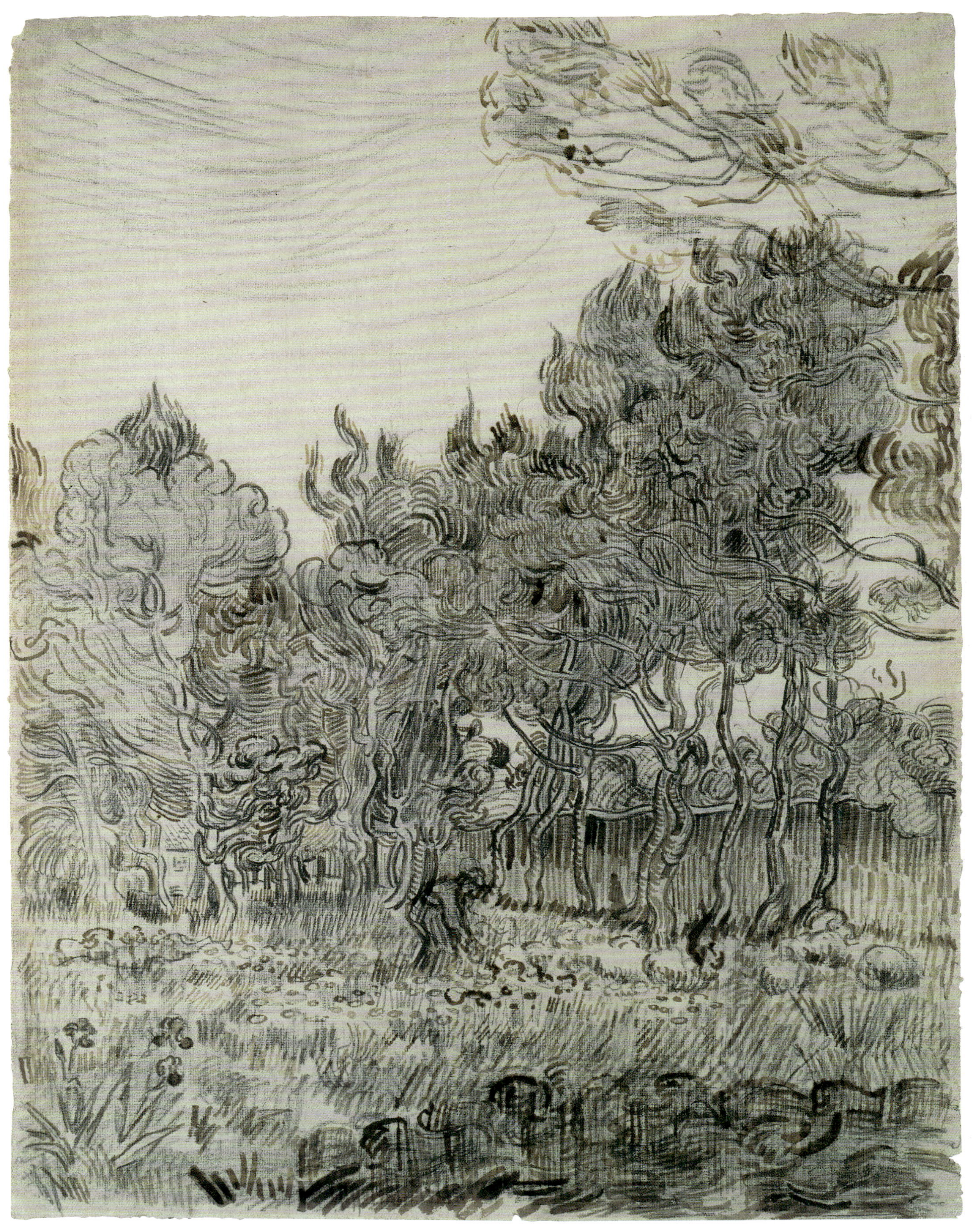

102. *Tree with Ivy in the Garden of the Asylum*

Last week of May–first week of June 1889
Reed pen, brush, and ink, graphite on laid paper watermarked AL (in banderole) PL BAS
61.8 x 47.1 cm (24 3/8 x 18 1/2 in.)
Inscribed on verso, in another hand: *217*
Van Gogh Museum, Amsterdam (Vincent van Gogh Foundation) (d 340 V/1962)
F1532, JH1696

Provenance: Theo van Gogh (d. 1891); by inheritance to his son, Vincent Willem van Gogh (1890–1978), as part of his collection, administered by his widow, Johanna van Gogh-Bonger (d. 1925), 1891; placed on loan at the Stedelijk Museum, Amsterdam, 1931–73; ownership transferred to the Vincent van Gogh Foundation, 1962; placed on permanent loan at the Van Gogh Museum, Amsterdam, 1973.

Selected exhibitions: Leiden 1893; Paris 1896–97; Amsterdam 1905, no. 357; Berlin 1910, no. 68; Frankfurt 1911; Amsterdam 1914–15, no. 188; London 1926–27, no. 40; Berlin 1927–28, no. 85; London–Birmingham–Glasgow 1947–48, no. 164; London 1962, no. 63; London 1968–69, no. 147; New York 1986–87, no. 2; Otterlo 1990, no. 216; Kyōto–Tokyo 1992, no. 28.

Summary of the literature: De la Faille (1928, no. 1532) dated the drawing to the Saint-Rémy period and titled it simply "Jardin." Cooper (in London–Birmingham–Glasgow 1947–48, no. 164) retained the neutral title but assigned a more precise date, summer 1889. This was accepted in London 1962 (pp. 13, 80, 81), where for the first time the title specifies that the work shows a view of the garden of the asylum; there is also some discussion of Van Gogh's fascination for ivy and moss. Bowness (in London 1968–69, no. 147) was the first to date the drawing to May 1889, which most subsequent scholars have followed. He based this date on the fact that Van Gogh was not allowed to leave the grounds of the asylum during his first weeks there. In De la Faille 1970/1992 (no. 1532), however, the drawing was situated in July 1889, without specification of why. Hulsker (1980/1996, no. 1696) underpinned the May dating with a reference to the sheet's similarities to F1522 (cat. 107), which, however, he considered might possibly have been executed in June. Heenk (1995, p. 184) was the most precise, suggesting the date adopted here. Pickvance (in New York 1986–87, no. 2) discussed the sheet in connection with the other pen drawings of this period, noted the Japanese influence, and mentioned Van Gogh's understanding of the dualism of ivy, which destroys its host but also creates "green nests for lovers" [592]. He assumed that the sheet was one of the "hasty studies made in the garden" [595] that Vincent sent to Theo ca. June 18, which he corrected in Otterlo 1990 (pp. 284–85, 296), noting Theo's reaction to the consignment in letter T12, which indicates that different drawings were sent. Van Uitert and Hoyle 1987, p. 456, no. 2.532; Feilchenfeldt and Veenenbos 1988, p. 136.

Soon after his arrival in Saint-Rémy, Van Gogh became fascinated with the ivy-covered trees in the garden of the asylum. He had already painted *sous-bois* in Paris (F306, F307, F308, F309, F309a), and in Saint-Rémy he would again explore the subject on canvas (F609; see F1522, cat. 107). A short time later he made this drawing, the first sheet to depict the subject. It is briskly and spontaneously executed, yet renders each element with its own distinct line. The tree trunk cutting across the foreground was undoubtedly inspired by Japanese prints and can be found in Van Gogh's paintings from both Paris (F371) and Arles (F450). The low wall across the middle ground marks the boundary of the raised southern section of the garden.

Van Gogh first sketched his subject in graphite, working up the composition in ink using reed pen and brush, although without exactly following the penciled lines (fig. 256). He used brushes of three different widths; one was frayed. The ink now exhibits a variety of brown tones; the heaviest lines are dark blue at the edges, which may indicate that they were originally in color. The artist filled almost the entire sheet—in places going right over the edge of the paper—giving the drawing a highly decorative quality.

MV

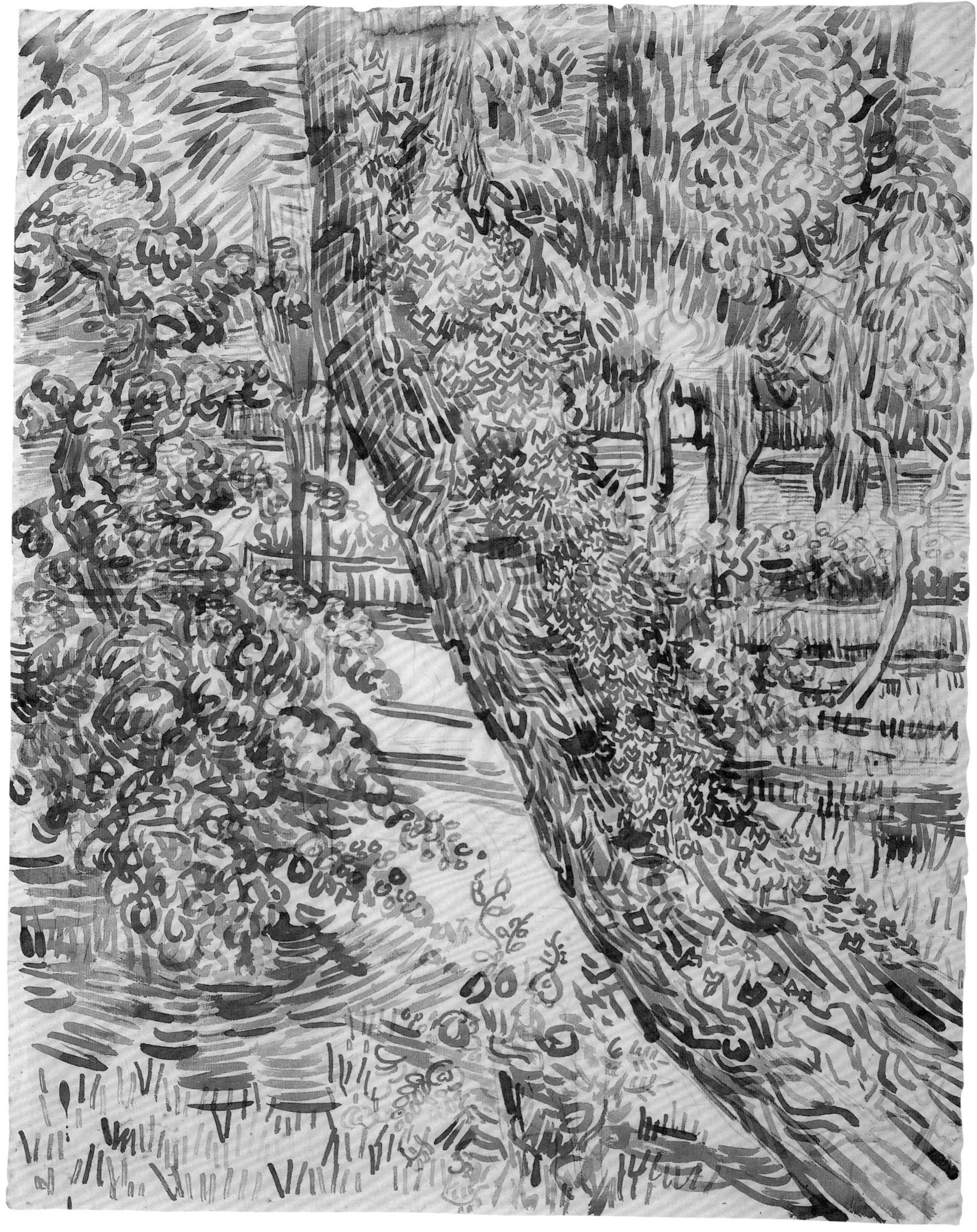

103. *Fountain in the Garden of the Asylum*

Last week of May–first week of June 1889
Reed pen, pen, and ink, brown chalk on wove paper
49.8 x 46.3 cm (19⅝ x 18¼ in.)
Inscribed on verso, in another hand: *no. 7*
Van Gogh Museum, Amsterdam (Vincent van Gogh Foundation) (d 440 V/1962)
F1531, JH1705
Letter T24

Provenance: Sent by the artist to Theo van Gogh (d. 1891), Paris, early January 1890 [T24]; by inheritance to his son, Vincent Willem van Gogh (1890–1978), as part of his collection, administered by his widow, Johanna van Gogh-Bonger (d. 1925), 1891; placed on loan at the Stedelijk Museum, Amsterdam, 1931–73; ownership transferred to the Vincent van Gogh Foundation, 1962; placed on permanent loan at the Van Gogh Museum, Amsterdam, 1973.

Selected exhibitions: Brussels 1891, no. 15; The Hague 1891; Rotterdam 1892; Antwerp 1892, no. 10; Amsterdam 1892–93; Copenhagen 1893, no. 195; Amsterdam 1905, no. 394; Berlin 1906, no. 52; Antwerp 1914, no. 93; Berlin 1914, no. 78; Cologne–Hamburg 1914; Amsterdam 1914–15, no. 143; Amsterdam 1915, no. 24; Utrecht 1923, no. 34; Rotterdam 1923; The Hague 1925; Berlin 1927–28, no. 82; New York and other cities 1935–36, no. 122; Paris 1937, no. 189; London–Birmingham–Glasgow 1947–48, no. 162; New York–Chicago 1949–50, no. 137; Arles–Saint-Rémy 1951 (shown in Saint-Rémy only), no. 94; London 1968–69, no. 148; Copenhagen 1984–85, no. 70; Otterlo 1990, no. 215.

Summary of the literature: Earliest reproductions are in *Elseviers Maandschrift* 30, no. 10 (1905), p. 228; Cohen-Gosschalk 1908, p. 233; Van Meurs 1910, no. 23; and *Lettres* 1911, pl. LXXVIII. In the last publication the drawing was first dated to Saint-Rémy. This was not adopted in the early exhibition catalogues, however: until Berlin 1927–28 (no. 82), the fountain was assumed to be in the garden of the hospital in Arles. Bremmer 1924, vol. 4, no. 28; Meier-Graefe 1928b, the first color reproduction. De la Faille (1928, no. 1531) titled the work "La fontaine dans le jardin de l'hôpital" and placed it among drawings from Saint-Rémy not mentioned in the letters. A more exact date, May 1889, was first suggested by Bowness (in London 1968–69, no. 148) and has not been disputed though it has also been given as May–June (De la Faille 1970, no. 1531; Heenk 1995, pp. 184, 185). Hulsker (1980/1996, no. 1705) compared the hatching with that in F1728 (cat. 106), a drawing he dated to the same time. In Copenhagen 1984–85 (pp. 121–23), Theo's fondness for the drawing is mentioned: in 1893 Johanna had an offer for the work, but on the grounds that it had been Theo's favorite, she refused to sell it for less than the asking price. Pickvance (in New York 1986–87, p. 82) identified five pen drawings Van Gogh made of the garden during this two-week period. In Otterlo 1990 (pp. 284–85), he described them in more detail but characterized F1531 (cat. 103) as executed on AL PL BAS paper and a pendant to F1537. Heenk (1995, pp. 184, 185) corrected these two assertions and was the first to point out a mention of the drawing in a letter from Theo to Vincent [T24]. Van Uitert and Hoyle 1987, p. 456, no. 2.530; Feilchenfeldt and Veenenbos 1988, p. 136; Stolwijk and Veenenbos 2002, p. 26.

Letter to Vincent from Theo van Gogh, January 8, 1890 [T24]: In one of the rolls there was also a superb pen drawing representing a fountain in a garden.

The drawing depicts the fountain in the garden of the asylum, located near the entrance to the north section of the men's ward, visible at the right, in which Van Gogh had his studio. The fountain, also seen in F1530 (cat. 115) and a painting, F732, spouts water from a carved basket of fruit. For the jet of water, the ink was scraped from the paper with a sharp object, a technique Van Gogh had not used before and would not again. The little bench behind the fountain looks as though it was made of thin slabs of stone, but a photograph shows it as really quite robust (fig. 226). The edges of the broad lines of ink are dark blue, possibly indicating that the drawing was done in color.

Van Gogh did not send the drawing to Theo until January 3, 1890 (when he also sent several paintings), more than six months after finishing it. According to Johanna van Gogh-Bonger, *Fountain in the Garden of the Asylum* was Theo's favorite drawing (letter to Octave Maus, February 7, 1891, Archief voor Hedendaagse Kunst, Brussels).

MV

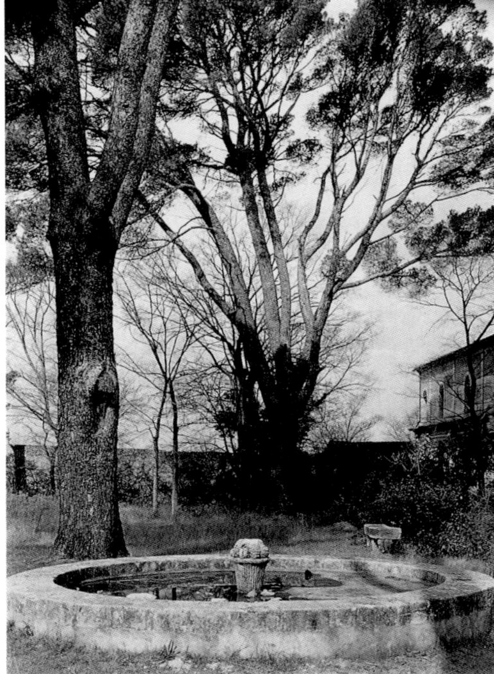

Fig. 226. Photograph of the Saint-Paul-de-Mausole garden with fountain, 1950s, from Tralbaut 1969, p. 283

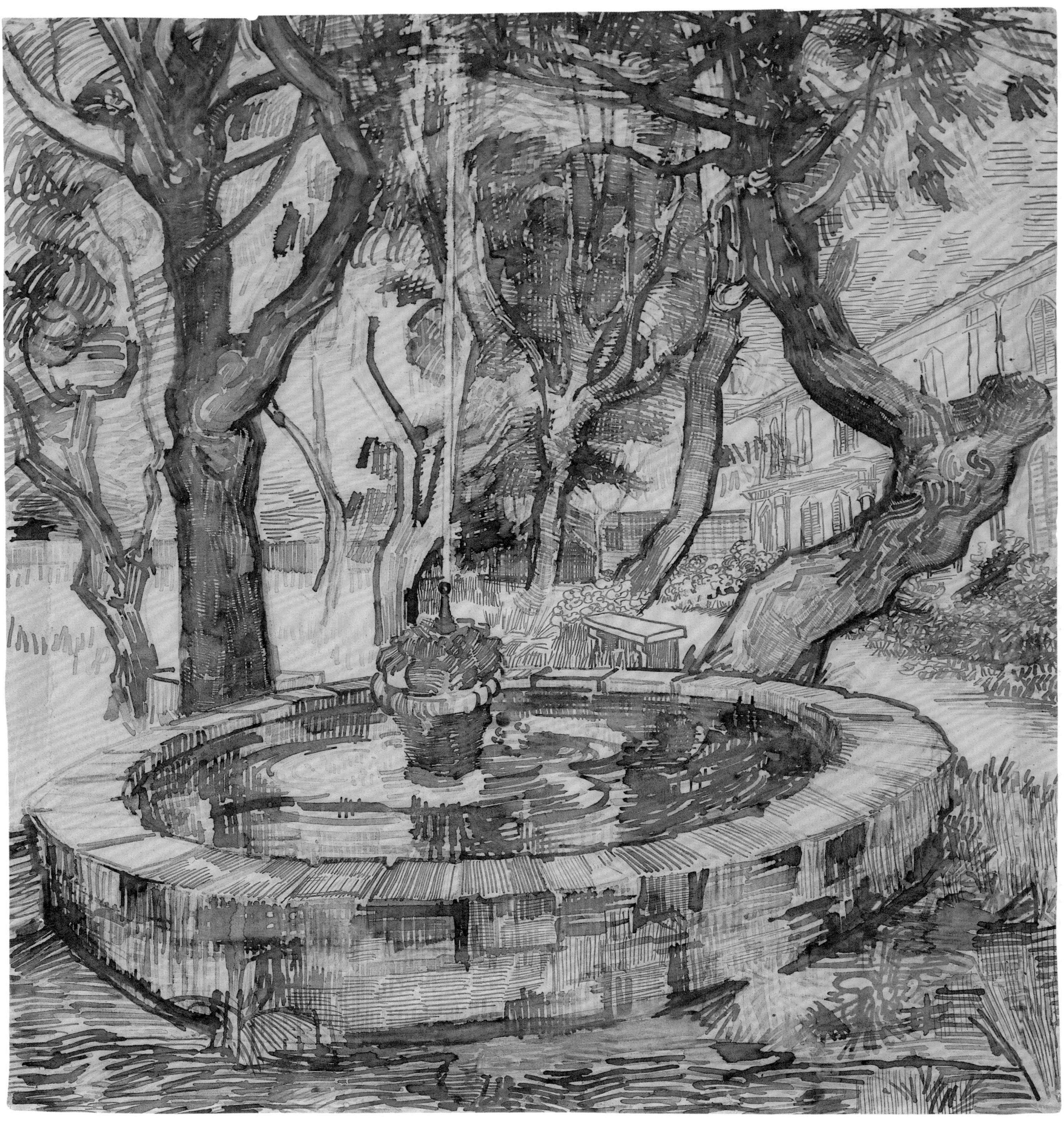

104. *Tree and Bushes in the Garden of the Asylum*

Last week of May–first week of June 1889
Brush, diluted oils, ink, and black chalk on wove paper
46.9 x 61.9 cm (18 1/2 x 24 3/8 in.)
Inscribed on verso, in another hand: *no. 7*
Van Gogh Museum, Amsterdam (Vincent van Gogh Foundation) (d 334 V/1962)
F1533, JH1710

Provenance: Theo van Gogh (d. 1891); by inheritance to his son, Vincent Willem van Gogh (1890–1978), as part of his collection, administered by his widow, Johanna van Gogh-Bonger (d. 1925), 1891; placed on loan at the Stedelijk Museum, Amsterdam, 1931–73; ownership transferred to the Vincent van Gogh Foundation, 1962; placed on permanent loan at the Van Gogh Museum, Amsterdam, 1973.

Selected exhibitions: Paris 1896–97; Amsterdam 1905, no. 356; Berlin 1906, no. 58; Munich and other cities 1909–10; Hamburg 1911–12; Dresden–Breslau 1912, no. 11; Berlin 1914, no. 60; Cologne–Hamburg 1914; Amsterdam 1914–15, no. 170; London 1926–27, no. 2; London–Birmingham–Glasgow 1947–48, no. 165; New York–Chicago 1949–50, no. 138; London 1968–69, no. 157; Otterlo 1990, no. 219.

Summary of the literature: De la Faille (1928, no. 1533) included the drawing among the works executed in Saint-Rémy and titled it simply "Parc." He believed the sheet was done in watercolor, an assumption followed by all later authors. In Amsterdam 1929 (no. 75), there is a more precise title, "Hospitaaltuin." Cooper (in London–Birmingham–Glasgow 1947–48, no. 165) was the first to date the sheet to the summer of 1889; Cooper (1955, pp. 80, 82, 83) revised this to May–early June. The same date was given in London 1968–69 (p. 103) and De la Faille 1970/1992 (no. 1533), while Hulsker (1980/1996, no. 1710) suggested May specifically. Pickvance (in New York 1986–87, p. 86) narrowed the date to two weeks, May 22–early June. This has now been widely accepted, with the exception of Van Uitert and Hoyle (1987, p. 456, no. 2.533), in which Hulsker's May dating was maintained. Pickvance (in New York 1986–87, p. 86) described the group of garden drawings as having been done in chalk, reed pen, and ink, with later additions of watercolor and gouache. He proposed (in Otterlo 1990, pp. 284–85, 297) that the works were pendants and suggested that the drawings might have been executed with the brushes Van Gogh ordered from Theo about this time. Heenk (1995, pp. 185, 186) also believed Van Gogh might have conceived the works as pendants. Feilchenfeldt and Veenenbos (1988, p. 136) provided additional information on the early exhibition history.

In addition to pen-and-ink drawings (see F1497, cat. 101; F1532, cat. 102; F1531, cat. 103), Van Gogh also executed seven views of the garden in diluted oil paint (three vertical and four horizontal) at the end of May or early June. In all of them, the artist's brushwork was swift and accurate, perfectly capturing the luxuriant atmosphere of the garden. Characteristic of this group is the close focus on one particular element: a tree, a bush, a staircase, or a stone bench. The sheets thus have little depth, which contributes to their highly modern feel. With one exception (F1537), each of the motifs appears in two sheets, which has led some scholars to assume they were intended as pendants.

Van Gogh sketched in the composition with black chalk and finished the scene with a variety of brushes and highly diluted oils, which until recently were believed to be watercolor. The brown lines that Pickvance (in New York 1986–87, p. 87; in Otterlo 1990, no. 219) interpreted as done with reed pen and ink were also made with brush and ink, which overlaps the paint, proving that the artist did not begin the work as a reed-pen drawing. The now-brown lines were probably done in aniline ink, which was available in bright colors but which fades quickly under exposure to light. Some of the brushstrokes appear dry and ragged, suggesting that Van Gogh used old brushes, not new ones as Pickvance proposed. It is possible the artist decided to order new brushes (see letter 593 of ca. June 2, 1889) while working on the group. By the time he actually received them, however (see letter 594 of ca. June 9), he had already turned his attention back to painting.

MV

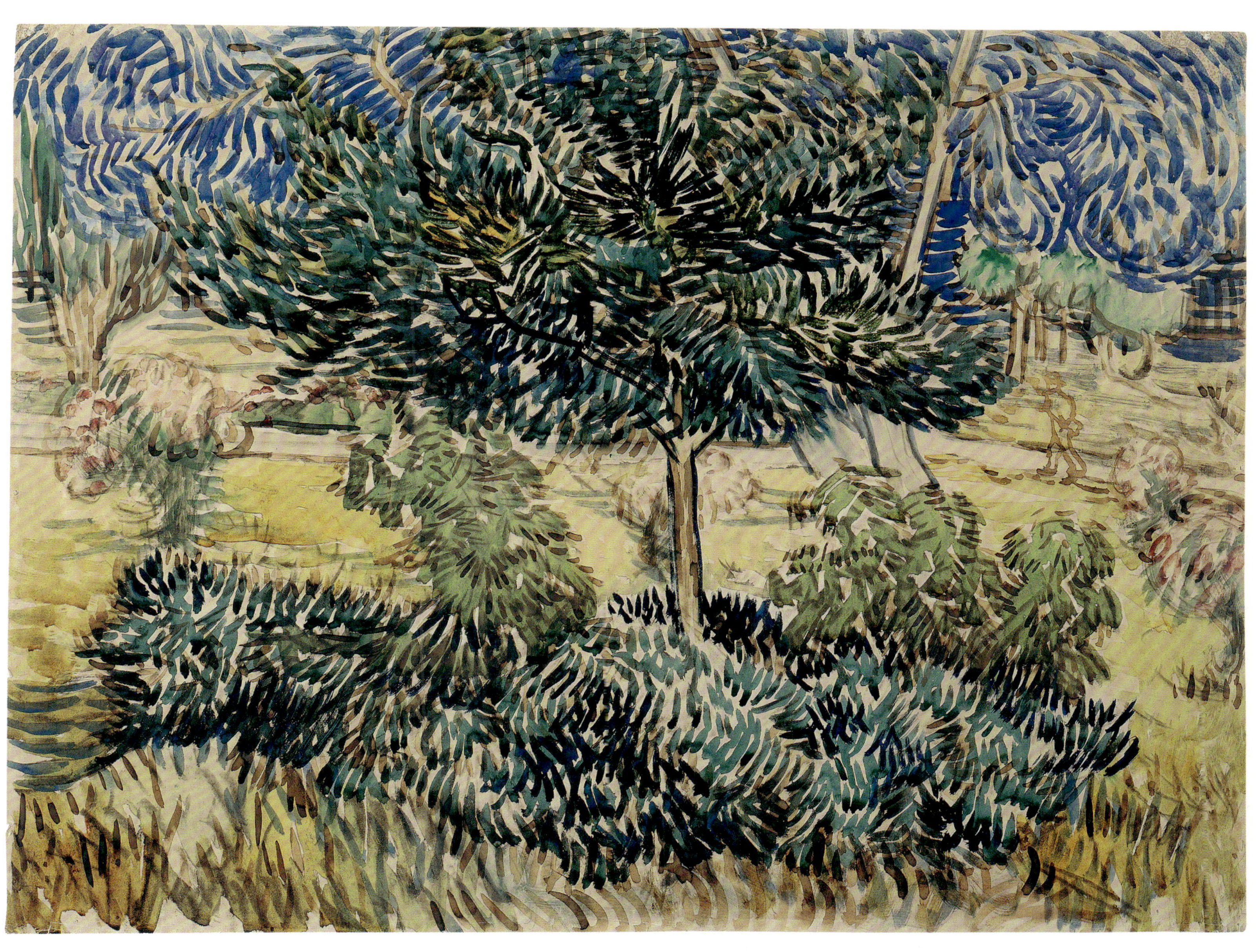

105. *Stairs in the Garden of the Asylum*

Last week of May–first week of June 1889
Brush, diluted oils, and ink, black chalk on thin cardboard
63.1 x 45.6 cm (24⅞ x 18 in.)
Inscribed on verso, in another hand: *no. 6*
Van Gogh Museum, Amsterdam (Vincent van Gogh Foundation) (d 438 V/1962)
F1535, JH1713

Provenance: Theo van Gogh (d. 1891); by inheritance to his son, Vincent Willem van Gogh (1890–1978), as part of his collection, administered by his widow, Johanna van Gogh-Bonger (d. 1925), 1891; placed on loan at the Stedelijk Museum, Amsterdam, 1931–73; ownership transferred to the Vincent van Gogh Foundation, 1962; placed on permanent loan at the Van Gogh Museum, Amsterdam, 1973.

Selected exhibitions: Amsterdam 1905, no. 418; Munich and other cities 1909–10; Berlin 1914, no. 59; Cologne–Hamburg 1914; Amsterdam 1914–15, no. 162; London–Birmingham–Glasgow 1947–48, no. 166; London 1968–69, no. 156; New York 1986–87, no. 3; Otterlo 1990, no. 218.

Summary of the literature: De la Faille (1928, no. 1535) included the drawing among the works executed in Saint-Rémy and gave it the neutral title "Parc." He believed the sheet was done in watercolor, an assumption followed by all later authors. Cooper (in London–Birmingham–Glasgow 1947–48, no. 166) was the first to date the sheet more exactly, to the autumn of 1889, based on the motifs in the paintings of that period (F640, F731); he repeated this in 1955 (pp. 86, 87) and referred to the drawing as a preliminary study for the canvases. Bowness (in London 1968–69, p. 103) dated this and five of the six related sheets to May–early June (he did not include F1537 in the series). In De la Faille 1970/1992 (no. 1535), it is dated to July, although no reasons were given. According to Hulsker (1980, no. 1713), who dated the drawing to May, the series in color consisted of seven works, while Pickvance (in New York 1986–87, pp. 84–86) included only six, arguing that F1534 is a pastiche. He narrowed the date to the two-week period May 22–early June, 1889. This has now been widely accepted. Van Uitert and Hoyle (1987, pp. 250, 251, 456, no. 2.534; apparently too far along to take account of this newer dating) gave a description of the technique and the discolorations. Pickvance (in New York 1986–87, p. 86) described the group of garden drawings as having been done in chalk, reed pen, and ink, with later additions of watercolor and gouache. He proposed (in Otterlo 1990, pp. 284–85, 297) that the works were pendants and suggested that the drawings might have been executed with the brushes Van Gogh ordered from Theo about this time. Heenk (1995, pp. 185, 186) also believed Van Gogh might have conceived the works as pendants. Feilchenfeldt and Veenenbos (1988, p. 137) provided additional information on the early exhibition history. In 1996, Hulsker (no. 1713) added a question mark after the date "May 1889," the meaning of which is not clear; he did not do this for the other drawings of the group.

The garden of the asylum had three levels, each linked to the next by stone steps. The steps in this drawing led from the central to the upper level, the part closest to the entrance to the complex (see F1497, cat. 101). As in F1533 (cat. 104), blue and green tones dominate. The same stairs, viewed from a greater distance, are also the central motif in the horizontal *Trees in the Garden of the Asylum* (F1536, fig. 227).

Van Gogh sketched the composition in black chalk and then brushed in diluted oils and colored ink (see F1533, cat. 104). The ink has discolored to brown, but bright colors can still be seen around the edges, where the mat overlapped the paper. The frayed character of some of the brushstrokes suggests that here, as in F1533, Van Gogh was using old, worn brushes.

MV

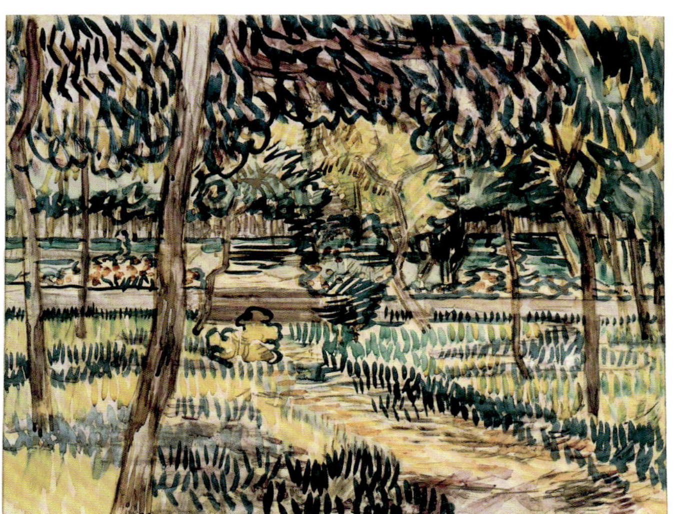

Fig. 227. *Trees in the Garden of the Asylum* (F1536), last week of May–first week of June 1889. Brush, diluted oils, and ink, 46.5 x 61.5 cm (18¼ x 24¼ in.). Private collection, courtesy Pierre Gianadda Foundation, Switzerland

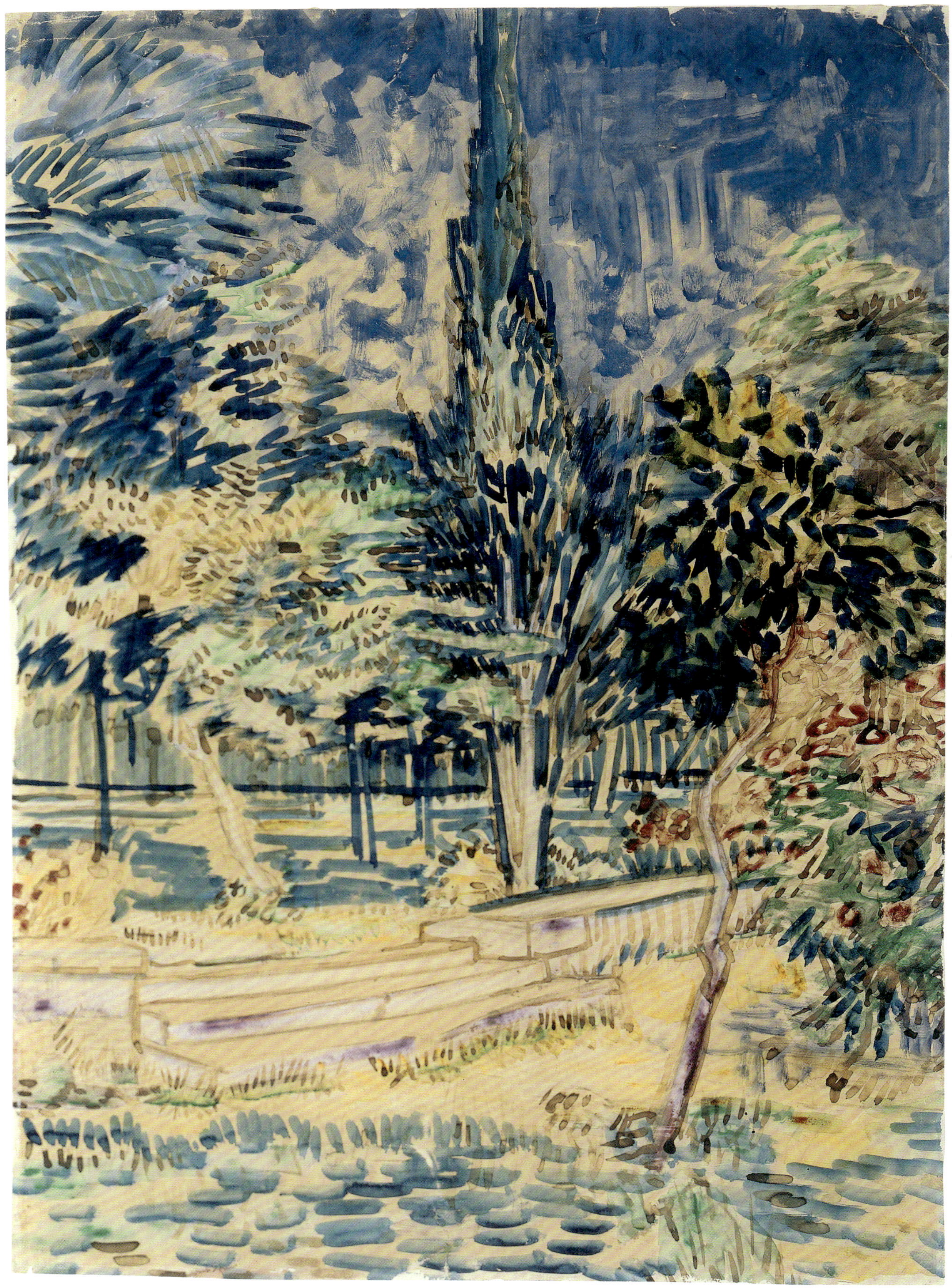

106. *Sun above the Walled Field*

Last week of May–first week of June 1889
Reed pen and ink, black chalk, white opaque watercolor on laid paper watermarked AL (in banderole)
47.5 x 56.6 cm (18¾ x 22¼ in.)
Kröller-Müller Museum, Otterlo (KM 125.482)
F1728, JH1706

Provenance: Theo van Gogh (d. 1891); by inheritance to his son, Vincent Willem van Gogh, as part of his collection, administered by his widow, Johanna van Gogh-Bonger, 1891, until 1901; acquired from her by E. D. van den Broecke, Middelburg (later Oostkapelle), during the Rotterdam Kunstkring exhibition of 1900–1901; her bequest to the Vereniging Het Kunstmuseum, Middelburg, 1932; donated to the Zeeuws Genootschap, which lent it to the Zeeuws Museum, Middelburg, 1962; purchased by the Kröller-Müller Museum, Otterlo, with support from the Vereniging Rembrandt, 1970.

Selected exhibitions: The Hague 1898, hors cat.; Rotterdam 1900–1901, no. 52; Paris–Albi 1966, no. 86; New York 1986–87, no. 39; Otterlo 1990, no. 225; Saint Louis–Frankfurt 2001, unnumbered; Bremen 2002–3, no. 16.

Summary of the literature: Between Rotterdam 1900–1901 (no. 52) and Paris–Albi 1966 (no. 86), F1728 was completely absent from the literature. It was added to the 1970 edition of De la Faille (no. 1728) and dated to autumn 1889; E. Joosten (1970) argued for this date on grounds of style and motif. The same date was given in Kröller-Müller Museum 1974 (pp. 67, 68) and 1980 (pp. 114, 115), but Hulsker (1980/1996, no. 1706) dated it to May 1889 on the basis of the detailed style and compared the hatching with that of F1531 (cat. 103). Pickvance (in New York 1986–87, p. 158; in Otterlo 1990, pp. 35, 284–86, 303) dated it to November–December 1889 on the evidence of the height of the wheat, which he concluded was the same as that in F737, and he considered the realistic style a reaction to Theo's criticism of Van Gogh's drawn copies from June–beginning of July. Wadley (1991, pp. 276, 277) concurred. Heenk (1995, p. 185) accepted Hulsker's dating, specifying May 22–June 9, the period between the first description of the view from Van Gogh's bedroom [592] and the description of the first painting depicting it (F611) [594], which she based on the precise drawing style and the height of the wheat. In Bremen 2002–3 (pp. 21, 78, 79), F1728 was dated to June, interpreted as an exploration of the motif in preparation for the related painting, and linked to a phrase in letter 595 of ca. June 18, 1889: "the fields and the olive trees." While the long-standing interpretation of the phrase as referring to two separate works is rightly disputed, identifying it with the drawing under discussion here, in which we see only one field and the olive trees play but a secondary role, does not seem plausible. Stolwijk and Veenenbos (2002, pp. 48, 144, 198) provided the information on the sale of the work by Johanna van Gogh-Bonger in 1901.

Van Gogh described his bedroom and the view from his window two weeks after his arrival in Saint-Rémy: "Through the iron-barred windows I can see a walled wheat field, a panoramic view as in a Van Goyen, above which I can, in the morning, see the sun rise in all its glory" [592]. He would depict this vista in both paintings and drawings. The present drawing, with its dramatic sky, is the only independent, highly finished large-size sheet among the drawings of this view. The same cloud-filled sky can be seen in the painting *Mountains beyond the Walled Field* (F611, fig. 228), executed during the first weeks of June. Van Gogh rendered the view again in autumn 1889 but in a quite different drawing style (F1552, cat. 116).

From 1901, when it was sold from the Van Gogh family collection and went into a private collection, until its exhibition in Paris in 1966, the present drawing was practically unknown. Its purchase by the Kröller-Müller Museum in 1970 and its inclusion that year in the new edition of De la Faille's catalogue raisonné ended its obscurity.

Van Gogh began this highly finished drawing with a sketch in black chalk, laying a sturdy ground for the clouds and the wall around the field. He then worked up the scene with a pen. Given the red-brown, green-gray, and blue tonalities of the now-brown ink, it seems possible the drawing was originally done in color. The blurred character of the lines forming the olive trees at the left, a phenomenon often seen in drawings done in aniline, would seem to confirm this. The sky is heightened with white opaque watercolor and the dark areas accentuated with black chalk applied over the ink.

MV

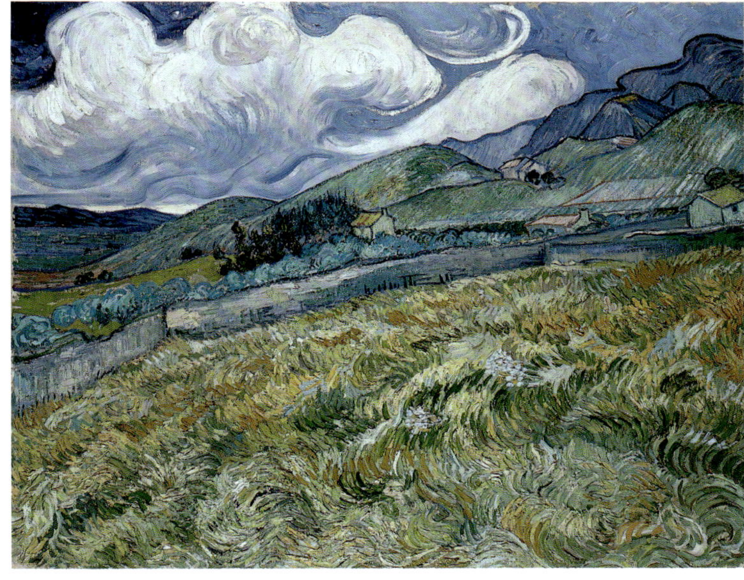

Fig. 228. *Mountains beyond the Walled Field* (F611), June 1889. Oil on canvas, 70.5 x 88.5 cm (27¾ x 34⅞ in.). Ny Carlsberg Glyptotek, Copenhagen

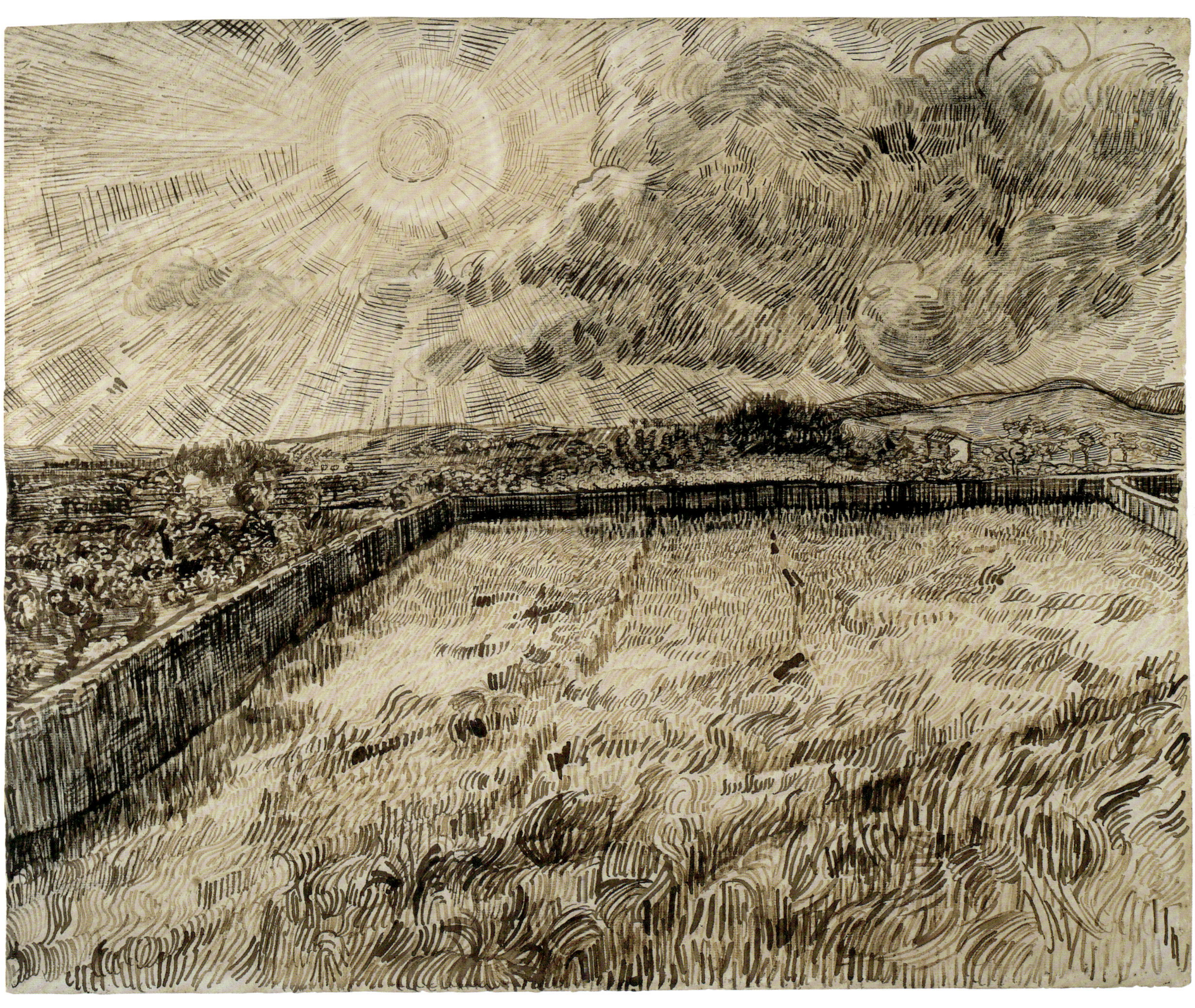

107. *Tree with Ivy in the Garden of the Asylum*

June–July 2, 1889
Reed pen, pen, and ink, graphite on wove paper blind stamped LATUNE ET CIE BLACONS
62.3 x 47.1 cm ($24^{1}/_{2}$ x $18^{1}/_{2}$ in.)
Inscribed on verso, in another hand: *160*
Van Gogh Museum, Amsterdam (Vincent van Gogh Foundation) (d 439 V/1962)
F1522, JH1695
Letters 597, W13, 603, T12

Amsterdam only

Provenance: Sent by the artist to Theo van Gogh (d. 1891), Paris, July 2, 1889 [597]; by inheritance to his son, Vincent Willem van Gogh (1890–1978), as part of his collection, administered by his widow, Johanna van Gogh-Bonger (d. 1925), 1891; placed on loan at the Stedelijk Museum, Amsterdam, 1931–73; ownership transferred to the Vincent van Gogh Foundation, 1962; placed on permanent loan at the Van Gogh Museum, Amsterdam, 1973.

Selected exhibitions: Groningen 1897; Paris 1902; Amsterdam 1905, no. 403; Berlin 1906, no. 80; Munich 1908, no. 75; Dresden 1908, no. 79; Frankfurt 1908, no. 86; The Hague–Amsterdam 1908, no. 91; Cologne–Frankfurt 1910; Amsterdam 1914–15, no. 189; Utrecht 1923, no. 45; Rotterdam 1923; Basel 1924, no. 94; Zürich 1924, no. 94; Stuttgart 1924, no. 7; The Hague 1925; Berlin 1927–28, no. 91; London–Birmingham–Glasgow 1947–48, no. 159; New York–Chicago 1949–50, no. 147; London 1968–69, no. 146; Otterlo 1990, no. 228.

Summary of the literature: The first reproduction of the drawing appeared in Bremmer 1910, vol. 11, no. 88. De la Faille (1928, no. 1522) dated it to May 1889 on the basis of letter 592 of May 22, 1889, in which Van Gogh gave both a written and a sketched description of the related painting (F609, fig. 228). Bowness (in London 1968–69, p. 100) accepted De la Faille's dating and is the first to suggest that the drawing was made after the painting. Hulsker (1980, no. 1695) was the first to include this sheet as among the several copy drawings sent to Paris in early July but was not able to tell whether Van Gogh did each drawing at the same time as the painting copied or whether the drawings were all executed in late June. According to Pickvance (in New York 1986–87, pp. 110–11), the sheet was made in late June–early July, and he noted that it is the only one of the copies that was done after a view of the garden from May. Van Uitert and Hoyle (1987, p. 456, no. 2.531) accepted the dating to May. Pickvance (in Otterlo 1990, pp. 286–87, 306) dated the sheet to before June 25, seeing a similarity in technique to F1525 (cat. 108), among others, a work about which Van Gogh wrote on June 25 [596]. In 1996, Hulsker repeated the information he gave in 1980 but in no. 1695 listed a discrepant date for the drawing—between May 15 and 20—while he dated the painting (and the letter sketch) to May 22. For early history, see Feilchenfeldt and Veenenbos 1988, p. 136.

Of the approximately ten drawings Van Gogh sent to Theo on July 2, 1889, this sheet is the only one not made after a painting he did in June, when he began working outside the walls of the asylum. He drew it instead after one of the canvases depicting the asylum garden that he had painted in May (F609, fig. 229). He described that painting to Theo in a letter of May 22: "Thick tree trunks covered in ivy, the ground also covered with ivy and periwinkle; a stone bench and a rose bush, with flowers that faded in the cool shade. In the foreground some plants with white calyxes. It is green, violet, and pink" [592]. He characterized it as depicting "eternal green nests for lovers" and drew a sketch in the letter. Van Gogh's selecting this painting to copy indicates his satisfaction with it. In his letter to Theo of November 17, 1889 [614], he wrote that this was one of the canvases he wanted to send to the 1890 annual exhibition of Les XX in Brussels.

For this sheet, as for most of the other copies made in June–July, Van Gogh first made an underdrawing in graphite. He then worked it up in pen and ink and further pencil work, filling the sheet with a decorative variety of strokes.

MV

Letter to Theo van Gogh, July 2, 1889 [597]: In order that you have some idea of what I am working on, I am sending you ten or so** [une dizaine] **drawings today, all from canvases I am working on. . . . The drawings seem to me to have little color this time, and the too-smooth paper is a little responsible for that. Anyway, the weeping tree and the courtyard of the Hospital at Arles have more color, but all the same this will give you an idea of what I am doing.

Letter to Wilhelmina van Gogh, July 2, 1889 [W13]: Today I've just sent Theo about twelve** [une douzaine] **drawings after canvases I am working on.

Letter to Theo van Gogh, July 6, 1889 [603]: Tell me, have you received those drawings of mine? I sent you half a dozen once by parcel post and ten or so later on. If by chance you have not received them yet they must have been lying at the station for days and for weeks.

Letter to Vincent from Theo van Gogh, July 16, 1889 [T12]: The last drawings give the impression of having been made in a fury, and are a bit removed from nature. I shall understand them better when I have seen one of these subjects in painting.

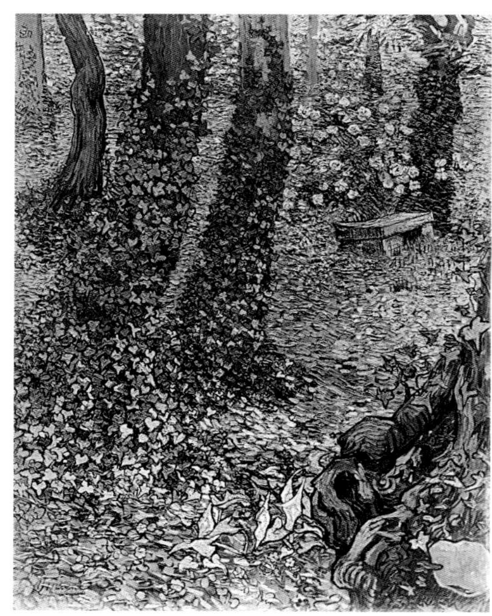

Fig. 229. *Trees with Ivy* (F609), May 1889. Oil on canvas, 92 x 72 cm ($36^{1}/_{4}$ x $28^{3}/_{8}$ in.). Present whereabouts unknown

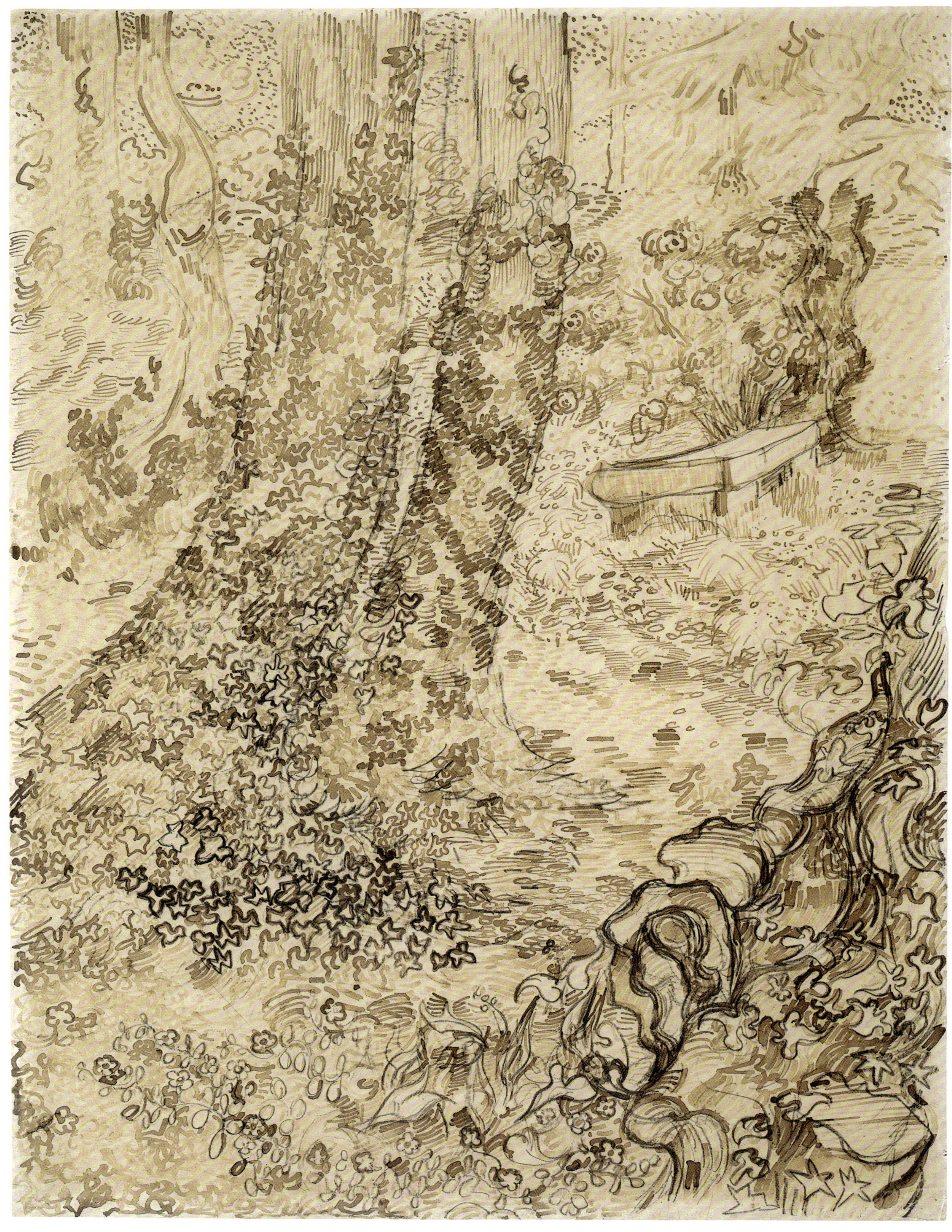

108. *Cypresses*

June 20–25, 1889
Reed pen, pen, and ink, graphite on wove paper blind-stamped LATUNE ET CIE BLACONS
62.2 x 47.1 cm (24½ x 18½ in.)
Inscribed on verso, in another hand: *221*
Brooklyn Museum, New York, Frank L. Babbott Fund and the A. Augustus Healy Fund (38.123)
F1525, JH1747
Letters 596, 597, W13, 603, T12

Provenance: Sent by the artist to Theo van Gogh (d. 1891), Paris, July 2, 1889 [597]; by inheritance to his son, Vincent Willem van Gogh, as part of his collection, administered by his widow, Johanna van Gogh-Bonger, 1891; sold by her to Sir Michael E. Sadler, Master of University College, Oxford, during the exhibition London 1923–24; German private collection, after 1927; M. Knoedler and Co., New York, 1935; acquired by the Brooklyn Museum, 1938.

Selected exhibitions: Amsterdam 1905, no. 420; Berlin 1909–10, no. 209; Berlin 1910, no. 65; Amsterdam 1914–15, no. 186; Utrecht 1923, no. 43; Rotterdam 1923; London 1923–24, no. 5; New York and other cities 1935–36, no. 119; New York 1943, no. 77; New York–Chicago 1949–50, no. 136; New York 1986–87, no. 18; Otterlo 1990, no. 231.

Summary of the literature: The first reproduction of the drawing was published in Du Quesne-Van Gogh 1911 (following p. 82); Pfister 1922, p. 41 (illus.). De la Faille (1928, no. 1525) linked the work to letter 596 and dated it to June 1889; the editors of De la Faille 1970 (no. 1525) stated that it was unclear which drawings of cypresses Van Gogh intended to send and that the drawing was done on colored paper. Hulsker 1980, no. 1747. Pickvance (in New York 1986–87, pp. 113–16) was the first to discuss several of the drawn copies of paintings (this work is examined on p. 113); in Otterlo 1990 (pp. 286–88), he devoted a separate paragraph to the group, asserting that the cypress copies were among the first of the copies after paintings from June–early July. Feilchenfeldt and Veenenbos 1988, p. 136. Kramer, Zieve, and Faunce (1993, p. 132) provided, among other information, a summary of the work's exhibition history. Heenk 1995, p. 186; Stolwijk and Veenenbos 2002, pp. 136, 164, 197.

Van Gogh first explored the cypress motif in June 1889. Initially, the tree was nothing more than a simple element in the landscape (F719; F717, cat. 111), but later in the month he executed two paintings in which cypresses are the principal subject (F613, cat. 109; F620). On June 25, he wrote to Theo of these canvases, noting that he had made drawings of them [596]. He described his fascination with the tall, slender trees: the shapes and proportions appealed to him, and their dark green color made a powerful contrast to the sun-drenched Provençal countryside. The impressive sheet in the Brooklyn Museum, with its whiplike lines, is based on the canvas in the Metropolitan Museum (F613, cat. 109), the composition Van Gogh regarded as the more successful of the two. Differences between the drawing and the painting may indicate Van Gogh continued working on the canvas after making the drawing. He sent the drawings to Theo on July 2, 1889, as part of a shipment of about ten copies of recent paintings [597].

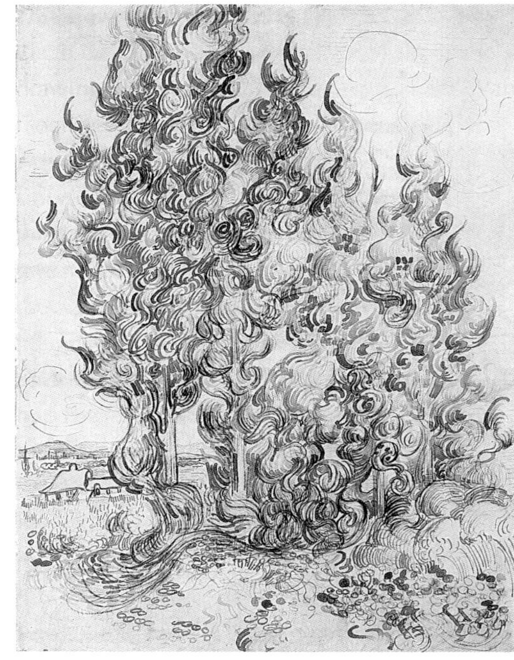

Fig. 230. *Cypresses* (F1524), June 1889. Reed pen, pen, and ink, graphite on wove paper, 62.5 x 47 cm (24⅝ x 18½ in.). The Art Institute of Chicago, Gift of Robert Allerton

This drawing was laid down in thin graphite lines and worked up in ink with a fine pen and a very broad reed pen. Van Gogh then used a sturdy graphite pencil over the lines of ink, accentuating the cypresses' dark character and giving them more depth, a technique he also used in F1524 (fig. 230). The delicate but also some rather coarse penciled lines can be seen clearly in the infrared reflectogram (fig. 257). Van Gogh situated the crescent moon somewhat more to the right and slightly higher in the finished drawing than in the pencil sketch. The way the thin ink lines faded, the blurry contours of some lines, and the ink's seepage onto the verso of the sheet indicate the kinds of inks he used (see "Technical Studies: Observations on the Drawing Materials Used by Van Gogh in Provence").

MV

Letter to Theo van Gogh, June 25, 1889 [596]: The cypresses are always occupying my thoughts, I should like to make something of them like the canvases of the sunflowers, because it astonishes me that they have not yet been done as I see them.

It is as beautiful of line and proportion as an Egyptian obelisk. And the green has a quality of such distinction.

It is a splash of* black *in a sunny landscape, but it is one of the most interesting black notes, and the most difficult to hit off exactly that I can imagine.

But then you must see them against the blue,* in *the blue rather. . . . I think that of the two canvases of cypresses, the one I am making this sketch of will be the best [fig. 231]. . . .

I will send you the drawings of it with two other drawings that I have done too.

For excerpts concerning this drawing from Van Gogh's letters to Theo of July 2, 1889 [597], to Wilhelmina of July 2 [W13], and to Theo of July 6 [603], and Theo's letter to Vincent of July 16 [T12], see cat. 107 (F1522).

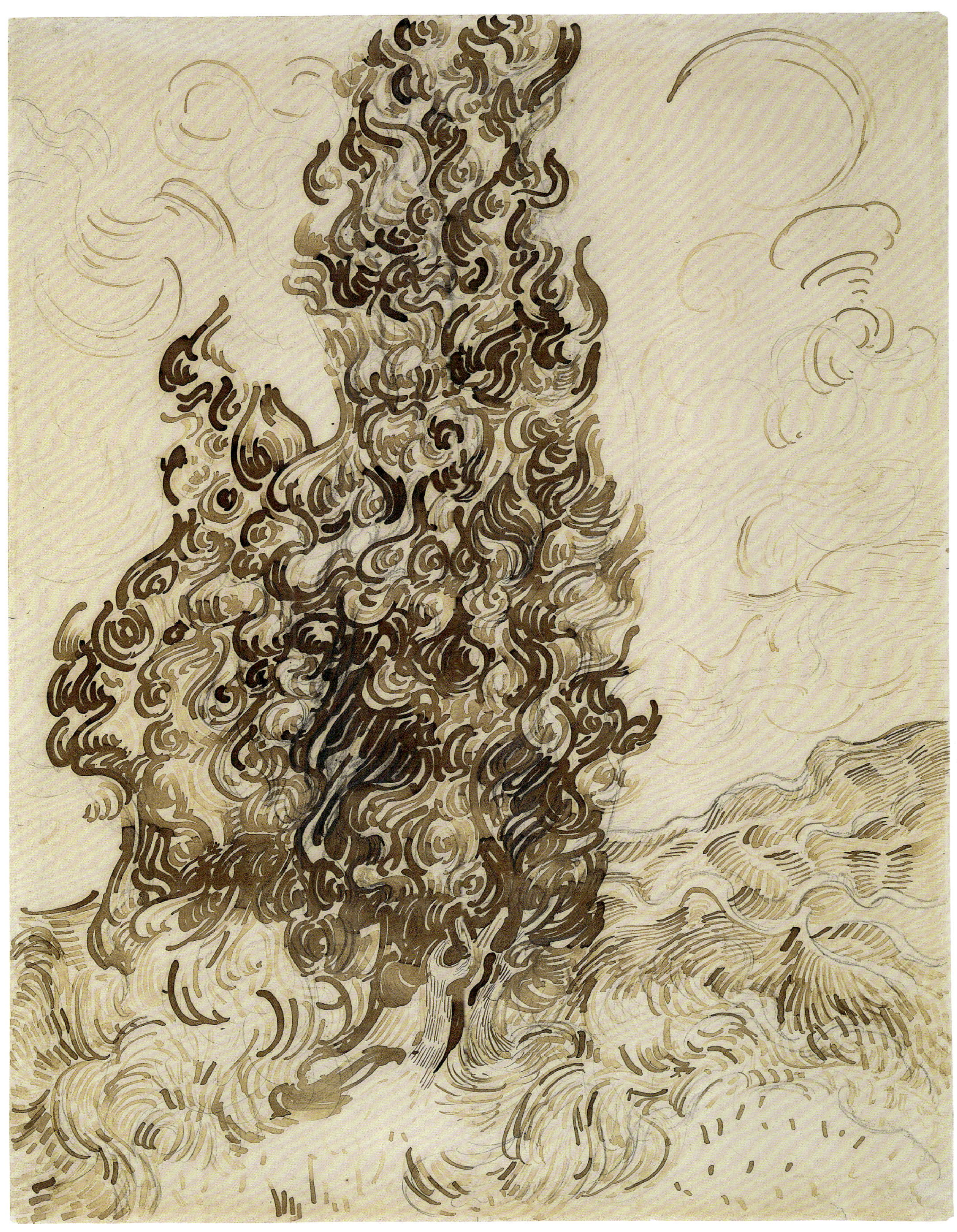

109. *Cypresses*

ca. June 25, 1889
Oil on canvas
93.3 x 74 cm (36¾ x 29⅛ in.)
The Metropolitan Museum of Art, New York, Rogers Fund, 1949 (49.30)
F613, JH1747
Letters 596, 608

New York only

***Letter to Theo van Gogh, June 25, 1889 [596]:** We have had some glorious days and I have set even more canvases going, so that there are twelve size 30 canvases in prospect. Two studies of cypresses of that difficult bottle-green hue [F613, cat. 109; F620]; I have worked their foregrounds with thick layers of white lead, which gives firmness to the ground. . . .*

The cypresses are always occupying my thoughts, I should like to make something of them like the canvases of the sunflowers, because it astonishes me that they have not yet been done as I see them.

It is as beautiful of line and proportion as an Egyptian obelisk. And the green has a quality of such distinction.

It is a splash of black *in a sunny landscape, but it is one of the most interesting black notes, and the most difficult to hit off exactly that I can imagine.*

But then you must see them against the blue, in *the blue rather. To paint nature here, as everywhere, you must be in it a long time. . . .*

I think that of the two canvases of cypresses, the one I am making this sketch of will be the best [fig. 231]. The trees in it are very big and massive. The foreground, very low with brambles and brushwood. Behind some violet hills, a sky green and pink with a crescent moon. The foreground especially is painted very thick, clumps of brambles with touches of yellow, violet and green.

I will send you the drawings of it with two other drawings that I have done too.

***Letter to Theo van Gogh, September 28, 1889 [608]:** I am writing you another letter to explain that there are three studies missing in the package of canvases you already have because the postage for the roll with these taken out was 3.50 fr. less. So I will send them at the next opportunity—or rather they are leaving today with other canvases—as follows:*
Wheat Field [F719]
Study of Cypresses [F613, cat. 109]
Wheat Field and Cypresses [F717, cat. 111]
Reaper [F617]
ditto [F615]
ditto [F618; fig. 221]
Ivy [F746]
Olives

Then also the three above mentioned—Poppies [F581]—Night Effect [F612, fig. 31]—Moonrise [F735].

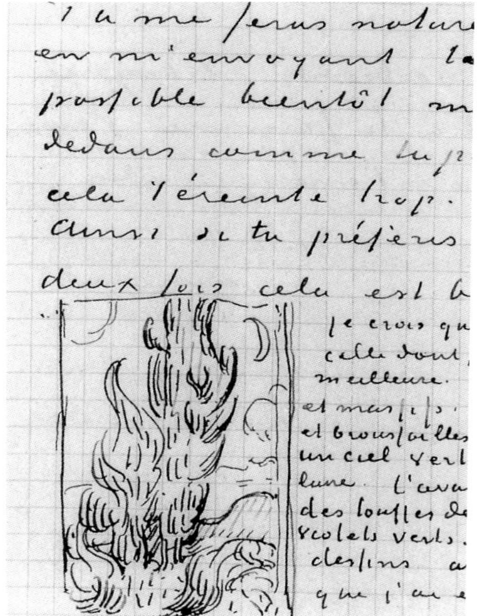
t a me ferais nature
en m'envoyant la
possible bientôt m
dedans comme lu
cela l'éreinte trop.
Ainsi si tu préfères
deux fois cela est
je crois qu
celle dont
meilleure.
et massifs.
et broussailles
un ciel vert
lune. L'ava
des touffes de
violets verts.
dessins a
que j'ai e

Fig. 231. Sketch in letter 596 to Theo van Gogh, June 25, 1889. Van Gogh Museum, Amsterdam (Vincent van Gogh Foundation)

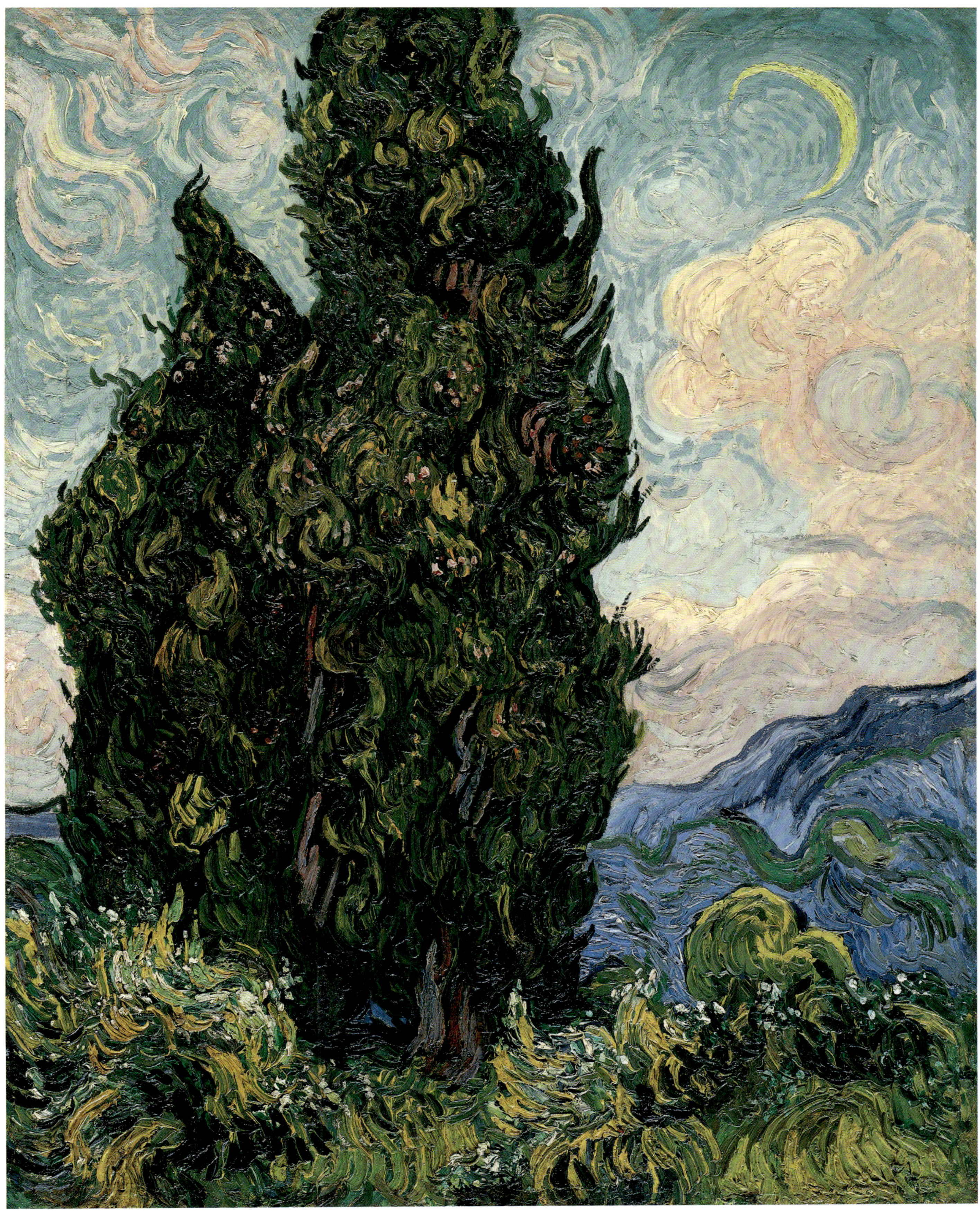

110. *Wheat Field with Cypresses*

Late June–July 2, 1889
Reed pen, pen, and ink, graphite on wove paper blind stamped LATUNE ET CIE BLACONS
47.1 x 62.3 cm (18½ x 24½ in.)
Inscribed on verso, in another hand: *100*
Van Gogh Museum, Amsterdam (Vincent van Gogh Foundation) (d 445 V/1962)
F1538, JH1757
Letters 597, W13, 603, T12

Provenance: Sent by the artist to Theo van Gogh (d. 1891), Paris, July 2, 1889 [597]; by inheritance to his son, Vincent Willem van Gogh (1890–1978), as part of his collection, administered by his widow, Johanna van Gogh-Bonger (d. 1925), 1891; placed on loan at the Stedelijk Museum, Amsterdam, 1931–73; ownership transferred to the Vincent van Gogh Foundation, 1962; placed on permanent loan at the Van Gogh Museum, Amsterdam, 1973.

Selected exhibitions: Groningen 1897; Paris 1902; Amsterdam 1905, no. 428; Munich 1908, no. 73; Dresden 1908, no. 77; Frankfurt 1908, no. 84; The Hague–Amsterdam 1908, no. 89; Berlin 1909–10, no. 210; Berlin 1910, no. 57; Frankfurt 1911; The Hague–Amsterdam 1912, no. 31; Amsterdam 1914–15, no. 185; Utrecht 1923, no. 58; Rotterdam 1923; Paris 1937, no. 179; London–Birmingham–Glasgow 1947–48, no. 167; London 1968–69, no. 160; Otterlo 1990, no. 232.

Summary of the literature: The drawing was first reproduced in Bremmer 1924 (vol. 4, pp. 31, 32, no. 32) and in color in Meier-Graefe 1928b (pl. IX). De la Faille (1928, no. 1538) dated the sheet to the Saint-Rémy period and called it "Le cyprès et l'arbre en fleurs"; it is not clear which tree he thought was flowering. Cooper (in London–Birmingham–Glasgow 1947–48, no. 167) dated the work to October 1889 and referred to it as "Cornfield and Cypress"; he noted a link with the painting F615. Bowness (in London 1968–69, p. 105), calling it "Wheat Field with Cypresses" and dating it to late June–early July 1889, provided an overview of the paintings of the same subject and a chronology, in which Van Gogh painted F717 and then executed the drawing. The editors of De la Faille 1970 (no. 1538) accepted Bowness's title and date but believed the drawing was copied from F615 or F743. Hulsker (1980, no. 1757) dated the sheet to June 1889 on the grounds of Van Gogh's fascination with cypresses at this time; he believed that in this drawing Van Gogh was copying F615. Van Uitert and Hoyle 1987, p. 460, no. 2.555. Pickvance (in New York 1986–87, p. 133; in Otterlo 1990, pp. 286, 310) followed Bowness in calling F717 the model for the drawing; since the canvas was finished at the end of the month, the drawing must date from the last days of June or the first two days of July. For Pickvance, the date is further validated by the technique. F717 is also identified as the model in Amsterdam 1990 (pp. 205–6) and Heenk (1995, p. 186). Feilchenfeldt and Veenenbos 1988, p. 137.

Before Van Gogh treated cypresses as the principal subject of his canvases (ca. June 25), he included them in two landscape paintings with wheat fields, of which one (F717, cat. 111) served as the model for this sheet. Every element in the drawing has its own formal style, which relates to the same element in the painting. For the sky he translated the different colors into a graphic language of long thin lines, small dots, and areas left blank. The olive trees at the back of the field at left and the Alpilles behind accentuate the Provençal character of the landscape. The artist executed two other paintings of the same composition (F615, F743), which has led to differences of opinion about which was the first version, that is, the one after which this drawing was made.

Van Gogh appears to have applied two shades of ink over his graphite underdrawing: a dark brown and a light brown. The tone of the light brown ink, the transparency of the lines, and the seepage onto the verso may indicate the drawing was originally made in color.

MV

For excerpts concerning this drawing from Van Gogh's letters to Theo of July 2, 1889 [597], to Wilhelmina of July 2 [W13], and to Theo of July 6 [603], and Theo's letter to Vincent of July 16 [T12], see cat. 107 (F1522).

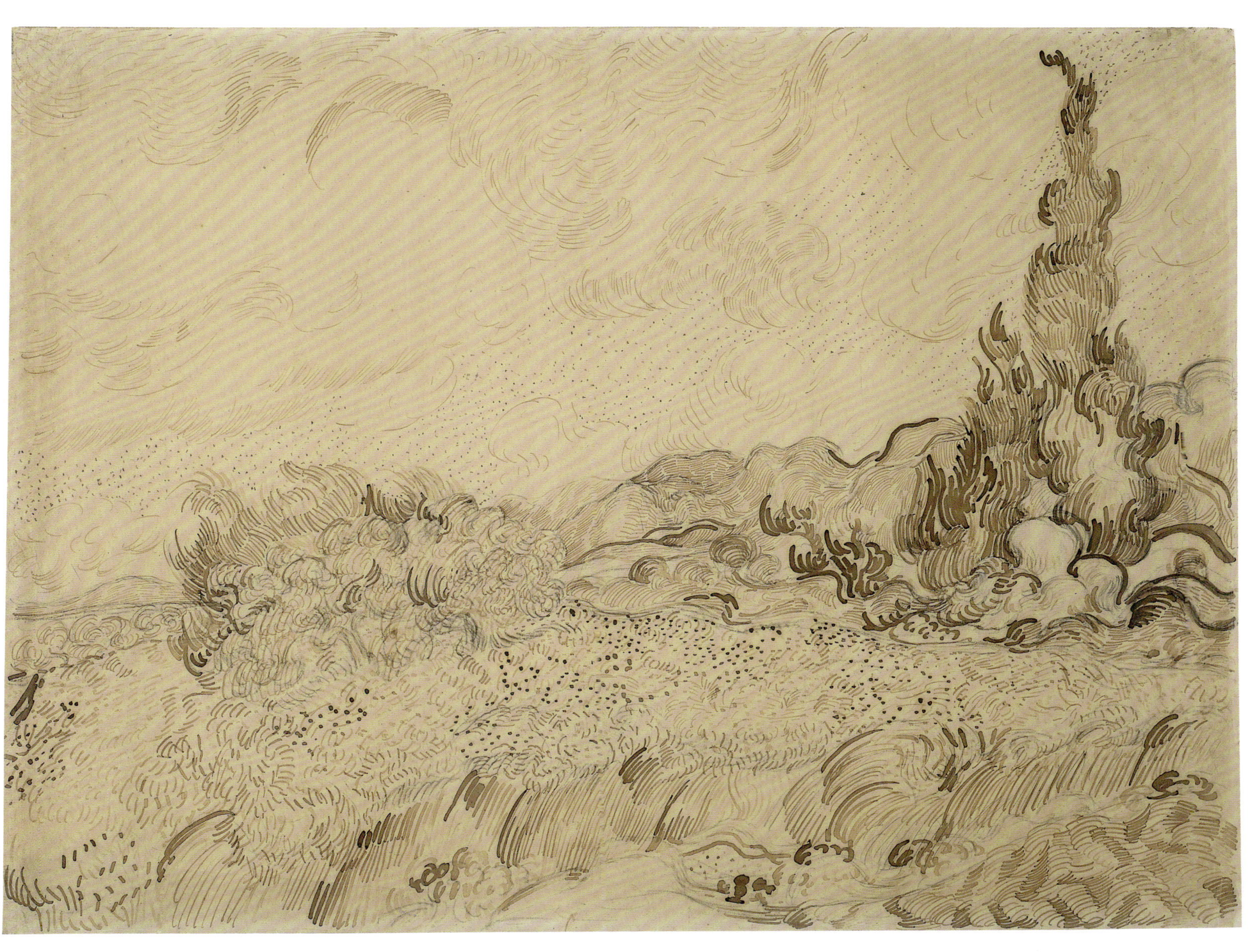

111. *Wheat Field with Cypresses*

June 1889
Oil on canvas
73 x 93.4 cm ($29^{3}/_{4}$ x $36^{3}/_{4}$ in.)
The Metropolitan Museum of Art, New York, Purchase, The Annenberg Foundation Gift, 1993 (1993.132)
F717, JH1756
Letters 597, 608

New York only

Letter to Theo van Gogh, July 2, 1889 [597]: I have a canvas of cypresses with some ears of wheat, some poppies, a blue sky like a piece of Scotch plaid; the former painted with a thick impasto like the Monticellis, and the wheat field in the sun, which represents the extreme heat, very thick too; I think that these would make it more or less clear to him [the dealer Alexander Reid] that he could not lose much by remaining friends with us.

Letter to Theo van Gogh, September 28, 1889 [608]: See cat. 109 (F613).

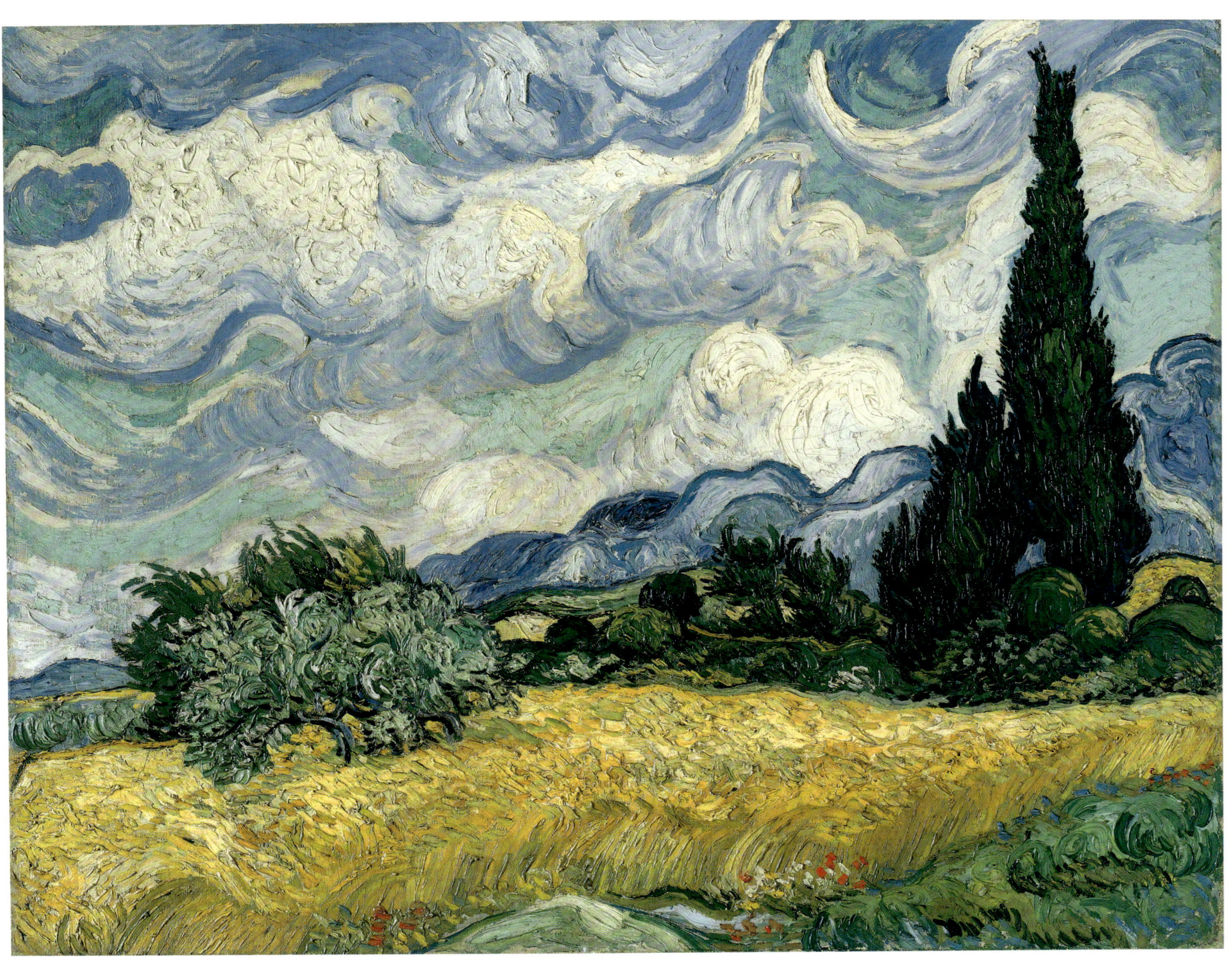

112. *Wild Vegetation*

Late June–July 2, 1889
Reed pen, pen, brush, and ink on wove paper blind stamped LATUNE ET CIE BLACONS
47.1 x 62.4 cm (18½ x 24⅝ in.)
Inscribed on verso, in another hand: *199*
Van Gogh Museum, Amsterdam (Vincent van Gogh Foundation) (d 177 V/1962)
F1542, JH1742
Letters 597, W13, 603, T12

Provenance: Sent by the artist to Theo van Gogh (d. 1891), Paris, possibly July 2, 1889 [597]; by inheritance to his son, Vincent Willem van Gogh (1890–1978), as part of his collection, administered by his widow, Johanna van Gogh-Bonger (d. 1925), 1891; placed on loan at the Stedelijk Museum, Amsterdam, 1931–73; ownership transferred to the Vincent van Gogh Foundation, 1962; placed on permanent loan at the Van Gogh Museum, Amsterdam, 1973.

Selected exhibitions: Basel 1924, no. 96; Zürich 1924, no. 96; Stuttgart 1924, no. 15; Berlin 1927–28, no. 87; Paris 1937, no. 166; Aix-en-Provence 1959, no. 54; London 1968–69, no. 161; Otterlo 1990, no. 236.

Summary of the literature: De la Faille (1928, no. 1542) gave no more specific date than within the Saint-Rémy period. In Aix-en-Provence 1959 (no. 54), the decorative rendering of the vegetation (see F609, fig. 229) was believed to suggest a date of May–June 1889. Bowness (in London 1968–69, pp. 105, 106) assumed that the sheet was executed in late June–early July 1889, i.e., in the period of the large drawn copies of paintings, noting that although there is no painting of the same motif, the fanciful mountains in the background do appear in Van Gogh's canvases from this time (e.g., F622). In De la Faille 1970 (no. 1542), the drawing was dated to July 1889. Hulsker (1980, no. 1742) suggested June 1889 based on stylistic similarities between the drawing and *Starry Night* (F1540, fig. 30) and *Olive Trees with the Alpilles in the Background* (F1544); he included the sheet among the drawings done after nature. In Van Uitert and Hoyle (1987, p. 460, no. 2.556), a somewhat broader dating, namely summer 1889, was suggested. Pickvance (in Otterlo 1990, pp. 284–85, 287, 314) pointed out that it is unclear whether the work was done from nature or if it is a copy after a now-lost painting, for in terms of style, technique, and materials, the drawing is in keeping with the copies; he also gave the date late June–early July. Heenk (1995, p. 186) believed the drawing to be a copy after a now-lost canvas.

Wild Vegetation is similar to the approximately ten drawings after paintings that Van Gogh did in Saint-Rémy in terms of materials, paper, and style, but no canvas is known from which it was copied. Van Gogh's comments on the shipment of those drawings to Theo do not indicate exactly how many were sent: he wrote of "une dizaine" (about ten [597]) and also of "une douzaine" (a dozen [W13]). Thus it is possible that *Wild Vegetation* was part of the group, which would then have consisted of a total of eleven works. As in two of the ten copies known (F1548, F1547), Van Gogh here drew directly in ink, with no previous sketching in graphite. This impressive drawing, like those in the group, is highly stylized, and the entire sheet is covered with a variety of pen lines, perhaps now carried to an even greater extreme than before.

MV

For excerpts concerning this drawing from Van Gogh's letters to Theo of July 2, 1889 [597], to Wilhelmina of July 2 [W13], and to Theo of July 6 [603], and Theo's letter to Vincent of July 16 [T12], see cat. 107 (F1522).

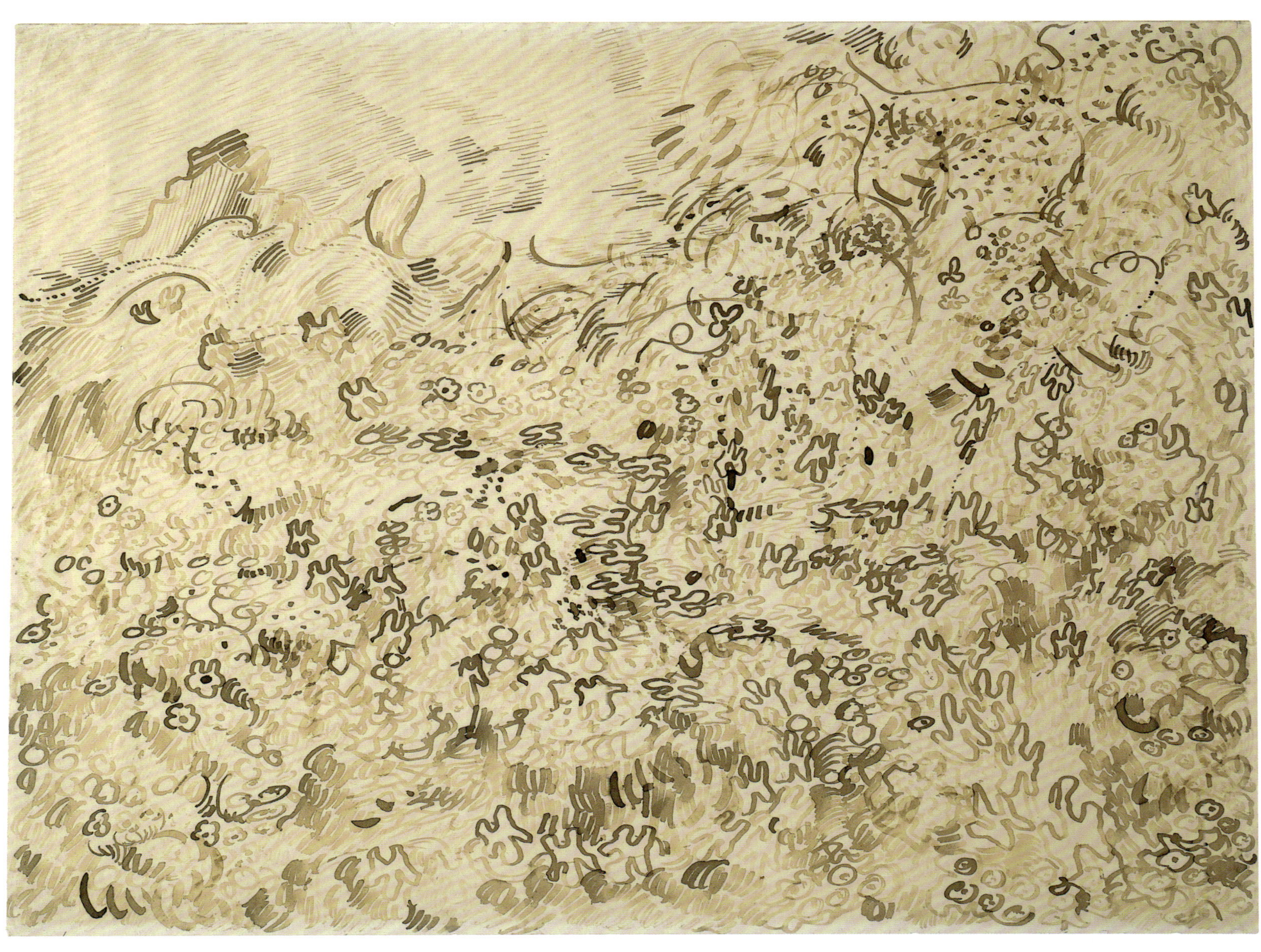

113. *Corridor in the Asylum*

September 1889
Brush and oils, black chalk on pink laid paper watermarked AL (in banderole) PL BAS
61.7 x 47.4 cm (24¼ x 18⅝ in.)
Inscribed on verso, in another hand: *No. 14*; in yet another hand: *Hospice à St-Remy*
The Metropolitan Museum of Art, New York, Bequest of Abby Aldrich Rockefeller, 1948 (48.190.2)
F1529, JH1808

Provenance: Theo van Gogh (d. 1891); by inheritance to his son, Vincent Willem van Gogh, as part of his collection, administered by his widow, Johanna van Gogh-Bonger, 1891, until 1927; sold to the Leicester Galleries, London, during the exhibition Edinburgh 1927; Mr. and Mrs. John D. Rockefeller, New York, 1929; her bequest to the Metropolitan Museum, 1948, with the stipulation that it be lent to the Museum of Modern Art, New York, for fifty years; transferred to the Metropolitan Museum, 1998.

Selected exhibitions: Amsterdam 1905, no. 363; Cologne–Frankfurt 1910; Amsterdam 1914–15, no. 156; New York 1920, no. 7; London 1926–27, no. 1; New York and other cities 1935–36, no. 120; New York 1955, no. 53; New York 1986–87, no. 6; Otterlo 1990, no. 221.

Summary of the literature: The first reproduction was published in *Onze Kunst* (Vogelsang 1905, p. 65); in London 1926–27 (no. 1), it was first noted that the drawing depicts the corridor of the asylum at Saint-Rémy, instead of the hospital in Arles, as previously thought. De la Faille (1928, no. 1529), listed V. W. van Gogh as still the owner. According to Cooper (1955, p. 84), Van Gogh's room was located on the corridor depicted here and the sheet was probably executed in June 1889. In De la Faille 1970 (no. 1529), the dating was given as May–early June. In Sydney–Melbourne–New York 1975 (pp. 72, 73), the influence of drawing with the reed pen on the form of the brushstrokes was first noted, although Cooper (1955) had mentioned something similar with regard to F1528 (cat. 114). Hulsker (1980, no. 1808) believed this sheet and the two other drawings of the interior (F1528, cat. 114; F1530, cat. 115) were executed between October 5 and 22, 1889 (see cat. 114 for his arguments). Elderfield 1983, pp. 30, 31. Pickvance (in New York 1986–87, pp. 88–91; in Otterlo 1990, pp. 284–85) maintained the dating to late May–early June and described the three works, which he thought were meant to form a triptych, as designed to give Theo an impression of the artist's new surroundings and also perhaps a form of acclimatization for Van Gogh; Pickvance believed the figure was a later addition. Feilchenfeldt and Veenenbos 1988 (p. 136). Heenk (1995, pp. 187, 188) dated the sheets to October on the evidence of the artworks depicted in F1528 (cat. 114) and the coloration; she was the first to state that oil paint was used (although that had been suggested for F1528, beginning with De la Faille in 1928).

Corridor in the Asylum is one of the three interior views Van Gogh executed in September 1889, during his recovery from his mid-July attack, the only works done in Saint-Rémy in which the asylum itself is the subject of the composition (see also F1528, cat. 114; F1530, cat. 115). It probably shows the ground floor of the north wing of the former monastery. The staircase starting in the lower right corner led to the second floor, where Van Gogh probably had his studio. Down the corridor, which is illuminated by sunlight flooding in the doorway off to the left (see F1530), a man is about to enter one of the rooms. A photograph from the 1950s (fig. 232) shows that Van Gogh rendered the corridor quite exactly, although it is not known whether the metal barriers in the photograph were there in Van Gogh's time.

While in terms of materials and technique, this sheet does form a suite with F1528 and F1530, that does not necessarily mean they were intended as a triptych, as Pickvance suggested (in New York 1986–87, no. 6, and Otterlo 1990, no. 221). Van Gogh first sketched the composition in black chalk, which he later partly erased—chalk still plays a role in the overall composition. He then painted over the sketch with oils, sometimes strongly diluted. The pink of the paper remains visible in some of the pilasters and in the second arch. The figure was added last.

There has always been a debate over the dating of the three interior views. When they were interpreted as the artist's initial exploration of his new surroundings, sent to Theo as a kind of report, they were situated in the period May–June 1889. October 1889 was suggested by Hulsker (1980/1996, no. 1808) based on similarities he saw between the work depicted at the upper right in F1528 and painting F731. That depiction, however, is far too sketchy for a specific identification. We suggest September: Van Gogh had recovered from his most recent attack, and he had begun painting again but did not feel strong enough to work outdoors. Possibly, in addition to the self-portraits (F626, F627, F629) and the copies of reproductions of work by other artists he was making at this time, he also thought of exploring his immediate surroundings on paper. The subdued oil colors used for these sheets correspond to those he used in his paintings done before and after his falling ill (F744, F525, F698, F618), paints (lead white, veronese green, ultramarine, cobalt, ocher-yellow, ocher-red, sienna, and bone black [594]) he had received by July 2 [597]. The large areas of color in these drawings further link them to the summer paintings. Dating the three sheets before June is contradicted by the appearance of a cypress in one of the works depicted in F1528; see catalogue entries 110 (F1538) and 108 (F1525).

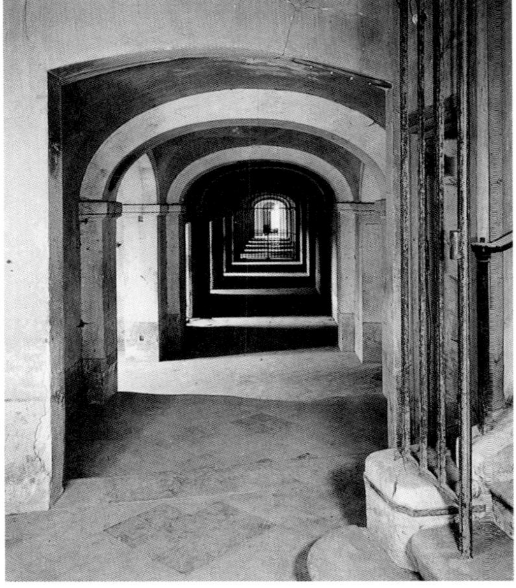

Fig. 232. Photograph of the asylum corridor, 1950s, from Tralbaut 1969, p. 289

MV

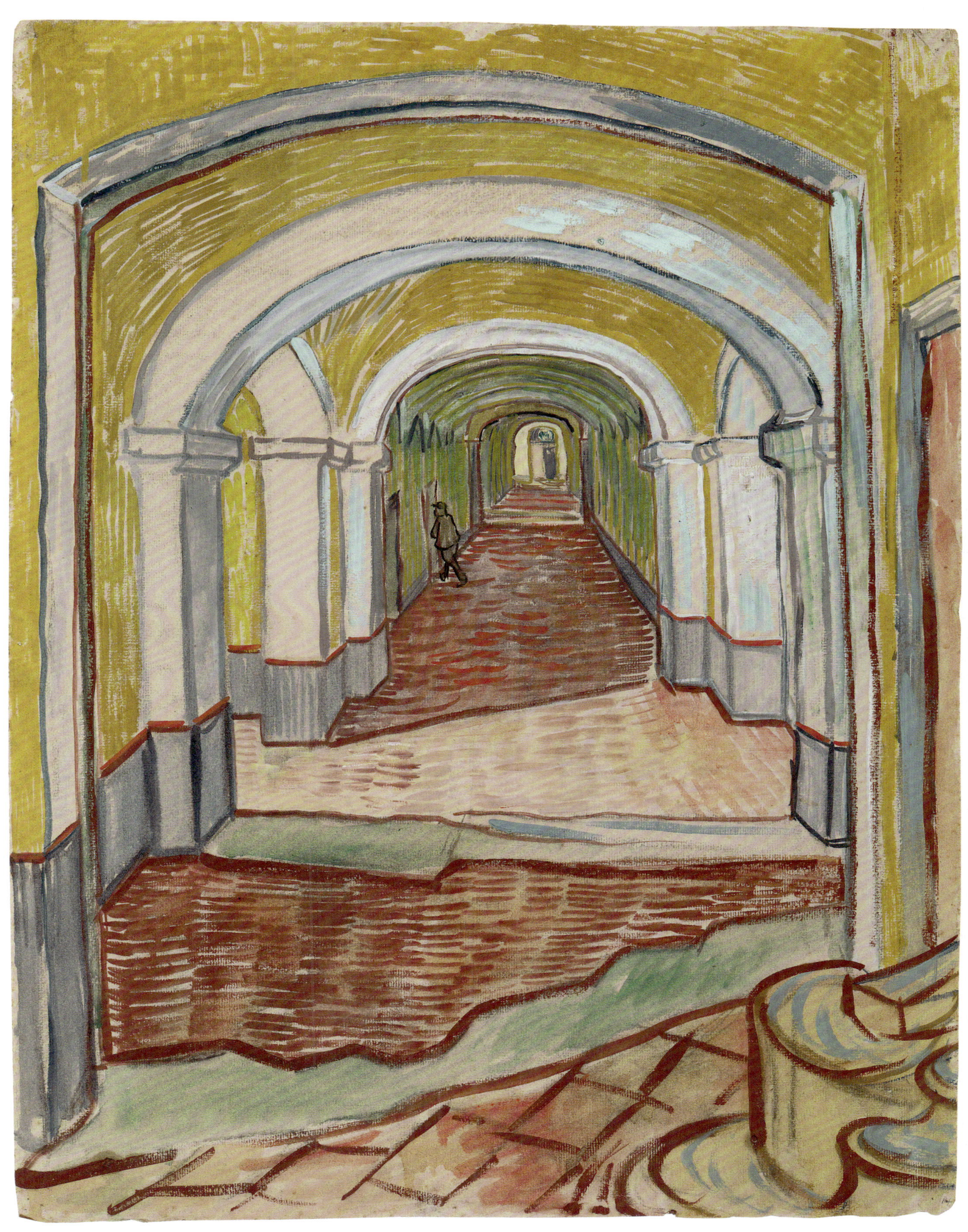

114. *Window in the Studio*

September 1889
Brush and oils, black chalk on pink laid paper watermarked AL (in banderole) PL BAS
62 x 47.6 cm (24⅜ x 18¾ in.)
Inscribed on verso, in another hand: *no. 12*
Van Gogh Museum, Amsterdam (Vincent van Gogh Foundation) (d 337 V/1962)
F1528, JH1807

Provenance: Theo van Gogh (d. 1891); by inheritance to his son, Vincent Willem van Gogh (1890–1978), as part of his collection, administered by his widow, Johanna van Gogh-Bonger (d. 1925), 1891; placed on loan at the Stedelijk Museum, Amsterdam, 1931–73; ownership transferred to the Vincent van Gogh Foundation, 1962; placed on permanent loan at the Van Gogh Museum, Amsterdam, 1973.

Selected exhibitions: Amsterdam 1914–15, no. 155; Amsterdam 1926, no. 56; London–Birmingham–Glasgow 1947–48, no. 161; New York–Chicago 1949–50, no. 145; London 1968–69, no. 154; Toronto–Amsterdam 1981, no. 36a; New York 1986–87, no. 7; Otterlo 1990, no. 223; Tokyo 2000, no. 27; Bremen 2002–3, no. 1.

Summary of the literature: The earliest attribution of the drawing to the Saint-Rémy period was in Amsterdam 1926 (no. 56); it had previously been considered to have been done in Arles. De la Faille (1928, no. 1528) also dated it to Saint-Rémy, gave a detailed description of the sheet but did not specify that it depicts Van Gogh's studio, and regarded the works to the right of the window as drawings. He mentioned oil paint in addition to watercolor and charcoal in his description of the medium. Cooper (1955, p. 84) suggested a date of June 1889. Tralbaut (1969, p. 281) indicated the location of the artist's studio—on the second floor, with a view of the garden. Bowness (in London 1968–69, p. 102) claimed the artist intended the three sheets (F1528–30) as an exploration of his new surroundings and thus dated them to May–early June 1889; he also mentioned oils as part of the medium. His dating was accepted in De la Faille 1970 (no. 1528); the use of oils, however, was not mentioned. Hulsker (1980/1996, no. 1807) dated the drawing to between October 5 and 22, when Van Gogh had run out of painting supplies. He based this dating on similarities between the drawing depicted hanging at the upper right and F731, a painting from October 1889. Hulsker (1980, no. 1807) described the studio as on the ground floor, however, and he was followed by many authors. Rosenblum (1975, p. 97) saw parallels between the works of Van Gogh and those of Caspar David Friedrich with their views from windows as "personal metaphors of an enclosed private world that is abruptly separated from something that lies beyond" and the works as symbolic self-portraits. Welsh-Ovcharov (in Toronto–Amsterdam 1981, pp. 152, 153) subscribed to the May–early June 1889 dating, mentioning the fresh-looking leaves visible through the window; she saw the works on the wall all as paintings, none identifiable, although she mentioned F640. Pickvance (in New York 1986–87, pp. 86, 88, 93; in Otterlo 1990, pp. 284–85, 301) retained the late May–early June dating and described F1528–30 as meant to form a triptych, as designed to give Theo an impression of the artist's new surroundings, and as also perhaps a form of acclimatization for Van Gogh; he suggested that one of the four unframed works on the wall was a view of the garden comparable to the already cited F731 and F640. Van Uitert and Hoyle (1987, pp. 266, 461 no. 2.560) followed Hulsker's October dating and noted the awkward perspective. Heenk (1995, pp. 187, 188) dated F1528–30 to October on the evidence of the artworks shown in F1528 and the coloration. She was the first since Bowness (in London 1968–69, no. 154) to note oils as part of the medium. The drawing's similarity of theme to *Window in the Bataille Restaurant* (F1392) was pointed out in Tokyo 2000 (pp. 90, 91, 177).

Two weeks after arriving in Saint-Rémy, Van Gogh described to Theo the various aspects of his life at the asylum: his bedroom and the view from its window, the food, the other patients, and the fact that he had been given an extra room for work [592]. The studio window, through which there was a view of the garden, is the subject of this drawing. That the studio was on the second floor of the north wing and not, as often stated, on the ground floor is demonstrated by comparing the view in the drawing with a photograph taken from a comparable window on the second floor (fig. 233). On the windowsill are various containers, including bottles, and on a table or cupboard at the lower right are three boxes, one holding brushes. Artworks hang on either side of the window—to the left, two unframed paintings, and to the right, two works consisting of black lines against light backgrounds that are undoubtedly drawings, both outlined with the brush and thus appearing framed. The one at the lower right clearly represents a landscape with cypresses, a motif Van Gogh first began

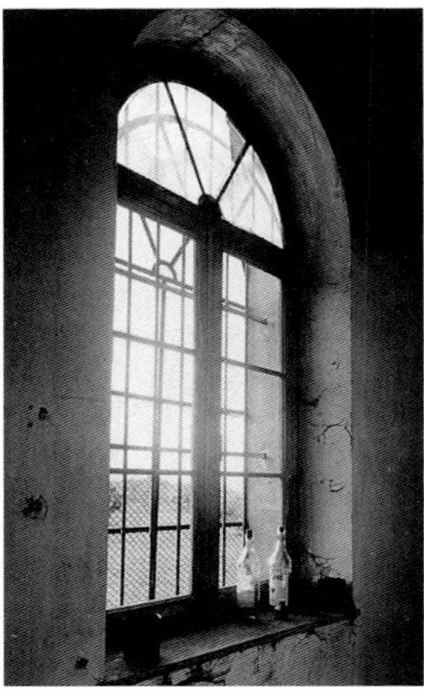

Fig. 233. Photograph of the window, 1950s, from Tralbaut 1969, p. 291

exploring in June and which he continued to work on in July and September (see F1538, cat. 110); thus a date for *Window in the Studio* of before the second half of June is impossible.

To the right of the window, the wall appears to curve away, making the perspective seem somewhat awkward. The scene, dominated by the barred window, has been interpreted as a symbol of Van Gogh's self-imposed incarceration, but given the other interior views of this period, it seems more likely the artist simply wanted to illustrate his surroundings. Moreover, the window motif had already appeared in works done in Paris and Arles (F1392, fig. 56; F389).

For a description of technique, see catalogue entry 113 (F1529). The bars on the window were first sketched in black chalk, then worked over with highly diluted oil paint, before the garden view through the windowpanes was painted in. However, in the lowest pane of the left casement, Van Gogh painted the bars over the garden view, and in the upper two panes of the right casement, he did not paint over the chalk lines of the bars with diluted oils and left the pink paper visible in the areas around the chalk lines.

MV

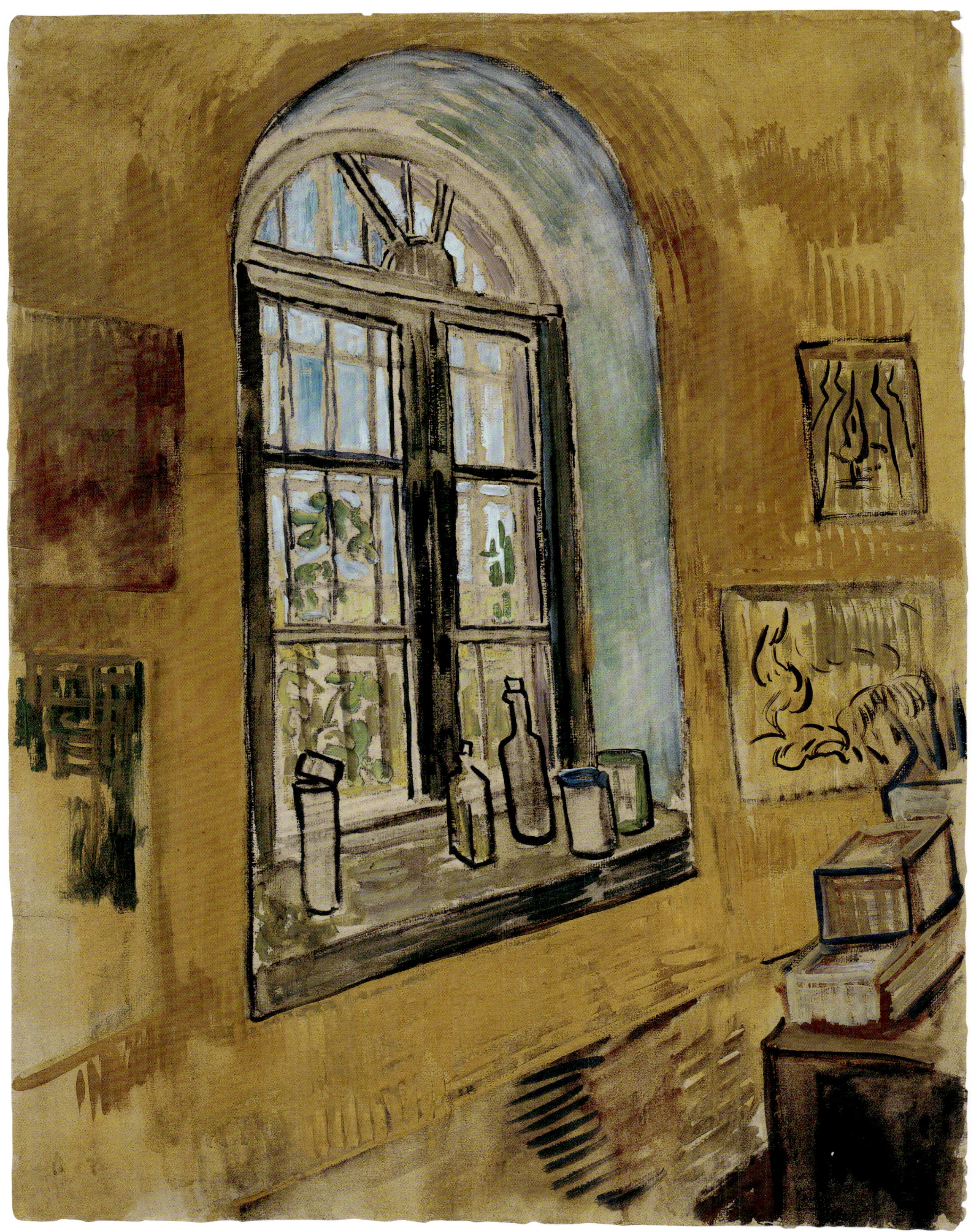

115. *Vestibule of the Asylum*

September 1889
Brush and oils, black chalk, on pink laid paper watermarked AL (in banderole) PL BAS
61.6 x 47.1 cm (24½ x 18½ in.)
Inscribed on verso, in another hand: *no. 13*; in yet another hand: *Hospice à Arles*
Van Gogh Museum, Amsterdam (Vincent van Gogh Foundation) (d 176 V/1962)
F1530, JH1806

Provenance: Theo van Gogh (d. 1891); by inheritance to his son, Vincent Willem van Gogh (1890–1978), as part of his collection, administered by his widow, Johanna van Gogh-Bonger (d. 1925), 1891; placed on loan at the Stedelijk Museum, Amsterdam, 1931–73; ownership transferred to the Vincent van Gogh Foundation, 1962; placed on permanent loan at the Van Gogh Museum, Amsterdam, 1973.

Selected exhibitions: Groningen 1897; Berlin 1909–10, no. 219; Amsterdam 1914–15, no. 154; Utrecht 1923, no. 25; Rotterdam 1923; Berlin 1927–28, no. 81; Paris 1937, no. 77; London–Birmingham–Glasgow 1947–48, no. 163; London 1968–69, no. 155; Toronto–Amsterdam 1981, no. 36b; New York 1986–87, no. 5; Otterlo 1990, no. 222; Tokyo 2000, no. 26.

Summary of the literature: Early exhibition catalogues assumed the sheet was executed in Arles, until Berlin 1927–28 (no. 81), which placed it among the works from Saint-Rémy. De la Faille (1928, no. 1530) followed this dating and provided a detailed description of the work and its colors. Cooper (1955, pp. 84, 85) suggested it was executed in June 1889 and noted the effect that Van Gogh's experience in drawing with a reed pen had on the appearance of the brushstrokes here. Bowness (in London 1968–69, p. 102) thought the artist had intended sheets F1528–30 as an exploration of his new surroundings and thus dated them to May–early June 1889. This dating was accepted in De la Faille 1970 (no. 1530). Hulsker (1980/1996, no. 1806) dated the three drawings to between October 5 and 22 (see cat. 114). Welsh-Ovcharov (in Toronto–Amsterdam 1981, pp. 152–53) followed the dating proposed by Bowness and in De la Faille 1970 (see cat. 114); she was the first to point out the painting and the portfolio propped against the wall at right. Pickvance (in New York 1986–87, no. 5; in Otterlo 1990, pp. 284–85, 300) retained the early dating, late May–early June (see cat. 114); he also mentioned the framed painting and suggested that the other was an unframed canvas. Van Uitert and Hoyle (1987, p. 461, no. 2.561) accepted Hulsker's October dating. Feilchenfeldt and Veenenbos 1988, p. 136. Heenk (1995, pp. 187, 188) dated the three sheets to October (see cat. 114). In Tokyo 2000 (pp. 88, 89, 176, 177), the rhythmic, parallel brushwork seen here and in some of the Paris paintings was linked to Van Gogh's desire to imitate Japanese prints.

When painting this sheet, Van Gogh stood in the hallway of the north wing of the asylum, facing the vestibule with its open doorway. The fountain he had drawn earlier (F1531, cat. 103) is visible beyond. The same doorway, seen from the garden, appears in paintings executed in the autumn of 1889 (see F653, fig. 234). Comparison of the drawing with these canvases indicates that the rectangle depicted in the drawing between the right side of the doorway and the fountain is part of the stone parapet on the stairs up to the entrance.

For a description of technique and discussion of dating, see catalogue entry 113.

MV

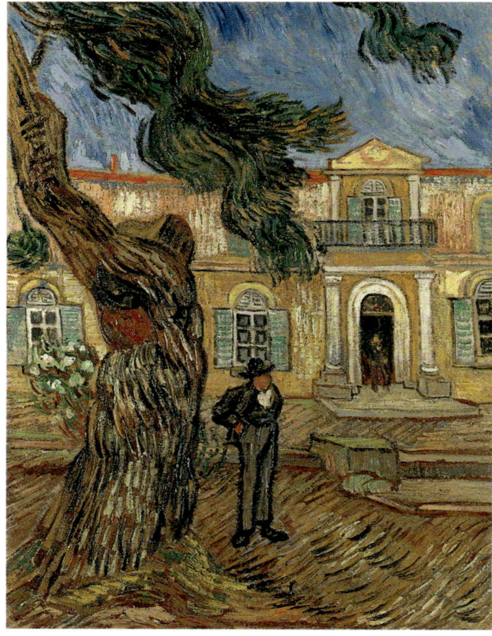

Fig. 234. *Pine Tree near the Entrance to the North Wing* (F653), autumn 1889. Oil on canvas, 58 x 45 cm (22⅞ x 17¾ in.). Musée d'Orsay, Paris (photo: Hervé Lewandowski—RMN/Art Resource, NY)

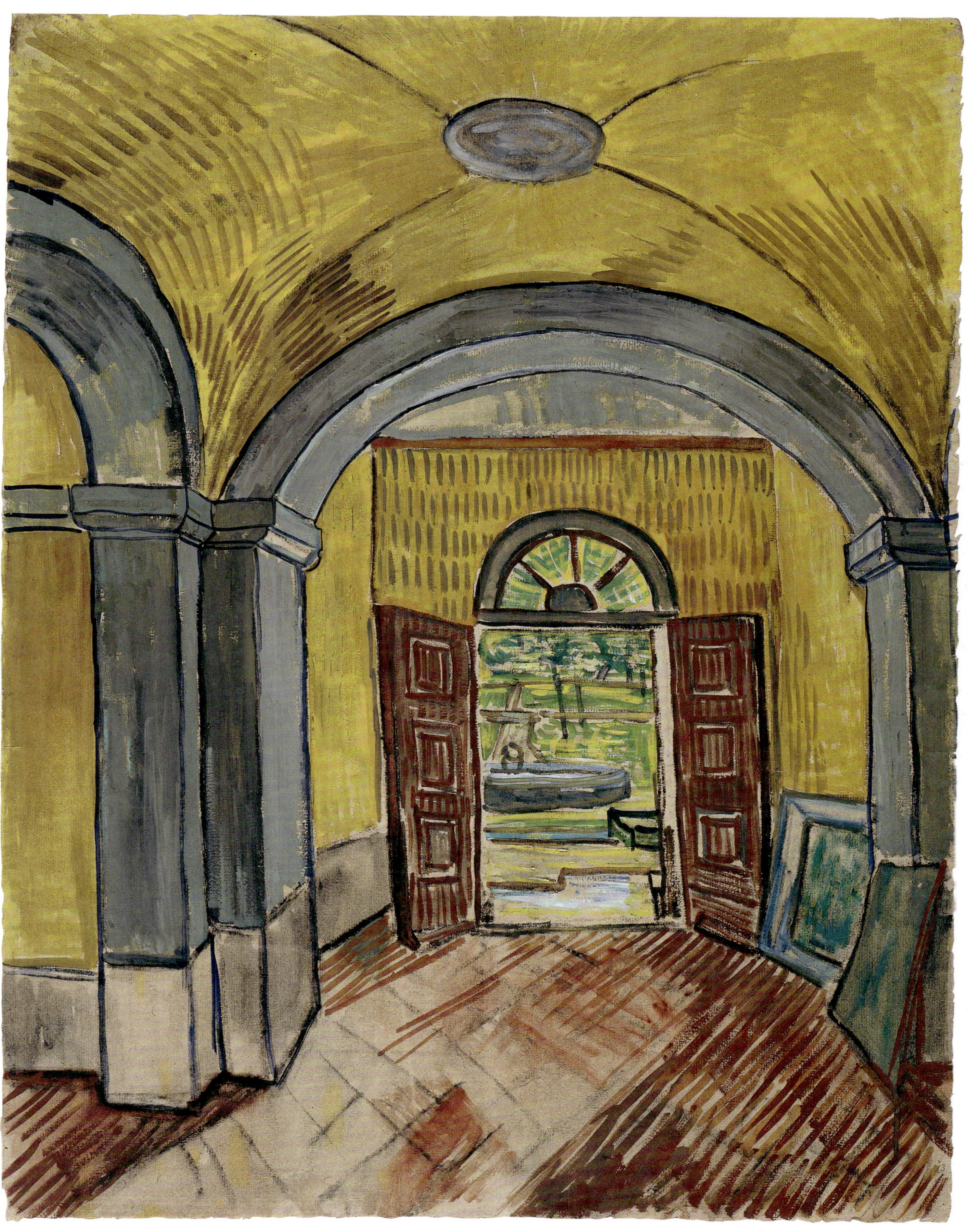

116. *Walled Wheat Field with Rising Sun*

Mid-November–mid-December 1889
Black chalk, reed pen, pen, and ink on pink laid paper watermarked AL (in banderole) PL BAS
47.4 x 62 cm (18⅝ x 24⅜ in.)
Staatliche Graphische Sammlung, Munich (44336Z)
F1552, JH1863

Provenance: Theo van Gogh (d. 1891); by inheritance to his son, Vincent Willem van Gogh, as part of his collection, administered by his widow, Johanna van Gogh-Bonger, 1891; sold by her through Paul Cassirer, Berlin, to Hugo von Tschudi (d. 1912), director of the Nationalgalerie, Berlin (with the support of the Jahrhundertausstellung), 1907; works from his collection purchased by a group of private individuals and donated to the Neue Pinakothek, Munich, 1912 (?); transferred to the Staatliche Graphische Sammlung, Munich, 1967.

Selected exhibitions: Amsterdam 1905, no. 424; Berlin 1907, hors cat.; Paris 1937, no. 76; Munich 1956, no. 140a; Munich 1961, no. 73; New York 1986–87, no. 38; Otterlo 1990, no. 237; Bremen 2002–3, no. 25.

Summary of the literature: The first color reproduction of the sheet was published in Hagen 1919, pl. 15; Meier-Graefe 1921, vol. 2, p. 63, illus. De la Faille (1928, no. 1552) dated it to the Saint-Rémy period; Martin 1962, p. 28; Wadley (1969, p. 39) situated it in the summer of 1889. In De la Faille 1970 (no. 1552) and Hulsker 1980 (no. 1863) it was dated to November and to December 1889, respectively. Hulsker suggested it was copied after painting F737 (fig. 235). Pickvance (in New York 1986–87, pp. 156–58; in Otterlo 1990, pp. 24, 288, 315) agreed, adjusted the dating to mid-November–mid-December, and suggested that the drawing was sent to Theo together with the painting ca. December 15. Heenk (1995, p. 186) accepted Pickvance's arguments; Feilchenfeldt and Veenenbos 1988, pp. 138, 155, 157. New information on the provenance was provided in Munich 1988, p. 25; Paul 1993, p. 392; and Berlin–Munich 1996–97, p. 148. Hulsker (1996, no. 1863) modified his 1980 date, now situating the drawing in November, and did not mention its relationship to the painting. Martigny 2000, pp. 101, 102; Stolwijk and Veenenbos 2002, p. 20. Hansen (in Bremen 2002–3, pp. 45, 96, 97) gave a date of October–November on the evidence of the height of the wheat. She suggested that the work was a study for the painting rather than a copy after it; she followed Pickvance's views on the shipment to Theo.

Van Gogh depicted the walled wheat field visible from his bedroom many times during the course of his stay in Saint-Rémy (see also F1728, cat. 106). In *Walled Wheat Field with Rising Sun* and the related painting (F737, fig. 235), the wheat—sown in mid-October—is visible and the furrows not yet completely hidden. The huge rising sun, surrounded by concentric circles of brilliance, is sufficiently low in the sky that a portion of the field is in shadow. Van Gogh's letters indicate that the painting was executed sometime between mid-November and mid-December, and the drawing was likely done about the same time though it is not clear which came first. Both exhibit the graphic style characterized by short, parallel strokes that was typical of Van Gogh's works from the autumn of 1889. When he sent the painting to Theo in the middle of December, Van Gogh wrote that he had included two drawings, and while it has often been claimed that *Walled Wheat Field with Rising Sun* was one of them, nothing of their subject matter was mentioned in the letter [617].

Van Gogh drew the scene in detail in black chalk and used it even over the pen and ink, which he applied in thick and thin lines. He rubbed the chalk to achieve the shadow effect near the wall.

MV

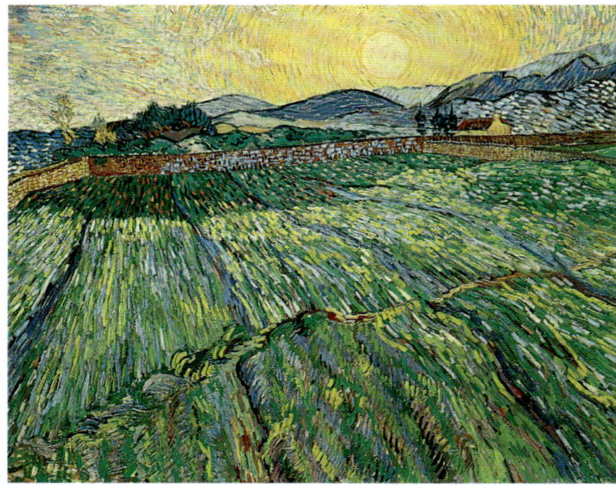

Fig. 235. *Walled Wheat Field with Rising Sun* (F737), mid-October–mid-November 1889. Oil on canvas, 71 x 90.5 cm (28 x 35⅝ in.). Private collection

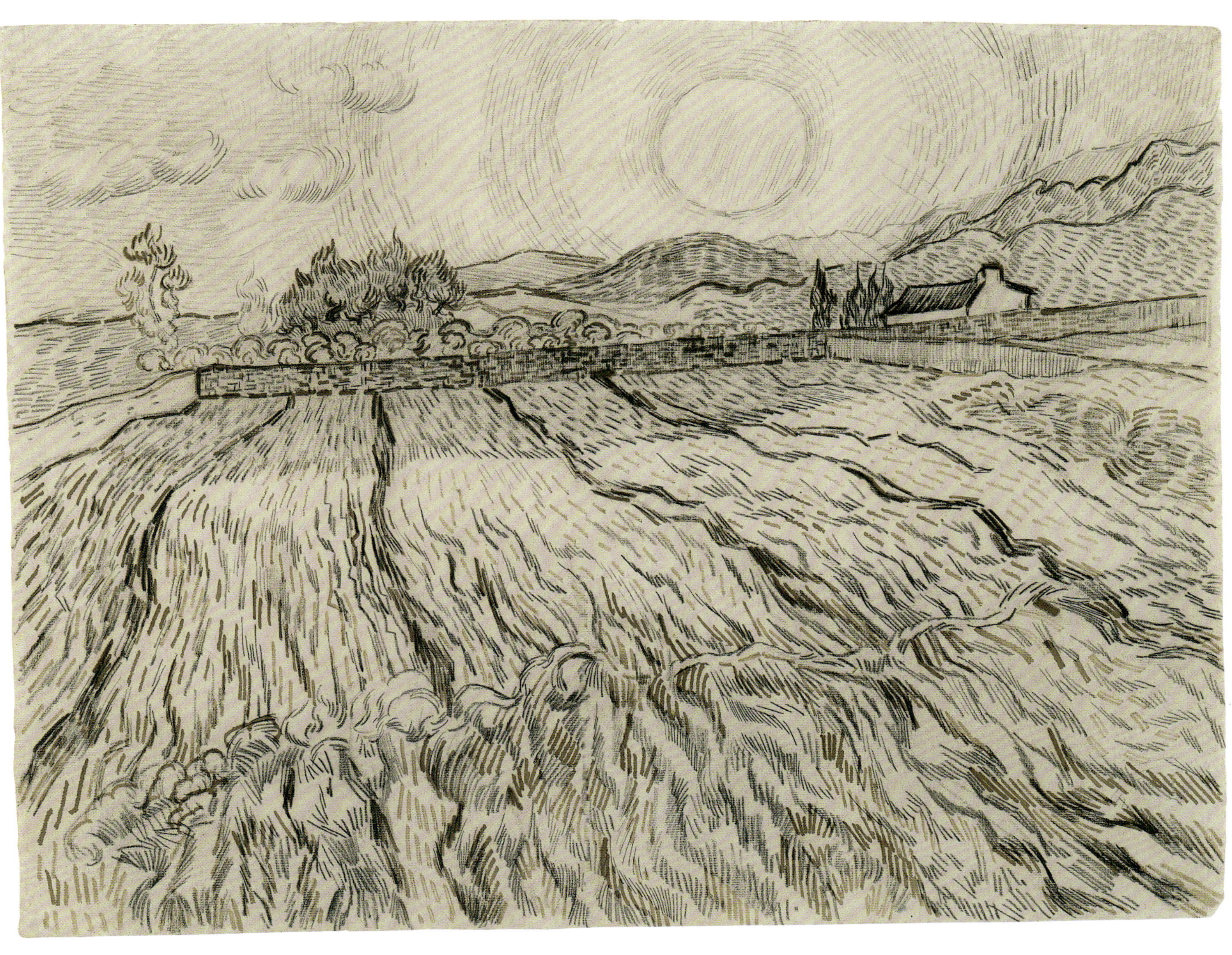

Auvers, 1890: Return to the North

Van Gogh believed that living among the mentally ill at Saint-Rémy had contributed to his own last bout of illness, and in early May he and Theo concluded that he should leave the asylum there. He decided to settle at an inn in Auvers-sur-Oise, a village near Paris. In early September 1889, following his first attack in Saint-Rémy, he had already expressed a desire to move back to the north of France [602, 605]. Then, there seemed to be no hurry and Van Gogh himself did not seriously contemplate moving until the spring of 1890, but from September 1889 onward Theo had been investigating where the painter might reside when he moved. Thanks to Camille Pissarro, the brothers learned of Paul-Ferdinand Gachet, a doctor in Auvers, who agreed to keep an eye on Van Gogh. On May 16, the artist left Saint-Rémy and arrived in Auvers on May 20, stopping on the way to visit with Theo and his family, in Paris.

Van Gogh was immediately enthusiastic about the landscape surrounding the little village on the Oise. He found old thatch-roofed farmhouses, which for him gave the environs a certain picturesqueness. Now that he had seen the south, he felt he could appreciate the north much better, and he was particularly excited about the colors he discovered in the landscape. He adapted his palette, now choosing bright, delicate tones. He worked hard and fast, executing about seventy-five paintings and fifty drawings during the remaining seventy days of his life.

The drawings are mainly quick chalk sketches; there is only a small group of more ambitious and finished works. These sheets, with their closely related colors, in many ways hark back to the artist's drawn color experiments during his time in Paris in 1887. He had already in Saint-Rémy recommenced this sort of exercise in a group of flower still lifes executed shortly before his departure: bouquets of irises and roses against backgrounds that formed either a complementary or a simultaneous contrast to the colors of the blossoms themselves.

Shortly after arriving in Auvers, Van Gogh made two drawings in watercolor and oils in which he created a simultaneous contrast in blue: *Old Vineyard with Peasant Woman* (F1624, cat. 117) and *Landscape with Houses* (F1640r, cat. 118). The *Landscape* is carried out entirely in shades of blue, while in the *Vineyard* Van Gogh added a complementary contrast by coloring the roofs of the houses orange (now faded to red-brown; see figs. 83, 84). We find a combination of both types of contrast in *Landscape with a Bridge over the Oise* (F1639, cat. 119; see "Metamorphoses: Van Gogh's Drawings Then and Now").

Although Van Gogh's palette, subject matter, and more secure style might lead one to suspect that he was somewhat happier in Auvers than in Saint-Rémy, he still felt that he was a failure and that there was little hope for the future. His depression only increased with the prospect of Theo leaving his position at Boussod et Valadon to become an independent art dealer, since Van Gogh believed this threatened his own financial security. The precise reason for Van Gogh's suicide at the end of July will likely never be known, but it brought an abrupt end to the short, productive life of a great artist and a brilliant draftsman.

MV

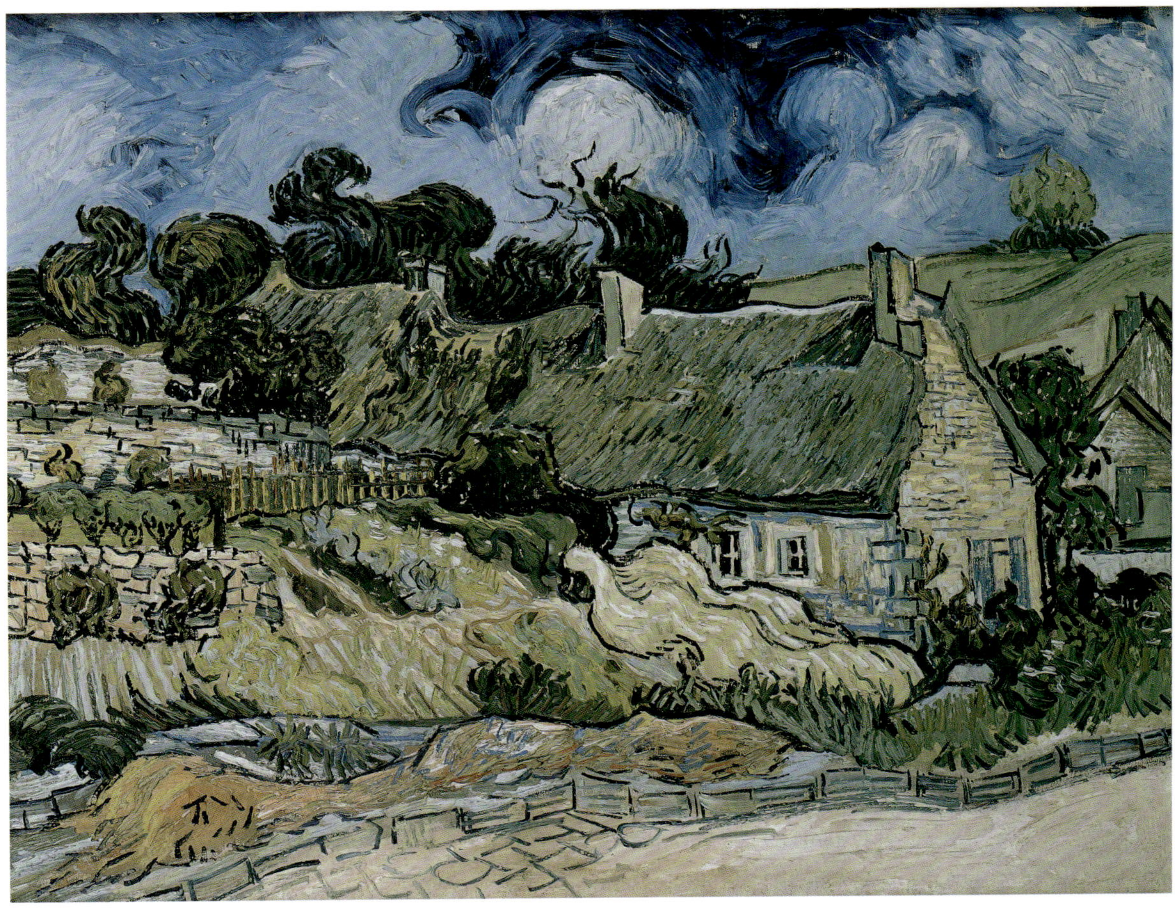

Fig 236. *Houses with Thatched Roofs, Cordeville* (F792), May 1890. Oil on canvas, 72 x 91 cm (20⅞ x 35⅞ in.). Musée d'Orsay, Paris, Gift of Paul Gachet

117. *Old Vineyard with Peasant Woman*

May 20–23, 1890
Brush, oils, and watercolor, graphite on laid paper watermarked DAMBRICOURT FRÈRES HALLINES
44.3 x 54 cm (17½ x 21¼ in.)
Inscribed on verso, in another hand: *213*
Van Gogh Museum, Amsterdam (Vincent van Gogh Foundation) (d 446 V/1962)
F1624, JH1985
Letters 648, 637

Provenance: Theo van Gogh (d. 1891); by inheritance to his son, Vincent Willem van Gogh (1890–1978), as part of his collection, administered by his widow, Johanna van Gogh-Bonger (d. 1925), 1891; placed on loan at the Stedelijk Museum, Amsterdam, 1931–73; ownership transferred to the Vincent van Gogh Foundation, 1962; placed on permanent loan at the Van Gogh Museum, Amsterdam, 1973.

Selected exhibitions: Paris 1896–97; Utrecht 1923, no. 29; Rotterdam 1923; The Hague 1925; Berlin 1927–28, no. 94; Paris 1937, no. 82; London–Birmingham–Glasgow 1947–48, no. 174; New York–Chicago 1949–50, no. 158; London 1968–69, no. 191; New York 1986–87, no. 57; Otterlo 1990, no. 242; Tokyo 2000, no. 29.

Summary of the literature: De la Faille (1928, no. 1624) linked the drawing to letter 648 but did not narrow down the date within the Auvers period. He titled the sheet "Jardin derrière des maisons" and listed the medium as charcoal, watercolor, and oil. Cooper (in London–Birmingham–Glasgow 1947–48, no. 174; 1955, pp. 90, 91) dated the drawing to June 1890 on the evidence of letter 648. Bowness (in London 1968–69, pp. 123, 124) assigned to letter 648 a date of ca. May 23, 1889; he believed the drawing was done at the end of the month, and he saw the influence of Millet in the figure at the right. Bowness substituted gouache for De la Faille's oil, which, until then, had been followed by all authors. In De la Faille 1970 (no. 1624), Bowness's dating was accepted. Hulsker (1980, no. 1985) also dated the drawing to May and linked it to letter 637 of May 25, 1889, in which Van Gogh also wrote about the drawing; Pickvance (in New York 1986–87, pp. 200, 201, 224–26, 236, 252) referred to both letters from the end of May and linked the drawing to painting F794, which shows the same vineyard from a different viewpoint. On the basis of the detailed underdrawing, he suggested that the work was begun outdoors and finished in the studio; in Otterlo 1990 (pp. 37, 318, 323), he added that the sheet forms a pair with F1640r (cat. 118), in which Van Gogh used the same medium and technique. Van Uitert and Hoyle (1987, pp. 288, 289, 474 no. 2.635) dated the drawing to May–June, Pickvance's suggestion that it was begun outdoors but completed in the studio was followed, and the proposal was made that the vineyard might be a biblical reference. Heenk (1994, p. 35; 1995, pp. 199, 200) linked the drawing to F1640r (cat. 118) and F1638, which are on the same type of paper and are both works related to paintings. From this, she concluded that there must once have been a painted version of F1624. Mothe (1994, pp. 48, 61, 319) did not link the drawing to the letters of May, dating the work instead to ca. July 11; he changed the title (location) of painting F794 from *Farm of Père Eloi* to *Farm of Gualbert Romaru*. Wilson and Young (1995, pp. 64, 65) support this identification with photographs and made a connection with the drawing. Hulsker (1996, no. 1985) dated the sheet to May 25, even though he certainly knew of the letter of May 23, in which it is also mentioned.

Vincent wrote to Theo three days after arriving in Auvers on May 20, 1889, that he had already completed four paintings and two drawings, among them *Old Vineyard with Peasant Woman* [648]. The farmhouse and vine-covered pergola, on the rue Carnot in Auvers, were owned by Gualbert Romaru. Chickens scratch in the shade of the vines, and to the right is a woman with a basket on her arm, a scarf on her head. Van Gogh was planning a large canvas of the subject, but it is not known if he ever carried it out; no such work is known today. However, Romaru's house and vines are seen again in a small painting (F794, fig. 237).

The drawing consists of sturdy, flowing lines and is thus typical of Van Gogh's work from Auvers. He began with a detailed pencil sketch; the sky was done in watercolor, with spaces left blank for the clouds. The rest of the drawing was built up of lines mostly in blue, giving it the appearance of having been done in pen and ink, but it was actually executed in oil, as indicated by the impasto application and the seepage to the verso.

MV

Letter to Theo and Johanna van Gogh, May 23, 1890 [648]: I'm doing very well these days, I am working hard and have four painted studies and two drawings. You will see a drawing of an old vineyard with the figure of a peasant woman. I intend to make a big canvas of it.

Letter to Theo and Johanna van Gogh, May 25, 1890 [637]: I have a drawing of an old vine, from which I intend to make a canvas of size 30, and a study of pink chestnuts and one of white chestnuts.

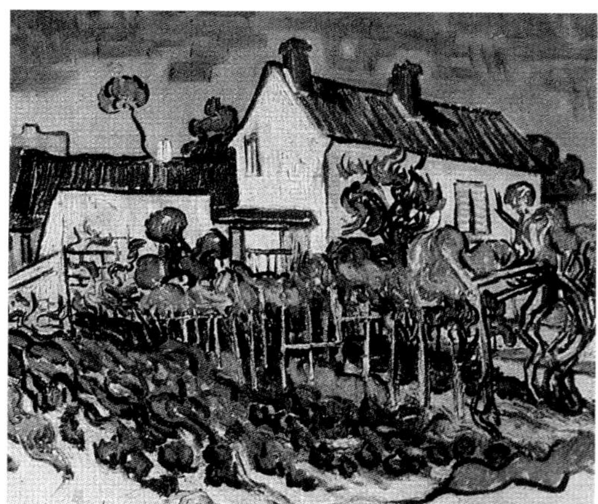

Fig. 237. *Group of Houses* (F794), late May 1890. Oil on canvas, 51 x 58 cm (20⅛ x 22⅞ in.). Present whereabouts unknown

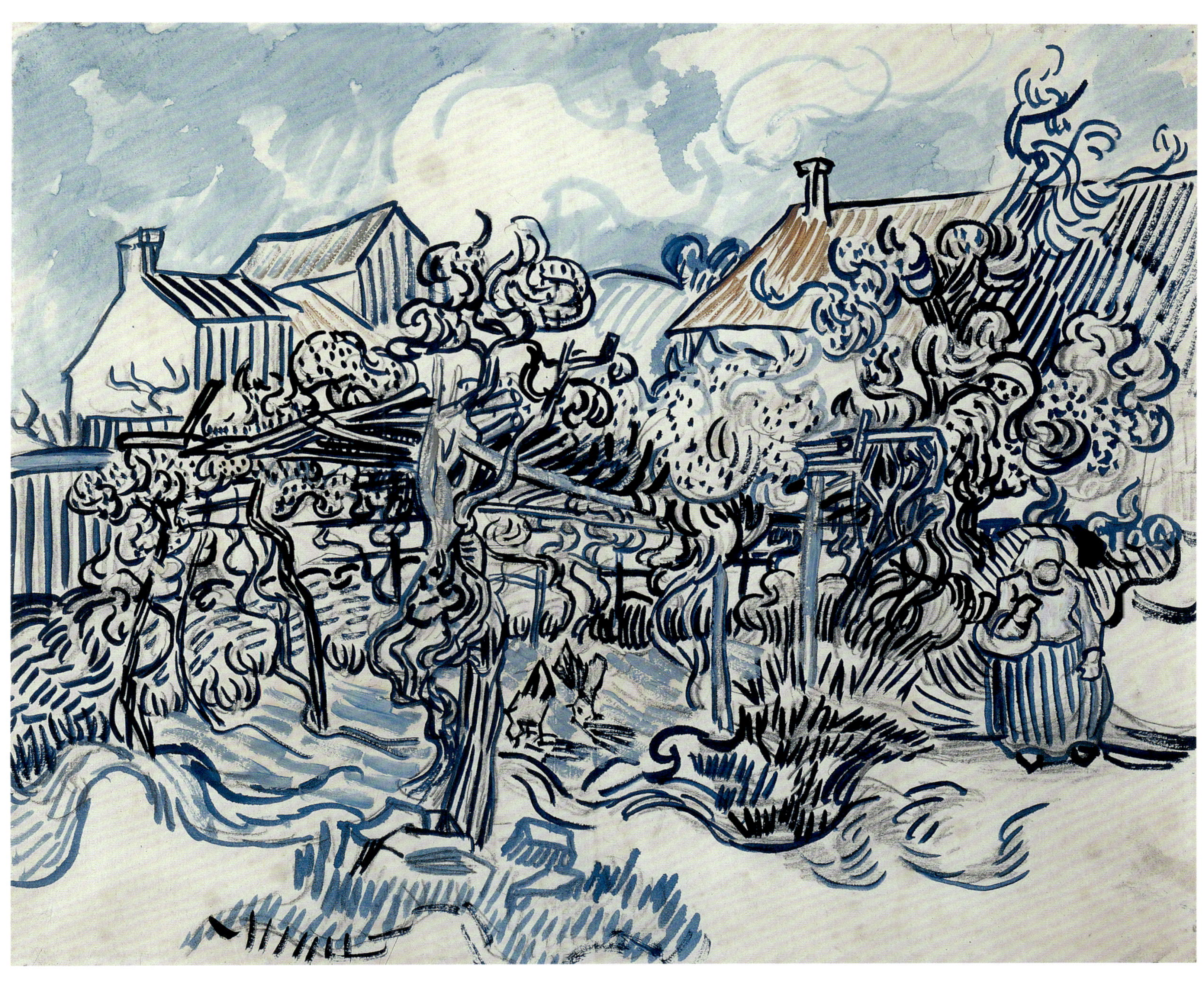

118. *Landscape with Houses*

ca. May 23, 1890
Brush, oils, and watercolor, graphite on laid paper watermarked DAMBRICOURT FRÈRES HALLINES
44 x 54.4 cm (17⅜ x 21⅜ in.)
Inscribed on verso, in another hand: *215*
Van Gogh Museum, Amsterdam (Vincent van Gogh Foundation) (d 332 V/1962)
F1640r, JH1986

Provenance: Theo van Gogh (d. 1891); by inheritance to his son, Vincent Willem van Gogh (1890–1978), as part of his collection, administered by his widow, Johanna van Gogh-Bonger (c. 1925), 1891; placed on loan at the Stedelijk Museum, Amsterdam, 1931–73; ownership transferred to the Vincent van Gogh Foundation, 1962; placed on permanent loan at the Van Gogh Museum, Amsterdam, 1973.

Selected exhibitions: Amsterdam 1905, no. 431; Berlin 1906, no. 64; Munich and other cities 1909–10; Cologne–Frankfurt 1910; Amsterdam 1911, no. 59; Hamburg 1911–12; Dresden–Breslau 1912, no. 16; Amsterdam 1914–15, no. 196; Utrecht 1923, no. 42; Rotterdam 1923; Basel 1924, no. 98; Zürich 1924, no. 98; Stuttgart 1924, no. 19; Paris 1925, unnumbered; Berlin 1927–28, no. 95; New York and other cities 1935–36, no. 125; Paris 1937, no. 79; London–Birmingham–Glasgow 1947–48, no. 177; New York–Chicago 1949–50, no. 156; London 1968–69, no. 192; Otterlo 1990, no. 241; Tokyo 2000, no. 28.

Summary of the literature: De la Faille (1928, no. 1640r) included the drawing among the works not mentioned in Van Gogh's letters from Auvers, called it "Paysage boisé," and described the medium as blue tempera and charcoal. In Liège–Brussels–Bergen 1946–47 (no. 138), the more exact date of June 1890 was proposed. Cooper (1955, p. 92) concurred and contended that the vehemence of the lines reflected the artist's state of mind; he mentioned painting F750, in which the same houses appear. Bowness (in London 1968–69, p. 124) dated the drawing to the end of May 1890, viewing it in connection with the series Souvenirs du Nord from Saint-Rémy. In De la Faille 1970 (no. 1640r), the drawing was dated to July 1890 with reasons not specified. Hulsker (1980, no. 1986) classified it among Van Gogh's works of May 1890. Based on the dating of the related painting, May 21, Pickvance (in New York 1986–87, pp. 200, 222, 223, 226, 249, 252) assumed that this sheet was also executed soon after Van Gogh's arrival in Auvers. He suggested that it is the second drawing mentioned in the letter of May 23 (see cat. 117). Given the underdrawing, he also believed the work was begun outdoors and finished in the studio. Van Uitert and Hoyle 1987, p. 473, no. 2.633. Feilchenfeldt and Veenenbos 1988, p. 138. Heenk (1994, p. 35; 1995, pp. 199, 200) considered the drawing an autonomous work despite its relationship to the painting (see also cat. 117). In 1995 she further suggested that the sketch on the verso (F1640v) was done first and left unfinished. Mothe (1994, pp. 47, 48, 317) dated both the painting and the drawing to May 22 and identified the locale. Hulsker (1996, no. 1986) now moved his dating to the end of May 1890. Martigny 2000, p. 110.

In terms of medium, paper, technique, and color relationships, *Landscape with Houses* strongly resembles *Old Vineyard with Peasant Woman* (F1624, cat. 117). It thus seems likely that the two works were made about the same time. In addition, Van Gogh referred to a second drawing in his letter to Theo of May 23 [648], which specifically mentions F1624, plausibly alluding to *Landscape with Houses* though he said nothing further about it.

On the verso is a drawing of a house with a chestnut tree (F1640v, fig. 238), a study for the painting *Blossoming Chestnut Tree* (F752) that Van Gogh referred to as finished in his May 25 letter to Theo [637]. This sketch was left incomplete, and the artist turned the sheet over for *Landscape with Houses*, which shows buildings in Gré, a hamlet between Four and Chaponval. The same houses appear in *A Group of Cottages* (F750, fig. 239), the first canvas he executed in Auvers. In the painting, a ridge of mountains rises up behind the houses.

In working up the sheet, Van Gogh did not follow the penciled underdrawing exactly, so that in places it remains clearly visible. As in F1624 (cat. 117), he worked in watercolor and oil, using two different brushes. The dark blue paint was applied last; it seeped through one of the tack holes left during Van Gogh's sketching on the verso, additional proof of the chronology of the two drawings.

MV

Fig. 238. *House with Chestnut Tree* (F1640v), May 20–25, 1890. Chalk and graphite on laid paper, 44 x 54.4 cm (17⅜ x 21⅜ in.). Van Gogh Museum, Amsterdam (Vincent van Gogh Foundation)

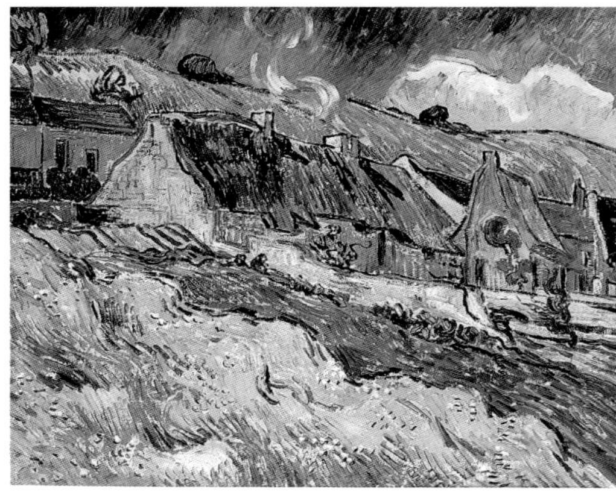

Fig. 239. *A Group of Cottages* (F750), May 21, 1890. Oil on canvas, 60 x 73 cm (23⅝ x 28¾ in.). The State Hermitage Museum, Saint Petersburg

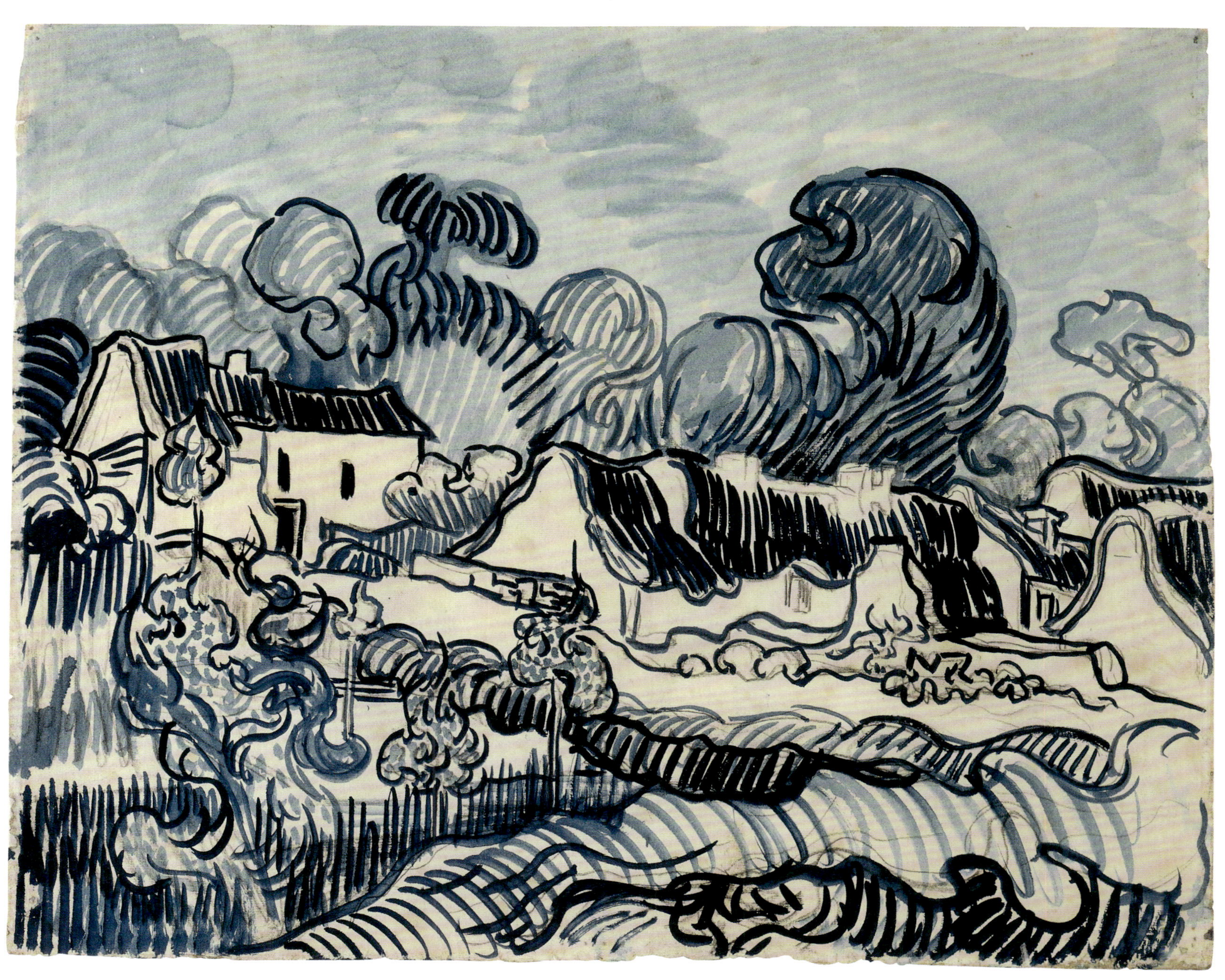

119. *Landscape with a Bridge over the Oise*

Late May–early June 1890
Brush, opaque watercolor, and oils, pen and ink, graphite on pink laid paper watermarked ED & CIE PL BAS
47.8 x 62.8 cm (18 7/8 x 24 3/4 in.)
Tate, London, Bequeathed By C. Frank Stoop, 1933 (NO 4714)
F1639, JH2023

Provenance: Theo van Gogh (d. 1891); by inheritance to his son, Vincent Willem van Gogh, administered by his widow, Johanna van Gogh-Bonger, as part of his collection, 1891; sold by her (together with F1242, cat. 24; F1497, cat. 101) through Kunsthandel C. M. van Gogh to Dutch stockbroker and collector C. F. Stoop, London, 1911; bequeathed by him to the Tate Gallery, 1933.

Selected exhibitions: Berlin 1909–10, no. 220; Amsterdam 1914–15, no. 197; London–Birmingham–Glasgow 1947–48, no. 176; Frankfurt 1970, no. 64; New York 1986–87, no. 74; Otterlo 1990, no. 245; Martigny 2000, no. 86; Toledo 2003, no. 19.

Summary of the literature: De la Faille (1928, no. 1639) included the drawing among the works not mentioned in Van Gogh's letters from Auvers and gave it the title "L'Oise"; he provided a detailed description of the original colors. Cooper (in London–Birmingham–Glasgow 1947–48, no. 176) dated the drawing to June 1890; in 1955 (p. 88), he shifted the date to May–June, just after the artist's arrival in Auvers. In Frankfurt 1970 (no. 64), the location, somewhere near Méry, was suggested. That and Cooper's dating of May–June were accepted in De la Faille 1970 (no. 1639). Hulsker (1980, no. 2023) gave a date of June. Alley (1981, pp. 293, 294) agreed; he suggested that Van Gogh positioned himself on the steep embankment along the railroad tracks and contended that the tall trees along the river were Van Gogh's invention although old postcards show that there were trees there. Alley also noted the discolorations; these are clearly visible in the color reproduction (including the original colors along the edges) in Mothe 1987 (p. 145). Mothe wrote that the view was taken from the rue Rajon. Pickvance (in New York 1986–87, pp. 252–53; in Otterlo 1990, pp. 319, 326) stressed the combination of rural and modern, industrial elements in the drawing and noted that this is the only sheet in which the river Oise plays a prominent role. Feilchenfeldt and Veenenbos 1988, p. 138. Heijbroek and Wouthuysen (1993, p. 206) gave the date of the sale to Stoop as January 1913. Heenk (1994, pp. 34, 35; 1995, pp. 198, 199, 201) linked the cows on this sheet with those on F1632. Stolwijk and Veenenbos 2002, pp. 53, 129, 150, 163, 198. In Toledo 2003 (no. 19) the style and subject were characterized as congruent with those of the artist's early Auvers period.

Van Gogh here depicted fields along the river Oise dotted with cows and with figures at work. To the right is the wrought-iron bridge that had opened just six months earlier. Across the river are two factories with tall chimneys, one hidden behind the enormous poplars. Undulating lines dominate the composition: the banks of the river, the hills on the horizon, and the line along the tops of the trees. The drawing was probably executed at the end of May or early June, based on the specific kind of color contrast (see F1624, cat. 117; F1640r, cat. 118) and on the sheet's similarities to *Landscape with a Coach and Train in the Background* (F760, fig. 240) of about June 12, 1890, in terms of the raised viewpoint, organization of pictorial elements, horizontal line cutting through the composition, and small details added to the landscape.

Van Gogh sketched the scene in graphite, then delineated some elements in pen and ink—the cows, the fence, the trees, and the factory behind them; he applied the watercolor and oil paints last. Van Gogh's use of oil paint in the sky is evidenced by the yellow film around the brushstrokes, where the oil has separated from the pigment.

MV

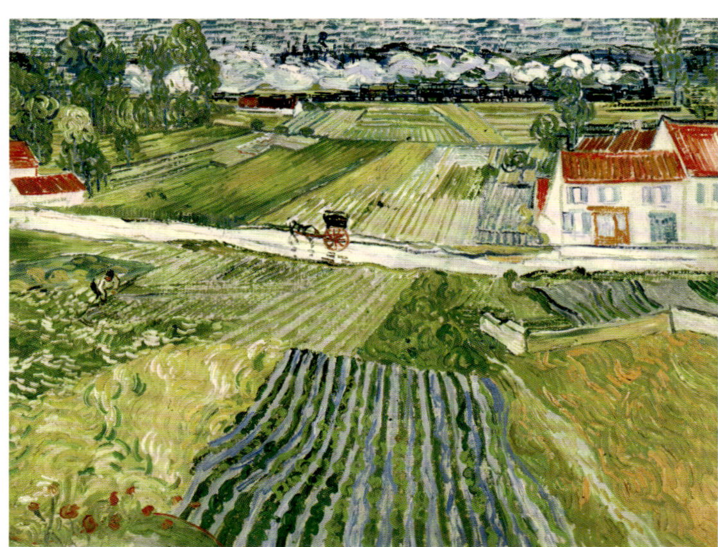

Fig. 240. *Landscape with a Coach and Train in the Background* (F760), ca. June 12, 1890. Oil on canvas, 72 x 90 cm (28 3/8 x 35 3/8 in.). Pushkin State Museum of Fine Arts, Moscow

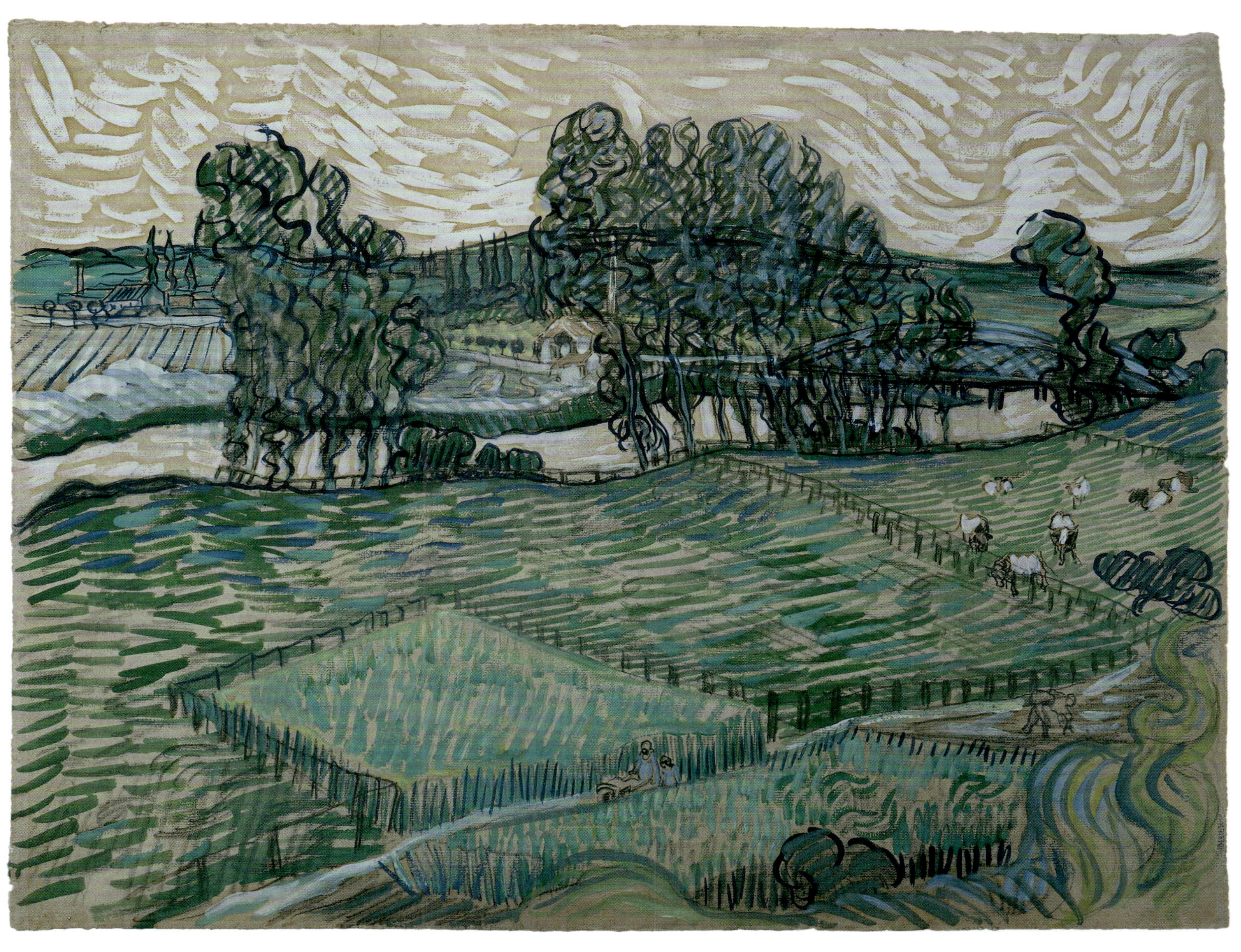

Infrared Reflectography: The Drawings under the Drawings

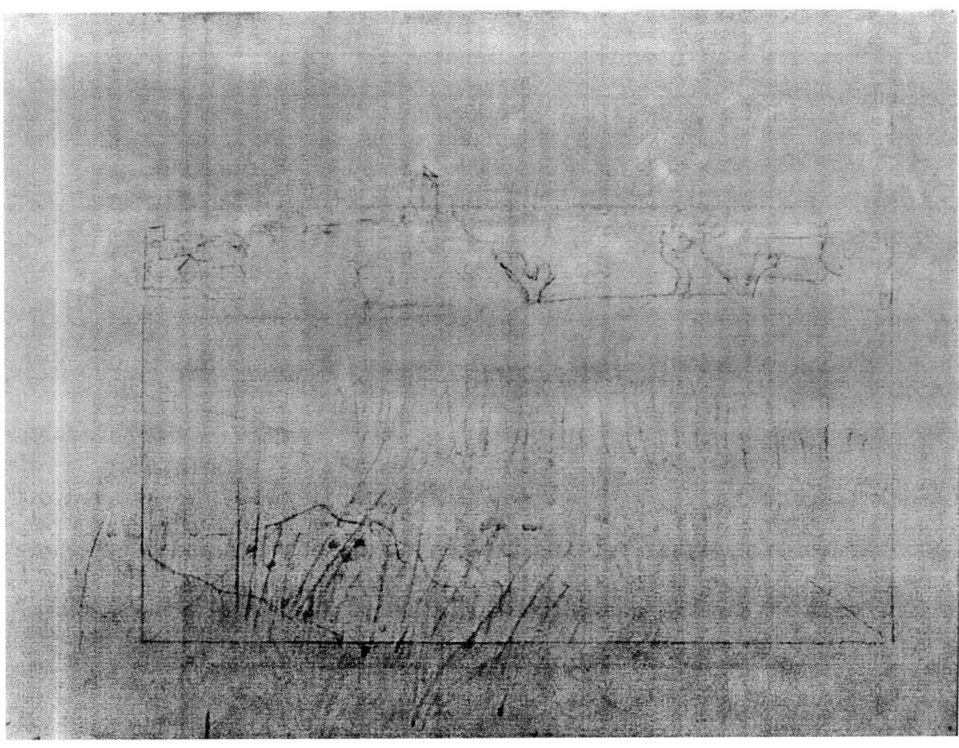

Fig. 241. Infrared reflectogram of *View of Arles with Irises in the Foreground* (F1416r), cat. 46

Infrared reflectography was used to investigate Van Gogh's working process in the drawings illustrated in the following pages. The technique, developed at the Sherman Fairchild Center for Works on Paper and Photograph Conservation of The Metropolitan Museum of Art under the direction of Marjorie Shelley, utilized a vidicon camera, which is sensitive in the near to middle infrared region of the spectrum, with a series of long pass filters. Because of the particular spectral response of different artists' materials at different wavelengths, it was possible (using 1000 and 1100nm filters) to penetrate the ink in each of these drawings and reveal their underlying graphite sketches. The imaging and assembly of these reflectograms was done by Alison Gilchrest.

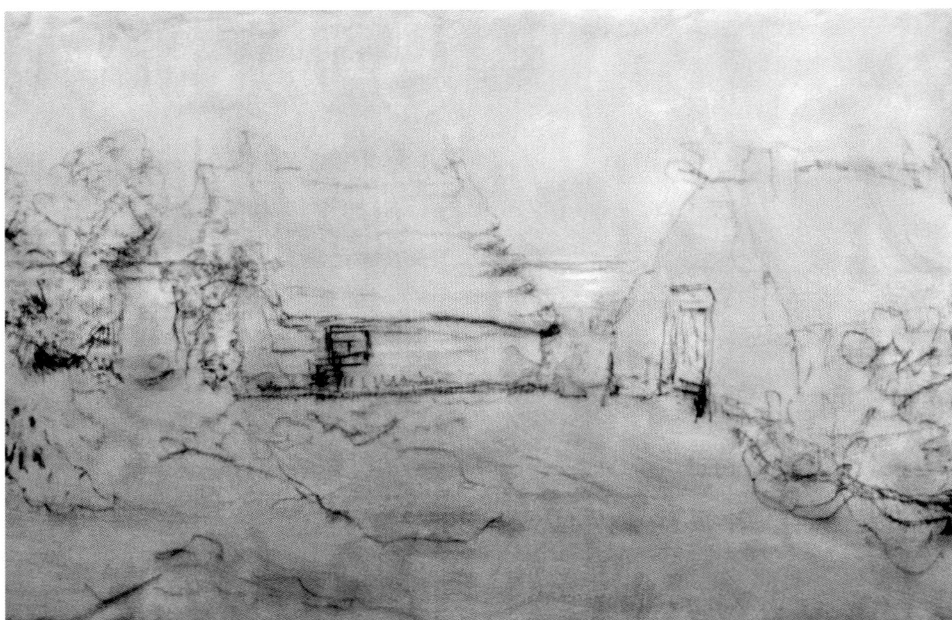

Fig. 242. Infrarec reflectogram of *Two Cottages, Saintes-Maries-de-la-Mer* (F1440), cat. 48

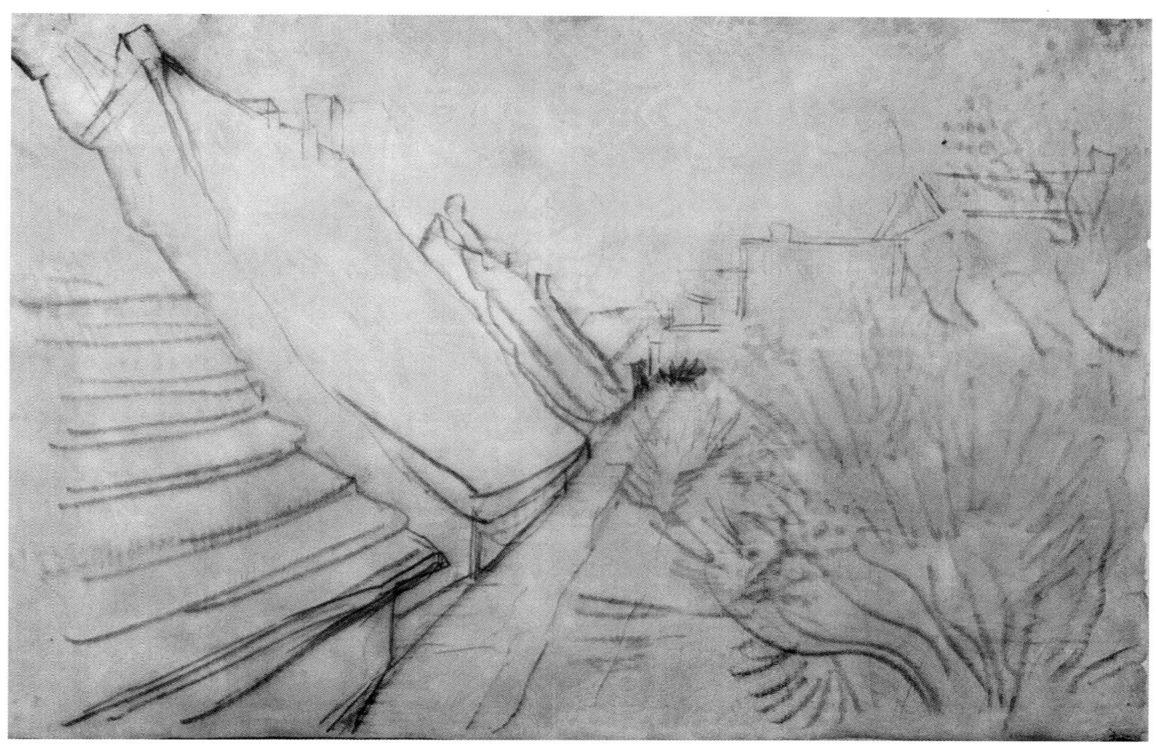

Fig. 243. Infrared reflectogram of *Street in Saintes-Maries-de-la-Mer* (F1434), cat. 50

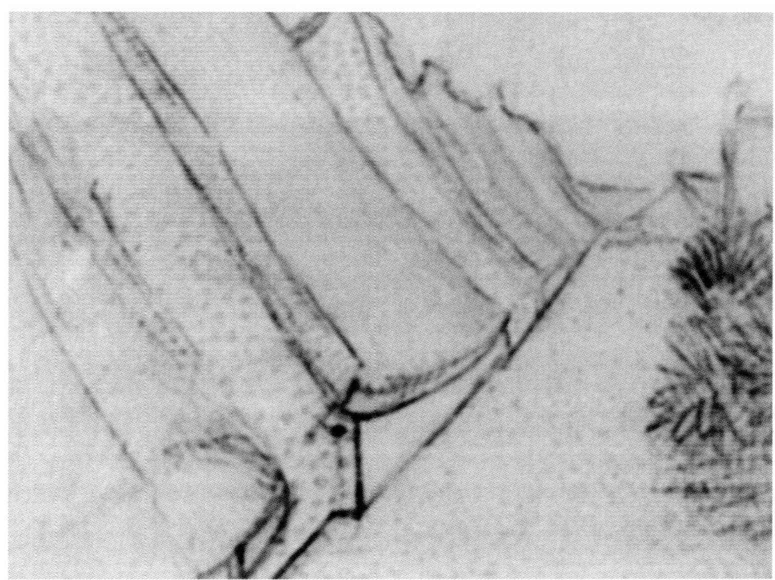

Fig. 244. Infrared reflectogram of the left side of *Street in Saintes-Maries-de-la-Mer* (F1435), cat. 53

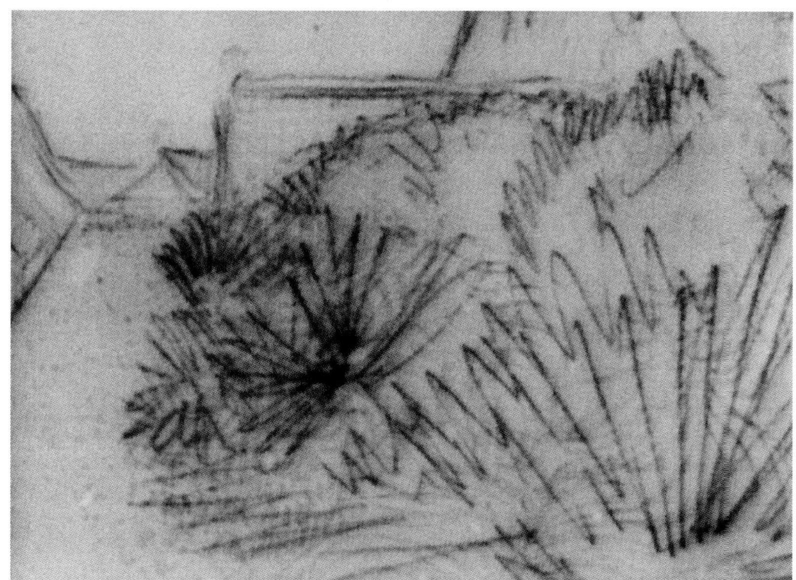

Fig. 245. Infrared reflectogram of the lower right corner of *Street in Saintes-Maries-de-la-Mer* (F1435), cat. 53

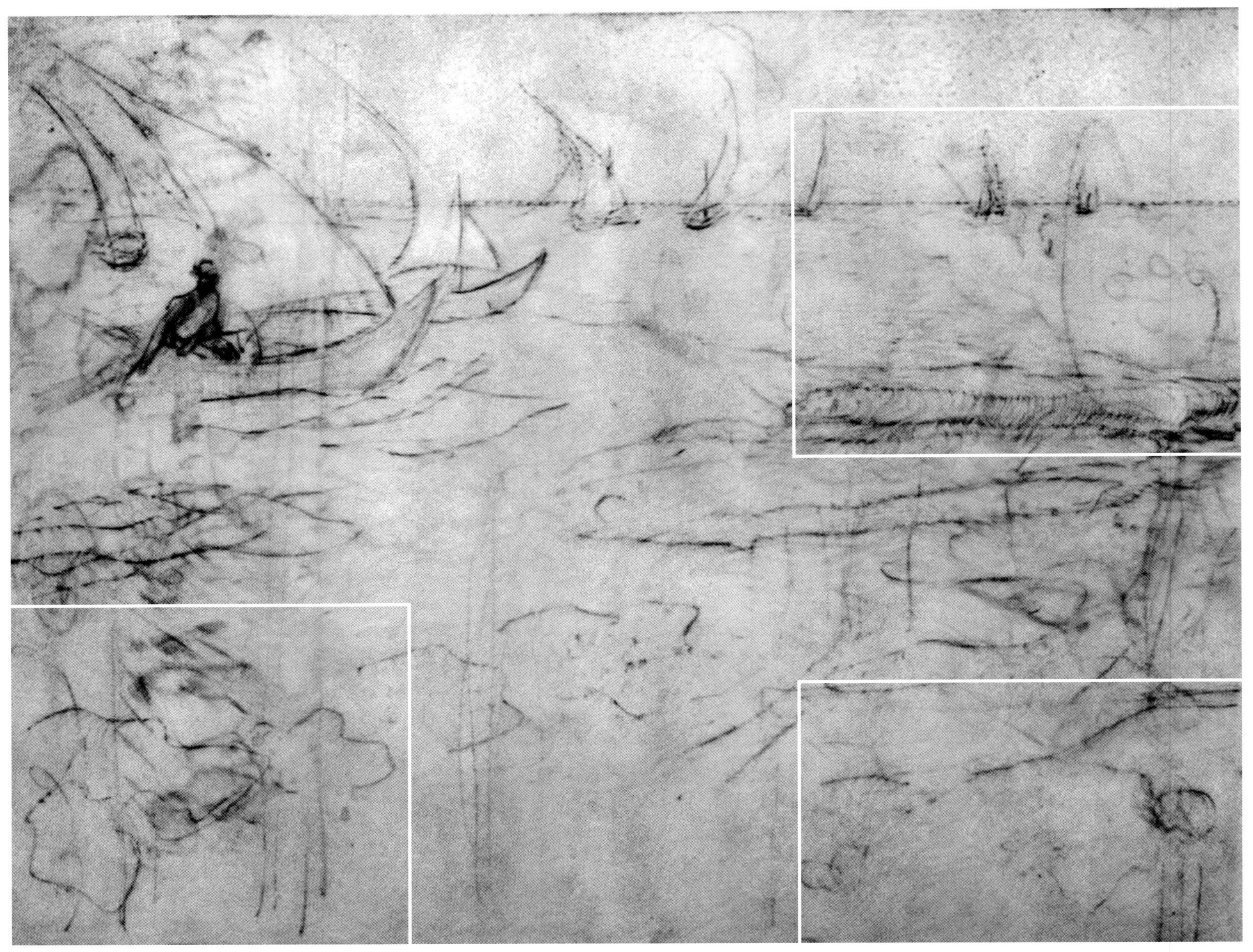

Fig. 246. Infrared reflectogram of *Boats at Sea, Saintes-Maries-de-la-Mer* (F1430a), cat. 58

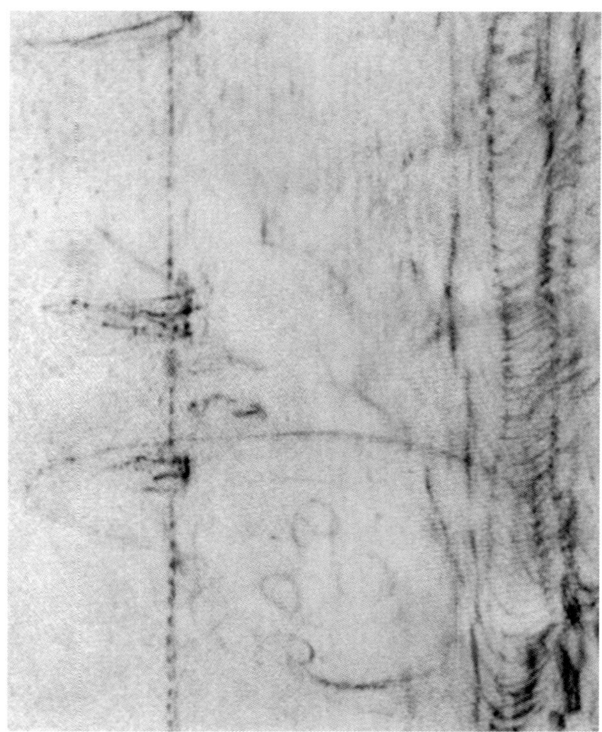

Fig. 247. Detail of fig. 246, figure study

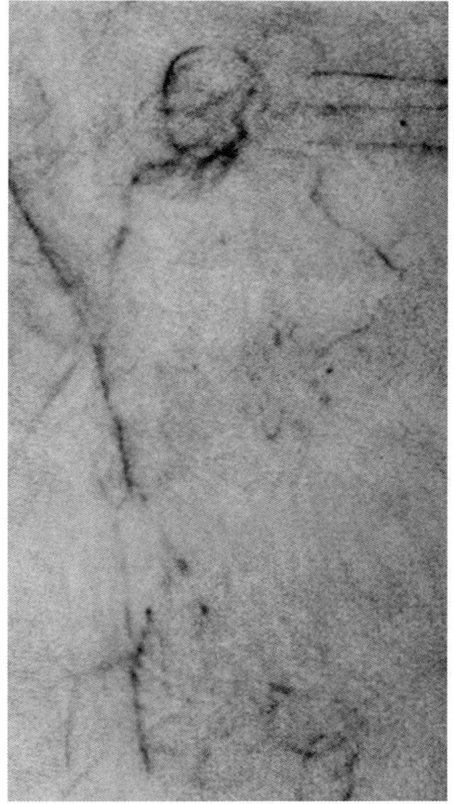

Fig. 249. Detail of fig. 246, figure study

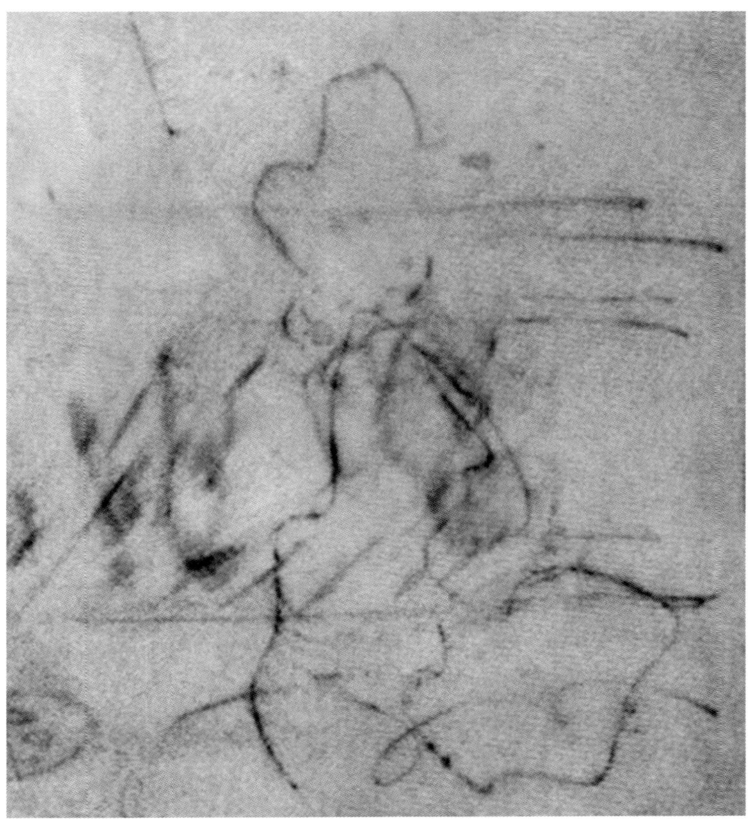

Fig. 248. Detail of fig. 246, figure study

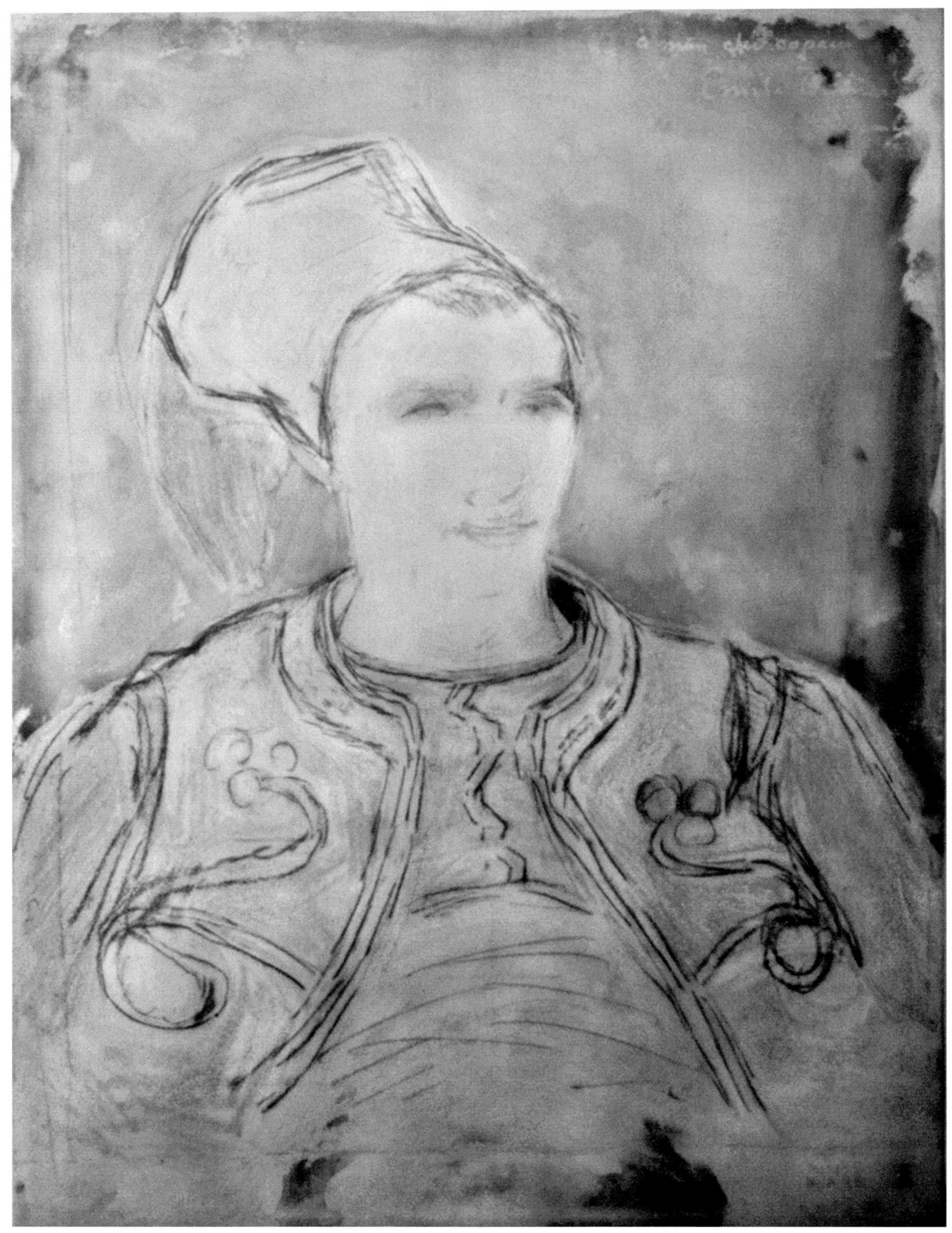

Fig. 250. Infrared reflectogram of *The Zouave* (F1482), cat. 77

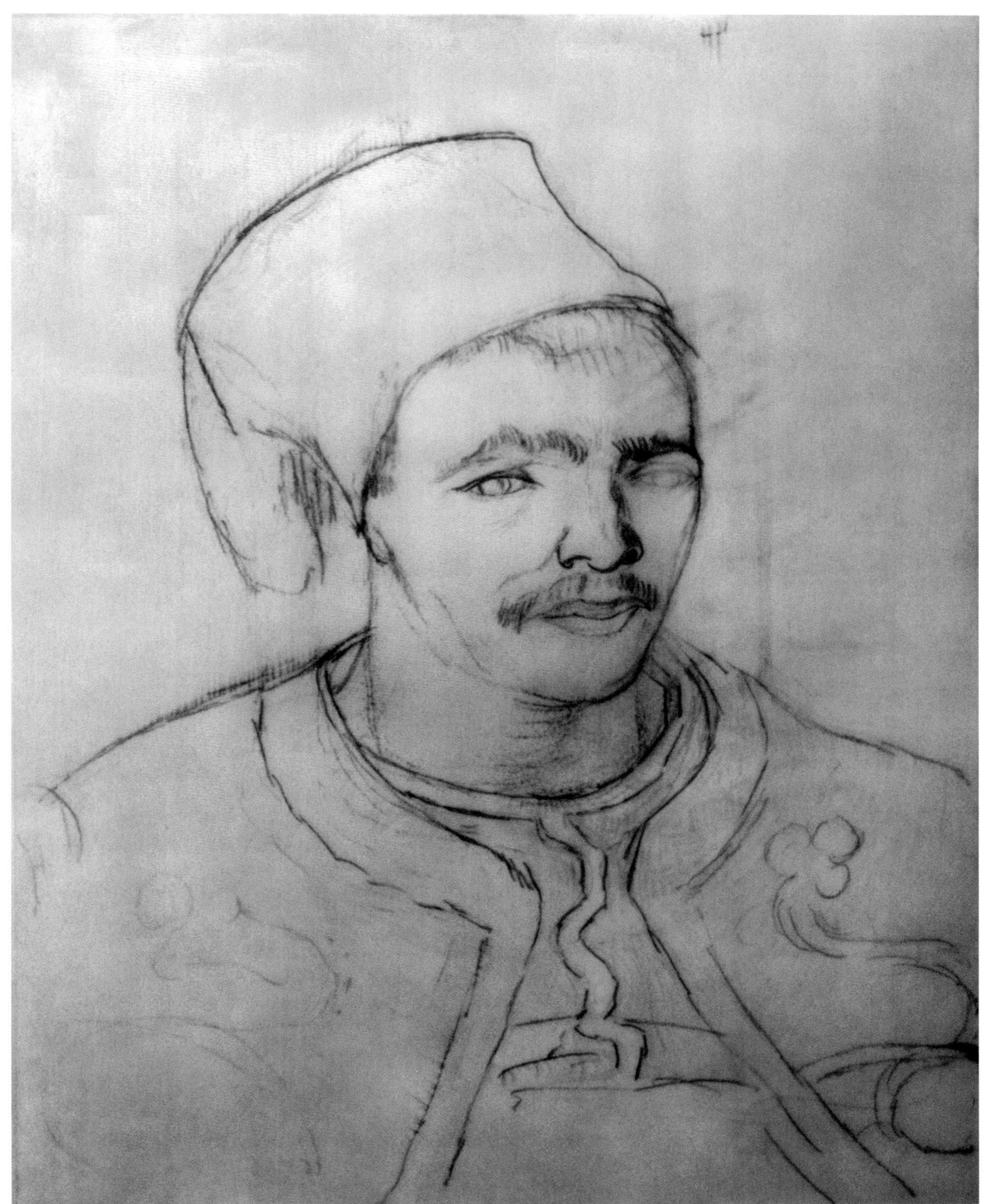

Fig. 251. Infrared reflectogram of *The Zouave* (F1482a), cat. 79

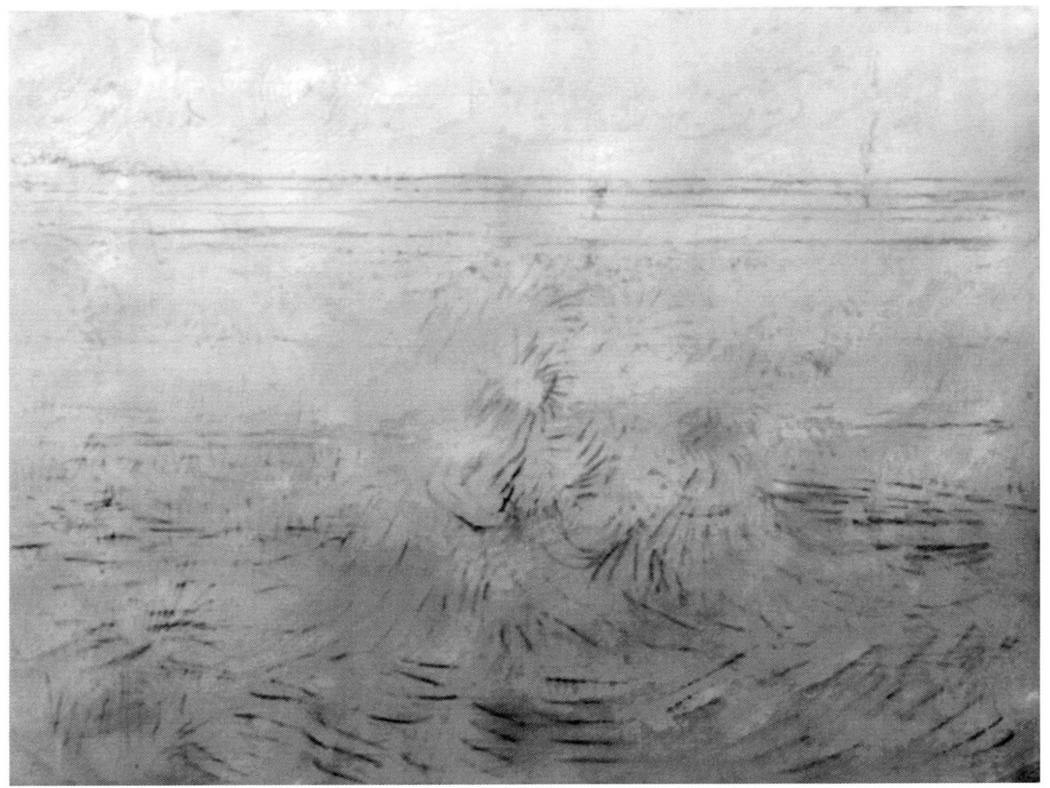

Fig. 252. Infrared reflectogram of *Wheat Field with Sheaves* (F1489), cat. 74

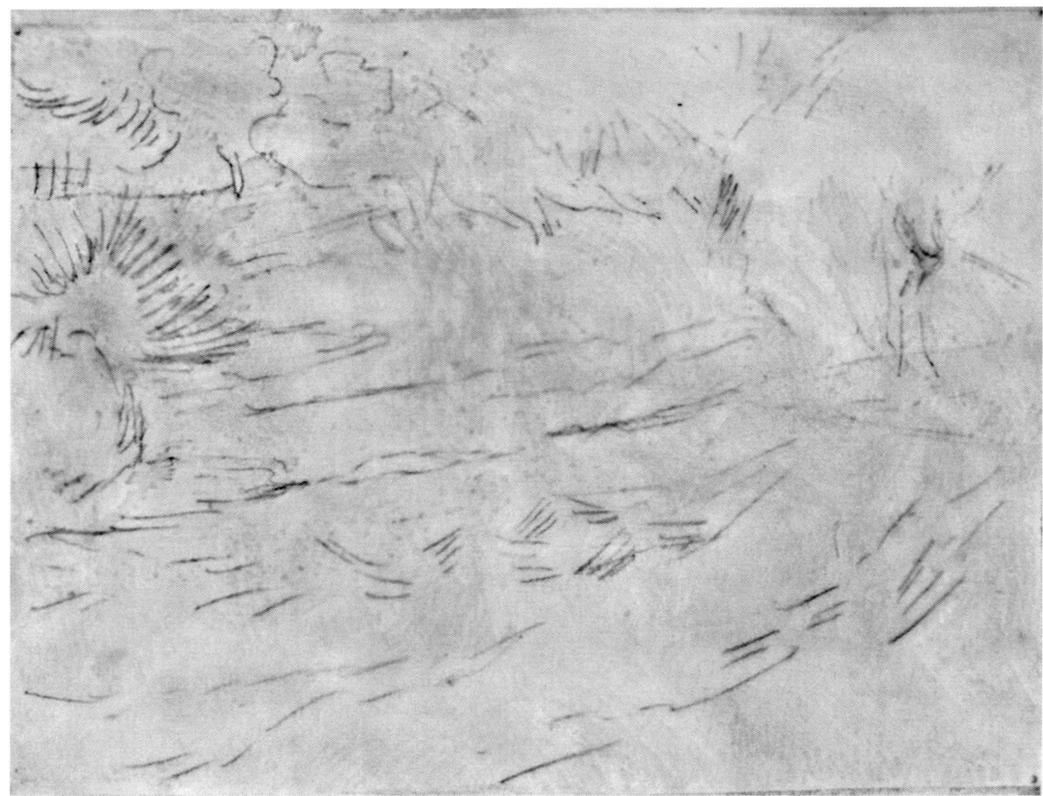

Fig. 253. Infrared reflectogram of *The Garden; A Corner of a Garden in the Place Lamartine* (F1450), cat. 88

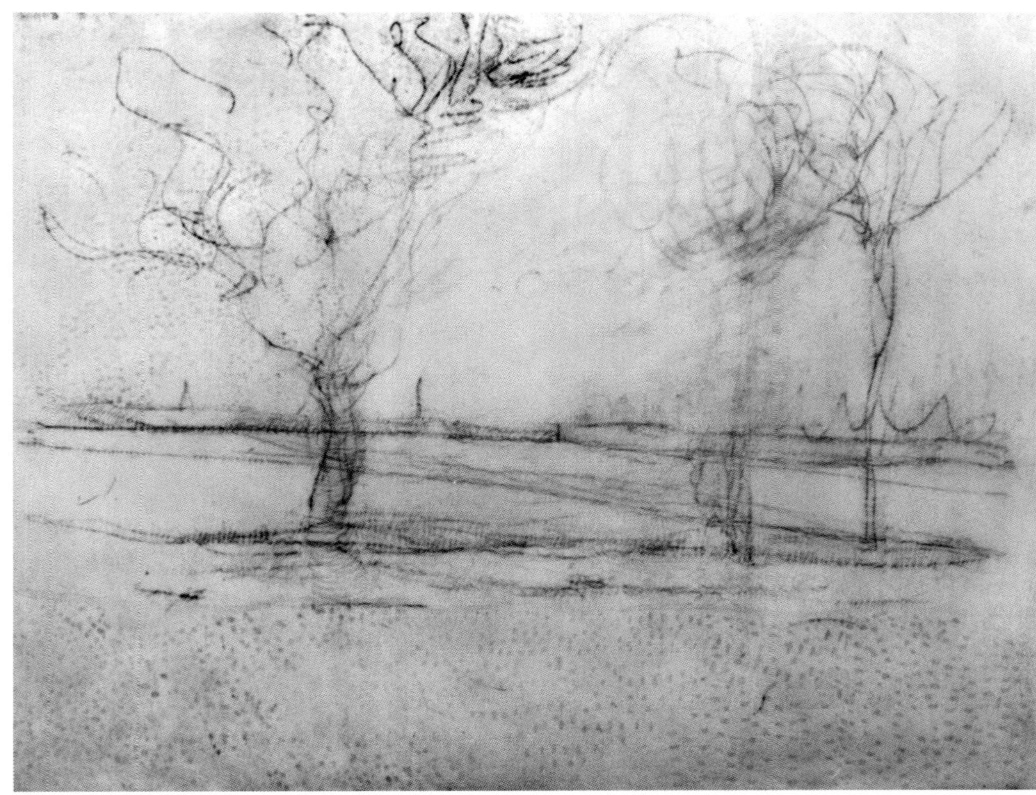

Fig. 254. Infrared reflectogram of *The Road to Tarascon* (F1502a), cat. 93

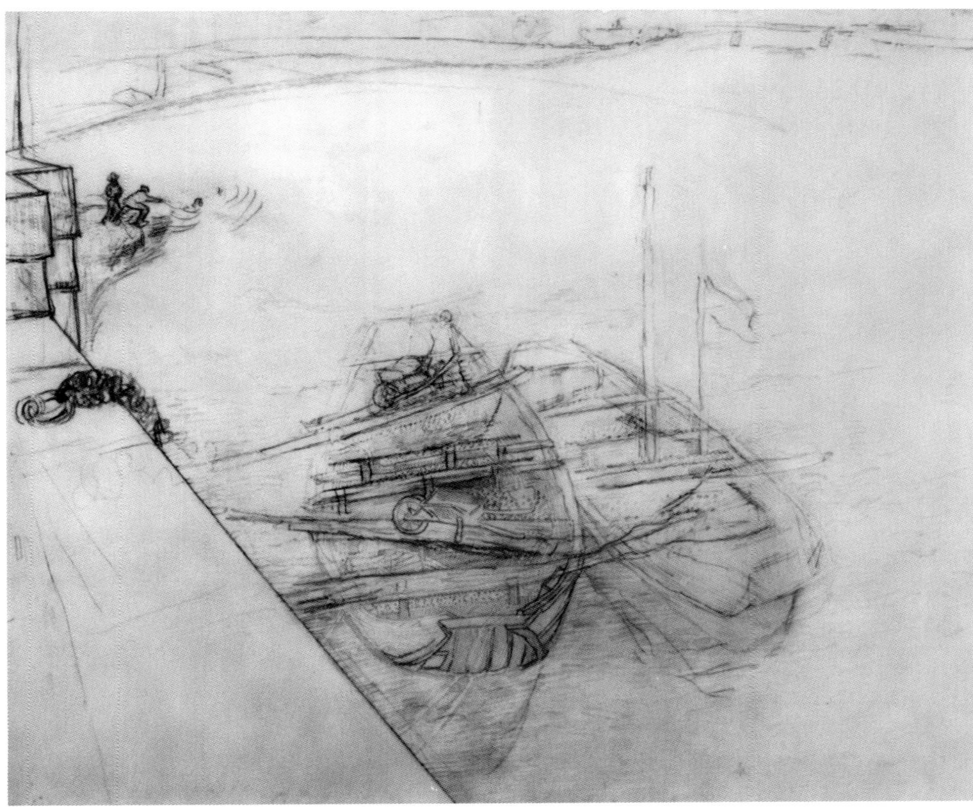

Fig. 255. Infrared reflectogram of *Sand Barges on the Rhône* (F1462), cat. 95

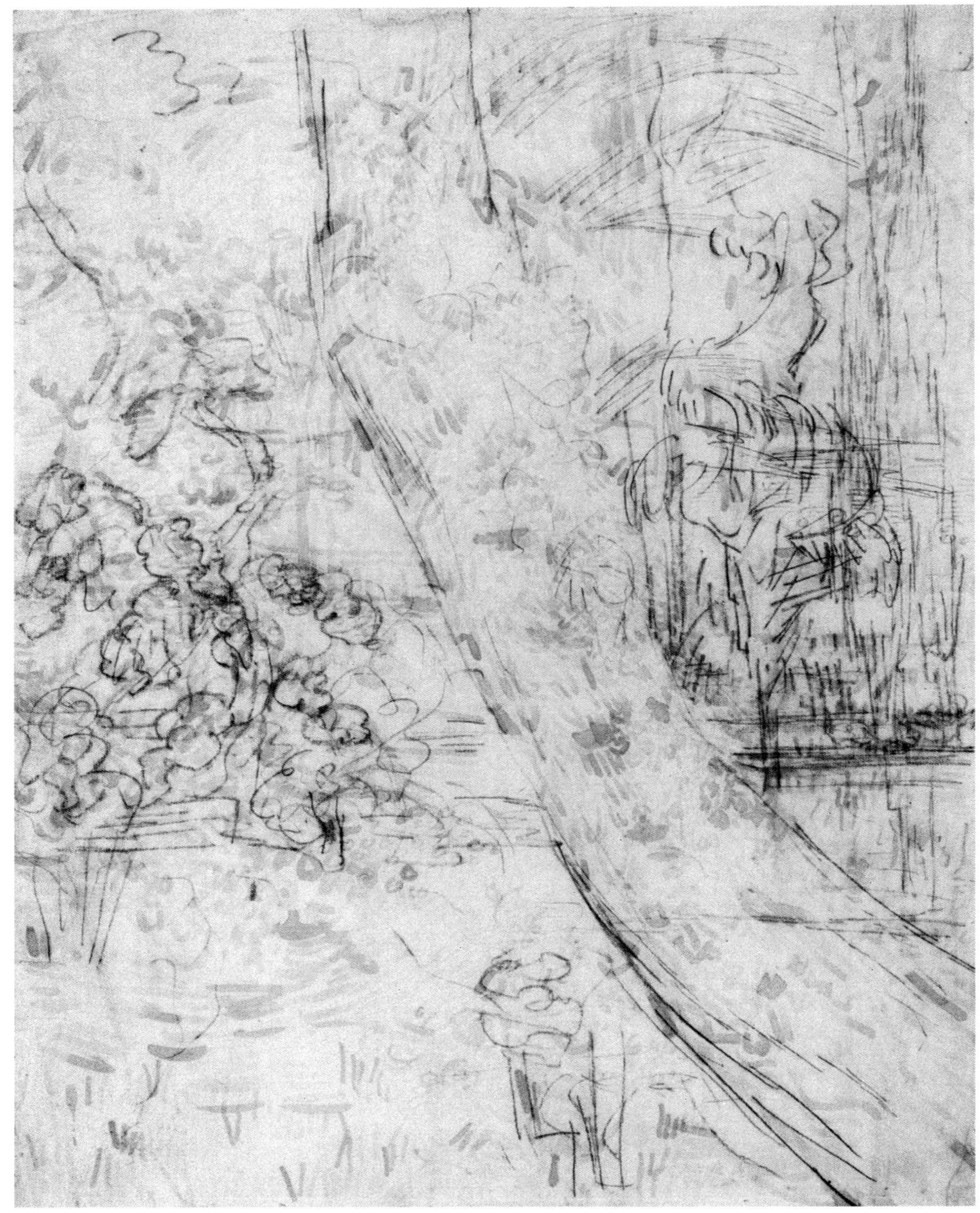

Fig. 256. Infrared reflectogram of *Tree with Ivy in the Garden of the Asylum* (F1532), cat. 102 (IRR: Nico Lingbeek)

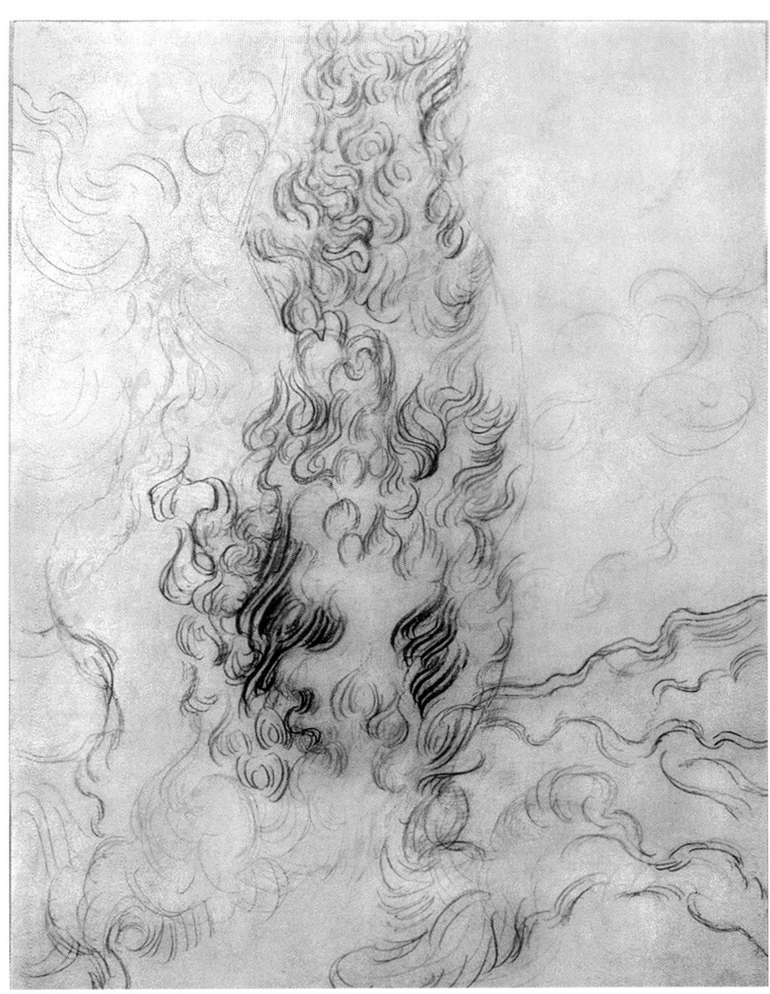

Fig. 257. Infrared reflectogram of *Cypresses* (F1525), cat. 108

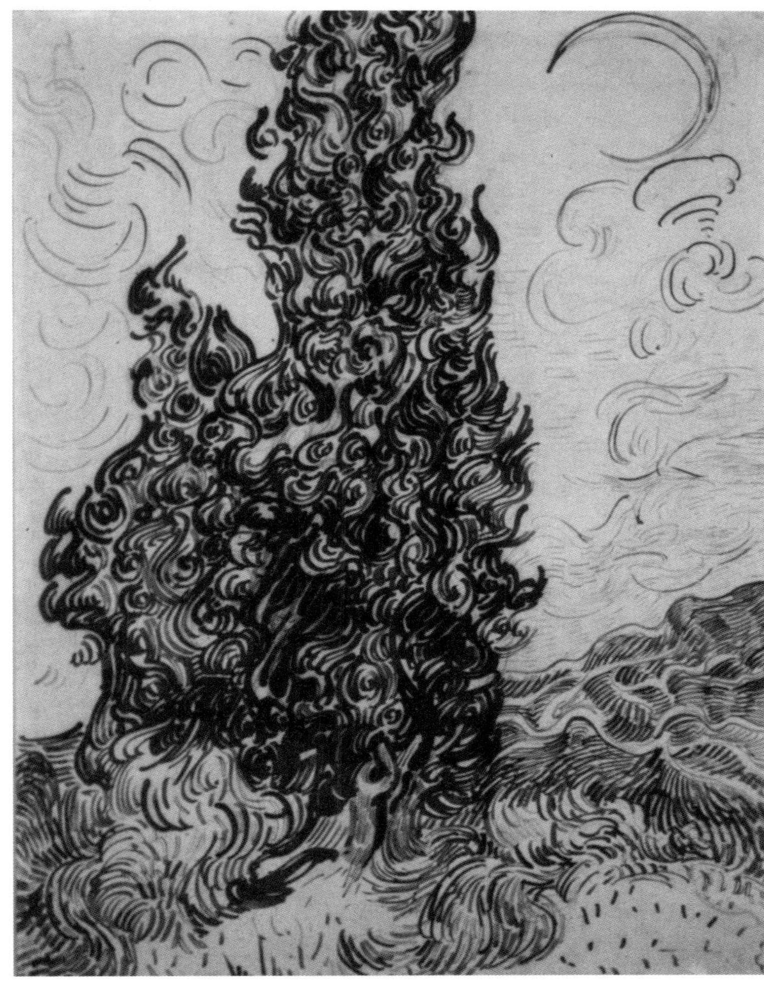

Fig. 258. Photograph taken under ultraviolet light of *Cypresses* (F1525), cat. 108

Technical Studies: Observations on the Drawing Materials Used by Van Gogh in Provence

Marjorie Shelley
with scientific analyses by
Silvia A. Centeno

BLACK AND WHITE: THE INKS

Throughout his correspondence, Van Gogh expressed his passion for pen-and-ink drawing. Letters from the early years of his work as an artist reveal his admiration for the English "black and white" illustrators, for various French draftsmen (among them Millet, Corot, Lhermitte), and for the old masters. These letters also document his desire to build a collection of illustrations as well as his interest in publishing his own drawings. From Cassagne's *Traité d'aquarelle*, which he purchased in 1881, he was able to gather information not only on watercolor but also on sepia and other inks [146, late June 1881]. By 1883 he would write with assurance about "Black and White," a method that "makes it possible to put on paper, relatively swiftly effects that would otherwise lose something of what is called 'spontaneity'" [R20, ca. February 4, 1883]. Later that year, he noted that "with the pen one can enter into such details as are impossible in painted studies" [326, September 22, 1883]. His many comments on the best types of pen provide a picture of the sustained importance he invested in such tools: an "ordinary writing pen" [R30, March 5, 1883]; a "reed pen to work up [his] pencil drawings" [146];[1] six special penholders and various nibs that he judged to be "rubbish," alongside praise for the satisfaction of the more fluent, bolder stroke of an ordinary quill [R30]; on sharpening "a reed the way you would a goose quill" [478, ca. April 20, 1888]; and a description of one of his drawings as done with "very thick reeds on thin Whatman paper," with finer quill strokes for the background [498a, May 29 or 30, 1888]. The significance of these tools is also revealed in acerbic comments, such as, "very fine pens, like very elegant people, are sometimes amazingly useless, and as I see, they often lack elasticity which the most ordinary pens just naturally have to a certain extent" [R30]; or in his lament that "perhaps there would be more pen drawings in the world if somebody invented a good pen for use outdoors with an inkstand to go with it" [195, May 1, 1882].[2] Van Gogh's absorption in the process of ink drawing is also evident in the range of inks he tried in the early 1880s: sepia, India ink, engraving, autographic, and lithographic ink, "ordinary" ink [R29, between ca. February 23 and 26, 1883; 279, ca. April 11, 1883], powdered ink, and lampblack [150, mid-September 1881; 256, December 31, 1882, and January 2, 1883]. In his experiments with these materials he sought to "bring a new kind of black" into his drawings [R8, May 28, 1882], often combining mixtures of them with dry black media-charcoal, black "mountain" chalk, or lithographic crayon [R36, ca. May 25, 1883; R37, ca. June 15, 1883], and diluting printer's ink with turpentine [278, ca. April 2, 1883].[3]

Despite this wealth of commentary on his early work in pen and ink, Van Gogh divulged little about the ink drawings he did in Arles or thereafter. Though he used a far simpler technique, dispensing with the multiple layers and admixtures of black media, water, fixing solutions, body color, bread crumbs, and scraping, the late drawings present a number of questions. Among them their original color and identity remain an enigma. Their coloration, ranging from blackish browns to reddish browns to grays and drab yellows, has led most viewers to believe these works were rendered in iron gall ink, which originally would have been black, but the darkest strokes in the works in this study reveal no evidence of corrosion and only minimal penetration through the paper, characteristics generally associated with this acidic material. We do not know the components of the "ordinary" ink that he referred to years before [279, April 11, 1883], or if it was an ink he used frequently. Similarly, the once protected margins of a few of the drawings reveal strokes rendered in purple ink, a color that is not generally associated with Van Gogh's works on paper. It is also not known if these drawings were produced by varying the concentration of one ink, or if several inks were used. Finally, the strokes in many of these drawings abruptly change tonality without evidence of inks of different compositions having been used.

The following observations seek to unravel some of these queries and also provide new insights into Van Gogh's inks. They draw upon a limited range of samples within a small group of drawings that were studied closely using nondestructive analysis, including high-powered magnification, X-ray fluorescence (XRF), Raman spectroscopy, and infrared reflectography. (Explanations of the testing procedures, the results of instrumental analysis, and the criteria for identification are presented in the appendixes.) They are supported by information on late-nineteenth-century ink technology. In order to ascertain the ink type, XRF was used to determine the elemental composition of the dark, medium, and light ink samples. The results indicated that different types of logwood inks were used in this group of drawings, and that in some sheets more than one logwood ink was used. Examination under stereo-binocular magnification and by Raman analysis also indicated the presence of a mixture containing carbonaceous particles or ink in several of the drawings. Infrared reflectography using a vidicom camera with a 1100 nm longpass filter, which revealed the presence of carbon in many of the strokes, also proved to be a valuable tool in revealing the graphite underdrawing by penetrating through the design layer.[4] Even with these resources, complete identification was not always possible. There are instrumental limitations in detecting certain organic compounds if samples are not removed from the drawings, while some inorganic constituents fall below detectable levels. Nonetheless, the findings presented here can be used as a point of departure for future research.

The drawings examined show that Van Gogh used several different inks. Each work was begun with a graphite sketch mapping out the essential elements that would subsequently be developed in pen. It was discovered that he did not use a traditional iron gall ink, which, in fact, was rapidly falling unto disuse,[5] but rather several formulations of a commercially available black writing ink made of logwood and a brightly hued aniline ink. It was also observed that in some drawings Van Gogh employed a very dark ink containing carbonaceous particles, possibly an autographic ink or India ink mixed with writing ink.[6]

Iron Gall and Logwood Inks

Iron gall ink, a material in continuous use for writing and drawing from at least the eleventh century until the end of the nineteenth,[7] was made from an aqueous solution of an iron salt, usually ferrous sulfate, and an organic compound derived from a decoction of oak galls or other vegetable matter rich in tannates.[8] Depending on the proportions of these ingredients the resultant ink was invariably a deep brownish or bluish black.[9] On aging it generally underwent a degradation process, fading to a range of dark brown, reddish brown, and gray brown, colors characteristic of Van Gogh's drawings today. In efforts to correct the ink's many shortcomings over the course of time, formulations for iron gall were modified by adding provisional colorants (such as indigo, carmine, and logwood) to increase chromatic intensity while the initial color formation process was taking place on paper.[10] By the nineteenth century, manufacturers sought to produce a writing ink that not only would assume full color intensity when first used rather than after several hours, days, or even weeks had elapsed, but also would not corrode the increasingly popular steel pen nib; that would flow readily; and that would penetrate the fibers of the paper (to ensure the document's permanence) but not pass through it or provoke deterioration of the support.

The logwood inks that were ultimately developed to rectify these problems were numerous and became widely available by the last quarter of the nineteenth century. Such inks were prepared from the red to dark brown extracts made from the wood of the campeachy tree combined with various substances including iron gall ink, an iron salt, potassium chromate, or an alum salt.[11] They were produced by many manufacturers and despite diverse recipes they were fairly similar in their writing properties, sedimentation, and intense black color. Since few of these inexpensive substances were sold under names indicative of their contents, it is unlikely that the user had any particular knowledge of their individual constituents and would have chosen one or another of them at random from those on the marketplace.[12] Elemental analysis revealed that Van Gogh used such inks in many of the drawings studied. Three types made with the components cited could be identified with certainty: chrome logwood ink and two logwoods made with other additives. Possibly the popular logwood–iron gall mixture, known as logwood tannin ink, was also used.[13] One of the inks examined had similar elemental constituents as an "ordinary ink" cited in a manual of 1902.[14] Since logwood inks were grouped as a broad class of common writing ink, it is likely that this designation was applied to most, if not all of these substances.[15] Hence, it is possible that Van Gogh's "ordinary ink" was a logwood. A discussion of the findings is presented below and a more detailed account of the constituents of the inks used by the artist follows in Appendix 1.

Chrome logwood inks

Chrome logwood inks, introduced in about 1848, became the most widespread among the logwoods by the latter part of the century.[16] Made by adding potassium chromate, an oxidizing agent, to the logwood extract, these inks turned a deep black color in the bottle or immediately upon drying. Chrome inks, like other logwoods containing iron, alum, or copper salts, tended gradually to form a precipitate, or sediment, upon standing; hence, the flow of the ink was subject to inconsistencies in viscosity.[17] However, the simplicity of their production and their good overall working properties accounted for their popularity. This type of ink was found in the greatest number of drawings in this study. The slight variations among the test sites probably reflect the different formulas of the many manufacturers producing this particular ink. Van Gogh's use of this ink is indicated in the XRF spectra by the presence of chromium and the absence of any other element in quantities above ones corresponding to the paper reserve in the following drawings:[18] *Two Cottages, Saintes-Maries-de-la-Mer* (F1440, cat. 48), *Street in Saintes-Maries-de-la-Mer* (F1435, cat. 53), and *The Zouave* (F1482, cat. 77). It is also indicated in the dark tone inks in *Wheat Field* (F1481, fig. 186), and the dark and light tone inks in the Saint-Rémy drawing *Cypresses* (F1525, cat. 108). In the last sheet, the different constituents in the medium brown sites (chromium, sulfur, and potassium) suggest a second ink, possibly an alum logwood ink.

Alum logwood inks

The presence of sulfur and chromium in three of the drawings suggests an ink composed of a chrome logwood recipe and an alum salt.[19] It was observed in the dark, medium, and light brown inks in *Boats at Sea, Saintes-Maries-de-la-Mer* (F1430a, cat. 58); in the dark tones in *The Trinquetaille Bridge* (F1507, fig. 182); and in the medium tones in *Cypresses.*

Iron logwood inks

A third subgroup of logwoods, distinguished by the presence of chromium and iron, was found in the dark and medium ink tones in *The Garden* (F1450, cat. 88). There were no characteristic sulfur signals beyond that present in the bare paper, suggesting that this ink was similar to chrome logwood ink but that it also included an iron salt not containing sulfates.

View of Arles with Irises in the Foreground (F1416r, cat. 46) is an example of a drawing in which the type of ink or ink mixture could not be conclusively determined. Chromium, iron, sulfur, and potassium were detected by XRF in the medium and richly hued dark inks. Chromium suggests that a chrome logwood ink was used; alternatively, the presence of iron and sulfur may indicate that this formulation was combined either with an iron salt (such as iron sulfate) or with iron gall ink. The combination of iron gall ink and logwood extract, known as logwood tannin ink, was one of the earliest and most popular types of

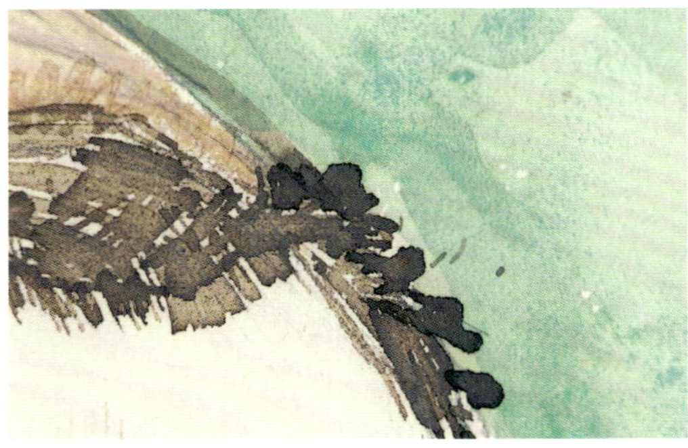

Fig. 259. Detail of *The Zouave* (F1482, cat. 77) showing strokes of the dark, lustrous carbonaceous and logwood ink mixture and of the transparent, faded, and matte brown logwood ink

logwood ink made. Unlike this drawing ink, the faded orangey signature and title yielded no information regarding its constituents, i.e., whether it is a pure logwood or an aniline derivative. Its unusual color and lack of similarity to the ink sampled elsewhere on this sheet point to the artist's use of at least two different inks in this drawing and perhaps may reflect a decision to add the inscription after the work had been completed.

In summary, elemental analysis of the inks in these drawings provides evidence of Van Gogh's use of logwood ink, though there are no visual clues distinguishing the different types of logwoods from one another or from the range of brown and reddish tones generally associated with iron gall ink. Although logwood inks were claimed not to penetrate a sheet of paper to its verso, some evidence to the contrary was found in this group of drawings among the darkest and most concentrated inks (for example, *The Zouave* [F1482, cat. 77], in which the ink in the dark collar area is visible on the back of the sheet). Yet even in these sites, there was no evidence of acid corrosion of the paper such as might occur in the presence of dark iron gall ink. Research needs to be undertaken on this long neglected material and its particular fading characteristics. Until such analysis is done, identification of logwood inks by eye alone is not possible.

Aniline Ink

The discovery in 1856 of aniline, a coal tar derivative, led to a virtual explosion in the commercial production of synthetic pigments and dyes and the marketing of a vast array of brilliantly hued inks by the following decade. The popularity of these new colors, particularly violet, mauve, and purple, also led to new formulations of logwood ink in these hues and in imitation of traditional colorants.[20] Unlike many natural inks, including some of the logwoods described above, these synthetics were made with a high proportion of water and did not form sediments and hence were free flowing, making them especially suitable for the newly popular stylographic and other fountain pens as well as for the quill, reed, or steel nib.[21] That Van Gogh never mentioned using these colorful inks in his letters is puzzling, but they would have presented little novelty to him as they were commonplace by the last quarter of the nineteenth century for writing and letter copying. Not least, since the late 1870s the family of violets, lilacs, and mauves had become the new coloring favored by the Impressionists.[22] With few exceptions, over the course of the twentieth century these synthetic inks, much like iron gall and the logwoods, faded to muted browns, reddish browns, and grays. These transformations resulted from the degradation of the constituents, the mode of preparation, and the long-term exposure to light and other adverse environmental factors. Once faded, these inks are difficult to distinguish from the logwoods on the basis of their colors.

From the time these colored inks were introduced, their fugitive nature was recognized by ink-makers and laymen,[23] but longevity played a secondary role to their enticing brilliance. We may surmise that it was the latter, as well as the ease of use and low cost, that attracted Van Gogh's attention. His love of vibrant tones is clearly demonstrated in the bright hues of paintings and colored drawings executed in 1888 (*Harvest in Provence* [F1484, fig. 141], *Harvest in Provence* [F1483, cat. 62], *The Langlois Bridge* [F1480, fig. 63], and *The Zouave* [F1482, cat. 77]). Though few violet drawings survive today, evidence exists that Van Gogh utilized such vivid substances on several occasions during his stay in Arles. Both *Montmajour* (F1423, fig. 67) and *Meadow* (F1493, fig. 72) were described about thirty years after their execution as having been rendered in purple ink.[24] Traces of this color remain in *Montmajour* in areas of the design and at the edges of the sheet where it was protected by a mat (see fig. 67). Microscopic samples of this colored ink extracted from fibers of the paper were tested by Raman spectroscopy and determined to be an organic compound derived from aniline.[25]

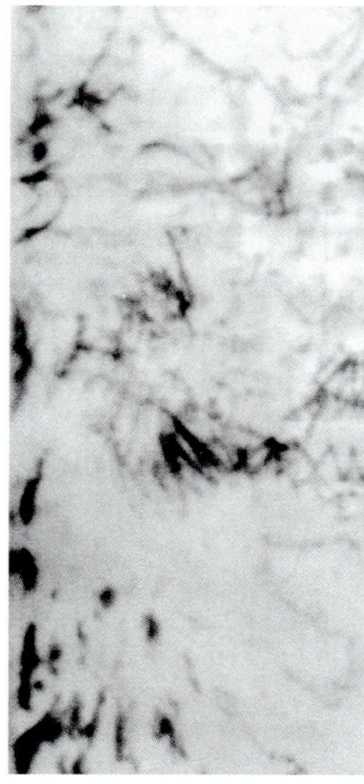

Fig. 260. Detail of an IR image of *Two Cottages, Saintes-Maries-de-la-Mer* (F1440, cat. 48). Because of the absorption of light by the carbonaceous component of the ink mixture, lines and marks appear relatively opaque, whereas the logwood ink becomes transparent when viewed at 1100nm

Writing Ink Combined with Carbonaceous Ink

Van Gogh occasionally used two inks on the same sheet.[26] Close inspection of several of the drawings revealed that many dark strokes were composed of a combination of a lustrous and somewhat viscous black ink and a typical brown writing ink that is matte and transparent with little textural relief (see figs. 259, 260). These characteristics appear, for example, in *Two Cottages, Saintes-Maries-de-la-Mer* (F1440, cat. 48), *Boats at Sea, Saintes-Maries-de-la-Mer* (F1430a, cat. 58), *The Road to Tarascon* (F1502a, cat. 93), and the two *Zouaves* (F1482, cat. 77; F1482a, cat. 79).[27]

Raman spectroscopy of the ink mixtures (Appendix 1) revealed the unequivocal presence of carbonaceous particles, components that would not be present in any of the conventional contemporary writing inks, such as iron gall or logwood. These results were also supported by infrared reflectography: inks containing carbon particles absorbed light and thus tended to appear as black strokes or marks, whereas logwood-based writing inks generally became transparent even when applied in multiple layers. The increase in absorption or opacity is seen, for example, in *The Road to Tarascon* (F1502a, cat. 93) and *Street in Saintes-Maries-de-la-Mer* (fig. 261). Under stereo-binocular magnification this ink mixture could be recognized by its rich black color; the somewhat thickened, lustrous, and opaque quality of the material; and the presence of minute carbonaceous particles in areas of transparent brown ink.[28]

These observations suggest the presence of a carbon-containing ink that appears to have been mixed with a writing ink. Although logwood inks, identified in most of the drawings studied, were black when ready for use, the incorporation of a carbon ink must have been generated by the artist's desire to enrich the depth of color of selected strokes or marks in these simple pen-and-ink drawings. Such experiments are evocative of Van Gogh's earlier, more painterly drawings, done in The Hague, in rich gradations of black, densely constructed with layers of charcoal worked over with brush and printer's ink, autographic or writing ink, a mixture that he described as having "some pith in it" [288].[29]

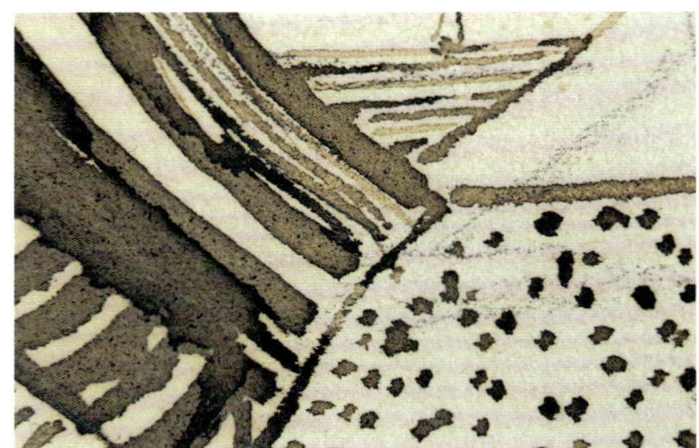

Fig. 261. Detail of *Street in Saintes-Maries-de-la-Mer* (F1435, cat. 53) showing the presence of carbonaceous particles in the ink mixture

Although the identity of this carbonaceous admixture remains uncertain, its visual characteristics and rounded particles or clusters suggest that it may be either an India ink[30] or an autographic ink, the latter being a material the artist had frequently described with great enthusiasm in the early 1880s.[31] Although it is not mentioned in Van Gogh's letters in the late 1880s, autographic ink may have had properties that suited his current purposes. It has similar constituents to lithographic ink,[32] which is solid and is applied directly to stone, but it is liquid and soluble in water and in the aqueous writing inks the artist used for his drawings. It thus required little dilution and preparation and, like an ordinary writing ink, could be used with a fine pen or a brush. Because its processing entailed burning multiple organic constituents to reduce them to carbonaceous material, this ink possessed a blackness that was unequaled in conventional writing inks. To Van Gogh its blackness would have evoked media he greatly admired: lithography, etching, and Japanese ukiyo-e prints and calligraphy. Unlike logwood or iron gall, writing inks incorporating such carbonaceous substances would also have retained their blackness, accounting for the relative depth of tone that these inks preserve.

Van Gogh's use of logwood ink and occasional use of ink mixtures, as suggested by these observations, possibly explains a puzzling feature of several of the drawings studied, namely, the abrupt alteration in many strokes along their length, from opacity to transparency, or from dark to light, without any indication that different inks were being employed or that his hand rested in the process of drawing. This alteration can be readily seen, for example, in *Cypresses* (fig. 262) and one of the earlier *Zouave* drawings (F1482a, cat. 79). It is possible, yet not conclusive, that these effects result from variations in the viscosity and sedimentation rate of the various types of logwoods he employed or the different inks present in a mixture, such as a combination of a logwood and a carbon-containing ink, that is, inks that either tended to form a precipitate before use or were not fully miscible, with the result that their sediments were deposited at different rates along the stroke. Sedimentation in commercial writing ink had long been considered a defect because it inhibited the smooth flow of the liquid and hence the rapidity of writing.[33] This defect might have been of little concern to Van Gogh, for the settling out of his ink mixtures would not have been evident when they were freshly applied and black. It was only with the passage of time that the respective constituents would have degraded and faded at different rates—with the thinner and more transparent inks more prone to alteration—resulting in the sharp changes in hue and density that are visible today.

ADDING COLOR: TWO CASE STUDIES

The Zouave

Van Gogh began this portrait study, *The Zouave* (ca. June 20, 1888; F1482, cat. 77),[34] with a conventional graphite pencil, such as the Fabers that he had discovered some years before and that, as he noted, were soft and of better quality than a carpenter's pencil [R37, ca. June 15, 1883]. Pencils were customarily graded on the basis of their hardness or darkness, which were inversely related, and the type he chose to use, suitable to his broad and vigorous manner of handling, did not require bearing down to leave a mark. Because of the relative darkness of this pencil and its wide stroke, graphite is visible through many of the subsequent layers of media. As revealed by infrared reflectography, the rendering of the sitter, which is far more summary than another *Zouave* (F1482a, cat. 79; fig. 251), appears to have been done with two different goals: one for the costume, the other for the sitter's face (see fig. 250). The jacket and its details were rendered in firm, yet somewhat broken or halting, strokes. Minor revisions in the lines of the hat are present as well as alterations in its scale and placement. The facial features were rendered far more lightly, with little emphasis on the physiognomy of the sitter: the nose barely discernible, the eyes and eyebrows not fully developed, the mustache absent, and the hair cursorily indicated. Also visible on the underdrawing is a vertical pencil line near the left edge of the sheet extending upward from the sitter's shoulder suggesting a plan, at an early stage of execution, to reorganize the space. Examination of the subsequent layers of media provides some insight as to this phase of the composition: Van Gogh's resolution of issues of color placement, sequence of media application, and the relationship of the sitter to his space.

Establishing the preliminary design in pencil provided the framework for Van Gogh to develop his composition in pen and ink. Using a broad-tipped reed pen[35] and long, continuous strokes, he followed the pencil outline of the figure rather closely, working up the contours of the face, adding the shadows at the collar, the hatching at the sleeves, and the cords of the tassel, and departing from his original plan only in the placement of the jacket decoration, which was now set lower. He did not redraw the folds of the cummerbund. The ink, analyzed by XRF, contains minor amounts of chromium, a constituent element of potassium chromate used in the black chrome logwood writing inks that were commonplace at the end of the nineteenth century.[36] Toward completion of the drawing, or as the final treatment, Van Gogh reworked most of these lines with a somewhat viscous and glossy opaque black ink, following them fairly precisely with occasional overlaps at the edges of the colored media. Based on its visual properties, Raman analysis, and infrared reflectography, this darker substance appears to be a mixture of writing ink and a carbonaceous ink, such as autographic ink or an India ink. This mixed ink is also present in several of the drawings examined.[37] Though both of the inks initially would have been black, over the course of time they have undergone varying degrees of color alteration as a result of oxidation. While the relative darkness of many of the strokes is attributable to the overlapping layers of colored media and ink, independent strokes containing carbonaceous material have undergone the least change on aging, and those rendered in ordinary writing ink (for instance, in the passementerie loops at the lower left and in facial details) have faded to a light transparent brown.

The emphatic ink lines and the strongly silhouetted form contribute a simplicity and boldness to

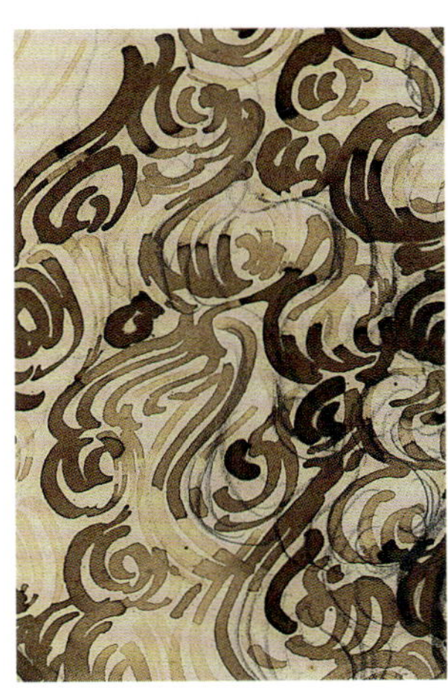

Fig. 262. Detail of *Cypresses* (F1525, cat. 108) showing abrupt changes in the color and the transparency of ink strokes. This is presumed to result from sedimentation owing to differences in density and the rate of settling out of the carbonaceous and logwood components of the ink mixture

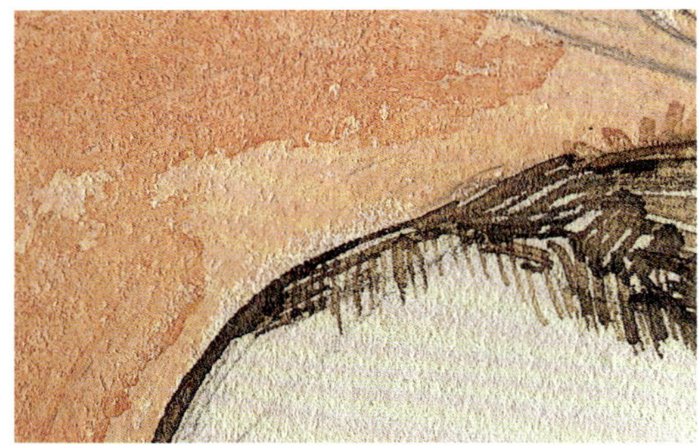

Fig. 263. Detail of the sitter's forehead and hat in *The Zouave* (F1482, cat. 77). The irregular striations and surface topography in the light pink area were produced by the action of the waxy crayon stroke and displacement of the medium. The fluid quality of the dark pink field results from the use of a solvent to dissolve the medium and spread the color

the composition that are balanced by the purposeful orchestration of the contrasting colors. The colors are circumscribed by ink outlines, and the palette is limited to pure flat tones of rose and green, blue and yellow: none is compounded, none is modulated or layered to produce an optical effect of another hue. Each is instead a bold, discrete unit. Despite the different requirements and properties of these colored media, which include watercolor and wax crayon, the artist applied each in tonally uniform passages. Many of these ideas, articulated in his correspondence, were perhaps inspired by the Japanese color woodcuts he collected.[38]

In *The Zouave*, Van Gogh achieved a successful combination of materials that were not fully compatible, applying them to a lightly sized wove support that was not equally suitable for each. In the process, he conveyed, as he wished, a sense of a drawing that had been executed with great rapidity. His mastery of watercolor, a technique with which he had often expressed frustration, is evident in the transparency of the green background and the yellow decoration, both of which he applied in moderately thin layers, thereby allowing the creamy tone of the sheet to confer an underlying brightness. In the background this effect is further enhanced by subtle variations in the diffuse green wash: the clearly defined strokes applied with a wide flat brush, the small areas of reserve interspersed between them, and the slight reticulation of the paint (upper right).[39] The pigments, emerald green and chrome yellow, synthetic colors introduced in the nineteenth century, are ones Van Gogh often used in his watercolors. The green was applied after the sitter's contour was rendered in chrome logwood ink, as it both follows and overlaps these lines. Van Gogh must have painted the cummerbund at the same time, as vague traces of the green remain at this site. It would have to have been painted prior to applying the vigorous blue crayon strokes, for the crayon's waxy binder would have repelled the aqueous paint. Evidence of color alteration, seen in the mat burn along the lower edge of the sheet, suggests that this area has markedly faded. The diffuse, yellowed effect, however, results from sponging off the watercolor.[40] Presumably he had second thoughts as to the placement of the green hue in that site. The amorphous tide line (the interface between wet and dry areas) on the right, which does not relate to his rather articulated watercolor strokes seen elsewhere, supports this as being the artist's correction and not the result of fading.

Clear traces of green and a touch of red remain in the eye, and pink is visible in the lips. It is not possible, however, to discern with certainty by either visual or scientific means whether a flesh tone was intended in the face but has now faded, as there are no pigment particles present.[41] Perhaps Van Gogh's intention was to leave the paper in reserve or to apply only the faintest flesh-toned wash. In a letter to Bernard, he wrote of the Japanese approach to "express[ing] the mat and pale complexion of a young girl and the piquant contrast of the black hair marvelously well by means of white paper and four strokes of the pen" [B6, ca. June 7, 1888].[42] If he had planned this effect in advance, it would account for the very lightly rendered graphite underdrawing in the face, as a more forceful sketch would have remained visible and diminished the effect of simplicity.[43]

It has proven difficult to identify by chemical means the rose pink medium used for the hat and jacket trim (fig. 263). Van Gogh experimented with "colored chalks," a term that has long been loosely applied to natural chalks, pastel, and wax crayon, in Antwerp, occasionally in Paris, and then in Arles in 1888 in brilliantly hued landscapes, such as *The Langlois Bridge* (F1480, fig. 63), as well as the two more restrained scenes *Harvest in Provence* (F1483, cat. 62; F1484, fig. 141). Based on visual properties under magnification, the rose pink color in *The Zouave* has the characteristics of wax crayon. Its striated texture results from the pressure of the stroke, which lightly displaces the soft medium by its action. Typical of wax crayon, which offers little modulation, this pink color is tonally uniform. In addition, magnification also revealed the slightly lustrous surface typical of wax media, and not of the particles associated with pastel. Although wax could not be identified analytically because of limitations in the sample size, a small percentage of kaolin, a low-cost extender, was present. Both substances were commonly employed in pastels to modify their working properties, as well as in wax crayons to give them greater opacity.[44] Analysis of the pigment also revealed the presence of red lead, combined with a coal tar dye, possibly the eosin vermilionette.[45]

Besides its appealing vibrant color and perhaps the desire to experiment, crayon was perfectly suited to working rapidly. Van Gogh applied his crayon directly by its point in the trim of the jacket, but for the broader area of the hat he dissolved it in a solvent (such as turpentine or petroleum spirits), which allowed him to brush it on as wash; he then intensified the hue in the central area by applying the dry color stick. Under magnification small bright red pigment particles remain visible, the same color seen in the tide line where the medium was dispersed in a solvent.[46] Such colors are known to lack permanence, thus explaining the difference between the cap in the drawing today and its strong red coloration in the oil painting of *The Zouave* (F423, cat. 78) and verifying De la Faille's observation in 1928 about the hue's intensity ("une chéchia d'un rouge vif et un costume bleu foncé à fleurs rouges").[47]

No doubt because of its chromatic limitations, there are relatively few instances of wax crayon being used or described in the literature at that time. By the end of the nineteenth century, however, inexpensive pigments bound with paraffin and kaolin mixtures were being commercially introduced and listed with some frequency in artist's catalogues.[48] Whereas Van Gogh's rose-colored crayon would appear to be this type of material, intended for artwork, the blue wax crayon he used for the sitter's jacket was possibly one manufactured for more utilitarian purposes.[49] Despite this function, such crayons were in fairly widespread use for drawing, and Van Gogh would have known about them from contemporary artist-printmakers such as Theophile Steinlen, or his friends Toulouse-Lautrec and Gauguin. Because of a long-standing interest in publishing his own drawings, in printed illustrations, and in photographs of artists' prints, he would also have been familiar with their use for certain reproductive processes.[50]

Van Gogh's choice of this simple medium must have been purposeful as it allowed for fast application and did not require time for drying. He must also have been attracted to its intensity and tonal uniformity, which, as is characteristic of all wax crayons, did not markedly vary in hue, however much pressure was exerted in drawing. In *The Zouave,* the variations in stroke, from the fine lines at the shoulders to the broader strokes at the lower edge of the jacket; and the grainy quality of the lightly applied strokes of the cummerbund that skip over the subtle texture of the paper, indicate that this transparent crayon, composed of Prussian blue, was relatively soft and that the point was wearing down as the artist worked the broad color mass. In the cummerbund these strokes were spaced more widely, creating a lighter area, thereby projecting the body close to the picture plane. If, in fact, the horizontal crease at the lower edge of the sheet (about 1.5 cm from the bottom) was done by Van Gogh following the completion of the drawing, it may indicate that he was experimenting with this particular effect, for when one envisions the support folded under, the overall space is reduced and the body is brought forward. As such its placement anticipates both the corresponding painted composition and the pen-and-ink drawing of this subject (F1482a, cat. 79).

From his experiences with lithographic crayon Van Gogh would have intuitively understood that waxy media repel aqueous ones. Hence, the blue crayon—the last in his sequence of colors—was applied after the green and yellow watercolor. His final reinforcement of the outlines was done in the viscous and more tenacious mixture of writing ink combined with autographic or India ink, and the inscription at the top right, *à mon cher copain / Emile Bernard / Vincent*, was written after the green watercolor had dried (as is indicated by the lack of bleeding at this site) but in an ordinary writing ink.

These firm marks of the crayon, as well as the graphite and pen lines, were well suited to the smooth texture of the creamy, off-white wove paper on which *The Zouave* was executed, a type support he often used at this time. Its dense and uniform surface allowed these media to glide rapidly, for his inks to flow without wicking into the fibers, and for strong contrasts. The support's moderate sizing and thinness, however, were not especially appropriate for water-based paint and limited the range of techniques that could be employed. Yet, despite certain incompatible properties, Van Gogh intuitively adapted his unconventional array of media to each other and to this rather ordinary paper, masterfully demonstrating his distinctive artistic brilliance.

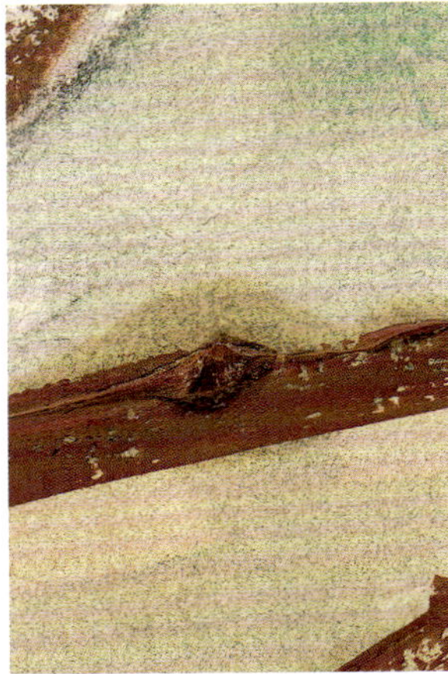

Fig. 264. Detail of *Corridor in the Asylum* (F1529, cat. 113) showing oil migration surrounding the lustrous, thickly applied paint, the thin green essence wash, and the charcoal underdrawing

Corridor in the Asylum

The propensity Van Gogh showed for working with heavily bodied paint on paper goes back to his earliest years as an artist, and he continually struggled to achieve luminous effects with transparent watercolor. Despite his efforts to follow the recommendations in Cassagne's *Traité d'aquarelle* or those offered by his cousin Anton Mauve, he often turned to the more forgiving medium of gouache.[51] He combined it with watercolor in several later works, including versions of *Harvest in Provence* (F1483, cat. 62; F1484, fig. 141). *Corridor in the Asylum* (F1529, cat. 113) has long been regarded as rendered in gouache, a material first purchased by Van Gogh in August 1882 [222]. Like oil, it was available in tubes, lending it to use with flat ferrule brushes. This feature contributed to its popularity from the middle of the nineteenth century as it allowed for imitating oil strokes in water-based paint. While *Corridor in the Asylum* has visual characteristics associated with gouache, close examination of the thick, yet fluid, strokes of color argues in favor of the medium's identification as oil and *essence*, or drained oil paint.

Distinguishing gouache and oil is often problematic since both are opaque and of full color saturation when squeezed from the tube. Because of reluctance to remove samples for testing the binders, assessment must rely on nondestructive means. Though gouache and oil are similar in their viscosity and adaptability to be applied in impasto, gouache yields a dry, matte, and almost pastelike surface, while the heavily laid-on strokes in this drawing display the slight luster associated with oil paint. Additionally, the small craters or dried burst bubbles that are often seen in gouache under magnification are absent in this drawing.[52] Other evidence supporting the presence of oil is the brown staining beneath the impasted dark red paint strokes in the foreground (fig. 264). On the verso, the staining that corresponds to the principal outlines has a yellowish fluorescence under ultraviolet light, also characteristic of oil. In areas where the paint was thinly applied (the foreground and green washes), the absence of staining on the verso suggests the presence of lean paint, such as drained oils, combined with large amounts of a volatile solvent, such as turpentine.

The sheet of pink Ingres paper on which *Corridor in the Asylum* is executed was not fully appropriate for Van Gogh's purposes. Its slightly fibrous and absorbent texture make it better suited for dry, direct media, such as charcoal or graphite, and its color did not provide the underlying luminosity for transparent washes, as would have a white or off-white support. Van Gogh was, nonetheless, able to override these limitations to suit the requirements of the media and his aesthetic goals. The lightly sized paper, like his primed canvases, served to absorb the excess oil from the colors, thereby yielding the matte, gouachelike effect that was so highly sought by Impressionists and subsequent generations of artists. Rather than utilizing the support as a source of light, he instead revealed areas of the pink reserve, thereby integrating its hue with the painted strokes.

Two other large-format landscapes on white paper done the previous year (*Harvest in Provence* [F1483, cat. 62; F1484, fig. 141]) were approached as ink drawings to which color (watercolor, gouache, pastel, and wax crayon) was added.[53] *Corridor in the Asylum*, in contrast, is a composition fully conceived in color. As in a painting, the support is copiously covered with brushwork; in a more draftsmanly manner, as noted, areas were left exposed to reveal the paper's hue. Van Gogh executed only a summary sketch in lightly applied "black chalk," mostly visible to the unaided eye in the foreground.[54] Diffuse smudges, which may be accidental, are present in the reserve of the large archway. There are, as well, a faint vertical ruled line in this medium in the approximate center and two small diagonal strokes nearby that may have served as guides in the initial conception; they do not appear to correspond to the perspective of the drawing.[55] Abandoning pen and ink altogether in this sheet, Van Gogh instead organized the space with painted outlines of blue, red, and gray, rendered with the point of the brush.[56] Some of the clearly demarcated units they circumscribe were first filled with broad washes. Van Gogh also used dilute color for the foreground elements (the base of the column in pale ocher, the small areas of blue wainscoting at the left foreground, the narrow band delineating the red door at the far right), for the wash underlying the entire length of the floor, and for the green and red passages at the entrance of the corridor. The irregularity of the green in particular—the darker zigzag surrounded by a pool of lighter tone—indicates how rapidly this lightly sized paper absorbed the paint, thus inhibiting its spreading uniformly and yielding a diffuse, dull color, the latter a consequence of the weak reflective powers of the thin washes and the middle-tone pink paper. Perhaps the limited control Van Gogh had with these fluid washes and their lack of chromatic strength prompted him to further develop the drawing with an additional layer of discrete strokes of a more heavily bodied paint. These wide, short parallel marks—the brilliant orange and white alongside dabs of acid blue-green—sit on the surface and reflect light more effectively. His intuitive grasp of the absorbent nature of this support and the need for relatively dry brushwork are also revealed by the unpainted hollows of the laid paper throughout the composition. It is this directness of application in viscous and lean strokes that gives *Corridor in the Asylum* its powerful expressive impact.

Multiple sites in eleven discrete pigments or color mixtures were analyzed nondestructively using Raman spectroscopy and X-ray fluorescence (see Appendix 3), and the results are consistent with what other researchers have found.[57] The colors are typical of Van Gogh's work in Provence and, more generally, similar to the colors discovered or introduced in the nineteenth century and used by French Impressionist painters. At least eight of the colors (zinc white, lead white ["flake white"], "chrome yellow 1," ultramarine blue, emerald green, vermilion, red ocher, and possibly "orange lead" [chrome yellow 3]) of the sixteen Van Gogh requested in his correspondence with Theo from May to September 1889 [592, 594, 604, 605, 608] are present in this drawing.[58] It could not be determined analytically if they were adulterated with organic pigments or dyes, as was often done by colormen (the manufacturers and sellers of pigments, paints, and artists' supplies) to modify hue.[59] The brushwork reveals that they are mostly pure undiluted tube colors and that many of the mixed colors are not thoroughly combined. The different brilliant yellows that predominate in the palette were produced by variations in one or more of the manufactured shades of chrome yellow. Zinc was found in conjunction with chrome yellow, which may indicate that zinc white was mixed with the yellow or that zinc yellow (yellow zinc chromate) is present in the chrome yellow.[60] Though Van Gogh had complained the previous year about the slow drying of zinc white [472], both it and lead ("flake") white were found in *Corridor in the Asylum,* the latter applied independently for the bold strokes along the archway and mixed with blue in the wainscoting (lower left). Both whites were separately combined with colored pigments to produce the high-keyed bluish green (upper right) and the blue on the left.[61] Vermilion was present in the bright orangey red. Other pigments found in this drawing that Van Gogh requested during this year were a red earth (red ocher) combined with chrome yellow, zinc white [592, May 22, 1889], and ultramarine blue—presumably French ultramarine rather than the extremely costly natural color—which was both mixed with lead white and used independently.[62] Emerald green was identified in combination with zinc white and, in another sample, mixed with chrome yellow and small amounts of ultramarine blue. These sharply juxtaposed colors are neither modulated in tone to produce a sense of volume nor fused by the eye, but are instead distinct entities surrounded by strong contours emphasizing the linear structure of the work. They are coloristically unified only by the blue-gray wainscoting. Another important chromatic element of this drawing is the paper, which was presumably dyed with one of the synthetic aniline colors frequently employed at this time. Unlike the customary watercolor practice in which areas of exposed paper functioned as heightening, a middle tone, or a source of luminosity beneath a transparent wash, the once vibrant hue of this sheet—as can be seen on its verso—served more simply as a lively counterpoint to the brilliant palette.

While at the asylum at Saint-Rémy in the fall of 1889, with his supplies greatly depleted, Van Gogh used what was at hand for his drawings, transposing his well-practiced techniques in opaque paint from gouache to oil. *Corridor in the Asylum* demonstrates his trials in manipulating this medium on paper to develop the composition and its imagery. By varying the opacity of his paint from fluid washes to solid color, its texture from smooth to thick, and by the repetition of both brushwork and striking color of unvarying intensity, he produced a powerful image of a rapidly receding, claustrophobic passageway.

1. On October 15, 1880 [137], he wrote that the pen was good for accentuating pencil drawings and that using it was good preparation in case one later wanted to learn etching. Between ca. July 15 and 20, 1881 [147], he noted that Ingres paper was especially well suited to pen drawing, especially to the reed.
2. Examination of *The Zouave* (F1482a, cat. 79) reveals clear evidence of his use of a steel pen for the jacket passementerie (along the opening and at the collar), in the hair, in areas of both eyes, and in the outline of the hat. The double-grooved ink line of the split nib is heavily impressed into the paper, far more so than would have been possible with a quill, which would have broken under the pressure required to produce this effect.
3. He clearly distinguished printer's ink from autographic ink [R33, ca. April 3, 1883].
4. Infrared reflectograms were produced by Alison Gilchrest. Under IR, iron gall and logwood inks tend to become transparent, while carbon-containing materials, including writing inks mixed with carbonaceous inks (such as India ink, lithographic ink, or lampblack), show degrees of opacity. Using filters, it was possible to subtract the pure writing inks found in these drawings, allowing full visibility of the underdrawings executed in graphite pencil, a carbon-based medium, as well as the presence of carbonaceous components of some of the inks.
5. Sigmund Lehner, *Ink Manufacture including Writing, Copying, Lithographic, Marking, Stamping, and Laundry Inks,* 2nd ed., trans. from German 5th ed. by Arthur Morris and Herbert Robson (1902; London, 1914), p. 10.
6. Although Van Gogh spoke of enhancing the deep tones of his drawings with lampblack applied with pen or ink [256, December 31, 1882, and January 2, 1883], neither it nor ground charcoal has the subtle luster characteristic of autographic ink or India ink. It is this characteristic that distinguishes the mixed inks described in this study. Hence, it is unlikely that either of these materials would have been combined with his writing inks to strengthen their darkness.
7. Examples of texts written in iron gall ink are found before the first millennium A.D., but the earliest known detailed recipe for using an iron salt with a tannin-containing compound (hawthorn wood bark) to intensify an ink's blackness is recorded in Theophilus, *De diversis artibus* (ca. 1120), chap. 38.
8. Iron gall inks are characterized under XRF by the presence of iron and sulfur as well as various elements present in lower percentages. The latter will often differ depending upon the formulation of the ink and its additives.
9. The process of color formation of iron gall inks begins with the reaction of gallic acid (present in galls) and ferrous sulfate. The process produces the colorless compound ferrous gallate. In the presence of air, this complex is oxidized to ferric gallate. Free ferric ions, present in the ferrous sulfate, catalyze the formation of the dark-colored ferric pyrogallate compound. This may have a slight hue of brown, violet, or blue depending on the source of tannates and the presence of various additives, such as copper sulfate. For penetration of the fibers, which ensured the ink's durability for documents, it was necessary that the full reaction, from colorless substance to colored ink, take place on the paper. A variety of degradation mechanisms, e.g., temperature and relative humidity, and reactions between the constituents of the ink and the paper carrier, may further produce discoloration of the ink. See Christoph Krekel, "The Chemistry of Historical Iron Gall Inks," *International Journal of Forensic Document Examiners* 5 (1999), pp. 54–58; V. Daniels, "The Chemistry of Iron Gall Ink," in *The Iron Gall Ink Meeting: 4–5 September 2000, the University of Northumbria Newcastle-upon-Tyne: Postprints,* edited by A. Jean E. Brown (Newcastle-upon-Tyne, 2000), pp. 31–36; C. Ainsworth Mitchell and Thomas Cradock Hepworth, *Inks: Their Composition and Manufacture* (London, 1904), p. 92.
10. Mitchell and Hepworth, *Inks,* pp. 97, 102–3; Lehner, *Ink Manufacture,* pp. 48–51. Such inks were often referred to as "added color" inks.
11. The campeachy tree (*Haematoxylon campechianum*), indigenous to Mexico, Central America, and the West Indies, yields a substance used in preparing logwood inks. Various recipes for logwood inks are given in Mitchell and Hepworth, *Inks,* pp. 99–109, and Lehner, *Ink Manufacture,* pp. 56–63. The metallic salts most often combined with logwood extract were ferrous sulfate, ferrous nitrate, or copper sulfate. (For logwood ink recipes containing copper sulfate, see Mitchell and Hepworth, *Inks,* pp. 104–5.) Various alum salts could be used, among them potassium aluminum sulfate, aluminum sulfate, or ammonium aluminum sulfate. Although these

constituents would impart a particular hue to the ink during its formation stage, depending on their composition logwood inks would turn jet black at different rates after their formation: some while standing, others upon drying (ibid., pp. 103–7). For the desirable properties of logwood ink, see ibid., p. 120.

12. David N. Carvalho, *Forty Centuries of Ink* (1904; Seattle: World Wide School e-book, 1999), chap. 14. It is perhaps because the identity of logwoods ceased to be known and differentiated from either iron gall or aniline inks by the time most had turned brown that only very general comments on the fading of these inks are to be found.
13. Logwood was added to iron gall inks for the purpose of enhancing their blackness; Lehner, *Ink Manufacture,* p. 39.
14. Ibid., p. 63. The recipe for "ordinary ink" contained pure logwood extract, alum, and an iron compound; Mitchell and Hepworth, *Inks,* p. 102.
15. Carvalho, *Forty Centuries of Ink,* chap. 12.
16. Joe Nickell, *Pen, Ink, and Evidence,* reprint (New Castle, Del., 2003), p. 40.
17. Lehner, *Ink Manufacture,* p. 60; Mitchell and Hepworth, *Inks,* p. 103. Descriptions of various types of logwood inks include remedies to counteract precipitation and coagulation; ibid., pp. 105–7.
18. XRF analysis can detect constituent elements such as chromium, sulfur, iron, or potassium that are present in logwood inks or iron gall inks, but the identity of the organic components (for example, the gallic acid complexing agent in iron gall ink) can only be assumed from the presence of the inorganic constituents. It is not possible to determine the source of the chromium by means of the analysis used in the present study.
19. Several alum salts could have been used, including potassium aluminum sulfate, aluminum sulfate, and ammonium aluminum sulfate. A logwood recipe using chrome alum, a double sulfate of chromium, and a univalent metal such as potassium or sodium is given in Mitchell and Hepworth, *Inks,* p. 107. Such inks, according to Mitchell, were "too pale and grey," which probably accounts for the more widespread use of recipes that included potassium chromate since they produced a darker ink.
20. August Wilhelm von Hofmann's "violet," discovered in 1863, was the first aniline-derived color used in ink making, specifically for copy ink; Mitchell and Hepworth, *Inks,* p. 116. For a listing of "aniline" inks, see ibid., pp. 116–18. Purple and violet logwood inks were also made at this time; see ibid., p. 114.
21. Mitchell and Hepworth, *Inks,* p. 13. Because synthetic inks did not require a gum they were not vulnerable to mold, another factor accounting for their popularity.
22. The widespread enthusiasm for violet, or "indigomania," was ridiculed and harshly criticized as a form of pathology; see Oscar Reutersvärd, "The 'Violettomania' of the Impressionists," *Journal of Aesthetics and Art Criticism* 9, no. 2 (Winter 1950), pp. 106–10.
23. With the exception of carbon inks, most inks were considered to be unstable. According to Lehner (*Ink Manufacture,* p. 9), few inks were known "to possess the property of keeping their color for a long time." According to Mitchell and Hepworth (*Inks,* pp. 103–4), the class of iron logwoods became unstable after two to three months, turning from black to brown. The same was said of aniline inks (ibid., p. 116). According to J. G. Vibert (*The Science of Painting,* 15th ed., retrans. and rev. [London, 1915], p. 170), "'Vegetable violets' obtained from Campeachy wood extract mixed with lead salts are fugitive."
24. New York 1920, nos. 11, 12, which Susan Stein brought to my attention. Sjraar van Heugten, "Metamorphoses: Van Gogh's Drawings Then and Now," in the present publication, refers to the original purple color of the drawings recorded by Johanna van Gogh-Bonger in 1907 and 1909 and to the critical acclaim for the artist's use of purple ink.
25. Conclusive identification of the ink as an aniline derivative substance by Raman analysis undertaken by Silvia Centeno (see Appendix 1) by comparison of the sample with a "purple aniline" reference sample from ca. 1872 (see fig. 267). No evidence of a violet chrome logwood ink (such as that made with copper acetate, gum arabic, and alum) was detected in the colored fiber. For recipes, see Mitchell and Hepworth, *Inks,* p. 114, and Lehner, *Ink Manufacture,* p. 62.
26. Van Heugten, "Metamorphoses."
27. Not every drawing executed by Van Gogh with erratic dark concentrations was necessarily made with a mixture of two inks. All inks composed of finely divided particles held in suspension tend to settle out despite the addition of a gum to counteract the formation of a precipitate on standing. Dark ink applied in heavy concentrations will appear more dense than thin applications of ink and will often retain greater intensity of color, despite exposure to light. In addition, evaporation of ink on paper can result in a somewhat darker, granular buildup of particles especially at the edges of the stroke.
28. These particles or clusters can be either a mixture of burnt organic material, as found in lithographic and autographic ink, or a soot, such as lampblack.
29. Van Gogh referred to drawings made with admixtures or layers of various black media in 1882 and 1883. The rich blackness of *Nursery on Schenkweg* (F930, cat. 8) is representative of the materials and techniques he employed, consisting of soft graphite pencil, two types of inks, two gouaches (one zinc and one calcium carbonate white), and sgrafitto.
30. India ink was used widely. It was praised by Joseph Pennell in his contemporary treatise (*Pen Drawing and Pen Draughtsmen: Their Work and Their Methods* [New York, 1889], p. 279), which also described the many types of carbon inks with which Van Gogh may have been familiar in the late 1880s.
31. Among Van Gogh's first references to autographic ink is in letter 241, November 5, 1882. See also letters 243, 245, 246, R18, R29, 250.
32. Lehner, *Ink Manufacture,* pp. 126, 127. Autographic inks were variants of lithographic inks but with different textural and handling properties. Recipes for lithographic ink consisted of the following ingredients or comparable substances: lampblack, soot, mastic, copal, pitch, linseed oil, tallow, soap, shellac, rosin, India rubber, and oil of turpentine. Autographic ink contained the same or similar ingredients but the mass was then combined with or rubbed up with water (ibid., pp. 122–29). The oxidation of some of these organic compounds may also account for the faint brown halo surrounding some of the concentrated strokes in these ink mixtures, such as is evident in a few sites in *The Zouave* (F1482, cat. 77); see Colin H. Bloy, *A History of Printing Ink, Balls, and Rollers, 1440–1850* (London, 1967), p. 89. Van Gogh was aware of the effects of aging on oil paint and believed he could counteract this process by applying paint in thick layers. Van Gogh may similarly have thought that the addition of a carbon black ink would forestall the inevitable discoloration of iron gall ink.
33. Lehner, *Ink Manufacture,* pp. 45, 53; Mitchell and Hepworth, *Inks,* pp. 105–7. The problems associated with the sedimentation of ink generated the formulation of numerous writing inks that kept the flocculent in suspension.
34. We wish to thank Marco Leona and Tony Frantz for contributing to the scientific analysis of this drawing carried out by Silvia Centeno.
35. Van Gogh first experimented with the reed pen in 1881 in Etten [146].
36. Mitchell and Hepworth, *Inks,* pp. 105–8; Lehner, *Ink Manufacture,* pp. 60–62. This same chrome ink was found in some of the other drawings analyzed (see Appendix 1), including *Two Cottages, Saintes-Maries-de-la-Mer* (F1440, cat. 48), *Street in Saintes-Maries-de-la-Mer* (F1435, cat. 53), *Boats at Sea, Saintes-Maries-de-la-Mer* (F1430a, cat. 58), *Wheat Field* (F1481, fig. 186), *The Trinquetaille Bridge* (F1507, fig. 182), and *Cypresses* (F1525, cat. 108).
37. *Street in Saintes-Maries-de-la-Mer* (F1435, cat. 53), *Boats at Sea, Saintes-Maries-de-la-Mer* (F1430a, cat. 58), *The Road to Tarascon* (F1502a cat. 93), *The Zouave* (F1482a, cat. 79), and *The Trinquetaille Bridge* (F1507, fig. 182).
38. He wrote to Émile Bernard: "I try to grasp what is essential in drawing—later I fill in the spaces which are bounded by contours . . . with tones that are also simplified" [B3, ca. April 12, 1888], and "the Japanese artist ignores reflected colors and paints the flat ones side by side with characteristic lines marking off the movement of the forms" [B4, April 19, 1888].
39. This unequal absorption of the paint probably resulted from irregularities in the paper sizing.
40. See letters 171 (ca. January 21, 1882) and 263 (February 3, 1883), in which he referred to sponging his watercolor and crayon drawing to soften the shadows.
41. XRF spectra present weak signals for iron, calcium, lead, and silica. Examination under stereo-binocular magnification suggests that a thin wash of pigment may be present in the face. The radiographic image is transparent in this area. We are grateful to Tony Frantz for carrying out this examination.
42. On May 27, 1888 [491], he noted he had "asked for some watercolors because I would like to make some pen drawings . . . to be washed afterward in flat tints like the Japanese prints."
43. In contrast, the underdrawing in *The Zouave* (F1482a, cat. 79) was rendered forcefully in graphite with well-defined and emphatic features that provided a foundation, but one that would be hidden by the subsequent heavily wrought drawing in pen and ink.
44. Typical ingredients of colored wax crayons consisted of kaolin, talc, or chalk as extenders, colorants (pigments or dyes), and wax (paraffin, beeswax, carnauba); Margaret Holben Ellis and H. Bridget Yeh, "The History, Use, and Characteristics of Wax-Based Drawing Media," *Paper Conservator* 22 (1998), p. 50.
45. Red lead was identified by Raman by Centeno and using XRF by Frantz. Kaolin was identified by Leona using FTIR. Vermilionettes or royal reds were eosine lakes made from acid coal tar colors and were generally precipitated on a lead acetate base, though alum was occasionally used. Introduced about 1885–87, this group of organic aniline colors was produced in a great variety of brilliant tints ranging from very pale pinkish red to a very deep scarlet that were used as cheap substitutes for quality artist's pigments and for lower-grade media including wax crayon; George H. Hurst, *Painters' Colours, Oils, and Varnishes: A Practical Manual,* 3rd ed., rev. (London, 1901), pp. 282–84. They were also recognized at the time as being highly fugitive (Mitchell and Hepworth, *Inks,* p. 116). In this study the presence of the eosine vermilionette is suggested but not confirmed by its characteristic brilliant pink fluorescence under UV. Although it was rarely used as a watercolor pigment by this time, red lead and other traditional pigments were occasionally combined with organic colorants. One study found evidence of red lead and an organic dye in a sample of red oil paint used by Van Gogh; it was identified as eosin lake with a small amount of vermilion. The study suggested that vermilion might have been included to improve the permanence of very fugitive pigments; Mette Marie Bang, "Van Gogh's Palette," in *A Closer Look: Technical and Art-Historical Studies on Works by Van Gogh and Gauguin,* edited by Cornelia Peres, M. Hoyle, and Louis van Tilborgh, Cahier Vincent, no. 3 (Zwolle, 1991), pp. 58, 60 n. 8. The presence of the red lead in the Zouave sample may have served the same purpose.
46. The formation of the precipitate—the bright red pigment particles in the central area and in the surrounding tide line—occurred when the solid coloring matter was dissolved in a volatile spirit, such as was used here.
47. De la Faille 1928, no. 1482; this reference was brought to my attention by Susan Stein.
48. For example, in Winsor and Newton's 1883 catalogue (Archives, Winsor and Newton, Harrow, U.K.); in 1890, four types of pastels and various crayons and chalks were offered for sale. The catalogues, which were reprinted about every five years and often without changes in the products, were bound with instruction books, e.g., in J. Scott Taylor, *A Descriptive Handbook of Modern Watercolour Pigments* (London: Winsor and Newton, 1890). The 1910 catalogue of the American firm Favor, Ruhl and

Co., New York, gave twelve pages (pp. 157–68) to these products.

49. Blue and black wax crayons intended for industrial marking purposes are listed in Frost and Adams Co.'s *Artists' Materials: Descriptive Catalogue* (Boston, [ca. 1905–11]), p. 207 (Holben Ellis and Yeh, "History . . . of Wax-Based Drawing Media," p. 54).
50. The orthochromatic properties of film at that time were insensitive to blue editing marks that were made in this type of crayon and would appear black on a negative and white in the final photographic print, a phenomenon of which Van Gogh was aware [R35].
51. Gouache, like watercolor, has a gum arabic binder but has a higher ratio of pigment to water and may contain fillers such as barites.
52. These bubbles result from the irregular particle size of the constituents and foaming from the brushwork, which in turn is due to a high proportion of gum binder.
53. For other ink drawings from Saint-Rémy to which color was added, see F1527 (fig. 219), F1533 (cat. 104), and F1535 (cat. 105).
54. Infrared reflectography did not reveal other sites executed in charcoal, which, if present, may be obscured because of the comparable absorption of the paint.
55. For Van Gogh's continued use of the perspective frame, see *View of Arles with Irises in the Foreground* (F1416r, cat. 46), and esp. IRR, fig. 241).
56. This approach recalls his intention in September of 1889 to dispense with charcoal underdrawing in his paintings: "I have deliberately arrived at the point where I will not draw a picture from charcoal. That's no use, you must attack drawing with the color itself in order to draw well" [539]. He did not follow this approach consistently.
57. J. H. Hofenk de Graaff, M. F. S. Karreman, M. de Keijzer, W. G. T. Roelofs, "Scientific Investigation," in *A Closer Look*, pp. 80 n. 4, 81–84, and Bang, "Van Gogh's Palette," pp. 57–60.
58. Three chrome yellows were identified, but their specific correspondence to commercial chromes cannot be ascertained. See Appendix 3.
59. Such admixtures may be below the Raman detection limit.
60. The color differences in the chrome yellows can be accounted for by the varying amounts of lead oxide and lead sulfate they contain. The colors were further modified by being mixed with other colors. See Appendix 3.
61. Other investigations revealing the presence of lead and zinc whites include one undertaken at the Fogg Art Museum of *Self-Portrait Dedicated to Paul Gauguin, Arles, Sept 1888* (F476) and three other Arles paintings discussed in Bang, "Van Gogh's Palette," p. 59.
62. Synthetic or French ultramarine and natural ultramarine differ in their particle morphology, which was not investigated in this study. Ultramarine blue has been identified in other paintings done in Arles and is mentioned in the artist's correspondence; ibid., p. 60 n. 15.

Appendixes: Summaries of Scientific Analyses of Drawing Materials

Silvia A. Centeno

APPENDIX 1

XRF AND RAMAN SPECTROSCOPIC ANALYSES ON TWELVE DRAWINGS MADE IN PROVENCE: SUMMARY OF FINDINGS

The drawings listed in the table below were analyzed by X-ray fluorescence (XRF), except for *The Zouave* (F1482a) and *Montmajour* (F1423), which were analyzed only by Raman spectroscopy. Raman spectroscopy was used in combination with XRF in *Street in Saintes-Maries-de-la-Mer* (F1434), *The Zouave* (F1482), and *Boats at Sea, Saintes-Maries-de-la-Mer* (F1430a).

All the XRF analyses were performed nondestructively with a Jordan Valley open-architecture 3600 system. Consistent experimental parameters were used in all the drawings for both the ink and the "bare" paper areas: direct unfiltered radiation from a Rh target, 30–40kV, 200 seconds for the preset time and medium throughput, with deadtimes between 35 and 40 percent. As many spots as possible in the different ink tones (dark, medium, light) and bare paper areas were probed in each drawing.

In many cases, the composition of the bare paper was found to be inhomogeneous; elements such as Si, S, K, Ca, and Fe were detected in several of these areas. The elements reported as ink components in Table 1 consistently showed peaks with intensities at least 30 percent above the corresponding peaks for the bare paper areas. Ti, Ca, and Cu were detected in some of the additional supports used to back the drawings during the XRF analysis.

In *Street in Saintes-Maries-de-la-Mer* (F1434), Pb was detected as a component of the ink (both the Pb L_α and M_α lines are observed in the spectrum as expected). The Jordan Valley XRF system used for the present study has limitations in separating the S K_α line at 2.308 keV and the Pb M_α line at .346 keV, respectively. Therefore if Pb is present, it is not possible to determine if S is present in the ink.

Cu was consistently detected in both ink and bare paper, though in all cases the intensity of the Cu peak superimposes for both areas, so the presence of Cu is not reported as an ink component in the table below, except for *The Zouave* (F1482), which showed a strong Cu signal. This, together with the characteristic peaks from As, is due to the

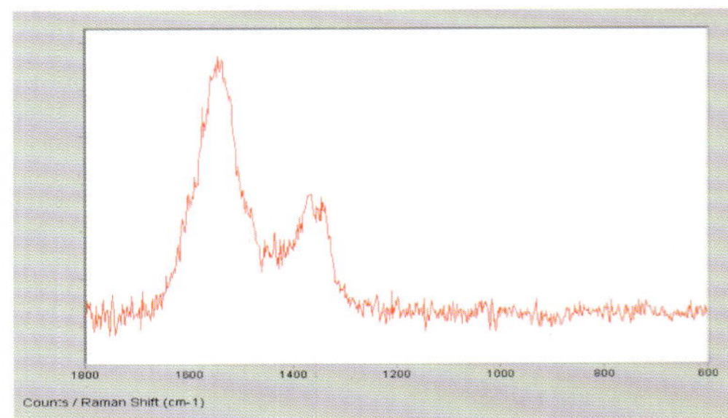

Fig. 265. Raman spectrum of carbonaceous particles in *Boats at Sea, Saintes-Maries-de-la-Mer* (F1430a, cat. 58)

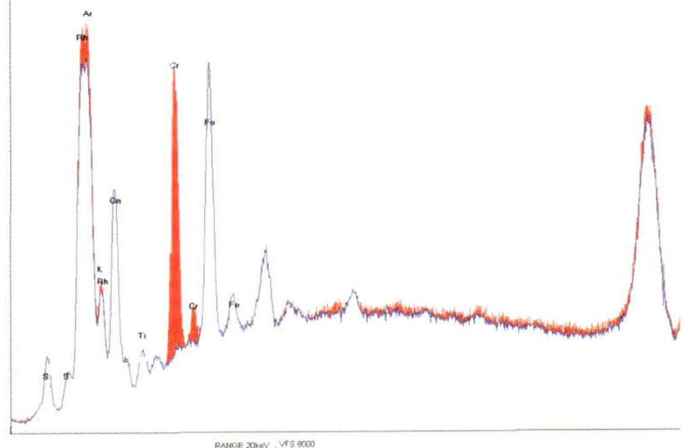

Fig 266. XRF spectra of medium-tone ink (red) and bare paper (blue) in *Street in Saintes-Maries-de-la-Mer* (F1435, cat. 53), showing the presence of Cr in the ink

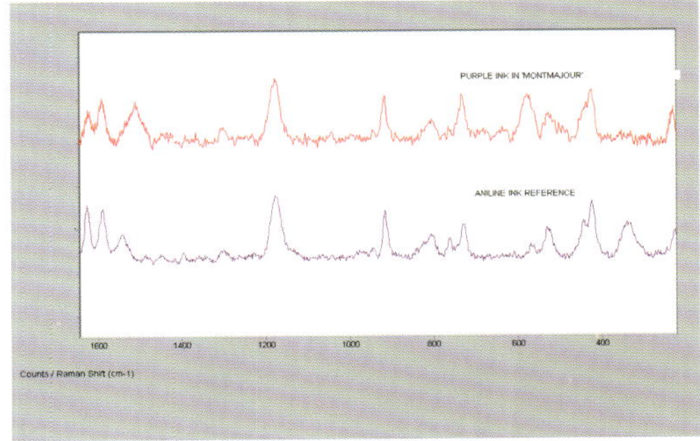

Fig. 267. Raman spectra of purple ink in *Montmajour* (F1423, fig. 67; top) and "purple aniline" reference sample ("Leamon's Genuine Aniline Dyes—Purple," Wells, Richardson, and Co., Burlington, Vt.. 1872; bottom)

Table 1. XRF and Raman Analysis of Elemental Composition of Inks in Twelve Van Gogh Drawings

Drawing	Composition of the inks
Two Cottages, Saintes-Maries-de-la-Mer (F1440, cat. 48)	dark, medium, and light tones: Cr (XRF)
Street in Saintes-Maries-de-la-Mer (F1434, cat. 50)	dark, medium, and light tones: Cr, K, Pb, S (?) (XRF) carbonaceous particles in the dark tones (Raman)
The Zouave (F1482, cat. 77)	Cr (XRF) carbonaceous component (Raman) Cu and As (XRF) from emerald green pigment, also detected by Raman
Boats at Sea, Saintes-Maries-de-la-Mer (F1430a, cat. 58)	dark, medium, and light tones: Cr and S (XRF) carbonaceous particles were detected in the dark-tone ink (Raman, fig. 265)
The Zouave (F1482a, cat. 79)	carbonaceous particles (Raman)
The Garden; A Corner of a Garden in the Place Lamartine (F1450, cat. 88)	dark and medium tones: Fe, Cr, Ca (XRF)
Wheat Field (F1481, fig. 186)	dark tones: Cr (XRF)
The Trinquetaille Bridge (F1507, fig. 182)	dark tone: Cr, S (XRF)
Street in Saintes-Maries-de-la-Mer (F1435, cat. 53)	dark, medium, and light tones: Cr (XRF, fig. 266)
Cypresses (F1525, cat. 108)	dark, medium, and light tones: Cr. Also S and K present in the medium tones (XRF)
Montmajour (F1423, fig. 67)	aniline-based ink (Raman, fig. 267)
View of Arles with Irises in the Foreground (F1416r, cat. 46)	dark and medium tones: S, Ca, K, Cr, Fe

presence of emerald green pigment in the ink area, also identified by Raman.

Raman spectroscopy was used to analyze the purple ink in *Montmajour* (F1423) and carbonaceous particles in other drawings.[1] The spectra were recorded with a Renishaw System 1000 spectrometer, using a 514 nm laser. The laser beam was focused on different areas of the drawings using a fiber optic probe equipped with x20 lens, which allowed spatial resolution on the order of 5 microns. Powers on the order of 1mW were used, with accumulation times between 40 and 600 seconds. In the particular case of *Montmajour*, the analysis was done by placing the purple ink sample in the stage of an optical Leica microscope coupled to the Raman spectrometer and focusing a 785 nm laser beam on the grains with a x50 objective lens. Identification of the materials was done by comparing the spectrum of the unknown with those of reference compounds. The composition of the "purple aniline" reference sample ("Leamon's Genuine Aniline Dyes—Purple," Wells, Richardson, and Co., Burlington, Vt., 1872) was also checked by Fourier transform infrared spectroscopy. Representative Raman and XRF spectra are shown in figures 265–67.

1. We are grateful to F. Haanen and E. Hendriks at the Van Gogh Museum for their generosity in providing and allowing us to test a purple fiber sample from *Montmajour*.

APPENDIX 2

PIGMENTS USED BY VAN GOGH IN *THE ZOUAVE*: SUMMARY OF RESULTS OF RAMAN ANALYSIS

In *The Zouave* (F1482, cat. 77), Raman spectra were recorded nondestructively with a Renishaw System 1000 spectrometer, using a 514 nm laser. The laser beam was focused on different areas of the drawing using a fiber optic probe equipped with an x20 lens, which allowed spatial resolution on the order of 5 microns. Powers on the order of 1 mW were used, with accumulation times between 40 and 600 seconds. Identification of the materials was done by comparing the spectra of the unknown with those of reference compounds.

Color	Pigment identification
blue in jacket	Prussian blue
yellow in jacket	chrome yellow
green on background	emerald green
light pink in hat	red lead
dark pink in hat	red lead

Though red lead was detected in both the light and the dark pink areas in the Zouave's hat, the difference in composition that would account for their different colors is below the detection limit of the Raman technique.

APPENDIX 3

SOME PIGMENTS USED BY VAN GOGH IN *CORRIDOR IN THE ASYLUM*: SUMMARY OF RESULTS OF RAMAN AND XRF ANALYSES

The pigments present in different passages of *Corridor in the Asylum* (F1529, cat. 113) were nondestructively analyzed by Raman spectroscopy and in some areas also by X-ray fluorescence (XRF). Raman spectra were recorded with a Renishaw System 1000 spectrometer, using a 514 nm laser. The laser beam was focused on different areas of the drawing using a fiber optic probe equipped with an x20 lens, which allowed spatial resolution on the order of 5 microns. Powers between 1 and 5 mW were used, with accumulation times between 40 and 600 seconds. Identification of the materials was done by comparing the spectra of the unknown with those of reference compounds.

X-ray fluorescence (XRF) elemental analyses were performed nondestructively with a Jordan Valley open-architecture 3600 system using unfiltered radiation from an Rh target.

Chrome yellow was detected in all the *yellow* areas by Raman. The wave numbers of the strongest Raman band [ν_1 (a_1) CrO_4^{2-}] observed were slightly different (ca. 2 cm^{-1}) for the three *yellow* areas probed. This difference may be due to a change in the proportion of PbO present in the $PbCrO_4$ lattice, which also affects the depth of color.[1] In addition, Zn was detected in the *yellow* areas analyzed. The presence of Zn may be due to zinc white, ZnO, or the pigment zinc yellow, with approximate composition $K_2O.4ZnCrO_4.3H_2O$,[2] though no bands for any of these compounds were detected in the Raman spectra. Zinc yellow was not included in Van Gogh's paint orders from 1889.[3]

In the *red 1* area, results from the XRF elemental analysis suggest the presence of a red earth. The Raman bands for this compound, which showed up alongside those due to chrome yellow, were found to be weak.

In the *red 2* areas, the spectrum of vermilion detected by Raman presented a strong fluorescent background. In addition, the materials detected in the *red 1* areas (red earth, chrome yellow, and possibly zinc white or zinc chromate) were also found to be present in the *red 2* spots by XRF, most likely as contaminants.

1. Ian M. Bell, Robin J. H. Clark, and Peter J. Gibbs, "Raman Spectroscopic Library of Natural and Synthetic Pigments (pre–1850 A.D.)," *Spectrochimica Acta*, part A 53A (1997), p. 2159.
2. H. Kühn and M. Curran, "Chrome Yellow and Other Chromate Pigments," in *Artists' Pigments: A Handbook of Their History and Characteristics, Volume 1*, edited by Robert L. Feller (Washington, 1986), p. 201.
3. Van Gogh's letters 592, 594, 604, 605, and 608 to Theo.

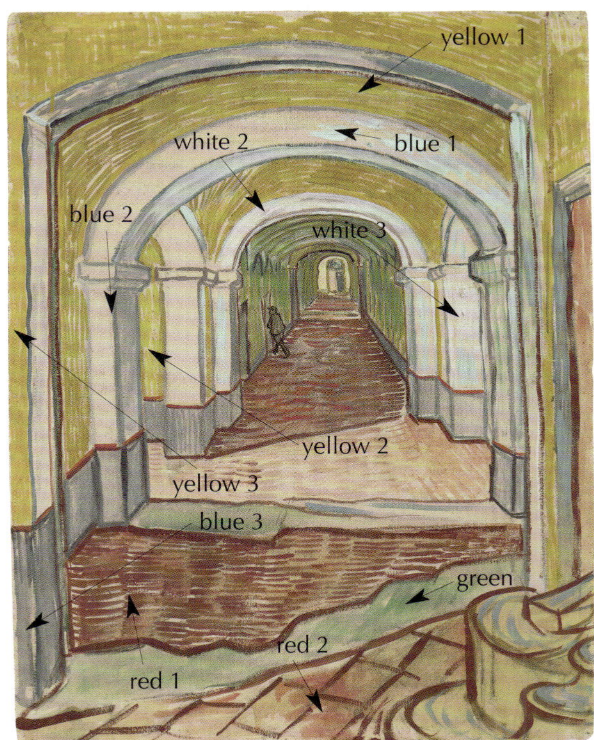

Fig. 268. Photograph of *Corridor in the Asylum* (F1529, cat. 113) with indications of the different areas probed by Raman either alone or combined with XRF. Several samples were analyzed within each of the eleven sites

Table 2. Summary of Results of Raman and XRF Analyses

Color area	XRF	Raman	Pigment(s)
blue 1	Cu, As, Zn	zinc white (white particles)	emerald green and zinc white
blue 2		ultramarine blue and lead white	ultramarine blue and lead white
blue 3		ultramarine blue	ultramarine blue
green		emerald green, chrome yellow, and ultramarine blue particles	emerald green, chrome yellow, and ultramarine blue particles
yellow 1	Cr, Pb, Zn	chrome yellow	chrome yellow and possibly zinc white or zinc yellow*
yellow 2	Cr, Pb, Zn	chrome yellow	chrome yellow and possibly zinc white or zinc yellow*
yellow 3	Cr, Pb, traces of Zn	chrome yellow	chrome yellow and possibly zinc white or zinc yellow*
red 1	Si, Ca, Fe, Pb, Cr, Zn	chrome yellow	red earth, chrome yellow, and possibly zinc white or zinc yellow*
red 2		vermilion	vermilion
white 2		lead white	lead white
white 3		lead white	lead white

* Zn was detected by XRF in these passages, but no Raman bands for zinc white or zinc yellow were observed in the corresponding areas.

List of Abbreviated Exhibitions and Publications

Ackerman 2003. Gerald Ackerman, with Graydon Parrish. *Charles Bargue Drawing Course*. With the collaboration of Jean-Léon Gérôme. Paris, 2003.

Aix-en-Provence 1959. *Vincent van Gogh en Provence*. Exhibition, Pavillon de Vendôme, October 3–November 30. Catalogue by H. J. Reinink. N.p., [1959].

Alley 1981. Ronald Alley. *Catalogue of the Tate Gallery's Collection of Modern Art Other than Works by British Artists*. London, 1981.

Amsterdam 1892. *Vincent van Gogh teekeningen*. Exhibition, Maatschappij Arti et Amicitiae, opened February 25. No catalogue known.

Amsterdam 1892–93. *Tentoonstelling der nagelaten werken van Vincent van Gogh*. Exhibition, Kunstzaal Panorama, December 17–February 5. Catalogue introduction by Richard N. Roland-Holst. Amsterdam, [1892].

Amsterdam 1901. *Tentoonstelling van teekeningen van Vincent van Gogh*. Exhibition, Sociëteit de Harmonie, March 10–15. No catalogue known.

Amsterdam 1905. *Tentoonstelling Vincent van Gogh*. Exhibition, Stedelijk Museum, July 15–September 1. Catalogue. Amsterdam, 1905. 13 paintings and 26 drawings were added to the exhibition on August 14. These are listed as nos. 433–74 on a supplementary page in the catalogue.

Amsterdam 1906. *Aquarellen en teekeningen van den heer Vincent van Gogh*. Exhibition, Genootschap Doctrina et Amicitia, February. No catalogue known.

Amsterdam 1911. *Tentoonstelling van schilderijen, aquarellen en teekeningen van Vincent van Gogh*. Exhibition, Larensche Kunsthandel, June 16–July. Brochure. Amsterdam, 1911.

Amsterdam 1914–15. *Teekeningen door Vincent van Gogh uit de verzameling van Mevrouw J. van Gogh-Bonger en den heer V. W. van Gogh*. Exhibition, Stedelijk Museum, December 22–January 12. No catalogue published. This exhibition also traveled to Kunstzalen d'Audretsch, The Hague, March; Gymnasium Gebouw, Arnhem, March–April.

Amsterdam 1915. *Vincent van Gogh, werken van genooten: Schilderijen, teekeningen en beeldhouwwerken*. Exhibition, Gebouw van het Genootschap van Kunstenaren Moderne Kunstkring, September 26–November 30. No catalogue known.

Amsterdam 1917. *Collectie De Bois*. Exhibition, J. H. de Bois, April 16–May 31. No catalogue known.

Amsterdam 1924. *Vincent van Gogh tentoonstelling*. Exhibition, Gebouw voor Beeldende Kunst, March–April. Catalogue by H. P. Bremmer, H. J. Haverman, and J. de Meester. Amsterdam, 1924.

Amsterdam 1926. *Vincent van Gogh tentoonstelling ter gelegenheid van het internationale jeugdfeest der S.J.I.* Exhibition, Stedelijk Museum, May 15–June 15. Catalogue. [Amsterdam], 1926.

Amsterdam 1929. *Teekeningen en aquarellen door Vincent van Gogh*. Exhibition, Stedelijk Museum, October 19–November 17. Brochure. N.p., [1929].

Amsterdam 1931. *Vincent van Gogh: Werken uit de verzameling van Ir. V. W. van Gogh, in bruikleen afgestaan aan de gemeente Amsterdam*. Exhibition, Stedelijk Museum, opened February 14. Catalogue by Willem Johannes Steenhoff. Amsterdam, 1931.

Amsterdam 1945. *Vincent van Gogh*. Exhibition, Stedelijk Museum, September 14–December 1. Catalogue. Amsterdam, 1945.

Amsterdam 1955. *Vincent van Gogh*. Exhibition, Stedelijk Museum, June 24–September. Catalogue, no. 134. [Amsterdam, 1955.]

Amsterdam 1958. *Vincent van Gogh: Leven en scheppen in beeld*. Exhibition, Stedelijk Museum, May 16–June 30. Catalogue, no. 187, by Vincent W. van Gogh and Marc Edo Tralbaut. [Amsterdam, 1958.]

Amsterdam 1963. *150 jaar Nederlandse kunst: Schilderijen, beelden, tekeningen, grafiek, 1813–1963*. Exhibition, Stedelijk Museum, July 6–September 29. Catalogue; sponsored by the Comité Nationale Herdenking, 1813–1963. [Amsterdam, 1963.]

Amsterdam 1963–64. *Hollandse kunstenaars en hun ontboezemingen*. Exhibition, Rijksmuseum, December 2–February 2. Catalogue titled *Drie perioden uit honderdvijftig jaar, 1813, 1888, 1963*, by J. W. Niemeijer, L. C. J. Frerichs, and J. Verbeek. [Amsterdam, 1963.]

Amsterdam 1976. *De notaris in de kunst / Le notaire dans l'art*. Exhibition, Rijksmuseum, January 24–February 15. Catalogue by Peter Schatborn and R. J. C. van Helden. Amsterdam, 1976.

Amsterdam 1980–81. *Vincent van Gogh in zijn Hollandse jaren: Kijk op stad en land door Van Gogh en zijn tijdgenoten, 1870–1890*. Exhibition, Van Gogh Museum, December 13–March 22. Catalogue by Griselda Pollock. Amsterdam, 1980.

Amsterdam 1988–89. *Van Gogh and Millet*. Exhibition, Van Gogh Museum, December 9–February 26. Catalogue by Sjraar van Heugten and Philip Conisbee; edited by Louis van Tilborgh; translated by Martin Cleaver. Zwolle and Amsterdam, 1989.

Amsterdam 1990. *Vincent van Gogh: Paintings*. Exhibition, Van Gogh Museum, March 30–July 29. Catalogue by Evert van Uitert, Louis van Tilborgh, and Sjraar van Heugten; translated by Martin Cleaver et al. Milan and Rome, 1990.

Amsterdam 1991. *Aanwinsten, 1986–1991 / Acquisitions, 1986–1991*. Exhibition, Van Gogh Museum, September 27–

January 5. Catalogue, with additional acquisitions. Zwolle and Amsterdam, 1991.

Amsterdam 1993. *Kunst, kennis en commercie: De kunsthandelaar J. H. de Bois (1878–1946).* Exhibition, Rijksmuseum, January 23–May 2. *See* Heijbroek and Wouthuysen 1993.

Amsterdam 1995. *The Graphic Work of Vincent van Gogh.* Exhibition, Van Gogh Museum, May 19–August 27. Catalogue by Sjraar van Heugten and Fieke Pabst. Cahier Vincent, no. 6. Zwolle, 1995.

Amsterdam 1996. *Vincent van Gogh Drawings: The Early Years, 1880–1883.* Exhibition, Van Gogh Museum, May 10–September 15. *See* Van Heugten 1996.

Amsterdam 1997. *Vincent van Gogh Drawings: Nuenen, 1883–1885.* Exhibition, Van Gogh Museum, June 20–October 12. *See* Van Heugten 1997.

Amsterdam 1997–98. *Langs velden en wegen: De verbeelding van het landschap in de 18de en 19de eeuw.* Exhibition, Rijksmuseum, November 28–March 3. Catalogue by Wiepke Loos, Robert-Jan te Rijdt, and Marjan van Heteren, with contributions by Alexander Bakker et al. Blaricum, 1997.

Amsterdam 2001–2. *Vincent van Gogh Drawings. Antwerp and Paris, 1885–1888.* Exhibition, Van Gogh Museum, September 28–January 6. *See* Vellekoop and Van Heugten 2001.

Amsterdam 2002. *Aquarellen van de Haagse School: De collectie Drucker-Fraser.* Exhibition, Rijksmuseum, July 29–October 27. Catalogue by Wiepke Loos. Amsterdam, 2002.

Amsterdam 2003. *Stad en land: Stedelijk Museum in De Nieuwe Kerk 2 / Town and Country: 19th Century Masterpieces from the Stedelijk Museum Collection.* Exhibition, De Nieuwe Kerk, May 25–October 10. Catalogue. Amsterdam, 2003.

Amsterdam–Boston 2000. *Rond 1900: Kunst op papier in Nederland.* Exhibition, Rijksmuseum, January 15–April 9; Museum of Fine Arts, July 25–November 5. Catalogue by Irene de Groot, Marijn Schapelhouman, and Carel Blotkamp. Zwolle, 2000. English ed.: *Van Gogh to Mondrian: Dutch Works on Paper.* Catalogue introduction by Carel Blotkamp. Zwolle, 2000.

Anonymous 1891. "Letteren en kunst." *Haarlems dagblad,* [December 1891], press clipping, Andries Bonger Plakboek BVG 311, Van Gogh Museum, Amsterdam.

Antwerp 1892. *Art d'aujourd'hui: 1ère exposition annuelle. Kunst van Heden.* Exhibition, Association pour l'Art, May–June. No catalogue known.

Antwerp 1914. *L'art contemporain: Salon 1914. Kunst van Heden. Tentoonstelling 1914.* Exhibition, Feestzaal, March 7–April 5. No catalogue known.

Antwerp 1955. *Vincent van Gogh.* Exhibition, Stad Antwerpen Feestzaal, May 7–June 19. Catalogue. [Antwerp, 1955.]

Arles 1989. *Van Gogh et Arles.* Exhibition, Ancien Hôpital Van Gogh, February 4–May 15. Catalogue by Ronald Pickvance. Arles, 1989.

Arles 2003. *Van Gogh à Arles: Dessins, 1888–1889.* Exhibition, Fondation Vincent van Gogh, Arles, July–October. Catalogue. Arles, 2003.

Arles–Saint-Rémy 1951 *Vincent van Gogh en Provence.* Exhibition, Musée Réattu, May 5–27; Hôtel de Sade, Saint-Rémy de Provence. Catalogue edited by Madeleine Jauneau; texts by Vincent W. van Gogh, René Jullian, and E. Leroy. Arles, 1951.

Arnhem and other cities 1930–31. *Tentoonstelling van teekeningen, aquarellen en schilderijen door Vincent van Gogh.* Exhibition, De Korenbeurs, December 12–26; Groningen Pictura, Groote Societeit, January 4–19; Friesch Museum, Leeuwarden, January 24–February 8; Openbare Leeszaal, Enschede, February 13–25. No catalogue known.

Baer 1994. Ann Baer. *A Catalogue of Marées Gesellschaft and Ganymed Press Facsimiles.* London, 1994.

Bailey 1992. Martin Bailey. "KGB's Secret Store of Looted Old Masters." *The Observer* (London), September 20, 1992.

Baltimore and other cities 1961–62. *Vincent van Gogh: Paintings, Watercolors and Drawings.* Exhibition, Baltimore Museum of Art, October 18–November 26; Cleveland Museum of Art, December 5–January 14; Albright Art Gallery, Buffalo, January 30–March 11; Museum of Fine Arts Boston, March 22–April 29. Catalogue. Baltimore, 1961.

Baltimore–San Francisco–Brooklyn 1970–71. *Vincent van Gogh: Paintings and Drawings.* Exhibition, Baltimore Museum of Art, October 11–November 29; M. H. de Young Memorial Museum, December 11–January 31; Brooklyn Museum, February 14–April 4. Catalogue. Amsterdam, 1970.

Baltimore–Worcester 1942. *Paintings by Van Gogh.* Exhibition, Baltimore Museum of Art, September 18–October 18; Worcester Art Museum, October 28– November 28. Catalogue by H. W. van Loon. Baltimore, 1942.

Bargue 1871. Charles Bargue. *Exercices au fusain, pour préparer à l'étude de l'Académie d'après nature.* Paris, 1871.

Bargue 1873. Charles Bargue, with the collaboration of Jean-Léon Gérôme. *Cours de dessin.* Paris, n.d. [ca. 1873].

Barnett 1978. Vivian Endicott Barnett. *The Guggenheim Museum, Justin K. Thannhauser Collection.* New York: Solomon R. Guggenheim Museum, 1978.

Basel 1924. *Vincent van Gogh.* Exhibition, Kunsthalle Basel, March 27–May 4. No catalogue known. This exhibition also traveled to Zürich.

Basel 1944. *Kunstwerke des neunzehnten Jahrhunderts aus Basler Privatbesitz.* Exhibition, Kunsthalle, May 1–July 4. Catalogue. Basel, 1944.

Basel 1945. *25. Werke von Vincent van Gogh.* Exhibition, Galerie M. Schulthess, June 23–August 19. Catalogue. Basel, 1945.

Basel 1947. *Vincent van Gogh, 1853–1890.* Exhibition, Kunsthalle Basel, October 11–November 23. Catalogue. Basel, 1947.

Bergen–Oslo 1948. *Vincent van Gogh.* Exhibition, Kunstforening, March 23–April 15; Kunstnernes Hus, April 24–May 15. Catalogue. Oslo, 1948.

Berlin 1906. *Zwölften Kunstausstellung der Berliner Secession, Zeichnende Künste.* Exhibition, Paul Cassirer, December. Catalogue. Berlin, 1906.

Berlin 1907. *Vierzehnte Kunstausstellung der Berliner Secession, Zeichnende Künste.* Exhibition, Paul Cassirer, December. Catalogue. Berlin, 1907.

Berlin 1908. Title unknown. Exhibition, Paul Cassirer, October. No catalogue published.

Berlin 1909–10. *Neunzehnten Ausstellung der Berliner Secession, Zeichnende Künste.* Exhibition, Ausstellungshaus am Kurfürstendamm, November 27–January 9. Catalogue. Berlin, 1909.

Berlin 1910. *III. Ausstellung: Vincent van Gogh, 1853–1890.* Exhibition, Paul Cassirer, October 25–November 20. Catalogue. Berlin, 1910.

Berlin 1914. *Vincent van Gogh: Zehnte Ausstellung.* Exhibition, Paul Cassirer, May–June. Catalogue. Berlin, 1914.

Berlin 1927–28. *Vincent van Gogh: Erste grosse Ausstellung seiner Zeichnungen und Aquarelle.* Exhibition, Otto Wacker, December 6–February 1. Catalogue by J.-B. de la Faille. Berlin, 1927.

Berlin–Munich 1996–97. *Manet bis Van Gogh: Hugo von Tschudi und der Kampf um die Moderne.* Exhibition, Nationalgalerie, Staatliche Museen zu Berlin, September 20–January 6; Neue Pinakothek, Bayerische Staatsgemäldesammlungen, January 24–May 11. Catalogue by Johann Georg Prinz von Hohenzollern and Peter-Klaus Schuster. Munich, 1996.

Bern 1954–55. *Vincent van Gogh.* Exhibition, Kunstmuseum Bern, November 27–January 30. Catalogue. Bern, 1954.

Bernard 1891a. Émile Bernard. "Vincent van Gogh." *Les hommes d'aujourd'hui* 8, no. 390 (1891). Published in translation in Stein 1986, pp. 282–85.

Bernard 1891b. Émile Bernard. "Vincent van Gogh." *La plume,* September 1, 1891. Published in translation in Stein 1986, p. 282.

Blanc 1867. Charles Blanc. *Grammaire des arts du dessin: Architecture, sculpture, peinture.* Paris, 1867.

Boele van Hensbroek 1892. P. A. M. Boele van Hensbroek. "De van Goghs." *De Nederlandsche spectator,* January 9, 1892. Published in translation in Stein 1986, p. 286.

Bordeaux 1972. *Vincent van Gogh: Collection du Musée National Vincent van Gogh à Amsterdam.* Exhibition, Musée des Beaux-Arts, April 21–June 20. Catalogue. Paris and Bordeaux, 1972.

Breda 2003–4. *Vincent van Gogh: Het mysterie van de Bredase kisten. Verloren vondsten.* Exhibition, Breda's Museum, November 22–February 1. Catalogue edited by Ron Dirven and Kees Wouters. Breda, 2003.

Bremen 2002–3. *Van Gogh: Fields.* The Field with Poppies *and the Artists' Dispute.* Exhibition, Kunsthalle Bremen,

November 9–January 26. Catalogue edited by Wulf Herzogenrath and Dorothee Hansen. Ostfildern-Ruit, 2002. A modified version of this exhibition traveled to Toledo, Ohio; *see* Toledo 2003.

Bremmer n.d. *Vincent van Gogh: Vier-en-twintig teekeningen uit zijn "Hollandsche periode." Verzameling Hidde Nijland.* Preface by H. P. Bremmer. Amsterdam: Versluys, n.d. [1907?].

Bremmer 1904. H. P. Bremmer, ed. *Moderne kunstwerken: Schilderijen, teekeningen en beeldhouwwerken* 2 (1904), vol. 10.

Bremmer 1910. H. P. Bremmer, ed. *Moderne kunstwerken: Schilderijen, teekeningen en beeldhouwwerken* 8 (1910), vol. 11.

Bremmer 1911. H. P. Bremmer. *Vincent van Gogh: Inleidende beschouwingen.* Amsterdam, 1911.

Bremmer 1917. H. P. Bremmer. *Catalogus van de schilderijen verzameling van Mevr. H. Kröller-Müller.* The Hague, [1917].

Bremmer 1918. H. P. Bremmer, ed. *Beeldende Kunst* 5 (1917–18), vol. 2.

Bremmer 1919. H. P. Bremmer. *Vincent van Gogh: Reproducties naar zijn werken in de verzameling van Mevrouw H. Kröller-Müller.* The Hague, 1919.

Bremmer 1921–28. H. P. Bremmer. *Verzameling van Mevrouw H. Kröller-Müller, The Hague.* 2 vols. The Hague, 1921–28.

Bremmer 1924. H. P. Bremmer, ed. *Beeldende Kunst* 11 (1923–24), vol. 4.

Bremmer 1926. H. P. Bremmer, ed. *Beeldende Kunst* 13 (1926), vols. 8, 11.

Bromig-Kolleritz 1954. Katharina Bromig-Kolleritz von Novisancz. "Die Selbstbildnisse Vincent van Goghs: Versuch einer kunsthistorischen Erfassung der Darstellungen." Ph.D. dissertation, Garmisch. Munich, 1954.

De Brouwer 2000. Ton de Brouwer. *De oude toren en Van Gogh in Nuenen.* Venlo, 2000.

Brussels 1890. *VIIe exposition annuelle des XX.* Exhibition, Musée d'Art Moderne, opened January 17. Catalogue. Brussels, 1890.

Brussels 1891. *VIIIe exposition annuelle des XX.* Exhibition, Musée d'Art Moderne, February 7–March 8. Catalogue. Brussels, 1891.

Carroy 1962. Christian Carroy. "Een panoramalandschap van Van Gogh." *Bulletin van het Rijksmuseum* 10, no. 4 (1962), pp. 139–42.

Cassagne n.d. Armand Cassagne. *Abécédaire du dessin / Abecedary of Drawing.* Ser. 7 of *Le dessin pour tous: Cahiers d'exercices élémentaires et progressifs.* Paris and London, [186-?].

Cassagne 1873. Armand Cassagne. *Guide pratique pour les différents genres de dessin: Dessin à la mine de plomb;—au crayon noir dit Conté;—à la sanguine;—au fusain;—à la plume;—au lavis;—à la sépia;—à la plume, relevé de couleur.* Paris, 1873.

Cassagne 1875. Armand Cassagne. *Traité d'aquarelle.* Paris, 1875.

Cassagne 1879. Armand Cassagne. *Traité pratique de perspective.* Paris, 1879.

Cassagne 1880. Armand Cassagne. *Guide de l'alphabet du dessin ou l'art d'apprendre et d'enseigner les principes rationnels du dessin d'après nature.* Paris, 1880.

Charleroi–Ghent 1965. *Vincent van Gogh: Schilderijen, aquarellen, tekeningen.* Exhibition, Palais des Beaux-Arts, January 9–February 9; Museum voor Schone Kunsten, February 19–March 21. Catalogue titled *Vincent van Gogh.* [Charleroi, 1965.]

Chetham 1976. Charles Chetham. *The Role of Vincent van Gogh's Copies in the Development of His Art.* New York and London, 1976.

Chicago–Amsterdam 2001–2. *Van Gogh and Gauguin: The Studio of the South.* Exhibition, Art Institute of Chicago, September 22–January 13; Van Gogh Museum, February 9–June 2. Catalogue by Douglas W. Druick and Peter Kort Zegers, with Britt Salvesen, Kristin Hoermann Lister, and Mary C. Weaver. Chicago, 2001.

Cleveland 1948. *Work by Vincent van Gogh.* Exhibition, Cleveland Museum of Art, November 3–December 12. Catalogue. Cleveland, 1948.

Cohen-Gosschalk 1908. Johan Cohen-Gosschalk. "Vincent van Gogh." *Zeitschrift für bildende Kunst* 43, no. 9 (1908), pp. 225–35.

Cologne 1912. *Internationale Kunst-Ausstellung des Sonderbundes westdeutschen Kunstfreunde und Künstler zu Cöln.* Exhibition, Städtische Ausstellungshalle am Aachener Tor, May 25–September 30. Catalogue. Cologne, 1912.

Cologne–Frankfurt 1910. *Zeichnungen von Vincent van Gogh.* Exhibition, Kunstverein, January; Moderne Kunsthandlung Marie Held, February. No catalogue published.

Cologne–Hamburg 1914. *V. van Gogh.* Exhibition, Kölner Kunstverein, July–August; Hamburg Galerie Commeter, September. No catalogue known.

Cooper 1955. Douglas Cooper. *Drawings and Watercolours* [by Vincent van Gogh]: *A Selection of 32 Plates in Colour.* With an essay by Hugo Hofmannsthal. New York, 1955.

Cooper 1974. Douglas Cooper. "The Yellow House." In *Van Gogh in Perspective,* edited by Bogomila Welsh-Ovcharov, pp. 149–55. Englewood Cliffs, N.J., 1974.

Copenhagen 1893. *Den Frie Udstilling.* Exhibition, Den Frie Udstilling, March 26–May. Catalogue titled *Fortegnelse over kunstvaerkerne paa den Frie Udstilling.* [Copenhagen], n.d. [1893].

Copenhagen 1938. *Vincent van Gogh. Malerier, tegninger, akvareller.* Exhibition, Charlottenborg, January. Catalogue by K. Flor. Copenhagen, 1938.

Copenhagen 1984–85. *Gauguin og Van Gogh i København i 1893 / Gauguin and Van Gogh in Copenhagen in 1893.* Exhibition, Ordrupgaard, December 12–February 10. Catalogue by Merete Bodelsen and Kirsten Olesen. Copenhagen, 1984.

Van Crimpen 1986. Han van Crimpen. "Landschap in Drente, met kanaal en zeilboot, Vincent van Gogh, 1853–1890." *Vereniging Rembrandt. Jaarverslag 1986,* pp. 70–71.

Van Crimpen 1987. H[an] v[an] C[rimpen]. "New Acquisition." *Van Gogh Bulletin* 2, no. 2 (1987), unpaged.

Dallas and other cities 1967–68. *Vincent van Gogh: Drawings and Watercolors.* Exhibition, Dallas Museum of Fine Arts, October 6–November 4; Philadelphia Museum of Art, November 17–December 31; Toledo Museum of Art, January 20–March 3; National Gallery of Canada, Ottawa, March 14–April 15. Catalogue. Amsterdam, [1967].

Daloze 1982. Marcel Daloze. "La découverte de l'oeuvre et de la personalité de Van Gogh en Belgique (1890–1914)." Doctoral dissertation, Université de Liège, 1982.

Davis 1997. Bruce Davis. *Master Drawings in the Los Angeles County Museum of Art.* Los Angeles: Los Angeles County Museum of Art, 1997.

Detroit–Boston–Philadelphia 2000–2001. *Van Gogh, Face to Face: The Portraits.* Exhibition, Detroit Institute of Arts, March 12–June 4; Museum of Fine Arts, July 2–September 24; Philadelphia Museum of Art, October 22–January 14. Catalogue by Roland Dorn et al.; chronology by Katherine Sachs. Detroit, 2000.

Dijk and Van der Sluis 2001. Wout J. Dijk and Meent W. van der Sluis. *De Drentse tijd van Vincent van Gogh: Een onderbelichte periode nader onderzocht.* Groningen, 2001.

Dordrecht 1897. *Expositie Vincent van Gogh: Collectie Hidde Nijland.* Exhibition, Dordrecht Pictura, February 18–25. No catalogue known.

Dordrecht 1905. *Vincent van Gogh: 100 teekeningen uit de verzameling Hidde Nijland.* Exhibition, Dordrechts Museum, dates unknown. *See* Nijland 1905.

Dorn 1987. Roland Dorn. "Als Zeichner unter Malern: Vincent van Gogh in Den Haag, 1881–1883." In John Sillevis et al., *Die Haager Schule: Meisterwerke der holländischen Malerei des 19. Jahrhunderts aus Haags Gemeentemuseum,* pp. 58–80. Exh. cat. Mannheim: Kunsthalle Mannheim, 1987.

Dorn 1997–98. Roland Dorn. "'Refiler à Saintes-Maries?': Pickvance and Hulsker Revisited." *Van Gogh Museum Journal* 1997–98, pp. 15–25.

Dorn 1999. Roland Dorn. "Vincent van Gogh *Soir d'été,* 1888." In *Van Gogh, Van Doesburg, de Chirico, Picasso, Guston, Weiner, Mangold, Richter: Texte zu Werken im Kunstmuseum Winterthur,* edited by Dieter Schwarz, pp. 11–41. Düsseldorf and Winterthur, 1999.

Douwes 1930. Willem F. Douwes. *Vincent van Gogh.* Amsterdam, [1930].

Dresden 1908. *Vincent van Gogh / Paul Cézanne.* Exhibition, Emil Richter, April–May. Catalogue. Dresden, 1908.

Dresden–Breslau 1912. *Ausstellung Vincent van Gogh, 1853–1890.* Exhibition, Galerie Ernst Arnold, February. Catalogue. Breslau, 1912.

Du Quesne-Van Gogh 1911. E. H. du Quesne-Van Gogh. *Persönliche Erinnerungen an Vincent van Gogh.* 2nd ed. Munich, 1911.

Van den Eerenbeemt 1924. [Herman van den Eerenbeemt]. "Vincent van Gogh." *Opgang* 4, no. 162 (1924), pp. 265, 268–82.

Elderfield 1983. John Elderfield. *The Modern Drawing: 100 Works on Paper from the Museum of Modern Art.* New York, 1983.

Elgar 1958. Frank Elgar. *Van Gogh.* Paris, 1958.

Enschede 1960. *Vincent van Gogh: Tekeningen.* Exhibition, Rijksmuseum Twenthe, February 6–March 20. Catalogue by Vincent W. van Gogh and C. C. W. J. Hijszeler. N.p., [1960].

Erpel 1964. Fritz Erpel. *Van Gogh: The Self-Portraits.* Oxford, 1964.

Essen 1957. *Vincent van Gogh (1853–1890), Leben und Schaffen: Dokumentation, Gemälde, Zeichnungen.* Exhibition, Villa Hügel, October 16–December 15. Catalogue. Essen, 1957.

Essen–Amsterdam 1990. *Vincent van Gogh and the Modern Movement, 1890–1914.* Exhibition, Museum Folkwang Essen, August 11–November 4; Van Gogh Museum, November 16–February 18. Catalogue edited by Georg-W. Költzsch, Ronald de Leeuw, and Inge Bodesohn-Vogel; contributions by Roland Dorn et al.; translated by Eileen Martin. Zwolle, 1990.

De la Faille 1928. J.-B. de la Faille. *L'oeuvre de Vincent van Gogh: Catalogue raisonné.* 4 vols. Paris and Brussels, 1928.

De la Faille 1970. J.-B. de la Faille. *The Works of Vincent van Gogh: His Paintings and Drawings.* Rev. ed. Amsterdam, 1970.

De la Faille 1992. J.-B. de la Faille. *Vincent van Gogh: The Complete Works on Paper. Catalogue Raisonné.* 2 vols. Reprint of De la Faille 1928, vol. 3 and a rev. suppl. ed. of the portion of 1970 concerning works on paper. San Francisco, 1992.

Feilchenfeldt and Veenenbos 1988. Walter Feilchenfeldt, with a catalogue of the drawings compiled by Han Veenenbos. *Vincent van Gogh and Paul Cassirer, Berlin: The Reception of Van Gogh in Germany from 1901 to 1914.* Cahier Vincent, no. 2. Zwolle, 1988.

Fels 1928. Florent Fels. *Vincent van Gogh.* Paris, 1928.

Findhammer 2002. Joost Findhammer. "Wat is er over van het landschap ten tijde van Van Gogh?" *De Drijehornickels* 11, no. 1 (April 2002), pp. 17–24.

Florence 1974. *Quarta biennale internazionale della grafica d'arte. La grafica dal realismo al simbolismo.* Exhibition, Palazzo Strozzi, May 11–June 30. Catalogue, vol. 2. Florence, 1974.

Florence 1996. *Da Van Gogh a Fontana: Opere su carta dello Stedelijk Museum Amsterdam.* Exhibition, Istituto Universitario Olandese di Storia dell'Arte, October 12–December 15. Catalogue. Florence, 1996.

Florence 1997. *Van Gogh in nero: La grafica.* Exhibition, Istituto Universitario Olandese di Storia dell'Arte, October 10–December 14. Catalogue. Florence, 1997.

Francis 1892. Francis. "Exposition Van Gogh chez Le Barc de Boutteville." *La vie moderne,* April 24, 1892. Published in translation in Stein 1986, p. 294.

Frankfurt 1908. *Vincent van Gogh.* Exhibition, Frankfurter Kunstverein, June 14–28. Catalogue. Frankfurt am Main, 1908.

Frankfurt 1911. Title unknown. Exhibition, Galerie Hermes Frankfurt am Main, January. No catalogue known.

Frankfurt 1970. *Vincent van Gogh: Zeichnungen und Aquarelle.* Exhibition, Frankfurter Kunstverein, April 30–June 21. Catalogue edited by Sylvia Rathke-Köhl. Frankfurt am Main, 1970.

Galbally 1977. Ann Galbally. *The Art of John Peter Russell.* South Melbourne, 1977.

Gans 1961. L. Gans. "Twee onbekende tekeningen uit Van Gogh's Hollandse Periode." *Museumjournaal* 7, no. 2 (July 1961), pp. 33–34.

Gauguin 1910. Paul Gauguin. "Vincent van Gogh." *Kunst und Kunstler* 8 (1910), p. 581.

Gaunt 1950. William Gaunt. "Van Gogh: The Man in His Time." *Artnews Annual* 19 (1950), pp. 51–64.

Van Gelder 1949. J. G. van Gelder. *De aardappeleters van Vincent van Gogh.* Amsterdam and Antwerp, 1949.

Van Gelder 1958. J. G. van Gelder. "Vincent van Gogh (1853–1890): Gezicht op een industriewijk te Paris." *Openbaar Kunstbezit* 2 (1958).

Geneva 1947. *172 oeuvres de Vincent van Gogh (1852–1890).* Exhibition, Musée Rath, March 22–April 20. Catalogue. Geneva, 1947.

Glasgow–Amsterdam 1990–91. *The Age of Van Gogh: Dutch Painting, 1880–1895.* Exhibition, Burrell Collection, November 10–February 10; Van Gogh Museum, March 1–May 26. Catalogue edited by Richard Bionda and Carel Blotkamp; contributions by Rieta Bergsma, Enno Endt, and Sanne Van Smoorenburg. Zwolle, 1990.

Van Gogh n.d. *40 Photocollographies d'après ses tableaux et dessins.* Amsterdam: W. Versluys, n.d. [1904].

Van Gogh Letters 1914. Vincent van Gogh. *Brieven aan zijn broeder; uitgegeven en toegelicht door zijn schoonzuster.* Preface and notes by Jo van Gogh-Bonger. 3 vols. Amsterdam, 1914. German ed.: Vincent van Gogh. *Briefe an seinen Bruder; zusammengestellt von seiner Schwägerin, J. van Gogh-Bonger.* Translated by Leo Klein-Diepold. Berlin, 1914.

Van Gogh Letters 1958. *The Complete Letters of Vincent van Gogh with Reproductions of All the Drawings in the Correspondence.* Introduction by Vincent W. van Gogh. 3 vols. Greenwich, Conn., 1958.

Van Gogh Letters 1990. *De brieven van Vincent van Gogh.* Edited by Han van Crimpen and Monique Berends-Albert. 4 vols. The Hague, 1990.

Gouda 1949. *Tekeningen van Vincent van Gogh.* Exhibition, Catharina Gasthuis, April 13–May 29. No catalogue known.

Groningen 1897. Title unknown. Exhibition, Groningsch Museum, March–April. No catalogue known.

De Gruyter 1961. W. Jos de Gruyter. *Tekeningen van Vincent van Gogh.* [Amsterdam, 1961.]

Haarlem 1956. *Vincent van Gogh.* Exhibition, Vishal, July 21–August 27. Catalogue. Haarlem, 1956.

Hagen 1912. *Moderne Kunst: Plastik, Malerei, Graphik.* Exhibition, Museum Folkwang, July. Catalogue edited by Kurt Freyer. Hagen, 1912.

Hagen 1919. Oskar Hagen. *Vincent van Gogh: Faksimiles nach Zeichnungen und Aquarellen.* Munich, 1919.

The Hague 1891. *Vincent van Gogh teekeningen.* Exhibition, Pulchri Studio, December. No catalogue known.

The Hague 1892. *Werken van Vincent van Gogh.* Exhibition, Haagsche Kunstkring (Buitenhof), May 16–June 6. *Catalogus der nagelaten werken van Vincent van Gogh.* The Hague, 1892.

The Hague 1895. *Tentoonstelling van teekeningen van Vincent van Gogh* [Hidde Nijland collection]. Exhibition, Haagsche Kunstkring, February 17–March 3. No catalogue known.

The Hague 1898. *Vincent van Gogh.* Exhibition, Arts and Crafts Gallery, November. *See* Plasschaert 1898.

The Hague 1918. *Tentoonstelling van aquarellen, teekeningen en schetsen van Vincent van Gogh: Verzameling Hidde Nijland.* Exhibition, Haagsche Kunstkring, April 6–29. Brochure. The Hague, 1918.

The Hague 1925. *Vincent van Gogh.* Exhibition, Pulchri Studio, March–April. No catalogue known.

The Hague 1948–49. *Vincent van Gogh: Collectie Ir. V. W. van Gogh.* Exhibition, Gemeentemuseum, October 12–January 10. Catalogue essay by W. Jos. de Gruyter. The Hague, 1948.

The Hague 1953. *Vincent van Gogh.* Exhibition, Gemeentemuseum, March 30–May 17. Catalogue by W. Jos de Gruyter. The Hague, 1953.

The Hague 1978. *Kunstenaren der idee: Symbolistische tendenzen in Nederland, ca. 1880–1930.* Exhibition, Gemeentemuseum, September 16–November 26. Catalogue by Carel Blotkamp, with contributions by Abraham Marie Hammacher and Dick Veeze. The Hague, 1978.

The Hague 1990. *Van Gogh en Den Haag.* Exhibition, Haags Historisch Museum, September 8–November 18. Catalogue edited by Michiel van der Mast and Charles Dumas. Zwolle, 1990.

The Hague–Amsterdam 1908. *Vincent van Gogh tentoonstelling.* Exhibition, Kunstzalen C. M. van Gogh, The Hague, dates unknown, no catalogue known; Kunstzalen C. M. van Gogh, Amsterdam, September 3–24. Catalogue. Amsterdam, 1908.

The Hague–Amsterdam 1912. *Tentoonstelling van teekeningen door Vincent van Gogh.* Exhibition, Artz en De Bois, July–August; Kunstzalen C. M. van Gogh, Autumn. Brochure. The Hague, 1912.

Hamburg 1911–12. No title known. Exhibition Galerie Commeter, November–January. No catalogue published.

Hamburg 1995. *Van Gogh: Die Pariser Selbstbildnisse.* Exhibition, Hamburger Kunsthalle, March 17–May 28. Catalogue by Uwe M. Schneede and Christoph Heinrich. Stuttgart, 1995.

Hamburg 2002. *Vincent van Gogh: Die Pariser Zeichnungen.* Exhibition, Hamburger Kunsthalle, March 22–June 9. Catalogue edited by Uwe M. Schneede. Hamburg, 2002.

Hansen 2002–3. Dorothee Hansen. "Outside Arles: Harvest in Provence, 1888." In Bremen 2002–3, pp. 110–33.

Havelaar 1915. Just Havelaar. *Vincent van Gogh.* Amsterdam, [1915].

Heenk 1994. Liesbeth Heenk. "Revealing Van Gogh: An Examination of His Papers." *Paper Conservator* 18 (1994), pp. 30–39.

Heenk 1995. Elizabeth Nicoline Heenk. "Vincent van Gogh's Drawings: An Analysis of Their Production and Uses." 2 vols. Ph.D. dissertation, Courtauld Institute of Art, University of London, 1995.

Heijbroek 1991. Jan F. Heijbroek. "Het Rijksmuseum voor Moderne Kunst van Willem Steenhoff: Werkelijkheid of utopie?" *Bulletin van het Rijksmuseum* 39 (1991), pp. 163–255.

Heijbroek and Wouthuysen 1993. Jan F. Heijbroek and Ester L. Wouthuysen. *Kunst, kennis en commercie: De kunsthandelaar J. H. de Bois (1878–1946).* Amsterdam, 1993. Published in conjunction with Amsterdam 1993.

Hengelo 1949. *Tekeningen van Vincent van Gogh.* Exhibition, Openbare Leeszaal, opened January 29. No catalogue known.

's Hertogenbosch 1987–88. *Van Gogh in Brabant: Paintings and Drawings from Etten and Nuenen.* Exhibition, Noordbrabants Museum, November 2–January 10. Catalogue edited by Evert van Uitert; with Trudy van Spaandonk, Antoinette Wildenberg, and Ank Mulder-Koenen. Zwolle, 1987.

Van Heugten 1996. Sjraar van Heugten. *Vincent van Gogh Drawings.* Vol. 1, *The Early Years, 1880–1883.* Amsterdam: Van Gogh Museum, 1996. Published in conjunction with Amsterdam 1996.

Van Heugten 1997. Sjraar van Heugten. *Vincent van Gogh Drawings.* Vol. 2, *Nuenen, 1883–1885.* Amsterdam: Van Gogh Museum, 1997. Published in conjunction with Amsterdam 1997.

Van Heugten 2003. Sjraar van Heugten. "Working in Black and White and Colour: Van Gogh's Regard for Tonality and Technique." In *Vincent's Choice: The Musée Imaginaire of Van Gogh,* edited by Chris Stolwijk et al., pp. 123–32. Exh. cat. Amsterdam: Van Gogh Museum, 2003.

Van Heugten and Pabst 1995. *See* Amsterdam 1995.

Hoensbroek 1953. *Vincent van Gogh.* Exhibition, Kasteel Hoensbroek, May 23–July 13. Catalogue. Hoensbroek, 1953.

Houston 1951. *Vincent van Gogh.* Exhibition, Contemporary Arts Museum, February 4–25. Catalogue. Houston, 1951.

Hulsker 1970. Jan Hulsker. "The Houses Where Van Gogh Lived in The Hague." *Vincent: Bulletin of the Rijksmuseum Vincent van Gogh* 1, no. 1 (1970), pp. 2–13.

Hulsker 1974. Jan Hulsker. "The Poet's Garden." *Vincent: Bulletin of the Rijksmuseum Vincent van Gogh* 3, no. 1 (1974), pp. 22–32.

Hulsker 1976. Jan Hulsker. "Van Gogh's First and Only Commission as an Artist." *Vincent: Bulletin of the Rijksmuseum Vincent van Gogh* 4, no. 4 (1976), pp. 5–19.

Hulsker 1980. Jan Hulsker. *The Complete Van Gogh: Paintings, Drawings, Sketches.* New York, 1980.

Hulsker 1993. Jan Hulsker. *Vincent van Gogh: A Guide to His Work and Letters.* Amsterdam, 1993.

Hulsker 1996. Jan Hulsker. *The New Complete Van Gogh: Paintings, Drawings, Sketches.* Rev. ed. Amsterdam and Philadelphia, 1996.

Humlebæk 1963. *Vincent van Gogh: Malerier og tegninger.* Exhibition, Louisiana Museum of Modern Art, October 24–December 8. Catalogue by Vincent W. van Gogh and K. W. Jensen. Amsterdam, [1962].

Humlebæk 1969. *Vincent van Gogh: Tegninger og akvareller.* Exhibition, Louisiana Museum of Modern Art, January 25–March 16. Catalogue. Amsterdam, 1969.

Humlebæk 1994. *Fra Van Gogh til Gerhard Richter: Hovedværker fra Museum Folkwang Essen.* Exhibition, Louisiana Museum of Modern Art, July 22–October 23. Catalogue. Humlebæk, 1994.

E. Joosten 1970. E. J. Joosten. "Gezicht uit het hospitaal Saint Paul." *Verslag van de Vereniging Rembrandt* 1970, pp. 31–32.

J. Joosten 1970. J. M. Joosten. "Deel 5: Het vervolg van de besprekingen van de Amsterdamse keuze-tentoonstelling van vroege tekeningen bij de kunsthandel Oldenzeel te Rotterdam en de Van Gogh tentoonstelling in het Panorama-gebouw te Amsterdam." *Museumjournaal* 15, no. 2 (1970), pp. 100–103.

Kerstens 1990. C. Kerstens. *Piet Kaufmann: Van Gogh's Model.* d'Hûskes, no. 19. Etten-Leur, 1990.

Knapp 1930. Fritz Knapp. *Vincent van Gogh.* Bielefeld and Leipzig, 1930.

Kōdera 1990. Tsukasa Kōdera. *Vincent van Gogh: Christianity versus Nature.* Oculi, vol. 3. Amsterdam and Philadelphia, 1990.

Kōdera 1991. Tsukasa Kōdera. "Van Gogh's Utopian Japonisme." In Van Rappard-Boon, Van Gulik, and Van Bremen-Ito 1991, pp. 11–45.

Kōdera 1993. Tsukasa Kōdera, ed.; Yvette Rosenberg, ed. for English. *The Mythology of Vincent van Gogh.* Tokyo, 1993.

Komanecky 1975. Michael K. Komanecky. "Vue d'Arles (View of Arles)." In *Selection V: French Watercolors and Drawings from the Museum's Collection, ca. 1800–1910,* pp. 83–87. Exh. cat. Providence: Museum of Art, Rhode Island School of Design, 1975.

Kramer, Zieve, and Faunce 1993. Linda Konheim Kramer, Karyn Zieve, and Sarah Faunce. *French Nineteenth-Century Drawings and Watercolors at the Brooklyn Museum.* New York, 1993.

Kress 1973. Annelise Kress. "Vincent van Gogh's 'Reality.'" *Vincent: Bulletin of the Rijksmuseum Vincent van Gogh* 2, no. 4 (1973), pp. 8–21.

Kröller-Müller Museum 1974. *Vincent van Gogh. Catalogue of 276 Works in the Collection of the Rijksmuseum Kröller-Müller, Otterlo.* [Otterlo, 1974.]

Kröller-Müller Museum 1980. *Vincent van Gogh: A Detailed Catalogue of the Paintings and Drawings by Vincent van Gogh in the Collection of the Kröller-Müller National Museum.* 4th ed. Otterlo, 1980.

Kröller-Müller Museum 2003. *The Paintings of Vincent van Gogh in the Collection of the Kröller-Müller Museum.* Catalogue by Jos ten Berge et al.; edited by Toos van Kooten and Mieke Rijnders. Otterlo, 2003.

Kröller-Müller Museum 2006. *Drawings by Vincent van Gogh in the Kröller-Müller Museum.* Otterlo, 2006. Forthcoming.

Kunsthalle Bremen 1991. *Dokumentation der durch Auslagerung im 2. Weltkrieg vermißten Kunstwerke der Kunsthalle Bremen.* Edited by Siegfried Salzmann. Bremen, 1991. In German and Russian.

Kunsthalle Bremen 1997. *A Catalogue of the Works of Art from the Collection of the Kunsthalle Bremen Lost during Evacuation in the Second World War.* Edited by Andreas Kruel and Anne Röver-Kann. 2nd ed. Bremen, 1997.

Kyōto–Tokyo 1992. *Gohho to Nihon ten / Vincent van Gogh and Japan.* Exhibition, National Museum of Modern Art, February 18–March 29; Setagaya Art Museum, April 4–May 24. Catalogue by Takeo Uchiyama et al. [Tokyo], 1992.

Larsson 1996. Håkan Larsson. *Flames from the South: On the Introduction of Vincent van Gogh to Sweden.* Eslöv, 1996.

Leiden 1893. *Teekeningen van Vincent van Gogh.* Exhibition, Stedelijk Museum De Lakenhal, April 25–May 1. No catalogue known.

Leiden 1901. *Teekeningen van Vincent van Gogh.* Exhibition, Stedelijk Museum De Lakenhal, January 18–25? No catalogue known.

Leiden 1909. *Teekeningen van Van Gogh.* Exhibition, Het Leidsche Volkshuis, opened November 3. No catalogue known.

Leiden 1910. *Schilderijen en tekeningen van Van Gogh.* Exhibition, Het Leidsche Volkshuis, opened November 14. No catalogue known.

Leiden 1913. *Teekeningen van Van Gogh.* Exhibition, Het Leidsche Volkshuis, opened January 21. No catalogue known.

Leprohon 1972. Pierre Leprohon. *Vincent van Gogh.* Paris, 1972.

***Lettres* 1911.** *Lettres de Vincent van Gogh à Émile Bernard publiées par Ambroise Vollard.* Paris, 1911.

Leurs and Tralbaut 1957. Stan Leurs and Mark Edo Tralbaut. "De verdwenen kerk van Nuenen. Door Vincent van Gogh levend gebleven in de herinnering." *Brabantia,* February 1, 1957, pp. 29–68.

Leymarie 1951. Jean Leymarie. *Van Gogh.* Paris, 1951.

Leymarie 1968. Jean Leymarie. *Qui était Van Gogh?* Geneva, 1968.

Liège 1968. *Vincent van Gogh: Dessins, aquarelles.* Exhibition, Musée des Beaux-Arts, September 3–30. Catalogue by Vincent W. van Gogh and M. A. M. Klompé. Amsterdam, 1968.

Liège–Brussels–Bergen 1946–47. *Vincent van Gogh.* Exhibition, Musée des Beaux-Arts, October 12–November 3; Palais des Beaux-Arts, November 9–December 19; Museum voor Schoone Kunsten, December 27–January. Catalogue [edited by E. Langui]. Brussels, 1946. *See also* Basel 1947; London–Birmingham–Glasgow 1947–48; Paris 1947.

Lille–Zürich 1967. *Vincent van Gogh: Dessins, aquarelles.* Exhibition, Palais des Beaux-Arts, January 14–March 13; Kunsthaus Zürich, April 5–June 4. Catalogue prefaces by Vincent W. van Gogh and Abraham Marie Hammacher. Lille, 1967. Also published in German.

Liverpool–Manchester–Newcastle-upon-Tyne 1955–56. *Vincent van Gogh: Paintings and Drawings, Mainly from the Collection of Ir. V. W. van Gogh.* Exhibition, Walker Art Gallery, October 29–December 10; Manchester City Art Gallery, December 17–February 4; Laing Art Gallery, February 11–March 24. Catalogue introduction by Philip James. [London, 1955.]

London 1910–11. *Manet and the Post-Impressionists.* Exhibition, Grafton Galleries, November 8–January 15. Catalogue. London, [1910].

London 1923–24. *Works by Vincent van Gogh.* Exhibition, Leicester Galleries, December 1–January 15. *Catalogue of an Exhibition of Works by Vincent van Gogh (1853–1890),* by M. Sadler. London, 1923.

London 1926–27. *Vincent van Gogh Exhibition.* Exhibition, Leicester Galleries, November 26–January 6. *Catalogue of an Exhibition of Works by Vincent van Gogh.* Exhibition no. 423. London, 1926.

London 1962. *Van Gogh's Life in His Drawings: Van Gogh's Relationship with Signac.* Exhibition, Marlborough Fine Art, May–June. Catalogue no. 100 by [A. M. Hammacher]. London, 1962.

London 1968–69. *Vincent van Gogh: Paintings and Drawings from the Collection of the Vincent van Gogh Foundation, Amsterdam.* Exhibition, Hayward Gallery, October 23–January 12. Catalogue compiled by Alan Bowness. London, 1968.

London 1992. *Van Gogh in England: Portrait of the Artist as a Young Man.* Exhibition, Barbican Art Gallery, February 27–May 4. Catalogue by Martin Bailey; essay by Debora Silverman. London, 1992.

London 1997. *Modern Art in Britain, 1910–1914.* Exhibition, Barbican Art Gallery, February 20–May 26. Catalogue by Anna Gruetzner Robins. London, 1997.

London–Birmingham–Glasgow 1947–48. *Vincent van Gogh, 1853–1890.* Exhibition, Tate Gallery, December 10–January 14; City Art Gallery, Birmingham, January 24–February 14; City Art Gallery, Glasgow, February 21–March 14. Catalogue by Roger Fry and Abraham Marie Hammacher. London, 1947.

Los Angeles 1957. *Vincent van Gogh: A Loan Exhibition of Paintings and Drawings.* Exhibition, Municipal Art Gallery, July 3–August 4. Catalogue introduction by John Rewald. Los Angeles, 1957.

Los Angeles and other cities 1969–70. *Vincent van Gogh: Paintings and Drawings.* Exhibition, Los Angeles County Museum of Art, October 14–December 1; City Art Museum of Saint Louis, December 20–February 1; Philadelphia Museum of Art, February 28–April 5 (paintings only); Columbus Gallery of Fine Arts, March 5–April 5 (drawings only). Catalogue. Los Angeles, 1969.

Lugt 1921, 1956. Fritz Lugt. *Les marques de collections de dessins et d'estampes. . . .* Amsterdam, 1921. *Supplément.* The Hague, 1956.

Luijten 2003. Hans Luijten. "'Rummaging among My Woodcuts': Van Gogh and the Graphic Arts." In *Vincent's Choice: The Musée Imaginaire of Van Gogh,* edited by Chris Stolwijk et al., pp. 110–12. Exh. cat. Amsterdam: Van Gogh Museum, 2003.

Lyon–Grenoble 1951. *Vincent van Gogh.* Exhibition, Musée de Lyon, February 5–March 27; Musée de Grenoble, March 30–May 2. Catalogue by Madeleine Jauneau. Lyon, 1951.

Maastricht–Heerlen 1946. *Vincent van Gogh.* Exhibition, Bonnefanten, January 13–27; Raadhuis Heerlen, February 8–24. Catalogue by F. Lodewick. Maastricht, 1946; Heerlen, 1946.

Malmö 1975. *Vincent van Gogh: 100 teckningar och akvareller / 100 Drawings and Water Colours.* Exhibition, Malmö Konsthall, June 6–August 10. Catalogue. Malmö, 1975.

Manchester 1932. *Vincent van Gogh. Loan Collection of Paintings and Drawings.* Exhibition, Manchester City Art Gallery, October 13–November 27. Catalogue by L. Haward. Manchester, 1932.

Marées-Gesellschaft, Piper & Co., Munich (publisher). *See* Hagen 1919 and Meier-Graefe 1928b.

Marseille 1957. *Vincent van Gogh.* Exhibition, Musée Cantini, March 12–April 28. Catalogue by C. Mauron. Marseille, [1957].

Martigny 2000. *Van Gogh.* Exhibition, Fondation Pierre Gianadda, June 21– November 26. Catalogue by Ronald Pickvance. Martigny, 2000.

Martin 1962. Kurt Martin. *Die Tschudi-Spende: Hugo von Tschudi zum Gedächtnis, 7. Februar 1851–26 November 1911.* Munich, 1962.

Mauclair 1892. Camille Mauclair [Séverin Faust]. "Galerie Le Barc de Boutteville." *La revue indépendante* 23 (April 1892). Quoted in translation in Stein 1986, pp. 294, 303.

Meier-Graefe 1910. Julius Meier-Graefe. *Vincent van Gogh.* 3rd ed. Munich, 1910.

Meier-Graefe 1921. Julius Meier-Graefe. *Vincent.* 2 vols. Munich, 1921.

Meier-Graefe 1928a. Julius Meier-Graefe. *Vincent van Gogh der Zeichner.* Berlin, 1928.

Meier-Graefe 1928b. Julius Meier-Graefe. *Vincent van Gogh: Faksimiles nach Aquarellen und Zeichnungen.* Munich, 1928.

Van Meurs 1910. Willem Jan Gerritt van Meurs. *Isographieën systeem W. van Meurs. Volledige geïllustreerde catalogus.* Amsterdam, [1910].

Milan 1952. *Vincent van Gogh: Dipinti e disegni.* Exhibition, Palazzo Reale, February–April. No catalogue known.

Millard 1974. Charles W. Millard. "A Chronology for Van Gogh's Drawings of 1888." *Master Drawings* 12, no. 2 (Summer 1974), pp. 156–65.

Montreal and other cities 1960–61. *Vincent van Gogh: Paintings–Drawings/Tableaux–dessins.* Exhibition, Montreal Museum of Fine Arts, October 6–November 6; National Gallery of Canada, Ottawa, November 17–December 18; Winnipeg Art Gallery, December 29–January 31; Art Gallery of Toronto, February 10–March 12. Catalogue. Montreal, 1960.

Moscow–Saint Petersburg 1992–93. *Zapadnoevropeiskii risunok XVI–XX vekov: Iz sobranii Kunstkhalle v Bremene / Westeuropäische Zeichnung XVI. bis XX. Jahrhundert: Kunsthalle Bremen / West European Drawing of XVI–XX Centuries: Kunsthalle Collection in Bremen.* Exhibition, State Museum of Architecture, opened November; Hermitage, opened March 19. Catalogue by Irina Sergeevna Grigoreva et al. Moscow, 1992.

Mothe 1987. Alain Mothe. *Vincent van Gogh à Auvers-sur-Oise.* Paris, 1987.

Mothe 1994. Alain Mothe. Commentary to *Les 70 jours de Van Gogh à Auvers: Essai d'éphéméride dans le décor de l'époque (20 mai–30 juillet 1890), d'après les lettres, documents, souvenirs et déductions, Auvers-sur-Oise,* by Paul Gachet. Paris, 1994.

Munich 1908. *Vincent van Gogh.* Exhibition, Moderne Kunsthandlung, March–April. Catalogue. Munich, 1908.

Munich 1909. *Vincent van Gogh.* Exhibition, Brakls Moderner Kunsthandlung, October 7–December. Catalogue. Munich, 1909.

Munich 1926. *Erste Allgemeine Kunst-Ausstellung.* Exhibition, Glaspalast, June 1–October 3. Catalogue. Munich, 1926.

Munich 1956. *Vincent van Gogh, 1853–1890.* Exhibition, Haus der Kunst, October–December. Catalogue by Louis Gans. Munich, 1956.

Munich 1961. *Vincent van Gogh: Zeichnungen und Aquarelle.* Exhibition, Städtische Galerie München, May 23–June 25. Catalogue. Munich, 1961.

Munich 1988. *Französiche Zeichnungen des 19. und frühen 20. Jahrhunderts aus eigenem Bestand.* Exhibition, Staatliche Graphische Sammlung München, May 1–July 3. Catalogue by Brigitte Buberl. Munich, 1988.

Munich and other cities 1909–10. *Vincent van Gogh.* Exhibition, Brakl, Munich, October–December; house of Mr. Marcus (director Frankfurter Kunstverein), Frankfurt am

Main, January; Galerie Ernst Arnold, Dresden, February–March; Kunstsalon Gerstenberger, Chemnitz, April. Catalogue. Munich, 1909.

Murray 1980. Ann Murray. "'Strange and Subtle Perspective . . .': Van Gogh, The Hague School, and the Dutch Landscape Tradition." *Art History* 3, no. 4 (December 1980), pp. 410–24.

Museum Folkwang 1929. Agnes Waldstein, comp. *Museum Folkwang.* Vol. 1, *Moderne Kunst, Malerei, Plastik, Grafik.* Essen, 1929.

Museum of Fine Arts 1976. Museum of Fine Arts, Boston. *Illustrated Handbook.* Boston, 1976.

New York 1913. *International Exhibition of Modern Art.* Exhibition, Armory of the Sixty-Ninth Infantry, February 17–March 15; smaller versions of the exhibition traveled to Art Institute of Chicago, March 24–April 16, and Copley Hall, Boston, April 28–May 19. *Catalogue of the International Exhibition of Modern Art.* New York, 1913.

New York 1920. *Vincent van Gogh Exhibition.* Exhibition, Montross Gallery, October 23–December. Catalogue. New York, 1920.

New York 1921. *French Prints and Drawings of the Last Hundred Years.* Exhibition, The Metropolitan Museum of Art, May 17–September 15. No catalogue published.

New York 1943. *The Art and Life of Vincent van Gogh: Loan Exhibition in Aid of American and Dutch War Relief.* Exhibition, Wildenstein & Co., October 6–November 7. Catalogue compiled by Georges de Batz; introduction by Alfred M. Frankfurter. New York, 1943.

New York 1955. *Vincent van Gogh: Loan Exhibition for the Benefit of the Public Education Association.* Exhibition, Wildenstein & Co., March 24–April 30. Catalogue. New York, 1955.

New York 1984. *Van Gogh in Arles.* Exhibition, The Metropolitan Museum of Art, October 18–December 30. Catalogue by Ronald Pickvance. New York, 1984.

New York 1986–87. *Van Gogh in Saint-Rémy and Auvers.* Exhibition, The Metropolitan Museum of Art, November 25–March 22. Catalogue by Ronald Pickvance. New York, 1986.

New York 1994–95. *The Thaw Collection: Master Drawings and New Acquisitions.* Exhibition, Pierpont Morgan Library, September 21–January 22. Catalogue by Cara D. Denison et al. New York, 1994.

New York and other cities 1935–36. *Vincent van Gogh.* Exhibition, Museum of Modern Art, November 5–January 5; Philadelphia Museum of Art, January 11–February 10; Museum of Fine Arts, Boston, February 19–March 15; Cleveland Museum of Art, March 25–April 19; California Palace of the Legion of Honor, San Francisco, April 28–May 24; William Rockhill Nelson Gallery of Art and Atkins Museum, Kansas City, June 9–July 10; Minneapolis Institute of Arts, July 20–August 17; Art Institute of Chicago, August 26–September 23; Detroit Institute of Arts, October 6–28. Catalogue introduction by Alfred H. Barr Jr. New York, 1935.

New York–Chicago 1949–50. *Vincent van Gogh, Paintings and Drawings: A Special Loan Exhibition.* Exhibition, The Metropolitan Museum of Art, October 21–January 15; Art Institute of Chicago, February 1–April 16. Catalogue. New York, 1949.

New York–Richmond 1985–86. *Drawings from the Collection of Mr. and Mrs. Eugene Victor Thaw: Part II.* Exhibition, Pierpont Morgan Library, September 3–November 10; Virginia Museum of Fine Arts, February 17–April 13. Catalogue by Cara D. Denison et al. New York, 1985.

Nicholas 1994. Lynn H. Nicholas. *The Rape of Europa: The Fate of Europe's Treasures in the Third Reich and the Second World War.* London, 1994.

Nijland 1905. J. Hidde Nijland. *Vincent van Gogh: 100 teekening van uit de verzameling Hidde Nijland in het Museum te Dordrecht.* Amsterdam: W. Versluys, 1905. Published in conjunction with Dordrecht 1905.

Nijmegen 1957. *Tekeningen en aquarellen van Vincent van Gogh.* Exhibition, Waaggebouw, March 13–April 15. Catalogue. N.p., [1957].

Nottingham and other cities 1974–75. *English Influence on Vincent van Gogh.* Exhibition, Nottingham University Art Gallery, November 5–30; Laing Art Gallery, Newcastle-upon-Tyne, December 7–January 12; Victoria and Albert Museum, London, January 30–February 23; Turnpike Gallery, Leigh, March 1–22; Graves Art Gallery, Sheffield, March 29–April 20; and other English cities. Catalogue by Ronald Pickvance. London, 1974.

Novotny 1936. Fritz Novotny. "Van Gogh's teekeningen van het *Straatje te Saintes-Maries.*" *Maandblad voor beeldende kunsten,* December 1936, pp. 370–80.

Novotny 1953. Fritz Novotny. "Reflections on a Drawing by Van Gogh: *Tile Factory Near Arles.*" Translated by Marguerite Kay. *Art Bulletin* 35 (March 1953), pp. 35–43.

Op de Coul 1975. Martha Op de Coul. "The Entrance to the 'Bank van Leening' (Pawnshop)." *Vincent: Bulletin of the Rijksmuseum Vincent van Gogh* 4, no. 2 (1975), pp. 28–30.

Op de Coul 1976. Martha Op de Coul. "De toegang tot de 'Bank van Leening' in Den Haag, getekend door Vincent van Gogh." *Oud Holland* 90, no. 1 (1976), pp. 65–68.

Op de Coul 1983. Martha Op de Coul. "Een mannenfiguur in 1882 door Vincent van Gogh getekend." *Oud Holland* 97, no. 3 (1983), pp. 196–200.

Op de Coul 2002. Martha Op de Coul. "In Search of Van Gogh's Nuenen Studio: The Oldenzeel Exhibitions of 1903." *Van Gogh Museum Journal* 2002, pp. 104–19.

Osaka 1986. *Van Gohho ten Oranda korekushon ni yoru: Shūkyō–ningen–shizen / Vincent van Gogh from Dutch Collections: Religion–Humanity–Nature.* Exhibition, National Museum of Art, February 21–March 31. Catalogue. [Tokyo?], 1986.

Oslo 1937. *Vincent van Gogh: Malerier, tegninger, akvareller.* Exhibition, Kunstnernes Hus, December 3–24. Catalogue. [Oslo, 1937.]

Ottawa 1999. *Van Gogh's Irises: Masterpiece in Focus.* Exhibition, National Gallery of Canada, June 11–September 19. Catalogue by Colin B. Bailey and John Collins. Ottawa, 1999.

Otterlo 1990. *Vincent van Gogh. Drawings.* Exhibition, Kröller-Müller Museum, March 30–July 29. Catalogue by Johannes van der Wolk, Ronald Pickvance, and E. B. F. Pey; translated by J. W. Watson. Milan, 1990.

Otterlo–Amsterdam 1953. *Eeuwfeest Vincent van Gogh.* Exhibition, Kröller-Müller Museum, May 24–July 19; Stedelijk Museum, July 23–September 20. Catalogue. Otterlo, 1953. This exhibition originated in The Hague.

Palm Beach–Miami–New Orleans 1955. *Vincent van Gogh, 1853–1890.* Exhibition, Society of the Four Arts, January 21–February 13; Lowe Gallery of the University of Miami, February 24–March 20; Isaac Delgado Museum, March 27–April 20. Catalogue. N.p., 1955.

Paris 1888. *Société des Artistes Indépendants: 4e exposition.* Exhibition, Pavillion de la Ville de Paris, Champs-Élysées, March 22–May 3. *Catalogue des oeuvres exposées 1888: Société des Artistes Indépendants.* Paris, 1888.

Paris 1889. *Société des Artistes Indépendants: 5e exposition.* Exhibition, Salle de la Société d'Horticulture, 84 rue de Grenelle, September 3–October 4. *Catalogue des oeuvres exposées 1889: Société des Artistes Indépendants.* Paris, 1889.

Paris 1890. *Société des Artistes Indépendants: 6e exposition.* Exhibition, Pavillion de la Ville de Paris, Champs-Élysées, March 20–April 27. *Catalogue des oeuvres exposées 1890: Société des Artistes Indépendants.* Paris, 1890.

Paris 1892. *Exposition Van Gogh.* Exhibition, Galerie Le Barc de Boutteville, April. Flyer by Émile Bernard (see fig. 41 in this publication). Reviews published in translation in Stein 1986, pp. 294–305.

Paris 1896–97. Title unknown. Exhibition, Galerie Vollard, November–January? No catalogue known. *See* Susan Alyson Stein, "The Paper Trail," in this publication.

Paris 1901. *Exposition d'oeuvres de Vincent van Gogh.* Exhibition, Galerie Bernheim-Jeune, March 15–31. Catalogue preface by Julien Leclercq. Paris, 1901.

Paris 1902. Title unknown. Exhibition, Galerie Moline, opened ca. February. No catalogue published.

Paris 1905. *Société des Artistes Indépendants: 21me exposition.* Exhibition, Grandes Serres de la Ville de Paris, Cours-de-la-Reine, March 24–April 30. Included a "Rétrospective Vincent van Gogh." Catalogue. Paris, 1905.

Paris 1908a. *Cent tableaux de Vincent van Gogh.* Exhibition, Galerie Bernheim-Jeune, January. Catalogue. Paris, 1908.

Paris 1908b. *Vincent van Gogh.* Exhibition, Galerie E. Druet, January 6–18. Catalogue. Paris, 1908.

Paris 1909. *Cinquante tableaux de Vincent van Gogh.* Exhibition, Galerie E. Druet, November 8–20. Catalogue. Paris, 1909.

Paris 1925. *Exposition rétrospective d'oeuvres de Vincent van Gogh (1853–1890).* Exhibition, Galerie Marcel Bernheim, January 5–24. Catalogue. Paris, 1925.

Paris 1928. *Aquarelles, dessins et pastels de Van Gogh (1853–1890).* Exhibition, Galerie Dru, June 23–July 12. Catalogue by J.-B. de la Faille. [Paris], 1928.

Paris 1937. *La vie et l'oeuvre de Van Gogh.* Exhibition, Les Nouveaux Musées, Quai de Tokyo, June–October. Catalogue by Wilhelm Uhde. Vienna, 1937.

Paris 1947. *Vincent van Gogh.* Exhibition, Musée de l'Orangerie, January 24–March 15. Catalogue by René Huyghe. Paris, 1947.

Paris 1960. *Vincent van Gogh, 1853–1890.* Exhibition, Musée Jacquemart-André, February–May. Catalogue by Marc Edo Tralbaut. Paris, 1960.

Paris 1963. *L'aquarelle néerlandaise au siècle dernier.* Exhibition, Institut Néerlandais, February 28–March 31. Catalogue by Victorine Bakker-Hefting. Paris, 1963.

Paris 1971–72. *Vincent van Gogh: Collection du Musée National Vincent van Gogh à Amsterdam.* Exhibition, Orangerie des Tuileries, December 21–April 10. Catalogue by Vincent W. van Gogh and Emil R. Meijer, with Han van Crimpen and Isabelle Plemp van Duiveland. Paris, 1971.

Paris 1977. *Vincent van Gogh.* Exhibition, Grand Palais, November 4–December 3. Catalogue. Paris, 1977.

Paris 1988. *Van Gogh à Paris.* Exhibition, Musée d'Orsay, February 2–May 15. Catalogue by Françoise Cachin and Bogomila Welsh-Ovcharov, with Monique Nonne; translations by J. C. Garcias et al. Paris, 1988.

Paris 1998–99. *Millet—Van Gogh.* Exhibition, Musée d'Orsay, September 14–January 3. Catalogue by Louis van Tilborgh et al. Paris, 1998.

Paris–Albi 1966. *Vincent van Gogh, dessinateur.* Exhibition, Institut Néerlandais, January 28–March 20; Musée Toulouse-Lautrec, May 27–August 31. Catalogue preface by Vincent W. van Gogh and Abraham Marie Hammacher. Paris, 1966.

Paris–New York 1991–92. *Georges Seurat, 1859–1891.* Exhibition, Galeries Nationales du Grand Palais, April 9–August 12; The Metropolitan Museum of Art, September 24–January 12. Catalogue by Robert Herbert et al. New York, 1991.

Paris–New York–Amsterdam 1999. *Cézanne to Van Gogh: The Collection of Doctor Gachet.* Exhibition, Grand Palais, January 28–April 26; The Metropolitan Museum of Art, May 25–August 15; Van Gogh Museum, September 24–December 5. Catalogue by Anne Distel and Susan Alyson Stein. New York, 1999.

Passantino 1985. Erika D. Passantino, ed. *The Phillips Collection: A Summary Catalogue.* Washington, 1985.

Pataky 1959. Dénes Pataky. *Master Drawings from the Collection of the Budapest Museum of Fine Arts: 19th and 20th Centuries.* New York, 1959.

Paul 1993. Barbara Paul. *Hugo von Tschudi und die moderne französische Kunst im Deutschen Kaiserreich.* Mainz am Rhein, 1993.

Pfister 1922. Kurt Pfister. *Van Gogh.* Potsdam, 1922.

Pickvance 2003. Ronald Pickvance. "Vincent van Gogh: *La Maison de Vincent à Arles.*" Offprint of *Impressionist and Modern Art,* lot 52. Sale cat. London: Christie's, June 24, 2003.

Pion 1971. Léonce Pion, with Irène Pion-Leblanc. *Catalogue du Musée des Beaux-Arts de Tournai.* Tournai, 1971.

Pittsburgh–Detroit–Kansas City 1962–63. *Vincent van Gogh: Paintings, Watercolors, and Drawings.* Exhibition, Carnegie Institute, October 18–November 4; Detroit Institute of Arts, December 11–January 29; William Rockhill Nelson Gallery of Art, Mary Atkins Museum of Fine Arts, February 7–March 26. Catalogue of paintings and drawings from the collection of Vincent W. van Gogh on loan to the Stedelijk Museum. Amsterdam, 1962.

Plasschaert 1898. Albert Plasschaert. *Vincent van Gogh.* The Hague, 1898. Published in conjunction with The Hague 1898.

Pollock 1980. Griselda F. S. Pollock. "Vincent van Gogh and Dutch Art: A Study of the Development of Van Gogh's Notion of Modern Art with Special Reference to the Critical and Artistic Revival of Seventeenth Century Dutch Art in Holland and France in the Nineteenth Century." 2 vols. Ph.D. dissertation, Courtauld Institute of Art, London University, 1980.

Pollock 1983. Griselda Pollock. "Stark Encounters: Modern Life and Urban Work in Van Gogh's Drawings of The Hague, 1881–3." *Art History* 6, no. 3 (1983), pp. 330–58.

Proust 1913. Antonin Proust. *Édouard Manet: Souvenirs.* Paris, 1913.

Van Rappard-Boon, Van Gulik, and Van Bremen-Ito 1991. Charlotte van Rappard-Boon, Willem van Gulik, and Keiko van Bremen-Ito. *Catalogue of the Van Gogh Museum's Collection of Japanese Prints.* Introduction by Tsukasa Kōdera. Amsterdam, 1991.

Richard 1988. Pierre Richard. "Vincent van Gogh's Montmartre." *Jong Holland* 4, no. 1 (1988), pp. 16–21.

Rome 1988. *Vincent van Gogh.* Exhibition, Galleria Nazionale d'Arte Moderna, January 28–April 4. Catalogue edited by Gianna Piantoni; contributions by Stefania Frezzotti et al. Milan, 1988.

Rosenblum 1975. Robert Rosenblum. *Modern Painting and the Northern Romantic Tradition: Friedrich to Rothko.* New York, 1975.

Roskill 1966. Mark W. Roskill. "Van Gogh's Blue Cart and His Creative Process." *Oud Holland* 81, no. 1 (1966), pp. 3–19.

Roskill 1970. Mark Roskill. *Van Gogh, Gauguin, and the Impressionist Circle.* Greenwich, Conn., 1970.

Roskill 1971. Mark W. Roskill. "Van Gogh's Exchanges of Work with Émile Bernard in 1888." *Oud Holland* 86, no. 2–3 (1971), pp. 142–79.

Rotterdam 1892. *Vincent van Gogh schilderijen en teekeningen.* Exhibition, Kunstzalen Oldenzeel, March. No catalogue known.

Rotterdam 1900–1901. *Tentoonstelling van teekeningen van Vincent van Gogh.* Exhibition, Rotterdamsche Kunstkring, December 23–February 10. Brochure. Rotterdam, 1900.

Rotterdam 1903a. *Vincent van Gogh.* Exhibition, Kunstzalen Oldenzeel, January 4–February 5. No catalogue known.

Rotterdam 1903b. *Vincent van Gogh: Letteren en kunst.* Exhibition, Kunstzalen Oldenzeel, November–December. No catalogue known.

Rotterdam 1904. *Tentoonstelling van werken door Vincent van Gogh.* Exhibition, Kunstzalen Oldenzeel, November 10–December 15. Catalogue. Rotterdam, 1904.

Rotterdam 1907–8. *Tentoonstelling van aquarellen, teekeningen en schetsen van Vincent van Gogh.* Exhibition, Rotterdamsche Kunstkring, December 22–January 12. No catalogue known.

Rotterdam 1923. *Vincent van Gogh. Teekeningencollectie van Mevr. J. van Gogh-Bonger.* Exhibition, Rotterdamsche Kunstkring, March 15–April 2. No catalogue known. This exhibition originated in Utrecht.

Rotterdam 1929–30. *Teekeningen en aquarellen door Vincent van Gogh uit het bezit van den heer Ir. V. W. van Gogh te Laren.* Exhibition, Rotterdamsche Kunstkring, December 21–January 12. Brochure. Rotterdam, 1929.

Rotterdam 1947. *Vincent van Gogh: Tekeningen uit de verzameling van V. W. van Gogh.* Exhibition, Museum Boymans, June 28–August. Catalogue. Rotterdam, 1947.

Saint Louis–Frankfurt 2001. *Vincent van Gogh and the Painters of the Petit Boulevard: Charles Angrand, Louis Anquetin, Émile Bernard, Paul Gauguin, Vincent van Gogh, Camille Pissarro, Lucien Pissarro, Paul Signac, Georges Seurat, Henri de Toulouse-Lautrec.* Exhibition, Saint Louis Art Museum, February 17–May 13; Städelsches Kunstinstitut und Städtisches Galerie, June 8–September 2. Catalogue by Cornelia Homburg, with essays by Elizabeth C. Childs, John House, and Richard Thomson; chronology by Lynn DuBard. Saint Louis, 2001. German ed.: *Vincent van Gogh und die Maler des Petit Boulevard.* Ostfildern-Ruit, 2001.

Saint Louis–Philadelphia–Toledo 1953–54. *Vincent van Gogh, 1853–1890.* Exhibition, City Art Museum of Saint Louis, October 17–December 13; Philadelphia Museum of Art, January 2–February 28; Toledo Museum of Art, March 7–April 30. Catalogue. N.p., [1953].

San Francisco and other cities 1958–59. *Vincent van Gogh. Paintings and Drawings.* Exhibition, M. H. de Young Memorial Museum, October 6–November 30; Los Angeles County Museum, December 10–January 18; Portland Art Museum, January 28–March 1; Seattle Art Museum, March 7–April 19. Catalogue. [Los Angeles, 1958.]

Sapporo–Kōbe 2002. *Gohho ten / Vincent and Theo van Gogh.* Exhibition, Hokkaidō Museum of Modern Art, July 5–August 25; Hyōgo Prefectural Museum of Modern Art, September 7–November 4. Catalogue. [Sapporo], 2002.

Saunier 1892. Charles Saunier. "Vincent van Gogh." *L'endehors,* April 24, 1892. Published in translation in Stein 1986, pp. 303–5.

Schwarz 1946. Heinrich Schwarz. "An Unnoticed Drawing by Vincent van Gogh." *Museum Notes, Museum of Art, Rhode Island School of Design, Providence* 4, no. 4 (April 1946), pp. 2–3.

Silverman 2000. Debora Silverman. *Van Gogh and Gauguin: The Search for Sacred Art.* New York, 2000.

Silverman 2001. Debora Silverman. "Framing Art and Sacred Realism: Van Gogh's Ways of Seeing Arles." *Van Gogh Museum Journal* 2001, pp. 45–62.

Soth 1994. Lauren Soth. "Van Gogh's Images of Women Sewing." *Zeitschrift für Kunstgeschichte* 57, no. 1 (1994), pp. 105–10.

Stedelijk Museum 1914. *Catalogus van schilderijen, teekeningen en beelden in het Stedelijk Museum bijeengebracht door de "Vereeniging tot het Vormen van eene Openbare Verzameling van Hedendaagsche Kunst" te Amsterdam.* Amsterdam, 1914.

Stein 1986. Susan Alyson Stein, ed. *Van Gogh: A Retrospective.* New York, 1986.

Stein 1989. Susan Alyson Stein. "Van Gogh and Millet." In *Treasures from The Metropolitan Museum of Art: French Art from the Middle Ages to the Twentieth Century,* pp. 39–44. Exh. cat. Yokohama: Yokohama Museum of Art, 1989.

Stein 2001. Susan Alyson Stein. "Passage du Puits-Bertin, Clichy." In *Signac, 1863–1935,* by Marina Ferretti-Bocquillon et al., pp. 118–19. Exh. cat. New York: The Metropolitan Museum of Art, 2001.

Stockholm and other cities 1957–58. *Vincent van Gogh: Akvareller, teckningar, oljestudier, brev.* Exhibition, Nationalmuseum, October 5–November 22; Shopping-center, Luleå, December 4–19; Norrmalmsskolan, Kiruna, December 29–January 13; Länsmuseet, Umeå, January 18–February 2; Konstmuseet, Östersund, February 8–23; Konsthallen, Sandviken. Catalogue by Carl Nordenfalk and Pontus Grate. Stockholm, 1957.

Stockholm–Göteborg 1965–66. *Vincent van Gogh: Målningar, akvareller, teckningar.* Exhibition, Moderna Museet, October 22–December 19; Göteborgs Konstmuseum, December 30–February 20. Catalogue edited by Carlo Derkert and Karin Bergqvist Lindegren. Stockholm, 1965.

Stockholm–Göteborg–Malmö 1946. *Vincent van Gogh: Utställning anordnad till förmån för svenska hollandshjälpen.* Exhibition, Nationalmuseum, March 8–April 28; Göteborgs Konstmuseum, May 3–26; Malmö Museum, May 29–June 16. Catalogue. Nationalmusei utställningskataloger, no. 118. Stockholm, 1946.

Stockholm–Oslo 1976. *Vincent van Gogh.* Exhibition, Gallieriet Kulturhuset, February 10–March 28; Munch Museet, April 5–June 15. Catalogue. Stockholm, 1976.

Stolwijk and Veenenbos 2002. Chris Stolwijk and Han Veenenbos. *Account Book of Theo van Gogh and Jo van Gogh-Bonger.* Cahier Vincent, no. 8. Amsterdam and Leiden, 2002.

Strasbourg–Bern 1972–73. *Vincent van Gogh: Collection du Musée National Vincent van Gogh à Amsterdam.* Exhibition, Musée d'Art Moderne, October 22–January 15; Kunstmuseum Bern, January 25–April 15. Catalogue by Vincent W. van Gogh. Amsterdam, 1972.

Stuttgart 1924. *Ausstellung Vincent van Gogh, 1853–1890.* Exhibition, Württembergischer Kunstverein, October 12–November 30. Brochure. [Stuttgart, 1924.]

Stuttgart–Utrecht 1980–81. *Van Gogh bis Cobra: Holländische Malerei, 1880–1950.* Exhibition, Württembergischer Kunstverein, November 23–January 18; Centraal Museum, February 14–April 20. Catalogue by Geurt Imanse et al. Stuttgart, [1980]. Dutch ed.: *Van Gogh tot Cobra: Nederlandse schilderkunst, 1880–1950.* Utrecht, 1981.

Sydney–Melbourne–New York 1975. *Modern Masters: Manet to Matisse.* Exhibition, Art Gallery of New South Wales, April 10–May 11; National Gallery of Victoria, May 28–June 22; Museum of Modern Art, August 4–September 1. Catalogue by William S. Lieberman. New York, 1975.

Tel Aviv–Haifa 1963. *Vincent van Gogh, 1853–1890* [from the collection of the Kröller-Müller Museum, Otterlo]. Exhibition, Tel Aviv Museum, Helena Rubenstein Pavilion, January–February; Municipal Museum of Modern Art, February–March. Catalogue. Tel Aviv, 1963.

Tellegen-Hoogendoorn 1964. Annet Tellegen-Hoogendoorn. "Geen panoramalandschap bij Van Gogh." *Bulletin van het Rijksmuseum* 12, no. 2 (1964), pp. 57–61.

Tellegen-Hoogendoorn 1967. Annet Tellegen-Hoogendoorn. "Van Gogh en Montmajour." *Bulletin Museum Boijmans-Van Beuningen* 18, no. 1 (1967), pp. 16–33.

Thannhauser 1938. Henry Thannhauser. "Van Gogh and John Russell: Some Unknown Letters and Drawings." *Burlington Magazine* 73, no. 426 (September 1938), pp. 95–104.

Thomson 1987. Richard Thomson. "Van Gogh in Paris: The Fortifications Drawings of 1887." *Jong Holland* 3, no. 3 (1987), pp. 14–25.

Van Tilborgh 1993. Louis van Tilborgh. *The Potato Eaters by Vincent van Gogh / De Aardappeleters van Vincent van Gogh.* Contributions by Dieuwertje Dekkers et al. Cahier Vincent, no. 5. Zwolle, 1993.

Tokyo 2000. *Vincent van Gogh Drawing Exhibition: Van Gogh and His Time from the Van Gogh Museum and the H. W. Mesdag Museum.* Exhibition, Seiji Togo Memorial Yasuda Kasai Museum of Art, September 14–November 13. Catalogue by Sjraar van Heugten, J. Leighton, and N. Senzoku. [Tokyo]: Yasuda Kasai Fine Art Foundation, 2000.

Tokyo–Kyōto–Nagoya 1976–77. *Vincent van Gogh Exhibition.* Exhibition, National Museum of Western Art, October 30–December 19; National Museum of Modern Art, January 6–February 20; Aichi Prefectural Art Gallery, February 24–March 14. Catalogue. Tokyo, 1976.

Tokyo–Nagoya 1985–86. *Gohho Ten / Vincent van Gogh Exhibition.* Exhibition, National Museum of Western Art, October 12–December 8; Nagoya City Museum, December 19–February 2. Catalogue. Tokyo, 1985.

Toledo 2003. *Van Gogh: Fields.* Exhibition, Toledo Museum of Art, February 23–May 18; organized in conjunction with the Kunsthalle Bremen. Catalogue by Dorothee Hansen, Lawrence W. Nichols, and Judy Sund. Toledo, 2003.

Toronto–Amsterdam 1981. *Vincent van Gogh and the Birth of Cloisonism.* Exhibition, Art Gallery of Ontario, January 24–March 22; Van Gogh Museum, April 9–June 14. Catalogue by Bogomila Welsh-Ovcharov. Toronto, 1981.

Tournai 1957. *Dessins et gravures inédits de la Collection van Cutsem.* Exhibition, Musée des Beaux-Arts, April. No catalogue known.

Tralbaut 1958. Marc Edo Tralbaut. *Van Gogh: Eine Bildbiographie.* Munich, 1958.

Tralbaut 1959. Marc Edo Tralbaut. *Vincent van Gogh in Drenthe.* Assen, 1959.

Tralbaut 1969. Marc Edo Tralbaut. *Van Gogh, le mal aimé.* Lausanne, 1969.

Van Uitert and Hoyle 1987. Evert van Uitert and Michael Hoyle, eds. *The Rijksmuseum Vincent van Gogh.* Amsterdam, 1987.

Utrecht 1923. *Vincent van Gogh: Teekeningencollectie van Mevr. J. van Gogh-Bonger.* Exhibition, Vereeniging "Voor de Kunst," January 28–February 25. No catalogue known. This exhibition also traveled to Rotterdam.

Utrecht 1959–60. *Vincent van Gogh: Schilderijen en tekeningen.* Exhibition, Centraal Museum, December 18–February 1. Catalogue by Vincent W. van Gogh and M. E. Houtzager. [Utrecht, 1959.]

Vanbeselaere 1937. Walther Vanbeselaere. *De Hollandsche periode (1880–1885) in het werk van Vincent van Gogh (1853–1890).* Amsterdam, [1937].

***Van nu en straks* 1893.** "Brieven en platen van Vincent van Gogh." *Van nu en straks,* no. 3 (1893). Contributions by Henry van de Velde, Richard N. Roland-Holst, Jan Toorop, Johan Thorn Prikker, et al.

Vellekoop and Van Heugten 2001. Marije Vellekoop and Sjraar van Heugten. *Vincent van Gogh Drawings.* Vol. 3, *Antwerp and Paris, 1885–1888.* Amsterdam: Van Gogh Museum, 2001. Published in conjunction with Amsterdam 2001–2.

Vellekoop and Zwikker 2006. Marije Vellekoop and Roelie Zwikker. *Vincent van Gogh Drawings.* Vol. 4, *Arles, Saint Rémy and Auvers-sur-Oise, 1888–1890.* Amsterdam: Van Gogh Museum, 2006. Forthcoming.

Versluys, W. (publisher). *See* Bremmer n.d.; Van Gogh n.d. [1904]; and Nijland 1905.

Vienna 1996. *Van Gogh und die Haager Schule.* Exhibition, Bank Austria Kunstforum, February 28–May 27. Catalogue by Roland Dorn, Klaus Albrecht Schröder, and John Sillevis. Vienna, 1996.

Vienna–Hannover 1928. *Vincent van Gogh. Aquarelle und Handzeichnungen.* Exhibition, Neue Galerie, February–March; Kestner-Gesellschaft, April 3–25. Catalogue. Vienna, 1928.

Visser 1973. W. J. A. Visser. "Vincent van Gogh en 's-Gravenhage." *Geschiedkundige Vereniging Die Haghe. Jaarboek 1973,* pp. 1–125.

Vogelsang 1905. W. Vogelsang. "Tentoonstelling Vincent van Gogh." *Onze Kunst* 4, 2nd semester (1905), pp. 59–68.

Wadley 1969. Nicholas Wadley. *The Drawings of Van Gogh.* London, 1969.

Wadley 1991. Nicholas Wadley. *Impressionist and Post-Impressionist Drawing.* London, 1991.

Walker 1982. John A. Walker. "Van Gogh's Drawing of La Crau from Mont Majour." *Master Drawings* 20 (Winter 1982), pp. 380–85.

Warsaw 1962. *Vincent van Gogh: Obrazy i rysunki. Wystawa dziel ze zbiorów Museów Holenderskich* (Vincent van Gogh: Paintings, Drawings, Etchings from the Collection of the Kröller-Müller Museum, Otterlo). Exhibition, Muzeum Narodowe w Warszawie, October 8–18. Catalogue edited by Krystyna Secomska. Warsaw, 1962.

Washington–Chicago–Los Angeles 1985. *Leonardo to Van Gogh: Master Drawings from Budapest.* Exhibition, National Gallery of Art, May 12–July 14; Art Institute of Chicago, July 27–September 22; Los Angeles County Museum of Art, October 10–December 8. Catalogue edited by Mary Yakush; translated by Janós Scholz. Chicago, 1985.

Washington–New York 1964. *Vincent van Gogh: Paintings, Watercolors, and Drawings.* Exhibition, Washington Gallery of Modern Art, February 2–March 19; Solomon R. Guggenheim Museum, April 2–June 28. Catalogue. Washington, 1964.

Weisbach 1949–51. Werner Weisbach. *Vincent van Gogh: Kunst und Schicksal.* 2 vols. Basel, 1949–51.

Willemstad 1954–55. *Vincent van Gogh.* Exhibition, Curaçaosch Museum, December 19–January 15. No catalogue known.

Wilson and Young 1995. Carol Wilson and Catherine Young. "Deux tableaux de Vincent van Gogh identifiés à Auvers-sur-Oise." *Vivre en Val-d'Oise,* no. 34 (November 1995), pp. 62–65.

Wolfsburg 1967. *Vincent van Gogh: Gemälde, Aquarelle, Zeichnungen.* Exhibition, Stadthalle Wolfsburg, February 18–April 2. Catalogue by Vincent W. van Gogh. [Wolfsburg, 1967.]

Van der Wolk 1987. Johannes van der Wolk. *The Seven Sketchbooks of Vincent van Gogh: A Facsimile Edition.* Translated by Claudia Swan. New York, 1987.

Wylie 1970. Anne Styles Wylie. "An Investigation of the Vocabulary of Line in Vincent van Gogh's Expression of Space." *Oud Holland* 85, no. 4 (1970), pp. 210–35.

Zemel 1985. Carol Zemel. "The 'Spook' in the Machine: Van Gogh's Pictures of Weavers in Brabant." *Art Bulletin* 67, no. 1 (1985), pp. 123–37.

Zemel 1987. Carol Zemel. "Sorrowing Women, Rescuing Men: Van Gogh's Images of Women and Family." *Art History* 10, no. 3 (1987), pp. 351–68.

Zundert 1953. *Vincent van Gogh in Zundert.* Exhibition, Parochiehuis, March 30–April 20. Catalogue by G. J. A. Manders. N.p., [1953].

Zundert 1964. *Tentoonstelling van tekeningen van Vincent van Gogh.* Exhibition, Parochiehuis, May 28–June 8. Catalogue by G. J. A. Manders and Ossip Zadkine. N.p., [1964].

Zürich 1924. *Vincent van Gogh.* Exhibition, Kunsthaus Zürich, July 3–August 10. Catalogue. Zürich, 1924. This exhibition originated in Basel.

Zürich 1953. *Zeichnungen und Aquarelle Van Gogh aus der Vincent van Gogh-Stiftung im Stedelijk Museum Amsterdam.* Exhibition, Kunsthaus Zürich, January 24–March 1. Zürich, 1953.

Index

Page references in **boldface type** refer to main entries for catalogue items. Page references in *italic type* refer to illustrations.

Index of Provenances